GATEWAY TO THE GREAT

D1480163

GATEWAY
TO THE
GREAT BOOKS

Gateway
to the
Great Books

ROBERT M. HUTCHINS, MORTIMER J. ADLER
Editors in Chief

CLIFTON FADIMAN
Associate Editor

---

10 ^{12882}

PHILOSOPHICAL

ESSAYS

Encyclopædia Britannica, Inc.

WILLIAM BENTON
Publisher

Chicago, London, Toronto, Geneva, Sydney, Tokyo, Manila

Portrait illustrations are by Fred Steffen

Contents
of Volume 10

John Erskine

1879–1951

If anyone can be called the "father" of the Great Books movement, it is John Erskine. It was he who organized the first Great Books discussion classes at Columbia University. He suggested such classes as early as 1916, but it was not until 1920 that they were first offered. Each student in these classes was required to read one great book each week and to meet for two hours with a group of twenty-five or thirty students to discuss it. The discussion groups also included two professors, whose role was not to lecture but to stimulate discussion. Among Erskine's original associates in the program were the co-editor of this set, Mortimer J. Adler, and Mark Van Doren.

John Erskine was born in New York City in 1879. He was educated at Columbia University, where he received his Ph.D. degree in 1903. He taught literature at Amherst College from 1903 to 1909 and then moved to Columbia, where he remained until his retirement in 1937. From the beginning of his career, he was dissatisfied with the prevailing methods of teaching literature. He was particularly distressed by the fact that most college students were almost completely ignorant of the great literature of the past. He proposed the idea of approaching great books as though they were recently published best sellers. This meant reading them straight through—without commentaries and without histories—and then meeting to discuss them. At first, his academic colleagues were strongly opposed to the idea, but eventually he was given permission to go ahead with it. The program was very successful, and it was later imitated by several other leading universities. In 1947 the Great Books Foundation was set up to foster discussion groups on a national scale, and in 1952 the fifty-four volume set of *Great Books of the Western World* was published—all of this the outgrowth of John Erskine's original idea.

Though he is well known for his role in the Great Books movement, Erskine is probably even more famous for his satirical retelling of classic myths. The first of these was *The Private Life of Helen of Troy,* published in 1925. It proved to be so popular that he followed it with modernized versions of the legends of Galahad, Adam and Eve, and Tristan and Isolde.

Erskine was also very much interested in music. He made his concert debut as a pianist when he was in his late forties. He went on to become president of the Juilliard School of Music from 1928 to 1937, and a member of the board of the Metropolitan Opera Association.

A prolific writer, Erskine wrote (in addition to the works already mentioned) several novels, scores of essays, lectures, poems, memoirs, and even opera librettos. He died in 1951.

Erskine points out in the following selection that for a number of reasons—a common language being probably the most important—the English have exerted a greater influence upon the United States than has any other people. The result is that Americans tend to see things in much the same light as the English do. However beneficial this influence may have been in general, John Erskine finds that, in at least one important respect, it has had a detrimental effect.

It is Erskine's view that the English have traditionally assumed that intelligence and morality are incompatible. A man is clever or he is virtuous, but he cannot be both. And since a choice must be made between the two, the English have consistently cultivated character at the expense of intelligence. They have readily excused stupid behavior, even if its consequences were disastrous, so long as it sprang from good motives.

Erskine regrets that this attitude spread from England to America, but he is encouraged by signs that intelligence is becoming less and less suspect. It is his opinion that intelligence and morality, far from

---

Notes from the artist: "The portrait of Erskine is set against a background design of piano keys, suggesting his career as a musician. The Greek figure at the right recalls his novel The Private Life of Helen of Troy.*"*

John Erskine

being incompatible, are inseparable. All virtues are subject to "the discipline of intelligence," and men have a moral obligation "to find out as far as possible whether a given action leads to a good or a bad end."

Erskine's point of view in this essay closely parallels that of W. K. Clifford in *The Ethics of Belief*.[1] Both insist that knowledge is not something we can choose to have or not to have, according to our individual whim. They argue that since others are affected by our actions, we owe it to others to make certain (as far as possible) that they will not be harmed through our ignorance. It is our *duty* to be intelligent.

---

[1] See Vol. 10, pp. 16–36, in this set.

The Moral Obligation to Be Intelligent

If a wise man should ask, What are the modern virtues? and should answer his own question by a summary of the things we admire; if he should discard as irrelevant the ideals which by tradition we profess, but which are not found outside of the tradition or the profession—ideals like meekness, humility, the renunciation of this world; if he should include only those excellences to which our hearts are daily given, and by which our conduct is motived, in such an inventory what virtues would he name?

This question is neither original nor very new. Our times await the reckoning up of our spiritual goods which is here suggested. We have at least this wisdom, that many of us are curious to know just what our virtues are. I wish I could offer myself as the wise man who brings the answer. But I raise this question merely to ask another—When the wise man brings his list of our genuine admirations, will intelligence be one of them? We might seem to be well within the old ideal of modesty if we claimed the virtue of intelligence. But before we claim the virtue, are we convinced that it is a virtue, not a peril?

The disposition to consider intelligence a peril is an old Anglo-Saxon inheritance. Our ancestors have celebrated this disposition in verse and prose. Splendid as our literature is, it has not voiced all the aspirations of humanity, nor could it be expected to voice an aspiration that has not characteristically belonged to the English race; the praise of intelligence is not one of its characteristic glories.

"Be good, sweet maid, and let who will be clever." Here is the startling alternative which to the English, alone among great nations, has not been startling but a matter of course. Here is the casual assumption that a choice must be made between goodness and intelligence; that stupidity is first cousin to moral conduct, and cleverness the first step into mischief; that reason and God are not on good terms with each other; that the mind and the heart are minor buckets in the well of truth, inexorably balanced—full mind, starved heart—stout heart, weak head.

Kingsley's line is a convenient text, but to establish the point that English literature voices a traditional distrust of the mind we must go to the masters. In Shakespeare's plays there are some highly intelligent men, but they are either villains or tragic victims. To be as intelligent as Richard or Iago or Edmund seems to involve some break with goodness; to be as wise as Prospero seems to imply some Faust-like traffic with the forbidden world; to be as thoughtful as Hamlet seems to be too thoughtful to live. In Shakespeare the prizes of life go to such men as Bassanio, or Duke Orsino, or Florizel—men of good conduct and sound character, but of no particular intelligence. There might, indeed, appear to be one general exception to this sweeping statement: Shakespeare does concede intelligence as a fortunate possession to some of his heroines. But upon even a slight examination those ladies, like Portia, turn out to have been among Shakespeare's importations—their wit was part and parcel of the story he borrowed; or, like Viola, they are English types of humility, patience, and loyalty, such as we find in the old ballads, with a bit of euphuism added, a foreign cleverness of speech. After all, these are only a few of Shakespeare's heroines. Over against them are Ophelia, Juliet, Desdemona, Hero, Cordelia, Miranda, Perdita—lovable for other qualities than intellect—and in a sinister group, Lady Macbeth, Cleopatra, Goneril, intelligent and wicked.

In *Paradise Lost* Milton attributes intelligence of the highest order to the devil. That this is an Anglo-Saxon reading of the infernal character may be shown by a reference to the book of Job, where Satan is simply a troublesome body, and the great wisdom of the story is from the voice of God in the whirlwind. But Milton makes his Satan so thoughtful, so persistent and liberty-loving, so magnanimous, and God so illogical, so heartless and repressive, that many perfectly moral readers fear lest Milton, like the modern novelists, may have known good and evil, but could not tell them apart. It is disconcerting to intelligence that it should be God's angel who cautions Adam not to wander in the earth, nor inquire concerning heaven's causes and ends, and that it should be Satan meanwhile who questions and explores. By Milton's reckoning of intelligence the theologian and scientist today alike take after Satan.

If there were time, we might trace this valuation of intelligence through the English novel. We should see how often the writers distinguished between intelligence and goodness, and have enlisted our affections for a kind of inexpert virtue. In Fielding or Scott, Thackeray or Dickens, the hero of the English novel is a well-meaning blunderer who in the last chapter is temporarily rescued by the grace of God from the mess he has made of his life. Unless he also dies in the last chapter, he will probably need rescue again. The dear woman whom the hero marries is, with a few notable exceptions, rather less intelligent than himself. When David Copperfield marries Agnes, his prospects of happiness, to the eyes of intelligence, look not very exhilarating. Agnes has more sense than Dora, but it is not even for that slight distinction that we must admire her; her great qualities are of the heart—patience, humility, faithfulness. These are the qualities also of Thackeray's good heroines, like Laura or Lady Castlewood. Beatrix Esmond and Becky Sharp, both highly intelligent, are of course a bad lot.

No less significant is the kind of emotion the English novelist invites towards his secondary or lower-class heroes—toward Mr. Boffin in *Our Mutual Friend,* for example, or Harry Foker in *Pendennis*. These characters amuse us, and we feel pleasantly superior to them, but we agree with the novelist that they are wholly admirable in their station. Yet if a Frenchman—let us say—Balzac—were presenting such types, he would make us feel, as in *Père Goriot* or *Eugénie Grandet,* not only admiration for the stable, loyal nature, but also deep pity that such goodness should be so tragically bound in unintelligence or vulgarity. This comparison of racial temperaments helps us to understand ourselves. We may continue the method at our leisure. What would Socrates have thought of Mr. Pickwick, or the Vicar of Wakefield, or David Copperfield, or Arthur Pendennis? For that matter, would he have felt admiration or pity for Colonel Newcome?

I hardly need confess that this is not an adequate account of English literature. Let me hasten to say that I know the reader is resenting this somewhat cavalier handling of the noble writers he loves. He probably is wondering how I can expect to increase his love of literature by such unsympathetic remarks. But just now I am not concerned about our love of literature; I take it for granted and use it as an instrument to prod us with. If we love Shakespeare and Milton and Scott and Dickens and Thackeray, and yet do not know what qualities their books hold out for our admiration, then—let me say it as delicately as possible—our admiration is not discriminating; and if we neither have discrimination nor are disturbed by our lack of it, then perhaps the wise man could not list intelligence among our virtues. Certainly it would be but a silly account of English literature to say only that it set little store by the things of the mind. I am aware that for the sake of my argument I have exaggerated, by insisting upon only one aspect of English literature. But our history betrays a peculiar warfare between character and intellect, such as to the Greek, for example, would have been incomprehensible. The great Englishman, like the most famous Greeks, had intelligence as well as character, and was at ease with them both. But whereas the notable Greek seems typical of his race, the notable Englishman usually seems an exception to his own people, and is often best appreciated in other lands. What is more singular—in spite of the happy combination in himself of character and intelligence, he often fails to recognize the value of that combination in his neighbors. When Shakespeare portrayed such amateurish statesmen as the Duke in *Measure for Measure,* Burleigh was guiding Elizabeth's empire, and Francis Bacon was soon to be King James's counselor. It was the young Milton who pictured the life of reason in *L'Allegro* and *Il Penseroso,* the most spiritual fruit of philosophy in *Comus;* and when he wrote his epic he was probably England's most notable example of that intellectual inquiry and independence which in his great poem he discouraged. There remain several well-known figures in our literary history who have both possessed and believed in intelligence—Byron and Shelley in what seems our own day, Edmund Spenser before Shakespeare's time. England has more or less neglected all three, but they must in fairness be counted to her credit. Some excuse might be offered for the neglect of Byron and Shelley by a nation that likes the proprieties; but the gentle Spenser, the noblest philosopher and most chivalrous gentleman in our literature, seems to be unread only because he demands a mind as well as a heart used to high things.

This will be sufficient qualification of any disparagement of English literature; no people and no literature can be great that are not intelligent, and England has produced not only statesmen and scientists of the first order, but also poets in whom the soul was fitly mated with a lofty intellect. But I am asking you to reconsider your reading in history and fiction, to reflect whether our race has usually thought highly of the intelligence by which it has been great; I suggest these nonintellectual aspects of our literature as commentary upon my question—and all this with the hope of pressing upon you the question as to what *you* think of intelligence.

Those of us who frankly prefer character to intelligence are therefore not without precedent. If we look beneath the history of the English people, beneath the ideas expressed in our literature, we find in the temper of our remotest ancestors a certain bias which still prescribes our ethics and still prejudices us against the mind. The beginnings of our conscience can be geographically located. It began in the German forests, and it gave its allegiance not to the intellect but the will. Whether or not the severity of life in a hard climate raised the value of that persistence by which alone life could be preserved, the Germans as Tacitus knew them, and the Saxons as they landed in England, held as their chief virtue that will power which makes character. For craft or strategy they had no use; they were already a bulldog race; they liked fighting, and they liked best to settle the matter hand to hand. The admiration for brute force which naturally accompanied this ideal of self-reliance, drew with it as naturally a certain moral sanction. A man was as good as his word, and he was ready to back up his word with a blow. No German, Tacitus says, would enter into a treaty of public or private business without his sword in his hand. When this emphasis upon the will became a social emphasis, it gave the direction to ethical feeling. Honor lay in a man's integrity, in his willingness and ability to keep his word; therefore the man became more important than his word or deed. Words and deeds were then easily interpreted, not in terms of absolute good and evil, but in terms of the man behind them. The deeds of a bad man were bad; the deeds of a good man were good. Fielding wrote *Tom Jones* to show that a good man sometimes does a bad action, consciously or unconsciously, and a bad man sometimes does good, intentionally or unintentionally. From the fact that *Tom Jones* is still popularly supposed to be as wicked as it is coarse, we may judge that Fielding did not convert all his readers. Some progress certainly has been made; we do not insist that the more saintly of two surgeons shall operate on us for appendicitis. But as a race we seem as far as possible from realizing that an action can intelligently be called good only if it contributes to a good end; that it is the moral obligation of an intelligent creature to find out as far as possible whether a given action leads to a good or a bad end; and that any system of ethics that excuses him from that obligation is vicious. If I give you poison, meaning to give you wholesome food, I have—to say the least—not done a good act; and unless I intend to throw overboard all pretense to intelligence, I must feel some responsibility for that trifling neglect to find out whether what I gave you was food or poison.

Obvious as the matter is in this academic illustration, it ought to have been still more obvious in Matthew Arnold's famous plea for culture. The purpose of culture, he said, is "to make reason and the will of God prevail." This formula he quoted from an Englishman. Differently stated, the purpose of culture, he said, is "to make an intelligent being yet more intelligent." This formula he borrowed from a Frenchman. The basis culture must have in character, the English resolution to make reason and the will of God prevail, Arnold took for granted; no man ever set a higher price on character—so far as character by itself will go. But he spent his life trying to sow a little suspicion that before we can make the will of God prevail we must find out what is the will of God.

I doubt if Arnold taught us much. He merely embarrassed us temporarily. Our race has often been so embarrassed when it has turned a sudden corner and come upon intelligence. Charles Kingsley himself, who would rather be good than clever—and had his wish—was temporarily embarrassed when in the consciousness of his own upright character he publicly called Newman a liar. Newman happened to be intelligent as well as good, and Kingsley's discomfiture is well known. But we discovered long ago how to evade the sudden embarrassments of intelligence. "Toll for the brave," sings the poet for those who went down in the *Royal George*. They were brave. But he might have sung, "Toll for the stupid." In order to clean the hull, brave Kempenfelt and his eight hundred heroes took the serious risk of laying the vessel well over on its side, while most of the crew were below. Having made the error, they all died bravely; and our memory passes easily over the lack of a virtue we never did think much of, and dwells on the English virtues of courage and discipline. So we forget the shocking blunder of the charge of the Light Brigade, and proudly sing the heroism of the victims. Lest we flatter ourselves that this trick of defense has departed with our fathers—this reading of stupidity in terms of the tragic courage that endures its results—let us reflect that recently, after full warning, we drove a ship at top speed through a field of icebergs. When we were thrilled to read how superbly those hundreds died, in the great English way, a man pointed out that they did indeed die in the English way, and that our pride was therefore ill-timed; that all that bravery was wasted; that the tragedy was in the shipwreck of intelligence. That discouraging person was an Irishman.

I have spoken of our social inheritance as though it were entirely English. Once more let me qualify my terms. Even those ancestors of ours who never left Great Britain were heirs of many civilizations—Roman, French, Italian, Greek. With each world-tide some love of pure intelligence was washed up on English shores, and enriched the soil, and here and there the old stock marveled at its own progeny. But to America, much as we may sentimentally deplore it, England seems destined to be less and less the source of culture, of religion and learning. Our land assimilates all races; with every ship in the harbor our old English ways of thought must crowd a little closer to make room for a new tradition. If some of us do not greatly err, these newcomers are chiefly driving to the wall our inherited criticism of the intellect. As surely as the severe northern climate taught our forefathers the value of the will, the social conditions from which these new citizens have escaped have taught them the power of the mind. They differ from each other, but against the Anglo-Saxon they are confederated in a Greek love of knowledge, in a Greek assurance that sin and misery are the fruit of ignorance, and that to know is to achieve virtue. They join forces at once with that earlier arrival from Greece, the scientific spirit, which like all the immigrants has done our hard work and put up with our contempt. Between this rising host that follow intelligence, and the old camp that put their trust in a stout heart, a firm will, and a strong hand, the fight is on. Our college men will be in the thick of it. If they do not take sides, they will at least be battered in the scuffle. At this moment they are readily divided into those who wish to be men—whatever that means—and those who wish to be intelligent men, and those who, unconscious of blasphemy or humor, prefer not to be intelligent, but to do the will of God.

When we consider the nature of the problems to be solved in our day, it seems—to many of us, at least—that these un-English arrivals are correct, that intelligence is the virtue we particularly need. Courage and steadfastness we cannot do without, so long as two men dwell on the earth; but it is time to discriminate in our praise of these virtues. If you want to get out of prison, what you need is the key to the lock. If you cannot get that, have courage and steadfastness. Perhaps the modern world has got into a kind of prison, and what is needed is the key to the lock. If none of the old virtues exactly fits, why should it seem ignoble to admit it? England for centuries has got on better by sheer character than some other nations by sheer intelligence, but there is after all a relation between the kind of problem and the means we should select to solve it. Not all problems are solved by will power. When England overthrew Bonaparte, it was not his intelligence she overthrew; the contest involved other things besides intelligence, and she wore him out in the matter of physical endurance. The enemy that comes to her as a visible host or armada she can still close with and throttle; but when the foe arrives as an arrow that flieth by night, what avail the old sinews, the old stoutness of heart! We Americans face the same problems, and are too much inclined to oppose to them similar obsolete armor. We make a moral issue of an economic or social question, because it seems ignoble to admit it is simply a question for intelligence. Like the medicine man, we use oratory and invoke our hereditary divinities, when the patient needs only a little quiet, or permission to get out of bed. We applaud those leaders who warm to their work—who, when they cannot open a door, threaten to kick it in. In the philosopher's words, we curse the obstacles of life as though they were devils. But they are not devils. They are obstacles.

Perhaps my question as to what you think of intelligence has been pushed far enough. But I cannot leave the subject without a confession of faith.

None of the reasons here suggested will explain the true worship of intelligence, whether we worship it as the scientific spirit, or as scholarship, or as any other reliance upon the mind. We really seek intelligence not for the answers it may suggest to the problems of life, but because we believe it is life, not for aid in making the will of God prevail, but because we believe it is the will of God. We love it as we love virtue, for its own sake, and we believe it is only virtue's other and more precise name. We believe that the virtues wait upon intelligence—literally wait, in the history of the race. Whatever is elemental in man—love, hunger, fear—has obeyed from the beginning the discipline of intelligence. We are told that to kill one's aging parents was once a demonstration of solicitude; about the same time men hungered for raw meat and feared the sun's eclipse. Filial love, hunger, and fear are still motives to conduct, but intelligence has directed them to other ends. If we no longer hang the thief or flog the schoolboy, it is not that we think less harshly of theft or laziness, but that intelligence has found a better persuasion to honesty and enterprise.

We believe that even in religion, in the most intimate room of the spirit, intelligence long ago proved itself the master virtue. Its inward office from the beginning was to decrease fear and increase opportunity; its outward effect was to rob the altar of its sacrifice and the priest of his mysteries. Little wonder that from the beginning the disinterestedness of the accredited custodians of all temples has been tested by the kind of welcome they gave to intelligence. How many hecatombs were offered on more shores than that of Aulis, by seamen waiting for a favorable wind, before intelligence found out a boat that could tack! The altar was deserted, the religion revised—fear of the uncontrollable changing into delight in the knowledge that is power. We contemplate with satisfaction the law by which in our long history one religion has driven out another, as one hypothesis supplants another in astronomy or mathematics. The faith that needs the fewest altars, the hypothesis that leaves least unexplained, survives; and the intelligence that changes most fears into opportunity is most divine.

We believe this beneficent operation of intelligence was swerving not one degree from its ancient course when under the name of the scientific spirit it once more laid its influence upon religion. If the shock here seemed too violent, if the purpose of intelligence here seemed to be not revision but contradiction, it was only because religion was invited to digest an unusually large amount of intelligence all at once. Moreover, it is not certain that devout people were more shocked by Darwinism than the pious mariners were by the first boat that could tack. Perhaps the sacrifices were not abandoned all at once.

But the lover of intelligence must be patient with those who cannot readily share his passion. Some pangs the mind will inflict upon the heart. It is a mistake to think that men are united by elemental affections. Our affections divide us. We strike roots in immediate time and space, and fall in love with our locality, the customs and the language in which we were brought up. Intelligence unites us with mankind, by leading us in sympathy to other times, other places, other customs; but first the prejudiced roots of affection must be pulled up. These are the old pangs of intelligence, which still comes to set a man at variance against his father, saying, "He that loveth father or mother more than me, is not worthy of me."

Yet, if intelligence begins in a pang, it proceeds to a vision. Through measureless time its office has been to make of life an opportunity, to make goodness articulate, to make virtue a fact. In history at least, if not yet in the individual, Plato's faith has come true, that sin is but ignorance, and knowledge and virtue are one. But all that intelligence has accomplished dwindles in comparison with the vision it suggests and warrants. Beholding this long liberation of the human spirit, we foresee, in every new light of the mind, one unifying mind, wherein the human race shall know its destiny and proceed to it with satisfaction, as an idea moves to its proper conclusion; we conceive of intelligence at last as the infinite order, wherein man, when he enters it, shall find himself.

Meanwhile he continues to find his virtues by successive insights into his needs. Let us cultivate insight.

> O Wisdom of the Most High,
> That reachest from the beginning to the end,
> And dost order all things in strength and grace,
> Teach us now the way of understanding.

William Kingdon Clifford [1]

1845–1879

In free societies, it is commonly held that a man has the right to believe anything he wants, no matter how foolish those beliefs may be. It is only if he is led by his beliefs to act in an undesirable manner that society can interfere. Even then, society cannot force him to change his beliefs—it can only hinder him from acting upon them. Thus, a man is at perfect liberty to believe that women are not intelligent enough to vote, but he must not attempt to prevent any of them from going to the polls.

In *The Ethics of Belief,* W. K. Clifford argues that a man does *not* have the right to believe anything he wants. On the contrary, he has the right to believe only those things that he has carefully investigated, and for which he has found ample evidence. Says Clifford, "It is wrong always, everywhere, and for anyone, to believe anything upon insufficient evidence." Men must recognize that they have a *duty* to examine all of their beliefs and to reject those for which they cannot find adequate support. Society cannot force them to do this, however. They must become aware of it as a moral obligation.

Clifford attacks the assumption that beliefs can be kept separate from actions. Though a particular foolish belief may not have any immediate results, each belief, "however trifling and fragmentary it may seem. . .prepares us to receive more of its like, confirms those which resembled it before, and weakens others; and so gradually it lays a stealthy train in our inmost thoughts, which may someday explode into overt action."

Once he has established that there is a "duty of inquiry," Clifford goes on to consider some of the important questions which arise

---

[1] For a biography of W. K. Clifford, see Vol. 9, pp. 239–241, in this set.

when the process of inquiry has begun. How much should we depend on the authority of others? How can we determine who is an authority? Is tradition reliable? How far can we extend inferences from our own experience?

Clifford's essay recalls a famous passage in Plato's *Meno* in which Socrates distinguishes between right opinion and knowledge.[2] The man who has right opinion knows what is true but cannot give any reasons for it. The man who has knowledge not only knows what is true but can say *why* it is true. For Socrates it makes no difference whether actions are based upon right opinion or knowledge. The results will be the same. But for Clifford the difference is crucial. He insists that each man has a responsibility to make sure that his actions are based upon knowledge and not upon what Socrates calls right opinion. The life of the man who will not accept that responsibility is "one long sin against mankind."

---

[2] See *Great Books of the Western World,* Vol. 7, pp. 188–189.

The Ethics of Belief

I. THE DUTY OF INQUIRY

A ship-owner was about to send to sea an emigrant ship. He knew that she was old, and not over-well built at the first; that she had seen many seas and climes, and often had needed repairs. Doubts had been suggested to him that possibly she was not seaworthy. These doubts preyed upon his mind, and made him unhappy; he thought that perhaps he ought to have her thoroughly overhauled and refitted, even though this should put him to great expense. Before the ship sailed, however, he succeeded in overcoming these melancholy reflections. He said to himself that she had gone safely through so many voyages and weathered so many storms that it was idle to suppose she would not come safely home from this trip also. He would put his trust in Providence, which could hardly fail to protect all these unhappy families that were leaving their fatherland to seek for better times elsewhere. He would dismiss from his mind all ungenerous suspicions about the honesty of builders and contractors. In such ways he acquired a sincere and comfortable conviction that his vessel was thoroughly safe and seaworthy; he watched her departure with a light heart, and benevolent wishes for the success of the exiles in their strange new home that was to be; and he got his insurance money when she went down in mid-ocean and told no tales.

What shall we say of him? Surely this, that he was verily guilty of the death of those men. It is admitted that he did sincerely believe in the soundness of his ship; but the sincerity of his conviction can in no wise help him, because *he had no right to believe on such evidence as was before him*. He had acquired his belief not by honestly earning it in patient investigation, but by stifling his doubts. And although in the end he may have felt so sure about it that he could not think otherwise, yet inasmuch as he had knowingly and willingly worked himself into that frame of mind, he must be held responsible for it.

16

Let us alter the case a little, and suppose that the ship was not unsound after all; that she made her voyage safely, and many others after it. Will that diminish the guilt of her owner? Not one jot. When an action is once done, it is right or wrong for ever; no accidental failure of its good or evil fruits can possibly alter that. The man would not have been innocent, he would only have been not found out. The question of right or wrong has to do with the origin of his belief, not the matter of it; not what it was, but how he got it; not whether it turned out to be true or false, but whether he had a right to believe on such evidence as was before him.

There was once an island in which some of the inhabitants professed a religion teaching neither the doctrine of original sin nor that of eternal punishment. A suspicion got abroad that the professors of this religion had made use of unfair means to get their doctrines taught to children. They were accused of wresting the laws of their country in such a way as to remove children from the care of their natural and legal guardians; and even of stealing them away and keeping them concealed from their friends and relations. A certain number of men formed themselves into a society for the purpose of agitating the public about this matter. They published grave accusations against individual citizens of the highest position and character, and did all in their power to injure these citizens in the exercise of their professions. So great was the noise they made, that a commission was appointed to investigate the facts; but after the commission had carefully inquired into all the evidence that could be got, it appeared that the accused were innocent. Not only had they been accused on insufficient evidence, but the evidence of their innocence was such as the agitators might easily have obtained, if they had attempted a fair inquiry. After these disclosures the inhabitants of that country looked upon the members of the agitating society, not only as persons whose judgment was to be distrusted, but also as no longer to be counted honourable men. For although they had sincerely and conscientiously believed in the charges they had made, yet *they had no right to believe on such evidence as was before them.* Their sincere convictions, instead of being honestly earned by patient inquiring, were stolen by listening to the voice of prejudice and passion.

Let us vary this case also, and suppose, other things remaining as before, that a still more accurate investigation proved the accused to have been really guilty. Would this make any difference in the guilt of the accusers? Clearly not; the question is not whether their belief was true or false, but whether they entertained it on wrong grounds. They would no doubt say, "Now you see that we were right after all; next time perhaps you will believe us." And they might be believed, but they would not thereby become honourable men. They would not be innocent, they would only be not found out. Every one of them, if he chose to examine himself *in foro conscientiae*, would know that he had acquired and nourished a belief, when he had no right to believe on such evidence as was before him; and therein he would know that he had done a wrong thing.

It may be said, however, that in both of these supposed cases it is not the belief which is judged to be wrong, but the action following upon it. The ship-owner might say, "I am perfectly certain that my ship is sound, but still I feel it my duty to have her examined, before trusting the lives of so many people to her." And it might be said to the agitator, "However convinced you were of the justice of your cause and the truth of your convictions, you ought not to have made a public attack upon any man's character until you had examined the evidence on both sides with the utmost patience and care."

In the first place, let us admit that, so far as it goes, this view of the case is right and necessary; right, because even when a man's belief is so fixed that he cannot think otherwise, he still has a choice in regard to the action suggested by it, and so cannot escape the duty of investigating on the ground of the strength of his convictions; and necessary, because those who are not yet capable of controlling their feelings and thoughts must have a plain rule dealing with overt acts.

But this being premised as necessary, it becomes clear that it is not sufficient, and that our previous judgment is required to supplement it. For it is not possible so to sever the belief from the action it suggests as to condemn the one without condemning the other. No man holding a strong belief on one side of a question, or even wishing to hold a belief on one side, can investigate it with such fairness and completeness as if he were really in doubt and unbiased; so that the existence of a belief not founded on fair inquiry unfits a man for the performance of this necessary duty.

Nor is that truly a belief at all which has not some influence upon the actions of him who holds it. He who truly believes that which prompts him to an action has looked upon the action to lust after it, he has committed it already in his heart. If a belief is not realized immediately in open deeds, it is stored up for the guidance of the future. It goes to make a part of that aggregate of beliefs which is the link between sensation and action at every moment of all our lives, and which is so organized and compacted together that no part of it can be isolated from the rest, but every new addition modifies the structure of the whole. No real belief, however trifling and fragmentary it may seem, is ever truly insignificant; it prepares us to receive more of its like, confirms those which resembled it before, and weakens others; and so gradually it lays a stealthy train in our inmost thoughts, which may some day explode into overt action, and leave its stamp upon our character for ever.

And no one man's belief is in any case a private matter which concerns himself alone. Our lives are guided by that general conception of the course of things which has been created by society for social purposes. Our words, our phrases, our forms and processes and modes of thought, are common property, fashioned and perfected from age to age; an heir-loom which every succeeding generation inherits as a precious deposit and a sacred trust to be handed on to the next one, not unchanged but enlarged and purified, with some clear marks of its proper handiwork. Into this, for good or ill, is woven every belief of every man who has speech of his fellows. An awful privilege, and an awful responsibility, that we should help to create the world in which posterity will live.

In the two supposed cases which have been considered, it has been judged wrong to believe on insufficient evidence, or to nourish belief by suppressing doubts and avoiding investigation. The reason of this judg-ment is not far to seek: it is that in both these cases the belief held by one man was of great importance to other men. But forasmuch as no belief held by one man, however seemingly trivial the belief, and however obscure the believer, is ever actually insignificant or without its effect on the fate of mankind, we have no choice but to extend our judgment to all cases of belief whatever. Belief, that sacred faculty which prompts the decisions of our will, and knits into harmonious working all the compacted energies of our being, is ours not for ourselves, but for humanity. It is rightly used on truths which have been established by long experience and waiting toil, and which have stood in the fierce light of free and fearless questioning. Then it helps to bind men together, and to strengthen and direct their common action. It is desecrated when given to unproved and unquestioned statements, for the solace and private pleasure of the believer; to add a tinsel splendour to the plain straight road of our life and display a bright mirage beyond it; or even to drown the common sorrows of our kind by a self-deception which allows them not only to cast down, but also to degrade us. Whoso would deserve well of his fellows in this matter will guard the purity of his belief with a very fanaticism of jealous care, lest at any time it should rest on an unworthy object, and catch a stain which can never be wiped away.

It is not only the leader of men, statesman, philosopher, or poet, that owes this bounden duty to mankind. Every rustic who delivers in the village alehouse his slow, infrequent sentences, may help to kill or keep alive the fatal superstitions which clog his race. Every hard-worked wife of an artisan may transmit to her children beliefs which shall knit society together, or rend it in pieces. No simplicity of mind, no obscurity of station, can escape the universal duty of questioning all that we believe.

It is true that this duty is a hard one, and the doubt which comes out of it is often a very bitter thing. It leaves us bare and powerless where we thought that we were safe and strong. To know all about anything is to know how to deal with it under all circumstances. We feel much happier and more secure when we think we know precisely what to do, no matter what happens, than when we have lost our way and do not know where to turn. And if we have supposed ourselves to know all about anything, and to be capable of doing what is fit in regard to it, we naturally do not like to find that we are really ignorant and powerless, that we have to begin again at the beginning, and try to learn what the thing is and how it is to be dealt with—if indeed anything can be learnt about it. It is the sense of power attached to a sense of knowledge that makes men desirous of believing, and afraid of doubting.

This sense of power is the highest and best of pleasures when the belief on which it is founded is a true belief, and has been fairly earned by investigation. For then we may justly feel that it is common property, and holds good for others as well as for ourselves. Then we may be glad, not that *I* have learned secrets by which I am safer and stronger, but that *we men* have got mastery over more of the world; and we shall be strong, not for ourselves, but in the name of man and in his strength. But if the belief has been accepted on insufficient evidence, the pleasure is a stolen one. Not only does it deceive ourselves by giving us a sense of power which we do not really possess, but it is sinful, because it is stolen in defiance of our duty to mankind. That duty is to guard ourselves from such beliefs as from a pestilence, which may shortly master our own body and then spread to the rest of the town. What would be thought of one who, for the sake of a sweet fruit, should deliberately run the risk of bringing a plague upon his family and his neighbours?

And, as in other such cases, it is not the risk only which has to be considered; for a bad action is always bad at the time when it is done, no matter what happens afterwards. Every time we let ourselves believe for unworthy reasons, we weaken our powers of self-control, of doubting, of judicially and fairly weighing evidence. We all suffer severely enough from the maintenance and support of false beliefs and the fatally wrong actions which they lead to, and the evil born when one such belief is entertained is great and wide. But a greater and wider evil arises when the credulous character is maintained and supported, when a habit of believing for unworthy reasons is fostered and made permanent. If I steal money from any person, there may be no harm done by the mere transfer of possession; he may not feel the loss, or it may prevent him from using the money badly. But I cannot help doing this great wrong towards man, that I make myself dishonest. What hurts society is not that it should lose its property, but that it should become a den of thieves; for then it must cease to be society. This is why we ought not to do evil that good may come; for at any rate this great evil has come, that we have done evil and are made wicked thereby. In like manner, if I let myself believe anything on insufficient evidence, there may be no great harm done by the mere belief; it may be true after all, or I may never have occasion to exhibit it in outward acts. But I cannot help doing this great wrong towards man, that I make myself credulous. The danger to society is not merely that it should believe wrong things, though that is great enough; but that it should become credulous, and lose the habit of testing things and inquiring into them; for then it must sink back into savagery.

The harm which is done by credulity in a man is not confined to the fostering of a credulous character in others, and consequent support of false beliefs. Habitual want of care about what I believe leads to habitual want of care in others about the truth of what is told to me. Men speak the truth to one another when each reveres the truth in his own mind and in the other's mind; but how shall my friend revere the truth in my mind when I myself am careless about it, when I believe things because I want to believe them, and because they are comforting and pleasant? Will he not learn to cry, "Peace," to me, when there is no peace? By such a course I shall surround myself with a thick atmosphere of falsehood and fraud, and in that I must live. It may matter little to me, in my cloud-castle of sweet illusions and darling lies; but it matters much to man that I have made my neighbours ready to deceive. The credulous man is father to the liar and the cheat; he lives in the bosom of this his family, and it is no marvel if he should become even as they are. So closely are our duties knit together, that whoso shall keep the whole law, and yet offend in one point, he is guilty of all.

To sum up: it is wrong always, everywhere, and for anyone, to believe anything upon insufficient evidence.

If a man, holding a belief which he was taught in childhood or persuaded of afterwards, keeps down and pushes away any doubts which arise about it in his mind, purposely avoids the reading of books and the company of men that call in question or discuss it, and regards as impious those questions which cannot easily be asked without disturbing it—the life of that man is one long sin against mankind.

If this judgment seems harsh when applied to those simple souls who have never known better, who have been brought up from the cradle with a horror of doubt, and taught that their eternal welfare depends on *what* they believe, then it leads to the very serious question, *Who hath made Israel to sin?*

It may be permitted me to fortify this judgment with the sentence of Milton [1]—

> A man may be a heretic in the truth; and if he believe things only because his pastor says so, or the assembly so determine, without knowing other reason, though his belief be true, yet the very truth he holds becomes his heresy.

And with this famous aphorism of Coleridge [2]—

> He who begins by loving Christianity better than Truth, will proceed by loving his own sect or Church better than Christianity, and end in loving himself better than all.

Inquiry into the evidence of a doctrine is not to be made once for all, and then taken as finally settled. It is never lawful to stifle a doubt; for either it can be honestly answered by means of the inquiry already made, or else it proves that the inquiry was not complete.

"But," says one, "I am a busy man; I have no time for the long course of study which would be necessary to make me in any degree a competent judge of certain questions, or even able to understand the nature of the arguments." Then he should have no time to believe.

II. THE WEIGHT OF AUTHORITY

Are we then to become universal sceptics, doubting everything, afraid always to put one foot before the other until we have personally tested the firmness of the road? Are we to deprive ourselves of the help and guidance of that vast body of knowledge which is daily growing upon the world, because neither we nor any other one person can possibly test a hundredth part of it by immediate experiment or observation, and because it would not be completely proved if we did? Shall we steal and tell lies because we have had no personal experience wide enough to justify the belief that it is wrong to do so?

---

1. *Areopagitica.*
2. *Aids to Reflection.*

There is no practical danger that such consequences will ever follow from scrupulous care and self-control in the matter of belief. Those men who have most nearly done their duty in this respect have found that certain great principles, and these most fitted for the guidance of life, have stood out more and more clearly in proportion to the care and honesty with which they were tested, and have acquired in this way a practical certainty. The beliefs about right and wrong which guide our actions in dealing with men in society, and the beliefs about physical nature which guide our actions in dealing with animate and inanimate bodies, these never suffer from investigation; they can take care of themselves, without being propped up by "acts of faith," the clamour of paid advocates, or the suppression of contrary evidence. Moreover there are many cases in which it is our duty to act upon probabilities, although the evidence is not such as to justify present belief; because it is precisely by such action, and by observation of its fruits, that evidence is got which may justify future belief. So that we have no reason to fear lest a habit of conscientious inquiry should paralyse the actions of our daily life.

But because it is not enough to say, "It is wrong to believe on unworthy evidence," without saying also what evidence is worthy, we shall now go on to inquire under what circumstances it is lawful to believe on the testimony of others; and then, further, we shall inquire more generally when and why we may believe that which goes beyond our own experience, or even beyond the experience of mankind.

In what cases, then, let us ask in the first place, is the testimony of a man unworthy of belief? He may say that which is untrue either knowingly or unknowingly. In the first case he is lying, and his moral character is to blame; in the second case he is ignorant or mistaken, and it is only his knowledge or his judgment which is in fault. In order that we may have the right to accept his testimony as ground for believing what he says, we must have reasonable grounds for trusting his *veracity*, that he is really trying to speak the truth so far as he knows it; his *knowledge*, that he has had opportunities of knowing the truth about this matter; and his *judgment*, that he has made proper use of those opportunities in coming to the conclusion which he affirms.

However plain and obvious these reasons may be, so that no man of ordinary intelligence, reflecting upon the matter, could fail to arrive at them, it is nevertheless true that a great many persons do habitually disregard them in weighing testimony. Of the two questions, equally important to the trustworthiness of a witness, "Is he dishonest?" and "May he be mistaken?" the majority of mankind are perfectly satisfied if *one* can, with some show of probability, be answered in the negative. The excellent moral character of a man is alleged as ground for accepting his statements about things which he cannot possibly have known. A Mohammedan, for example, will tell us that the character of his Prophet was so noble and majestic that it commands the reverence even of those who do not believe in his mission. So admirable was his moral teaching, so wisely put together the great social machine which he created, that his precepts have not only been accepted by a great portion of mankind, but have actually been obeyed. His institutions have on the one hand rescued the Negro from savagery, and on the other hand have taught civilization to the advancing West; and although the races which held the highest forms of his faith, and most fully embodied his mind and thought, have all been conquered and swept away by barbaric tribes, yet the history of their marvellous attainments remains as an imperishable glory to Islam. Are we to doubt the word of a man so great and so good? Can we suppose that this magnificent genius, this splendid moral hero, has lied to us about the most solemn and sacred matters? The testimony of Mohammed is clear, that there is but one God, and that he, Mohammed, is his prophet; that if we believe in him we shall enjoy everlasting felicity, but that if we do not we shall be damned. This testimony rests on the most awful of foundations, the revelation of heaven itself; for was he not visited by the angel Gabriel, as he fasted and prayed in his desert cave, and allowed to enter into the blessed fields of paradise? Surely God is God and Mohammed is the Prophet of God.

What should we answer to this Mussulman? First, no doubt, we should be tempted to take exception against his view of the character of the Prophet and the uniformly beneficial influence of Islam: before we could go with him altogether in these matters it might seem that we should have to forget many terrible things of which we have heard or read. But if we chose to grant him all these assumptions, for the sake of argument, and because it is difficult both for the faithful and for infidels to discuss them fairly and without passion, still we should have something to say which takes away the ground of his belief, and therefore shows that it is wrong to entertain it. Namely this: the character of Mohammed is excellent evidence that he was honest and spoke the truth so far as he knew it; but it is no evidence at all that he knew what the truth was. What means could he have of knowing that the form which appeared to him to be the angel Gabriel was not a hallucination, and that his apparent visit to paradise was not a dream? Grant that he himself was fully persuaded and honestly believed that he had the guidance of heaven, and was the vehicle of a supernatural revelation, how could he know that this strong conviction was not a mistake? Let us put ourselves in his place; we shall find that the more completely we endeavour to realize what passed through his mind, the more clearly we shall perceive that the Prophet could have had no adequate ground for the belief in his own inspiration. It is most probable that he himself never doubted of the matter, or thought of asking the question; but we are in the position of those to whom the question has been asked, and who are bound to answer it. It is known to medical observers that solitude and want of food are powerful means of producing delusion and of fostering a tendency to mental disease. Let us suppose, then, that I, like Mohammed, go into desert places to fast and pray; what things can happen to me which will give me the right to believe that I am divinely inspired? Suppose that I get information, apparently from a celestial visitor, which upon being tested is found to be correct. I cannot be sure, in the first place, that the celestial visitor is not a figment of my own mind, and that the information did not come to me, unknown at the time to my consciousness, through some subtle channel of sense. But if my visitor were a real visitor, and for a long time gave me information which was found to be trustworthy, this would indeed be good ground for trusting him in the future as to such matters as fall within human powers of verification; but it would not be ground for trusting his testimony as to any other matters. For although his tested character would justify me in believing that he spoke the truth so far as he knew, yet the same question would present itself—what ground is there for supposing that he knows?

Even if my supposed visitor had given me such information, subsequently verified by me, as proved him to have means of knowledge about verifiable matters far exceeding my own; this would not justify me in believing what he said about matters that are not at present capable of verification by man. It would be ground for interesting conjecture, and for the hope that, as the fruit of our patient inquiry, we might by and by attain to such a means of verification as should rightly turn conjecture into belief. For belief belongs to man, and to the guidance of human affairs: no belief is real unless it guide our actions, and those very actions supply a test of its truth.

But, it may be replied, the acceptance of Islam as a system is just that action which is prompted by belief in the mission of the Prophet, and which will serve for a test of its truth. Is it possible to believe that a system which has succeeded so well is really founded upon a delusion? Not only have individual saints found joy and peace in believing, and verified those spiritual experiences which are promised to the faithful, but nations also have been raised from savagery or barbarism to a higher social state.

Surely we are at liberty to say that the belief has been acted upon, and that it has been verified.

It requires, however, but little consideration to show that what has really been verified is not at all the supernal character of the Prophet's mission, or the trustworthiness of his authority in matters which we ourselves cannot test, but only his practical wisdom in certain very mundane things. The fact that believers have found joy and peace in believing gives us the right to say that the doctrine is a comfortable doctrine, and pleasant to the soul; but it does not give us the right to say that it is true. And the question which our conscience is always asking about that which we are tempted to believe is not, "Is it comfortable and pleasant?" but, "Is it true?" That the Prophet preached certain doctrines, and predicted that spiritual comfort would be found in them, proves only his sympathy with human nature and his knowledge of it; but it does not prove his superhuman knowledge of theology.

And if we admit for the sake of argument (for it seems that we cannot do more) that the progress made by Moslem nations in certain cases was really due to the system formed and sent forth into the world by Mohammed, we are not at liberty to conclude from this that he was inspired to declare the truth about things which we cannot verify. We are only at liberty to infer the excellence of his moral precepts, or of the means which he devised for so working upon men as so get them obeyed, or of the social and political machinery which he set up. And it would require a great amount of careful examination into the history of those nations to determine which of these things had the greater share in the result. So that here again it is the Prophet's knowledge of human nature, and his sympathy with it, that are verified; not his divine inspiration, or his knowledge of theology.

If there were only one Prophet, indeed, it might well seem a difficult and even an ungracious task to decide upon what points we would trust him, and on what we would doubt his authority; seeing what help and furtherance all men have gained in all ages from those who saw more clearly, who felt more strongly, and who sought the truth with more single heart than their weaker brethren. But there is not only one Prophet; and while the consent of many upon that which, as men, they had real means of knowing and did know, has endured to the end, and been honourably built into the great fabric of human knowledge, the diverse witness of some about that which they did not and could not know remains as a warning to us that to exaggerate the prophetic authority is to misuse it, and to dishonour those who have sought only to help and further us after their power. It is hardly in human nature that a man should quite accurately gauge the limits of his own insight; but it is the duty of those who profit by his work to consider carefully where he may have been carried beyond it. If we must needs embalm his possible errors along with his solid achievements, and use his authority as an excuse for believing what he cannot have known, we make of his goodness an occasion to sin.

To consider only one other such witness: the followers of the Buddha have at least as much right to appeal to individual and social experience in support of the authority of the Eastern saviour. The special mark of his religion, it is said, that in which it has never been surpassed, is the comfort and consolation which it gives to the sick and sorrowful, the tender sympathy with which it soothes and assuages all the natural griefs of men. And surely no triumph of social morality can be greater or nobler than that which has kept nearly half the human race from persecuting in the name of religion. If we are to trust the accounts of his early followers, he believed himself to have come upon earth with a divine and cosmic mission to set rolling the wheel of the law. Being a prince, he divested himself of his kingdom, and of his free will became acquainted with misery, that he might learn how to meet and subdue it. Could such a man speak falsely about solemn things? And as for his knowledge, was he not a man miraculous with powers more than man's? He was born of woman without the help of man; he rose into the air and was transfigured before his kinsmen; at last he went up bodily into heaven from the top of Adam's Peak. Is not his word to be believed in when he testifies of heavenly things?

If there were only he, and no other, with such claims! But there is Mohammed with his testimony; we cannot choose but listen to them both. The Prophet tells us that there is one God, and that we shall live for ever in joy or misery, according as we believe in the Prophet or not. The Buddha says that there is no God, and that we shall be annihilated by and by if we are good enough. Both cannot be infallibly inspired; one or the other must have been the victim of a delusion, and thought he knew that which he really did not know. Who shall dare to say which? And how can we justify ourselves in believing that the other was not also deluded?

We are led, then, to these judgments following. The goodness and greatness of a man do not justify us in accepting a belief upon the warrant of his authority, unless there are reasonable grounds for supposing that he knew the truth of what he was saying. And there can be no grounds for supposing that a man knows that which we, without ceasing to be men, could not be supposed to verify.

If a chemist tells me, who am no chemist, that a certain substance can be made by putting together other substances in certain proportions and subjecting them to a known process, I am quite justified in believing this upon his authority, unless I know anything against his character or his judgment. For his professional training is one which tends to encourage veracity and the honest pursuit of truth, and to produce a dislike of hasty conclusions and slovenly investigation. And I have reasonable ground for supposing that he knows the truth of what he is saying, for although I am no chemist, I can be made to understand so much of the methods and processes of the science as makes it conceivable to me that, without ceasing to be man, I might verify the statement. I may never actually verify it, or even see any experiment which goes towards verifying it; but still I have quite reason enough to justify me in believing that the verification is within the reach of human appliances and powers, and in particular that it has been actually performed by my informant. His result, the belief to which he has been led by his inquiries, is valid not only for himself but for others; it is watched and tested by those who are working in the same ground, and who know that no greater service can be rendered to science than the purification of accepted results from the errors which may have crept into them. It is in this way that the result becomes common property, a right object of belief, which is a social affair and matter of public business. Thus it is to be observed that his authority is valid because there are those who question it and verify it; that it is precisely this process of examining and purifying that keeps alive among investigators the love of that which shall stand all possible tests, the sense of public responsibility as of those whose work, if well done, shall remain as the enduring heritage of mankind.

But if my chemist tells me that an atom of oxygen has existed unaltered in weight and rate of vibration throughout all time, I have no right to believe this on his authority, for it is a thing which he cannot know without ceasing to be man. He may quite honestly believe that this statement is a fair inference from his experiments, but in that case his judgment is at fault. A very simple consideration of the character of experiments would show him that they never can lead to results of such a kind; that being themselves only approximate and limited, they cannot give us knowledge which is exact and universal. No eminence of character and genius can give a man authority enough to justify us in believing him when he makes statements implying exact or universal knowledge.

Again, an Arctic explorer may tell us that in a given latitude and longitude he has experienced such and such a degree of cold, that the sea was of such a depth, and the ice of such a character. We should be quite right to believe him, in the absence of any stain upon his veracity. It is conceivable that we might, without ceasing to be men, go there and verify his statement; it can be tested by the witness of his companions, and there is adequate ground for supposing that he knows the truth of what he is saying. But if an old whaler tells us that the ice is three hundred feet thick all the way up to the Pole, we shall not be justified in believing him. For although the statement may be capable of verification by man, it is certainly not capable of verification by *him*, with any means and appliances which he has possessed; and he must have persuaded himself of the truth of it by some means which does not attach any credit to his testimony. Even if, therefore, the matter affirmed is within the reach of human knowledge, we have no right to accept it upon authority unless it is within the reach of our informant's knowledge.

What shall we say of that authority, more venerable and august than any individual witness, the time-honoured tradition of the human race? An atmosphere of beliefs and conceptions has been formed by the labours and struggles of our forefathers, which enables us to breathe amid the various and complex circumstances of our life. It is around and about us and within us; we cannot think except in the forms and processes of thought which it supplies. Is it possible to doubt and to test it? And if possible, is it right?

We shall find reason to answer that it is not only possible and right, but our bounden duty; that the main purpose of the tradition itself is to supply us with the means of asking questions, of testing and inquiring into things; that if we misuse it, and take it as a collection of cut and dried statements, to be accepted without further inquiry, we are not only injuring ourselves here, but by refusing to do our part towards the building up of the fabric which shall be inherited by our children, we are tending to cut off ourselves and our race from the human line.

Let us first take care to distinguish a kind of tradition which especially requires to be examined and called in question, because it especially shrinks from inquiry. Suppose that a medicine man in Central Africa tells his tribe that a certain powerful medicine in his tent will be propitiated if they kill their cattle; and that the tribe believe him. Whether the medicine was propitiated or not, there are no means of verifying, but the cattle are gone. Still the belief may be kept up in the tribe that propitiation has been effected in this way; and in a later generation it will be all the easier for another medicine man to persuade them to a similar act. Here the only reason for belief is that everybody has believed the thing for so long that it must be true. And yet the belief was founded on fraud, and has been propagated by credulity. That man will undoubtedly do right, and be a friend of men, who shall call it in question and see that there is no evidence for it, help his neighbours to see as he does, and even, if need be, go into the holy tent and break the medicine.

The rule which should guide us in such cases is simple and obvious enough: that the aggregate testimony of our neighbours is subject to the same conditions as the testimony of any one of them. Namely, we have no right to believe a thing true because everybody says so, unless there are good grounds for believing that some one person at least has the means of knowing what is true, and is speaking the truth so far as he knows it. However many nations and generations of men are brought into the witness-box, they cannot testify to anything which they do not know. Every man who has accepted the statement from somebody else, without himself testing and verifying it, is out of court; his word is worth nothing at all. And when we get back at last to the true birth and beginning of the statement, two serious questions must be disposed of in regard to him who first made it: was he mistaken in thinking that he *knew* about this matter, or was he lying?

This last question is unfortunately a very actual and practical one even to us at this day and in this country. We have no occasion to go to La Salette, or to Central Africa, or to Lourdes, for examples of immoral and debasing superstition. It is only too possible for a child to grow up in London surrounded by an atmosphere of beliefs fit only for the savage, which have in our own time been founded in fraud and propagated by credulity.

Laying aside, then, such tradition as is handed on without testing by successive generations, let us consider that which is truly built up out of the common experience of mankind. This great fabric is for the guidance of our thoughts, and through them of our actions, both in the moral and in the material world. In the moral world, for example, it gives us the conceptions of right in general, of justice, of truth, of beneficence, and the like. These are given as conceptions, not as statements or propositions; they answer to certain definite instincts, which are certainly within us, however they came there. That it is right to be beneficent is matter of immediate personal experience; for when a man retires within himself and there finds something, wider and more lasting than his solitary personality, which says, "I want to do right," as well as, "I want to do good to man," he can verify by direct observation that one instinct is founded upon and agrees fully with the other. And it is his duty so to verify this and all similar statements.

The tradition says also, at a definite place and time, that such and such actions are just, or true, or beneficent. For all such rules a further inquiry is necessary, since they are sometimes established by an authority other than that of the moral sense founded on experience. Until recently, the moral tradition of our own country—and indeed of all Europe—taught that it was beneficent to give money indiscriminately to beggars. But the questioning of this rule, and investigation into it, led men to see that true beneficence is that which helps a man to do the work which he is most fitted for, not that which keeps and encourages him in idleness; and that to neglect this distinction in the present is to prepare pauperism and misery for the future. By this testing and discussion, not only has practice been purified and made more beneficent, but the very conception of beneficence has been made wider and wiser. Now here the great social heirloom consists of two parts: the instinct of beneficence, which makes a certain side of our nature, when predominant, wish to do good to men; and the intellectual conception of beneficence, which we can compare with any proposed course of conduct and ask, "Is this beneficent or not?" By the continual asking and answering of such questions the conception grows in breadth and distinctness, and the instinct becomes strengthened and purified. It appears then that the great use of the conception, the intellectual part of the heirloom, is to enable us to ask questions; that it grows and is kept straight by means of these questions; and if we do not use it for that purpose we shall gradually lose it altogether, and be left with a mere code of regulations which cannot rightly be called morality at all.

Such considerations apply even more obviously and clearly, if possible, to the store of beliefs and conceptions which our fathers have amassed for us in respect of the material world. We are ready to laugh at the rule of thumb of the Australian, who continues to tie his hatchet to the side of the handle, although the Birmingham fitter has made a hole on purpose for him to put the handle in. His people have tied up hatchets so for ages: who is he that he should set himself up against their wisdom? He has sunk so low that he cannot do what some of them must have done in the far distant past—call in question an established usage, and invent or learn something better. Yet here, in the dim beginning of knowledge, where science and art are one, we find only the same simple rule which applies to the highest and deepest growths of that cosmic tree; to its loftiest flower-tipped branches as well as to the profoundest of its hidden roots;

the rule, namely, that what is stored up and handed down to us is rightly used by those who act as the makers acted, when they stored it up; those who use it to ask further questions, to examine, to investigate; who try honestly and solemnly to find out what is the right way of looking at things and of dealing with them.

A question rightly asked is already half answered, said Jacobi; we may add that the method of solution is the other half of the answer, and that the actual result counts for nothing by the side of these two. For an example let us go to the telegraph, where theory and practice, grown each to years of discretion, are marvellously wedded for the fruitful service of men. Ohm found that the strength of an electric current is directly proportional to the strength of the battery which produces it, and inversely as the length of the wire along which it has to travel. This is called Ohm's law; but the result, regarded as a statement to be believed, is not the valuable part of it. The first half is the question: what relation holds good between these quantities? So put, the question involves already the conception of strength of current, and of strength of battery, as quantities to be measured and compared; it hints clearly that these are the things to be attended to in the study of electric currents. The second half is the method of investigation; how to measure these quantities, what instruments are required for the experiment, and how are they to be used? The student who begins to learn about electricity is not asked to believe in Ohm's law: he is made to understand the question, he is placed before the apparatus, and he is taught to verify it. He learns to do things, not to think he knows things; to use instruments and to ask questions, not to accept a traditional statement. The question which required a genius to ask it rightly is answered by a tyro. If Ohm's law were suddenly lost and forgotten by all men, while the question and the method of solution remained, the result could be rediscovered in an hour. But the result by itself, if known to a people who could not comprehend the value of the question or the means of solving it, would be like a watch in the hands of a savage who could not wind it up, or an iron steamship worked by Spanish engineers.

In regard, then, to the sacred tradition of humanity, we learn that it consists, not in propositions or statements which are to be accepted and believed on the authority of the tradition, but in questions rightly asked, in conceptions which enable us to ask further questions, and in methods of answering questions. The value of all these things depends on their being tested day by day. The very sacredness of the precious deposit imposes upon us the duty and the responsibility of testing it, of purifying and enlarging it to the utmost of our power. He who makes use of its results to stifle his own doubts, or to hamper the inquiry of others, is guilty of a sacrilege which centuries shall never be able to blot out. When the labours and questionings of honest and brave men shall have built up the fabric of known truth to a glory which we in this generation can neither hope for nor imagine, in that pure and holy temple he shall have no part nor lot, but his name and his works shall be cast out into the darkness of oblivion for ever.

III. THE LIMITS OF INFERENCE

The question in what cases we may believe that which goes beyond our experience, is a very large and delicate one, extending to the whole range of scientific method, and requiring a considerable increase in the application of it before it can be answered with anything approaching to completeness. But one rule, lying on the threshold of the subject, of extreme simplicity and vast practical importance, may here be touched upon and shortly laid down.

A little reflection will show us that every belief, even the simplest and most fundamental, goes beyond experience when regarded as a guide to our actions. A burnt child dreads the fire, because it believes that the fire will burn it to-day just as it did yesterday; but this belief goes beyond experience, and assumes that the unknown fire of to-day is like the known fire of yesterday. Even the belief that the child was burnt yesterday goes beyond *present* experience, which contains only the memory of a burning, and not the burning itself; it assumes, therefore, that this memory is trustworthy, although we know that a memory may often be mistaken. But if it is to be used as a guide to action, as a hint of what the future is to be, it must assume something about that future, namely, that it will be consistent with the supposition that the burning really took place yesterday; which is going beyond experience. Even the fundamental "I am," which cannot be doubted, is no guide to action until it takes to itself "I shall be," which goes beyond experience. The question is not, therefore, "May we believe what goes beyond experience?" for this is involved in the very nature of belief; but "How far and in what manner may we add to our experience in forming our beliefs?"

And an answer, of utter simplicity and universality, is suggested by the example we have taken: a burnt child dreads the fire. We may go beyond experience by assuming that what we do not know is like what we do know; or, in other words, we may add to our experience on the assumption of a uniformity in nature. What this uniformity precisely is, how we grow in the knowledge of it from generation to generation, these are questions which for the present we lay aside, being content to examine two instances which may serve to make plainer the nature of the rule.

From certain observations made with the spectroscope, we infer the existence of hydrogen in the sun. By looking into the spectroscope when the sun is shining on its slit, we see certain definite bright lines: and experiments made upon bodies on the earth have taught us that when these bright lines are seen hydrogen is the source of them. We assume, then, that the unknown bright lines in the sun are like the known bright lines of the laboratory, and that hydrogen in the sun behaves as hydrogen under similar circumstances would behave on the earth.

But are we not trusting our spectroscope too much? Surely, having found it to be trustworthy for terrestrial substances, where its statements can be verified by man, we are justified in accepting its testimony in other like cases; but not when it gives us information about things in the sun, where its testimony cannot be directly verified by man.

Certainly, we want to know a little more before this inference can be justified; and fortunately we do know this. The spectroscope testifies to exactly the same thing in the two cases; namely, that light vibrations of a certain rate are being sent through it. Its construction is such that if it were wrong about this in one case, it would be wrong in the other. When we come to look into the matter, we find that we have really assumed the matter of the sun to be like the matter of the earth, made up of a certain number of distinct substances; and that each of these, when very hot, has a distinct rate of vibration, by which it may be recognized and singled out from the rest. But this is the kind of assumption which we are justified in using when we add to our experience. It is an assumption of uniformity in nature, and can only be checked by comparison with many similar assumptions which we have to make in other such cases.

But is this a true belief, of the existence of hydrogen in the sun? Can it help in the right guidance of human action?

Certainly not, if it is accepted on unworthy grounds, and without some understanding of the process by which it is got at. But when this process is taken in as the ground of the belief, it becomes a very serious and practical matter. For if there is no hydrogen in the sun, the spectroscope—that is to say, the measurement of rates of vibration—must be an uncertain guide in recognizing different substances; and consequently it ought not to be used in chemical analysis—in assaying, for example—to the great saving of time, trouble, and money. Whereas the acceptance of the spectroscopic method as trustworthy has enriched us not only with new metals, which is a great thing, but with new processes of investigation, which is vastly greater.

For another example, let us consider the way in which we infer the truth of an historical event—say the siege of Syracuse in the Peloponnesian War. Our experience is that manuscripts exist which are said to be and which call themselves manuscripts of the history of Thucydides; that in other manuscripts, stated to be by later historians, he is described as living during the time of the war; and that books, supposed to date from the revival of learning, tell us how these manuscripts had been preserved and were then acquired. We find also that men do not, as a rule, forge books and histories without a special motive; we assume that in this respect men in the past were like men in the present; and we observe that in this case no special motive was present. That is, we add to our experience on the assumption of a uniformity in the characters of men. Because our knowledge of this uniformity is far less complete and exact than our knowledge of that which obtains in physics, inferences of the historical kind are more precarious and less exact than inferences in many other sciences.

But if there is any special reason to suspect the character of the persons who wrote or transmitted certain books, the case becomes altered. If a group of documents give internal evidence that they were produced among people who forged books in the names of others, and who, in describing events, suppressed those things which did not suit them, while they amplified such as did suit them; who not only committed these crimes, but gloried in them as proofs of humility and zeal; then we must say that upon such documents no true historical inference can be founded, but only unsatisfactory conjecture.

We may, then, add to our experience on the assumption of a uniformity in nature; we may fill in our picture of what is and has been, as experience gives it us, in such a way as to make the whole consistent with this uniformity. And practically demonstrative inference—that which gives us a right to believe in the result of it—is a clear showing that in no other way than by the truth of this result can the uniformity of nature be saved.

No evidence, therefore, can justify us in believing the truth of a statement which is contrary to, or outside of, the uniformity of nature. If our experience is such that it cannot be filled up consistently with uniformity, all we have a right to conclude is that there is something wrong somewhere; but the possibility of inference is taken away; we must rest in our experience, and not go beyond it at all. If an event really happened which was not a part of the uniformity of nature, it would have two properties:

no evidence could give the right to believe it to any except those whose actual experience it was; and no inference worthy of belief could be founded upon it at all.

Are we then bound to believe that nature is absolutely and universally uniform? Certainly not; we have no right to believe anything of this kind. The rule only tells us that in forming beliefs which go beyond our experience, we may make the assumption that nature is practically uniform so far as we are concerned. Within the range of human action and verification, we may form, by help of this assumption, actual beliefs; beyond it, only those hypotheses which serve for the more accurate asking of questions.

To sum up:

We may believe what goes beyond our experience, only when it is inferred from that experience by the assumption that what we do not know is like what we know.

We may believe the statement of another person, when there is reasonable ground for supposing that he knows the matter of which he speaks, and that he is speaking the truth so far as he knows it.

It is wrong in all cases to believe on insufficient evidence; and where it is presumption to doubt and to investigate, there it is worse than presumption to believe.

"The Ethics of Belief" is from a collection of Clifford's essays entitled LECTURES AND ESSAYS.

William James [1]

1842–1910

William James was both a philosopher and a psychologist. His greatest work, the *Principles of Psychology*,[2] makes major contributions to both fields. The *Principles* was published in 1890.

Earlier than that, he had begun writing articles for the learned journals and lecturing to an ever-increasing public. The first volume of his lectures to be collected appeared in 1897 under the title of the first lecture, *The Will to Believe*. His study of religious belief, already manifest in this volume, found fullest expression in *The Varieties of Religious Experience*, 1902. His most important philosophical works are *Pragmatism*, 1907, *A Pluralistic Universe* and *The Meaning of Truth*, both of which appeared in 1909, and *Essays in Radical Empiricism*, 1912.

One attraction of James the psychologist lies in his continually going beyond the bounds of his science to raise the broader questions of philosophy. Yet it is no less true that a large part of the fascination of James the philosopher is found in his psychological interest and insight. In *The Sentiment of Rationality*, reprinted here from *The Will to Believe*, James raises what is fundamentally a problem of meaning and method: what is to count as an explanation? Other men have written about method, notably Aristotle in the *Posterior Analytics* and Descartes in the *Discourse on Method*. But neither of them raises, as James does, the question of what feeling an explanation has to satisfy and whether temperament predisposes a person to favor one type of explanation over another. Thus in this essay James analyzes idealism and materialism in terms of the sentiments which they appeal to and satisfy. This leads him later on, in *Pragmatism*, to pro-

---

[1] For a biography of William James, see Vol. 7, pp. 137–138, in this set.
[2] See *Great Books of the Western World*, Vol. 53.

pose that all philosophies can be divided into the tender and the tough-minded. However, since both sentiments are to be found in man, he claims that a true and sound philosophy will somehow have to satisfy both.

Recognizing the influence in the fixing of belief of "passional tendencies" or "our willing nature," James attacks what he considers the crudity of scientists who would dismiss all religious belief for not being based on rational evidence. With Pascal, whom he quotes, he appeals to the reasons of the heart "which the reason does not understand." These, he argues, enter into the judgments of science as well as into those of religion. In this, he emphasizes what more recently has come to be called personal as distinguished from abstractive and objective knowledge.

Another side to his defense of religious belief leads to the philosophy of pragmatism. *The Will to Believe* is dedicated to James's old friend Charles Sanders Peirce, to whom he attributes the original idea of pragmatism. A simplified version of the pragmatic principle, but one from which James himself would not shrink, might be expressed thus: *A belief is true if it works.* James accordingly asks us to test our beliefs by looking to their effects or consequences. Such, he points out, is the ordinary procedure by which science tests a hypothesis. From this James goes on to emphasize the importance of the practical in even our most theoretical beliefs.

James also insists upon the practical importance of theoretical beliefs. This is reflected in his conviction that philosophy is too important to be left to the experts. It is an enterprise in which every man is engaged. The two essays printed here James calls "essays in popular philosophy." They are popular not only or mainly because they are written in a fairly nontechnical and even racy style, but because they reflect James's deep conviction that philosophy is every man's business.

The Will to Believe

In the recently published *Life* by Leslie Stephen of his brother, Fitzjames, there is an account of a school to which the latter went when he was a boy. The teacher, a certain Mr. Guest, used to converse with his pupils in this wise: "Gurney, what is the difference between justification and sanctification? Stephen, prove the omnipotence of God!" etc. In the midst of our Harvard freethinking and indifference we are prone to imagine that here at your good old orthodox College conversation continues to be somewhat upon this order; and to show you that we at Harvard have not lost all interest in these vital subjects, I have brought with me tonight something like a sermon on justification by faith to read to you—I mean an essay in justification *of* faith, a defense of our right to adopt a believing attitude in religious matters, in spite of the fact that our merely logical intellect may not have been coerced. "The Will to Believe," accordingly, is the title of my paper.

I have long defended to my own students the lawfulness of voluntarily adopted faith; but as soon as they have got well imbued with the logical spirit, they have as a rule refused to admit my contention to be lawful philosophically, even though in point of fact they were personally all the time chock-full of some faith or other themselves. I am all the while, however, so profoundly convinced that my own position is correct, that your invitation has seemed to me a good occasion to make my statements more clear. Perhaps your minds will be more open than those with which I have hitherto had to deal. I will be as little technical as I can, though I must begin by setting up some technical distinctions that will help us in the end.

Let us give the name of *hypothesis* to anything that may be proposed to our belief; and just as the electricians speak of live and dead wires, let us speak of any hypothesis as either *live* or *dead*. A live hypothesis is one which appeals as a real possibility to him to whom it is proposed. If I ask you to believe in the Mahdi, the notion makes no electric connection with your nature—it refuses to scintillate with any credibility at all. As a hypothesis it is completely dead. To an Arab, however (even if he be not one of the Mahdi's followers), the hypothesis is among the mind's possibilities: it is alive. This shows that deadness and liveness in a hypothesis are not intrinsic properties, but relations to the individual thinker. They are measured by his willingness to act. The maximum of liveness in a hypothesis means willingness to act irrevocably. Practically, that means belief; but there is some believing tendency wherever there is willingness to act at all.

Next, let us call the decision between two hypotheses an *option*. Options may be of several kinds. They may be—1, *living* or *dead;* 2, *forced* or *avoidable;* 3, *momentous* or *trivial;* and for our purposes we may call an option a *genuine* option when it is of the forced, living, and momentous kind.

1. A living option is one in which both hypotheses are live ones. If I say to you: "Be a theosophist or be a Mohammedan," it is probably a dead option, because for you neither hypothesis is likely to be alive. But if I say: "Be an agnostic or be a Christian," it is otherwise: trained as you are, each hypothesis makes some appeal, however small, to your belief.

2. Next, if I say to you: "Choose between going out with your umbrella or without it," I do not offer you a genuine option, for it is not forced. You can easily avoid it by not going out at all. Similarly, if I say, "Either love me or hate me," "Either call my theory true or call it false," your option is avoidable. You may remain indifferent to me, neither loving nor hating, and you may decline to offer any judgment as to my theory. But if I say, "Either accept this truth or go without it," I put on you a forced option, for there is no standing place outside of the alternative. Every dilemma based on a complete logical disjunction, with no possibility of not choosing, is an option of this forced kind.

3. Finally, if I were Dr. Nansen and proposed to you to join my North Pole expedition, your option would be momentous; for this would probably be your only similar opportunity, and your choice now would either exclude you from the North Pole sort of immortality altogether or put at least the chance of it into your hands. He who refuses to embrace a unique opportunity loses the prize as surely as if he tried and failed. Per contra, the option is trivial when the opportunity is not unique, when the stake is insignificant, or when the decision is reversible if it later prove unwise. Such trivial options abound in the scientific life. A chemist finds a hy-

pothesis live enough to spend a year in its verification: he believes in it to that extent. But if his experiments prove inconclusive either way, he is quit for his loss of time, no vital harm being done.

It will facilitate our discussion if we keep all these distinctions well in mind.

The next matter to consider is the actual psychology of human opinion. When we look at certain facts, it seems as if our passional and volitional nature lay at the root of all our convictions. When we look at others, it seems as if they could do nothing when the intellect had once said its say. Let us take the latter facts up first.

Does it not seem preposterous on the very face of it to talk of our opinions being modifiable at will? Can our will either help or hinder our intellect in its perceptions of truth? Can we, by just willing it, believe that Abraham Lincoln's existence is a myth, and that the portraits of him in McClure's Magazine are all of someone else? Can we, by any effort of our will, or by any strength of wish that it were true, believe ourselves well and about when we are roaring with rheumatism in bed, or feel certain that the sum of the two one-dollar bills in our pocket must be a hundred dollars? We can *say* any of these things, but we are absolutely impotent to believe them; and of just such things is the whole fabric of the truths that we do believe in made up—matters of fact, immediate or remote, as Hume said, and relations between ideas, which are either there or not there for us if we see them so, and which if not there cannot be put there by any action of our own.

In Pascal's *Thoughts* there is a celebrated passage known in literature as Pascal's wager. In it he tries to force us into Christianity by reasoning as if our concern with truth resembled our concern with the stakes in a game of chance. Translated freely his words are these: You must either believe or not believe that God is—which will you do? Your human reason cannot say. A game is going on between you and the nature of things which at the day of judgment will bring out either heads or tails. Weigh what your gains and your losses would be if you should stake all you have on heads, or God's existence: if you win in such case, you gain eternal beatitude; if you lose, you lose nothing at all. If there were an infinity of chances, and only one for God in this wager, still you ought to stake your all on God; for though you surely risk a finite loss by this procedure, any finite loss is reasonable, even a certain one is reasonable, if there is but the possibility of infinite gain. Go, then, and take holy water, and have masses said; belief will come and stupefy your scruples—*Cela vous fera croire et vous abêtira*. Why should you not? At bottom, what have you to lose?

You probably feel that when religious faith expresses itself thus, in the language of the gaming table, it is put to its last trumps. Surely Pascal's own personal belief in masses and holy water had far other springs; and this celebrated page of his is but an argument for others, a last desperate snatch at a weapon against the hardness of the unbelieving heart. We feel that a faith in masses and holy water adopted wilfully after such a mechanical calculation would lack the inner soul of faith's reality; and if we were ourselves in the place of the Deity, we should probably take particular pleasure in cutting off believers of this pattern from their infinite reward. It is evident that unless there be some pre-existing tendency to believe in masses and holy water, the option offered to the will by Pascal is not a living option. Certainly no Turk ever took to masses and holy water on its account; and even to us Protestants these means of salvation seem such foregone impossibilities that Pascal's logic, invoked for them specifically, leaves us unmoved. As well might the Mahdi write to us, saying, "I am the Expected One whom God has created in his effulgence. You shall be infinitely happy if you confess me; otherwise you shall be cut off from the light of the sun. Weigh, then, your infinite gain if I am genuine against your finite sacrifice if I am not!" His logic would be that of Pascal; but he would vainly use it on us, for the hypothesis he offers us is dead. No tendency to act on it exists in us to any degree.

The talk of believing by our volition seems, then, from one point of view, simply silly. From another point of view it is worse than silly, it is vile. When one turns to the magnificent edifice of the physical sciences, and sees how it was reared; what thousands of disinterested moral lives of men lie buried in its mere foundations; what patience and postponement, what choking down of preference, what submission to the icy laws of outer fact are wrought into its very stones and mortar; how absolutely impersonal it stands in its vast augustness—then how besotted and contemptible seems every little sentimentalist who comes blowing his voluntary smoke wreaths, and pretending to decide things from out of his private dream! Can we wonder if those bred in the rugged and manly school of science should feel like spewing such subjectivism out of their mouths? The whole system of loyalties which grow up in the schools of science go dead against its toleration; so that it is only natural that those who have caught the scientific fever should pass over to the opposite extreme, and write sometimes as if the incorruptibly truthful intellect

ought positively to prefer bitterness and unacceptableness to the heart in
its cup.

> It fortifies my soul to know
> That, though I perish, Truth is so—

sings Clough, while Huxley exclaims: "My only consolation lies in the reflection that, however bad our posterity may become, so far as they hold
by the plain rule of not pretending to believe what they have no reason to
believe, because it may be to their advantage so to pretend [the word
'pretend' is surely here redundant], they will not have reached the lowest
depth of immorality." And that delicious *enfant terrible* Clifford writes:
"Belief is desecrated when given to unproved and unquestioned statements for the solace and private pleasure of the believer. . . . Whoso
would deserve well of his fellows in this matter will guard the purity of
his belief with a very fanaticism of jealous care, lest at any time it should
rest on an unworthy object, and catch a stain which can never be wiped
away. . . . If [a] belief has been accepted on insufficient evidence
[even though the belief be true, as Clifford on the same page explains]
the pleasure is a stolen one. . . . It is sinful because it is stolen in defiance
of our duty to mankind. That duty is to guard ourselves from such beliefs
as from a pestilence which may shortly master our own body and then
spread to the rest of the town. . . . It is wrong always, everywhere, and
for every one, to believe anything upon insufficient evidence."

All this strikes one as healthy, even when expressed, as by Clifford, with
somewhat too much of robustious pathos in the voice. Free will and simple
wishing do seem, in the matter of our credences, to be only fifth wheels
to the coach. Yet if any one should thereupon assume that intellectual insight is what remains after wish and will and sentimental preference have
taken wing, or that pure reason is what then settles our opinions, he
would fly quite as directly in the teeth of the facts.

It is only our already dead hypotheses that our willing nature is unable
to bring to life again. But what has made them dead for us is for the most
part a previous action of our willing nature of an antagonistic kind. When
I say "willing nature," I do not mean only such deliberate volitions as may
have set up habits of belief that we cannot now escape from—I mean all
such factors of belief as fear and hope, prejudice and passion, imitation
and partisanship, the circumpressure of our caste and set. As a matter of
fact we find ourselves believing, we hardly know how or why. Mr. Balfour
gives the name of "authority" to all those influences, born of the intellectual

climate, that make hypotheses possible or impossible for us, alive or dead. Here in this room, we all of us believe in molecules and the conservation of energy, in democracy and necessary progress, in Protestant Christianity and the duty of fighting for "the doctrine of the immortal Monroe," all for no reasons worthy of the name. We see into these matters with no more inner clearness, and probably with much less, than any disbeliever in them might possess. His unconventionality would probably have some grounds to show for its conclusions; but for us, not insight, but the *prestige* of the opinions, is what makes the spark shoot from them and light up our sleeping magazines of faith. Our reason is quite satisfied, in nine hundred and ninety-nine cases out of every thousand of us, if it can find a few arguments that will do to recite in case our credulity is criticized by someone else. Our faith is faith in someone else's faith, and in the greatest matters this is most the case. Our belief in truth itself, for instance, that there is a truth, and that our minds and it are made for each other—what is it but a passionate affirmation of desire, in which our social system backs us up? We want to have a truth; we want to believe that our experiments and studies and discussions must put us in a continually better and better position towards it; and on this line we agree to fight out our thinking lives. But if a Pyrrhonistic skeptic asks us *how we know* all this, can our logic find a reply? No! certainly it cannot. It is just one volition against another—we willing to go in for life upon a trust or assumption which he, for his part, does not care to make.

As a rule we disbelieve all facts and theories for which we have no use. Clifford's cosmic emotions find no use for Christian feelings. Huxley belabors the bishops because there is no use for sacerdotalism in his scheme of life. Newman, on the contrary, goes over to Romanism, and finds all sorts of reasons good for staying there, because a priestly system is for him an organic need and delight. Why do so few "scientists" even look at the evidence for telepathy, so called? Because they think, as a leading biologist, now dead, once said to me, that even if such a thing were true, scientists ought to band together to keep it suppressed and concealed. It would undo the uniformity of nature and all sorts of other things without which scientists cannot carry on their pursuits. But if this very man had been shown something which as a scientist he might *do* with telepathy, he might not only have examined the evidence, but even have found it good enough. This very law which the logicians would impose upon us—if I may give the name of logicians to those who would rule out our willing nature here—is based on nothing but their own natural wish to exclude all elements for which they, in their professional quality of logicians, can find no use.

Evidently, then, our nonintellectual nature does influence our convictions. There are passional tendencies and volitions which run before and others which come after belief, and it is only the latter that are too late for the fair; and they are not too late when the previous passional work has been already in their own direction. Pascal's argument, instead of being powerless, then seems a regular clincher, and is the last stroke needed to make our faith in masses and holy water complete. The state of things is evidently far from simple; and pure insight and logic, whatever they might do ideally, are not the only things that really do produce our creeds.

Our next duty, having recognized this mixed-up state of affairs, is to ask whether it be simply reprehensible and pathological, or whether, on the contrary, we must treat it as a normal element in making up our minds. The thesis I defend is, briefly stated, this: *Our passional nature not only lawfully may, but must, decide an option between propositions, whenever it is a genuine option that cannot by its nature be decided on intellectual grounds; for to say, under such circumstances, "Do not decide, but leave the question open," is itself a passional decision—just like deciding yes or no—and is attended with the same risk of losing the truth.* The thesis thus abstractly expressed will, I trust, soon become quite clear. But I must first indulge in a bit more of preliminary work.

It will be observed that for the purposes of this discussion we are on "dogmatic" ground—ground, I mean, which leaves systematic philosophical skepticism altogether out of account. The postulate that there is truth, and that it is the destiny of our minds to attain it, we are deliberately resolving to make, though the skeptic will not make it. We part company with him, therefore, absolutely, at this point. But the faith that truth exists, and that our minds can find it, may be held in two ways. We may talk of the *empiricist* way and of the *absolutist* way of believing in truth. The absolutists in this matter say that we not only can attain to knowing truth, but we can *know when* we have attained to knowing it; while the empiricists think that although we may attain it, we cannot infallibly know when. To *know* is one thing, and to know for certain *that* we know is another. One may hold to the first being possible without the second; hence the empiricists and the absolutists, although neither of them is a skeptic in the usual philosophic sense of the term, show very different degrees of dogmatism in their lives.

If we look at the history of opinions, we see that the empiricist tendency has largely prevailed in science, while in philosophy the absolutist tendency has had everything its own way. The characteristic sort of happiness, indeed, which philosophies yield has mainly consisted in the conviction felt by each successive school or system that by it bottom-certitude had been attained. "Other philosophies are collections of opinions, mostly false; *my* philosophy gives standing ground forever"—who does not recognize in this the keynote of every system worthy of the name? A system, to be a system at all, must come as a *closed* system, reversible in this or that detail, perchance, but in its essential features never!

Scholastic orthodoxy, to which one must always go when one wishes to find perfectly clear statement, has beautifully elaborated this absolutist conviction in a doctrine which it calls that of "objective evidence." If, for example, I am unable to doubt that I now exist before you, that two is less than three, or that if all men are mortal then I am mortal too, it is because these things illumine my intellect irresistibly. The final ground of this objective evidence possessed by certain propositions is the *adaequatio intellectus nostri cum re* [the equating of our minds with the thing]. The certitude it brings involves an *aptitudinem ad extorquendum certum assensum* [aptitude for extracting clear and positive assent] on the part of the truth envisaged, and on the side of the subject a *quietem in cognitione* [repose in apprehension], when once the object is mentally received, that leaves no possibility of doubt behind; and in the whole transaction nothing operates but the *entitas ipsa* [existence itself] of the object and the *entitas ipsa* of the mind. We slouchy modern thinkers dislike to talk in Latin—indeed, we dislike to talk in set terms at all; but at bottom our own state of mind is very much like this whenever we uncritically abandon ourselves: You believe in objective evidence, and I do. Of some things we feel that we are certain: we know, and we know that we do know. There is something that gives a click inside of us, a bell that strikes twelve, when the hands of our mental clock have swept the dial and meet over the meridian hour. The greatest empiricists among us are only empiricists on reflection: when left to their instincts, they dogmatize like infallible popes. When the Cliffords tell us how sinful it is to be Christians on such "insufficient evidence," insufficiency is really the last thing they have in mind. For them the evidence is absolutely sufficient, only it makes the other way. They believe so completely in an anti-Christian order of the universe that there is no living option: Christianity is a dead hypothesis from the start.

But now, since we are all such absolutists by instinct, what in our quality of students of philosophy ought we to do about the fact? Shall we espouse and indorse it? Or shall we treat it as a weakness of our nature from which we must free ourselves, if we can?

I sincerely believe that the latter course is the only one we can follow as reflective men. Objective evidence and certitude are doubtless very fine ideals to play with, but where on this moonlit and dream-visited planet are they found? I am, therefore, myself a complete empiricist so far as my theory of human knowledge goes. I live, to be sure, by the practical faith that we must go on experiencing and thinking over our experience, for only thus can our opinions grow more true; but to hold any one of them —I absolutely do not care which—as if it never could be reinterpretable or corrigible, I believe to be a tremendously mistaken attitude, and I think that the whole history of philosophy will bear me out. There is but one indefectibly certain truth, and that is the truth that Pyrrhonistic skepticism itself leaves standing—the truth that the present phenomenon of consciousness exists. That, however, is the bare starting point of knowledge, the mere admission of a stuff to be philosophized about. The various philosophies are but so many attempts at expressing what this stuff really is. And if we repair to our libraries what disagreement do we discover! Where is a certainly true answer found? Apart from abstract propositions of comparison (such as two and two are the same as four), propositions which tell us nothing by themselves about concrete reality, we find no proposition ever regarded by anyone as evidently certain that has not either been called a falsehood, or at least had its truth sincerely questioned by someone else. The transcending of the axioms of geometry, not in play but in earnest, by certain of our contemporaries (as Zöllner and Charles H. Hinton), and the rejection of the whole Aristotelian logic by the Hegelians, are striking instances in point.

No concrete test of what is really true has ever been agreed upon. Some make the criterion external to the moment of perception, putting it either in revelation, the *consensus gentium,* the instincts of the heart, or the systematized experience of the race. Others make the perceptive moment its own test—Descartes, for instance, with his clear and distinct ideas guaranteed by the veracity of God; Reid with his "common sense"; and Kant with his forms of synthetic judgment a priori. The inconceivability of the opposite; the capacity to be verified by sense; the possession of complete organic unity or self-relation, realized when a thing is its own other, are standards which, in turn, have been used. The much lauded objective evidence is never triumphantly there; it is a mere aspiration or *Grenzbegriff,* marking the infinitely remote ideal of our thinking life. To claim that certain truths now possess it is simply to say that when you think them true and they *are* true, then their evidence is objective, otherwise it is not. But practically one's conviction that the evidence one goes by is of the real objective brand, is only one more subjective opinion added to the lot. For what a contradictory array of opinions have objective evidence and absolute certitude been claimed! The world is rational through and through—its existence is an ultimate brute fact; there is a personal God—a personal God is inconceivable; there is an extramental physical world immediately known—the mind can only know its own ideas; a moral imperative exists—obligation is only the resultant of desires; a permanent spiritual principle is in every one—there are only shifting states of mind; there is an endless chain of causes—there is an absolute first cause; an eternal necessity—a freedom; a purpose—no purpose; a primal One—a primal Many; a universal continuity—an essential discontinuity in things; an infinity—no infinity. There is this—there is that; there is indeed nothing which someone has not thought absolutely true, while his neighbor deemed it absolutely false; and not an absolutist among them seems ever to have considered that the trouble may all the time be essential, and that the intellect, even with truth directly in its grasp, may have no infallible signal for knowing whether it be truth or no. When, indeed, one remembers that the most striking practical application to life of the doctrine of objective certitude has been the conscientious labors of the Holy Office of the Inquisition, one feels less tempted than ever to lend the doctrine a respectful ear.

But please observe, now, that when as empiricists we give up the doctrine of objective certitude, we do not thereby give up the quest or hope of truth itself. We still pin our faith on its existence, and still believe that we gain an ever better position towards it by systematically continuing to roll up experiences and think. Our great difference from the scholastic lies in the way we face. The strength of his system lies in the principles, the origin, the *terminus a quo* of his thought; for us the strength is in the outcome, the upshot, the *terminus ad quem*. Not where it comes from but what it leads to is to decide. It matters not to an empiricist from what quarter a hypothesis may come to him: he may have acquired it by fair means or by foul; passion may have whispered or accident suggested it; but if the total drift of thinking continues to confirm it, that is what he means by its being true.

One more point, small but important, and our preliminaries are done. There are two ways of looking at our duty in the matter of opinion—ways entirely different, and yet ways about whose difference the theory of knowledge seems hitherto to have shown very little concern. *We must know the truth;* and *we must avoid error*—these are our first and great commandments as would-be knowers; but they are not two ways of stating an identical commandment, they are two separable laws. Although it may indeed happen that when we believe the truth A, we escape as an incidental consequence from believing the falsehood B, it hardly ever happens that by merely disbelieving B we necessarily believe A. We may in escaping B fall into believing other falsehoods, C or D, just as bad as B; or we may escape B by not believing anything at all, not even A.

Believe truth! Shun error! These, we see, are two materially different laws; and by choosing between them we may end by coloring differently our whole intellectual life. We may regard the chase for truth as paramount, and the avoidance of error as secondary; or we may, on the other hand, treat the avoidance of error as more imperative, and let truth take its chance. Clifford, in the instructive passage which I have quoted, exhorts us to the latter course. Believe nothing, he tells us, keep your mind in suspense forever, rather than by closing it on insufficient evidence incur the awful risk of believing lies. You, on the other hand, may think that the risk of being in error is a very small matter when compared with the blessings of real knowledge, and be ready to be duped many times in your investigation rather than postpone indefinitely the chance of guessing true. I myself find it impossible to go with Clifford. We must remember that these feelings of our duty about either truth or error are in any case only expressions of our passional life. Biologically considered, our minds are as ready to grind out falsehood as veracity, and he who says, "Better go without belief forever than believe a lie!" merely shows his own preponderant private horror of becoming a dupe. He may be critical of many of his desires and fears, but this fear he slavishly obeys. He cannot imagine anyone questioning its binding force. For my own part, I have also a horror of being duped; but I can believe that worse things than being duped may happen to a man in this world: so Clifford's exhortation has to my ears a thoroughly fantastic sound. It is like a general informing his soldiers that it is better to keep out of battle forever than to risk a single wound. Not so are victories either over enemies or over nature gained. Our errors are surely not such awfully solemn things. In a world where we are so certain to incur them in spite of all our caution, a certain lightness of heart seems healthier than this excessive nervousness on their behalf. At any rate, it seems the fittest thing for the empiricist philosopher.

And now, after all this introduction, let us go straight at our question. I have said, and now repeat it, that not only as a matter of fact do we find our passional nature influencing us in our opinions, but that there are some options between opinions in which this influence must be regarded both as an inevitable and as a lawful determinant of our choice.

I fear here that some of you my hearers will begin to scent danger, and lend an inhospitable ear. Two first steps of passion you have indeed had to admit as necessary—we must think so as to avoid dupery, and we must think so as to gain truth; but the surest path to those ideal consummations, you will probably consider, is from now onwards to take no further passional step.

Well, of course, I agree as far as the facts will allow. Wherever the option between losing truth and gaining it is not momentous, we can throw the chance of *gaining truth* away, and at any rate save ourselves from any chance of *believing falsehood*, by not making up our minds at all till objective evidence has come. In scientific questions, this is almost always the case; and even in human affairs in general, the need of acting is seldom so urgent that a false belief to act on is better than no belief at all. Law courts, indeed, have to decide on the best evidence attainable for the moment, because a judge's duty is to make law as well as to ascertain it, and (as a learned judge once said to me) few cases are worth spending much time over: the great thing is to have them decided on *any* acceptable principle, and got out of the way. But in our dealings with objective nature we obviously are recorders, not makers, of the truth; and decisions for the mere sake of deciding promptly and getting on to the next business would be wholly out of place. Throughout the breadth of physical nature facts are what they are quite independently of us, and seldom is there any such hurry about them that the risks of being duped by believing a premature theory need be faced. The questions here are always trivial options, the hypotheses are hardly living (at any rate not living for us spectators), the choice between believing truth or falsehood is seldom forced. The attitude of skeptical balance is therefore the absolutely wise one if we would escape mistakes. What difference, indeed, does it make to most of us whether we have or have not a theory of the Röntgen rays, whether we believe or not in mind stuff, or have a conviction about the causality of conscious states? It makes no difference. Such options are not forced on us. On every account it is better not to make them, but still keep weighing reasons *pro et contra* with an indifferent hand.

I speak, of course, here of the purely judging mind. For purposes of discovery such indifference is to be less highly recommended, and science would be far less advanced than she is if the passionate desires of individuals to get their own faiths confirmed had been kept out of the game. See for example the sagacity which Spencer and Weismann now display.

On the other hand, if you want an absolute duffer in an investigation, you must, after all, take the man who has no interest whatever in its results: he is the warranted incapable, the positive fool. The most useful investigator, because the most sensitive observer, is always he whose eager interest in one side of the question is balanced by an equally keen nervousness lest he become deceived.[1] Science has organized this nervousness into a regular *technique,* her so-called method of verification; and she has fallen so deeply in love with the method that one may even say she has ceased to care for truth by itself at all. It is only truth as technically verified that interests her. The truth of truths might come in merely affirmative form, and she would decline to touch it. Such truth as that, she might repeat with Clifford, would be stolen in defiance of her duty to mankind. Human passions, however, are stronger than technical rules. "Le coeur a ses raisons," as Pascal says, "que la raison ne connaît pas [The heart has its reasons which the reason does not understand]"; and however indifferent to all but the bare rules of the game the umpire, the abstract intellect, may be, the concrete players who furnish him the materials to judge of are usually, each one of them, in love with some pet "live hypothesis" of his own. Let us agree, however, that wherever there is no forced option, the dispassionately judicial intellect with no pet hypothesis, saving us, as it does, from dupery at any rate, ought to be our ideal.

The question next arises: Are there not somewhere forced options in our speculative questions, and can we (as men who may be interested at least as much in positively gaining truth as in merely escaping dupery) always wait with impunity till the coercive evidence shall have arrived? It seems a priori improbable that the truth should be so nicely adjusted to our needs and powers as that. In the great boarding house of nature, the cakes and the butter and the sirup seldom come out so even and leave the plates so clean. Indeed, we should view them with scientific suspicion if they did.

Moral questions immediately present themselves as questions whose solution cannot wait for sensible proof. A moral question is a question not of what sensibly exists, but of what is good, or would be good if it did exist. Science can tell us what exists; but to compare the *worths,* both of what exists and of what does not exist, we must consult not science, but what Pascal calls our heart. Science herself consults her heart when she

---

1. Cf. Wilfrid Ward's essay, "The Wish to Believe," in his *Witnesses to the Unseen,* Macmillan & Co., 1893.

lays it down that the infinite ascertainment of fact and correction of false belief are the supreme goods for man. Challenge the statement, and science can only repeat it oracularly, or else prove it by showing that such ascertainment and correction bring man all sorts of other goods which man's heart in turn declares. The question of having moral beliefs at all or not having them is decided by our will. Are our moral preferences true or false, or are they only odd biological phenomena, making things good or bad for *us*, but in themselves indifferent? How can your pure intellect decide? If your heart does not *want* a world of moral reality, your head will assuredly never make you believe in one. Mephistophelian skepticism, indeed, will satisfy the head's play instincts much better than any rigorous idealism can. Some men (even at the student age) are so naturally coolhearted that the moralistic hypothesis never has for them any pungent life, and in their supercilious presence the hot young moralist always feels strangely ill at ease. The appearance of knowingness is on their side, of naïveté and gullibility on his. Yet, in the inarticulate heart of him, he clings to it that he is not a dupe, and that there is a realm in which (as Emerson says) all their wit and intellectual superiority is no better than the cunning of a fox. Moral skepticism can no more be refuted or proved by logic than intellectual skepticism can. When we stick to it that there *is* truth (be it of either kind), we do so with our whole nature, and resolve to stand or fall by the results. The skeptic with his whole nature adopts the doubting attitude; but which of us is the wiser, Omniscience only knows.

Turn now from these wide questions of good to a certain class of questions of fact, questions concerning personal relations, states of mind between one man and another. *Do you like me or not?* for example. Whether you do or not depends, in countless instances, on whether I meet you halfway, am willing to assume that you must like me, and show you trust and expectation. The previous faith on my part in your liking's existence is in such cases what makes your liking come. But if I stand aloof, and refuse to budge an inch until I have objective evidence, until you shall have done something apt, as the absolutists say, *ad extorquendum assensum meum* [at extorting my assent], ten to one your liking never comes. How many women's hearts are vanquished by the mere sanguine insistence of some man that they *must* love him! He will not consent to the hypothesis that they cannot. The desire for a certain kind of truth here brings about that special truth's existence; and so it is in innumerable cases of other sorts. Who gains promotions, boons, appointments, but the man in whose life they are seen to play the part of live hypotheses, who discounts them, sacrifices other things for their sake before they have come, and takes risks for them in advance? His faith acts on the powers above him as a claim, and creates its own verification.

A social organism of any sort whatever, large or small, is what it is because each member proceeds to his own duty with a trust that the other members will simultaneously do theirs. Wherever a desired result is achieved by the co-operation of many independent persons, its existence as a fact is a pure consequence of the precursive faith in one another of those immediately concerned. A government, an army, a commercial system, a ship, a college, an athletic team, all exist on this condition, without which not only is nothing achieved, but nothing is even attempted. A whole train of passengers (individually brave enough) will be looted by a few highwaymen, simply because the latter can count on one another, while each passenger fears that if he makes a movement of resistance, he will be shot before any one else backs him up. If we believed that the whole carful would rise at once with us, we should each severally rise, and train robbing would never even be attempted. There are, then, cases where a fact cannot come at all unless a preliminary faith exists in its coming. *And where faith in a fact can help create the fact,* that would be an insane logic which should say that faith running ahead of scientific evidence is the "lowest kind of immorality" into which a thinking being can fall. Yet such is the logic by which our scientific absolutists pretend to regulate our lives!

In truths dependent on our personal action, then, faith based on desire is certainly a lawful and possibly an indispensable thing.

But now, it will be said, these are all childish human cases, and have nothing to do with great cosmical matters, like the question of religious faith. Let us then pass on to that. Religions differ so much in their accidents that in discussing the religious question we must make it very generic and broad. What then do we now mean by the religious hypothesis? Science says things are; morality says some things are better than other things; and religion says essentially two things.

First, she says that the best things are the more eternal things, the overlapping things, the things in the universe that throw the last stone, so to speak, and say the final word. "Perfection is eternal"—this phrase of Charles Secrétan seems a good way of putting this first affirmation of religion, an affirmation which obviously cannot yet be verified scientifically at all.

The second affirmation of religion is that we are better off even now if we believe her first affirmation to be true.

Now, let us consider what the logical elements of this situation are *in case the religious hypothesis in both its branches be really true.* (Of course, we must admit that possibility at the outset. If we are to discuss the question at all, it must involve a living option. If for any of you religion be a hypothesis that cannot, by any living possibility, be true, then you need go no farther. I speak to the "saving remnant" alone.) So proceeding, we see, first, that religion offers itself as a *momentous* option. We are supposed to gain, even now, by our belief, and to lose by our nonbelief, a certain vital good. Secondly, religion is a *forced* option, so far as that good goes. We cannot escape the issue by remaining skeptical and waiting for more light, because, although we do avoid error in that way *if religion be untrue,* we lose the good, *if it be true,* just as certainly as if we positively chose to disbelieve. It is as if a man should hesitate indefinitely to ask a certain woman to marry him because he was not perfectly sure that she would prove an angel after he brought her home. Would he not cut himself off from that particular angel possibility as decisively as if he went and married someone else? Skepticism, then, is not avoidance of option; it is option of a certain particular kind of risk. *Better risk loss of truth than chance of error*—that is your faith vetoer's exact position. He is actively playing his stake as much as the believer is; he is backing the field against the religious hypothesis, just as the believer is backing the religious hypothesis against the field. To preach skepticism to us as a duty until "sufficient evidence" for religion be found is tantamount therefore to telling us, when in presence of the religious hypothesis, that to yield to our fear of its being error is wiser and better than to yield to our hope that it may be true. It is not intellect against all passions, then; it is only intellect with one passion laying down its law. And by what, forsooth, is the supreme wisdom of this passion warranted? Dupery for dupery, what proof is there that dupery through hope is so much worse than dupery through fear? I, for one, can see no proof; and I simply refuse obedience to the scientist's command to imitate his kind of option, in a case where my own stake is important enough to give me the right to choose my own form of risk. If religion be true and the evidence for it be still insufficient, I do not wish, by putting your extinguisher upon my nature (which feels to me as if it had after all some business in this matter), to forfeit my sole chance in life of getting upon the winning side—that chance depending, of course, on my willingness to run the risk of acting as if my passional need of taking the world religiously might be prophetic and right.

All this is on the supposition that it really may be prophetic and right, and that, even to us who are discussing the matter, religion is a live hypothesis which may be true. Now, to most of us religion comes in a still further way that makes a veto on our active faith even more illogical. The more perfect and more eternal aspect of the universe is represented in our religions as having personal form. The universe is no longer a mere *It* to us, but a *Thou*, if we are religious; and any relation that may be possible from person to person might be possible here. For instance, although in one sense we are passive portions of the universe, in another we show a curious autonomy, as if we were small active centers on our own account. We feel, too, as if the appeal of religion to us were made to our own active good will, as if evidence might be forever withheld from us unless we met the hypothesis halfway. To take a trivial illustration: just as a man who in a company of gentlemen made no advances, asked a warrant for every concession, and believed no one's word without proof would cut himself off by such churlishness from all the social rewards that a more trusting spirit would earn, so here, one who should shut himself up in snarling logicality and try to make the gods extort his recognition willy-nilly, or not get it at all, might cut himself off forever from his only opportunity of making the gods' acquaintance. This feeling, forced on us we know not whence, that by obstinately believing that there are gods (although not to do so would be so easy both for our logic and our life) we are doing the universe the deepest service we can seems part of the living essence of the religious hypothesis. If the hypothesis *were* true in all its parts, including this one, then pure intellectualism, with its veto on our making willing advances, would be an absurdity; and some participation of our sympathetic nature would be logically required. I, therefore, for one, cannot see my way to accepting the agnostic rules for truth seeking, or willfully agree to keep my willing nature out of the game. I cannot do so for this plain reason, that *a rule of thinking which would absolutely prevent me from acknowledging certain kinds of truth if those kinds of truth were really there would be an irrational rule.* That for me is the long and short of the formal logic of the situation, no matter what the kinds of truth might materially be.

I confess I do not see how this logic can be escaped. But sad experience makes me fear that some of you may still shrink from radically saying with me, *in abstracto,* that we have the right to believe at our own risk any hypothesis that is live enough to tempt our will. I suspect, however, that if this is so, it is because you have got away from the abstract logical point of view altogether, and are thinking (perhaps without realizing it) of some particular religious hypothesis which for you is dead. The freedom to "believe what we will" you apply to the case of some patent superstition; and the faith you think of is the faith defined by the schoolboy when he said, "Faith is when you believe something that you know ain't true." I can only repeat that this is misapprehension. *In concreto,* the freedom to believe can only cover living options which the intellect of the individual cannot by itself resolve; and living options never seem absurdities to him who has them to consider. When I look at the religious question as it really puts itself to concrete men, and when I think of all the possibilities which both practically and theoretically it involves, then this command that we shall put a stopper on our heart, instincts, and courage, and *wait*—acting of course meanwhile more or less as if religion were *not* true [2] till doomsday, or till such time as our intellect and senses working together may have raked in evidence enough—this command, I say, seems to me the queerest idol ever manufactured in the philosophic cave. Were we scholastic absolutists, there might be more excuse. If we had an infallible intellect with its objective certitudes, we might feel ourselves disloyal to such a perfect organ of knowledge in not trusting to it exclusively, in not waiting for its releasing word. But if we are empiricists, if we believe that no bell in us tolls to let us know for certain when truth is in our grasp, then it seems a piece of idle fantasticality to preach so solemnly our duty of waiting for the bell. Indeed we *may* wait if we will—I hope you do not think that I am denying that—but if we do so, we do so at our peril as much as if we believed. In either case we *act*, taking our life in our hands. No one of us ought to issue vetoes to the other, nor should we bandy words of abuse. We ought, on the contrary, delicately and profoundly to respect one another's mental freedom: then only shall we bring about the intellectual republic; then only shall we have that spirit of inner tolerance without which all our outer tolerance is soulless, and which is empiricism's glory; then only shall we live and let live, in speculative as well as in practical things.

I began by a reference to Fitzjames Stephen; let me end by a quotation from him. "What do you think of yourself? What do you think of the world? . . . These are questions with which all must deal as it seems good to them. They are riddles of the Sphinx, and in some way or other

---

2. Since belief is measured by action, he who forbids us to believe religion to be true, necessarily also forbids us to act as we should if we did believe it to be true. The whole defense of religious faith hinges upon action. If the action required or inspired by the religious hypothesis is in no way different from that dictated by the naturalistic hypothesis, then religious faith is a pure superfluity, better pruned away, and controversy about its legitimacy is a piece of idle trifling, unworthy of serious minds. I myself believe, of course, that the religious hypothesis gives to the world an expression which specifically determines our reactions, and makes them in a large part unlike what they might be on a purely naturalistic scheme of belief.

we must deal with them. . . . In all important transactions of life we have to take a leap in the dark. . . . If we decide to leave the riddles unanswered, that is a choice; if we waver in our answer, that, too, is a choice: but whatever choice we make, we make it at our peril. If a man chooses to turn his back altogether on God and the future, no one can prevent him; no one can show beyond reasonable doubt that he is mistaken. If a man thinks otherwise and acts as he thinks, I do not see that any one can prove that *he* is mistaken. Each must act as he thinks best; and if he is wrong, so much the worse for him. We stand on a mountain pass in the midst of whirling snow and blinding mist, through which we get glimpses now and then of paths which may be deceptive. If we stand still we shall be frozen to death. If we take the wrong road we shall be dashed to pieces. We do not certainly know whether there is any right one. What must we do? 'Be strong and of a good courage.' Act for the best, hope for the best, and take what comes. . . . If death ends all, we cannot meet death better." [3]

3. *Liberty, Equality, Fraternity*, p. 353, 2d edition, London, 1874.

The Sentiment of Rationality

What is the task which philosophers set themselves to perform; and why do they philosophize at all? Almost everyone will immediately reply: They desire to attain a conception of the frame of things which shall on the whole be more rational than that somewhat chaotic view which every one by nature carries about with him under his hat. But suppose this rational conception attained, how is the philosopher to recognize it for what it is, and not let it slip through ignorance? The only answer can be that he will recognize its rationality as he recognizes everything else, by certain subjective marks with which it affects him. When he gets the marks, he may know that he has got the rationality.

What, then, are the marks? A strong feeling of ease, peace, rest is one of them. The transition from a state of puzzle and perplexity to rational comprehension is full of lively relief and pleasure.

But this relief seems to be a negative rather than a positive character. Shall we then say that the feeling of rationality is constituted merely by the absence of any feeling of irrationality? I think there are very good grounds for upholding such a view. All feeling whatever, in the light of certain recent psychological speculations, seems to depend for its physical condition not on simple discharge of nerve currents, but on their discharge under arrest, impediment, or resistance. Just as we feel no particular pleasure when we breathe freely, but a very intense feeling of distress when the respiratory motions are prevented—so any unobstructed tendency to action discharges itself without the production of much cogitative accompaniment, and any perfectly fluent course of thought awakens but little feeling; but when the movement is inhibited, or when the thought meets with difficulties, we experience distress. It is only when the distress is upon us that we can be said to strive, to crave, or to aspire. When enjoying plenary freedom either in the way of motion or of thought, we are in a sort of anesthetic state in which we might say with Walt Whitman, if we cared to say anything about ourselves at such times, "I am sufficient as I am." This feeling of the sufficiency of the present moment, of its absoluteness—this absence of all need to explain it, account for it, or justify it—is what I call the Sentiment of Rationality. As soon, in short, as we are enabled from any cause whatever to think with perfect fluency, the thing we think of seems to us *pro tanto* rational.

Whatever modes of conceiving the cosmos facilitate this fluency, produce the sentiment of rationality. Conceived in such modes, being vouches for itself and needs no further philosophic formulation. But this fluency may be obtained in various ways; and first I will take up the theoretic way.

The facts of the world in their sensible diversity are always before us, but our theoretic need is that they should be conceived in a way that reduces their manifoldness to simplicity. Our pleasure at finding that a chaos of facts is the expression of a single underlying fact is like the relief of the musician at resolving a confused mass of sound into melodic or harmonic order. The simplified result is handled with far less mental effort than the original data; and a philosophic conception of nature is thus in no metaphorical sense a labor-saving contrivance. The passion for parsimony, for economy of means in thought, is the philosophic passion *par excellence;* and any character or aspect of the world's phenomena which gathers up their diversity into monotony will gratify that passion, and in the philosopher's mind stand for that essence of things compared with which all their other determinations may by him be overlooked.

More universality or extensiveness is, then, one mark which the philosopher's conceptions must possess. Unless they apply to an enormous number of cases they will not bring him relief. The knowledge of things by their causes, which is often given as a definition of rational knowledge, is useless to him unless the causes converge to a minimum number, while still producing the maximum number of effects. The more multiple then are the instances, the more flowingly does his mind rove from fact to fact. The phenomenal transitions are no real transitions; each item is the same old friend with a slightly altered dress.

Who does not feel the charm of thinking that the moon and the apple are, as far as their relation to the earth goes, identical; of knowing respiration and combustion to be one; of understanding that the balloon rises by the same law whereby the stone sinks; of feeling that the warmth in one's palm when one rubs one's sleeve is identical with the motion which the friction checks; of recognizing the difference between beast and fish to be only a higher degree of that between human father and son; of believing our strength when we climb the mountain or fell the tree to be no other than the strength of the sun's rays which made the corn grow out of which we got our morning meal?

But alongside of this passion for simplification there exists a sister passion, which in some minds—though they perhaps form the minority—is its rival. This is the passion for distinguishing; it is the impulse to be *acquainted* with the parts rather than to comprehend the whole. Loyalty to clearness and integrity of perception, dislike of blurred outlines, of vague identifications, are its characteristics. It loves to recognize particulars in their full completeness, and the more of these it can carry the happier it is. It prefers any amount of incoherence, abruptness, and fragmentariness (so long as the literal details of the separate facts are saved) to an abstract way of conceiving things that, while it simplifies them, dissolves away at the same time their concrete fullness. Clearness and simplicity thus set up rival claims, and make a real dilemma for the thinker.

A man's philosophic attitude is determined by the balance in him of these two cravings. No system of philosophy can hope to be universally accepted among men which grossly violates either need, or entirely subordinates the one to the other. The fate of Spinoza, with his barren union of all things in one substance, on the one hand; that of Hume, with his equally barren "looseness and separateness" of everything, on the other— neither philosopher owning any strict and systematic disciples today, each being to posterity a warning as well as a stimulus—show us that the only possible philosophy must be a compromise between an abstract monotony and a concrete heterogeneity. But the only way to mediate between diversity and unity is to class the diverse items as cases of a common essence which you discover in them. Classification of things into extensive "kinds" is thus the first step; and classification of their relations and conduct into extensive "laws" is the last step, in their philosophic unification. A completed theoretic philosophy can thus never be anything more than a completed classification of the world's ingredients; and its results must always be abstract, since the basis of every classification is the abstract essence embedded in the living fact—the rest of the living fact being for the time ignored by the classifier. This means that none of our explanations are complete. They subsume things under heads wider or more familiar; but the last heads, whether of things or of their connections, are mere abstract genera, data which we just find in things and write down.

When, for example, we think that we have rationally explained the connection of the facts A and B by classing both under their common attribute x, it is obvious that we have really explained only so much of these items as *is* x. To explain the connection of chokedamp and suffocation by the lack of oxygen is to leave untouched all the other peculiarities both of chokedamp and of suffocation, such as convulsions and agony on the one hand, density and explosibility on the other. In a word, so far as A and B contain *l, m, n,* and *o, p, q,* respectively, in addition to x, they are not explained by x. Each additional particularity makes its distinct appeal. A single explanation of a fact only explains it from a single point of view. The entire fact is not accounted for until each and all of its characters have been classed with their likes elsewhere. To apply this now to the case of the universe, we see that the explanation of the world by molecular movements explains it only so far as it actually *is* such movements. To invoke the "Unknowable" explains only so much as is unknowable, "Thought" only so much as is thought, "God" only so much as is God. *Which* thought? *Which* God? are questions that have to be answered by bringing in again the residual data from which the general term was abstracted. All those data that cannot be analytically identified with the attribute invoked as universal principle, remain as independent kinds or natures, associated empirically with the said attribute but devoid of rational kinship with it.

Hence the unsatisfactoriness of all our speculations. On the one hand, so far as they retain any multiplicity in their terms, they fail to get us out of the empirical sand-heap world; on the other, so far as they eliminate multiplicity the practical man despises their empty barrenness. The most they can say is that the elements of the world are such and such, and that each is identical with itself wherever found; but the question Where is it found? the practical man is left to answer by his own wit. Which, of all the essences, shall here and now be held the essence of this concrete thing, the fundamental philosophy never attempts to decide. We are thus led to the conclusion that the simple classification of things is, on the one hand, the best possible theoretic philosophy, but is, on the other, a most miserable and inadequate substitute for the fullness of the truth. It is a monstrous abridgment of life, which, like all abridgments is got by the absolute loss and casting out of real matter. This is why so few human beings truly care for philosophy. The particular determinations which she ignores are the real matter exciting needs, quite as potent and authoritative as hers. What does the moral enthusiast care for philosophical ethics? Why does the *Aesthetik* of every German philosopher appear to the artist an abomination of desolation?

*Grau, theurer Freund, ist alle Theorie
Und grün des Lebens goldner Baum.*

[Gray, dear friend, is all theory
And green the golden tree of life.]

The entire man, who feels all needs by turns, will take nothing as an equivalent for life but the fullness of living itself. Since the essences of things are as a matter of fact disseminated through the whole extent of time and space, it is in their spread outness and alternation that he will enjoy them. When weary of the concrete clash and dust and pettiness, he will refresh himself by a bath in the eternal springs, or fortify himself by a look at the immutable natures. But he will only be a visitor, not a dweller in the region; he will never carry the philosophic yoke upon his shoulders, and when tired of the gray monotony of her problems and insipid spaciousness of her results, will always escape gleefully into the teeming and dramatic richness of the concrete world.

So our study turns back here to its beginning. Every way of classifying a thing is but a way of handling it for some particular purpose. Conceptions, "kinds," are teleological instruments. No abstract concept can be a valid substitute for a concrete reality except with reference to a particular interest in the conceiver. The interest of theoretic rationality, the relief of identification, is but one of a thousand human purposes. When others rear their heads, it must pack up its little bundle and retire till its turn recurs. The exaggerated dignity and value that philosophers have claimed for their solutions is thus greatly reduced. The only virtue their theoretic conception need have is simplicity, and a simple conception is an equivalent for the world only so far as the world is simple—the world meanwhile, whatever simplicity it may harbor, being also a mightily complex affair. Enough simplicity remains, however, and enough urgency in our craving to reach it, to make the theoretic function one of the most invincible of human impulses. The quest of the fewest elements of things is an ideal that some will follow, as long as there are men to think at all.

But suppose the goal attained. Suppose that at last we have a system unified in the sense that has been explained. Our world can now be conceived simply, and our mind enjoys the relief. Our universal concept has made the concrete chaos rational. But now I ask, Can that which is the ground of rationality in all else be itself properly called rational? It would seem at first sight that it might. One is tempted at any rate to say that, since the craving for rationality is appeased by the identification of one thing with another, a datum which left nothing else outstanding might quench that craving definitively, or be rational *in se*. No otherness being left to annoy us, we should sit down at peace. In other words, as the theoretic tranquillity of the boor results from his spinning no further considerations about his chaotic universe, so any datum whatever (provided it were simple, clear, and ultimate) ought to banish puzzle from the universe of the philosopher and confer peace, inasmuch as there would then be for him absolutely no further considerations to spin.

This in fact is what some persons think. Professor Bain says—

> A difficulty is solved, a mystery unriddled, when it can be shown to resemble something else; to be an example of a fact already known. Mystery is isolation, exception, or it may be apparent contradiction: the resolution of the mystery is found in assimilation, identity, fraternity. When all things are assimilated, so far as assimilation can go, so far as likeness holds, there is an end to explanation; there is an end to what the mind can do, or can intelligently desire. . . . The path of science as exhibited in modern ages is toward generality, wider and wider, until we reach the highest, the widest laws of every department of things; there explanation is finished, mystery ends, perfect vision is gained.

But, unfortunately, this first answer will not hold. Our mind is so wedded to the process of seeing an *other* beside every item of its experience, that when the notion of an absolute datum is presented to it, it goes through its usual procedure and remains pointing at the void beyond, as if in that lay further matter for contemplation. In short, it spins for itself the further positive consideration of a nonentity enveloping the being of its datum; and as that leads nowhere, back recoils the thought toward its datum again. But there is no natural bridge between nonentity and this particular datum, and the thought stands oscillating to and fro, wondering "Why was there anything but nonentity; why just this universal datum and not another?" and finds no end, in wandering mazes lost. Indeed, Bain's words are so untrue that in reflecting men it is just when the attempt to fuse the manifold into a single totality has been most successful, when the conception of the universe as a unique fact is nearest its perfection, that the craving for further explanation, the ontological wonder-sickness, arises in its extremest form. As Schopenhauer says, "The uneasiness which keeps the never-resting clock of metaphysics in motion, is the consciousness that the nonexistence of this world is just as possible as its existence."

The notion of nonentity may thus be called the parent of the philosophic craving in its subtilest and profoundest sense. Absolute existence is absolute mystery, for its relations with the nothing remain unmediated to our understanding. One philosopher only has pretended to throw a logical bridge over this chasm. Hegel, by trying to show that nonentity and concrete being are linked together by a series of identities of a synthetic kind, binds everything conceivable into a unity, with no outlying notion to disturb the free rotary circulation of the mind within its bounds. Since such unchecked movement gives the feeling of rationality, he must be held, if he has succeeded, to have eternally and absolutely quenched all rational demands.

But for those who deem Hegel's heroic effort to have failed, nought remains but to confess that when all things have been unified to the supreme degree, the notion of a possible other than the actual may still haunt our imagination and prey upon our system. The bottom of being is left logically opaque to us, as something which we simply come upon and find, and about which (if we wish to act) we should pause and wonder as little as possible. The philosopher's logical tranquillity is thus in essence no other than the boor's. They differ only as to the point at which each refuses to let further considerations upset the absoluteness of the data he assumes. The boor does so immediately, and is liable at any moment to the ravages of many kinds of doubt. The philosopher does not do so till unity has been reached, and is warranted against the inroads of those considerations, but only practically, not essentially, secure from the blighting breath of the ultimate Why? If he cannot exorcise this question, he must ignore or blink it, and, assuming the data of his system as something given, and the gift as ultimate, simply proceed to a life of contemplation or of action based on it. There is no doubt that this acting on an opaque necessity is accompanied by a certain pleasure. See the reverence of Carlyle for brute fact: "There is an infinite significance in fact." "Necessity," says Dühring, and he means not rational but given necessity, "is the last and highest point that we can reach. . . . It is not only the interest of ultimate and definitive knowledge, but also that of the feelings, to find a last repose and an ideal equilibrium in an uttermost datum which can simply not be other than it is."

Such is the attitude of ordinary men in their theism, God's fiat being in physics and morals such an uttermost datum. Such also is the attitude of all hard-minded analysts and *Verstandesmenschen* [persons ruled by the intellect]. Lotze, Renouvier, and Hodgson promptly say that of experience as a whole no account can be given, but neither seek to soften the abruptness of the confession nor to reconcile us with our impotence.

But mediating attempts may be made by more mystical minds. The peace of rationality may be sought through ecstasy when logic fails. To religious persons of every shade of doctrine moments come when the world, as it is, seems so divinely orderly, and the acceptance of it by the heart so rapturously complete, that intellectual questions vanish; nay, the intellect itself is hushed to sleep—as Wordsworth says, "thought is not; in enjoyment it expires." Ontological emotion so fills the soul that ontological speculation can no longer overlap it and put her girdle of interrogation marks round existence. Even the least religious of men must have felt with Walt Whitman, when loafing on the grass on some transparent summer morning, that "swiftly arose and spread round him the peace and knowledge that pass all the argument of the earth." At such moments of energetic living we feel as if there were something diseased and contemptible, yea vile, in theoretic grubbing and brooding. In the eye of healthy sense the philosopher is at best a learned fool.

Since the heart can thus wall out the ultimate irrationality which the head ascertains, the erection of its procedure into a systematized method would be a philosophic achievement of first-rate importance. But as used by mystics hitherto it has lacked universality, being available for few persons and at few times, and even in these being apt to be followed by fits of reaction and dryness; and if men should agree that the mystical method is a subterfuge without logical pertinency, a plaster but no cure, and that the idea of nonentity can never be exorcised, empiricism will be the ultimate philosophy. Existence then will be a brute fact to which as a whole the emotion of ontologic wonder shall rightfully cleave, but remain eternally unsatisfied. Then wonderfulness or mysteriousness will be an essential attribute of the nature of things, and the exhibition and emphasizing of it will continue to be an ingredient in the philosophic industry of the race. Every generation will produce its Job, its Hamlet, its Faust, or its Sartor Resartus.

With this we seem to have considered the possibilities of purely theoretic rationality. But we saw at the outset that rationality meant only unimpeded mental function. Impediments that arise in the theoretic sphere might perhaps be avoided if the stream of mental action should leave that sphere betimes and pass into the practical. Let us therefore inquire what constitutes the feeling of rationality in its *practical* aspect. If thought is not to stand forever pointing at the universe in wonder, if its movement is to be diverted from the issueless channel of purely theoretic contemplation, let us ask what conception of the universe will awaken active impulses capable of effecting this diversion. A definition of the world which will give back to the mind the free motion which has been blocked in the purely contemplative path may so far make the world seem rational again.

Well, of two conceptions equally fit to satisfy the logical demand, that one which awakens the active impulses, or satisfies other aesthetic demands better than the other, will be accounted the more rational conception, and will deservedly prevail.

There is nothing improbable in the supposition that an analysis of the world may yield a number of formulas, all consistent with the facts. In physical science different formulas may explain the phenomena equally well—the one-fluid and the two-fluid theories of electricity, for example. Why may it not be so with the world? Why may there not be different points of view for surveying it, within each of which all data harmonize, and which the observer may therefore either choose between, or simply cumulate one upon another? A Beethoven string quartet is truly, as someone has said, a scraping of horses' tails on cats' bowels, and may be exhaustively described in such terms; but the application of this description in no way precludes the simultaneous applicability of an entirely different description. Just so a thoroughgoing interpretation of the world in terms of mechanical sequence is compatible with its being interpreted teleologically, for the mechanism itself may be designed.

If, then, there were several systems excogitated, equally satisfying to our purely logical needs, they would still have to be passed in review, and approved or rejected by our aesthetic and practical nature. Can we define the tests of rationality which these parts of our nature would use?

Philosophers long ago observed the remarkable fact that mere familiarity with things is able to produce a feeling of their rationality. The empiricist school has been so much struck by this circumstance as to have laid it down that the feeling of rationality and the feeling of familiarity are one and the same thing, and that no other kind of rationality than this exists. The daily contemplation of phenomena juxtaposed in a certain order begets an acceptance of their connection, as absolute as the repose engendered by theoretic insight into their coherence. To explain a thing is to pass easily back to its antecedents; to know it is easily to foresee its consequents. Custom, which lets us do both, is thus the source of whatever rationality the thing may gain in our thought.

In the broad sense in which rationality was defined at the outset of this essay, it is perfectly apparent that custom must be one of its factors. We said that any perfectly fluent and easy thought was devoid of the sentiment of irrationality. Inasmuch then as custom acquaints us with all the relations of a thing, it teaches us to pass fluently from that thing to others, and *pro tanto* tinges it with the rational character.

Now, there is one particular relation of greater practical importance than all the rest—I mean the relation of a thing to its future consequences. So long as an object is unusual, our expectations are baffled; they are fully determined as soon as it becomes familiar. I therefore propose this as the first practical requisite which a philosophic conception must satisfy: *It must, in a general way at least, banish uncertainty from the future.* The permanent presence of the sense of futurity in the mind has been strangely ignored by most writers, but the fact is that our consciousness at a given moment is never free from the ingredient of expectancy. Everyone knows how when a painful thing has to be undergone in the near future, the vague feeling that it is impending penetrates all our thought with uneasiness and subtly vitiates our mood even when it does not control our attention; it keeps us from being at rest, at home in the given present. The same is true when a great happiness awaits us. But when the future is neutral and perfectly certain, "we do not mind it," as we say, but give an undisturbed attention to the actual. Let now this haunting sense of futurity be thrown off its bearings or left without an object, and immediately uneasiness takes possession of the mind. But in every novel or unclassified experience this is just what occurs; we do not know what will come next; and novelty per se becomes a mental irritant, while custom per se is a mental sedative, merely because the one baffles while the other settles our expectations.

Every reader must feel the truth of this. What is meant by coming "to feel at home" in a new place, or with new people? It is simply that, at first, when we take up our quarters in a new room, we do not know what drafts may blow in upon our back, what doors may open, what forms may enter, what interesting objects may be found in cupboards and corners. When after a few days we have learned the range of all these possibilities, the feeling of strangeness disappears. And so it does with people, when we have got past the point of expecting any essentially new manifestations from their character.

The utility of this emotional effect of expectation is perfectly obvious; "natural selection," in fact, was bound to bring it about sooner or later. It is of the utmost practical importance to an animal that he should have prevision of the qualities of the objects that surround him, and especially that he should not come to rest in presence of circumstances that might be fraught either with peril or advantage—go to sleep, for example, on the brink of precipices, in the dens of enemies, or view with indifference some new-appearing object that might, if chased, prove an important addition to the larder. Novelty *ought* to irritate him. All curiosity has thus a practical genesis. We need only look at the physiognomy of a dog or a horse when a new object comes into his view, his mingled fascination and fear, to see that the element of conscious insecurity or perplexed expectation lies at the root of his emotion. A dog's curiosity about the movements of his master or a strange object only extends as far as the point of deciding what is going to happen next. That settled, curiosity is quenched. The dog quoted by Darwin, whose behavior in presence of a newspaper moved by the wind seemed to testify to a sense "of the supernatural," was merely exhibiting the irritation of an uncertain future. A newspaper which could move spontaneously was in itself so unexpected that the poor brute could not tell what new wonders the next moment might bring forth.

To turn back now to philosophy. An ultimate datum, even though it be logically unrationalized, will, if its quality is such as to define expectancy, be peacefully accepted by the mind; while if it leave the least opportunity for ambiguity in the future, it will to that extent cause mental uneasiness if not distress. Now, in the ultimate explanations of the universe which the craving for rationality has elicited from the human mind, the demands of expectancy to be satisfied have always played a fundamental part. The term set up by philosophers as primordial has been one which banishes the incalculable. "Substance," for example, means, as Kant says, *das Beharrliche,* which will be as it has been, because its being is essential and eternal. And although we may not be able to prophesy in detail the future phenomena to which the substance shall give rise, we may set our minds at rest in a general way, when we have called the substance God, Perfection, Love, or Reason, by the reflection that whatever is in store for us can never at bottom be inconsistent with the character of this term; so that our attitude even toward the unexpected is in a general sense defined. Take again the notion of immortality, which for common people seems to be the touchstone of every philosophic or religious creed: what is this but a way of saying that the determination of expectancy is the essential factor of rationality? The wrath of science against miracles, of certain philosophers against the doctrine of free will, has precisely the same root—dislike to admit any ultimate factor in things which may rout our prevision or upset the stability of our outlook.

Antisubstantialist writers strangely overlook this function in the doctrine of substance: "If there be such a *substratum,*" says Mill, "suppose it at this instant miraculously annihilated, and let the sensations continue to occur in the same order, and how would the *substratum* be missed? By what signs should we be able to discover that its existence had terminated? Should we not have as much reason to believe that it still existed as we now have? And if we should not then be warranted in believing it, how can we be so now?" Truly enough, if we have already securely bagged our facts in a certain order, we can dispense with any further warrant for that order. But with regard to the facts yet to come the case is far different. It does not follow that if substance may be dropped from our conception of the irrecoverably past, it need be an equally empty complication to our notions of the future. Even if it were true that, for aught we know to the contrary, the substance might develop at any moment a wholly new set of attributes, the mere logical form of referring things to a substance would still (whether rightly or wrongly) remain accompanied by a feeling of rest and future confidence. In spite of the acutest nihilistic criticism, men will therefore always have a liking for any philosophy which explains things *per substantiam.*

A very natural reaction against the theosophizing conceit and hidebound confidence in the upshot of things, which vulgarly optimistic minds display, has formed one factor of the skepticism of empiricists, who never cease to remind us of the reservoir of possibilities alien to our habitual experience which the cosmos may contain, and which, for any warrant we have to the contrary, may turn it inside out tomorrow. Agnostic substantialism like that of Mr. Spencer, whose Unknowable is not merely the unfathomable but the absolute irrational, on which, if consistently represented in thought, it is of course impossible to count, performs the same function of rebuking a certain stagnancy and smugness in the manner in which the ordinary philistine feels his security. But considered as anything else than as reactions against an opposite excess, these philosophies of uncertainty cannot be acceptable; the general mind will fail to come to rest in their presence, and will seek for solutions of a more reassuring kind.

We may then, I think, with perfect confidence lay down as a first point gained in our inquiry that a prime factor in the philosophic craving is the desire to have expectancy defined; and that no philosophy will definitively triumph which in an emphatic manner denies the possibility of gratifying this need.

We pass with this to the next great division of our topic. It is not sufficient for our satisfaction merely to know the future as determined, for it may be determined in either of many ways, agreeable or disagreeable. For a philosophy to succeed on a universal scale it must define the future *congruously with our spontaneous powers.* A philosophy may be unimpeachable in other respects, but either of two defects will be fatal to its universal acceptance. First, its ultimate principle must not be one that essentially baffles and disappoints our dearest desires and most cherished powers. A pessimistic principle like Schopenhauer's incurably vicious Will-substance, or Hartmann's wicked Jack-of-all-trades the Unconscious, will perpetually call forth essays at other philosophies. Incompatibility of the future with their desires and active tendencies is, in fact, to most men a source of more fixed disquietude than uncertainty itself. Witness the attempts to overcome the "problem of evil," the "mystery of pain." There is no "problem of good."

But a second and worse defect in a philosophy than that of contradicting our active propensities is to give them no object whatever to press against. A philosophy whose principle is so incommensurate with our most intimate powers as to deny them all relevancy in universal affairs, as to annihilate their motives at one blow, will be even more unpopular than pessimism. Better face the enemy than the eternal Void! This is why materialism will always fail of universal adoption, however well it may fuse things into an atomistic unity, however clearly it may prophesy the future eternity. For materialism denies reality to the objects of almost all the impulses which we most cherish. The real *meaning* of the impulses, it says, is something which has no emotional interest for us whatever. Now, what is called "extradition" is quite as characteristic of our emotions as of our senses: both point to an object as the cause of the present feeling. What an intensely objective reference lies in fear! In like manner an enraptured man and a dreary-feeling man are not simply aware of their subjective states; if they were, the force of their feelings would all evaporate. Both believe there is outward cause why they should feel as they do: either, "It is a glad world! how good life is!" or, "What a loathsome tedium is existence!" Any philosophy which annihilates the validity of the reference by explaining away its objects or translating them into terms of no emotional pertinency leaves the mind with little to care or act for. This is the opposite condition from that of nightmare, but when acutely brought home to consciousness it produces a kindred horror. In nightmare we have motives to act, but no power; here we have powers, but no motives. A nameless *unheimlichkeit* [uneasiness] comes over us at the thought of there being nothing eternal in our final purposes, in the objects of those loves and aspirations which are our deepest energies. The monstrously lopsided equation of the universe and its knower, which we postulate as the ideal of cognition, is perfectly paralleled by the no less lopsided equation of the universe and the *doer*. We demand in it a character for which our emotions and active propensities shall be a match. Small as we are, minute as is the point by which the cosmos impinges upon each one of us, each one desires to feel that his reaction at that point is congruous with the demands of the vast whole—that he balances the latter, so to speak, and is able to do what it expects of him. But as his abilities to do lie wholly in the line of his natural propensities, as he enjoys reacting with such emotions as fortitude, hope, rapture, admiration, earnestness, and the like, and as he very unwillingly reacts with fear, disgust, despair, or doubt—a philosophy which should only legitimate emotions of the latter sort would be sure to leave the mind a prey to discontent and craving.

It is far too little recognized how entirely the intellect is built up of practical interests. The theory of evolution is beginning to do very good service by its reduction of all mentality to the type of reflex action. Cognition, in this view, is but a fleeting moment, a cross section at a certain point, of what in its totality is a motor phenomenon. In the lower forms of life no one will pretend that cognition is anything more than a guide to appropriate action. The germinal question concerning things brought for the first time before consciousness is not the theoretic "What is that?" but the practical "Who goes there?" or rather, as Horwicz has admirably put it, "What is to be done?"—"*Was fang' ich an?*" In all our discussions about the intelligence of lower animals, the only test we use is that of their *acting* as if for a purpose. Cognition, in short, is incomplete until discharged in act; and although it is true that the later mental development, which attains its maximum through the hypertrophied cerebrum of man, gives birth to a vast amount of theoretic activity over and above that which is immediately ministerial to practice, yet the earlier claim is only postponed, not effaced, and the active nature asserts its rights to the end.

When the cosmos in its totality is the object offered to consciousness, the relation is in no whit altered. React on it we must in some congenial way. It was a deep instinct in Schopenhauer which led him to reinforce his pessimistic argumentation by a running volley of invective against the practical man and his requirements. No hope for pessimism unless he is slain!

Helmholtz' immortal works on the eye and ear are to a great extent little more than a commentary on the law that practical utility wholly determines which parts of our sensations we shall be aware of, and which parts we shall ignore. We notice or discriminate an ingredient of sense only so far as we depend upon it to modify our actions. We *comprehend* a thing when we synthetize it by identity with another thing. But the other great department of our understanding, *acquaintance* (the two departments being recognized in all languages by the antithesis of such words as *wissen* [to know] and *kennen* [to be acquainted with]; *scire* [to know] and *noscere* [to be acquainted with], etc.), what is that also but a synthesis—a synthesis of a passive perception with a certain tendency to reaction? We are acquainted with a thing as soon as we have learned how to behave towards it, or how to meet the behavior which we expect from it. Up to that point it is still "strange" to us.

If there be anything at all in this view, it follows that however vaguely a philosopher may define the ultimate universal datum, he cannot be said to leave it unknown to us so long as he in the slightest degree pretends that our emotional or active attitude toward it should be of one sort rather than another. He who says "life is real, life is earnest," however much he may speak of the fundamental mysteriousness of things, gives a distinct definition to that mysteriousness by ascribing to it the right to claim from us the particular mood called seriousness—which means the willingness to live with energy, though energy bring pain. The same is true of him who says that all is vanity. For indefinable as the predicate "vanity" may be *in se*, it is clearly something that permits anesthesia, mere escape from suffering, to be our rule of life. There can be no greater incongruity than for a disciple of Spencer to proclaim with one breath that the substance of things is unknowable, and with the next that the thought of it should inspire us with awe, reverence, and a willingness to add our co-operative push in the direction toward which its manifestations seem to be drifting. The unknowable may be unfathomed, but if it make such distinct demands upon our activity we surely are not ignorant of its essential quality.

If we survey the field of history and ask what feature all great periods of revival, of expansion of the human mind, display in common, we shall find, I think, simply this: that each and all of them have said to the human being, "The inmost nature of the reality is congenial to *powers* which you possess." In what did the emancipating message of primitive Christianity consist but in the announcement that God recognizes those weak and tender impulses which paganism had so rudely overlooked? Take repentance: the man who can do nothing rightly can at least repent of his failures. But for paganism this faculty of repentance was a pure supernumerary, a straggler too late for the fair. Christianity took it, and made it the one power within us which appealed straight to the heart of God. And after the night of the Middle Ages had so long branded with obloquy even the generous impulses of the flesh, and defined the reality to be such that only slavish natures could commune with it, in what did the *sursum corda* of the Platonizing renaissance lie but in the proclamation that the archetype of verity in things laid claim on the widest activity of our whole aesthetic being? What were Luther's mission and Wesley's but appeals to powers which even the meanest of men might carry with them—faith and self-despair—but which were personal, requiring no priestly intermediation, and which brought their owner face to face with God? What caused the wildfire influence of Rousseau but the assurance he gave that man's nature was in harmony with the nature of things, if only the paralyzing corruptions of custom would stand from between? How did Kant and Fichte, Goethe and Schiller inspire their time with cheer, except by saying, "Use all your powers; that is the only obedience the universe exacts"? And Carlyle with his gospel of work, of fact, of veracity, how does he move us except by saying that the universe imposes no tasks upon us but such as the most humble can perform? Emerson's creed that everything that ever was or will be is here in the enveloping now; that man has but to obey himself—"He who will rest in what he *is* is a part of destiny"—is in like manner nothing but an exorcism of all skepticism as to the pertinency of one's natural faculties.

In a word, "Son of Man, *stand upon thy feet* and I will speak unto thee!" is the only revelation of truth to which the solving epochs have helped the disciple. But that has been enough to satisfy the greater part of his rational need. *In se* and per se the universal essence has hardly been more defined by any of these formulas than by the agnostic *x;* but the mere assurance that my powers, such as they are, are not irrelevant to it, but pertinent; that it speaks to them and will in some way recognize their reply; that I can be a match for it if I will, and not a footless waif, suffices to make it rational to my feeling in the sense given above. Nothing could be more absurd than to hope for the definitive triumph of any philosophy which should refuse to legitimate, and to legitimate in an emphatic manner, the more powerful of our emotional and practical tendencies. Fatalism, whose solving word in all crises of behavior is "all striving is vain," will never reign supreme, for the impulse to take life strivingly is indestructible in the race. Moral creeds which speak to that impulse will be widely successful in spite of inconsistency, vagueness, and shadowy determination of expectancy. Man needs a rule for his will, and will invent one if one be not given him.

But now observe a most important consequence. Men's active impulses are so differently mixed that a philosophy fit in this respect for Bismarck will almost certainly be unfit for a valetudinarian poet. In other words, although one can lay down in advance the rule that a philosophy which utterly denies all fundamental ground for seriousness, for effort, for hope, which says the nature of things is radically alien to human nature, can never succeed, one cannot in advance say what particular dose of hope, or of Gnosticism of the nature of things, the definitely successful philosophy shall contain. In short, it is almost certain that personal temperament will here make itself felt, and that although all men will insist on being spoken to by the universe in some way, few will insist on being spoken to in just the same way. We have here, in short, the sphere of what Matthew Arnold likes to call *Aberglaube* [superstition], legitimate, inexpugnable, yet doomed to eternal variations and disputes.

Take idealism and materialism as examples of what I mean, and suppose for a moment that both give a conception of equal theoretic clearness and consistency, and that both determine our expectations equally well. Idealism will be chosen by a man of one emotional constitution, materialism by another. At this very day all sentimental natures, fond of conciliation and intimacy, tend to an idealistic faith. Why? Because idealism gives to the nature of things such kinship with our personal selves. Our own thoughts are what we are most at home with, what we are least afraid of. To say then that the universe essentially is thought is to say that I myself, potentially at least, am all. There is no radically alien corner, but an all-pervading *intimacy*. Now, in certain sensitively egotistic minds this conception of reality is sure to put on a narrow, close, sickroom air. Everything sentimental and priggish will be consecrated by it. That element in reality which every strong man of common sense willingly feels there because it calls forth powers that he owns—the rough, harsh sea wave, north-wind element, the denier of persons, the democratizer—is banished because it jars too much on the desire for communion. Now, it is the very enjoyment of this element that throws many men upon the materialistic or agnostic hypothesis, as a polemic reaction against the contrary extreme. They sicken at a life wholly constituted of intimacy. There is an overpowering desire at moments to escape personality, to revel in the action of forces that have no respect for our ego, to let the tides flow, even though they flow over us. The strife of these two kinds of mental temper will, I think, always be seen in philosophy. Some men will keep insisting on the reason, the atonement, that lies in the heart of things, and that we can act *with;* others, on the opacity of brute fact that we must react *against.*

Now, there is one element of our active nature which the Christian religion has emphatically recognized, but which philosophers as a rule have with great insincerity tried to huddle out of sight in their pretension to found systems of absolute certainty. I mean the element of faith. Faith means belief in something concerning which doubt is still theoretically possible; and as the test of belief is willingness to act, one may say that faith is the readiness to act in a cause the prosperous issue of which is not certified to us in advance. It is in fact the same moral quality which we call courage in practical affairs; and there will be a very widespread tendency in men of vigorous nature to enjoy a certain amount of uncertainty in their philosophic creed, just as risk lends a zest to worldly activity. Absolutely certified philosophies seeking the *inconcussum* [unshaken] are fruits of mental natures in which the passion for identity (which we saw to be but one factor of the rational appetite) plays an abnormally exclusive part. In the average man, on the contrary, the power to trust, to risk a little beyond the literal evidence, is an essential function. Any mode of conceiving the universe which makes an appeal to this generous power, and makes the man seem as if he were individually helping to create the actuality of the truth whose metaphysical reality he is willing to assume, will be sure to be responded to by large numbers.

The necessity of faith as an ingredient in our mental attitude is strongly insisted on by the scientific philosophers of the present day; but by a singularly arbitrary caprice they say that it is only legitimate when used in the interests of one particular proposition—the proposition, namely, that the course of nature is uniform. That nature will follow tomorrow the same laws that she follows today is, they all admit, a truth which no man can *know;* but in the interests of cognition as well as of action we must postulate or assume it. As Helmholtz says: *"Hier gilt nur der eine Rath: vertraue und handle* [Here it is a matter of only one kind of advice: Have faith and act]!" And Professor Bain urges: "Our only error is in proposing to give any reason or justification of the postulate, or to treat it as otherwise than begged at the very outset."

With regard to all other possible truths, however, a number of our most influential contemporaries think that an attitude of faith is not only illogical but shameful. Faith in a religious dogma for which there is no outward proof, but which we are tempted to postulate for our emotional interests, just as we postulate the uniformity of nature for our intellectual interests, is branded by Professor Huxley as "the lowest depth of immorality." Citations of this kind from leaders of the modern *Aufklärung* [enlightenment] might be multiplied almost indefinitely. Take Professor Clifford's article on the *Ethics of Belief*. He calls it "guilt" and "sin" to believe even the truth without "scientific evidence." But what is the use of being a genius, unless *with the same scientific evidence* as other men, one can reach more truth than they? Why does Clifford fearlessly proclaim his belief in the conscious-automaton theory, although the "proofs" before him are the same which make Mr. Lewes reject it? Why does he believe in primordial units of "mind-stuff" on evidence which would seem quite worthless to Professor Bain? Simply because, like every human being of the slightest mental originality, he is peculiarly sensitive to evidence that bears in some one direction. It is utterly hopeless to try to exorcise such sensitiveness by calling it the disturbing subjective factor, and branding it as the root of all evil. "Subjective" be it called! and "disturbing" to those whom it foils! But if it helps those who, as Cicero says, "*vim naturae magis sentiunt* [feel more strongly the force of nature]," it is good and not evil. Pretend what we may, the whole man within us is at work when we form our philosophical opinions. Intellect, will, taste, and passion co-operate just as they do in practical affairs; and lucky it is if the passion be not something as petty as a love of personal conquest over the philosopher across the way. The absurd abstraction of an intellect verbally formulating all its evidence and carefully estimating the probability thereof by a vulgar fraction by the size of whose denominator and numerator alone it is swayed is ideally as inept as it is actually impossible. It is almost incredible that men who are themselves working philosophers should pretend that any philosophy can be, or ever has been, constructed without the help of personal preference, belief, or divination. How have they succeeded in so stultifying their sense for the living facts of human nature as not to perceive that every philosopher, or man of science either, whose initiative counts for anything in the evolution of thought, has taken his stand on a sort of dumb conviction that the truth must lie in one direction rather than another, and a sort of preliminary assurance that his notion can be made to work; and has borne his best fruit in trying to make it work? These mental instincts in different men are the spontaneous variations upon which the intellectual struggle for existence is based. The fittest conceptions survive, and with them the names of their champions shining to all futurity.

The coil is about us, struggle as we may. The only escape from faith is mental nullity. What we enjoy most in a Huxley or a Clifford is not the professor with his learning, but the human personality ready to go in for what it feels to be right, in spite of all appearances. The concrete man has but one interest—to be right. That for him is the art of all arts, and all means are fair which help him to it. Naked he is flung into the world, and between him and nature there are no rules of civilized warfare. The rules of the scientific game, burdens of proof, presumptions, *experimenta crucis*, complete inductions, and the like, are only binding on those who enter that game. As a matter of fact we all more or less do enter it, because it helps us to our end. But if the means presume to frustrate the end and call us cheats for being right in advance of their slow aid, by guesswork or by hook or crook, what shall we say of them? Were all of Clifford's works, except the *Ethics of Belief*, forgotten, he might well figure in future treatises on psychology in place of the somewhat threadbare instance of the miser who has been led by the association of ideas to prefer his gold to all the goods he might buy therewith.

In short, if I am born with such a superior general reaction to evidence that I can guess right and act accordingly, and gain all that comes of right action, while my less gifted neighbor (paralyzed by his scruples and waiting for more evidence which he dares not anticipate, much as he longs to) still stands shivering on the brink, by what law shall I be forbidden to reap the advantages of my superior native sensitiveness? Of course I yield to my belief in such a case as this or distrust it, alike at my peril, just as I do in any of the great practical decisions of life. If my inborn faculties are good, I am a prophet; if poor, I am a failure: nature spews me out of her mouth, and there is an end of me. In the total game of life we stake our persons all the while; and if in its theoretic part our persons will help us to a conclusion, surely we should also stake them there, however inarticulate they may be.[1]

But in being myself so very articulate in proving what to all readers with a sense for reality will seem a platitude, am I not wasting words? We cannot live or think at all without some degree of faith. Faith is synonymous with working hypothesis. The only difference is that while some hypotheses can be refuted in five minutes, others may defy ages. A chemist who conjectures that a certain wallpaper contains arsenic, and has faith enough to lead him to take the trouble to put some of it into a hydrogen bottle, finds out by the results of his action whether he was right or wrong. But theories like that of Darwin, or that of the kinetic constitution of matter, may exhaust the labors of generations in their corroboration, each tester of their truth proceeding in this simple way, that he acts as if it were

---

1. At most, the command laid upon us by science to believe nothing not yet verified by the senses is a prudential rule intended to maximize our right thinking and minimize our errors *in the long run*. In the particular instance we must frequently lose truth by obeying it; but on the whole we are safer if we follow it consistently, for we are sure to cover our losses with our gains. It is like those gambling and in- surance rules based on probability, in which we secure ourselves against losses in detail by hedging on the total run. But this hedging philosophy requires that long run should be there; and this makes it inapplicable to the question of religious faith as the latter comes home to the individual man. He plays the game of life not to escape losses, for he brings nothing with him to lose; he plays it for gains; and it is now or never with him, for the long run which exists indeed for humanity is not there for him. Let him doubt, believe, or deny, he runs his risk, and has the natural right to choose which one it shall be.

true, and expects the result to disappoint him if his assumption is false. The longer disappointment is delayed, the stronger grows his faith in his theory.

Now, in such questions as God, immortality, absolute morality, and free will, no nonpapal believer at the present day pretends his faith to be of an essentially different complexion; he can always doubt his creed. But his intimate persuasion is that the odds in its favor are strong enough to warrant him in acting all along on the assumption of its truth. His corroboration or repudiation by the nature of things may be deferred until the day of judgment. The uttermost he now means is something like this: "I *expect* then to triumph with tenfold glory; but if it should turn out, as indeed it may, that I have spent my days in a fool's paradise, why, better have been the dupe of *such* a dreamland than the cunning reader of a world like that which then beyond all doubt unmasks itself to view." In short, we *go in* against materialism very much as we should *go in*, had we a chance, against the Second French Empire or the Church of Rome, or any other system of things toward which our repugnance is vast enough to determine energetic action, but too vague to issue in distinct argumentation. Our reasons are ludicrously incommensurate with the volume of our feeling, yet on the latter we unhesitatingly act.

Now, I wish to show what to my knowledge has never been clearly pointed out, that belief (as measured by action) not only does and must continually outstrip scientific evidence, but that there is a certain class of truths of whose reality belief is a factor as well as a confessor; and that as regards this class of truths faith is not only licit and pertinent, but essential and indispensable. The truths cannot become true till our faith has made them so.

Suppose, for example, that I am climbing in the Alps, and have had the ill luck to work myself into a position from which the only escape is by a terrible leap. Being without similar experience, I have no evidence of my ability to perform it successfully; but hope and confidence in myself make me sure I shall not miss my aim, and nerve my feet to execute what without those subjective emotions would perhaps have been impossible. But suppose that, on the contrary, the emotions of fear and mistrust preponderate; or suppose that, having just read the *Ethics of Belief*, I feel it would be sinful to act upon an assumption unverified by previous experience—why, then I shall hesitate so long that at last, exhausted and trembling, and launching myself in a moment of despair, I miss my foothold and roll into the abyss. In this case (and it is one of an immense class) the part of wisdom clearly is to believe what one desires; for the belief is one of the indispensable preliminary conditions of the realization of its object. *There are then cases where faith creates its own verification.* Believe, and you shall be right, for you shall save yourself; doubt, and you shall again be right, for you shall perish. The only difference is that to believe is greatly to your advantage.

The future movements of the stars or the facts of past history are determined now once for all, whether I like them or not. They are given irrespective of my wishes, and in all that concerns truths like these subjective preference should have no part; it can only obscure the judgment. But in every fact into which there enters an element of personal contribution on my part, as soon as this personal contribution demands a certain degree of subjective energy which, in its turn, calls for a certain amount of faith in the result, so that, after all, the future fact is conditioned by my present faith in it, how trebly asinine would it be for me to deny myself the use of the subjective method, the method of belief based on desire!

In every proposition whose bearing is universal (and such are all the propositions of philosophy), the acts of the subject and their consequences throughout eternity should be included in the formula. If M represent the entire world *minus* the reaction of the thinker upon it, and if $M + x$ represent the absolutely total matter of philosophic propositions (x standing for the thinker's reaction and its results), what would be a universal truth if the term x were of one complexion might become egregious error if x altered its character. Let it not be said that x is too infinitesimal a component to change the character of the immense whole in which it lies imbedded. Everything depends on the point of view of the philosophic proposition in question. If we have to define the universe from the point of view of sensibility, the critical material for our judgment lies in the animal kingdom, insignificant as that is, quantitatively considered. The moral definition of the world may depend on phenomena more restricted still in range. In short, many a long phrase may have its sense reversed by the addition of three letters, *n-o-t;* many a monstrous mass have its unstable equilibrium discharged one way or the other by a featherweight that falls.

Let us make this clear by a few examples. The philosophy of evolution offers us today a new criterion to serve as an ethical test between right and wrong. Previous criteria, it says, being subjective, have left us still floundering in variations of opinion and the *status belli.* Here is a criterion which is objective and fixed: *That is to be called good which is destined to prevail or survive.* But we immediately see that this standard can only remain objective by leaving myself and my conduct out. If what prevails and survives does so by my help, and cannot do so without that help; if something else will prevail in case I alter my conduct, how can I possibly now, conscious of alternative courses of action open before me, either of which I may suppose capable of altering the path of events, decide which course to take by asking what path events will follow? If they follow my direction, evidently my direction cannot wait on them. The only possible manner in which an evolutionist can use his standard is the obsequious method of forecasting the course society would take *but for him*, and then putting an extinguisher on all personal idiosyncrasies of desire and interest, and with bated breath and tiptoe tread following as straight as may be at the tail, and bringing up the rear of everything. Some pious creatures may find a pleasure in this; but not only does it violate our general wish to lead and not to follow (a wish which is surely not immoral if we but lead aright), but if it be treated as every ethical principle must be treated, namely, as a rule good for all men alike, its general observance would lead to its practical refutation by bringing about a general deadlock. Each good man hanging back and waiting for orders from the rest, absolute stagnation would ensue. Happy, then, if a few unrighteous ones contribute an initiative which sets things moving again!

All this is no caricature. That the course of destiny may be altered by individuals no wise evolutionist ought to doubt. Everything for him has small beginnings, has a bud which may be "nipped," and nipped by a feeble force. Human races and tendencies follow the law, and have also small beginnings. The best, according to evolution, is that which has the biggest endings. Now, if a present race of men, enlightened in the evolutionary philosophy, and able to forecast the future, were able to discern in a tribe arising near them the potentiality of future supremacy; were able to see that their own race would eventually be wiped out of existence by the newcomers if the expansion of these were left unmolested, these present sages would have two courses open to them, either perfectly in harmony with the evolutionary test: strangle the new race *now*, and ours survives; help the new race, and *it* survives. In both cases the action is right as measured by the evolutionary standard—it is action for the winning side.

Thus the evolutionist foundation of ethics is purely objective only to the herd of nullities whose votes count for zero in the march of events. But for others, leaders of opinion or potentates, and in general those to whose actions position or genius gives a far-reaching import, and to the rest of us, each in his measure, whenever we espouse a cause we contribute to the determination of the evolutionary standard of right. The truly wise disciple of this school will then admit faith as an ultimate ethical factor. Any philosophy which makes such questions as, What is the ideal type of humanity? What shall be reckoned virtues? What conduct is good? depend on the question, What is going to succeed? must needs fall back on personal belief as one of the ultimate conditions of the truth. For again and again success depends on energy of act; energy again depends on faith that we shall not fail; and that faith in turn on the faith that we are right, which faith thus verifies itself.

Take as an example the question of optimism or pessimism, which makes so much noise just now in Germany. Every human being must sometime decide for himself whether life is worth living. Suppose that in looking at the world and seeing how full it is of misery, of old age, of wickedness and pain, and how unsafe is his own future, he yields to the pessimistic conclusion, cultivates disgust and dread, ceases striving, and finally commits suicide. He thus adds to the mass M of mundane phenomena, independent of his subjectivity, the subjective complement x, which makes of the whole an utterly black picture illumined by no gleam of good. Pessimism completed, verified by his moral reaction and the deed in which this ends, is true beyond a doubt. $M + x$ expresses a state of things totally bad. The man's belief supplied all that was lacking to make it so, and now that it is made so the belief was right.

But now suppose that with the same evil facts M, the man's reaction x is exactly reversed; suppose that instead of giving way to the evil he braves it, and finds a sterner, more wonderful joy than any passive pleasure can yield in triumphing over pain and defying fear; suppose he does this successfully, and however thickly evils crowd upon him proves his dauntless subjectivity to be more than their match, will not everyone confess that the bad character of the M is here the *conditio sine qua non* of the good character of the x? Will not everyone instantly declare a world fitted only for fair-weather human beings susceptible of every passive enjoyment, but without independence, courage, or fortitude, to be from a moral point of view incommensurably inferior to a world framed to elicit from the man every form of triumphant endurance and conquering moral energy? As James Hinton says—

> Little inconveniences, exertions, pains—these are the only things in which we rightly feel our life at all. If these be not there, existence becomes worthless, or worse; success in putting them all away is fatal. So it is men engage in athletic sports, spend their holidays in climbing up mountains, find nothing so enjoyable as that which taxes their endurance

and their energy. This is the way we are made, I say. It may or may not be a mystery or a paradox; it is a fact. Now, this enjoyment in endurance is just according to the intensity of life: the more physical vigor and balance, the more endurance can be made an element of satisfaction. A sick man cannot stand it. The line of enjoyable suffering is not a fixed one; it fluctuates with the perfectness of the life. That our pains are, as they are, unendurable, awful, overwhelming, crushing, not to be borne save in misery and dumb impatience, which utter exhaustion alone makes patient—that our pains are thus unendurable means not that they are too great, but that *we are sick*. We have not got our proper life. So you perceive pain is no more necessarily an evil, but an essential element of the highest good.

But the highest good can be achieved only by our getting our proper life; and that can come about only by help of a moral energy born of the faith that in some way or other we shall succeed in getting it if we try pertinaciously enough. This world *is* good, we must say, since it is what we make it—and we shall make it good. How can we exclude from the cognition of a truth a faith which is involved in the creation of the truth? M has its character indeterminate, susceptible of forming part of a thoroughgoing pessimism on the one hand, or of a meliorism, a moral (as distinguished from a sensual) optimism on the other. All depends on the character of the personal contribution x. Wherever the facts to be formulated contain such a contribution, we may logically, legitimately, and inexpugnably believe what we desire. The belief creates its verification. The thought becomes literally father to the fact, as the wish was father to the thought.[2]

Let us now turn to the radical question of life—the question whether this be at bottom a moral or an unmoral universe—and see whether the method of faith may legitimately have a place there. It is really the question of materialism. Is the world a simple brute actuality, an existence *de facto* about which the deepest thing that can be said is that it happens so to be; or is the judgment of *better* or *worse*, of *ought*, as intimately pertinent to phenomena as the simple judgment *is* or *is not?* The materialistic theorists say that judgments of worth are themselves mere matters of

---

2. Observe that in all this not a word has been said of free will. It all applies as well to a predetermined as to an indeterminate universe. If $M + x$ is fixed in advance, the belief which leads to x and the desire which prompts the belief are also fixed. But fixed or not, these subjective states form a phenomenal condition necessarily preceding the facts; necessarily constitutive, therefore, of the truth $M + x$ which we seek. If, however, free acts be possible, a faith in their possibility, by augmenting the moral energy which gives them birth, will increase their frequency in a given individual.

fact; that the words "good" and "bad" have no sense apart from subjective passions and interests which we may, if we please, play fast and loose with at will, so far as any duty of ours to the nonhuman universe is concerned. Thus, when a materialist says it is better for him to suffer great inconvenience than to break a promise, he only means that his social interests have become so knit up with keeping faith that, those interests once being granted, it *is* better for him to keep the promise in spite of everything. But the interests themselves are neither right nor wrong, except possibly with reference to some ulterior order of interests which themselves again are mere subjective data without character, either good or bad.

For the absolute moralists, on the contrary, the interests are not there merely to be felt—they are to be believed in and obeyed. Not only is it best for my social interests to keep my promise, but best for me to have those interests, and best for the cosmos to have this me. Like the old woman in the story who described the world as resting on a rock, and then explained that rock to be supported by another rock, and finally when pushed with questions said it was rocks all the way down, he who believes this to be a radically moral universe must hold the moral order to rest either on an absolute and ultimate *should,* or on a series of *shoulds* all the way down.[3]

The practical difference between this objective sort of moralist and the other one is enormous. The subjectivist in morals, when his moral feelings are at war with the facts about him, is always free to seek harmony by toning down the sensitiveness of the feelings. Being mere data, neither good nor evil in themselves, he may pervert them or lull them to sleep by any means at his command. Truckling, compromise, time-serving, capitulations of conscience are conventionally opprobrious names for what, if successfully carried out, would be on his principles by far the easiest and most praiseworthy mode of bringing about that harmony between inner and outer relations which is all that he means by good. The absolute moralist, on the other hand, when his interests clash with the world, is not free to gain harmony by sacrificing the ideal interests. According to him, these latter should be as they are and not otherwise. Resistance then, poverty, martyrdom if need be, tragedy in a word, such are the solemn feasts of his inward faith. Not that the contradiction between the two men occurs every day; in commonplace matters all moral schools agree. It is

3. In either case, . . . the *should* which the moralist regards as binding upon *him* must be rooted in the feeling of some other thinker, or collection of thinkers, to whose demands he individually bows.

only in the lonely emergencies of life that our creed is tested: then routine maxims fail, and we fall back on our gods. It cannot then be said that the question, Is this a moral world? is a meaningless and unverifiable question because it deals with something nonphenomenal. Any question is full of meaning to which, as here, contrary answers lead to contrary behavior. And it seems as if in answering such a question as this we might proceed exactly as does the physical philosopher in testing an hypothesis. He deduces from the hypothesis an experimental action, x; this he adds to the facts M already existing. It fits them if the hypothesis be true; if not, there is discord. The results of the action corroborate or refute the idea from which it flowed. So here: the verification of the theory which you may hold as to the objectively moral character of the world can consist only in this, that if you proceed to act upon your theory it will be reversed by nothing that later turns up as your action's fruit; it will harmonize so well with the entire drift of experience that the latter will, as it were, adopt it, or at most give it an ampler interpretation, without obliging you in any way to change the essence of its formulation. If this be an objectively moral universe, all acts that I make on that assumption, all expectations that I ground on it, will tend more and more completely to interdigitate with the phenomena already existing. $M + x$ will be in accord; and the more I live, and the more the fruits of my activity come to light, the more satisfactory the consensus will grow. While if it be not such a moral universe, and I mistakenly assume that it is, the course of experience will throw ever new impediments in the way of my belief, and become more and more difficult to express in its language. Epicycle upon epicycle of subsidiary hypothesis will have to be invoked to give to the discrepant terms a temporary appearance of squaring with each other; but at last even this resource will fail.

If, on the other hand, I rightly assume the universe to be not moral, in what does my verification consist? It is that by letting moral interests sit lightly, by disbelieving that there is any duty about *them* (since duty obtains only as *between* them and other phenomena), and so throwing them over if I find it hard to get them satisfied—it is that by refusing to take up a tragic attitude, I deal in the long run most satisfactorily with the facts of life. "All is vanity" is here the last word of wisdom. Even though in certain limited series there may be a great appearance of seriousness, he who in the main treats things with a degree of good-natured skepticism and radical levity will find that the practical fruits of his epicurean hypothesis verify it more and more, and not only save him from pain but do honor to his sagacity. While, on the other hand, he who contrary to reality stiffens himself in the notion that certain things absolutely should be, and rejects the truth that at bottom it makes no difference what is, will find himself evermore thwarted and perplexed and bemuddled by the facts of the world, and his tragic disappointment will, as experience accumulates, seem to drift farther and farther away from that final atonement or reconciliation which certain partial tragedies often get.

Anesthesia is the watchword of the moral skeptic brought to bay and put to his trumps. *Energy* is that of the moralist. Act on my creed, cries the latter, and the results of your action will prove the creed true, and that the nature of things is earnest infinitely. Act on mine, says the epicurean, and the results will prove that seriousness is but a superficial glaze upon a world of fundamentally trivial import. You and your acts and the nature of things will be alike enveloped in a single formula, a universal *vanitas vanitatum* [vanity of vanities].

For the sake of simplicity I have written as if the verification might occur in the life of a single philosopher, which is manifestly untrue, since the theories still face each other, and the facts of the world give countenance to both. Rather should we expect that, in a question of this scope, the experience of the entire human race must make the verification, and that all the evidence will not be "in" till the final integration of things, when the last man has had his say and contributed his share to the still unfinished x. Then the proof will be complete; then it will appear without doubt whether the moralistic x has filled up the gap which alone kept the M of the world from forming an even and harmonious unity, or whether the nonmoralistic x has given the finishing touches which were alone needed to make the M appear outwardly as vain as it inwardly was.

But if this be so, is it not clear that the facts M, taken per se, are inadequate to justify a conclusion either way in advance of my action? My action is the complement which, by proving congruous or not, reveals the latent nature of the mass to which it is applied. The world may in fact be likened unto a lock, whose inward nature, moral or unmoral, will never reveal itself to our simply expectant gaze. The positivists, forbidding us to make any assumptions regarding it, condemn us to eternal ignorance, for the "evidence" which they wait for can never come so long as we are passive. But nature has put into our hands two keys, by which we may test the lock. If we try the moral key *and it fits,* it is a moral lock. If we try the unmoral key and *it* fits, it is an unmoral lock. I cannot possibly conceive of any other sort of "evidence" or "proof" than this. It is quite true that the co-operation of generations is needed to educe it. But in these matters the solidarity (so called) of the human race is a patent fact. The essential thing to notice is that our active preference is a legitimate part of the game —that it is our plain business as men to try one of the keys, and the one in which we most confide. If then the proof exist not till I have acted, and I must needs in acting run the risk of being wrong, how can the popular science professors be right in objurgating in me as infamous a "credulity" which the strict logic of the situation requires? If this really be a moral universe; if by my acts I be a factor of its destinies; if to believe where I may doubt be itself a moral act analogous to voting for a side not yet sure to win, by what right shall they close in upon me and steadily negate the deepest conceivable function of my being by their preposterous command that I shall stir neither hand nor foot, but remain balancing myself in eternal and insoluble doubt? Why, doubt itself is a decision of the widest practical reach, if only because we may miss by doubting what goods we might be gaining by espousing the winning side. But more than that! It is often practically impossible to distinguish doubt from dogmatic negation. If I refuse to stop a murder because I am in doubt whether it be not justifiable homicide, I am virtually abetting the crime. If I refuse to bale out a boat because I am in doubt whether my efforts will keep her afloat, I am really helping to sink her. If in the mountain precipice I doubt my right to risk a leap, I actively connive at my destruction. He who commands himself not to be credulous of God, of duty, of freedom, of immortality, may again and again be indistinguishable from him who dogmatically denies them. Skepticism in moral matters is an active ally of immorality. Who is not for is against. The universe will have no neutrals in these questions. In theory as in practice, dodge or hedge, or talk as we like about a wise skepticism, we are really doing volunteer military service for one side or the other.

Yet obvious as this necessity practically is, thousands of innocent magazine readers lie paralyzed and terrified in the network of shallow negations which the leaders of opinion have thrown over their souls. All they need to be free and hearty again in the exercise of their birthright is that these fastidious vetoes should be swept away. All that the human heart wants is its chance. It will willingly forego certainty in universal matters if only it can be allowed to feel that in them it has that same inalienable right to run risks which no one dreams of refusing to it in the pettiest practical affairs. And if I, in these last pages, like the mouse in the fable, have gnawed a few of the strings of the sophistical net that has been binding down its lion-strength, I shall be more than rewarded for my pains.

To sum up: No philosophy will permanently be deemed rational by all men which (in addition to meeting logical demands) does not to some degree pretend to determine expectancy, and in a still greater degree make a direct appeal to all those powers of our nature which we hold in highest esteem. Faith, being one of these powers, will always remain a factor not to be banished from philosophic constructions, the more so since in many ways it brings forth its own verification. In these points, then, it is hopeless to look for literal agreement among mankind.

The ultimate philosophy, we may therefore conclude, must not be too strait laced in form, must not in all its parts divide heresy from orthodoxy by too sharp a line. There must be left over and above the propositions to be subscribed, *ubique, semper, et ab omnibus* [everywhere, always, and apart from all], another realm into which the stifled soul may escape from pedantic scruples and indulge its own faith at its own risks; and all that can here be done will be to mark out distinctly the questions which fall within faith's sphere.

The foregoing essays are taken from William James's
THE WILL TO BELIEVE AND OTHER ESSAYS IN POPULAR PHILOSOPHY.

John Dewey

1859–1952

John Dewey, thought by many to be the foremost philosopher the United States has produced, was born in Burlington, Vermont, in 1859. He was educated in the local public schools and at the University of Vermont, graduating with a bachelor's degree in 1879. After teaching school for two years, he entered Johns Hopkins University to do graduate work. He received his Ph.D. degree in 1884, and for the next ten years he taught philosophy at Michigan and Minnesota universities. In 1894 he was invited to the University of Chicago to become head of the combined departments of philosophy, psychology, and pedagogy.

It was at the University of Chicago that Dewey engaged in the educational experiments that were to bring him international recognition. With funds obtained from interested private citizens, he established an experimental elementary school known as "The Laboratory School." This school provided him with the opportunity to make firsthand observations of children in various classroom situations. On the basis of these observations, he developed the revolutionary educational theories that inspired the "progressive education" movement.

Dewey's influential and widely read book *The School and Society* was published in 1899. It was followed by *The Child and the Cur-*

Notes from the artist: "A detailed study of the head of Dewey is ornamented with a bunch of grapes, symbolizing the long quotation from Art as Experience.*"*

Etymologically, an act of expression is a squeezing out, a pressing forth. Juice is expressed when grapes are crushed in the wine press; to use a more prosaic comparison, lard and oil are rendered when certain fats are subjected to heat and pressure. Nothing is pressed forth except from original raw or natural material. But it is equally true that the mere issuing forth or discharge of raw material is not expression. Through interaction with something external to it, the wine press, or the treading foot of man, juice results. Skin and seeds are separated and retained; only when the apparatus is defective are they discharged. Even in the most mechanical modes of expression there is interaction and a consequent transformation of the primitive material which stands as raw material for a product of art, in relation to what is actually pressed out. It takes the wine press as well as grapes to ex-press juice, and it takes environing and resisting objects as well as internal emotion and impulsion to constitute an *expression* of emotion.

JOHN DEWEY

riculum in 1902. His other major works on education, *How We Think* and *Democracy and Education,* were published several years later. In all of these works, he argued for greater emphasis upon the needs and interests of the students, and less upon formal subject matter. He insisted that there should be a close relationship between school experiences and life outside the school. He maintained that the primary aim of education is to train students to think through problematic situations, not to memorize isolated facts or abstract formulas.

Dewey resigned from the University of Chicago in 1904 as the result of a dispute with the university administration over Laboratory School policy. He then accepted a position at Columbia University, where he remained until his retirement in 1930.

Though Dewey is best known for his contributions to educational theory, he wrote extensively on almost all philosophical subjects, including logic, epistemology, ethics, politics, and aesthetics. His philosophy, usually referred to as Instrumentalism, is closely related to the pragmatism of William James. It is perhaps best described as the application of the scientific method to all areas of human inquiry.

Dewey's activities were not confined to the academy. He took part in several political campaigns and was active in a number of political action groups. A vigorous man even in his old age, Dewey remarried when he was eighty-seven (his first wife died in 1927). Dewey had six children by his first wife and with her adopted one child; with his second wife he adopted two children. He died in New York City in 1952.

A theory of education must be based upon a theory of knowledge. Before we can make any useful recommendations concerning how people should be *taught,* we must first have some conception of how people *learn. How We Think* is an attempt to describe the learning process and to suggest some methods for stimulating and guiding it.

Though *How We Think* is essentially a work of description and analysis, it can also be read as "A Guide to Effective Thinking." In analyzing the process which leads from inquiry to knowledge, Dewey finds it necessary to consider some of the obstacles to clear thinking. After listing these obstacles, he goes on to suggest ways of overcoming them through the cultivation of proper attitudes.

How We Think begins with an examination of the various types of thinking, and an explanation of why some are more valuable than others. According to Dewey, only one type—reflective thinking—leads to genuine knowledge. As defined by him, reflective thinking is the "active, persistent, and careful consideration of any belief or supposed form of knowledge in the light of the grounds that support it and the further conclusions to which it tends." After discussing the value of reflective thinking, Dewey considers some of the factors hindering it. He insists that these hindrances can be removed (or their effect lessened) by the development of the attitudes of "open-mindedness," "wholeheartedness," and "responsibility."

The main section of *How We Think* is a detailed analysis of the various phases of reflective thinking. Dewey knew very well how complex a process thinking is, and he made no attempt to gloss over its complexities. He shows how facts and ideas are continually being modified by each other, how analysis and synthesis are inseparably related, how meanings and concepts undergo subtle changes, etc. In the course of his analysis of thinking, he explains what ideas are, what it means to make judgments, what concepts are and how they arise, how things acquire meaning, and why method is important in thinking.

How We Think concludes with some observations about the thought processes in children, the relationships between play, work, and education, the differences between practical and theoretical thinking, the role of language in thought, and the importance of developing the ability to make precise observations. All in all, *How We Think* is an extraordinarily illuminating and useful analysis of thinking by one of the greatest psychologists of the twentieth century.

The Process of Thought
from *How We Think*

WHAT IS THINKING?

I

DIFFERENT MEANINGS
OF THOUGHT

The Best Way of Thinking

N o one can tell another person in any definite way how he *should* think, any more than how he ought to breathe or to have his blood circulate. But the various ways in which men *do* think can be told and can be described in their general features. Some of these ways are better than others; the reasons why they are better can be set forth. The person who understands what the better ways of thinking are and why they are better can, if he will, change his own personal ways until they become more effective; until, that is to say, they do better the work that thinking can do and that other mental operations cannot do so well. The better way of thinking that is to be considered in this book is called reflective thinking: the kind of thinking that consists in turning a subject over in the mind and giving it serious and consecutive consideration. Before we take up this main theme, we shall, however, first take note briefly of some other mental processes to which the name *thought* is sometimes given.

The "Stream of Consciousness." All the time we are awake and sometimes when we are asleep, something is, as we say, going through our heads. When we are asleep we call that kind of sequence "dreaming." We also have daydreams, reveries, castles built in the air, and mental streams that are even more idle and chaotic. To this uncontrolled coursing of ideas through our heads the name of "thinking" is sometimes given. It is automatic and unregulated. Many a child has attempted to see whether he could not "stop thinking"—that is, stop this procession of mental states through his mind—and in vain. More of our waking life than most of us would care to admit is whiled away in this inconsequential trifling with mental pictures, random recollections, pleasant but unfounded hopes, flitting, half-developed impressions. Hence it is that he who offers "a penny for your thoughts" does not expect to drive any great bargain if his offer is taken; he will only find out what happens to be "going through the mind" and what "goes" in this fashion rarely leaves much that is worth while behind.

Reflective Thought Is a Chain. In this sense, silly folk and dullards *think.* The story is told of a man in slight repute for intelligence, who, desiring to be chosen selectman in his New England town, addressed a knot of neighbors in this wise: "I hear you don't believe I know enough to hold office. I wish you to understand that I am thinking about something or other most of the time." Now, reflective thought is like this random coursing of things through the mind in that it consists of a succession of things thought of, but it is unlike in that the mere chance occurrence of any chance "something or other" in an irregular sequence does not suffice. Reflection involves not simply a sequence of ideas, but a *con*-sequence—a consecutive ordering in such a way that each determines the next as its proper outcome, while each outcome in turn leans back on, or refers to, its predecessors. The successive portions of a reflective thought grow out of one another and support one another; they do not come and go in a medley. Each phase is a step from something to something—technically speaking, it is a *term* of thought. Each term leaves a deposit that is utilized in the next term. The stream or flow becomes a train or chain. There are in any reflective thought definite units that are linked together so that there is a sustained movement to a common end.

Thinking Usually Restricted to Things Not Directly Perceived. The second meaning of thinking limits it to things not sensed or directly perceived, to things *not* seen, heard, touched, smelled, or tasted. We ask the man telling a story if he saw a certain incident happen, and his reply may be, "No, I only thought of it." A note of invention, as distinct from faithful record of observation, is present. Most important in this class are successions of imaginative incidents and episodes that have a certain coherence, hang together on a continuous thread, and thus lie between kaleidoscopic flights of fancy and considerations deliberately employed to establish a conclusion. The imaginative stories poured forth by children possess all degrees of internal congruity; some are disjointed, some are articulated. When connected, they simulate reflective thought; indeed, they usually occur in minds of logical capacity. These imaginative enterprises often precede thinking of the close-knit type and prepare the way for it. In this sense, a thought or idea is a mental picture of something not actually present, and thinking is the succession of such pictures.

Reflective Thinking Aims at a Conclusion. In contrast, reflective thinking has a purpose beyond the entertainment afforded by the train of agreeable mental inventions and pictures. The train must lead somewhere; it must tend to a conclusion that can be substantiated outside the course of the images. A story of a giant may satisfy merely because of the story itself; a reflective conclusion that a giant lived at a certain date and place on the earth would have to have some justification outside of the chain of ideas in order to be a valid or sound conclusion. This contrasting element is probably best conveyed in the ordinary saying: "Think it *out.*" The phrase suggests an entanglement to be straightened out, something obscure to be cleared up through the application of thought. There is a goal to be reached, and this end sets a task that controls the sequence of ideas.

Thinking as Practically Synonymous with Believing. A third meaning of thought is practically synonymous with *belief.* "I think it is going to be colder tomorrow" or "I think Hungary is larger than Yugoslavia" is equivalent to "I believe so-and-so." When we say, "Men used to think the world was flat," we obviously refer to a belief that was held by our ancestors. This meaning of thought is narrower than those previously mentioned. A belief refers to something beyond itself by which its value is tested; it makes an assertion about some matter of fact or some principle or law. It means that a specified state of fact or law is accepted or rejected, that it is something proper to be affirmed or at least acquiesced in. It is hardly necessary to lay stress upon the importance of belief. It covers all the matters of which we have no sure knowledge and yet which we are sufficiently confident of to act upon and also the matters that we now accept as certainly true, as knowledge, but which nevertheless may be questioned in the future—just as much that passed as knowledge in the past has now passed into the limbo of mere opinion or of error.

There is nothing in the mere fact of thought as identical with belief that reveals whether the belief is well founded or not. Two different men say, "I believe the world is spherical." One man, if challenged, could produce little or no evidence for thinking as he does. It is an idea that he has picked up from others and that he accepts because the idea is generally current, not because he has examined into the matter and not because his own mind has taken any active part in reaching and framing the belief.

Such "thoughts" grow up unconsciously. They are picked up—we know not how. From obscure sources and by unnoticed channels they insinuate themselves into the mind and become unconsciously a part of our mental furniture. Tradition, instruction, imitation—all of which depend upon authority in some form, or appeal to our own advantage, or fall in with a strong passion—are responsible for them. Such thoughts are prejudices; that is, prejudgments, not conclusions reached as the result of personal mental activity, such as observing, collecting, and examining evidence. Even when they happen to be correct, their correctness is a matter of accident as far as the person who entertains them is concerned.

Reflective Thinking Impels to Inquiry. Thus we are brought again, by way of contrast, to the particular kind of thinking that we are to study in this volume, *reflective thinking.* Thought, in the two first senses mentioned, may be harmful to the mind because it distracts attention from the real world, and because it may be a waste of time. On the other hand, if indulged in judiciously these thoughts may afford genuine enjoyment and also be a source of needed recreation. But in either case they can make no claim to truth; they cannot hold themselves up as something that the mind should accept, assert, and be willing to act upon. They may involve a kind of emotional commitment, but not intellectual and practical commitment. Beliefs, on the other hand, do involve precisely this commitment and consequently sooner or later they demand our investigation to find out upon what grounds they rest. To think of a cloud as a whale or a camel—in the sense of to "fancy"—does not commit one to the conclusion that the person having the idea would ride the camel or extract oil from the whale. But when Columbus "thought" the world was round, in the sense of "believed it to be so," he and his followers were thereby committed to a series of other beliefs and actions: to beliefs about routes to India, about what would happen if ships traveled far westward on the Atlantic, etc., precisely as thinking that the world was flat had committed those who held it to belief in the impossibility of circumnavigation, and in the limitation of the earth to regions in the small civilized part of it Europeans were already acquainted with, etc.

The earlier thought, belief in the flatness of the earth, had some foundation in evidence; it rested upon what men could see easily within the limits of their vision. But this evidence was not further looked into; it was not checked by considering other evidence; there was no search for new evidence. Ultimately the belief rested on laziness, inertia, custom, absence of courage and energy in investigation. The later belief rests upon careful and extensive study, upon purposeful widening of the area of observation, upon reasoning out the conclusions of alternative conceptions to see what would follow in case one or the other were adopted for belief. As distinct from the first kind of thinking there was an orderly chain of ideas; as distinct from the second, there was a controlling purpose and end; as distinct from the third, there was personal examination, scrutiny, inquiry.

Because Columbus did not accept unhesitatingly the current traditional theory, because he doubted and inquired, he arrived at his thought. Skeptical of what, from long habit, seemed most certain, and credulous of what seemed impossible, he went on thinking until he could produce evidence for both his confidence and his disbelief. Even if his conclusion had finally turned out wrong, it would have been a different sort of belief from those it antagonized, because it was reached by a different method. *Active, persistent, and careful consideration of any belief or supposed form of knowledge in the light of the grounds that support it and the further conclusions to which it tends* constitutes reflective thought. Any one of the first three kinds of thought may elicit this type; but once begun, it includes a conscious and voluntary effort to establish belief upon a firm basis of evidence and rationality.

II
THE CENTRAL FACTOR IN THINKING

The Suggestion of Something Not Observed. There are, however, no sharp lines of demarcation between the various operations just outlined. The problem of attaining correct habits of reflection would be much easier than it is did not the different modes of thinking blend insensibly into one another. So far, we have considered rather extreme instances of each kind in order to get the field clearly before us. Let us now reverse this operation; let us consider a rudimentary case of thinking, lying between careful examination of evidence and a mere irresponsible stream of fancies. A man is walking on a warm day. The sky was clear the last time he observed it; but presently he notes, while occupied primarily with other things, that the air is cooler. It occurs to him that it is probably going to rain; looking up, he sees a dark cloud between him and the sun, and he then quickens his steps. What, if anything, in such a situation can be called thought? Neither the act of walking nor the noting of the cold is a thought. Walking is one direction of activity; looking and noting are other modes of activity. The likelihood that it will rain is, however, something *suggested*. The pedestrian *feels* the cold; first he *thinks* of clouds, then he looks and perceives them, and then he thinks of something he does not see: a storm. This *suggested possibility* is the idea, the thought. If it is believed in as a genuine possibility which may occur, it is the kind of thought which falls within the scope of knowledge and which requires reflective consideration.

Up to a certain point there is the same sort of situation as when one who looks at a cloud is reminded of a human figure and face. Thinking in both of these cases (the cases of belief and of fancy) involves noting or perceiving a fact, followed by something else that is not observed but that is brought to mind, suggested by the thing seen. One thing reminds us, as we say, of the other. Side by side, however, with this factor of agreement in the two cases of suggestion is a factor of marked disagreement. We do not *believe* in the face suggested by the cloud; we do not consider at all the probability of its being a fact. There is no *reflective* thought. The danger of rain, on the contrary, presents itself to us as a genuine possibility—a fact of the same nature as the observed coolness. Put differently, we do not regard the cloud as meaning or indicating a face, but merely as suggesting it, while we do consider that the coolness may *mean* rain. In the first case, on seeing an object, we just happen, as we say, to think of something else; in the second, we consider the *possibility and nature of the connection between the object seen and the object suggested.* The seen thing is regarded as in some way *the ground or basis of belief* in the suggested thing; it possesses the quality of *evidence.*

The Function of Signifying. This function whereby one thing signifies or indicates another, thus leading us to consider how far the one may be regarded as warrant for belief in the other, is, then, the central factor in all reflective or distinctively intellectual thinking. By calling up various situations to which such terms as *signifies* and *indicates* apply, the student will realize for himself the actual facts denoted. Synonyms for these terms are: points to, tells of, betokens, prognosticates, represents, stands for, implies.[1] We also say one thing portends another, is ominous of another, or a symptom of it, or a key to it, or (if the connection is quite obscure) that it gives a hint, clue, or intimation. Reflection is not identical with the mere fact that one thing indicates, means, another thing. It commences when we begin to inquire into the reliability, the worth, of any particular indication; when we try to test its value and see what guarantee there is that the existing data *really* point to the idea that is suggested in such a way as to *justify* acceptance of the latter.

---

1. *Implies* is more often used when a principle or general truth brings about belief in some other truth; the other phrases are more frequently used to denote the cases in which a fact or event leads us to believe in some other fact or in a law.

Reflection Implies Belief on Evidence. Reflection thus implies that something is believed in (or disbelieved in), not on its own direct account, but through something else which stands as witness, evidence, proof, voucher, warrant; that is, as *ground of belief.* At one time, rain is actually felt or directly experienced; at another time, we *infer* that it has rained from the appearance of the grass and trees, or that it is going to rain because of the condition of the air or the state of the barometer. At one time, we see a man (or suppose we do) without any intermediary fact; at another time, we are not quite sure what we see, and hunt for accompanying facts that will serve as signs, indications, tokens of what we are to believe.

Thinking, for the purposes of this inquiry, is accordingly defined as *that operation in which present facts suggest other facts (or truths) in such a way as to induce belief in what is suggested on the ground of real relation in the things themselves,* a relation between what suggests and what is suggested. A cloud *suggests* a weasel or a whale; it does not *mean* the latter, because there is no tie, or bond, in the things themselves between what is seen and what is suggested. Ashes not merely suggest a previous fire, but they signify there has been a fire, because ashes are produced by combustion and, if they are genuine ashes, only by combustion. It is an objective connection, the link in actual things, that makes one thing the ground, warrant, evidence, for believing in something else.

III
PHASES OF REFLECTIVE THINKING

We may carry our account further by noting that *reflective* thinking, in distinction from other operations to which we apply the name of thought, involves (1) a state of doubt, hesitation, perplexity, mental difficulty, in which thinking originates, and (2) an act of searching, hunting, inquiring, to find material that will resolve the doubt, settle and dispose of the perplexity.

The Importance of Uncertainty and of Inquiry. In our illustration, the shock of coolness generated confusion and suspended belief, at least momentarily. Because it was unexpected, it was a shock or an interruption needing to be accounted for, identified, or placed. To say that the abrupt occurrence of the change of temperature constitutes a problem may sound forced and artificial; but if we are willing to extend the meaning of the word *problem* to whatever—no matter how slight and commonplace in character—perplexes and challenges the mind so that it makes belief at all uncertain, there is a genuine problem, or question, involved in an experience of sudden change.

The turning of the head, the lifting of the eyes, the scanning of the heavens are activities adapted to bring to recognition facts that will answer the question presented by the sudden coolness. The facts as they first presented themselves were perplexing; they suggested, however, clouds. The act of looking was an act to discover whether this suggested explanation held good. It may again seem forced to speak of this looking, almost automatic, as an act of research, or inquiry. But once more, if we are willing to generalize our conceptions of our mental operations to include the trivial and ordinary as well as the technical and recondite, there is no good reason for refusing to give this title to the act of looking. For the result of the act is to bring facts before the mind that enable a person to reach a conclusion on the basis of evidence. In so far, then, as the act of looking was deliberate, was performed with the intention of getting an external basis on which to rest a belief, it exemplifies in an elementary way the operation of hunting, searching, inquiring involved in any reflective operation.

Another instance, commonplace also, yet not quite so trivial, may enforce this lesson. A man traveling in an unfamiliar region comes to a branching of the road. Having no sure knowledge to fall back upon, he is brought to a standstill of hesitation and suspense. Which road is right? And how shall his perplexity be resolved? There are but two alternatives: he must either blindly and arbitrarily take his course, trusting to luck for the outcome, or he must discover grounds for the conclusion that a given road is right. Any attempt to decide the matter by thinking will involve inquiring into other facts, whether brought to mind by memory, or by further observation, or by both. The perplexed wayfarer must carefully scrutinize what is before him and he must cudgel his memory. He looks for evidence that will support belief in favor of either of the roads—for evidence that will weight down one suggestion. He may climb a tree; he may go first in this direction, then in that, looking, in either case, for signs, clues, indications. He wants something in the nature of a signboard or a map, and *his reflection is aimed at the discovery of facts that will serve this purpose.*

The foregoing illustration may be generalized. Thinking begins in what may fairly enough be called a *forked-road* situation, a situation that is ambiguous, that presents a dilemma, that proposes alternatives. As long as our activity glides smoothly along from one thing to another, or as long as we permit our imagination to entertain fancies at pleasure, there is no call for reflection. Difficulty or obstruction in the way of reaching a belief brings us, however, to a pause. In the suspense of uncertainty, we metaphorically climb a tree; we try to find some standpoint from which we may survey additional facts and, getting a more commanding view of the situation, decide how the facts stand related to one another.

The Regulation of Thinking by Its Purpose. Demand for the solution of a perplexity is the steadying and guiding factor in the entire process of reflection. Where there is no question of a problem to be solved or a difficulty to be surmounted, the course of suggestions flows on at random; we have the first type of thought described. If the stream of suggestions is controlled simply by their emotional congruity, their fitting agreeably into a single picture or story, we have the second type. But a question to be answered, an ambiguity to be resolved, sets up an end and holds the current of ideas to a definite channel. Every suggested conclusion is tested by its reference to this regulating end, by its pertinence to the problem in hand. This need of straightening out a perplexity also controls the kind of inquiry undertaken. A traveler whose end is the most beautiful path will look for other signs and will test suggestions on another basis than if he wishes to discover the way to a given city. *The nature of the problem fixes the end of thought,* and *the end controls the process of thinking.*

IV

SUMMARY

We may recapitulate by saying that the origin of thinking is some perplexity, confusion, or doubt. Thinking is not a case of spontaneous combustion; it does not occur just on "general principles." There is something that occasions and evokes it. General appeals to a child (or to a grownup) to think, irrespective of the existence in his own experience of some difficulty that troubles him and disturbs his equilibrium, are as futile as advice to lift himself by his bootstraps.

Given a difficulty, the next step is suggestion of some way out—the formation of some tentative plan or project, the entertaining of some theory that will account for the peculiarities in question, the consideration of some solution for the problem. The data at hand cannot supply the solution; they can only suggest it. What, then, are the sources of the suggestion? Clearly, past experience and a fund of relevant knowledge at one's command. If the person has had some acquaintance with similar situations, if he has dealt with material of the same sort before, suggestions more or less apt and helpful will arise. But unless there has been some analogous experience, confusion remains mere confusion. Even when a child (or a grownup) has a problem, it is wholly futile to urge him to think when he has no prior experiences that involve some of the same conditions.

There may, however, be a state of perplexity and also previous experience out of which suggestions emerge, and yet thinking need not be reflective. For the person may not be sufficiently *critical* about the ideas that occur to him. He may jump at a conclusion without weighing the grounds on which it rests; he may forego or unduly shorten the act of hunting, inquiring; he may take the first "answer," or solution, that comes to him because of mental sloth, torpor, impatience to get something settled. One can think reflectively only when one is willing to endure suspense and to undergo the trouble of searching. To many persons both suspense of judgment and intellectual search are disagreeable; they want to get them ended as soon as possible. They cultivate an overpositive and dogmatic habit of mind, or feel perhaps that a condition of doubt will be regarded as evidence of mental inferiority. It is at the point where examination and test enter into investigation that the difference between reflective thought and bad thinking comes in. To be genuinely thoughtful, we must be willing to sustain and protract that state of doubt which is the stimulus to thorough inquiry, so as not to accept an idea or make positive assertion of a belief until justifying reasons have been found.

WHY REFLECTIVE THINKING
MUST BE AN EDUCATIONAL AIM

I
THE VALUES OF THINKING

It Makes Possible Action with a Conscious Aim. We all acknowledge, in words at least, that ability to think is highly important; it is regarded as the distinguishing power that marks man off from the lower animals. But since our ordinary notions of how and why thinking is important are vague, it is worthwhile to state explicitly the values possessed by reflective thought. In the first place, it emancipates us from merely impulsive and merely routine activity. Put in positive terms, thinking enables us to direct our activities with foresight and to plan according to ends in view, or purposes of which we are aware. It enables us to act in deliberate and intentional fashion to attain future objects or to come into command of what is now distant and lacking. By putting the consequences of different ways and lines of action before the mind, it enables us to *know what we are about* when we act. *It converts action that is merely appetitive, blind, and impulsive into intelligent action.* A brute animal, as far as we know, is pushed on from behind; it is moved in accordance with its present physiological state by some present external stimulus. The being who can think is moved by remote considerations, by results that can be attained perhaps only after a lapse of years—as when a young person sets out to gain a professional education to fit himself for a career in years to come.

For example, an animal without thought will go into its hole when rain threatens, because of some immediate stimulus to its organism. But a thinking being will perceive that certain given facts are probable signs of a future rain and will take steps in the light of this anticipated future. To plant seeds, to cultivate the soil, to harvest grain are intentional acts, possible only to a being who has learned to subordinate the immediately felt elements of an experience to those values which these elements hint at and prophesy. Philosophers have made much of the phrases "book of nature," "language of nature." Well, it is in virtue of thought that given things are significant of absent things and that nature speaks a language which may be interpreted. To a being who thinks, things are records of their past, as fossils tell of the prior history of the earth, and are prophetic of their future, as from the present positions of heavenly bodies remote eclipses are foretold. Shakespeare's "tongues in trees, books in the running brooks" expresses literally enough the power superadded to existences when they are used by a thinking being. Only when things about us have meaning for us, only when they signify consequences that can be reached by using them in certain ways, is any such thing as intentional, deliberate control of them possible.

It Makes Possible Systematic Preparations and Inventions. By thought man also develops and arranges artificial signs to remind him in advance of consequences and of ways of securing and avoiding them. As the trait just mentioned makes the difference between savage man and brute, so this trait makes the difference between civilized man and savage. A savage who has been shipwrecked on a river may note certain things that serve him as signs of danger in the future. But civilized man deliberately *makes* such signs; he sets up in advance of any particular shipwreck warning buoys, and builds lighthouses where he sees signs that such an event may occur. A savage reads weather signs with great expertness; civilized man institutes a weather service by which signs are artificially secured and information is distributed in advance of the appearance of any signs that could be detected without special methods. A savage finds his way skillfully through a wilderness by reading certain obscure indications; civilized man builds a highway that shows the road to all. The savage learns to detect the signs of fire and thereby to invent methods of producing flame; civilized man discovers illuminating gas and oils, and invents lamps, electric lights, stoves, furnaces, central heating plants, etc. The very essence of civilized culture is that we deliberately erect monuments and memorials, lest we forget; and deliberately institute, in advance of the happening of various contingencies and emergencies of life, devices for detecting their approach and registering their nature, for warding off what is unfavorable, or at least for protecting ourselves from its full impact and for making more secure and extensive what is favorable. All forms of artificial apparatus are intentional modifications of natural things so designed that they may serve better than in their natural estate to indicate the hidden, the absent, and the remote.

It Enriches Things with Meanings. Finally, thought confers upon physical events and objects a very different status and value from those which they possess to a being that does not reflect. These words are mere scratches, curious variations of light and shade, to one to whom they are not linguistic signs. To him for whom they are signs of other things, the collection of marks stands for some idea or object. We are so used to the fact that things have meaning for us, that they are not mere excitations of sense organs, that we fail to recognize that they are charged with the significance they have only because in the past absent things have been suggested to us by what is present and these suggestions have been confirmed in subsequent experience. If we stumble against something in the dark, we may react to it and get out of the way to save ourselves a bruise or a tumble without recognizing what particular *object* it is. We react almost automatically to many stimuli; they have no meaning for us or are not definite individual objects. For an *object* is more than a mere *thing;* it is a thing having a definite significance.

The distinction we are making can be most readily understood if the reader will call to mind things and events that are strange to him and compare them with the same things and events as they appear to persons having expert knowledge of them; or if he will compare a thing or event as it is *before,* with what it is *after,* he has obtained intellectual mastery over it. To a layman a particular body of water may signify only something to wash with or to drink; to another person it may stand for a union of two chemical elements, themselves not liquids but gases; or it may signify something that should *not* be drunk because of danger of typhoid fever. To a baby things are at first only patterns of color and light, sources of sound; they acquire meaning only as they become signs of possible, but not yet present and actual, experiences. To the learned scientific man, the range of meanings possessed by ordinary things is much widened. A stone is not merely a stone; it is a stone of a given mineralogical type, from a particular geological stratum, etc. It tells him something about what happened millions of years ago, and helps paint the picture of the earth's history.

Control and Enriched Value. The first two values mentioned are of a practical sort; they give increased power of *control*. The value just mentioned is an enrichment of meaning apart from added control—a certain event in the heavens cannot be warded off just because we know it is an eclipse and how it is produced, but it does have a significance for us that it did not have before. We may not need to do any thinking now when some event occurs, but if we have thought about it before, the outcome of that thinking is funded as a directly added and deepened meaning of the event. The great reward of exercising the power of thinking is that there are no limits to the possibility of carrying over, into the objects and events of life, meanings originally acquired by thoughtful examination, and hence no limit to the continual growth of meaning in human life. A child today may see meanings in things that were hidden from Ptolemy and Copernicus because of the results of reflective investigations that have occurred in the meantime.

Various values of the power of thought are summed up in the following quotation from John Stuart Mill.

> To draw inferences has been said to be the great business of life. Everyone has daily, hourly, and momentary need of ascertaining facts which he has not directly observed: not from any general purpose of adding to his stock of knowledge, but because the facts themselves are of importance to his interests or to his occupations. The business of the magistrate, of the military commander, of the navigator, of the physician, of the agriculturist, *is merely to judge of evidence and to act accordingly.* . . . As they do this well or ill, so they discharge well or ill the duties of their several callings. *It is the only occupation in which the mind never ceases to be engaged.*[2]

Two Reasons for Training Thought. These three values, in their cumulative effect, make the difference between a truly human and rational life and the existence lived by those animals that are immersed in sensation and appetite. Beyond a somewhat narrow limit, enforced by the necessi-

---

2. Mill, *System of Logic*, Introduction, § 5.

ties of life, the values that have been described do not, however, automatically realize themselves. For anything approaching their adequate realization, thought needs careful and attentive educational direction. Nor is that the whole story. Thinking may develop in positively wrong ways and lead to false and harmful beliefs. The need of systematic training would be less than it is if the only danger to be feared were lack of any development; the evil of the wrong kind of development is even greater.

An earlier writer than Mill, John Locke (1632–1704), brings out the importance of thought for life and the need of training so that its best and not its worst possibilities will be realized, in the following words:

> No man ever sets himself about anything but upon some view or other, which serves him for a reason for what he does; and whatsoever faculties he employs, the understanding with such light as it has, well or ill informed, constantly leads; and by that light, true or false, all his operative powers are directed. . . . Temples have their sacred images, and we see what influence they have always had over a great part of mankind. But in truth the ideas and images in men's minds are the invisible powers that constantly govern them, and to these they all, universally, pay a ready submission. It is therefore of the highest concernment that great care should be taken of the understanding, to conduct it aright in the search of knowledge and in judgments it makes.[3]

While the power of thought, then, frees us from servile subjection to instinct, appetite, and routine, it also brings with it the occasion and possibility of error and mistake. In elevating us above the brute, it opens the possibility of failures to which the animal, limited to instinct, cannot sink.

II

TENDENCIES NEEDING CONSTANT REGULATION

Physical and Social Sanctions of Correct Thinking. Up to a certain point, the necessities of life enforce a fundamental and persistent discipline of thought for which the most cunningly devised artifices would be ineffective substitutes. The burned child dreads the fire; a painful consequence emphasizes the need of correct inference much more than would learned discourses on the properties of heat. Social conditions also put a premium on correct inference in matters where action based on valid thought is socially important. These sanctions of proper thinking may affect life itself, or at least a life reasonably free from perpetual discomfort.

---

3. Locke, *The Conduct of the Understanding,* first paragraph.

The signs of enemies, of shelter, of food, of the main social conditions have to be correctly apprehended.

But this disciplinary training, efficacious as it is within certain limits, does not carry us far. Logical attainment in one direction is no bar to extravagant conclusions in another. A savage who is expert in judging the movements and location of the animals that he hunts will accept and gravely narrate the most preposterous yarns concerning the origin of their habits and peculiarities of structure. When there is no direct appreciable reaction of the inference upon the security and prosperity of life, there are no natural checks to the acceptance of wrong beliefs. Conclusions may be accepted merely because the suggestions are vivid and interesting, while a large accumulation of dependable data may fail to suggest a proper conclusion because of opposition from existing customs. Then there is a "primitive credulity," a natural tendency to believe anything that is suggested unless there is overpowering evidence to the contrary. It sometimes seems, upon surveying the history of thought, that men exhausted pretty much all wrong forms of belief before they hit upon the right conceptions. The history of scientific beliefs also shows that, when a wrong theory once gets general acceptance, men will expend ingenuity of thought in buttressing it with additional errors rather than surrender it and start in a new direction: witness for example the elaborate pains taken to preserve the Ptolemaic theory of the solar system. Even today correct beliefs about the constitution of nature are held by the great multitude merely because they are current and popular rather than because the multitude understands the reasons upon which they rest.

Superstition Is as Natural as Science. As to the mere function of suggestion, there is no difference between the power of a column of mercury to portend rain and that of the entrails of an animal or the flight of birds to foretell the fortunes of war. For all anybody can tell in advance, the spilling of salt is as likely to import bad luck as the bite of a mosquito to import malaria. Only systematic regulation of the conditions under which observations are made and severe discipline of the habits of entertaining suggestions can secure a decision that one type of belief is vicious and the other sound. The substitution of scientific for superstitious habits of inference has not been brought about by any improvement in the acuteness of the senses or in the natural workings of the function of suggestion. It is the result of regulation *of the conditions* under which observation and inference take place. When such regulation is absent, dreams, the position of stars, the lines of the hand are regarded as valuable signs, and the fall of cards as an inevitable omen, while natural events of the most crucial significance go disregarded. Hence beliefs in portents of various kinds, now mere nook-and-cranny superstitions, were once universal. A long discipline in exact science was required for their conquest.

The General Causes of Bad Thinking: Bacon's "Idols." It is instructive to note some of the attempts that have been made to classify the main sources of error in reaching beliefs. Francis Bacon, for example, at the beginning of modern scientific inquiry, enumerated four such classes, under the somewhat fantastic title of "idols" (Gr. εἴδωλα, images), spectral forms that allure the mind into false paths. These he called the idols, or phantoms, of (*a*) the tribe, (*b*) the market place, (*c*) the cave or den, and (*d*) the theatre; or, less metaphorically, (*a*) standing erroneous methods (or at least temptations to error) that have their roots in human nature generally, (*b*) those that come from intercourse and language, (*c*) those that are due to causes peculiar to a specific individual, and finally, (*d*) those that have their sources in the fashion or general current of a period. Classifying these causes of fallacious belief somewhat differently, we may say that two are intrinsic and two are extrinsic. Of the intrinsic, one is common to all men alike (such as the universal tendency to notice instances that corroborate a favorite belief more readily than those that contradict it), while the other resides in the specific temperament and habits of the given individual. Of the extrinsic, one proceeds from generic social conditions—like the tendency to suppose that there is a fact wherever there is a word, and no fact where there is no linguistic term—while the other proceeds from local and temporary social currents.

Locke on Typical Forms of Wrong Belief. Locke's method of dealing with typical forms of wrong belief is less formal and may be more enlightening. We can hardly do better than quote his forcible and quaint language when, enumerating different classes of men, he shows different ways in which thought goes wrong:

> (*a*) The first is of those who seldom reason at all, but do and think according to the example of others, whether parents, neighbors, ministers, or whom else they are pleased to make choice of to have an implicit faith in, for the saving of themselves the pains and troubles of thinking and examining for themselves.
>
> (*b*) This kind is of those who put passion in the place of reason, and being resolved that shall govern their actions and arguments, neither use their own, nor hearken to other people's reason, any farther than it suits their humor, interest, or party.[4]

---

4. In another place Locke says: "Men's prejudices and inclinations impose often upon themselves. . . . Inclination suggests and slides into discourse favorable terms, which introduce favorable ideas; till at last by this means that is concluded clear

(*c*) The third sort is of those who readily and sincerely follow reason, but for want of having that which one may call large, sound, roundabout sense, have not a full view of all that relates to the question. . . . They converse but with one sort of men, they read but one sort of books, they will not come in the hearing but of one sort of notions. . . . They have a pretty traffic with known correspondents in some little creek . . . but will not venture out into the great ocean of knowledge. [Men of originally equal natural parts may finally arrive at very different stores of knowledge and truth] when all the odds between them has been the different scope that has been given to their understandings to range in, for the gathering up of information and furnishing their heads with ideas and notions and observations, whereon to employ their mind.[5]

In another portion of his writings,[6] Locke states the same ideas in slightly different form.

1. That which is inconsistent with our *principles* is so far from passing for probable with us that it will not be allowed possible. The reverence borne to these principles is so great, and their authority so paramount to all other, that the testimony not only of other men but the evidence of our own senses are often rejected when they offer to vouch anything contrary to these *established rules*. . . . There is nothing more ordinary than children's receiving into their minds propositions . . . from their parents, nurses, or those about them; which being insinuated in their unwary as well as unbiased understandings, and fastened by degrees, are at last (and this whether true or false) riveted there by long custom and education, beyond all possibility of being pulled out again. For men, when they are grown up, reflecting upon their opinions and finding those of this sort to be as ancient in their minds as their very memories, not having observed their early insinuation, nor by what means they got them, they are apt to reverence them as sacred things, and not to suffer them to be profaned, touched, or questioned. [They take them as standards] to be the great and unerring deciders of truth and falsehood, and the judges to which they are to appeal in all manner of controversies.

2. Secondly, next to these are men whose understandings are cast into a mold, and fashioned just to the size of a received hypothesis. [Such men, while not denying the existence of facts and evidence, cannot be convinced even by the evidence that would decide them if their minds were not so closed by adherence to fixed belief.]

---

and evident, thus dressed up, which, taken in its native state, by making use of none but precise determined ideas, would find no admittance at all."
5. *The Conduct of the Understanding*, § 3.
6. *Essay Concerning Human Understanding*, Bk. IV, Ch. XX, "Of Wrong Assent or Error." [See *Great Books of the Western World*, Vol. 35, pp. 388–394 (Ed.).]

3. Predominant Passions. Thirdly, probabilities which cross men's appetites and prevailing passions run the same fate. Let ever so much probability hang on one side of a covetous man's reasoning, and money on the other, it is easy to foresee which will outweigh. Earthly minds, like mud walls, resist the strongest batteries.

4. Authority. The fourth and last wrong measure of probability I shall take notice of, and which keeps in ignorance or error more people than all the others together, is the giving up our assent to the common received opinions, either of our friends or party, neighborhood or country.

Importance of Attitudes. We have quoted from influential thinkers of the past. But the facts to which they refer are familiar in our everyday experience. Any observant person can note any day, both in himself and in others, the tendency to believe that which is in harmony with desire. We take that to be true which we should like to have so, and ideas that go contrary to our hopes and wishes have difficulty in getting lodgment. We all jump to conclusions; we all fail to examine and test our ideas because of our personal attitudes. When we generalize, we tend to make sweeping assertions; that is, from one or only a few facts we make a generalization covering a wide field. Observation also reveals the powerful influence wielded by social influences that have actually nothing to do with the truth or falsity of what is asserted and denied. Some of the dispositions that give these irrelevant influences power to limit and mislead thought are good in themselves, a fact that renders the need of training the more important. Reverence for parents and regard for those placed in authority are in the abstract surely valuable traits. Yet, as Locke points out, they are among the chief forces that determine beliefs apart from and even contrary to the operations of intelligent thought. The desire to be in harmony with others is in itself a desirable trait. But it may lead a person too readily to fall in with the prejudices of others and may weaken his independence of judgment. It even leads to an extreme partisanship that regards it as disloyal to question the beliefs of a group to which one belongs.

Because of the importance of attitudes, ability to train thought is not achieved merely by knowledge of the best forms of thought. Possession of this information is no guarantee for ability to think well. Moreover, there are no set exercises in correct thinking whose repeated performance will cause one to be a good thinker. The information and the exercises are both of value. But no individual realizes their value except as he is personally animated by certain dominant attitudes in his own character. It was once almost universally believed that the mind had faculties, like memory and attention, that could be developed by repeated exercise, as gymnastic exercises are supposed to develop the muscles. This belief is now generally discredited in the large sense in which it was once held. Similarly it is highly questionable whether the practice of thinking in accordance with some logical formula results in creation of a general habit of thinking; namely, one applicable over a wide range of subjects. It is a matter of common notice that men who are expert thinkers in their own special fields adopt views on other matters without doing the inquiring that they know to be necessary for substantiating simpler facts that fall within their own specialities.

The Union of Attitude and Skilled Method. What can be done, however, is to cultivate those *attitudes* that are favorable to the use of the best methods of inquiry and testing. Knowledge of the methods alone will not suffice; there must be the desire, the will, to employ them. This desire is an affair of personal disposition. But on the other hand the disposition alone will not suffice. There must also be understanding of the forms and techniques that are the channels through which these attitudes operate to the best advantage. Since these forms and techniques will be taken up for discussion later, we shall here mention the attitudes that need to be cultivated in order to secure their adoption and use.

(a) *Open-mindedness.* This attitude may be defined as freedom from prejudice, partisanship, and such other habits as close the mind and make it unwilling to consider new problems and entertain new ideas. But it is something more active and positive than these words suggest. It is very different from empty-mindedness. While it *is* hospitality to new themes, facts, ideas, questions, it is not the kind of hospitality that would be indicated by hanging out a sign: "Come right in; there is nobody at home." It includes an active desire to listen to more sides than one; to give heed to facts from whatever source they come; to give full attention to alternative possibilities; to recognize the possibility of error even in the beliefs that are dearest to us. Mental sluggishness is one great factor in closing the mind to new ideas. The path of least resistance and least trouble is a mental rut already made. It requires troublesome work to undertake the alteration of old beliefs. Self-conceit often regards it as a sign of weakness to admit that a belief to which we have once committed ourselves is wrong. We get so identified with an idea that it is literally a "pet" notion and we rise to its defense and stop our mental eyes and ears to anything different. Unconscious fears also drive us into purely defensive attitudes that operate like a coat of armor not only to shut out new conceptions but even to prevent us from making a new observation. The cumulative effect of these forces is to shut in the mind, and to create a withdrawal from new intellectual contacts that are needed for learning. They can best be fought by cultivating that alert curiosity and spontaneous outreaching for the new which is the essence of the open mind. The mind that is open merely in the sense that it passively permits things to trickle in and through will not be able to resist the factors that make for mental closure.

(b) *Wholeheartedness.* When anyone is thoroughly interested in some object and cause, he throws himself into it; he does so, as we say, "heartily," or with a whole heart. The importance of this attitude or disposition is generally recognized in practical and moral affairs. But it is equally important in intellectual development. There is no greater enemy of effective thinking than divided interest. This division unfortunately is often produced in school. A pupil gives an external, perfunctory attention to the teacher and to his book and lesson while his inmost thoughts are concerned with matters more attractive to him. He pays attention with ear or eye, but his brain is occupied with affairs that make an immediate appeal. He feels obliged to study because he has to recite, to pass an examination, to make a grade, or because he wishes to please his teacher or his parents. But the material does not hold him by its own power. His approach is not straightforward and single-minded. This point may in some cases seem trivial. But in others it may be very serious. It then contributes to the formation of a general habit or attitude that is most unfavorable to good thinking.

When a person is absorbed, the subject carries him on. Questions occur to him spontaneously; a flood of suggestions pour in on him; further inquiries and readings are indicated and followed; instead of having to use his energy to hold his mind to the subject (thereby lessening that which is available for the subject, itself, and creating a divided state of mind), the material holds and buoys his mind up and gives an onward impetus to thinking. A genuine enthusiasm is an attitude that operates as an intellectual force. A teacher who arouses such an enthusiasm in his pupils has done something that no amount of formalized method, no matter how correct, can accomplish.

(c) *Responsibility.* Like sincerity or wholeheartedness, responsibility is usually conceived as a moral trait rather than as an intellectual resource. But it is an attitude that is necessary to win the adequate support of desire for new points of view and new ideas and of enthusiasm for and capacity for absorption in subject matter. These gifts may run wild, or at least they may lead the mind to spread out too far. They do not of themselves ensure that centralization, that unity, which is essential to good thinking. To be intellectually responsible is to consider the consequences of a projected step; it means to be willing to adopt these consequences when they follow reasonably from any position already taken. Intellectual responsibility secures integrity; that is to say, consistency and harmony in belief. It is not uncommon to see persons continue to accept beliefs whose logical consequences they refuse to acknowledge. They profess certain beliefs but are unwilling to commit themselves to the consequences that flow from them. The result is mental confusion. The "split" inevitably reacts upon the mind to blur its insight and weaken its firmness of grasp; no one can use two inconsistent mental standards without losing some of his mental grip. When pupils study subjects that are too remote from their experience, that arouse no active curiosity, and that are beyond their power of understanding, they begin to use a measure of value and of reality for school subjects different from the measure they employ for affairs of life that make a vital appeal. They tend to become intellectually irresponsible; they do not ask for the *meaning* of what they learn, in the sense of what difference it makes to the rest of their beliefs and to their actions.

The same thing happens when such a multitude of subjects or disconnected facts is forced upon the mind that the student does not have time and opportunity to weigh their meaning. He fancies he is accepting them, is believing them, when in fact his belief is of a totally different kind and implies a different measure of reality from that which operates in his life and action out of school. He then becomes mentally mixed; mixed not only about particular things but also about the basic reasons that make things worthy of belief. Fewer subjects and fewer facts and more responsibility for thinking the material of those subjects and facts through to realize what they involve would give better results. To carry something through to completion is the real meaning of thoroughness, and power to carry a thing through to its end or conclusion is dependent upon the existence of the attitude of intellectual responsibility.

The Bearing of These Personal Attitudes upon Readiness to Think. The three attitudes that have been mentioned, open-mindedness, wholehearted or absorbed interest, responsibility in facing consequences, are of themselves personal qualities, traits of character. They are not the only attitudes that are important in order that the *habit* of thinking in a reflective way may be developed. But the other attitudes that might be set forth are also traits of character, attitudes that, in the proper sense of the word, are *moral*, since they are traits of personal character that have to be cultivated. Any person thinks at times on particular subjects that arouse him. Other persons have habits of thinking quite persistently in special fields of interest; on matters, for example, that are their professional concern. A thoroughgoing habit of thinking is, however, more extended in its scope. No one can think about everything, to be sure; no one can think about *anything* without experience and information about it. Nevertheless, there is such a thing as *readiness* to consider in a thoughtful way the subjects that do come within the range of experience—a readiness that contrasts strongly with the disposition to pass judgment on the basis of mere custom, tradition, prejudice, etc., and thus shun the task of thinking. The personal attitudes that have been named are essential constituents of this general readiness.

If we were compelled to make a choice between these personal attitudes and knowledge about the principles of logical reasoning together with some degree of technical skill in manipulating special logical processes, we should decide for the former. Fortunately no such choice has to be made, because there is no opposition between personal attitudes and logical processes. We only need to bear in mind that, with respect to the aims of education, no separation can be made between impersonal, abstract principles of logic and moral qualities of character. What is needed is to weave them into unity.

ANALYSIS
OF REFLECTIVE THINKING

I

FACTS AND IDEAS

When a situation arises containing a difficulty or perplexity, the person who finds himself in it may take one of a number of courses. He may dodge it, dropping the activity that brought it about, turning to something else. He may indulge in a flight of fancy, imagining himself powerful or wealthy, or in some other way in possession of the means that would enable him to deal with the difficulty. Or, finally, he may face the situation. In this case, he begins to reflect.

Reflection Includes Observation. The moment he begins to reflect, he begins of necessity to observe in order to take stock of conditions. Some of these observations are made by direct use of the senses; others by recollecting observations previously made either by himself or by others. The person who had the engagement to keep notes with his eyes his present location, recalls the place where he should arrive at one o'clock, and brings back to mind the means of transportation with which he is acquainted and their respective locations. In this way he gets as clear and distinct a recognition as possible of the nature of the situation with which he has to deal. Some of the conditions are obstacles and others are aids, resources. No matter whether these conditions come to him by direct perception or by memory, they form the "*facts* of the case." They are the things that are *there*, that have to be reckoned with. Like all facts, they are stubborn. They cannot be got out of the way by magic just because they are disagreeable. It is no use to *wish* they did not exist or were different. They must be taken for just what they are. Hence observation and recollection must be used to the full so as not to glide over or to mistake important features. Until the habit of thinking is well formed, facing the situation to discover the facts requires an effort. For the mind tends to dislike what is unpleasant and so to sheer off from an adequate notice of that which is especially annoying.

Reflection Includes Suggestions. Along with noting the conditions that constitute the facts to be dealt with, suggestions arise of possible courses of action. Thus the person of our illustration thinks of surface cars, elevated trains, and the subway. These alternative suggestions compete with one another. By comparison he judges which alternative is best, which one is the more likely to give a satisfactory solution. The comparison takes place indirectly. The moment one thinks of a possible solution and holds it in suspense, he turns back to the facts. He has now a point of view that leads him to new observations and recollections and to a reconsideration of observations already made in order to test the worth of the suggested way out. Unless he uses the suggestion so as to guide to new observations instead of exercising suspended judgment, he accepts it as soon as it presents itself. Then he falls short of truly reflective thought. The newly noted facts may (and in any complex situation surely will) cause new suggestions to spring up. These become clues to further investigation of conditions. The results of this survey test and correct the proposed inference or suggest a new one. This continuous interaction of the facts disclosed by observation and of the suggested proposals of solution and the suggested methods of dealing with conditions goes on till some suggested solution meets all the conditions of the case and does not run counter to any discoverable feature of it.

Data and Ideas Are Correlative and Indispensable Factors in Reflection. A technical term for the observed facts is *data*. The data form the material that has to be interpreted, accounted for, explained; or, in the case of deliberation as to what to do or how to do it, to be managed and utilized. The suggested solutions for the difficulties disclosed by observation form *ideas*. Data (facts) and ideas (suggestions, possible solutions) thus form the two indispensable and correlative factors of all reflective activity. The two factors are carried on by means respectively of *observation* (in which for convenience is included memory of prior observations of similar cases) and *inference*. The latter runs beyond what is actually noted, beyond what is found, upon careful examination, to be actually present. It relates, therefore, to what is *possible*, rather than to what is actual. It proceeds by anticipation, supposition, conjecture, imagination. All foresight, prediction, planning, as well as theorizing and speculation, are characterized by excursion from the actual into the possible. Hence (as we have already seen) what is inferred demands a double test: first, the process of forming the idea or supposed solution is checked by constant cross reference to the conditions observed to be actually present; secondly, the idea *after* it is formed is tested by *acting* upon it, overtly if possible, otherwise in imagination. The consequences of this action confirm, modify, or refute the idea.

We shall illustrate what has been said by a simple case. Suppose you are walking where there is no regular path. As long as everything goes smoothly, you do not have to think about your walking; your already formed habit takes care of it. Suddenly you find a ditch in your way. You think you will jump it (supposition, plan); but to make sure, you survey it with your eyes (observation), and you find that it is pretty wide and that the bank on the other side is slippery (facts, data). You then wonder if the ditch may not be narrower somewhere else (idea), and you look up and down the stream (observation) to see how matters stand (test of idea by observation). You do not find any good place and so are thrown back upon forming a new plan. As you are casting about, you discover a log (fact again). You ask yourself whether you could not haul that to the ditch and get it across the ditch to use as a bridge (idea again). You judge that idea is worth trying, and so you get the log and manage to put it in place and walk across (test and confirmation by overt action).

If the situation were more complicated, thinking would of course be more elaborate. You can imagine a case in which making a raft, constructing a pontoon bridge, or making a dugout would be the ideas that would finally come to mind and have to be checked by reference to conditions of action (facts). Simple or complicated, relating to what to do in a practical predicament or what to infer in a scientific or philosophic problem, there will always be the two sides: the conditions to be accounted for, dealt with, and the ideas that are plans for dealing with them or are suppositions for interpreting and explaining the phenomena.

In predicting an eclipse, for example, a multitude of observed facts regarding position and movements of earth, sun, and moon comes in on one side, while on the other side the ideas employed to predict and explain involve extensive mathematical calculations. In a philosophic problem, the facts or data may be remote and not susceptible of direct observation by the senses. But still there will be data, perhaps of science, or of morals, art, or the conclusions of past thinkers, that supply the subject matter to be dealt with and by which theories are checked. On the other side, there are the speculations that come to mind and that lead to search for additional subject matter which will both develop the proposed theories as ideas and test their value. Mere facts or data are dead, as far as mind is concerned, unless they are used to suggest and test some idea, some way out of a difficulty. Ideas, on the other hand, are *mere* ideas, idle speculations, fantasies, dreams, unless they are used to guide new observations of, and reflections upon, actual situations, past, present, or future. Finally, they must be brought to some sort of check by actual given material or else remain ideas. Many ideas are of great value as material of poetry, fiction, or the drama, but not as the stuff of knowledge. However, ideas may be of intellectual use to a penetrating mind even when they do not find any immediate reference to actuality, provided they stay in the mind for use when new facts come to light.

II
THE ESSENTIAL FUNCTIONS OF REFLECTIVE ACTIVITY

We now have before us the material for the analysis of a complete act of reflective activity. In the preceding chapter we saw that the two limits of every unit of thinking are a perplexed, troubled, or confused situation at the beginning and a cleared-up, unified, resolved situation at the close. The first of these situations may be called *pre*-reflective. It sets the problem to be solved; out of it grows the question that reflection has to answer. In the final situation the doubt has been dispelled; the situation is *post*-reflective; there results a direct experience of mastery, satisfaction, enjoyment. Here, then, are the limits within which reflection falls.

Five Phases, or Aspects, of Reflective Thought. In between, as states of thinking, are (1) *suggestions,* in which the mind leaps forward to a possible solution; (2) an intellectualization of the difficulty or perplexity that has been *felt* (directly experienced) into a *problem* to be solved, a question for which the answer must be sought; (3) the use of one suggestion after another as a leading idea, or *hypothesis*, to initiate and guide observation and other operations in collection of factual material; (4) the mental elaboration of the idea or supposition as an idea or supposition (*reasoning*, in the sense in which reasoning is a part, not the whole, of inference); and (5) testing the hypothesis by overt or imaginative action.

We shall now take up the five phases, or functions, one by one.

The First Phase, Suggestion. The most "natural" thing for anyone to do is to go ahead; that is to say, to *act* overtly. The disturbed and perplexed situation arrests such direct activity temporarily. The tendency to continue *acting* nevertheless persists. It is diverted and takes the form of an idea or a suggestion. The *idea* of what to do when we find ourselves "in a hole" is a substitute for direct action. It is a vicarious, anticipatory way of acting, a kind of dramatic rehearsal. Were there only one suggestion popping up, we should undoubtedly adopt it at once. But where there are two or more, they collide with one another, maintain the state of suspense, and produce further inquiry. The first suggestion in the instance recently cited was to jump the ditch, but the perception of conditions inhibited that suggestion and led to the occurrence of other ideas.

Some inhibition of *direct* action is necessary to the condition of hesitation and delay that is essential to thinking. Thought is, as it were, conduct turned in upon itself and examining its purpose and its conditions, its resources, aids, and difficulties and obstacles.

The Second Phase, Intellectualization. We have already noted that it is artificial, so far as thinking is concerned, to start with a ready-made problem, a problem made out of whole cloth or arising out of a vacuum. In reality such a "problem" is simply an assigned *task*. There is not at first a situation *and* a problem, much less just a problem and no situation. There is a troubled, perplexed, trying situation, where the difficulty is, as it were, spread throughout the entire situation, infecting it as a whole. If we knew just what the difficulty was and where it lay, the job of reflection would be much easier than it is. As the saying truly goes, a question well put is half answered. In fact, we know what the problem *exactly* is simultaneously with finding a way out and getting it resolved. Problem and solution stand out *completely* at the same time. Up to that point, our grasp of the problem has been more or less vague and tentative.

A blocked suggestion leads us to reinspect the conditions that confront us. Then our uneasiness, the shock of disturbed activity, gets stated in some degree on the basis of observed conditions, of objects. The width of the ditch, the slipperiness of the banks, not the mere presence of a ditch, is the trouble. The difficulty is getting located and defined; it is becoming a true problem, something intellectual, not just an annoyance at being held up in what we are doing. The person who is suddenly blocked and troubled in what he is doing by the thought of an engagement to keep at a time that is near and a place that is distant has the suggestion of getting there at once. But in order to carry this suggestion into effect, he has to find means of transportation. In order to find them he has to note his present position and its distance from the station, the present time, and the interval at his disposal. Thus the perplexity is more precisely located: just so much ground to cover, so much time to do it in.

The word "problem" often seems too elaborate and dignified to denote what happens in minor cases of reflection. But in every case where reflective activity ensues, there is a process of *intellectualizing* what at first is merely an *emotional* quality of the whole situation. This conversion is effected by noting more definitely the conditions that constitute the trouble and cause the stoppage of action.

The Third Phase, the Guiding Idea, Hypothesis. The first suggestion occurs spontaneously; it comes to mind automatically; it *springs* up; it "pops," as we have said, "into the mind"; it flashes upon us. There is no direct control of its occurrence; the idea just comes or it does not come; that is all that can be said. There is nothing *intellectual* about its occurrence. The intellectual element consists in *what we do with it,* how we use it, *after* its sudden occurrence as an idea. A controlled use of it is made possible by the state of affairs just described. In the degree in which we define the difficulty (which is effected by stating it in terms of objects), we get a better idea of the kind of solution that is needed. The facts or data set the problem before us, and insight into the problem corrects, modifies, expands the suggestion that originally occurred. In this fashion the suggestion becomes a definite supposition or, stated more technically, a *hypothesis.*

Take the case of a physician examining a patient or a mechanic inspecting a piece of complicated machinery that does not behave properly. There is something wrong, so much is sure. But how to remedy it cannot be told until it is known *what* is wrong. An untrained person is likely to make a wild guess—the suggestion—and then proceed to act upon it in a random way, hoping that by good luck the right thing will be hit upon. So some medicine that appears to have worked before or that a neighbor has recommended is tried. Or the person fusses, monkeys, with the machine, poking here and hammering there on the chance of making the right move. The trained person proceeds in a very different fashion. He *observes* with unusual care, using the methods, the techniques, that the experience of physicians and expert mechanics in general, those familiar with the structure of the organism or the machine, have shown to be helpful in detecting trouble.

The idea of the solution is thus controlled by the diagnosis that has been made. But if the case is at all complicated, the physician or mechanic does not foreclose further thought by assuming that the suggested method of remedy is certainly right. He proceeds to act upon it tentatively rather than decisively. That is, he treats it as a guiding idea, a working hypothesis, and is led by it to make more observations, to collect more facts, so as to see if the *new* material is what the hypothesis calls for. He reasons that *if* the disease is typhoid, *then* certain phenomena will be found; and he looks particularly to see if *just* these conditions are present. Thus both the first and second operations are brought under control; the sense of the problem becomes more adequate and refined and the suggestion ceases to be a *mere* possibility, becoming a *tested* and, if possible, a *measured* probability.

The Fourth Phase, Reasoning (in the Narrower Sense). Observations pertain to what exists in nature. They constitute the facts, and these facts both regulate the formation of suggestions, ideas, hypotheses, and test their probable value as indications of solutions. The ideas, on the other hand, occur, as we say, in our heads, in our minds. They not only occur there, but are capable, as well, of great development there. Given a fertile suggestion occurring in an experienced, well-informed mind, that mind is capable of elaborating it until there results an idea that is quite different from the one with which the mind started.

. . . In more complex cases, there are long trains of reasoning in which one idea leads up to another idea known by previous test to be related to it. The stretch of links brought to light by reasoning depends, of course, upon the store of knowledge that the mind is already in possession of. And this depends not only upon the prior experience and special education of the individual who is carrying on the inquiry, but also upon the state of culture and science of the age and place. Reasoning helps extend knowledge, while at the same time it depends upon what is already known and upon the facilities that exist for communicating knowledge and making it a public, open resource.

A physician today can develop, by reasoning from his knowledge, the implications of the disease that symptoms suggest to him as probable in a way that would have been impossible even a generation ago; just as, on the other hand, he can carry his observation of symptoms much farther because of improvement in clinical instruments and the technique of their use.

Reasoning has the same effect upon a suggested solution that more intimate and extensive observation has upon the original trouble. Acceptance of a suggestion in its first form is prevented by looking into it more thoroughly. Conjectures that seem plausible at first sight are often found unfit or even absurd when their full consequences are traced out. Even when reasoning out the bearings of a supposition does not lead to its rejection, it develops the idea into a form in which it is more apposite to the problem. Only when, for example, the conjecture that a pole was an index pole had been thought out in its implications could its particular applicability to the case in hand be judged. Suggestions at first seemingly remote and wild are frequently so transformed by being elaborated into what follows from them as to become apt and fruitful. The development of an idea through reasoning helps supply intervening or intermediate terms which link together into a consistent whole elements that at first seemingly conflict with each other, some leading the mind to one inference and others to an opposed one.

Mathematics as Typical Reasoning. Mathematics affords the typical example of how far can be carried the operation of relating ideas to one another, without having to depend upon the observations of the senses. In geometry we start with a few simple conceptions, line, angle, parallel, surfaces formed by lines meeting, etc., and a few principles defining equalities. Knowing something about the equality of angles made by parallel lines when they intersect a straight line, and knowing, by definition, that a perpendicular to a straight line forms two right angles, by means of a combination of these ideas we readily determine that the sum of the interior angles of a triangle is equal to two right angles. By continuing to trace the implications of theorems already demonstrated, the whole subject of plane figures is finally elaborated. The manipulation of algebraic symbols so as to establish a series of equations and other mathematical functions affords an even more striking example of what can be accomplished by developing the relation of ideas to one another.

When the hypothesis indicated by a series of scientific observations and experiments can be stated in mathematical form, that idea can be transformed to almost any extent, until it assumes a form in which a problem can be dealt with most expeditiously and effectively. Much of the accomplishment of physical science depends upon an intervening mathematical elaboration of ideas. It is not the mere presence of measurements in quantitative form that yields scientific knowledge, but that particular kind of mathematical statement which can be developed by reasoning into other and more fruitful forms—a consideration which is fatal to the claim to scientific standing of many educational measurements merely because they have a quantitative form.

The Fifth Phase, Testing the Hypothesis by Action. The concluding phase is some kind of testing by overt action to give *experimental corroboration,* or *verification,* of the conjectural idea. Reasoning shows that *if* the *idea* be adopted, certain consequences follow. So far the conclusion is hypothetical or conditional. If when we look we find present all the conditions demanded by the theory, and if we find the characteristic traits called for by rival alternatives to be lacking, the tendency to believe, to accept, is almost irresistible. Sometimes direct observation furnishes corroboration, as in the case of the pole on the boat. In other cases, as in that of the bubbles, experiment is required; that is, *conditions are deliberately arranged in accord with the requirements of an idea or hypothesis to see whether the results theoretically indicated by the idea actually occur.* If it is found that the experimental results agree with the theoretical, or rationally deduced, results, and if there is reason to believe that *only* the conditions in question would yield such results, the confirmation is so strong as to induce a conclusion—at least until contrary facts shall indicate the advisability of its revision.

Of course, verification does not always follow. Sometimes consequences show failure to confirm instead of corroboration. The idea in question is refuted by the court of final appeal. But a great advantage of possession of the habit of reflective activity is that failure is not *mere* failure. It is instructive. The person who really thinks learns quite as much from his failures as from his successes. For a failure indicates to the person whose thinking has been involved in it, and who has not come to it by mere blind chance, what further observations should be made. It suggests to him what modifications should be introduced in the hypothesis upon which he has been operating. It either brings to light a new problem or helps to define and clarify the problem on which he has been engaged. Nothing shows the trained thinker better than the use he makes of his errors and mistakes. What merely annoys and discourages a person not accustomed to thinking, or what starts him out on a new course of aimless attack by mere cut-and-try methods, is a stimulus and a guide to the trained inquirer.

The Sequence of the Five Phases Is Not Fixed. The five phases, terminals, or functions of thought that we have noted do not follow one another in a set order. On the contrary, each step in genuine thinking does something to perfect the formation of a suggestion and promote its change into a leading idea or directive hypothesis. It does something to promote the location and definition of the problem. Each improvement in the idea leads to new observations that yield new facts or data and help the mind judge more accurately the relevancy of facts already at hand. The elaboration of the hypothesis does not wait until the problem has been defined and adequate hypothesis has been arrived at; it may come in at any intermediate time. And as we have just seen, any particular overt test need not be final; it may be introductory to new observations and new suggestions, according to what happens in consequence of it.

There is, however, an important difference between test by overt action in practical deliberations and in scientific investigations. In the former the practical commitment involved in overt action is much more serious than in the latter. An astronomer or a chemist performs overt actions, but they are for the sake of knowledge; they serve to test and develop his conceptions and theories. In practical matters, the main result desired lies outside of knowledge. One of the great values of thinking, accordingly, is that it defers the commitment to action that is irretrievable, that, once made, cannot be revoked. Even in moral and other practical matters, therefore, a thoughtful person treats his overt deeds as experimental so far as possible; that is to say, while he cannot call them back and must stand their consequences, he gives alert attention to what they teach him about his conduct as well as to the nonintellectual consequences. He makes a problem out of consequences of conduct, looking into the causes from which they probably resulted, especially the causes that lie in his own habits and desires.

In conclusion, we point out that the five phases of reflection that have been described represent only in outline the indispensable traits of reflective thinking. In practice, two of them may telescope, some of them may be passed over hurriedly, and the burden of reaching a conclusion may fall mainly on a single phase, which will then require a seemingly disproportionate development. No set rules can be laid down on such matters. The way they are managed depends upon the intellectual tact and sensitiveness of the individual. When things have come out wrong, it is, however, a wise practice to review the methods by which the unwise decision was reached, and see where the misstep was made.

One Phase May Be Expanded. In complicated cases some of the five phases are so extensive that they include definite subphases within themselves. In this case it is arbitrary whether the minor functions are regarded as parts or are listed as distinct phases. There is nothing especially sacred about the number five. For example, in matters of practical deliberation where the object is to decide what to do, it may be well to undertake a scrutiny of the underlying desires and motives that are operating; that is, instead of asking what ends and means will best satisfy one's wish, one may turn back to the attitudes of which the wish is the expression. It is a matter of indifference whether this search be listed as an independent problem, having its own phases, or as an additional phase in the original problem.

Reference to the Future and to the Past. Again, it has been suggested that reflective thinking involves a look into the future, a forecast, an anticipation, or a prediction, and that this should be listed as a sixth aspect, or phase. As a matter of fact, every intellectual suggestion or idea is anticipatory of some possible future experience, while the final solution gives a definite set toward the future. It is both a record of something accomplished and an assignment of a future method of operation. It helps set up an enduring habit of procedure. When a physician, for example, has diagnosed a case, he usually makes also a *prognosis*, a forecast, of the probable future course of the disease. And not only is his treatment a verification—or the reverse—of the idea or hypothesis about the disease upon which he has proceeded, but the result also affects his treatment of future patients. In some cases, the future reference may be so important as to require special elaboration. In this case, it may be presented as an added, distinct phase. Some of the investigations of an astronomical expedition to watch an eclipse of the sun may be directly intended, for example, to get material bearing on Einstein's theory. But the theory, itself, is so important that its confirmation or refutation will give a decided turn to the future of physical science, and this consideration is likely to be uppermost in the minds of scientists.

Of equal importance is the reference to the *past* involved in reflection. Of course, suggestions are dependent in any case upon one's past experience; they do not arise out of nothing. But while sometimes we go ahead with the suggestion without stopping to go back to the original experience of which it is the fruit, at other times we go consciously over the past experience in considerable detail as part of the process of testing the value of the suggestion.

For example, it occurs to a man to invest in real estate. Then he recalls that a previous investment of this kind turned out unfortunately. He goes over the former case, comparing it bit by bit with the present, to see how far the two cases are alike or unlike. Examination of the past may be the chief and decisive factor in thought. The most valuable reference to the past is likely, however, to come at the time the conclusion is reached. We noted earlier the importance of a final survey to secure a net formulation of the exact result and of the premises upon which it logically depends. This is not only an important part of the process of *testing*, but, as was stated in the earlier discussion, is almost necessary if good habits are to be built up. Ability to *organize* knowledge consists very largely in the habit of reviewing previous facts and ideas and relating them to one another on a new basis; namely, that of the conclusion that has been reached. A certain amount of this operation is included in the testing phase that has been described. But its influence upon the attitude of students is so important that it may be well at times so to emphasize it that it becomes a definite function, or phase, on its own account.

THE PLACE OF JUDGMENT
IN REFLECTIVE ACTIVITY

I
THREE FACTORS IN JUDGING

We have been dealing so far with the act of reflection as an entirety. There are subordinate unities within the process upon whose character the efficiency of the whole undertaking depends.

Judgments, the Constituent Units of Thought. From one point of view the whole process of thinking consists of making a series of judgments that are so related as to support one another in leading to a final judgment—the conclusion. In spite of this fact, we have treated reflective activity as a whole, first, because judgments do not occur in isolation but in connection with the solution of a problem, the clearing away of something obscure and perplexing, the resolution of a difficulty; in short, as units in reflective activity. The purpose of solving a problem determines what kind of judgments should be made. If I were suddenly to announce that it would take twenty-two and a half yards of carpet to cover a certain floor, it might be a perfectly correct statement, but as a *judgment* it would be senseless if it did not bear upon some question that had come up. Judgments need to be *relevant* to an issue as well as correct. Judging is the act of selecting and weighing the bearing of facts and suggestions as they present themselves, as well as of deciding whether the alleged facts are really facts and whether the idea used is a sound idea or merely a fancy. We may say, for short, that a person of sound judgment is one who, in the idiomatic phrase, has "horse sense"; he is a good judge of *relative values;* he can estimate, appraise, evaluate, with tact and discernment.

It follows that the heart of a good habit of thought lies in the power to pass judgments *pertinently* and *discriminatingly.* We sometimes meet men with little schooling whose advice is greatly relied upon and who are spontaneously looked to when an emergency arises, men who are conspicuously successful in conducting vital affairs. They are the persons of sound judgment. A man of sound judgment in any set of affairs is an *educated* man as respects those affairs, whatever his schooling or academic standing. And if our schools turn out their pupils in that attitude of mind which is conducive to good judgment in any department of affairs in which the pupils are placed, they have done more than if they sent out their pupils possessed *merely* of vast stores of information or high degrees of skill in specialized branches.

The Features of Judgment. The significant traits of judgment may be gathered from a consideration of the operations to which the word *judgment* was originally applied; namely, the authoritative decision of matters in a legal controversy—the procedure of the *judge on the bench.* There are three such features: (1) a controversy, consisting of opposite claims regarding the same objective situation; (2) a process of defining and elaborating these claims and of sifting the facts adduced to support them; (3) a final decision, or sentence, closing the particular matter in dispute while also serving as a rule or principle for deciding future cases.

It Arises from Doubt and Controversy. (1) Unless there is something doubtful, the situation is read off at a glance; it is taken in on sight; *i.e.,* there is merely perception, recognition, not judgment. If the matter is wholly doubtful, if it is dark and obscure throughout, there is a blind mystery and again no judgment occurs. But if it suggests, however vaguely, different meanings, rival possible interpretations, there is some *point at issue,* some *matter at stake.* Doubt takes the form of discussion, of controversy within the mind. Different sides compete for a conclusion in their favor. Cases brought to trial before a judge illustrate neatly and unambiguously this strife of alternative interpretations; but any attempt to clear up intellectually a doubtful situation exemplifies the same traits. A moving blur catches our eye in the distance; we ask ourselves: "What is it? Is it a cloud of whirling dust? a tree waving its branches? a man signaling to us?" Something in the total situation suggests each of these possible meanings. Only one of them can possibly be correct; perhaps none of them is appropriate; yet *some* meaning the thing in question surely has.

Which of the alternative suggested meanings has the rightful claim? What does the perception really mean? How is it to be interpreted, estimated, appraised, placed? Every judgment proceeds from some such situation.

It Defines the Issue by Selecting Evidential Facts and Appropriate Principles. (2) The hearing of the controversy, the trial, the weighing of alternative claims, divides into two branches, either of which, in a given case, may be more conspicuous than the other. In the consideration of a legal dispute these two branches are sifting the evidence and selecting the rules that are applicable; they are "the facts" and "the law" of the case. In ordinary judgment they are (*a*) the determination of the data that are important in the given case, and (*b*) the elaboration of the conceptions or meanings suggested by the crude data. They are concerned with the two questions: (*a*) What portions or aspects of the situation are significant in controlling the formation of the interpretation? (*b*) Just what is the full meaning and bearing of the idea used as a method of interpretation? These questions are strictly correlative; the answer to each depends upon the answer to the other. We may, however, for convenience, consider them separately.

(*a*) *Selecting the Facts.* In every actual occurrence there are many details that are part of the total occurrence, but nevertheless are not significant in relation to the point at issue. All parts of an experience are equally present, but they are very far from being equally valuable as signs or as evidences. Nor is there any tag, or label, on any trait saying: "This is important" or "This is trivial." Nor is intensity, or vividness, or conspicuousness a safe measure of indicative and proving value. The glaring thing may be totally insignificant in this particular situation, and the key to the understanding of the whole matter may be modest or hidden. Features that are not significant are distracting; they insist upon their claim to be regarded as clues and cues to interpretation, while traits that are really significant do not appear on the surface at all. Hence, judgment is required *even in reference to the situation* or event that is present to the senses; elimination or rejection, selection, discovery, or bringing to light must take place. Till we have reached a final conclusion, rejection and selection must be tentative or conditional. We select the things that we hope or trust are cues to meaning. But if they do not suggest a situation that accepts and includes them, we reconstitute our data, the facts of the case; for we mean, intellectually, by the facts of the case *those traits that are used as evidence in reaching a conclusion or forming a decision.*

No hard and fast rules for this operation of selecting and rejecting, or fixing upon significant evidential facts, can be given. It all comes back, as we say, to the good judgment, the good sense, of the one judging. To be a good judge is to have a sense of the relative indicative or signifying values of the various features of the perplexing situation; to know what to let go as of no account; what to eliminate as irrelevant; what to retain as conducive to the outcome; what to emphasize as a clue to the difficulty. This power in ordinary matters we call *knack, tact, cleverness;* in more important affairs, *insight, discernment.* In part it is instinctive or inborn, but it also represents the funded outcome of long familiarity with like operations in the past. Possession of this ability to seize what is evidential or significant and to let the rest go is the mark of the expert, the connoisseur, the *judge,* in any matter.

Mill cites the following case, which is worth noting as an instance of the extreme delicacy and accuracy to which may be developed this power of sizing up the significant factors of a situation.

> A Scotch manufacturer procured from England, at a high rate of wages, a working dyer, famous for producing very fine colors, with a view of teaching to his other workmen the same skill. The workman came; but his method of proportioning the ingredients, in which lay the secret of the effects he produced, was by taking them up in handfuls, while the common method was to weigh them. The manufacturer sought to make him turn his handling system into an equivalent weighing system, that the general principles of his peculiar mode of proceeding might be ascertained. This, however, the man found himself quite unable to do, and could therefore impart his own skill to nobody. He had, from individual cases of his own experience, established a connection in his mind between fine effects of color and tactual perceptions in handling his dyeing materials; and from these perceptions he could, in any particular case, *infer the means to be employed* and the effects which would be produced.

Long brooding over conditions, intimate contact associated with keen interest, thorough absorption in a multiplicity of allied experiences tend to bring about those judgments which we then call "intuitive"; but they are true judgments, because they are based on intelligent selection and estimation, with solution of a problem as the controlling standard. Possession of this capacity makes the difference between the artist and the intellectual bungler.

Such is ability to judge in its completest form. But in any case there is a certain feeling after the way to be followed; a tentative picking out of certain qualities to see what emphasis upon them would lead to; a willingness to hold final appraisal in suspense; willingness to reject the factors entirely or relegate them to a different position in the evidential scheme if other features yield more solvent suggestions. Alertness, flexibility, curiosity are the essentials; dogmatism, rigidity, prejudice, caprice, arising from routine, passion, and flippancy are fatal.

(*b*) *Selecting the Principles.* This selection of data is, of course, for the sake of controlling the *development and elaboration of the suggested meaning in the light of which they are to be interpreted.* Evolution of conceptions thus goes on simultaneously with determination of the facts; one possible meaning after another is held before the mind, considered in relation to the data to which it is applied, is developed into its more detailed bearings, is dropped or tentatively accepted and used. We do not approach any problem with a wholly naïve or virgin mind; we approach it with certain acquired habitual modes of understanding, with a certain store of previously evolved meanings or at least of experiences from which meanings may be educed.

If a habit is checked, and so inhibited from easy application, a possible meaning for the facts in question comes to the mind. No hard and fast rules decide whether a meaning suggested is the right and proper meaning to follow up. The individual's own good (or bad) judgment is the guide. There is no label, on any given idea or principle, that says automatically, "Use me in this situation"—as the magic cakes of Alice in Wonderland were inscribed "Eat me." The thinker has to decide, to choose; and there is always a risk, so that the prudent thinker selects warily—subject, that is, to confirmation or frustration by later events. If one is not able to estimate wisely what is relevant to the interpretation of a given perplexing or doubtful issue, it avails little that arduous learning has built up a large stock of concepts. For learning is not wisdom; information does not guarantee good judgment. Memory may provide a refrigerator in which to store a stock of meanings for future use, but judgment selects and adopts the one to be used in an emergency—and without an emergency (some crisis, slight or great) there is no call for judgment. No conception, even if it is carefully and firmly established in the abstract, can at first safely be more than a *candidate* for the office of interpreter. Only greater success than that of its rivals in clarifying dark spots, untying hard knots, reconciling discrepancies can elect it and prove it to be a valid idea for the given situation. In short, thinking is a continual appraising of both data and ideas. Unless the pertinence and force of each seemingly evidential fact and seemingly explanatory idea is *judged*, appraised, the mind goes on a wild-goose chase.

It Terminates in a Decision. (3) The judgment when formed is a *decision;* it closes, or concludes, the question at issue. This determination not only settles that particular case, but it also helps fix a rule or method for deciding similar matters in the future; as the sentence of the judge on the bench both terminates that dispute and also forms a precedent for future decisions. If the interpretation settled upon is not controverted by subsequent events, a presumption is built up in favor of similar interpretation in other cases where the features are not so obviously unlike as to make it inappropriate. In this way, principles of judging are gradually built up; a certain manner of interpretation gets weight, authority. In short, meanings get *standardized;* they become logical concepts.

II
ANALYSIS AND SYNTHESIS:
THE TWO FUNCTIONS OF JUDGMENT

Through judging, confused data are cleared up, and seemingly incoherent and disconnected facts are brought together. The clearing up is *analysis*. The bringing together, or unifying, is *synthesis*. Things may have a peculiar feeling for us; they may make a certain indescribable impression upon us: the thing may *feel* round (that is, present a quality which we afterwards define as "round"); an act may seem rude; yet this impression, this quality, may be lost, absorbed, blended in the total situation. Only as we need to use just that aspect of the original situation as a tool of grasping something perplexing or obscure in another situation, do we detach the quality so that it becomes individualized. Only because we need to characterize the shape of some new object or the moral quality of some new act, does the element of roundness or rudeness in the old experience detach itself and so stand out as a distinctive feature. If the element thus selected clears up what is otherwise obscure in the new experience, if it settles what is uncertain, it thereby gains in positiveness and definiteness of meaning. This point will meet us again in the following chapter; here we speak of the matter only as it bears upon the question of analysis and synthesis.

Mental Analysis Is Not like Physical Division. Even when it is definitely stated that intellectual and physical analyses are different sorts of operations, intellectual analysis is often treated after the analogy of physical, as if it were the breaking up of a whole into all its constituent parts in the mind instead of in space. As nobody can possibly tell what breaking a whole into its parts in the mind means, this conception leads to the further notion that logical analysis is a mere enumeration and listing of all conceivable qualities and relations. The influence upon education of this conception has been very great. Every subject in the curriculum has passed through—or still remains in—what may be called the phase of "anatomical" or "morphological" method: the stage in which understanding the subject is thought to consist of multiplying distinctions of quality, form, relation, and so on, and attaching some name to each distinguished element. In normal growth, specific properties are emphasized and so individualized only when they serve to clear up a present difficulty. Only as they are involved in judging some specific situation is there any motive or use for analyses, for emphasis upon some element or relation as peculiarly significant.

The same putting the cart before the horse, the product before the process, is found in that overconscious formulation of methods of procedure so current in elementary instruction. The method that is employed in discovery, in reflective inquiry, cannot possibly be identified with the method that emerges *after* the discovery is made. In the genuine operation of inference, the mind is in the attitude of *search*, of *hunting*, of *projection*, of *trying this and that;* when the conclusion is reached, the search is at an end. The Greeks used to discuss: "How is learning (or inquiry) possible? For either we know already what we are after, and then we do not learn or inquire; or we do not know, and then we cannot inquire, for we do not know what to look for." The dilemma is at least suggestive, for it points to the true alternative: the use in inquiry of doubt, of tentative suggestion, of experimentation. After we have reached the conclusion, a reconsideration of the steps of the process to see what is helpful, what is harmful, what is merely useless assists in dealing more promptly and efficaciously with analogous problems in the future. In this way the method of *organizing* thought is built up.

Conscious Method and Unconscious Logical Attitude. The common assumption that, unless the pupil from the outset *consciously recognizes and explicitly states* the method logically implied in the result he is to reach, he will have *no* method and his mind will work confusedly or anarchically is fallacious. It is equally erroneous to believe that, if he accompanies his performance with conscious statement of some form of procedure (outline, topical analysis, list of headings and subheadings, uniform formula), his mind is safeguarded and strengthened. As a matter of fact, the gradual, largely unconscious, development of *logical attitude and habit* comes first. A conscious setting forth of the method logically adapted for reaching an end is possible only after the result has first been reached by unconscious and tentative methods. Such conscious setting forth of the method is valuable when a review of the method that achieved success in a given case will throw light upon a new similar case. The ability to fasten upon and single out (abstract, analyze) those features of one experience that are logically best is hindered by premature insistence upon their explicit formulation. Repeated use is what gives a *method* definiteness; given this definiteness, precipitation into formulated statement should follow naturally. But because teachers find that the things that they themselves best understand are marked off and defined in clear-cut ways, our schoolrooms are pervaded with the superstition that children are to *begin* with crystallized formulas of method.

As analysis is conceived to be a sort of picking to pieces, so synthesis is thought to be a sort of physical piecing together. When it is so imagined, it too becomes a mystery. In fact, synthesis takes place wherever we grasp the bearing of facts on a conclusion or of a principle on facts. As analysis is *emphasis*, so synthesis is *placing;* the one causes the emphasized fact or property to stand out as significant; the other puts what is selected in its *context*, its connection with what is signified. It unites it with some other meaning to give both increased significance. When quicksilver was linked to iron, tin, etc., as a *metal*, all these objects obtained new intellectual value. Every judgment is analytic in so far as it involves discernment, discrimination, marking off the trivial from the important, the irrelevant from what points to a conclusion; and it is synthetic in so far as it leaves the mind with an inclusive situation within which selected facts are placed.

Analysis and Synthesis in Educational Procedure. Educational methods that pride themselves on being exclusively analytic or exclusively synthetic are (so far as they carry out their boasts) incompatible with normal operations of judgment. Discussions have taken place, for example, as to whether the teaching of geography should be analytic or synthetic. The synthetic method is supposed to begin with the partial, limited portion of the earth's surface already familiar to the pupil, and then gradually piece on adjacent regions (the county, the country, the continent, and so on) till an idea of the entire globe is reached, or of the solar system that includes the globe. The analytic method is supposed to begin with the physical whole, the solar system or globe, and to work down through its constituent portions till the immediate environment is reached. The underlying conceptions here deal with physical wholes and physical parts. As a matter of fact, we cannot assume that the portion of the earth already familiar to the child is such a definite object, mentally, that he can safely start with and from his present idea of it. His knowledge of it is misty and vague as well as incomplete. Accordingly, mental progress will involve analysis of *it*—emphasis of features that are significant till they will stand out clearly. Moreover, his own locality is not sharply marked off, neatly bounded, and measured. His experience of it is already an experience that involves sun, moon, and stars as parts of the scene he surveys; it involves a changing horizon line as he moves about. In short, even his more limited and local experience involves far-reaching factors that take his imagination out beyond his own street and village. Connection, relationship with a larger whole, is already involved. But understanding of these relations is inadequate, vague, incorrect. He needs to define the features of the local environment in order to clarify and enlarge his conceptions of the larger geographical scene to which they belong. At the same time, not till he has grasped the larger scene will many of even the commonest features of his local environment become intelligible. Analysis leads to synthesis, while synthesis perfects analysis. As the pupil grows in comprehension of the vast complicated earth in its setting in space, he also sees more definitely the meaning of familiar local details. This intimate interaction between selective emphasis and interpretation through a context of what is selected is found wherever reflection proceeds normally. Hence the folly of trying to set analysis and synthesis over against each other.

Whenever we appraise, we both select and emphasize a particular quality or feature, and we link together things that, from an intellectual point of view, were previously separate. In appraising the value of land, the appraiser not only causes its monetary property to stand out, but he also places it in a scale of the land values of the whole community. Something of this sort happens in all judgment.

UNDERSTANDING:
IDEAS AND MEANINGS

I

IDEAS AS SUGGESTIONS AND CONJECTURES

We see something moving, hear a sound unexpectedly, smell an unusual odor, and we ask: What is it? What does what we see, hear, smell *mean?* When we have found out what it signifies, a squirrel running, two persons conversing, an explosion of gunpowder, we say that we *understand*. To understand is to grasp meaning. Until we understand, we are, if we have curiosity, troubled, baffled, and hence moved to inquire. After we understand, we are, comparatively at least, intellectually at home. There is a time during our investigation when meaning is only suggested; when we hold it in suspense as a possibility rather than accept it as an actuality. Then the meaning is an *idea*. An idea thus stands midway between assured understanding and mental confusion and bafflement. While a meaning is *conditionally* accepted, accepted for use and trial, it is an idea, a supposal. When it is *positively* accepted, some object or event is understood.

Ideas Are Elements in Judgments, Tools of Interpretation. An idea is thus not a unity like judgment, but rather a unit element in forming a judgment. We may compare a complete reflection to a paragraph; then the judgment is like a sentence in the structure of the paragraph, and an idea is like a word in the sentence. That ideas are necessary constituents of inference, we have already seen. Positive inference can be deferred and kept in process of development and test only while a meaning is *not* asserted and believed in. Moreover, ideas are indispensable to inference because they direct observations and regulate the collection and inspection of data. Without a guiding idea, facts would be heaped up like grains of sand; they would not be organized into intellectual unity. In discussing ideas we are not, accordingly, introducing a new topic, but are, as in the discussion of judgment, going into detail regarding an element in the whole already considered.

Let us take the instance of a blur in motion at a distance. We wonder what the *thing is;* that is, what the *blur means.* A man waving his arms, a friend beckoning to us are suggested as possibilities. To accept at once either alternative is to arrest judgment. But if we treat what is suggested as only a suggestion, a supposition, a possibility, it becomes an idea, having the following traits: (*a*) As merely a suggestion, it is a conjecture, a guess, which in cases of greater dignity we call a "hypothesis" or a "theory." That is to say, it is *a possible, but as yet doubtful, mode of interpretation.* (*b*) Even though doubtful, it has an office to perform; namely, that of directing inquiry and examination. If this blur means a friend beckoning, then careful observation should show certain other traits. If it is a man driving unruly cattle, certain other traits should be found. Let us look and see if these traits are found. Taken merely as a doubt, an idea would paralyze inquiry. Taken merely as a certainty, it would arrest inquiry. Taken as a doubtful possibility, it affords a standpoint, a platform, a method of inquiry.

Ideas, then, are not genuine ideas unless they are tools with which to search for material to solve a problem. Suppose it is desired that the pupil grasp *the idea* of the sphericity of the earth. This is different from teaching him its sphericity *as a fact.* He may be shown (or reminded of) a ball or a globe and be told that the earth is round like those things; he may then be made to repeat that statement day after day till the shape of the earth and the shape of the ball are welded together in his mind. But he has not thereby acquired an *idea* of the earth's sphericity; at most, he has had a

certain image of a sphere and has finally managed to image the earth after
the analogy of his ball image. To grasp "sphericity" as an idea, the pupil
must first have realized certain confusing features in observed facts and
have had the idea of spherical shape suggested to him as a possible way of
accounting for such phenomena as tops of masts being seen at sea after
the hulls have disappeared, the shape of shadows of the earth in an
eclipse, etc. Only by use as a method of interpreting data so as to give
them fuller meaning does sphericity become a genuine idea. There may be
a vivid image and no idea; or there may be a fleeting, obscure image and
yet an idea, if that image performs the function of instigating and directing the observation and relation of facts.

Logical ideas are like keys that are shaped with reference to opening a
lock. Pike, separated by a glass partition from the fish upon which they
ordinarily prey, will—so it is said—butt their heads against the glass until
it is literally beaten into them that they cannot get at their food. Animals
learn (when they learn at all) by a "cut-and-try" method, by doing at
random first one thing then another thing and continuing the things that
happen to succeed. This procedure is followed by human beings when
they do not operate on the basis of ideas, when they "monkey," to use a
term derived from the random activity of one of the most intelligent of the
lower animals. Action directed consciously by ideas—by suggested meanings accepted for the sake of experimenting with them—is the sole alternative both to bullheaded stupidity and to learning bought from that dear
teacher—chance experience.

It is significant that many words for intelligence suggest the idea of
circuitous, evasive activity—often with a sort of intimation of even moral
obliquity. The bluff, hearty man goes straight (and stupidly, it is implied)
at some work. The intelligent man is cunning, shrewd (crooked), wily,
subtle, crafty, artful, designing—the idea of indirection is involved. An
idea is a method of evading, circumventing, or surmounting through
reflection obstacles that otherwise would have to be attacked by brute
force. But ideas may lose their intellectual quality because of habitual use.
When a child was first learning to recognize, in some hesitating suspense,
cats, dogs, houses, marbles, trees, shoes, and other objects, ideas—conscious and tentative meanings—intervened as methods of identification.
Now, as a rule, the thing and the meaning are so completely fused that
there is no idea proper, but only automatic recognition. On the other
hand, things which are so familiar, so known already, that they are
recognized without an intervening idea may appear in an unusual context
and give rise to a problem that necessitates intermediate ideas in order
that the object be understood. For example, a person drawing a room will

be compelled to form a new idea of the corner of the room formed by the meeting of two walls and the ceiling, since now that corner has to be represented on a plane surface. A child has practical familiarity with squares and spheres in the context of daily life, as shapes of toys and utensils. But when they present themselves in a definitely geometrical connection, he is obliged to use mental effort to form ideas of them.

Ideas Are Logical Instruments, Not Psychic Compounds. It will be noted that an idea in its logical significance is something quite different from ideas as they are often treated in psychological texts. An idea, logically speaking, is not a faded perception of an object, nor is it a compound of a number of sensations. You would not get the peculiar meaning that is attached to, say, "chair" by having a mental picture of one. A savage might be able to form an image of poles and wires, and a layman of a complex scientific diagram. But unless the savage knew something about telegraphy, he would have no idea, or at least no correct idea, of the poles and wires, while the most accurate mental reproduction of the diagram would leave the layman totally without understanding of its meaning, and hence without an idea of it, even though he could list all *its* qualities one by one. The fact is that an idea, intellectually, cannot be defined by its structure, but only by its function and use. Whatever in a doubtful situation or undecided issue helps us to form a judgment and to bring inference to a conclusion by means of anticipating a possible solution is an idea, and nothing else is. It is an idea because of what it *does* in clearing up a perplexity or in harmonizing what is otherwise fragmentary, not because of its psychical make-up.

II
THINGS AND MEANINGS

An idea normally terminates in giving understanding, so that an event or thing acquires meaning. A thing understood, a thing with a meaning, is different from both an idea, which is a doubtful and still unattached meaning, and from a mere brute, physical thing. I can stumble against something in the dark and get hurt without any understanding of what the thing is. So far, it is *merely* a thing, a something or other. If I get a light and investigate, I learn that the thing is a stool, or a coal hod, or a log of firewood. Now it is a *known* object, a thing understood, a thing with a meaning—all three being synonymous expressions.

To Understand Is to Grasp Meaning. If a person comes suddenly into your room and calls out "Paper," various alternatives are possible. If you do not understand the English language, there is simply a noise that may act as a physical stimulus or irritant. But the noise is not an intellectual object; it does not have intellectual value. It is the mere brute thing just spoken of. If, first, the cry is the usual accompaniment of the delivery of the morning paper, the sound will have meaning, intellectual content; you will understand it. Or if, second, you are eagerly awaiting the receipt of some important document, you may assume that the cry means an announcement of its arrival. If, third, you understand the English language, but no context suggests itself from your habits and expectations, the *word* has meaning, but not the whole event. You are then perplexed and incited to think out, to hunt for, some explanation of the apparently meaningless occurrence. If you find something that accounts for the performance, it gets meaning; you come to understand it. As intelligent beings, we presume the existence of meaning, and its absence is an anomaly. Hence, if it should turn out that the person merely meant to inform you that there was a scrap of paper on the sidewalk, or that paper existed somewhere in the universe, you would think him crazy or yourself the victim of a stupid joke. To grasp the meaning of a thing, an event, or a situation is to see it in its *relations* to other things: to note how it operates or functions, what consequences follow from it, what causes it, what uses it can be put to. In contrast, what we have called the brute thing, the thing without meaning to us, is something whose relations are not grasped.

Since all knowing, including all scientific inquiry, aims at clothing things and events with meaning—at understanding them—it always proceeds by taking the thing inquired into out of its isolation. Search is continued until the thing is discovered to be a related part in some larger whole. Thus a piece of rock may be understood by referring it to a sedimentary stratum known to have been formed under certain conditions, or a suddenly appearing light in the heavens may be understood when identified as the return of Halley's Comet. Suppose that the rock has peculiar markings on it. They may be contemplated purely esthetically, as curiosities. But they may arouse inquiry. If so, the resulting investigation will have for its purpose the removal of the apparent isolation, the non-connectedness, of the markings. Finally, they are explained as glacial scratches. They no longer stand alone. They have been brought into connection with a past era of the earth's history in which great masses of slow-moving ice descended into regions now temperate, carrying with them grit and rocks that ground and scratched other rocks imbedded in place.

Interaction of Two Modes of Understanding. In these illustrations two types of grasp of meaning have been exemplified. When the English language is understood, the person grasps at once the meaning of "paper." He may not, however, see any meaning or sense in the performance as a whole. Similarly, the person identifies the object on sight as a stone; there is no secret, no mystery, no perplexity about that. But he does not understand the markings on it. They have some meaning, but what is it? In one case, owing to familiar acquaintance, the thing and its meaning, up to a certain point, are one; in the other, the thing and its meaning are, temporarily at least, sundered, and meaning has to be sought in order to understand the thing. In one case understanding is direct, prompt, immediate; in the other, it is roundabout and delayed.

Most languages have two sets of words to express these two modes of understanding; one for the direct taking in or grasp of meaning, the other for its circuitous apprehension, thus: γνῶναι and εἰδέναι in Greek; *noscere* and *scire* in Latin; *kennen* and *wissen* in German; *connaître* and *savoir* in French; while in English *to be acquainted with* and *to know of or about* have been suggested as equivalents.[7] Now, our intellectual life consists of a peculiar interaction between these two types of understanding. All judgment, all reflective inference, presupposes some lack of understanding, a partial absence of meaning. We reflect in order that we may get hold of the full and adequate significance of what happens. Nevertheless, *something* must be already understood, the mind must be in possession of some meaning that it has mastered, or else thinking is impossible. We think in order to grasp meaning, but nonetheless every extension of knowledge makes us aware of blind and opaque spots, where with less knowledge all had seemed obvious and natural. A scientist brought into a new district will find many things that he does not understand, while the native savage or rustic will be wholly oblivious to any meanings beyond those directly apparent. Some Indians brought to a large city remained stolid at the sight of mechanical wonders of bridge, trolley, and telephone, but were held spellbound by the sight of workmen climbing poles to repair wires. Increase of the store of meanings makes us conscious of new problems, while only through translation of the new perplexities into what is already familiar and plain do we understand or solve these problems. This is the constant spiral movement of knowledge.

Intellectual Progress a Rhythm. Our progress in genuine knowledge always consists *in part in the discovery of something not understood in what had previously been taken for granted as plain, obvious, matter-of-course, and in part in using meanings that are directly grasped as*

---

7. James, *Principles of Psychology.* To *know* and to *know that* are perhaps more precise equivalents; compare "I know him" and "I know *that* he has gone home." The former expresses a fact simply; for the latter, evidence might be demanded and supplied. [See *Great Books of the Western World,* Vol. 53, p. 144 (Ed.).]

instruments for getting hold of obscure and doubtful meanings. No object is so familiar, so obvious, so commonplace that it may not unexpectedly present, in a novel situation, some problem, and thus arouse reflection in order to understand it. No object or principle is so strange, peculiar, or remote that it may not be dwelt upon till its meaning becomes familiar—taken in on sight without reflection. We may come to *see, perceive, recognize, grasp, seize, lay hold of* principles, laws, abstract truths—*i.e.*, to understand their meaning in an immediate fashion. Our intellectual progress consists, as has been said, in a rhythm of direct understanding—technically called *ap*prehension—with indirect, mediated understanding—technically called *com*prehension.

III

THE PROCESS BY WHICH THINGS ACQUIRE MEANING

The first problem that comes up in connection with direct understanding is how a store of directly recognized meanings is built up. How do we learn to view things on sight as significant members of a situation or as having, as a matter of course, specific meanings? Our chief difficulty in answering this question lies in the thoroughness with which the lesson of familiar things has been learned. Thought can more easily traverse an unexplored region than it can undo what has been so thoroughly done as to be ingrained in unconscious habit. We apprehend chairs, tables, books, trees, horses, clouds, stars, rain so promptly and directly that it is hard to realize that once these objects were mere brute things, as alien to our understanding as the sounds of the Choctaw language would be if we now suddenly heard them.

Vague Wholes Are Antecedent to Understanding. In an often quoted passage, Mr. James has said: "The baby, assailed by eyes, ears, nose, skin, and entrails at once, feels it all as one great blooming, buzzing confusion." [8] Mr. James is speaking of a baby's world taken as a whole; the description, however, is equally applicable to the way any new thing strikes an adult, so far as the thing is really new and strange. To the traditional "cat in a strange garret," everything is blurred and confused; the usual marks that label things so as to separate them from one another are lacking. Foreign languages that we do not understand always seem jabberings, babblings, in which it is impossible to fix a definite, clear-cut, individualized group of

---

8. *Principles of Psychology.* [See *Great Books of the Western World*, Vol. 53, p. 318 (Ed.).]

sounds. The countryman in the crowded city street, the landlubber at sea, the ignoramus in sport at a contest between experts in a complicated game are instances. Put an unexperienced man in a factory, and at first the work seems to him a meaningless medley. All strangers of another race proverbially look alike to the visiting foreigner. Only gross differences of size or color are perceived by an outsider in a flock of sheep, each of which is perfectly individualized to the shepherd. A diffusive blur and indiscriminate shifting characterize what we do not understand. The problem of the acquisition of meaning by things, or (stated in another way) of forming habits of simple apprehension, is thus the problem of introducing (*a*) *definiteness,* or *distinction* and (*b*) *consistency, coherence, constancy,* or *stability* of meaning into what is otherwise vague and wavering.

Practical Responses Clarify the Vague. The acquisition of definiteness and of consistency of meanings is derived primarily from practical activities. By rolling an object, the child makes its roundness appreciable; by bouncing it, he singles out its elasticity; by lifting it, he makes weight its conspicuous distinctive factor. Not through the senses, but by means of the reaction, the responsive adjustment, is an impression given a character marked off from qualities that call out unlike reactions. Children, for example, are usually quite slow in apprehending differences in color. Differences from the standpoint of the adult so glaring that it is impossible not to note them are recognized and recalled by the young with great difficulty. Doubtless colors do not all *feel* alike, but there is no intellectual recognition of what constitutes the difference. The redness or greenness or blueness of the object does not call out a reaction that is sufficiently peculiar to give prominence or distinction to the color trait. Gradually, however, certain characteristic habitual responses associate themselves with certain things; the white becomes the sign, say, of milk and sugar, to which the child reacts favorably; blue becomes the sign of a dress that the child likes to wear, and so on; and the distinctive reactions tend to single out color qualities from other things in which they had been submerged.

Take another example. We have little difficulty in distinguishing from one another rakes, hoes, plows and harrows, shovels and spades. Each has its own associated characteristic use and function. A student of botany or chemistry may have, however, great difficulty in recalling the difference between serrate and dentate, ovoid and obovoid, in the shapes and edges of leaves, or between acids in *ic* and in *ous.* There is some difference; but just what? Or, he knows what the difference is; but which is which?

Variations in form, size, color, and arrangement of parts have much less to do, and the uses, purposes, and functions of things and of their parts much more to do, with distinctness of character and meaning than we should be likely to think. What misleads us is the fact that the qualities of form, size, color, and so on, are *now* so distinct that we fail to see that the problem is precisely to account for the way in which they originally obtained their definiteness and conspicuousness. As long as we sit passive before objects, they are not distinguished out of the vague blur that swallows them all. Differences in the pitch and intensity of sounds leave behind a different feeling, but until we assume different attitudes toward them, or *do* something special in reference to them, their vague difference cannot be *intellectually* gripped and retained.

Illustrations from Drawing and Language. Children's drawings afford a further exemplification of the same principle. Perspective does not exist, for the child's interest is not in *pictorial representation,* but in the *values* of the things represented; and while perspective is essential to the former, it is no part of the characteristic use and function of the things themselves. The house is drawn with transparent walls, because the rooms, chairs, beds, people inside are the important things in the house meaning; smoke always comes out of the chimney—otherwise, why have a chimney at all? At Christmas time, the stockings may be drawn almost as large as the house or even so large that they have to be put outside of it—in any case, it is the scale of values in use that furnishes the scale for their qualities. The drawings are diagrammatic reminders of these values, not impartial records of physical and sensory qualities. One of the chief difficulties felt by most persons in learning the art of pictorial representation is that habitual uses and results of use have become so intimately read into the character of things that it is practically impossible to shut them out at will.

The acquiring of meaning by sounds, in virtue of which they become words, is perhaps the most striking illustration that can be found of the way in which mere sensory stimuli acquire definiteness and constancy of meaning and are thereby themselves defined and interconnected for purposes of recognition. Language is a specially good example because there are hundreds or even thousands of words in which meaning is now so thoroughly consolidated with physical qualities as to be directly understood. In the case of words it is easier to recognize that this connection has been gradually and laboriously acquired than in the case of physical objects, such as chairs, tables, buttons, trees, stones, hills, flowers, and so on, where it seems as if the union of intellectual meaning with physical fact were aboriginal. It now seems to be thrust upon us rather than acquired through active explorations. But in the case of the meaning of words, we see readily that it is by making sounds and noting the results that follow, by listening to the sounds of others and watching the activities that accompany them, that a given sound finally becomes the stable bearer of a meaning.

Meaning and Context. In the case of the meaning of words, we are aware by watching children and by our own experience in learning French or German that happenings, like sounds, which originally were devoid of significance acquire meaning by use, and that this use always involves a *context*. With children just learning to understand and use speech, the context is largely that of objects and acts. A child associates *hat* with putting something on his head when he is going outdoors; *drawer* with pulling something out of a table, etc. Single words, because of the direct presence of a context of actions performed with objects, then have the force that complete sentences have to an older person. Gradually other words that originally gained meaning by use in a context of overt actions become capable of supplying the context, so that the mind can dispense with the context of things and deeds. Speaking in sentences marks obviously a *linguistic* gain. But the more important matter is that it shows a person has made a great *intellectual* advance. He can now think by putting together verbal signs of things that are not present to the senses and are not accompanied by any overt actions on his part. As he understands similar combinations made by others, he has a new resource that extends his otherwise narrow personal experience indefinitely. When he learns to read, arbitrary marks on paper acquire meaning for him, and he gains possession of the means of still further extending his experience so as to include what others, far remote from him in space and time, have experienced.

As was indicated a short time ago, it is not easy to grasp the fact that things had at first no significance in our experience, and that significance was acquired in their case, as in that of sounds, by entering into a context of use, by bringing help and enjoyment to us—articles of food, furniture, and wearing apparel—or by bringing harm and suffering—like fire approached too closely, pins that scratch, hammers that hit fingers instead of nails.

Take, for example, a little spark of light appearing at night in the heavens, and compare the original mere sight of it with the discriminating and extensive knowledge of it that the expert astronomer has. He identifies it, say, as planet, asteroid, satellite, or fixed star that is the sun of some other system. Each one of these things carries an immense store of mean-

ings with it—distance, rate of movement, chemical composition, indeed all
the things that one finds in a bulky volume upon astronomy. The change
from a mere spark to an immensely significant object illustrates the acquisition of meaning which has taken place in the case of everything that we
understand or know. It illustrates also the fact that the acquisition of
ability to understand (which is the same as the acquisition of significance
by things) is immensely furthered by language and by elaboration of a
series of meanings and through reasoning. This latter process is itself
dependent upon possession of some kind of linguistic sign system—for we
must remember that mathematical symbols are also a kind of language.

The Means-Consequence Relation and Its Educational Significance.
We may sum up by stating that things gain meaning when they are used
as *means to bring about consequences* (or as means to prevent the occurrence of undesired consequences), or as standing for *consequences* for
which we have to discover *means.* The relation of *means-consequence* is
the center and heart of all understanding. The operations by which things
become understood as chairs, tables, shoes, hats, food illustrate the
means-consequence relation from the "means" side. The relation beginning with the "consequence," or result-sought, side is illustrated in any
invention. Edison thought of producing light by the use of electricity; he
then had to discover the conditions of things and relations that would
produce it—the means for it. The same obtained with Langley and the
Wright brothers after they conceived the idea, as a desired end, of a
machine to fly in the air. It is illustrated in all cases of ordinary planning.
We think of something needful or desirable, and then we have to seek out
materials and methods for bringing it to pass. Every time we have to solve
a problem of this kind, things enter into the means-consequence relation
and in doing so take on added meaning, just as carbon filaments obtained
a new significance through the production of electric light, and as gaso-
line, once almost a waste by-product, secured new meaning when the
internal-combustion engine was invented.

The educational bearing of this principle is almost too obvious for
mention. One of the chief causes for failure in school to secure that gain in
ability to understand that is a precious educational result is the neglecting
to set up the conditions for active use as a means in bringing consequences
to pass—the neglecting to provide projects that call out the inventiveness
and ingenuity of pupils in proposing aims to realize, or finding means to
realize, consequences already thought of. All routine and all externally
dictated activity fail to develop ability to understand, even though they
promote skill in external doing. Too many so-called "problems," in reality

assigned tasks, call at best simply for a kind of mechanical dexterity in applying set rules and manipulating symbols. In short, there is a challenge to understanding only when there is either a desired consequence for which means have to be found by inquiry, or things (including symbols in the degree in which experience has matured) are presented under conditions where reflection is required to see what consequences can be effected by their use.

It is assumed too frequently that subject matter is understood when it has been stored in memory and can be reproduced upon demand. The net outcome of our discussion is that nothing is really known except in so far as it is understood.

UNDERSTANDING: CONCEPTION AND DEFINITION

I

THE NATURE OF CONCEPTIONS

In the preceding chapter we discussed meaning from two points of view, and we suggested a third aspect of it that we shall consider more fully in this chapter. The two aspects that were discussed were (1) meaning as doubtful, as a hypothetical possibility; in short as an *idea* (which, as was pointed out, is not a mere psychological complex but is an object or situation that has a status of being *supposed* instead of being accepted), and (2) meaning as a property of things and events. It was shown in that connection how things *acquire* meaning and how finally meaning is so consolidated with a thing that we do not dream of separating the thing from its significance.

They Are Established Meanings. The aspect of meaning that was indicated in passing is the fact that an idea, after it has been used as a guide to observation and action, may be confirmed and so acquire an accepted status on its own behalf. Afterwards it is employed, not tentatively and conditionally, but with assurance as an instrumentality of understanding and explaining things that are still uncertain and perplexing. These established meanings, taken to be secure and warranted, are *conceptions*. They are means of judgment because they are *standards of reference*. They may be best described as "standardized meanings." Every common noun that is familiar and so well understood in itself that it can be used to judge other things expresses a concept. Table, stone, sunset, grass, animal, moon, and on through the list of common nouns that are solid and dependable, are concepts in their meaning. We see an object that looks strange; we are told that it is the kind of bed used by a certain folk. The thing in question is no longer unfamiliar in meaning; to us its significance is settled.

They Enable Us to Generalize. Concepts enable us to *generalize*, to extend and carry over our understanding from one thing to another. If we know what "bed" means in general, we at least can tell what *kind* or what *sort* of thing the individual thing is. It is plain that conceptions, since they represent the whole class or set of things, economize our intellectual efforts tremendously. Sometimes of course we are especially interested in the peculiar traits of an object, in what is unique about it, what makes it an *individual.* But for practical purposes it is often enough to know what *kind* of thing it is; knowing that fact, we can bring into play the habits of thought and behavior that belong to every member of the entire class. The concept calls into play whatever is appropriate to a large number of cases previously known, thus freeing thought from preoccupation with finding out what *this* is.

They Standardize Our Knowledge. Conceptions *standardize* our knowledge. They introduce solidity into what would otherwise be formless, and *permanence* into what would otherwise be shifting. If pounds arbitrarily changed their weight and foot rules their length while we were using them, weighing and measuring would, obviously, amount to nothing. What would it signify to say that a piece of cloth was a yard and a half wide, or that a bulk of sugar weighed twenty pounds? The standard of reference must remain the same to be of any use. The concept signifies that a meaning has been stabilized and remains the same in different contexts. Sometimes when persons are discussing a controversial matter, the argument gets confused and the debaters misled because, as they go along, they unconsciously shift the meanings of the terms they use. Reflection and new discoveries may, to be sure, change the meaning of an old concept, just as people may change from the foot-pound system of measurement to the metric system. But they should know what they are about and deliberately note that they are using a changed meaning unless they are to get hopelessly mixed up.

When persons are said to have come to an understanding with each other, it is meant that they have arrived at an *agreement* or *settlement* of some affair or issue that has been under discussion between them. This fact indicates that standardized and stable meanings are a condition of effective communication. When two persons speak languages that are not mutually understood, they can still communicate to some extent, provided there are gestures which have *identical meanings for both parties.* Indeed, the social necessity of meanings that are the same for two persons in spite of differences in their experiences and their conditions of life is one of the chief forces in standardizing meanings. After they are socially stabilized, an individual has the ability to keep his own thinking steady because some of his thoughts remain constant in what they refer to; "chair" always signifies the same; so do "sun," "water," "earth," etc. Each of our entire list of common nouns always refers to the same objects, in spite of differences of place, time, and other conditions of experience.

They Help Identify the Unknown and Supplement the Sensibly Present. Stating the matter somewhat differently, conceptions, or standard meanings, are instruments of (*a*) identification, (*b*) supplementation, and (*c*) placing an object in a system. Suppose a little speck of light hitherto unseen is detected in the heavens. Unless there is a store of meanings to fall back upon in reasoning, that speck of light will remain just what it is to the senses—a mere speck of light. For all that it leads to intellectually, it might as well be a mere irritation of the optic nerve. Given, however, the stock of meanings built up in prior experience, this speck of light is mentally attacked by means of appropriate concepts. Does it indicate asteroid, or comet, or a new-forming sun, or a nebula resulting from some cosmic collision or disintegration? Each of these conceptions has its own specific and differentiating characters, which are then sought for by minute and persistent inquiry. As a result, then, the speck is identified, we will say, as a comet. Through a standard meaning it gets identity and stability of character. Supplementation then takes place. All the known qualities of comets are read into this particular thing, even though they have not been as yet observed. All that the astronomers of the past have learned about the paths and structure of comets becomes available capital with which to interpret the speck of light. Finally, this comet meaning is, itself, not isolated; it is a related portion of the whole system of astronomic knowledge. Suns, planets, satellites, nebulae, comets, meteors, star dust—all these conceptions have a certain mutuality of reference and interaction, and when the speck of light is identified as meaning a comet, it is at once adopted as a full member in this vast kingdom of beliefs.

Darwin, in an autobiographical sketch, says that when a youth he told the geologist Sidgwick of finding a tropical shell in a certain gravel pit. Thereupon Sidgwick said it must have been thrown there by some person, adding: "But if it were really embedded there, it would be the greatest misfortune to geology, because it would overthrow all that we know about the superficial deposits of the Midland Counties"—since these were glacial. And then Darwin adds: "I was then utterly astonished at Sidgwick not being delighted at so wonderful a fact as a tropical shell being found near the surface in the middle of England. Nothing before had made me thoroughly realize *that science consists in grouping facts so that general laws or conclusions may be drawn from them.*" This instance (which might, of course, be duplicated from any branch of science) indicates how scientific notions make explicit the systematizing tendency involved in all use of concepts.

The Educational Significance of Concepts. It follows that it would be impossible to overestimate the educational importance of arriving at conceptions: that is, of meanings that are *general* because applicable in a great variety of different instances in spite of their difference; that are constant, uniform, or self-identical in what they refer to, and that are standardized, known points of reference by which to get our bearings when we are plunged into the strange and unknown.

Young children cannot of course acquire and employ the same conceptions that persons of riper experience use. But at *every* stage of development, each lesson, in order to be educative, should lead up to a certain amount of conceptualizing of impressions and ideas. Without this conceptualizing or intellectualizing, nothing is gained that can be carried over to the better understanding of new experiences. The *deposit* is what counts, educationally speaking. No amount of transient interest, however absorbing and exciting it may be, can compensate for failure to achieve an intellectual deposit.

The very importance of concepts has led, however, to great mistakes in the conduct of teaching. What we earlier termed the false use of the "logical" had its roots in the belief that somehow definite and general meanings, or concepts, can be presented to pupils and absorbed by them *ready-made,* thus promoting the rapidity and efficiency of acquisition of knowledge. In consequence, failure to observe the conditions that are essential for the formation of conceptions left most pupils with only *verbal* formulas. Concepts were often presented that were so remote from the understanding and experience of students as to be positively confusing in their artificiality.

The reaction of education in experimental schools against the arbitrary imposition of indigestible material has often, however, been a reaction to the opposite extreme. A variety of worthwhile experiences and activities with real materials is introduced, but pains are not taken to make sure that the activities terminate in that which makes them *educationally* worthwhile, as distinct from an agreeable passing of the time—namely, the achievement of a fairly definite *intellectualization* of the experience. This intellectualization is the deposit of an *idea* that is both definite and general. Education in its intellectual aspect and getting an idea from what is experienced are synonymous. What does having an experience amount to unless, as it ceases to exist, it leaves behind an increment of meaning, a better understanding of something, a clearer future plan and purpose of action: in short, an idea? With respect to teaching there is no more important topic than the question of the way in which genuine concepts are formed. To that question we now turn.

II
HOW CONCEPTIONS ARISE

They Are Not Formed by Extracting Common Traits from Ready-Made Objects. It is convenient in discussing this question to begin with the negative side, with the mistaken character of some current beliefs about the way in which conceptions come into existence. They are *not* derived by taking a number of things, each of which is already well understood and definite in meaning, and then comparing them one with another, point by point, till all different qualities are excluded and there remains a core of what is common to all. The origin of concepts is sometimes described to be as if a child began with a lot of different particular things, say particular dogs: his own Fido, his neighbor's Carlo, his cousin's Tray. Having all these different objects before him, he analyzes them into a lot of different qualities, say (a) color, (b) size, (c) shape, (d) number of legs, (e) quantity and quality of hair, (f) foods eaten, and so on; and then strikes out all the unlike qualities (such as color, size, shape, hair), retaining traits, such as quadruped and domesticated, which they all have in common.

They Begin with Experiences. As a matter of fact, the child begins with whatever significance he has got out of some one dog he has seen, heard, and played with. He carries over from his experience of this one object to his subsequent experiences expectations of characteristic modes of behavior: he expects them before they show themselves. He assumes this attitude of anticipation whenever an object gives him any excuse for it. Thus he may call cats "little dogs" or horses "big dogs." But finding that other expected traits and modes of behavior are not fulfilled, he is forced to throw out certain traits from the dog meaning, while by contrast some other traits are selected and emphasized. As he further applies the meaning to other animals, the dog meaning gets still further defined and refined. He does not begin with a lot of ready-made objects from which he extracts a common meaning; he tries to apply in every new experience whatever result of his old experience will help him understand and deal with it.

They Become More Definite with Use. It is not true that the child's idea of each individual dog is clear and definite to begin with, and that his own dog is perceived by him with its full equipment of distinct qualities. Rather his original idea of Fido is vague and pulpy, wavering, as long as Fido is the only dog (and much more so if the only animal) he knows. By observing the family cat, he is led to discriminate the particular qualities that characterize each of them. As he makes acquaintance with other animals, the horse, pig, etc., the definite properties that belong to a dog are still further demarcated. Thus, even without much comparison with other *dogs*, a dog concept is gradually built up. In just the extent to which he is aware of the qualities that make his Fido a *dog*, rather than a cat, horse, or any other animal, he has a standardized point of reference for assimilating and sorting out other animals as he makes acquaintance with them. During the whole process he has been trying to fit his idea, vague or definite according to his stage of experience, on all animals that are at all similar to dogs, applying it when he can, becoming aware of differences whenever it won't fit. By these processes, his idea gets body, steadiness, distinction; it becomes a concept.

They Become General with Use. By the same processes, a vague, more or less formless idea acquires *generality*. Conceptions, that is to say, are general because of use and application, not because of their ingredients. The view that a conception originates in an impossible sort of analysis has its counterpart in the idea that it is made up out of all the like elements that remain after dissection of a number of individuals. Not so; the moment a meaning is gained, it is a working tool of further apprehensions, an instrument of understanding other things. Thereby the meaning is *extended* as well as defined. Generality resides in application to the comprehension of new cases, not in the constituent parts of a notion. A collection of traits left as the common residuum, the *caput mortuum* of a million objects, would be merely a collection, an inventory or aggregate, not a *general idea*. Any striking trait emphasized in an experience that afterward serves as an aid in understanding some other experience becomes, in virtue of that application, in so far general.

What has just been said may be compared with the earlier statements about analysis and synthesis. The analysis that results in giving an idea the solidity and definiteness of a concept is simply emphasis upon that which gives a clue for dealing with some uncertainty. If a child identifies a dog seen at a distance by the way in which the animal wags its tail, then that particular trait, which may never have been *consciously* singled out before, becomes distinct—it is analyzed out of its vague submergence in the animal as a whole. The only difference between such a case and the analysis effected by a scientific inquirer in chemistry or botany is that the latter is alert for clues that will serve for the purpose of sure identification in the *widest possible area* of cases; he wants to find the signs by which he can identify an object as one of a definite kind or class even should it present itself under very unusual circumstances and in an obscure and disguised form. The idea that the selected trait is already plain to the mind and then is merely isolated from other traits equally definite puts the cart before the horse. It is selection as evidence or as a clue that gives a trait distinctness it did not possess before.

Synthesis is the operation that gives extension and generality to an idea, as analysis makes the meaning distinct. Synthesis is correlative to analysis. As soon as any quality is definitely discriminated and given a special meaning of its own, the mind at once looks around for other cases to which that meaning may be applied. As it is applied, cases that were previously separated in meaning become assimilated, identified, in their significance. They now belong to the same *kind* of thing. Even a young child, as soon as he masters the meaning of a word, tries to find occasion to use it; if he gets the idea of a cylinder, he sees cylinders in stovepipes, logs, etc. In principle this is not different from Newton's procedure in the story about the origin in his mind of the concept of gravitation. Having the idea suggested by the falling of an apple, he at once extended it in imagination to the moon as something also tending to fall towards the earth, and then to the movements of the planets in relation to the sun, to the movement of the ocean in the tides, etc. In consequence of this application of an idea that was discriminated, made definite in some one case, to other events, a large number of phenomena that previously were believed to be disconnected from one another were integrated into a consistent system. In other words, there was a comprehensive synthesis.

It would be a great mistake, however, as just indicated, to confine the idea of synthesis to important cases like Newton's generalization. On the contrary, when anyone carries over any meaning from one object to another object that had previously seemed to be of a different kind, synthesis occurs. It is synthesis when a lad associates the gurgling that takes place when water is poured into what he had thought was an empty bottle with the existence and pressure of air; when he learns to interpret the siphoning of water and the sailing of a boat in connection with the same fact. It is synthesis when things themselves as different as clouds, meadow, brook, and rocks are so brought together as to be composed into a picture. It is synthesis when iron, tin, and mercury are conceived to be of the same kind in spite of individual differences.

III
DEFINITION AND ORGANIZATION OF MEANINGS

The Harmful Consequences of Vagueness. A being that cannot understand at all is at least protected from *mis*-understandings. But beings that get knowledge by means of inferring and interpreting, by judging what things signify in relation to one another, are constantly exposed to the danger of *mis*-apprehension, *mis*-understanding, *mis*-taking—taking of a thing amiss. A constant source of misunderstanding and mistake is indefiniteness of meaning. Because of vagueness of meaning we misunderstand other people, things, and ourselves; because of ambiguity we distort and pervert. Conscious distortion of meaning may be enjoyed as nonsense; erroneous meanings, if clear-cut, may be followed up and got rid of. But vague meanings are too gelatinous to offer matter for analysis and too pulpy to afford support to other beliefs. They evade testing and responsibility. Vagueness disguises the unconscious mixing together of different meanings, and facilitates the substitution of one meaning for another, and covers up the failure to have any precise meaning at all. It is the aboriginal logical sin—the source from which flow most bad intellectual consequences. Totally to eliminate indefiniteness is impossible; to reduce it in extent and in force requires sincerity and vigor.

Meaning as Intension and as Extension. To be clear or perspicuous, a meaning must be detached, single, self-contained, homogeneous as it were, throughout. The technical name for any meaning that is thus individualized is *intension*. The process of arriving at such units of meaning (and of stating them when reached) is *definition*. The intension of the terms "man," "river," "honesty," "supreme court" is the meaning that *exclusively* and *characteristically* attaches to those terms. This meaning is set forth in *definition* of these units of meaning.

The test of the distinctness of a meaning is that it successfully marks off a group of things that exemplify the meaning from other groups, especially from those objects that convey nearly allied meanings. The river meaning (or character) must serve to *designate* the Rhone, the Rhine, the Mississippi, the Hudson, the Wabash, in spite of their varieties of place, length, quality of water; and must be such as *not* to suggest ocean currents, ponds, or brooks. This use of a meaning to mark off and group together a variety of distinct existences constitutes its *extension*.

As definition sets forth intension, so division (or the reverse process, classification) expounds extension. Intension and extension, definition and division, are clearly correlative; in language previously used, *intension* is meaning as a principle of identifying particulars; extension is the group of particulars identified and distinguished. Meaning, as extension, would be wholly in the air or unreal did it not point to some object or group of objects; while objects would be as isolated and independent intellectually as they seem to be spatially were they not bound into groups or classes on the basis of characteristic meanings they suggest and exemplify in a uniform way.

Together, definition and division put us in possession of definite meanings and also indicate the group of objects to which they refer, the *kind* of things indicated and its various subclasses. They typify the fixation and the organization of meanings. In the degree in which the meanings of any set of experiences are so cleared up as to serve as principles for grouping those experiences in relation to one another, that set of particulars becomes a science; *i.e.*, definition and classification are the marks of a science, as distinct from unrelated heaps of miscellaneous information and from habits that introduce coherence into our experience without our being aware of their operation.

Three Types of Definitions. Definitions are of three types, *denotative, expository, scientific*. Of these, the first and third are logically important, while the expository type is socially and pedagogically important as an intervening step.

(*a*) *Denotative.* A blind man can never have an adequate understanding of the meaning of *color* and *red;* a seeing person can acquire the knowledge only by having certain things designated in such a way as to fix attention upon some of their qualities. This method of delimiting a meaning by calling out a certain attitude toward objects may be called *denotative*, or *indicative*. It is required for all sense qualities—sounds, tastes, colors—and equally for all emotional and moral qualities. The meanings of "honesty," "sympathy," "hatred" must be grasped by having them presented in an individual's firsthand experience. The reaction of educational reformers against linguistic and bookish training has always taken the form of demanding recourse to personal experience. However advanced the person is in knowledge and in scientific training, understanding of a new subject, or of a new aspect of an old subject, must always be through acts of experiencing directly or in imagination the existence of the quality in question.

(*b*) *Expository*. Given a certain store of meanings that have been directly or denotatively marked out, language becomes a resource by which imaginative combinations and variations may be built up. A color may be defined to one who has not experienced it as lying between green and blue; a tiger may be defined (*i.e.*, the idea of it made more definite) by selecting some qualities from known members of the cat tribe and combining them with ideas of size and weight derived from other objects. Illustrations are of the nature of expository definitions; so are the accounts of meanings given in a dictionary. By taking better-known meanings and associating them, the attained store of meanings of the community in which one resides is put at one's disposal. But in themselves these definitions are secondhand and conventional; there is danger that instead of inciting one to effort after personal experiences that will exemplify and verify them, they will be accepted on authority as *substitutes* for direct observation and experiment.

(*c*) *Scientific*. Even popular definitions serve as rules for identifying and classifying individuals, but the purpose of such identifications and classifications is mainly practical and social, not intellectual. To conceive the whale as a fish does not interfere with the success of whalers, nor does it prevent recognition of a whale when seen, while to conceive it not as a fish but as a mammal serves the practical end equally well, and also furnishes a much more valuable principle for scientific identification and classification. Popular definitions select certain fairly obvious traits as keys to classification. Scientific definitions select *conditions of causation, production, and generation* as their characteristic material. The traits used by the popular definition do not help us to understand why an object has its common meanings and qualities; they simply state the fact that it does have them. Causal and genetic definitions settle on the way an object is constructed as giving the key to its belonging to a certain *kind* of objects. They explain why it has its class or common traits on the basis of its manner of production.

If, for example, a layman of considerable practical experience were asked what he meant or understood by *metal*, he would probably reply in terms of the qualities useful in recognizing any given metal and in the arts. Smoothness, hardness, glossiness, and brilliancy, heavy weight for its size would probably be included in his definition, because such traits enable us to identify specific things when we see and touch them; the serviceable properties of capacity for being hammered and pulled without breaking, of being softened by heat and hardened by cold, of retaining the shape and form given, of resistance to pressure and decay would probably be included—whether or not such terms as "malleable" or "fusible" were used. Now a scientific conception, instead of using, even with additions, traits of this kind, determines meaning on a different basis. The present definition of metal is about like this: Metal means any chemical element that enters into combination with oxygen so as to form a base; *i.e.*, a compound that combines with an acid to form a salt. This scientific definition is founded, not on directly perceived qualities nor on directly useful properties, but on the *way in which certain things are causally related to other things; i.e.,* it denotes a relation. As chemical concepts become more and more those of relationships of interaction in constituting other substances, so physical concepts express more and more relations of operation: mathematical, functions of dependence and order of grouping; biological, relations of differentiation of descent, effected through adjustment of various environments; and so on through the sphere of the sciences. In short, our conceptions attain a maximum of definite individuality and of generality (or applicability) in the degree to which they show how things depend upon one another or influence one another, instead of expressing the qualities that objects possess statistically. The ideal of a system of scientific conceptions is to attain continuity, freedom, and flexibility of transition in passing from any fact and meaning to any other; this demand is met in the degree in which we lay hold of the dynamic ties that hold things together in a continuously changing process—a principle that gives insight into mode of production or growth.

SYSTEMATIC METHOD: CONTROL OF DATA AND EVIDENCE

I

METHOD AS DELIBERATE TESTING OF FACTS AND IDEAS

Judgment, understanding, conception are all of them constituents of the reflective process in which a perplexing, confused, unsettled situation is transformed into one that is coherent, clear, and decided or settled. In discussing them we have introduced nothing new in principle but have amplified what was illustrated in the three cases . . . analyzed in some detail [in the chapter on "Analysis of Reflective Thinking"]. We shall now return to the original account and utilize the added knowledge we have obtained to discuss the method of reflective activity when it is regulated in a technical and elaborate way. We saw . . . that reflection is an operation in which facts on one side and meaning on the other are elicited through constant interaction with each other. Each newly discovered fact develops, tests, and modifies an idea, and every new idea and new shade of an idea lead to further inquiry, which brings to light new facts, modifying our understanding of facts previously observed.

The discussion in which we are now engaging accordingly has two sides. One side concerns method as it operates in gathering and testing the *data* that form the evidence upon which an inference must rest to be properly supported—method of control of observation and memory, which supply the facts upon which inference proceeds. The other side concerns the formation and development of method as it operates in arriving at the *ideas* that are used to interpret the data, to solve problems, and to elaborate and apply concepts. The two functions, as we have seen, accompany each other. The improved selection and discrimination of pertinent data gives a better clue to ideas that are fruitful when employed and to the tests to which they must be submitted. The improvement of ideas in turn stimulates the performance of new observations and the collection of new data.

The Need for Systematized Method. Method of a systematic sort is required in order to safeguard the operations by which we move from one to the other, from facts to ideas, and back again from ideas to the facts that will test them. Without adequate method a person grabs, as it were, at the first facts that offer themselves; he does not examine them to see whether they are truly facts or whether, even though they be real facts, they are relevant to the inference that needs to be made. On the other side, we are given to jumping at the first solution that occurs to us, accepting it as a conclusion without examination and test. We are given also to generalizing an idea far beyond support by evidence. We extend it to new cases without careful study to see whether these cases may not be so different as not to justify the generalization. Method is particularly needed in complex cases and cases of generalization, in order to safeguard us from falling into these errors.

We shall first give an illustration of the way in which the discovery of relevant facts on which to base, and by which to support and test, an inferred solution goes on in company with the formation and use of ideas to interpret the facts.

A man who has left his room in order finds it upon his return in a state of confusion, articles being scattered at random. Automatically, the notion comes to his mind that burglary would account for the disorder. He has not seen the burglars; their presence is not a fact of observation; it is a thought, an idea. The state of the room is a *fact*, certain, speaking for itself; the presence of burglars is a possibility that may explain the facts. Moreover, the man has no special burglar in mind. The state of his room is perceived and is particular, definite—exactly as it is; a burglar is inferred. But no particular individual is thought of; merely some indefinite, unspecified, member of a class.

The original fact, the room as it is first observed, does not by any means *prove* the fact of burglary. The latter conjecture may be correct, but evidence to justify accepting it positively is lacking. The total "fact" as given contains both too much and too little; too much, because there are many features in it that are irrelevant to inference, that are therefore *logically* superfluous. Too little, because the considerations that are crucial—that, if they were ascertained, would be decisive—do not appear on the surface. Thoughtful search for the *kind* of facts that are clues is therefore necessitated. If the illustration were followed out beyond the judgment as to whether there had been a burglary to the question of who the criminal was and how he was to be discovered and the crime brought home to him, the need for extensive and careful examination of the fact side of the case would be even clearer.

Observation Valuable When Guided by Hypotheses. This search needs guidance. If it is conducted purely at random a multitude of facts will be turned up, but they will be so unrelated that their very number will add to the difficulty of the case. It is quite possible for thinking to be swamped by the mere multiplicity and diversity of facts. The real problem is: What facts are *evidence* in this case? The search for evidential facts is best conducted when some suggested *possible* meaning is used as a guide in exploring facts, especially in instituting a hunt for some fact that would point conclusively to one explanation and exclude all others. So the person entertains various hypotheses. Besides burglary, there is the possibility that some member of the family had an urgent need to find some article and, being in a hurry, had not taken the time to put things in order again. There are children also in the family, and they are not above mischief on occasion. Each of these conjectured possibilities is developed to some extent. *If* it were a burglar, or an adult in a hurry, or mischief on the part of children, *then* certain features characteristic of each particular cause would be present. *If* it were a case of burglary, *then* articles of value would be missing. Guided by this idea, the person looks again, not any longer at the scene as a whole, but analytically, with reference to this one item. He finds jewelry gone; he finds that some silver articles have been twisted and bent, and left behind as merely plated wear. These data are incompatible with any hypothesis except burglary. Looking further, he finds data that are most naturally interpreted to mean that a window has been tampered with—a fact consistent only with the action of a burglar. Under any ordinary circumstances these data would give adequate evidence of the visit of a burglar; if the conditions were very unusual, there would be nothing but to continue thinking of further possibilities and looking for further facts as data by which to test them. The instance is taken from ordinary life. Scientific method represents the same sort of thing carried on with greater elaborateness, by means especially of instruments and apparatus devised for the purpose and of mathematical calculations.

II

THE IMPORTANCE OF METHOD IN JUDGING DATA

From what has been said it is clear that the formation of the idea or hypothesis that is employed to interpret data and to unify them into a coherent situation is indirect. Fundamentally, suggestions just occur or do not occur, depending, as we have seen, on the state of culture and knowledge at the time; upon the discernment and experience and native genius of the individual; upon his recent activities; to some extent upon chance; for many of the most pregnant inventions and discoveries have come about almost accidentally, although these happy accidents never happen except to persons especially prepared by interest and prior thought. But while the original happening of a suggestion, whether it be brilliant or stupid, is not *directly* controlled, the acceptance and use of the suggestion is capable of control, given a person of a thoughtful habit of mind.

The primary method of control is that indicated in the illustration. The person who is confronted with the situation that has to be thought through returns upon, revises, extends, analyzes, and makes more precise and definite the facts of the case. He strives to convert them into just those data which will test the suggestions that occur to mind. This testing will take place, as in the burglary incident, by finding upon examination traits that are *incompatible* with some suggested possibility and consistent with some other. They are just what *should* be there in fact *if* that particular hypothesis is correct. The ideal of course is discovery of traits that could be present *only* upon a particular hypothesis. This type of evidence can rarely be found in fact, but it is approximated by the methods of control of observation and collection of data that have been found to work well in scientific inquiry.

The Interrelations of Observation and Thought. It will be noted, then, that observation is not an operation that is opposed to thought or that is even independent of it. On the contrary, *thoughtful* observing is at least one half of thinking, the other half being the entertaining and elaboration of multiple hypotheses. Features that are glaringly conspicuous often need to be ignored; hidden traits need to be brought to light; obscure characteristics to be emphasized and cleared up.

Consider, for example, how a physician makes his diagnosis, his interpretation. If he is scientifically trained, he suspends—postpones—reaching a conclusion in order that he may not be led by superficial occurrences into a snap judgment. There are some facts that are given in an obvious way to his observation. But what is obvious may be, *when regarded as an evidential sign,* most misleading; the evidential facts, the real data, may show themselves only after a prolonged search involving artificial apparatus and a technique that expresses the methods found useful by a whole body of experts.

Conspicuous phenomena may forcibly suggest typhoid, but the physician avoids a conclusion or even any strong preference for this or that conclusion until he has both greatly *enlarged* the scope of his data and also rendered them more *minute.* He not only questions the patient as to his feelings and as to his acts prior to the disease, but by various manipulations with his hands (and with instruments made for the purpose) brings to light a large number of facts of which the patient is quite unaware. The state of temperature, respiration, and heart action is accurately noted, and their fluctuations from time to time are exactly recorded. Until this examination has worked *out* toward a wider collection and *in* toward a minuter scrutiny of details, inference is deferred.

Regulative Features of Scientific Method. Scientific method includes, in short, *all the processes by which the observing and amassing of data are regulated with a view to facilitating the formation of explanatory conceptions and theories.* These devices are all directed toward selecting the precise facts to which weight and significance shall attach in forming suggestions or ideas. Specifically, this selective determination involves operations of (1) elimination by analysis of what is likely to be misleading and irrelevant, (2) emphasis of the important by collection and comparison of cases, and (3) deliberate construction of data by experimental variation.

Elimination of Irrelevant Meanings. (1) It is a common saying that one must learn to discriminate between observed facts and judgments based upon them. Taken literally, such advice cannot be carried out; in every

observed thing there is—if the thing have any meaning at all—some con-
solidation of meaning with what is sensibly and physically present, such
that, if this were entirely excluded, what is left would have no sense. A
says: "I saw my brother." The term *brother,* however, involves a relation
that cannot be sensibly or physically observed; it is inferential in status. If
A contents himself with saying, "I saw a man," the factor of classification,
of intellectual reference, is less complex, but still exists. If, as a last resort,
A were to say, "Anyway, I saw a colored object," some relationship, though
more rudimentary and undefined, still subsists. Theoretically, it is possible
that no object was there, only abnormal nerve stimulation. Nonetheless,
the advice to discriminate what is observed from what is inferred is sound
practical advice. Its working import is that one should eliminate or exclude *those* inferences as to which experience has shown that there is
greatest liability to error. This, of course, is a relative matter. Under
ordinary circumstances no reasonable doubt would attach to the observation, "I see my brother"; it would be pedantic and silly to resolve this
recognition back into a more elementary form. Under other circumstances
it might be a perfectly genuine question as to whether A saw even a
colored *thing,* or whether the color was due to a stimulation of the sensory
optical apparatus (like "seeing stars" upon a blow) or to a disordered
circulation. In general, the scientific man is one who knows that he is
likely to be hurried to a conclusion and that part of this precipitancy is
due to certain habits that tend to make him "read" certain meanings into
the situation that confronts him, so that he must be on the lookout against
errors arising from his interests, habits, and current preconceptions.

The technique of scientific inquiry thus consists in various processes
that tend to exclude overhasty "reading in" of meanings; devices that aim
to give a purely "objective," unbiased rendering of the data to be interpreted. Flushed cheeks usually mean heightened temperature; paleness
means lowered temperature. The clinical thermometer records automatically the actual temperature and hence checks up the habitual associations
that might lead to error in a given case. All the instrumentalities of
observation—the various -meters and -graphs and -scopes—fulfill a part of
their scientific role in helping to eliminate meanings supplied because of
habit, prejudice, the strong momentary preoccupation of excitement and
anticipation, and by the vogue of existing theories. Photographs, phono-
graphs, kymographs, actinographs, seismographs, plethysmographs, and
the like, moreover, give records that are permanent, so that they can be
employed by different persons, and by the same person in different states

of mind; *i.e.*, under the influence of varying expectations and dominant beliefs. Thus purely personal prepossessions (due to habit, to desire, to aftereffects of recent experience) may be largely eliminated. In ordinary language, the facts are *objectively*, rather than *subjectively*, determined. In this way tendencies to premature interpretation are held in check.

Collection of Sufficient Instances. (2) Another important method of control consists in the multiplication of cases or instances. If I doubt whether a certain handful gives a fair sample or one representative, for purposes of judging value, of a whole carload of grain, I take a number of handfuls from various parts of the car and compare them. If they agree in quality, well and good; if they disagree, we try to get enough samples so that when they are thoroughly mixed the result will be a fair basis for an evaluation. This illustration represents roughly the value of that aspect of scientific method that insists upon multiplying observations instead of basing the conclusion upon one or a few cases.

So prominent, indeed, is this aspect of method at a certain stage of its development that it is frequently treated as constituting induction. It is supposed that all controlled inference as to matters of fact is based upon collecting and comparing a number of like cases. Actually such comparison and collection is a secondary development within the process of securing a correct conclusion in some single case. If a man infers from one sample of grain as to the grade of wheat of the car as a whole, it is induction and, under certain circumstances, namely, if the entire bulk has been thoroughly mixed, it is a *sound* induction. Other cases are resorted to simply for the sake of rendering a suggested inference more guarded, and more probably correct. In like fashion, the reasoning that led up to the burglary idea in the instance already cited, the particulars upon which the general meaning (or relation) of burglary was grounded, were simply the sum total of the unlike items and qualities that made up the one case examined. Had this case presented very great obscurities and difficulties, recourse might *then* have been had to examination of a number of similar cases. But this comparison would not introduce scientific method into a process that was not previously of that character; it would only render inference more wary and adequate. *The object of bringing into consideration a multitude of cases is to facilitate the selection of the evidential or significant features upon which to base inference in some single case.*

Unlikeness as Important as Likeness in These Instances. Accordingly, points of *unlikeness* are as important as points of *likeness* among the cases examined. *Comparison*, without *contrast*, does not amount to anything logically. In the degree in which other cases observed or remembered merely duplicate the case in question, we are no better off for purposes of inference than if we had permitted our single original fact to dictate a conclusion. In the case of various samples of grain, it is the fact that samples are *different*, at least as to the place of the carload from which they are taken, that is important. Were it not for this difference, likeness in quality would be of no avail in controlling inference.[9] If we are endeavoring to get a child to regulate his conclusions about the germination of a seed by taking into account a number of instances, very little is gained if the conditions in all these instances closely approximate one another. But if one seed is placed in pure sand, another in loam, and another on blotting paper, and if in each case there are two conditions, one with and another without moisture, the unlike factors tend to throw into relief the factors that are significant (or "essential") for reaching a conclusion. Unless, in short, the observer takes care to have the differences in the observed cases as extreme as conditions allow, and unless he notes unlikenesses as carefully as likenesses, he has no way of determining the evidential force of the data that confront him.

Another way of bringing out this importance of unlikeness is the emphasis put by the scientist upon *negative* cases—upon instances that, it would seem, ought to fall into line but that, as a matter of fact, do not. Anomalies, exceptions, things that agree in most respects but disagree in some crucial point, are so important that many of the devices of scientific technique are designed purely to detect, record, and impress upon memory contrasting cases. Darwin remarked that, so easy is it to pass over cases that oppose a favorite generalization, he had made it a habit, not merely to hunt for contrary instances, but also to write down any exception he noted or thought of—as otherwise it was almost sure to be forgotten.

Experimental Variation of Conditions. (3) We have already touched upon this factor of control of method, the one that is the most important of all wherever it is feasible. Theoretically, one sample case *of the right kind* will be as good a basis for an inference as a thousand cases; but cases of the right kind rarely turn up spontaneously. We have to search for them, and we may have to *make* them. If we take cases just as we find them—whether one case or many cases—they contain much that is irrelevant to the problem in hand, while much that is relevant is obscure, hidden.

---

9. In terms of the phrases used in logical treatises, the so-called "methods of agreement" (comparison) and "difference" (contrast) must accompany each other or constitute a "joint method" in order to be of logical use.

The object of experimentation is the *construction, by regular steps taken on the basis of a plan thought out in advance, of a typical, crucial case,* a case formed with express reference to throwing light on the difficulty in question. All methods on the fact side rest, as already stated, upon regulation of the conditions of observation and memory; experiment is simply the most adequate regulation of these conditions that is possible. We try to make the observation such that every factor entering into it, together with the mode and the amount of its operation, may be open to recognition. Making observations open, overt, precise constitutes experiment.

Three Advantages of Experiment. Such observations have many and obvious advantages over observations—no matter how extensive—with respect to which we simply wait for an event to happen or an object to present itself. Experiment overcomes defects due to (*a*) the *rarity,* (*b*) the *subtlety* and minuteness (or the violence), and (*c*) the rigid *fixity* of facts as we ordinarily experience them. The following quotations from Jevons' *Elementary Lessons in Logic* bring out all these points:

> We might have to wait years or centuries to meet accidentally with facts which we can readily produce at any moment in a laboratory; and it is probable that most of the chemical substances now known and many excessively useful products would never have been discovered at all by waiting till nature presented them spontaneously to our observation.

This quotation refers to the infrequency, or rarity, of certain facts of nature, even very important ones. The passage then goes on to speak of the minuteness of many phenomena that makes them escape ordinary experience:

> Electricity doubtless operates in every particle of matter, perhaps at every moment of time; and even the ancients could not but notice its action in the loadstone, in lightning, in the aurora borealis, or in a piece of rubbed amber. But in lightning electricity was too intense and dangerous; in the other cases it was too feeble to be properly understood. The science of electricity and magnetism could only advance by getting regular supplies of electricity from the common electric machine or the galvanic battery and by making powerful electromagnets. Most, if not all, the effects which electricity produces must go on in nature, but altogether too obscurely for observation.

Jevons then deals with the fact that, under ordinary conditions of experience, phenomena that can be understood only by seeing them under varying conditions are presented in a fixed and uniform way.

Thus carbonic acid is only met in the form of a gas, proceeding from the combustion of carbon; but when exposed to extreme pressure and cold, it is condensed into a liquid, and may even be converted into a snowlike solid substance. Many other gases have in like manner been liquefied or solidified, and there is reason to believe that every substance is capable of taking all three forms of solid, liquid, and gas, if only the conditions of temperature and pressure can be sufficiently varied. Mere observation of nature would have led us, on the contrary, to suppose that nearly all substances were fixed in one condition only, and could not be converted from solid into liquid and from liquid into gas.

Many volumes would be required to describe in detail all the methods that investigators have developed in various subjects for analyzing and restating the facts of ordinary experience so that we may escape from capricious and routine suggestions and may get the facts in such a form and in such a light (or context) that exact and far-reaching explanations may be suggested in place of vague and limited ones. But these various devices of inductive inquiry all have one goal in view: the indirect regulation of the function of suggestions, or formation of ideas; and, in the main, they will be found to reduce to some combination of the three types of selecting and arranging subject matter just described.

SYSTEMATIC METHOD:
CONTROL OF REASONING AND CONCEPTS

I
THE VALUE OF SCIENTIFIC CONCEPTIONS

We have already called attention to the fact that control of observation and memory so as to select and give proper weight to data as evidence depends upon the possession of a store of standardized meanings, or conceptions. If, in the case of the disordered room, the person did not have in hand fairly definite conceptions of burglary, mischief, etc., he would have been as much at a loss in interpreting the scene that met his eyes as a little child would have been. Conceptions are the intellectual instrumentalities that are brought to bear upon the material of sense perception and of recollection in order to clarify the obscure, to bring order into seeming conflict, and unity into the fragmentary. In the case of the physician's diagnosis, dependence upon the fund of already possessed knowledge is even more evident as well as complete. It is an old story that we know *with* what we already know or have mastered intellectually. And "achieved understanding," "established and solid meaning," and "conception" are synonymous terms. Hence the necessity for the regulated control of their formation.

The Basic Importance of System in Concepts. We dealt previously with the way in which conceptions come into existence. We have now to consider the method by which a secure serial development of conceptions, one leading to another in regular sequence, is brought about. The important consideration here is the basic importance of relations between conceptions, of *system*.

A concept may be excellent for the purpose of identifying events that frequently recur in our experience, even if it is not placed in a system or related body of concepts. Thus a person can identify a given four-legged animal as a dog, even though the concept of "dog" is not part of a system of concepts such as forms the science of zoology. But there are other problems of animal life that cannot possibly be solved by the everyday conception of "dog," problems that require a serial order of concepts: wolf family, vertebrate, mammal, and a knowledge of the relations of mammal to birds, reptiles, etc.

The importance of the connections that bind concepts together into a whole is indicated by the words that we use to express the relation of premises and conclusions to each other. (1) The premises are called grounds, foundations, bases, and are said to underlie, uphold, support the conclusion. (2) We "descend" from the premises to the conclusion, and "ascend" in the opposite direction—as a river may be continuously traced from source to sea or vice versa. So the conclusion springs, flows, or is drawn from its premises. (3) The conclusion—as the word itself implies—closes, shuts in, locks up together the various factors stated in the premises. We say that the premises "contain" the conclusion, and that the conclusion "contains" the premises, thereby marking our sense of the inclusive and comprehensive unity in which the elements of reasoning are bound tightly together.

Popular concepts, like the ordinary one of a dog, are based on fairly obvious qualities, qualities that anyone having the normal use of his senses can readily perceive. But these popular concepts do not take us very far; they are extended or generalized to include cases outwardly different only with great risk. They are responsible for such generalizations as calling a bat a "bird," and a whale a "fish." They not only lead us astray, but they also stop far short of such generalizations as those that are basic and almost commonplace in science—electron, atom, molecule, mass, energy, etc. And it is this latter kind of concept that furthers discovery, invention, and the control of the forces of nature.

Value of the Concepts of Quantity. One of the great conquests of natural science has been effected by the development of mathematical concepts in a form applicable to observation and interpretation of natural events. Take for example the concepts of quantity and measurement. We can unite from the point of view of the popular concept such qualities as red, green, blue, etc., by bringing them together in the concept of color. But we can make much more exact and extensive inferences regarding color when we use the concept of rates of vibration. We can then relate color phenomena to other events apparently of a totally different kind—infrared and ultraviolet, radioactive phenomena, sound, electromagnetism, etc. Through the use of the concepts of quantity we can ignore the differences of quality which mark off things from one another and hence arrest inference. Consequently we can go from one fact to another to an almost indefinite extent if we treat them all as exhibiting measured differences of quantity.

Distinctive Standard Concepts Established in Each Science. Every branch of science, geology, zoology, chemistry, physics, astronomy, as well as the different branches of mathematics, arithmetic, algebra, calculus, etc., aims at establishing its own specialized set of concepts that are keys to understanding the phenomena that are classified in each field. In this way there is provided for every typical branch of subject matter a set of meanings and principles so closely interknit that any one implies some other, according to definite conditions, that, under certain other conditions, implies another, and so on. In this way, substitutions of equivalent meanings are possible, and reasoning, without having recourse to specific observations, can trace out very remote consequences of any principle that is suggested. Definition, general formulas, and classification are the devices by which the fixation of a meaning and its elaboration into its ramifications are carried on. They are not ends in themselves—as they are frequently regarded even in elementary education—but instrumentalities for facilitating understanding, aids to the interpretation of the obscure and the explanation of the puzzling. Moreover, a conception that, in the form in which it first presents itself, is not applicable to the situation may have implied meanings that are readily applicable—as the rise of water or mercury in a vacuum is explained by developing the implications of weight and of the fact that air has weight. Again, the original concept may be quite limited in its application, while energy will be conserved if the implied ideas traced out by reasoning have wider application than the original idea had.

Playing with Concepts. To the specialist, conceptual meanings become a subject matter of their own. It is an intellectual satisfaction to develop them in their logical relations of interdependence, of implication, without any reference at all to their immediate or even ulterior application to actual existence. To the trained mathematician, for example, nothing is more fascinating than to follow out the relations of concepts and, by discovering unexpected relations among them, see them unfold into a harmonious system whose contemplation gives great esthetic satisfaction. There is such a thing as *playing with ideas.*

It is possible for this form of sport to become much more absorbing than is playing games with things. No one, it is safe to say, has ever become distinguished as a thinker in any field of science or philosophy who did not have an absorbing interest in the relations of ideas for their own sake. Many children are much more capable of playing with ideas (provided they are within the range of their understanding) than is usually believed. Constraint arising from external imposition dulls this power and often turns into concealed daydreaming and fantasy building what, under happier circumstances, would be an interest in connecting meanings with one another and a delight in coming upon unexpected combinations. One of the great values of creative work, as in writing, painting, or any art, is that it promotes a constructive, although unconscious, playing with meanings in their relations.

Need of Final Test of Concepts. Although conceptions are capable of development without reference to direct observation, and although the habit of tracing their connection with one another as just ideas or meaning is absolutely indispensable to the growth of science and to high personal intellectual cultivation, yet the final test lies in the data furnished by experimental observation. Elaboration by reasoning may make a suggested idea very rich and very plausible, but it will not settle the validity of that idea. Only when facts are observed (by methods either of collection or of experimentation) that agree in detail and without exception with theoretical results, are we justified in accepting the rational conclusion as a conclusion that is valid for actual things. Thinking, in short, must end as well as begin in the domain of concrete observations if it is to be complete thinking. And the ultimate educative value of all deductive processes is measured by the degree to which they become working tools in the creation and development of new experiences.

II

SIGNIFICANT APPLICATIONS TO EDUCATION:
CHARACTERISTIC INADEQUACIES

Some of the points that have been made may be clinched by considering their bearing upon instruction and learning. We shall go back to the statement made earlier about the correlative character of fact and meaning, observation and conception. For most of the educational mistakes about concepts, definition, and generalization result from making a false separation between facts and meanings. In this separation, "facts" become a dead weight of undigested, mechanical, largely verbal, so-called "information," while ideas become so remote from objects and acts of experience that they are empty. Instead of being means for better understanding, they become themselves incomprehensible mysteries, which for some unexplained reason haunt the schoolroom but do not belong anywhere else.

Isolation of Facts from Meaning. In some school subjects and in many topics and lessons, pupils are immersed in mere details. Their minds are loaded with disconnected piecemeal items that are accepted on hearsay or authority. They may even be drawn from observation in so-called "object-lessons" if what is observed stands as an isolated thing, and no attempt is made to interpret it by placing it in relation to what it does, how it was caused, and what it stands for. It is not enough to load the memory with statement of facts and laws and then hope that later in life by some magic the mind will find a use for them. Even general principles, when merely memorized, stand on the same level as bare particular facts. Since they are not used either in understanding actual objects and events or in giving rise, through what they imply, to other conceptual meanings, they are, to the mind that memorizes them (falsely called *learning*), mere arbitrary items of information.

In laboratory instruction in higher education as well as in object lessons in elementary education, the subject is often so treated that the student fails to "see the forest on account of the trees." Things and their qualities are retailed and detailed, without reference to a more general character that they stand for and mean. In the laboratory the student becomes engrossed in the processes of manipulation, irrespective of the reason for their performance, without recognizing a typical problem for the solution of which they afford the appropriate method. Only deduction or reasoning brings out and emphasizes consecutive relationships, and only when *rela-*

tionships are held in view does learning become more than a miscellaneous scrap bag.

Failure to Follow Up by Reasoning. Again, the mind is allowed to hurry on to a vague notion of the whole of which the fragmentary facts are portions, without any attempt to become conscious of *how* they are bound together as parts of this whole. The student feels that "in a general way," as we say, the facts of the history or geography lesson are related thus and so; but "in a general way" here stands only for "in a vague way," somehow or other, with no clear recognition of just how.

The pupil may be encouraged to form, on the basis of the particular facts, a general notion, a conception of how they stand related, but no pains be taken to make the student follow up the notion, to elaborate it and see just what its bearings are upon the case in hand and upon similar cases. The inductive inference, the guess, is formed by the student; if it happens to be correct, it is at once accepted by the teacher; or if it is false, it is rejected. If any amplification of the idea occurs, it is quite likely carried through by the teacher, who thereby assumes the responsibility for its intellectual development. But a complete, an integral, act of thought requires that the person making the suggestion (the guess) be responsible also for reasoning out its bearings upon the problem in hand, for developing the suggestion enough at least to indicate the ways in which it applies to and accounts for the specific data of the case. Too often when a recitation does not consist in simply testing the ability of the student to display some form of technical skill or to repeat facts and principles accepted on authority, the teacher goes to the opposite extreme; and after calling out the spontaneous reflections of the pupils, their guesses or ideas about the matter, merely accepts or rejects them, assuming himself the responsibility for their elaboration. In this way, the function of suggestion and of interpretation is excited, but it is not directed and trained. Suggestion is stimulated but is not carried over into the *reasoning* phase necessary to complete it.

In other subjects and topics, the reasoning phase is isolated, and is treated as if it were complete in itself. This false isolation may show itself in either (and both) of two points; namely, at the beginning or at the end of the resort to general intellectual procedure.

Isolation of Deduction by Commencing with It. Beginning with definitions, rules, general principles, classifications, and the like, is a common form of the first error. This method has been such a uniform object of attack on the part of all educational reformers that it is not necessary to dwell upon it further than to note that the mistake is, logically, due to the

attempt to introduce deductive considerations without first making acquaintance with the particular facts that create a need for definition and
generalization. Unfortunately, the reformer sometimes carries his objection too far or, rather, locates it in the wrong place. He is led into a tirade
against *all* definition, all systematization, all use of general principles,
instead of confining himself to pointing out their futility and their deadness when not properly motivated by familiarity with concrete experiences. Moreover, a flat statement of a general principle may properly
come at the beginning, provided it is used to challenge attention and not
to close inquiry.

Isolation of Conceptions from Direction of New Observations. The
isolation of general ideas is found at the other end wherever there is
failure to clinch and test the results of the general reasoning processes by
application to new concrete cases. The final point of the rational devices
lies in their use in assimilating and comprehending individual cases. No
one understands a general principle fully—no matter how adequately he
can demonstrate it, to say nothing of repeating it—till he can employ it in
the mastery of new situations, which, if they *are* new, differ in manifestation from the cases used in reaching the generalization. Too often the
student and teacher are contented with a series of somewhat perfunctory
examples and illustrations, and the student is not forced to carry the
principle that he has formulated over into further cases of his own experience. In so far, the principle is inert and dead; it does not move into new
facts or ideas.

Failure to Provide for Experimentation. It is only a variation upon this
same theme to say that every complete act of reflective inquiry makes
provision for experimentation—for testing suggested and accepted principles by employing them for the active construction of new cases, in
which new qualities emerge. Only slowly do our schools accommodate
themselves to the general advance of scientific method. From the scientific
side, it is demonstrated that effective and integral thinking is possible only
where the experimental method in some form is used. Some recognition of
this principle is evinced in higher institutions of learning, colleges, and
high schools. But in elementary education, it is still assumed, for the most
part, that the pupil's natural range of observations, supplemented by what
he accepts on hearsay, is adequate for intellectual growth. Of course it is
not necessary that laboratories shall be introduced under that name, much
less that elaborate apparatus be secured; but the entire scientific history of
humanity demonstrates that the conditions for complete mental activity
do not exist unless adequate provision is made for carrying on activities

that actually modify physical conditions, and that books, pictures, and even objects, that are passively observed but not manipulated do not furnish the required provision.

The counterpart error has already been touched upon. In some "progressive" schools, continual outward activity, even though of a somewhat random and disconnected character, is treated as if it were experimentation. In truth, every genuine experiment involves a problem in which something must be found out and where overt action must be guided by an idea used as a working hypothesis so as to give action purpose and point.

Failure to Summarize Net Accomplishment. In such schools there is also a tendency to overlook the need of constant review, in the sense of looking back over what has been done and has been found out, so as to formulate the net outcome, thus getting mentally rid of debris, of all material and acts that do not sustain the outcome. Just because too explicit formulation and organization should *not* come at the beginning, it is so much the more necessary that the ongoing process of experience should be periodically arrested to make a survey of what has been going on and to secure a summary of its *net* accomplishment. Otherwise loose and disorderly habits are promoted.

ACTIVITY
AND THE TRAINING OF THOUGHT

In this chapter we shall gather together and amplify considerations that have already been advanced, in various passages of the preceding pages, concerning the relation of *action to thought*. We shall follow, though not with exactness, the order of development in the unfolding of a human being.

I
THE EARLY STAGE OF ACTIVITY

"What Is the Baby Thinking About?" The sight of a baby often calls out the question: "What do you suppose he is thinking about?" By the nature of the case, the question is unanswerable in detail; but, also by the nature of the case, we may be sure about a baby's chief interest. His primary problem is mastery of his body as a tool of securing comfortable and effective adjustments to his surroundings, physical and social. The child has to learn to do almost everything: to see, to hear, to reach, to handle, to

balance the body, to creep, to walk, and so on. Even if it be true that human beings have even more instinctive reactions than lower animals, it is also true that instinctive tendencies are much less perfect in men, and that most of them are of little use till they are intelligently combined and directed. A little chick just out of the shell will after a few trials peck at and grasp grains of food with its beak as well as at any later time. This involves a complicated co-ordination of the eye and the head. An infant does not even begin to reach definitely for things that the eye sees till he is several months old, and even then several weeks' practice is required before he learns the adjustment so as neither to overreach nor to under-reach. It may not be literally true that the child will grasp for the moon, but it is true that he needs much practice before he can tell whether an object is within reach or not. The arm is thrust out instinctively in response to a stimulus from the eye, and this tendency is the origin of the ability to reach and grasp exactly and quickly; but nevertheless final mastery re-quires observing and selecting the successful movements and arranging them in view of an end. *These operations of conscious selection and ar-rangement constitute thinking*, though of a rudimentary type.

Mastery of the Body Is an Intellectual Problem. Since mastery of the bodily organs is necessary for all later developments, such problems are both interesting and important, and solving them supplies a very genuine training of thinking power. The joy the child shows in learning to use his limbs, to translate what he sees into what he handles, to connect sounds with sights, sights with taste and touch, and the rapidity with which intelligence grows in the first year and a half of life (the time during which the more fundamental problems of the use of the organism are mastered) are sufficient evidence that the development of physical control is not a physical, but an intellectual, achievement.

Social Adjustments Soon Become Important. Although in the early months the child is mainly occupied in learning to use his body to accom-modate himself to physical conditions in a comfortable way and to use things skillfully and effectively, yet social adjustments are very impor-tant. In connection with parents, nurse, brother, and sister, the child learns the signs of satisfaction of hunger, of removal of discomfort, of the approach of agreeable light, color, sound, and so on. His contact with physical things is regulated by persons, and he soon distinguishes persons as the most important and interesting of all the objects with which he has to do.

Speech, the accurate adaptation of sounds heard to the movements of tongue and lips, is, however, the great instrument of social adaptation;

and with the development of speech (usually in the second year) adaptation of the baby's activities to and with those of other persons gives the keynote of mental life. His range of possible activities is indefinitely widened as he watches what other persons do, and as he tries to understand and to do what they encourage him to attempt. The outline pattern of mental life is thus set in the first four or five years. Years, centuries, generations of invention and planning may have gone to the development of the performances and occupations of the adults surrounding the child. Yet for him their activities are direct stimuli; they are part of his natural environment; they are carried on in physical terms that appeal to his eye, ear, and touch. He cannot, of course, appropriate their meaning directly through his senses; but they furnish stimuli to which he responds, so that his attention is focused upon a higher order of materials and of problems. Were it not for this process by which the achievements of one generation form the stimuli that direct the activities of the next, the story of civilization would be writ in water, and each generation would have laboriously to make for itself, if it could, its way out of savagery. In learning to understand and make words, children learn a great deal more than the words themselves. They gain a habit that opens a new world to them.

The Role of Imitation. Imitation is one, though only one, of the means by which the activities of adults supply stimuli that are so interesting, so varied, so complex, and so novel as to occasion a rapid progress of thought. Mere imitation, however, would not give rise to thinking; if we could learn like parrots by simply copying the outward acts of others, we should never have to think; nor should we know, after we had mastered the copied act, what was the meaning of the thing we had done. Educators (and psychologists) have often assumed that acts that reproduce the behavior of others are acquired merely by imitation. But a child rarely learns by conscious imitation, and to say that his imitation is unconscious is to say that it is not, from his standpoint, imitation at all. The word, the gesture, the act, the occupation of another, falls in line with *some impulse already active* and suggests some satisfactory mode of expression, some end in which it may find fulfillment. Having this end of his own, the child then notes other persons, as he notes natural events, to get further suggestions as to means of its realization. He selects some of the means he observes, tries them on, finds them successful or unsuccessful, is confirmed or weakened in his belief in their value, and so continues selecting, arranging, adapting, testing, till he can accomplish what he wishes. The onlooker may then observe the resemblance of this act to some act of an adult and conclude that it was acquired by imitation, while as a matter of fact it was acquired by attention, observation, selection, experimentation, and confirmation by results. Only because this method is employed is there intellectual discipline and an educative result. The presence of adult activities plays an enormous role in the intellectual growth of the child because they add to the natural stimuli of the world new stimuli that are more exactly adapted to the needs of a human being, that are richer, better organized, more complex in range, permitting more flexible adaptations, and calling out novel reactions. But in utilizing these stimuli, the child follows the same methods that he uses when he is forced to think in order to master his body.

II

PLAY, WORK, AND ALLIED FORMS OF ACTIVITY

The Significance of Play and of Playfulness. When things become signs, when they gain a representative capacity as standing for other things, play is transformed from mere physical exuberance into an activity involving a mental factor. A little girl who had broken her doll was seen to perform with the leg of the doll all the operations of washing, putting to bed, and fondling that she had been accustomed to perform with the entire doll. The part stood for the whole; she reacted, not to the stimulus sensibly present, but to the meaning suggested by the sense object. So children use a stone for a table, leaves for plates, acorns for cups. So they use their dolls, their trains, their blocks, their other toys. In manipulating them, they are living not with the physical things, but in the large world of meanings, natural and social, evoked by these things. So when children play horse, play store, play house or making calls, they are subordinating the physically present to the ideally signified. In this way, a world of meanings, a store of concepts (so fundamental in all intellectual achievement), is defined and built up.

Moreover, not only do meanings thus become familiar acquaintances, but they are organized, arranged in groups, made to cohere in connected ways. A play and a story blend insensibly into each other. The most fanciful plays of children rarely lose all touch with the mutual fitness and pertinency of various meanings to one another; the "freest" plays observe some principles of coherence and unification. They have a beginning, middle, and end. In games, rules of order run through various minor acts and bind them into a connected whole. The rhythm, the competition, and the co-operation involved in most plays and games also introduce organization. There is, then, nothing mysterious or mystical in the discovery made by Plato and remade by Froebel that play is the chief, almost the only, mode of education for the child in the years of later infancy.

Playfulness is a more important consideration than play. The former is an attitude of mind; the latter is a passing outward manifestation of this attitude. When things are treated simply as vehicles of suggestion, what is suggested overrides the thing. Hence the playful attitude is one of freedom. The person is not bound to the physical traits of things, nor does he care whether a thing really "means" what he takes it to represent. When the child plays horse with a broom and cars with chairs, the fact that the broom does not really represent a horse or a chair a locomotive is of no account. In order, then, that playfulness may not terminate in arbitrary fancifulness and in building up an imaginary world alongside the world of actual things, it is necessary that the play attitude should gradually pass into a work attitude.

The Significance of Work. What is work—work not as mere external performance, but as attitude of mind? In the natural course of growth, children come to find irresponsible, make-believe plays inadequate. A fiction is too easy a way out to afford contentment, not stimulus enough to call forth satisfactory mental response. When this point is reached, the ideas that things suggest are applied to the things with some regard to fitness. A small cart, resembling a "real" cart, with "real" wheels, tongue, and body, meets the mental demand better than merely making believe that anything that comes to hand is a cart. Occasionally to take part in setting a "real" table with "real" dishes brings more reward than forever to make believe a flat stone is a table and that leaves are dishes. The interest may still center in the meanings; things may be of importance only as furthering a certain meaning. So far the attitude is one of play. But meaning becomes of such a character that it must find embodiment, or at least expression, in actual things.

The dictionary does not permit us to call such activities work. Nevertheless, they represent a passage of play into work. For work (as a mental attitude, not as mere external performance) *means interest in the adequate embodiment of a meaning* (a suggestion, purpose, aim) *in objective form through the use of appropriate materials and appliances.* Such an attitude takes advantage of the meanings aroused and built up in free play, but *controls their development by seeing to it that they are applied to things in ways consistent with the observable structure of things themselves.*

The word "work" is not very satisfactory. For it is often used to denote routine activity that accomplishes useful results with but a minimum of thoughtful selection of means, deliberate adjustment to produce desired consequences. We view work from the outside when we think of it as simply doing things that need to be done. But it may also be looked at from the inside; it must be so looked at when we are thinking of it in relation to education. Then work signifies activity directed by ends that thought sets before the person as something to be accomplished; it signifies ingenuity and inventiveness in selecting proper means and making plans, and thus, finally, signifies that expectations and ideas are tested by actual results.

A child, like an adult, may make or do something following the dictation of others, working mechanically from oral or printed instructions, or stereotyped blueprints. There is then next to no thought; his activity is not truly reflective. But as we have already noted, the means-consequence relation is the heart of all meaning. "Work," in the sense of *intelligent action,* is therefore highly educative, because it continually builds up meanings while at the same time it tests them by application to actual conditions. It is necessary, however, that the adult do not judge the value of such an activity on the part of the young by his familiar adult standards about the value of the *product;* if he does, the activity will usually seem to him to amount to little. He must judge from the standpoint of the planning, invention, ingenuity, observation exercised by the young, remembering always that what is an old story to him may arouse emotion and thought in the child.

The True Distinction between Play and Work. The point of the distinction between play and work may be cleared up by comparing it with a more usual way of stating the difference. In play activity, it is said, the interest is in the activity for its own sake; in work, it is in the product or result in which the activity terminates. Hence the former is purely free, while the latter is tied down by the end to be achieved. When the difference is stated in this sharp fashion, there is almost always introduced a false, unnatural separation between process and product, between activity and its achieved outcome. The true distinction is not between an interest in activity for its own sake and interest in the external result of that activity, but between an interest in an activity just as it flows on from moment to moment and an interest in an activity as tending to a culmination, to an outcome, and therefore possessing a thread of continuity binding together its successive stages. Both may equally exemplify interest in an activity "for its own sake"; but in the one case the activity in which the interest resides is more or less casual, following the accident of circumstance and whim, or of dictation; in the other, the activity is enriched by the sense that it leads somewhere, that it amounts to something.

Were it not that the false theory of the relation of the play and the work attitudes has been connected with unfortunate modes of school practice, insistence upon a truer view might seem an unnecessary refinement. But the sharp break that so often prevails between the kindergarten and the grades is evidence that the theoretical distinction has practical implications. Under the title of "play" the former is rendered unduly symbolic, fanciful, sentimental, and arbitrary; while under the antithetical caption of "work" the latter contains many *tasks externally assigned*. The former has no end; the latter an end so remote that only the educator, not the child, is aware that it is an end.

There comes a time when children must extend and make more exact their acquaintance with existing things, must conceive ends and consequences with sufficient definiteness to guide their actions by them, and must acquire some technical skill in selecting and arranging means to realize these ends. Unless these factors are gradually introduced in the earlier play period, they must later be introduced abruptly and arbitrarily, to the manifest disadvantage of both the earlier and the later stages.

Correlative False Notions of Imagination and Utility. The sharp opposition of play and work is usually associated with false notions of utility and imagination. Activity that is directed upon matters of home and neighborhood interest is depreciated as merely utilitarian. To let the child wash dishes, set the table, engage in cooking, cut and sew dolls' clothes, make boxes that will hold "real things," and construct his own playthings by using hammer and nails excludes (so it is said) the aesthetic and appreciative factor, eliminates imagination, and subjects the child's development to material and practical concerns; while (so it is said) to reproduce symbolically the domestic relationships of birds and other animals, of human father and mother and child, of workman and tradesman, of knight, soldier, and magistrate secures a liberal exercise of mind that is of great moral as well as intellectual value. It has even been stated that it is overphysical and utilitarian if a child plants seeds and takes care of growing plants in the kindergarten; whereas if he reproduces dramatically the operations of planting, cultivating, reaping, and so on, with no physical materials or with symbolic representatives, he educates imagination and his spiritual appreciation. Toy dolls, trains or cars, boats, and engines are rigidly excluded, but cubes, balls, and other symbols for representing his social activities are recommended. The more unfitted the physical object for its imagined purpose, such as a cube for a boat, the greater is the supposed appeal to the imagination.

There are several fallacies in this way of thinking.

First, the healthy imagination deals not with the unreal, but with the mental realization of what is suggested. Its exercise is not a flight into the purely fanciful and ideal, but a method of expanding and filling in what is real. To the child the homely activities going on about him are not utilitarian devices for accomplishing physical ends; they exemplify a wonderful world, the depths of which he has not sounded, a world full of the mystery and promise that attend all the doings of the grownups whom he admires. However prosaic this world may be to the adults who find its duties routine affairs, to the child it is fraught with social meaning. To engage in it is to exercise the imagination in constructing an experience of wider value than any the child has yet mastered.

Second, educators sometimes think children are reacting to a great moral or spiritual truth when the children's reactions are largely physical and sensational. Children have great powers of dramatic simulation, and their physical bearing may seem (to adults prepossessed with a philosophic theory) to indicate they have been impressed with some lesson of chivalry, devotion, or nobility when the children, themselves, are occupied only with transitory physical excitations. To symbolize great truths far beyond the child's range of actual experience is an impossibility, and to attempt it is to invite love of momentary stimulation.

Third, just as the opponents of play in education always conceive of play as mere amusement, so the opponents of direct and useful activities confuse occupation with labor. The adult is acquainted with responsible labor upon which serious financial results depend. Consequently he seeks relief, relaxation, amusement. Unless children have prematurely worked for hire, unless they have come under the blight of child labor, no such division exists for them. Whatever appeals to them at all appeals directly on its own account. There is no contrast between doing things for utility and for fun. Their life is more united and more wholesome. To suppose that activities customarily performed by adults only under the pressure of utility may not be done perfectly freely and joyously by children indicates a lack of imagination. Not the thing done, but the quality of mind that goes into the doing, settles what is utilitarian and what is unconstrained and creative.

III

CONSTRUCTIVE OCCUPATIONS

The Sciences Grew Out of Occupations. The history of culture shows that mankind's scientific knowledge and technical abilities have developed, especially in all their earlier stages, out of the fundamental problems of life. Anatomy and physiology grew out of the practical needs of keeping healthy and active; geometry and mechanics out of demands for measuring land, for building, and for making labor-saving machines; astronomy has been closely connected with navigation, keeping record of the passage of time; botany grew out of the requirements of medicine and of agronomy; chemistry has been associated with dyeing, metallurgy, and other industrial pursuits. In turn, modern industry is almost wholly a matter of applied science; year by year the domain of routine and crude empiricism is narrowed by the translation of scientific discovery into industrial invention. The trolley, the telephone, the electric light, the steam engine, with all their revolutionary consequences for social intercourse and control, are the fruits of science.

School Occupations Offer Intellectual Possibilities. These facts are full of educational significance. Most children are pre-eminently active in their tendencies. The schools have also taken on—largely from utilitarian, rather than from strictly educative, reasons—a large number of active pursuits commonly grouped under the head of manual training, including also school gardens, excursions, and various graphic arts. Perhaps the most pressing problem of education at the present moment is to organize and relate these subjects so that they will become instruments for forming alert, persistent, and fruitful *intellectual* habits. That they take hold of the more primary and native equipment of children (appealing to their desire to do) is generally recognized; that they afford great opportunity for training in self-reliant and efficient social service is gaining acknowledgment. But they may also be used for presenting *typical problems to be solved by personal reflection and experimentation and by acquiring definite bodies of knowledge leading later to more specialized scientific knowledge.* There is indeed no magic by which mere physical activity or deft manipulation will secure intellectual results. Manual subjects may be taught by routine, by dictation, or by convention as readily as bookish subjects. But intelligent consecutive work in gardening, cooking, or weaving, or in elementary wood and iron, may be so planned that it will inevitably result not only in students' amassing information of practical and scientific importance in botany, zoology, chemistry, physics, and other sciences, but also (what is more significant) in their becoming versed in methods of experimental inquiry and proof.

That the elementary curriculum is overloaded is a common complaint. The only alternative to a reactionary return to the educational traditions of the past lies in working out the intellectual possibilities resident in various arts, crafts, and occupations, and reorganizing the curriculum accordingly. Here, more than elsewhere, are found the means by which the blind and routine experience of the race may be transformed into illuminated and emancipated experiment.

Conditions to Be Met to Render "Projects" Educative. Constructive occupations have in recent years found their way increasingly into the schoolroom. They are usually known as "projects." In order that they may be truly educative, there are certain conditions that should be fulfilled.

The first condition, that of interest, is usually met. Unless the activity lays hold on the emotions and desires, unless it offers an outlet for energy that means something to the individual himself, his *mind* will turn in aversion from it, even though externally he keeps at it. But interest is not enough. Given interest, the important matter is *what kind of object and action* enlists it. Is it something transitory or is it enduring? Is the interest mainly one of excitement or is thought involved?

Hence the second condition to be met is that the activity be worthwhile intrinsically. This statement does not signify, as we have just seen in another connection, that its outcome be something externally useful from the adult point of view. But it does mean that merely trivial activities, those that are of no consequence beyond the immediate pleasure that engaging in them affords, should be excluded. It is not difficult to find projects that are enjoyable while at the same time they stand for something valuable in life itself.

The third condition (really only an amplification of the point just made) is that the project in the course of its development present problems that awaken new curiosity and create a demand for information. There is nothing educative in an activity, however agreeable it may be, that does not lead the mind out into new fields. The new field cannot be entered unless the mind is led to ask questions that it had not thought of before and unless the presence of these questions creates a thirst for additional information to be obtained by observation, by reading, by consulting persons expert in that particular field.

Finally, as a fourth condition, the project must involve a considerable time span for its adequate execution. The plan and the object to be gained must be capable of development, one thing leading on naturally to another. Unless it does so, new fields cannot be entered. It is the province of the adult to look ahead and see whether one stage of achievement will suggest something else to be looked into and done. An occupation has continuity. It is not a succession of unrelated acts, but is a consecutively ordered activity in which one step prepares the need for the next one and that one adds to, and carries further in a cumulative way, what has already been done.

FROM THE CONCRETE
TO THE ABSTRACT

I
WHAT IS THE CONCRETE?

The maxim enjoined upon teachers, "proceed from the concrete to the abstract," is familiar rather than wholly intelligible. Few who read and hear it gain a clear conception of the starting point, the concrete; of the nature of the goal, the abstract; and of the exact nature of the path to be traversed in going from one to the other. At times the injunction is positively misunderstood, being taken to mean that education should advance from things to thought—as if any dealing with things in which thinking is not involved could possibly be educative. So understood, the maxim encourages mechanical routine or sensuous excitation at one end of the educational scale—the lower—and academic and unapplied learning at the upper end.

Actually, all dealing with things, even the child's, is immersed in inference; things are clothed with the suggestions they arouse. They are significant as challenges to interpretation or as evidences to substantiate a belief. Nothing could be more unnatural than instruction in things without thought, in sense perceptions without judgments connected with them. And if the abstract to which we are to proceed denotes thought apart from things, the goal is formal and empty, for effective thought always refers, more or less directly, to things.

Relation to Direct and Indirect Meaning. Yet the maxim has a meaning which, understood and supplemented, states the direction of logical development. What is this meaning? "Concrete" denotes a meaning definitely marked off from other meanings so that it is readily apprehended by itself. When we hear the words, *table, chair, stove, coat,* we do not have to reflect in order to grasp what is meant. The terms convey meaning so directly that no effort at translation is needed. The meaning of some terms and things, however, is grasped only by first calling to mind more familiar things and then tracing out connections between them and what we do not understand. Roughly speaking, the former kind of meaning is concrete; the latter is abstract.

Dependence on the Intellectual Status of the Individual. To one who is thoroughly at home in physics and chemistry, the notions of *atom* and *molecule* are fairly concrete. They are constantly used without involving any labor of thought in apprehending what they mean. But the layman and the beginner in science have to remind themselves of things with which they already are well acquainted, and then go through a process of slow translation. Moreover the terms *atom* and *molecule* lose their hard-won meaning only too easily if familiar things and the line of transition from them to the strange drop out of mind. The same difference is illustrated by any technical terms: *coefficient* and *exponent* in algebra, *triangle* and *square* in their geometric as distinct from their popular meanings; *capital* and *value* in political economy, and so on.

The difference as noted is purely relative to the intellectual progress of an individual; what is abstract at one period of growth is concrete at another; or even the contrary, as one finds that things supposed to be thoroughly familiar involve strange factors and unsolved problems. There is, nevertheless, a general line of cleavage that decides upon the whole what things fall within, and what fall without, the limits of familiar acquaintance. This line accordingly marks off the concrete and the abstract in a fairly permanent way. *The limits are fixed mainly by the demands of practical life.* Things such as sticks and stones, meat and potatoes, houses and trees are constant features of the environment of which we have to take account in order to live. Hence their important meanings are soon learned and are indissolubly associated with objects. We are acquainted with a thing (or it is familiar to us) when we have so much to do with it that its strange and troublesome corners are rubbed off. The necessities of social intercourse convey to adults a like concreteness upon such terms as *taxes, elections, wages, the law,* and so on. Things the meaning of which I personally do not take in directly, appliances of cook, carpenter, or weaver, for example, are nevertheless unhesitatingly classed as concrete, since they are directly connected with our common social life.

Relation to Thinking as a Means and as an End. By contrast, the abstract is the *theoretical,* that not intimately associated with practical concerns. The abstract thinker (the "man of pure science," as he is sometimes called) deliberately abstracts from application in life; that is, he leaves practical uses out of account. This, however, is a merely negative statement. What remains when connections with use and application are excluded? *Evidently only what has to do with knowing considered as an end in itself.* Many notions in science are abstract, not only because they cannot be understood without a long apprenticeship in the science (which is equally true of technical matters in the arts), but also because the whole content of their meaning has been framed for the sole purpose of facilitating further knowledge, inquiry, and speculation. *When thinking is used as a means to some end, good, or value beyond itself, it is concrete; when it is employed simply as a means to more thinking, it is abstract.* To a theorist an idea is adequate and self-contained just because it engages and rewards thought; to a medical practitioner, an engineer, an artist, a merchant, a politician, it is complete only when employed in the furthering of some interest in life—health, wealth, beauty, goodness, success, or what you will.

Depreciation of "Mere Theory." The great majority of men under ordinary circumstances find the practical exigencies of life almost, if not quite, coercive. Their main business is the proper conduct of their affairs. Whatever is of significance only as affording scope for thinking is pallid and remote—almost artificial. Hence the contempt felt by the practical and successful executive for the "mere theorist"; hence his conviction that certain things may be all very well in theory, but that they will not do in practice; hence, in general, the depreciatory way in which he uses the terms *abstract, theoretical,* and *intellectual.*

This attitude is justified, of course, under certain conditions. But depreciation of theory does not contain the whole truth, as common or practical sense recognizes. There is such a thing, even from the common-sense standpoint, as being "too practical," as being so intent upon the immediately practical as not to see beyond the end of one's nose or as to cut off the limb upon which one is sitting. The question is one of limits, of degrees and adjustments, rather than one of absolute separation. Truly practical men give their minds free play about a subject without asking too closely at every point for any advantage to be gained. Exclusive preoccupation with matters of use and application narrows the horizon and in the long run defeats itself. It does not pay to tether one's thoughts to the post of use with too short a rope. Power in action requires largeness of vision, which can be had only through the use of imagination. Men must at least have enough interest in thinking for the sake of thinking to escape the limitations of routine and custom. Interest in knowledge for the sake of knowledge, in thinking for the sake of the free play of thought, is necessary to the *emancipation* of practical life— to making it rich and progressive.

We now recur to the pedagogic maxim of going from the concrete to the abstract and call attention to three aspects of the process.

Beginning with Practical Manipulations. (1) Since the *concrete* denotes thinking applied to activities for the sake of dealing with difficulties that present themselves practically, "begin with the concrete" signifies that we should, at the outset of any new experience in learning, make much of what is already familiar, and if possible connect the new topics and principles with the pursuit of an end in some active occupation. We do not "follow the order of nature" when we multiply mere sensations or accumulate physical objects. Instruction in number is not concrete merely because splints or beans or dots are employed. Whenever the use and bearing of number relations are clearly perceived, a number idea is concrete even if figures alone are used. Just what sort of symbol it is best to use at a given time—whether blocks, or lines, or figures—is entirely a matter of adjustment to the given case. If the physical things used in teaching number or geography or anything else do not leave the mind illuminated with recognition of a *meaning* beyond themselves, the instruction that uses them is as abstruse as that which doles out ready-made definitions and rules, for it distracts attention from ideas to mere physical excitations.

The notion that we have only to put physical objects before the senses in order to impress ideas upon the mind amounts almost to a superstition. The introduction of object lessons and sense training scored a distinct advance over the prior method of linguistic symbols, but this advance tended to blind educators to the fact that only a halfway step had been taken. Things and sensations develop the child, indeed, but only when he *uses* them in mastering his body and co-ordinating his actions. Continuous occupations involve the use of natural materials, tools, modes of energy, and do it in a way that compels thinking as to how they are related to one another and to the realization of ends. But the mere isolated presentation of things to sense remains barren and dead. A few generations ago the great obstacle in the way of reform of primary education was belief in the almost magical efficacy of the symbols of language (including number) to produce mental training; at present, belief in the efficacy of objects just as objects blocks the way. As frequently happens, the better is an enemy of the best.

Transferring Interest to Intellectual Matters. (2) The interest in results, in the successful carrying on of an activity, should be gradually transferred to the *study* of objects—their properties, consequences, structures, causes, and effects. The adult when at work in his life calling is rarely free to devote time or energy—beyond the necessities of his immediate action—to the study of what he deals with. The educative activities of childhood should be so arranged that the activity creates a demand for attention to matters that have only an indirect and an intellectual connection with the original activity. To take an instance to which reference has already been made, the direct interest in carpentering or shopwork should gradually pass into an interest in geometric and mechanical problems. The interest in cooking should grow into an interest in chemical experimentation and the physiology and hygiene of bodily growth. The original casual making of pictures should pass to an interest in the technique of representation of perspective, the handling of brush, pigments, etc. This development is what the term "go" signifies in the maxim "go from the concrete to the abstract"; it represents the dynamic and educative phase of the process.

Developing Delight in Thinking. (3) The outcome, the *abstract* to which education is to proceed, is an interest in intellectual matters for their own sake, a delight in thinking for the sake of thinking. It is an old story that acts and processes that at the outset are incidental to something else develop and maintain an absorbing value of their own. So it is with thinking and with knowledge; at first incidental to results and adjustments beyond themselves, they attract more and more attention to themselves till they become ends, not means. Children engage, unconstrainedly and continually, in reflective inspection and testing for the sake of what they are interested in doing. Habits of thinking thus generated may increase in amount till they become of importance on their own account. It is part of the business of a teacher to lead students to extricate and dwell upon the distinctively intellectual side of what they do until there develops a spontaneous interest in ideas and their relations with one another—that is, a genuine power of abstraction, of rising from engrossment in the present to the plane of ideas.

II
WHAT IS THE ABSTRACT?

Examples of the Transition from Concrete to Abstract. The three instances cited [previously [10]] represent an ascending cycle from the concrete to the abstract. Taking thought to keep a personal engagement is obviously of the concrete kind. Endeavoring to work out the meaning of a certain part of a boat is an instance of an intermediate kind. The original reason for the existence and position of the pole is practical, so that to the designer the problem was purely concrete—the maintenance of a certain system of action. But for the passenger on the boat, the problem was theoretical, more or less speculative. It made no difference to his reaching

10. Chapter VI, which is not reprinted here [Ed.].

his destination whether he worked out the meaning or not. The third case, that of the appearance and movement of the bubbles, illustrates a strictly abstract case. No overcoming of physical obstacles, no adjustment of external means to ends, is at stake. Curiosity, intellectual curiosity, is challenged by a seemingly anomalous occurrence; and thinking tries simply to account for an apparent exception in terms of recognized principles. Intellectual means are adjusted to an intellectual result.

Abstract Thinking Not the Whole End and Not Congenial to Most Persons. Abstract thinking, it should be noted, represents *an* end, not *the* end. The power of sustained thinking on matters remote from direct use is an outgrowth of thinking on practical and immediate matters, but not a substitute for it. The educational end is not the destruction of power to think practically in overcoming obstacles, utilizing resources, and achieving ends; it is not its replacement by abstract reflection. Nor is theoretical thinking a higher type of thinking than practical. A person who has at command both types of thinking is of a higher order than he who possesses only one. Methods that, in developing abstract intellectual abilities, weaken habits of practical or concrete thinking fall as much short of the educational ideal as do the methods that, in cultivating ability to plan, to invent, to arrange, to forecast, fail to secure some delight in thinking, irrespective of practical consequences.

Educators should also note the very great individual differences that exist; they should not try to force one pattern and model upon all. In many (probably the majority) the executive tendency, the habit of mind that thinks for purposes of conduct and achievement, not for the sake of knowing, remains dominant to the end. Engineers, lawyers, doctors, merchants are much more numerous in adult life than scientists and philosophers. While education should strive to make men who, however prominent their professional interests and aims, partake of the spirit of the scholar, philosopher, and scientist, no good reason appears why education should esteem the one mental habit inherently superior to the other and deliberately try to transform the type from concrete to abstract. Have not our schools been one-sidedly devoted to the more abstract type of thinking, thus doing injustice to the majority of pupils? Has not the idea of a "liberal" and "humane" education tended too often in practice to the production of technical, because overspecialized, thinkers?

Education Should Aim to Secure a Working Balance. The aim of education should be to secure a balanced interaction of the two types of mental attitude, having sufficient regard to the disposition of the individual not to hamper and cripple whatever powers are naturally strong in him. The narrowness of individuals of strong concrete bent needs to be liberalized. Every opportunity that occurs within practical activities for developing curiosity and susceptibility to intellectual problems should be seized. Violence is not done to natural disposition; rather the latter is broadened. Otherwise, the concrete becomes narrowing and deadening. As regards the smaller number of those who have a taste for abstract, purely intellectual topics, pains should be taken to multiply opportunities for the application of ideas, for translating symbolic truths into terms of everyday and social life. Every human being has both capabilities, and every individual will be more effective and happier if both powers are developed in easy and close interaction with each other. Otherwise the abstract becomes identical with the academic and pedantic.

LANGUAGE
AND THE TRAINING OF THOUGHT

I
LANGUAGE AS THE TOOL OF THINKING

Language has such a peculiarly intimate connection with thought as to require special discussion. The very word logic, coming from logos (λόγος), means indifferently both word or speech and thought or reason. Yet "words, words, words" denote intellectual barrenness, a sham of thought. Schooling has language as its chief instrument (and often as its chief subject matter) of study. Yet educational reformers have for centuries brought their severest indictments against the current use of language in the schools. The conviction that language is necessary to thinking (is even identical with it) is met by the contention that language perverts and conceals thought. There is a genuine problem here.

Views of the Relation of Thought and Language. Three typical views have been maintained regarding the relation of thought and language: first, that they are identical; second, that words are the garb, or clothing, of thought, necessary not for thought but only for conveying it; and third (the view we shall here maintain), that, while language is not thought, it is necessary for thinking as well as for communication. When it is said, however, that thinking is impossible without language, we must recall that language includes much more than oral and written speech. Gestures, pictures, monuments, visual images, finger movements—anything deliberately and artificially employed as a *sign* is, logically, language. To say that language is necessary for thinking is to say that signs are necessary.

Thought deals not with bare things, but with their *meanings,* their suggestions; and meanings, in order to be apprehended, must be embodied in
sensible and particular existences. Without meaning, things are nothing
but blind stimuli, brute things, or chance sources of pleasure and pain;
and since meanings are not themselves tangible things, they must be
anchored by attachment to some physical existence. Existences that are
especially set aside to fixate and convey meanings are *symbols.* If a man
moves toward another to throw him out of the room, his movement is not
a sign. If, however, the man points to the door with his hand, or utters the
sound *go,* his act becomes a vehicle of meaning: it is a sign, not a complete
thing in itself. In the case of signs we care nothing for what they are in
themselves, but everything for what they signify and represent. *Canis,
Hund, chien, dog*—it makes no difference what the outward thing is, so
long as the meaning is presented.

Natural objects are signs of other things and events. Clouds stand for
rain; a footprint represents game or an enemy; a projecting rock serves to
indicate minerals below the surface. The limitations of *natural* signs are,
however, great. First, physical or direct sense excitation tends to distract
attention from what is meant or indicated. Almost everyone will recall
pointing out to a kitten or puppy an object of food, only to have the
animal devote himself to the hand pointing, not to the thing pointed at.
Second, where natural signs alone exist, we are mainly at the mercy of
external happenings; we have to wait until the natural event presents
itself in order to be warned or advised of the possibility of some other
event. Third, natural signs, not being originally intended to be signs, are
cumbrous, bulky, inconvenient, unmanageable. A symbol, on the contrary,
is intended and invented, like any artificial tool and utensil, for the
purpose of conveying meaning.

Aspects of Artificial Signs That Favor Their Use to Represent Meanings.
It is therefore indispensable for any high development of thought that
there exist intentional signs. Language supplies the requirement. Gestures,
sounds, written or printed forms are strictly physical existences, but their
native value is intentionally subordinated to the value they acquire as
representative of meanings. There are three aspects of artificial signs that
favor their use as representatives of meanings:

First, the direct and sensible value of faint sounds and minute written
or printed marks is very slight. Accordingly, attention is not distracted
from their *representative* function.

Second, their production is under our direct control, so that they may
be produced when needed. When we can make the word *rain,* we do not

have to wait for some physical forerunner of rain to call our thoughts in that direction. We cannot make the cloud; we can make the sound, and as a token of meaning the sound serves the purpose as well as the cloud.

Third, arbitrary linguistic signs are convenient and easy to manage. They are compact, portable, and delicate. As long as we live we breathe, and modifications by the muscles of throat and mouth of the volume and quality of the air are simple, easy, and indefinitely controllable. Bodily postures and gestures of the hand and arm are also employed as signs, but they are coarse and unmanageable compared with modifications of breath to produce sounds. No wonder that oral speech has been selected as the main stuff of intentional intellectual signs. Sounds, while subtle, refined, and easily modifiable, are transitory. This defect is met by the system of written and printed words, appealing to the eye. *Litera scripta manet* [The written word remains].

Bearing in mind the intimate connection of meanings and signs (or language), we may note in more detail what language does (1) for specific meanings, and (2) for the organization of meanings.

Language Selects, Preserves, and Applies Specific Meanings. In the case of specific meanings a verbal sign (*a*) selects, detaches, a meaning from what is otherwise a vague flux and blur; (*b*) retains, registers, stores that meaning; and (*c*) applies it, when needed, to the comprehension of other things. Combining these various functions in a mixture of metaphors, we may say that a linguistic sign is a fence, a label, and a vehicle—all in one.

(*a*) *The Word as a Fence.* Everyone has experienced how learning an appropriate name for what was dim and vague cleared up and crystallized the whole matter. Some meaning seems almost within reach, but is elusive; it refuses to condense into definite form; the attaching of a word somehow (just how, it is almost impossible to say) puts limits around the meaning, draws it out from the void, makes it stand out as an entity on its own account. When Emerson said that he would almost rather know the true name, the poet's name, for a thing, than to know the thing itself, he presumably had this irradiating and illuminating function of language in mind. The delight that children take in demanding and learning the names of everything about them indicates that meanings are becoming concrete individuals to them, so that their commerce with things is passing from the physical to the intellectual plane. It is hardly surprising that savages attach a magical efficacy to words. To name anything is to give it a title, to dignify and honor it by raising it from a mere physical occurrence to a meaning that is distinct and permanent. To know the names of people and things and to be able to manipulate these names are, in savage lore, to be in possession of their dignity and worth, to master them.

(*b*) *The Word as a Label.* Things come and go, or we come and go, and either way things escape our notice. Our direct sensible relation to things is very limited. The suggestion of meanings by natural signs is limited to occasions of direct contact or vision. But a meaning fixed by a linguistic sign is conserved for future use. Even if the thing is not there to represent the meaning, the word may be produced so as to evoke the meaning. Since intellectual life depends on possession of a store of meanings, the importance of language as a tool of preserving meanings cannot be overstated. To be sure, the method of storage is not wholly aseptic; words often corrupt and modify the meanings they are supposed to keep intact, but liability to infection is a price paid by every living thing for the privilege of living.

(*c*) *The Word as a Vehicle.* When a meaning is detached and fixed by a sign, it is possible to use that meaning in a new context and situation. This transfer and reapplication is the key to all judgment and inference. It would little profit a man to recognize that a given particular cloud was the premonitor of a given particular rainstorm if his recognition ended there, for he would then have to learn over and over again, since the next cloud and the next rain are different events. No cumulative growth of intelligence would occur. Experience might form habits of physical adaptation but it would not *teach* anything, for we should not be able to use an old experience consciously to anticipate and regulate a new experience. To be able to use the past to judge and infer the new and unknown implies that, although the past thing has gone, its *meaning* abides in such a way as to be applicable in determining the character of the new. Speech forms are our great carriers, the easy-running vehicles by which meanings are transported from experiences that no longer concern us to those that are as yet dark and dubious.

Language Signs Are Instruments for Organizing Meanings. In emphasizing the importance of signs in relation to specific meanings, we have overlooked another aspect, equally valuable. Signs not only mark off specific or individual meanings, but they are also instruments of grouping meanings in relation to one another. Words are not only names or titles of single meanings; they also form *sentences* in which meanings are organized in relation to one another. When we say "That book is a dictionary," or "That blur of light in the heavens is Halley's Comet," we express a *logical* connection—an act of classifying and defining that goes beyond the physical thing into the logical region of genera and species, things and attributes. Propositions, sentences bear the same relation to judgments that distinct words, built up mainly by analyzing propositions in their various types, bear to meanings or conceptions; and just as words imply a sentence, so a sentence implies a larger whole of consecutive discourse into which it fits. As is often said, grammar expresses the unconscious logic of the popular mind. *The chief intellectual classifications that constitute the working capital of thought have been built up for us by our mother tongue.* Our very lack of explicit consciousness, when using language, that we are then employing the intellectual systematizations of the race shows how thoroughly accustomed we have become to its logical distinctions and groupings.

II
THE ABUSE OF LINGUISTIC METHODS IN EDUCATION

Teaching Things Alone, the Negation of Education. Taken literally, the maxim, "Teach things, not words," or "Teach things before words," would be the negation of education; it would reduce mental life to mere physical and sensible adjustments. Learning, in the proper sense, is not learning things, but the *meanings* of things, and this process involves the use of signs, or language in its generic sense. In like fashion, the warfare of some educational reformers against symbols, if pushed to extremes, involves the destruction of intellectual life, since this lives, moves, and has its being in those processes of definition, abstraction, generalization, and classification that are made possible by symbols alone. Nevertheless, these contentions of educational reformers have been needed. The liability of a thing to abuse is in proportion to the value of its right use.

The Limitations and Dangers of Symbols in Relation to Meanings. Symbols themselves, as already pointed out, are particular, physical, sensible existences, like any other things. They are symbols only by virtue of what they suggest and represent; *i.e.*, meanings.

In the first place, they stand for these meanings to any individual only when he has had *experience* of some situation to which these meanings are actually relevant. Words can detach and preserve a meaning only when the meaning has been first involved in our own direct intercourse with things. To attempt to give a meaning through a word alone without any dealings with a thing is to deprive the word of intelligible signification; against this attempt, a tendency only too prevalent in education, reformers have protested. Moreover, there is a tendency to assume that, whenever there is a definite word or form of speech, there is also a definite idea; while, as a matter of fact, adults and children alike are capable of using even formulas that are verbally precise with only the vaguest and most confused sense of what they mean. Genuine ignorance is more profitable because it is likely to be accompanied by humility, curiosity, and open-mindedness; whereas ability to repeat catch phrases, cant terms, familiar propositions gives the conceit of learning and coats the mind with a varnish waterproof to new ideas.

In the second place, although new combinations of words without the intervention of physical things may supply new ideas, there are limits to this possibility. Lazy inertness causes individuals to accept ideas that have currency about them without personal inquiry and testing. A man uses thought, perhaps, to find out what others believe, and then stops. The ideas of others as embodied in language become substitutes for one's own ideas. The use of linguistic studies and methods to halt the human mind on the level of the attainments of the past, to prevent new inquiry and discovery, to put the authority of tradition in place of the authority of natural facts and laws, to reduce the individual to a parasite living on the secondhand experience of others—these things have been the source of the reformers' protest against the pre-eminence assigned to language in schools.

In the third place, words that originally stood for ideas come, with repeated use, to be mere counters; they become physical things to be manipulated according to certain rules or reacted to by certain operations without consciousness of their meaning. Mr. Stout (who has called such terms "substitute signs") remarks that "algebraical and arithmetical signs are to a great extent used as mere substitute signs. . . . It is possible to use signs of this kind whenever fixed and definite rules of operation can be derived from the nature of the things symbolized, so as to be applied in manipulating the signs, without further reference to their signification. A word is an instrument for thinking about the meaning which it expresses; a substitute sign is a means of *not* thinking about the meaning which it symbolizes." The principle applies, however, to ordinary words, as well as to algebraic signs; they also enable us to use meanings so as to get results without thinking. In many respects, signs that are means of not thinking are of great advantage; standing for the familiar, they release attention for meanings that, being novel, require conscious interpretation. Nevertheless, the premium put in the schoolroom upon attainment of technical facility, upon skill in producing external results, often changes this advantage into a positive detriment. In manipulating symbols so as to recite well, to get and give correct answers, to follow prescribed formulas of analysis, the pupil's attitude becomes mechanical, rather than thoughtful; verbal memorizing is substituted for inquiry into the meaning of things. This danger is perhaps the one uppermost in mind when verbal methods of education are attacked.

III

THE USE OF LANGUAGE IN ITS EDUCATIONAL BEARINGS

Language stands in a twofold relation to the work of education. On the one hand, it is continually used in all studies as well as in all the social discipline of the school; on the other, it is a distinct object of study. We shall consider only the ordinary use of language, since its effects upon habits of thought are much deeper than those of conscious linguistic study, for the latter only makes explicit what speech already contains.

The common statement that "language is the expression of thought" conveys only a half-truth, and a half-truth that is likely to result in positive error. Language does express thought, but not primarily, nor, at first, even consciously. The primary motive for language is to influence (through the expression of desire, emotion, and thought) the activity of others; its secondary use is to enter into more intimate sociable relations with them; its employment as a conscious vehicle of thought and knowledge is a tertiary, and relatively late, formation. The contrast is well brought out by the statement of John Locke that words have a double use, "civil" and "philosophical." "By their civil use, I mean such a communication of thoughts and ideas by words as may serve for the upholding of common conversation and commerce about the ordinary affairs and conveniences of civil life. . . . By the philosophical use of words, I mean such a use of them as may serve to convey the precise notions of things and to express in general propositions certain and undoubted truths."

Education Has to Transform Language into an Intellectual Tool. This distinction of the practical and social from the intellectual use of language throws much light on the problem of the school in respect to speech. That problem is *to direct pupils' oral and written speech, used primarily for practical and social ends, so that gradually it shall become a conscious tool of conveying knowledge and assisting thought.* How without checking the spontaneous, natural motives—motives to which language owes its vitality, force, vividness, and variety—are we to modify speech habits so as to render them accurate and flexible *intellectual* instruments? It is comparatively easy to encourage the original spontaneous flow and not make language over into a servant of reflective thought; it is comparatively easy to check and almost destroy (so far as the schoolroom is concerned) native aim and interest and to set up artificial and formal modes of expression in some isolated and technical matters. The difficulty lies in making over habits that have to do with "ordinary affairs and conveniences" into habits concerned with "precise notions." The successful accomplishing of the transformation requires (*a*) enlarging the pupil's vocabulary, (*b*) rendering its terms more precise and accurate, and (*c*) forming habits of consecutive discourse.

(*a*) *Enlarging the Vocabulary.* This takes place, of course, by wider intelligent contact with things and persons, and also vicariously, by gathering the meanings of words from the context in which they are heard or read. To grasp by either method a word in its meaning is to exercise intelligence, to perform an act of intelligent selection or analysis, and it is also to widen the fund of meanings or concepts readily available in further intellectual enterprises. It is usual to distinguish between one's active and one's passive vocabulary, the latter being composed of the words that are understood when they are heard or seen, the former of words that are used intelligently. The fact that the passive is very much larger than the active vocabulary indicates power not controlled or utilized by the individual. Failure to use meanings that are understood may reveal dependence upon external stimulus and lack of intellectual initiative. This condition is to some extent an artificial product of education. Small children usually attempt to put to use every new word they get hold of, but when they learn to read they are introduced to a large variety of terms that they have no opportunity to use. The result is a kind of mental suppression, if not smothering. Moreover, the meaning of words not actively used in building up and conveying ideas is never quite clear-cut or complete. Action is required to make them definite.

While a limited vocabulary may be due to a limited range of experience, to a sphere of contact with persons and things so narrow as not to suggest or require a full store of words, it is also due to carelessness and vagueness. A happy-go-lucky frame of mind makes the individual averse to clear discriminations, either in perception or in his own speech. Words are used loosely in an indeterminate kind of reference to things, and speech approaches a condition where practically everything is just a "thing-um-bob" or a "what-do-you-call-it," a condition that reacts to make thought hopelessly loose and vague. Paucity of vocabulary on the part of those with whom the child associates, triviality and meagerness in the child's reading matter (as frequently even in his school readers and textbooks) tend to shut down the area of mental vision. Even technical terms become clear when they are used to make either an idea or an object clearer in meaning. Every self-respecting mechanic will call the parts of an automobile by their right names because that is the way to distinguish them. Simplicity should mean intelligibility, but not an approach to baby talk.

We must note also the great difference between flow of words and command of language. Volubility is not necessarily a sign of a large vocabulary; much talking or even ready speech is quite compatible with moving round and round in a circle of moderate radius. Most schoolrooms suffer from a lack of materials and appliances save perhaps books—and even these are "written down" to the supposed capacity, or incapacity, of children. Occasion and demand for an enriched vocabulary are accordingly restricted. The vocabulary of things studied in the schoolroom is very largely isolated; it does not link itself organically to the range of the ideas and words that are in vogue outside the school. Hence the enlargement that takes place is often nominal, adding to the inert, rather than to the active, fund of meanings and terms.

(b) *Rendering the Vocabulary More Precise.* One way in which the fund of words and concepts is increased is by discovering and naming shades of meaning—that is to say, by making the vocabulary more precise. Increase in definiteness is as important relatively as is the enlargement of the capital stock absolutely.

The first meanings of terms, since they are due to superficial acquaintance with things, are "general"—in the sense of being vague. The little child calls all men "papa"; acquainted with a dog, he may call the first horse he sees "big dog." Differences of quantity and intensity are noted, but the fundamental meaning is so vague that it covers things that are far apart. To many persons trees are just trees, being discriminated only into deciduous trees and evergreens, with perhaps recognition of one or two kinds of each. Such vagueness tends to persist and to become a barrier to the advance of thinking. Terms that are miscellaneous in scope are clumsy tools at best; in addition they are frequently treacherous, for their ambiguous reference causes us to confuse things that should be distinguished.

The growth of precise terms out of original vagueness takes place normally in two directions: first, toward words that stand for relationships, and second, toward words that stand for highly individualized traits; the first is associated with abstract, the second with concrete, thinking. Some Australian tribes are said to have no words for *animal* or for *plant*, while they have specific names for every variety of plant and animal in their neighborhoods. This minuteness of vocabulary represents progress toward definiteness, but in a one-sided way. Specific properties are distinguished, but not relationships.[11] On the other hand, students of philosophy and of the general aspects of natural and social science are apt to acquire a store of terms that signify relations, without balancing them up with terms that designate specific individuals and traits. The ordinary use of such terms as *causation, law, society, individual, capital* illustrates this tendency.

In the history of language we find both aspects of the growth of vocabulary illustrated by changes in the sense of words: some words originally wide in their application are narrowed to denote shades of meaning; others originally specific are widened to express relationships. The term *vernacular*, now meaning mother speech, has been generalized from the word *verna*, meaning a slave born in the master's household. *Publication* has evolved its meaning of communication by means of print through restricting an earlier meaning of any kind of communication—although the wider meaning is retained in legal procedure, as publishing a libel. The sense of the word *average* has been generalized from a use connected with dividing loss by shipwreck proportionately among various sharers in an enterprise.

These historical changes assist the educator to appreciate the changes that occur in individuals with advance in intellectual resources. In studying geometry, a pupil must learn both to narrow and to extend the meanings of such familiar words as *line, surface, angle, square, circle*—to narrow them to the precise meanings involved in demonstrations, to extend them to cover generic relations not expressed in ordinary usage. Qualities of color and size must be excluded; relations of direction, of variation in direction, of limit must be definitely seized. Thus in generalized geometry the idea of *line* does not carry any connotation of *length*. To it, what is ordinarily called a line is only a *section* of a line. A like transformation occurs in every subject of study. Just at this point lies the danger, alluded to above, of simply overlaying common meanings with new and isolated meanings instead of effecting a genuine working over of popular and practical meanings into logical concepts.

Terms used with intentional exactness so as to express a meaning, the whole meaning, and only the meaning are called *technical*. For educational purposes, a technical term indicates something relative, not absolute; for a term is technical, not because of its verbal form or its unusual-

---

11. The term *general* is itself an ambiguous term, meaning (in its best logical sense) the related and also (in its natural usage) the indefinite, the vague. *General*, in the first sense, denotes the discrimination of a principle or generic relation; in the second sense, it denotes the absence of discrimination of specific or individual properties.

ness, but because it is employed to fix a meaning precisely. Ordinary words get a technical quality when used intentionally for this end. Whenever thought becomes more accurate, a (relatively) technical vocabulary grows up. Teachers are apt to oscillate between extremes in regard to technical terms. On the one hand, these are multiplied in every direction, seemingly on the assumption that learning a new piece of terminology, accompanied by verbal description or definition, is equivalent to grasping a new idea. On the other hand, when it is seen how largely the net outcome is the accumulation of an isolated set of words, a jargon or scholastic cant, and to what extent the natural power of judgment is clogged by this accumulation, there is a reaction to the opposite extreme. Technical terms are banished; "name words" exist, but not nouns: "action words," but not verbs; pupils may "take away," but not subtract; they may tell what four fives are, but not what four times five are, and so on. A sound instinct underlies this reaction—aversion to words that give the pretense, but not the reality, of meaning. Yet the fundamental difficulty is not with the word, but with the idea. If the idea is not grasped, nothing is gained by using a more familiar word; if the idea is grasped, the use of the term that exactly names it may assist in fixing the idea. Terms denoting highly exact meanings should be introduced only sparingly—that is, a few at a time; they should be led up to gradually, and great pains should be taken to secure the circumstances that render precision of meaning significant.

(c) *Forming Habits of Consecutive Discourse.* As we saw, language connects and organizes meanings as well as selects and fixes them. As every meaning is set in the context of some situation, so every word in concrete use belongs to some sentence (it may itself represent a condensed sentence); and the sentence, in turn, belongs to some larger story, description, or reasoning process. It is unnecessary to repeat what has been said about the importance of continuity and ordering of meanings. We may, however, note some ways in which school practices tend to interrupt consecutiveness of language and thereby interfere harmfully with systematic reflection.

First, teachers have a habit of monopolizing continued discourse. Many, if not most, instructors would be surprised if informed at the end of the day of the amount of time they have talked as compared with any pupil. Children's conversation is often confined to answering questions in brief phrases or in single disconnected sentences. Expatiation and explanation are reserved for the teacher, who often admits any hint at an answer on the part of the pupil, and then amplifies what he supposes the child must have meant. The habits of sporadic and fragmentary discourse thus promoted have inevitably a disintegrating intellectual influence.

Second, assignment of too short lessons, when accompanied (as it usually is in order to pass the time of the recitation period) by minute "analytic" questioning, has the same effect. This evil is usually at its height in such subjects as history and literature, where not infrequently the material is so minutely subdivided as to break up the unity of meaning belonging to a given portion of the matter, to destroy perspective, and in effect to reduce the whole topic to an accumulation of disconnected details all upon the same level. More often than the teacher is aware, *his* mind carries and supplies the background of unity of meaning against which pupils project isolated scraps.

Third, insistence upon avoiding error instead of attaining power tends also to interruption of continuous discourse and thought. Children who begin with something to say and with intellectual eagerness to say it are sometimes made so conscious of minor errors in substance and form that the energy that should go into constructive thinking is diverted into anxiety not to make mistakes, and even, in extreme cases, into passive quiescence as the best method of minimizing error. This tendency is especially marked in connection with the writing of compositions, essays, and themes. It has even been gravely recommended that little children should always write on trivial subjects and in short sentences because in that way they are less likely to make mistakes. The teaching of high-school and college students occasionally reduces itself to a technique for detecting and designating mistakes. Self-consciousness and constraint follow. Students lose zest for writing. Instead of being interested in what they have to say and in how it is said as a means of adequate formulation and expression of their own thought, interest is drained off. Having to say something is a very different matter from having something to say.

OBSERVATION AND INFORMATION IN THE TRAINING OF MIND

Thinking is ordering of subject matter with reference to discovering what it signifies or indicates. Thinking no more exists apart from this arranging of subject matter than digestion occurs apart from the assimilating of food. The way in which the subject matter is supplied and assimilated is, therefore, of fundamental importance. If the subject matter is provided in too scanty or too profuse fashion, if it comes in disordered array or in isolated scraps, the effect upon habits of thought is detrimental. If personal observation and the communication of information by others (whether in books or speech) are rightly conducted, half the logical battle is won, for these are the channels of obtaining subject matter, and the method in which they are carried on directly affects the habit of thinking. The effect is often deeper because it is so unconscious. The best digestion can be ruined by innutritious foodstuffs, by eating at the wrong time, too much at a time, or having an unbalanced diet—that is, one the materials of which are badly arranged.

I

THE NATURE AND VALUE OF OBSERVATION

Observation Not an End in Itself. The protest, mentioned in the last chapter, of educational reformers against the exaggerated and false use of language insisted upon personal and direct observation as the alternative course. The reformers felt that the current emphasis upon the linguistic factor eliminated all opportunity for firsthand acquaintance with real things; hence they appealed to sense perception to fill the gap. It is not surprising that this enthusiastic zeal frequently failed to ask how and why observation is educative, and hence fell into the error of making observation an end in itself and hence was satisfied with any kind of material under any kind of conditions. Such isolation of observation is still manifested in the statement that this faculty develops first, then that of memory and imagination, and finally the faculty of thought. From this point of view, observation is regarded as furnishing crude masses of raw material, to which, later on, reflective processes may be applied. Our previous pages should have made obvious the fallacy of this point of view by bringing out the fact that simple concrete thinking attends all our intercourse with things that is not on a purely physical level.

Observation Impelled by Sympathetic Interest in Extending Acquaintance. All persons have a natural desire—akin to curiosity—for a widening of their range of acquaintance with persons and things. The sign in art galleries that forbids the carrying of canes and umbrellas is obvious testimony to the fact that simply to see is not enough for many people; there is a feeling of lack of acquaintance until some direct contact is made. This demand for fuller and closer knowledge is quite different from conscious interest in observation for its own sake. Desire for expansion, for "self-realization," is its motive. The interest is sympathetic, socially and aesthetically sympathetic, rather than cognitive. While the interest is especially keen in children (because their actual experience is so small and their possible experience so large), it still characterizes adults when routine has not blunted its edge. This sympathetic interest provides the medium for carrying and binding together what would otherwise be a multitude of items, diverse, disconnected, and of no intellectual use. The result is a social and aesthetic organization rather than one consciously intellectual; but it provides the natural opportunity and supplies the material for conscious intellectual explorations. Some educators have recommended that nature study in the elementary schools be conducted with a love of nature and a cultivation of aesthetic appreciation in view rather than in a purely analytic spirit. Others have urged making much of the care of animals and plants. Both of these important recommendations have grown out of experience, not out of theory, but they afford an excellent exemplification of the point just made.

Analytic Observation Impelled by Need Arising in Activity: Some Fallacies about Sense Training. In normal development, specific analytic observations are originally connected almost exclusively with the imperative need for noting means and ends in carrying on activities. When one is *doing* something *intelligently,* one is compelled, if the work is to succeed (unless it is purely routine), to use eyes, ears, and sense of touch as guides to action. Without a constant and alert exercise of the senses, not even plays and games can go on; in any form of work, materials, obstacles, appliances, failures, and successes must be intently watched. Sense perception does not occur for its own sake or for purposes of training, but because it is an indispensable factor of success in doing what one is trying to do. Although it is not designed for sense training, this method effects sense training in the most economical and thoroughgoing way. Various schemes have been designed by teachers for cultivating sharp and prompt observation of forms, as by writing words (even in an unknown language), making arrangements of figures and geometrical forms, and having pupils reproduce them after a momentary glance. Children often attain great skill in quick seeing and full reproducing of even complicated meaningless combinations. But such methods of training, however valuable as occasional games and diversions, compare very unfavorably with the training of eye and hand that comes as an incident of work with tools in wood or metals, or such activities as gardening, cooking, or the care of animals. Training by isolated exercises leaves no deposit, leads nowhere; and even the technical skill acquired has little radiating power or transferable value. Criticism made upon the training of observation, on the ground that many persons cannot correctly reproduce the forms and arrangement of the figures on the face of their watches, misses the point, because persons do not look at a watch to find out whether four o'clock is indicated by IIII or by IV, but to find out what time it is, and if observation decides this fact, noting other details is irrelevant and a waste of time. In the training of observation the question of purpose and result is all-important.

Observation Impelled by Solving Theoretical Problems. The further intellectual or scientific development of observation follows the line of the growth of practical into theoretical reflection already traced. As problems emerge and are dwelt upon, observation is directed less to facts that bear upon a practical aim and more to what bears upon a problem as a problem. What often makes observation in schools intellectually ineffective is (more than anything else) that it is carried on without a sense of a problem that it helps define and solve. The evil of this isolation is seen through the entire educational system, from the kindergarten through the elementary and high schools to the college. Almost everywhere may be found, at some time, recourse to observations as if they were of complete and final value in themselves, instead of being means for getting the data that test an idea or plan and that make the felt difficulty into a question that guides subsequent thinking. Moreover, intellectual method is violated because observations are not aroused and guided by any idea of the *purpose* they are to serve.

In the kindergarten observations are heaped up regarding geometrical forms, lines, surfaces, cubes, colors, and so on. In the elementary school, under the name of "object lessons," the form and properties of objects—apple, orange, chalk—selected almost at random are minutely noted, while under the name of "nature study" similar observations are directed upon leaves, stones, insects, selected in almost equally arbitrary fashion. In the high school and college, laboratory and microscopic observations are carried on as if the accumulation of observed facts and the acquisition of skill in manipulation were educational ends in themselves.

Observation in Scientific Work. Compare with these methods of isolated observations the statement of Jevons that observation as conducted by scientific men is effective "only when excited and guided by hope of verifying a theory"; and again, "the number of things which can be observed and experimented upon are infinite, and if we merely set to work to record facts without any distinct purpose, our records will have no value." Strictly speaking, the first statement of Jevons is too narrow. Scientific men institute observations not merely to test an idea (or suggested explanatory meaning), but also to locate a problem or even create one and thereby guide the formation of a hypothesis. But the principle of his remark—namely, that scientific men never make the accumulation of observations an end in itself, but always a means to a general intellectual conclusion—is absolutely sound. Until the force of this principle is adequately recognized in education, observation will be largely a matter of uninteresting dead work or of acquiring forms of technical skill that are not available as intellectual resources.

II

METHODS AND MATERIALS OF OBSERVATION
IN THE SCHOOLS

The best methods already in use in schools furnish many suggestions for giving observation its right place in mental training. Three features of these methods deserve mention.

Observation Should Involve Active Exploration. First, they rest upon the sound assumption that observation is an *active* process. Observation is exploration, inquiry for the sake of discovering something previously hidden and unknown, this something being needed in order to reach some end, practical or theoretical. Observation is to be discriminated from recognition, the perception of what is familiar. The identification of something already understood is, indeed, an indispensable function of further investigation; but it is relatively automatic and passive, while observation demands the mind to be alert, on the *qui vive*, searching and probing. Recognition deals with the already mastered; observation is concerned with delving into the unknown. The common notions that perception is like writing on a blank piece of paper or like impressing an image on the mind as a seal is imprinted on wax or as a picture is formed on a photographic plate (notions that have played a disastrous role in educational methods) arise from a failure to distinguish between automatic recognition and live observation.

Observation Should Introduce the Dramatic Element of Suspense, of "Plot Interest." Second, much assistance in the selection of appropriate material for observation may be derived from considering the eagerness and closeness of observation that attend the following of a story or drama. Alertness of observation is at its height wherever there is "plot interest." Why? Because of the balanced combination of the old and the new, of the familiar and the unexpected. We hang on the lips of the storyteller because of the element of mental suspense. Alternatives are suggested, but are left ambiguous, so that our whole being questions: What befell next? Which way did things turn out? Contrast the ease and fullness with which a child notes all the salient traits of a story, with the labor and inadequacy of his observation of some dead and static thing where nothing raises a question or suggests alternative outcomes.

When an individual is engaged in doing or making something (the activity not being of such a mechanical and habitual character that its outcome is assured), there is an analogous situation. Something is going to come of what is present to the sense, but just what is doubtful. The plot is unfolding toward success or failure, but just when or how is uncertain. Hence the keen and tense observation of conditions and results that attends constructive manual operations. Where the subject matter is of a more impersonal sort, the same principle of movement toward a denouement may apply. It is a commonplace that what is moving attracts notice when that which is at rest escapes it. Yet too often it would seem as if pains were taken to deprive the material of school observations of all life and dramatic quality, to reduce it to a dead and inert form. Mere change is not enough, however. Vicissitude, alteration, motion excite observation; but if they merely excite it, there is no thought. The changes must (like the incidents of a well-arranged story or plot) take place in a certain cumulative order; each successive change must at once remind us of its predecessor and arouse interest in its successor if observations of change are to be intellectually ordered and thus are to aid in forming a logical attitude.

Observation of Structure and Function. Living beings, plants and animals, fulfill the twofold requirement to an extraordinary degree. Where there is growth, there is motion, change, process; and there is also arrangement of the changes in a cycle. The first arouses thought; the second organizes it. Much of the extraordinary interest that children take in planting seeds and watching the stages of their growth is due to the fact that a drama is enacting before their eyes; there is something doing, each step of which is important in the destiny of the plant. The great practical improvements that have occurred of late years in the teaching of botany and zoology will be found, upon inspection, to involve treating plants and animals as beings that act, that do something, instead of as mere inert specimens having static properties to be inventoried, named, and registered. Treated in the latter fashion, observation is inevitably reduced to the falsely "analytic," to mere enumeration and cataloguing.

There is, of course, a place, and an important place, for observation of the static qualities of objects. When, however, the primary interest is in *function,* in what the object does and how it operates, there is a motive for more minute analytic study, for observation of *structure.* Interest in noting an activity passes insensibly into noting how the activity is carried on; the interest in what is done passes over into an interest in the organs by which it is done. But when the beginning is made with the morphological, the anatomical, the noting of peculiarities of form, size, color, and distribution of parts, the material is cut off from significance and becomes dead and dull. It is as natural for children to look intently for the *stomata* of a plant after they have learned that, like animals, it breathes, and so must have something corresponding in function to lungs. It is repulsive to attend minutely to them when they are presented for study as mere items of structure, and no idea of their action and use is conveyed.

Observation Should Become Scientific in Nature. Third, observation that is carried on at first to help out a practical purpose or for the mere fun of seeing and hearing comes to be conducted for an intellectual purpose. Pupils learn to observe for the sake (*a*) of finding out what sort of perplexity confronts them; (*b*) of conjecturing and inventing hypothetical explanations for the puzzling features revealed by observation; and (*c*) of testing the ideas thus suggested.

In short, observation becomes scientific in nature. Of such observations it may be said that they should follow a rhythm between the extensive and the intensive. Problems become definite, and suggested explanations significant, by an alternation between a wide and loose soaking in of relevant facts and a minutely accurate study of a few selected facts. The wider, less exact observation is necessary to give the student a feeling for the reality of the field of inquiry, a sense of its bearings and possibilities, and to store his mind with materials that imagination may transform into suggestions. The intensive study is necessary for limiting the problem and for securing the conditions of experimental testing. As the latter by itself is too specialized and technical to arouse intellectual growth, the former by itself is too superficial and scattering for control of intellectual development. In the sciences of life, field study, excursions, acquaintance with living things in their natural habitats may alternate with microscopic and laboratory observation. In the physical sciences, phenomena of light, of heat, of electricity, of moisture, of gravity, in their broad setting in nature—their physiographic setting—should prepare for an exact study of selected facts under conditions of laboratory control. In this way, the student gets the benefit of technical scientific methods of discovery and testing, while he retains his sense of the identity of the laboratory modes of energy with large out-of-door realities, thereby avoiding the impression (that so often accrues) that the facts studied are peculiar to the laboratory. Scientific observation does not, however, merely replace observation that is enjoyed for its own sake. The latter, sharpened by the purpose of contributing to an art like writing, painting, singing, becomes truly aesthetic, and the persons who enjoy seeing and hearing will be the best observers.

III

COMMUNICATION OF INFORMATION

When all is said and done, the field of fact open to any one observer by himself is narrow. Into every one of our beliefs, even those that we have worked out under the conditions of utmost personal, firsthand acquaintance, much has insensibly entered from what we have heard or read of the observations and conclusions of others. In spite of the great extension of direct observation in our schools, the vast bulk of educational subject matter is derived from other sources—from textbook, lecture, and viva voce interchange. No educational question is of greater import than how to get *intellectual* good out of what persons and books have to communicate.

How to Make an Intellectual Asset of Learning through Communicated Information. Doubtless the chief meaning associated with the word *instruction* is this conveying and instilling of the results of the observations and inferences of others. Doubtless the undue prominence in education of the ideal of amassing information has its source in the prominence of the learning of other persons. The problem, then, is how to convert this form of learning into an intellectual asset. In logical terms, the material supplied from the experience of others is *testimony:* that is to say, *evidence* submitted by others that is to be employed by one's own judgment in reaching a conclusion. How shall we treat subject matter that is supplied by textbook and teacher so that it shall rank as material of reflective inquiry, not as ready-made intellectual pabulum to be accepted and swallowed just as if it were something bought at a shop?

In reply to this question, we may say first that communication of material should be *needed.* That is to say, it should be such as cannot readily be attained by personal observation. For teacher or book to cram pupils with facts which, with little more trouble, they could discover by direct inquiry is to violate their intellectual integrity and to cultivate mental servility. This does not mean that the material supplied through communication of others should be meager or scanty. With the utmost range of the senses, the world of nature and history stretches out almost infinitely beyond. But fields within which direct observation is practicable should be carefully chosen and sacredly protected. Curiosity should not be dulled by making its satisfaction cheap and stale.

Second, material should be supplied by way of stimulus, not with dogmatic finality and rigidity. When pupils get the notion that any field of study has been definitely surveyed, that knowledge about it is exhaustive and final, they may become docile pupils, but they cease to be students. All thinking whatsoever—so be it *is* thinking—contains a phase of originality. This originality does not imply that the student's conclusion varies from the conclusions of others, much less that it is a radically novel conclusion. His originality is not incompatible with large use of materials and suggestions contributed by others. Originality means personal interest in the question, personal initiative in turning over the suggestions furnished by others, and sincerity in following them out to a tested conclusion. Literally, the phrase "Think for yourself" is tautological; any thinking is thinking for one's self.

Third, the material furnished by way of information should be relevant to a question that is vital in the student's own experience. What has been said about the evil of observations that begin and end in themselves may be transferred without change to communicated learning. Instruction in subject matter that does not fit into an interest already stirring in the student's own experience or that is not presented in such a way as to arouse a problem is worse than useless for intellectual purposes. In that it fails to enter into any process of reflection, it is useless; in that it remains in the mind as so much lumber and debris, it is a barrier, an obstruction, in the way of effective thinking when a problem arises.

Another way of stating the same principle is that material furnished by communication must be such as to enter into some existing system or organization of experience. All students of psychology are familiar with the principle of apperception—that we assimilate new material with what we have digested and retained from prior experiences. Now the apperceptive basis of material furnished by teacher and textbook should be found, as far as possible, in what the learner has derived from more direct forms of his own experience. There is a tendency to connect material of the schoolroom simply with the material of prior school lessons, instead of linking it to what the pupil has acquired in his out-of-school experience. The teacher says, "Do you not remember what we learned from the book last week?"—instead of saying, "Do you not recall such and such a thing that you have seen or heard?" As a result, there are built up detached and independent systems of school knowledge that inertly overlay the ordinary systems of experience instead of reacting to enlarge and refine them. Pupils are taught to live in two separate worlds, one the world of out-of-school experience, the other the world of books and lessons. Then we stupidly wonder why what is studied in school counts so little outside.

SOME GENERAL CONCLUSIONS

We shall conclude our survey of how we think and how we should think by presenting some factors of thinking that should balance each other, but that constantly tend to become so isolated that they work against each other instead of co-operating to make reflective inquiry efficient.

I

THE UNCONSCIOUS AND THE CONSCIOUS

Implicit and Explicit Context. It is significant that one meaning of the term "understood" is something so thoroughly mastered, so completely agreed upon, as to be *assumed;* that is to say, something taken as a matter of course without explicit statement. The familiar "it goes without saying" means "it is understood." If two persons can converse intelligently with each other, it is because a common experience supplies a background of mutual understanding upon which their respective remarks are projected. To dig up and to formulate this common background would be imbecile; it is "understood"; that is, it is silently sup-plied and im-plied as the taken-for-granted medium of intelligent exchange of ideas.

If, however, the two persons find themselves at cross purposes, it is necessary to dig up and compare the presuppositions, the implied context, on the basis of which each is speaking. The im-plicit is made ex-plicit; what was unconsciously assumed is exposed to the light of conscious day. In this way, the root of the misunderstanding is removed. Some such rhythm of the unconscious and the conscious, of going ahead and of analysis, is involved in all fruitful thinking. A person in pursuing a consecutive train of thoughts takes some system of ideas for granted (which accordingly he leaves unexpressed, "unconscious") as surely as he does in conversing with others. Some context, some situation, some controlling purpose, dominates his explicit ideas so thoroughly that it does not need to be consciously formulated and expounded. Explicit thinking goes on within the limits of what is implied or understood. Yet the fact that reflection originates in a problem makes it necessary *at some points* consciously to inspect and examine this familiar background. We have to turn upon some unconscious assumption and make it explicit.

No rules can be laid down for attaining the due balance and rhythm of these two phases of mental life. No ordinance can prescribe at just what point the spontaneous working of some unconscious attitude and habit is to be checked till we have made explicit what is implied in it. No one is wise enough to tell in detail just when and how far analytic inspection and conscious statement should be engaged in. We can say that they must be carried far enough so that the individual will know what he is about and be able to guide his thinking; but in a given case just how far is that? We can say that they must be carried far enough to detect and guard against the source of some false perception or reasoning, and to get a leverage on an investigation; but such statements only restate the original difficulty. Since our reliance must be upon the disposition and tact of the individual in the particular case, there is no test of the success of an education more important than whether it nurtures a type of mind that maintains a balance of the unconscious and the conscious.

The ways of teaching criticized in the foregoing pages as false "analytic" methods of instruction all reduce themselves to the mistake of directing explicit attention and formulation to what would work better if left an unconscious attitude and working assumption. To pry into the familiar, the usual, the automatic, simply for the sake of making it conscious, simply for the sake of formulating it, is both an impertinent interference and a source of boredom. To be forced to dwell consciously upon the accustomed is the essence of ennui. Methods of instruction that have that tendency dull curiosity.

On the other hand, what has been said in criticism of merely routine forms of skill, what has been said about the importance of having a genuine problem, of introducing the novel, and of reaching a deposit of general meaning, weighs on the other side of the scales. It is fatal to good thinking to fail to make conscious the standing source of some error or recurring failure as well as to pry needlessly into what works smoothly. To oversimplify, to exclude the novel for the sake of prompt skill, to avoid obstacles for the sake of averting errors, is as detrimental as to try to get pupils to formulate everything they know and to state every step of the procedure by which a result was obtained. Where the shoe pinches, analytic examination is indicated. When a topic is to be clinched so that knowledge of it will carry over and be an effective resource in further topics, conscious summarizing and organization are imperative. In the early stage of acquaintance with a subject, a good deal of unconstrained unconscious mental play about it may be permitted, even at the risk of some random experimenting; in the later stages, conscious formulation and review may be encouraged. Projection and reflection, going directly ahead and turning back in scrutiny, should alternate. Unconsciousness gives spontaneity and freshness; consciousness, command and control.

An Illustration from Control of Reflective Thinking. The point may be illustrated by the analysis in this volume of the phases of reflective activity. Some readers may get the idea that it is intended that students in their study and recitation should be made consciously to note and formulate these various phases as a means of intellectual control. Such a notion is, however, foreign to the spirit of the analysis. For it holds that fundamental control is effected by means of the *conditions* under which students work—the provision of a real situation that arouses inquiry, suggestion, reasoning, testing, etc. The chief value of the analysis that has been given is therefore to suggest to teachers the ways in which reflective thought may be best secured in students without the latter being made conscious at every step of their own attitudes and processes. It is also true that, *after* the instructor has once provided the conditions most likely to call out and direct thinking, the student's subsequent activity, while conscious of ends and means, may be unconscious with respect to his own personal attitudes and procedures. The familiar fact that creative work in the arts, writing, painting, music, etc., is largely unconscious as to the motives and attitudes of the artist, his mind being fixed on the objects he is dealing with or constructing, suggests the adoption of a like course in both study and teaching. The artist should be taken as a model rather than the activities of one painfully conscious at every step of just how he is operating. Control should be exercised by the setup of the situation itself. Yet in conditions of unusual perplexity or repeated error it will usually be a help if conscious attention goes back to such causes as lie in the attitudes and processes of the learner.

Absorption and Incubation. It is a common experience that after prolonged preoccupation with an intellectual topic, the mind ceases to function readily. It apparently has got into a rut; the "wheels go around" in the head, but they do not turn out any fresh grist. New suggestions cease to occur. The mind is, as the apt expression goes, "fed up." This condition is a warning to turn, as far as conscious attention and reflection are concerned, to something else. Then after the mind has ceased to be intent on the problem, and consciousness has relaxed its strain, a period of incubation sets in. Material rearranges itself; facts and principles fall into place; what was confused becomes bright and clear; the mixed up becomes orderly, often to such an extent that the problem is essentially solved. Many persons having a complicated practical question to decide find it advisable to sleep on the matter. Often they awake in the morning to find that, while they were sleeping, things have wonderfully straightened themselves out. A subtle process of incubation has resulted in hatching a decision and a plan. But this bringing forth of inventions, solutions, and discoveries rarely occurs except to a mind that has previously steeped itself consciously in material relating to its question, has turned matters off and over, weighed pros and cons. Incubation, in short, is one phase of a rhythmic process.

II
PROCESS AND PRODUCT

Play and Work Again. A like balance in mental life characterizes process and product. We met one important phase of this adjustment in considering play and work. In play, interest centers in activity, without much reference to its outcome. The sequence of deeds, images, emotions suffices on its own account. In work, the end holds attention and controls the notice given to means. Since the difference is one of direction of interest, the contrast is one of emphasis, not of cleavage. When comparative prominence in consciousness of activity or outcome is transformed into isolation of one from the other, play degenerates into fooling, and work into drudgery.

Play Should Not Be Fooling. By "fooling" we understand a series of disconnected temporary overflows of energy dependent upon whim and accident. When all reference to outcome is eliminated from the sequence of ideas and acts that make play, each member of the sequence is cut loose from every other and becomes fantastic, arbitrary, aimless; mere fooling follows. There is some inveterate tendency to fool in children as well as in animals; the tendency is not wholly evil, for it militates against falling into ruts. Even indulgence in dreaming and fancies *may* give mind a start in a new direction. But when they are excessive in amount, dissipation and disintegration follow; and the only way of preventing this result is to see to it that the children look ahead and forecast, to some extent, the ends of their activity, the effects it is likely to produce.

Work Should Not Be Drudgery. However, *exclusive* interest in a result alters work to drudgery. For by drudgery is meant those activities in which the interest in the outcome does not suffuse the process of getting the result. Whenever a piece of work becomes drudgery, the process of doing loses all value for the doer; he cares solely for what is to be had at the end of it. The work itself, the putting forth of energy, is hateful; it is just a necessary evil, since without it some important end would be missed. Now, it is a commonplace that in the work of the world many things have to be done, the doing of which is not intrinsically very interesting. However, the argument that children should be kept doing drudgery tasks because thereby they acquire power to be faithful to distasteful duties is wholly fallacious. Repulsion, shirking, and evasion are the consequences of having the repulsive imposed—not loyal love of duty. Willingness to work for ends by means of acts not naturally attractive is best attained by securing an appreciation of the value of the end, so that a sense of its value is transferred to its means of accomplishment. Not interesting in themselves, they borrow interest from the result with which they are associated.

Balance of the Work Attitude and the Play Attitude. The intellectual harm accruing from divorce of work and play, product and process, is evidenced in the proverb, "All work and no play makes Jack a dull boy." That the obverse is true is perhaps sufficiently signalized in the fact that fooling is so near to foolishness. To be playful and serious at the same time is possible, and it defines the ideal mental condition. Absence of dogmatism and prejudice, presence of intellectual curiosity and flexibility are manifest in the free play of the mind upon a topic. To give the mind this free play is not to encourage toying with a subject, but is to be interested in the unfolding of the subject on its own account, apart from any subservience to a preconceived belief or habitual aim. Mental play is open-mindedness, faith in the power of thought to preserve its own integrity without external supports and arbitrary restrictions. Hence free mental play involves seriousness, the earnest following of the development of subject matter. It is incompatible with carelessness or flippancy, for it exacts accurate noting of every result reached in order that every conclusion may be put to further use. What is termed the "interest in truth for its own sake" is certainly a serious matter, yet this pure interest in truth coincides with love of the free play of thought in inquiry.

In spite of many appearances to the contrary—usually due to social conditions either of superfluity of means that induces idle fooling or of undue economic pressure that compels drudgery—childhood normally realizes the ideal of conjoint free mental play and thoughtfulness. Successful portrayals of children have always made their wistful intentness at least as obvious as their lack of worry for the morrow. To live in the present is compatible with condensation of far-reaching meanings in the present. Such enrichment of the present for its own sake is the just heritage of childhood and the best insurer of future growth. The child forced into premature concern with economic remote results may develop a surprising sharpening of wits in a particular direction, but there is danger that this precocious specialization will be paid for by later apathy and dullness.

The Attitude of the Artist. That art originated in play is a common saying. Whether or not the saying is historically correct, it suggests a harmony of mental playfulness and seriousness that describes the artistic ideal. When the artist is preoccupied overmuch with means and materials, he may achieve wonderful technique, but not the artistic spirit par excellence. When the animating idea is in excess of the command of method, aesthetic feeling may be indicated, but the art of presentation is too defective to express the feeling thoroughly. When the thought of the end becomes so adequate that it compels translation into the means that embody it, or when attention to means is inspired by recognition of the end they serve, we have the attitude typical of the artist, an attitude that may be displayed in all activities, even though they are not conventionally designated "arts."

The Teacher as an Artist. That teaching is an art and the true teacher an artist is a familiar saying. Now the teacher's own claim to rank as an artist is measured by his ability to foster the attitude of the artist in those who study with him, whether they be youth or little children. Some succeed in arousing enthusiasm, in communicating large ideas, in evoking energy. So far, well; but the final test is whether the stimulus thus given to wider aims succeeds in transforming itself into power; that is to say, into the attention to detail that ensures mastery over means of execution. If not, the zeal flags, the interest dies out, the ideal becomes a clouded memory. Other teachers succeed in training facility, skill, mastery of the technique of subjects. Again it is well—so far. But unless enlargement of mental vision, power of increased discrimination of final values, a sense for ideas, for principles, accompanies this training, forms of skill ready to be put indifferently to any end may be the result. Such modes of technical skill may display themselves, according to circumstances, as cleverness in serving self-interest, as docility in carrying out the purposes of others, or as unimaginative plodding in ruts. To nurture inspiring aim and executive means into harmony with each other is at once the difficulty and the reward of the teacher.

III

THE FAR AND THE NEAR

"Familiarity Breeds Contempt." Teachers who have heard that they should avoid matters foreign to pupils' experience are frequently surprised

to find pupils wake up when something beyond their ken is introduced, while they remain apathetic in considering the familiar. In geography the child upon the plains seems perversely irresponsive to the intellectual charms of his local environment, but fascinated by whatever concerns mountains or the sea. Teachers who have struggled with little avail to extract from pupils essays describing the details of things with which they are well acquainted sometimes find them eager to write on lofty or imaginary themes. A woman of education, who has recorded her experience as a factory worker, tried retelling *Little Women* to some factory girls during their working hours. They cared little for it, saying, "Those girls had no more interesting experience than we have," and demanded stories of millionaires and society leaders. A man interested in the mental condition of those engaged in routine labor asked a Scotch girl in a cotton factory what she thought about all day. She replied that, as soon as her mind was free from starting the machinery, she married a duke, and their fortunes occupied her for the remainder of the day.

Naturally, these incidents are not told in order to encourage methods of teaching that appeal to the sensational, the extraordinary, or the incomprehensible. They are told, however, to enforce the point that the familiar and the near do not excite or repay thought on their own account, but only as they are adjusted to mastering the strange and remote. It is a commonplace of psychology that we do not attend to the old or consciously mind that to which we are thoroughly accustomed. For this there is good reason; to devote attention to the old, when new circumstances are constantly arising to which we should adjust ourselves, would be wasteful and dangerous. Thought must be reserved for the new, the precarious, the problematic. Hence the mental constraint, the sense of being lost, that comes to pupils when they are invited to turn their thoughts upon that with which they are already familiar. The old, the near, the accustomed, is not that *to* which but that *with* which we attend; it does not furnish the material of a problem, but of its solution.

Balancing the New and the Old. The last sentence has brought us to the balancing of new and old, of the far and that close by, involved in reflection. The more remote supplies the stimulus and the motive; the nearer at hand furnishes the point of approach and the available resources. This principle may also be stated in this form: the best thinking occurs when the easy and the difficult are duly proportioned to each other. The easy and the familiar are equivalents, as are the strange and the difficult. Too much that is easy gives no ground for inquiry; too much that is hard renders inquiry hopeless.

The necessity of the interaction of the near and the far follows directly from the nature of thinking. Where there is thought, something present suggests and indicates something absent. Accordingly, unless the familiar is presented under conditions that are in some respect unusual, there is no jog to thinking; no demand is made upon hunting out something new and different. And if the subject presented is totally strange, there is no basis upon which it may suggest anything serviceable for its comprehension. When a person first has to do with fractions, for example, they will be wholly baffling so far as they do not signify to him some relation that he has already mastered in dealing with whole numbers. When fractions have become thoroughly familiar, his perception of them acts simply as a signal to do certain things; they are a "substitute sign," to which he can react without thinking. If, nevertheless, the situation as a whole presents something novel and hence uncertain, the entire response is not mechanical, because this mechanical operation is put to use in solving a problem. There is no end to this spiral process: foreign subject matter transformed through thinking into a familiar possession becomes a resource for judging and assimilating additional foreign subject matter.

Observation Supplies the Near, Imagination the Remote. The need for both imagination and observation in every mental enterprise illustrates another aspect of the same principle. Teachers who have tried object lessons of the conventional type have usually found that, when the lessons were new, pupils were attracted to them as a diversion, but as soon as they became matters of course, they were as dull and wearisome as was ever the most mechanical study of mere symbols. Imagination could not play about the objects so as to enrich them. The feeling that instruction in "facts, facts" produces a narrow Gradgrind is justified, not because facts in themselves are limiting, but because facts are dealt out as hard and fast ready-made articles. No room is left to imagination. Let the facts be presented so as to stimulate imagination, and culture ensues naturally enough. The converse is equally true. The imaginative is not necessarily the imaginary; that is, the unreal. The proper function of imagination is vision of realities and possibilities that cannot be exhibited under existing conditions of sense perception. Clear insight into the remote, the absent, the obscure is its aim. History, literature, and geography, the principles of science, nay, even geometry and arithmetic, are full of matters that must be imaginatively realized if they are realized at all. Imagination supplements and deepens observation; only when it turns into the fanciful does it become a substitute for observation and lose logical force.

A final exemplification of the required balance between near and far is found in the relation that obtains between the narrower field of experience realized in an individual's own contact with persons and things, and the wider experience of the race that may become his through communication. Instruction always runs the risk of swamping the pupil's own vital, though narrow, experience under masses of communicated material. The mere instructor ceases and the vital teacher begins at the point where communicated matter stimulates into fuller and more significant life that which has entered by the strait and narrow gate of sense perception and motor activity. Genuine communication involves contagion; its name should not be taken in vain by terming communication that which produces no community of thought and purpose between the child and the race of which he is the heir.

---

*The foregoing consists
of Chapters I–II, VII–XII, XIV–XVII, and XIX
from John Dewey's* HOW WE THINK.

Epicurus

c. 341–*c.* 270 B.C.

Lucretius in his poem *On the Nature of Things*[1] extols Epicurus as the "glory of the Greek race" and ranks him among the gods for his services to mankind. Yet in the word "epicure" this Greek philosopher has provided the name for a devotee of the pleasures of the flesh.

His life, from what we now know of it, was uneventful. He was born about 341 B.C. on the Aegean island of Samos. He thus belongs to the generation immediately following Plato, who died in 347, and was approaching his twentieth year when Aristotle died in 322. Although he must have known of these philosophers, his work contains little sign of any direct influence. Epicurus, whose father was an Athenian, went to Athens when he was eighteen. He remained there only a year and for the next fourteen years taught in various Greek cities and gathered about him a group of disciples. In 306 he returned to Athens, where he lived and taught for the rest of his life; he died about 270 B.C.

The scene of his life and teaching was a garden on the outskirts of Athens. This has given rise to his being called the philosopher of the Garden, as Plato is known for the Academy and Zeno for the Porch. It was there that Epicurus gathered about him a society of men and women. Although the relations between the sexes may not have been what is often referred to as Platonic, there seems to be little ground for the charges of licentiousness that were sometimes made. Rabelais may well have taken the society as the prototype for his Abbey of Thélème.[2]

---

[1] See *Great Books of the Western World*, Vol. 12, pp. 1–97.
[2] See *Great Books of the Western World*, Vol. 24, pp. 60–65.

Although Epicurus was a prolific writer, with but one exception nothing but fragments of his works remains extant. The exception consists of three letters in which he provided a summary of his most important teaching. These have been preserved in a work on the lives and teachings of the philosophers compiled about the beginning of the third century A.D. by Diogenes Laërtius. The *Letter to Pythoclese,* omitted here, deals with questions of astronomy and meteorology.

The *Letter to Herodotus* (who is not to be confused with the historian) contains a digest of the teaching of Epicurus on the constitution and structure of the universe. It sets forth his main arguments for the theory of the atomic structure of the world. The *Letter to Menoeceus* provides a summary of the Epicurean moral theory that pleasure and peace of mind constitute the main aim of human life. The two letters thus give us in brief a picture of the Epicurean philosophy. Epicureanism was one of the four great philosophical systems of the ancient world, the others being Platonism, Aristotelianism, and the Stoicism of Epictetus and Marcus Aurelius. From them we have inherited not only problems and methods of dealing with problems, but also in many cases the general form of the solutions to be applied.

Epicurus provides one classic statement of the issue between science and religion. He looks upon the two as rival views of the world competing for man's allegiance. Religion is for him nothing but superstition. Besides being false, it is pernicious, since it gives rise to false fears which turn human life into wretchedness. Religion is for Epicurus, and Lucretius after him, the very opposite of an "opiate of the people," as it is according to Marx. It is the destroyer of peace of mind. For all this, it is significant that Epicurus is not an atheist. He still declares that the gods exist. But it is not at all clear that they have any function. The arrangements of material atoms moving in space is sufficient, according to his theory, to account for everything there is.

Yet for all his praise of science Epicurus is more of a moralist than a scientist. He seeks pleasure and peace of mind and is willing to countenance many different scientific explanations of the same event so long as they enable him to avoid the fears that religion arouses in him. The pleasure that he calls the "beginning and end of the blessed life" is far from luxurious. He is no epicure, and the life he recommends is simple, even austere.

Letter to Herodotus

For those who are unable, Herodotus, to work in detail through all that I have written about nature, or to peruse the larger books which I have composed, I have already prepared at sufficient length an epitome of the whole system, that they may keep adequately in mind at least the most general principles in each department, in order that as occasion arises they may be able to assist themselves on the most important points, in so far as they undertake the study of nature. But those also who have made considerable progress in the survey of the main principles ought to bear in mind the scheme of the whole system set forth in its essentials. For we have frequent need of the general view, but not so often of the detailed exposition. Indeed it is necessary to go back on the main principles, and constantly to fix in one's memory enough to give one the most essential comprehension of the truth. And in fact the accurate knowledge of details will be fully discovered if the general principles in the various departments are thoroughly grasped and borne in mind; for even in the case of one fully initiated the most essential feature in all accurate knowledge is the capacity to make a rapid use of observation and mental apprehension, and this can be done if everything is summed up in elementary principles and formulae. For it is not possible for any one to abbreviate the complete course through the whole system if he cannot embrace in his own mind by means of short formulae all that might be set out with accuracy in detail. Wherefore since the method I have described is valuable to all those who are accustomed to the investigation of nature, I, who urge upon others the constant occupation in the investigation of nature, and find my own peace chiefly in a life so occupied, have composed for you another epitome on these lines, summing up the first principles of the whole doctrine.

First of all, Herodotus, we must grasp the ideas attached to words, in order that we may be able to refer to them and so to judge the inferences of opinion or problems of investigation or reflection, so that we may not either leave everything uncertain and go on explaining to infinity or use words devoid of meaning. For this purpose it is essential that the first mental image associated with each word should be regarded, and that there should be no need of explanation, if we are really to have a standard to which to refer a problem of investigation or reflection or a mental inference. And besides we must keep all our investigations in accord with our sensations, and in particular with the immediate apprehensions whether of the mind or of any one of the instruments of judgment, and likewise in accord with the feelings existing in us, in order that we may have indications whereby we may judge both the problem of sense-perception and the unseen.

Having made these points clear, we must now consider things imperceptible to the senses. First of all, that nothing is created out of that which does not exist: for if it were, everything would be created out of everything with no need of seeds. And again, if that which disappears were destroyed into that which did not exist, all things would have perished, since that into which they were dissolved would not exist. Furthermore, the universe always was such as it is now, and always will be the same. For there is nothing into which it changes: for outside the universe there is nothing which could come into it and bring about the change.

Moreover, the universe is bodies and space: for that bodies exist, sense itself witnesses in the experience of all men, and in accordance with the evidence of sense we must of necessity judge of the imperceptible by reasoning, as I have already said. And if there were not that which we term void and place and intangible existence, bodies would have nowhere to exist and nothing through which to move, as they are seen to move. And besides these two nothing can even be thought of either by conception or on the analogy of things conceivable such as could be grasped as whole existences and not spoken of as the accidents or properties of such existences. Furthermore, among bodies some are compounds, and others those of which compounds are formed. And these latter are indivisible and unalterable (if, that is, all things are not to be destroyed into the non-existent, but something permanent is to remain behind at the dissolution of compounds): they are completely solid in nature, and can by no means be dissolved in any part. So it must needs be that the first-beginnings are indivisible corporeal existences.

Moreover, the universe is boundless. For that which is bounded has an extreme point, and the extreme point is seen against something else. So that as it has no extreme point, it has no limit; and as it has no limit, it must be boundless and not bounded. Furthermore, the infinite is boundless both in the number of the bodies and in the extent of the void. For if on the one hand the void were boundless, and the bodies limited in number, the bodies could not stay anywhere, but would be carried about and scattered through the infinite void, not having other bodies to support them and keep them in place by means of collisions. But if, on the other hand, the void were limited, the infinite bodies would not have room wherein to take their place.

Besides this the indivisible and solid bodies, out of which too the compounds are created and into which they are dissolved, have an incomprehensible number of varieties in shape; for it is not possible that such great varieties of things should arise from the same atomic shapes if they are limited in number. And so in each shape the atoms are quite infinite in number, but their differences of shape are not quite infinite, but only incomprehensible in number.

And the atoms move continuously for all time, some of them falling straight down, others swerving, and others recoiling from their collisions. And of the latter, some are borne on, separating to a long distance from one another, while others again recoil and recoil, whenever they chance to be checked by the interlacing with others, or else shut in by atoms interlaced around them. For on the one hand the nature of the void which separates each atom by itself brings this about, as it is not able to afford resistance, and on the other hand the hardness which belongs to the atoms makes them recoil after collision to as great a distance as the interlacing permits separation after the collision. And these motions have no beginning, since the atoms and the void are the cause.

These brief sayings, if all these points are borne in mind, afford a sufficient outline for our understanding of the nature of existing things.

Furthermore, there are infinite worlds both like and unlike this world of ours. For the atoms being infinite in number, as was proved already, are borne on far out into space. For those atoms, which are of such nature that a world could be created out of them or made by them, have not been used up either on one world or on a limited number of worlds, nor again on all the worlds which are alike, or on those which are different from these. So that there nowhere exists an obstacle to the infinite number of the worlds.

Moreover, there are images like in shape to the solid bodies, far surpassing perceptible things in their subtlety of texture. For it is not impossible that such emanations should be formed in that which surrounds the objects, nor that there should be opportunities for the formation of such hollow and thin frames, nor that there should be effluences which preserve the respective position and order which they had before in the solid bodies: these images we call idols.

Next, nothing among perceptible things contradicts the belief that the images have unsurpassable fineness of texture. And for this reason they have also unsurpassable speed of motion, since the movement of all their atoms is uniform, and besides nothing or very few things hinder their emission by collisions, whereas a body composed of many or infinite atoms is at once hindered by collisions. Besides this, nothing contradicts the belief that the creation of the idols takes place as quick as thought. For the flow of atoms from the surface of bodies is continuous, yet it cannot be detected by any lessening in the size of the object because of the constant filling up of what is lost. The flow of images preserves for a long time the position and order of the atoms in the solid body, though it is occasionally confused. Moreover, compound idols are quickly formed in the air around, because it is not necessary for their substance to be filled in deep inside: and besides there are certain other methods in which existences of this sort are produced. For not one of these beliefs is contradicted by our sensations, if one looks to see in what way sensation will bring us the clear visions from external objects, and in what way again the corresponding sequences of qualities and movements.

Now we must suppose too that it is when something enters us from external objects that we not only see but think of their shapes. For external objects could not make on us an impression of the nature of their own colour and shape by means of the air which lies between us and them, nor again by means of the rays or effluences of any sort which pass from us to them—nearly so well as if models, similar in colour and shape, leave the objects and enter according to their respective size either into our sight or into our mind, moving along swiftly, and so by this means reproducing the image of a single continuous thing and preserving the corresponding sequence of qualities and movements from the original object as the result of their uniform contact with us, kept up by the vibration of the atoms deep in the interior of the concrete body.

And every image which we obtain by an act of apprehension on the part of the mind or of the sense-organs, whether of shape or of properties, this image is the shape or the properties of the concrete object, and is produced by the constant repetition of the image or the impression it has left. Now falsehood and error always lie in the addition of opinion with regard to what is waiting to be confirmed or not contradicted, and then is not confirmed or is contradicted. For the similarity between the things which exist, which we call real, and the images received as a likeness of things and produced either in sleep or through some other acts of apprehension on the part of the mind or the other instruments of judgment, could never be unless there were some effluences of this nature actually brought into

contact with our senses. And error would not exist unless another kind of
movement too were produced inside ourselves, closely linked to the apprehension of images, but differing from it; and it is owing to this, supposing
it is not confirmed, or is contradicted, that falsehood arises; but if it is
confirmed or not contradicted, it is true. Therefore we must do our best to
keep this doctrine in mind, in order that on the one hand the standards of
judgment dependent on the clear visions may not be undermined, and on
the other error may not be as firmly established as truth and so throw all
into confusion.

Moreover, hearing, too, results when a current is carried off from the
object speaking or sounding or making a noise, or causing in any other
way a sensation of hearing. Now this current is split up into particles, each
like the whole, which at the same time preserve a correspondence of
qualities with one another and a unity of character which stretches right
back to the object which emitted the sound: this unity it is which in most
cases produces comprehension in the recipient, or, if not, merely makes
manifest the presence of the external object. For without the transference
from the object of some correspondence of qualities, comprehension of
this nature could not result. We must not then suppose that the actual air
is moulded into shape by the voice which is emitted or by other similar
sounds—for it will be very far from being so acted upon by it—but that the
blow which takes place inside us when we emit our voice causes at once a
squeezing out of certain particles, which produce a stream of breath, of
such a character as to afford us the sensation of hearing.

Furthermore, we must suppose that smell, too, just like hearing, could
never bring about any sensation unless there were certain particles carried
off from the object of suitable size to stir this sense-organ, some of them in
a manner disorderly and alien to it, others in a regular manner and akin in
nature.

Moreover, we must suppose that the atoms do not possess any of the
qualities belonging to perceptible things, except shape, weight, and size,
and all that necessarily goes with shape. For every quality changes; but
the atoms do not change at all, since there must needs be something which
remains solid and indissoluble at the dissolution of compounds, which can
cause changes; not changes into the non-existent or from the non-existent,
but changes effected by the shifting of position of some particles, and by
the addition or departure of others. For this reason it is essential that the
bodies which shift their position should be imperishable and should not
possess the nature of what changes, but parts and configuration of their
own. For thus much must needs remain constant. For even in things per-

ceptible to us which change their shape by the withdrawal of matter it is seen that shape remains to them, whereas the qualities do not remain in the changing object, in the way in which shape is left behind, but are lost from the entire body. Now these particles which are left behind are sufficient to cause the differences in compound bodies, since it is essential that some things should be left behind and not be destroyed into the non-existent.

Moreover, we must not either suppose that every size exists among the atoms, in order that the evidence of phenomena may not contradict us, but we must suppose that there are some variations of size. For if this be the case, we can give a better account of what occurs in our feelings and sensations. But the existence of atoms of every size is not required to explain the differences of qualities in things, and at the same time some atoms would be bound to come within our ken and be visible; but this is never seen to be the case, nor is it possible to imagine how an atom could become visible.

Besides this we must not suppose that in a limited body there can be infinite parts or parts of every degree of smallness. Therefore, we must not only do away with division into smaller and smaller parts to infinity, in order that we may not make all things weak, and so in the composition of aggregate bodies be compelled to crush and squander the things that exist into the non-existent, but we must not either suppose that in limited bodies there is a possibility of continuing to infinity in passing even to smaller and smaller parts. For if once one says that there are infinite parts in a body or parts of any degree of smallness, it is not possible to conceive how this should be, and indeed how could the body any longer be limited in size? (For it is obvious that these infinite particles must be of some size or other; and however small they may be, the size of the body too would be infinite.) And again, since the limited body has an extreme point, which is distinguishable, even though not perceptible by itself, you cannot conceive that the succeeding point to it is not similar in character, or that if you go on in this way from one point to another, it should be possible for you to proceed to infinity marking such points in your mind. We must notice also that the least thing in sensation is neither exactly like that which admits of progression from one part to another, nor again is it in every respect wholly unlike it, but it has a certain affinity with such bodies, yet cannot be divided into parts. But when on the analogy of this resemblance we think to divide off parts of it, one on the one side and another on the other, it must needs be that another point like the first meets our view. And we look at these points in succession starting from the first, not within the limits of the same point nor in contact part with part, but yet by means of their own proper characteristics measuring the size of bodies, more in a greater body and fewer in a smaller. Now we must suppose that the least part in the atom too bears the same relation to the whole; for though in smallness it is obvious that it exceeds that which is seen by sensation, yet it has the same relations. For indeed we have already declared on the ground of its relation to sensible bodies that the atom has size, only we placed it far below them in smallness. Further, we must consider these least indivisible points as boundary-marks, providing in themselves as primary units the measure of size for the atoms, both for the smaller and the greater, in our contemplation of these unseen bodies by means of thought. For the affinity which the least parts of the atom have to the homogeneous parts of sensible things is sufficient to justify our conclusion to this extent, but that they should ever come together as bodies with motion is quite impossible.

Furthermore, in the infinite we must not speak of "up" or "down," as though with reference to an absolute highest or lowest—and indeed we must say that, though it is possible to proceed to infinity in the direction above our heads from wherever we take our stand, the absolute highest point will never appear to us—nor yet can that which passes beneath the point thought of to infinity be at the same time both up and down in reference to the same thing: for it is impossible to think this. So that it is possible to consider as one single motion that which is thought of as the upward motion to infinity and as another the downward motion, even though that which passes from us into the regions above our heads arrives countless times at the feet of beings above and that which passes downwards from us at the head of beings below; for none the less the whole motions are thought of as opposed, the one to the other, to infinity.

Moreover, the atoms must move with equal speed when they are borne onwards through the void, nothing colliding with them. For neither will the heavy move more quickly than the small and light, when, that is, nothing meets them; nor again the small more quickly than the great, having their whole course uniform, when nothing collides with them either; nor is the motion upwards or sideways owing to blows quicker, nor again that downwards owing to their own weight. For as long as either of the two motions prevails, so long will it have a course as quick as thought, until something checks it either from outside or from its own weight counteracting the force of that which dealt the blow. Moreover, their passage through the void, when it takes place without meeting any bodies which might collide, accomplishes every comprehensible distance in an inconceivably short time. For it is collision and its absence which take the outward appearance of slowness and quickness. Moreover, it will be said that in compound bodies too one atom is faster than another, though as a matter of fact all are equal in speed: this will be said because even in the least period of continuous time all the atoms in aggregate bodies move towards one place, even though in moments of time perceptible only by thought they do not move towards one place but are constantly jostling one against another, until the continuity of their movement comes under the ken of sensation. For the addition of opinion with regard to the unseen, that the moments perceptible only by thought will also contain continuity of motion, is not true in such cases; for we must remember that it is what we observe with the senses or grasp with the mind by an apprehension that is true. Nor must it either be supposed that in moments perceptible only by thought the moving body too passes to the several places to which its component atoms move (for this too is unthinkable, and in that case, when it arrives all together in a sensible period of time from any point that may be in the infinite void, it would not be taking its departure from the place from which we apprehend its motion); for the motion of the whole body will be the outward expression of its internal collisions, even though up to the limits of perception we suppose the speed of its motion not to be retarded by collision. It is of advantage to grasp this first principle as well.

Next, referring always to the sensations and the feelings, for in this way you will obtain the most trustworthy ground of belief, you must consider that the soul is a body of fine particles distributed throughout the whole structure, and most resembling wind with a certain admixture of heat, and in some respects like to one of these and in some to the other. There is also the part which is many degrees more advanced even than these in fineness of composition, and for this reason is more capable of feeling in harmony with the rest of the structure as well. Now all this is made manifest by the activities of the soul and the feelings and the readiness of its movements and its processes of thought and by what we lose at the moment of death. Further, you must grasp that the soul possesses the chief cause of sensation, yet it could not have acquired sensation unless it were in some way enclosed by the rest of the structure. And this in its turn having afforded the soul this cause of sensation acquires itself too a share in this contingent capacity from the soul. Yet it does not acquire all the capacities which the soul possesses; and therefore when the soul is released from the body, the body no longer has sensation. For it never possessed this power in itself, but used to afford opportunity for it to another existence, brought into being at the same time with itself; and this existence, owing to the power now consummated within itself as a result of motion, used spontaneously to produce for itself the capacity of sensation and then to communicate it to the body as well, in virtue of its contact and correspondence of movement, as I have already said. Therefore, so long as the soul remains in the body, even though some other part of the body be lost, it will never lose sensation; nay more, whatever portions of the soul may perish too, when that which enclosed it is removed either in whole or in part, if the soul continues to exist at all, it will retain sensation. On the other hand the rest of the structure, though it continues to exist either as a whole or in part, does not retain sensation, if it has once lost that sum of atoms, however small it be, which together goes to produce the nature of the soul. Moreover, if the whole structure is dissolved, the soul is dispersed and no longer has the same powers nor performs its movements, so that it does not possess sensation either. For it is impossible to imagine it with sensation, if it is not in this organism and cannot effect these movements, when what encloses and surrounds it is no longer the same as the surroundings in which it now exists and performs these movements. Furthermore, we must clearly comprehend as well that the incorporeal in the general acceptation of the term is applied to that which could be thought of as such as an independent existence. Now it is impossible to conceive the incorporeal as a separate existence, except the void; and the void can neither act nor be acted upon, but only provides opportunity of motion through itself to bodies. So that those who say that the soul is incorporeal are talking idly. For it would not be able to act or be acted on in any respect if it were of this nature. But as it is, both these occurrences are clearly distinguished in respect of the soul. Now if one refers all these reasonings about the soul to the standards of feeling and sensation and remembers what was said at the outset, he will see that they are sufficiently embraced in these general formulae to enable him to work out with certainty on this basis the details of the system as well.

Moreover, as regards shape and colour and size and weight and all other things that are predicated of body, as though they were concomitant properties either of all things or of things visible or recognizable through the sensation of these qualities, we must not suppose that they are either independent existences (for it is impossible to imagine that), nor that they absolutely do not exist, nor that they are some other kind of incorporeal existence accompanying body, nor that they are material parts of body; rather we should suppose that the whole body in its totality owes its own permanent existence to all these, yet not in the sense that it is composed of properties brought together to form it (as when, for instance, a larger structure is put together out of the parts which compose it, whether the first units of size or other parts smaller than itself, whatever it is), but only, as I say, that it owes its own permanent existence to all of them. All these properties have their own peculiar means of being perceived and distinguished, provided always that the aggregate body goes along with them and is never wrested from them, but in virtue of its comprehension as an aggregate of qualities acquires the predicate of body.

Furthermore, there often happen to bodies and yet do not permanently accompany them accidents, of which we must suppose neither that they do not exist at all nor that they have the nature of a whole body, nor that they can be classed among unseen things nor as incorporeal. So that when according to the most general usage we employ this name, we make it clear that accidents have neither the nature of the whole, which we comprehend in its aggregate and call body, nor that of the qualities which permanently accompany it, without which a given body cannot be conceived. But as the result of certain acts of apprehension, provided the aggregate body goes along with them, they might each be given this name, but only on occasions when each one of them is seen to occur, since accidents are not permanent accompaniments. And we must not banish this clear vision from the realm of existence, because it does not possess the nature of the whole to which it is joined nor that of the permanent accompaniments, nor must we suppose that such contingencies exist independently (for this is inconceivable both with regard to them and to the permanent properties), but, just as it appears in sensation, we must think of them all as accidents occurring to bodies, and that not as permanent accompaniments, or again as having in themselves a place in the ranks of material existence; rather they are seen to be just what our actual sensation shows their proper character to be.

Moreover, you must firmly grasp this point as well: we must not look for time, as we do for all other things which we look for in an object, by referring them to the general conceptions which we perceive in our own minds, but we must take the direct intuition, in accordance with which we speak of "a long time" or "a short time," and examine it, applying our intuition to time as we do to other things. Neither must we search for expressions as likely to be better, but employ just those which are in common use about it. Nor again must we predicate of time anything else as having the same essential nature as this special perception, as some people do, but we must turn our thoughts particularly to that only with which we associate this peculiar perception and by which we measure it. For indeed this requires no demonstration, but only reflection, to show that it is with days and nights and their divisions that we associate it, and likewise also with internal feelings or absence of feeling, and with movements and states of rest; in connection with these last again we think of this very perception as a peculiar kind of accident, and in virtue of this we call it time.

And in addition to what we have already said we must believe that worlds, and indeed every limited compound body which continuously exhibits a similar appearance to the things we see, were created from the infinite, and that all such things, greater and less alike, were separated off from individual agglomerations of matter; and that all are again dissolved, some more quickly, some more slowly, some suffering from one set of causes, others from another. And further we must believe that these worlds were neither created all of necessity with one configuration nor yet with every kind of shape. Furthermore, we must believe that in all worlds there are living creatures and plants and other things we see in this world; for indeed no one could prove that in a world of one kind there might or might not have been included the kinds of seeds from which living things and plants and all the rest of the things we see are composed, and that in a world of another kind they could not have been.

Moreover, we must suppose that human nature too was taught and constrained to do many things of every kind merely by circumstances; and that later on reasoning elaborated what had been suggested by nature and made further inventions, in some matters quickly, in others slowly, at some epochs and times making great advances, and lesser again at others. And so names too were not at first deliberately given to things, but men's natures according to their different nationalities had their own peculiar feelings and received their peculiar impressions, and so each in their own way emitted air formed into shape by each of these feelings and impressions, according to the differences made in the different nations by the places of their abode as well. And then later on by common consent in each nationality special names were deliberately given in order to make their meanings less ambiguous to one another and more briefly demonstrated. And sometimes those who were acquainted with them brought in things hitherto unknown and introduced sounds for them, on some occasions being naturally constrained to utter them, and on others choosing them by reasoning in accordance with the prevailing mode of formation, and thus making their meaning clear.

Furthermore, the motions of the heavenly bodies and their turnings and eclipses and risings and settings, and kindred phenomena to these, must not be thought to be due to any being who controls and ordains or has ordained them and at the same time enjoys perfect bliss together with immortality (for trouble and care and anger and kindness are not consistent with a life of blessedness, but these things come to pass where there is weakness and fear and dependence on neighbours). Nor again must we believe that they, which are but fire agglomerated in a mass, possess blessedness, and voluntarily take upon themselves these movements. But we must preserve their full majestic significance in all expressions which we apply to such conceptions, in order that there may not arise out of them opinions contrary to this notion of majesty. Otherwise this very contradiction will cause the greatest disturbance in men's souls. Therefore we must believe that it is due to the original inclusion of matter in such agglomerations during the birth-process of the world that this law of regular succession is also brought about.

Furthermore, we must believe that to discover accurately the cause of the most essential facts is the function of the science of nature, and that blessedness for us in the knowledge of celestial phenomena lies in this and in the understanding of the nature of the existences seen in these celestial phenomena, and of all else that is akin to the exact knowledge requisite for our happiness; in knowing too that what occurs in several ways or is capable of being otherwise has no place here, but that nothing which suggests doubt or alarm can be included at all in that which is naturally immortal and blessed. Now this we can ascertain by our mind is absolutely the case. But what falls within the investigation of risings and settings and turnings and eclipses, and all that is akin to this, is no longer of any value for the happiness which knowledge brings, but persons who have perceived all this, but yet do not know what are the natures of these things and what are the essential causes, are still in fear, just as if they did not know these things at all; indeed, their fear may be even greater, since the wonder which arises out of the observation of these things cannot discover any solution or realize the regulation of the essentials. And for this very reason, even if we discover several causes for turnings and settings and risings and eclipses and the like, as has been the case already in our investigation of detail, we must not suppose that our inquiry into these things has not reached sufficient accuracy to contribute to our peace of mind and happiness. So we must carefully consider in how many ways a similar phenomenon is produced on earth, when we reason about the causes of celestial phenomena and all that is imperceptible to the senses; and we must despise those persons who do not recognize either what exists or comes into being in one way only, or that which may occur in several ways in the case of things which can only be seen by us from a distance, and further are not aware under what conditions it is impossible to have peace of mind. If, therefore, we think that a phenomenon probably occurs in some such particular way, and that in circumstances under which it is equally possible for us to be at peace, when we realize that it may occur in several ways, we shall be just as little disturbed as if we know that it occurs in some particular way.

And besides all these matters in general we must grasp this point, that the principal disturbance in the minds of men arises because they think that these celestial bodies are blessed and immortal, and yet have wills and actions and motives inconsistent with these attributes; and because they are always expecting or imagining some everlasting misery, such as is depicted in legends, or even fear the loss of feeling in death as though it would concern them themselves; and, again, because they are brought to this pass not by reasoned opinion, but rather by some irrational presentiment, and therefore, as they do not know the limits of pain, they suffer a disturbance equally great or even more extensive than if they had reached this belief by opinion. But peace of mind is being delivered from all this, and having a constant memory of the general and most essential principles.

Wherefore we must pay attention to internal feelings and to external sensations in general and in particular, according as the subject is general or particular, and to every immediate intuition in accordance with each of the standards of judgment. For if we pay attention to these, we shall rightly trace the causes whence arose our mental disturbance and fear, and, by learning the true causes of celestial phenomena and all other occurrences that come to pass from time to time, we shall free ourselves from all which produces the utmost fear in other men.

Here, Herodotus, is my treatise on the chief points concerning the nature of the general principles, abridged so that my account would be easy to grasp with accuracy. I think that, even if one were unable to proceed to all the detailed particulars of the system, he would from this obtain an unrivalled strength compared with other men. For indeed he will clear up for himself many of the detailed points by reference to our general system, and these very principles, if he stores them in his mind, will constantly aid him. For such is their character that even those who are at present engaged in working out the details to a considerable degree, or even completely, will be able to carry out the greater part of their investigations into the nature of the whole by conducting their analysis in reference to such a survey as this. And as for all who are not fully among those on the way to being perfected, some of them can from this summary obtain a hasty view of the most important matters without oral instruction so as to secure peace of mind.

Letter to Menoeceus

L et no one when young delay to study philosophy, nor when he is old grow weary of his study. For no one can come too early or too late to secure the health of his soul. And the man who says that the age for philosophy has either not yet come or has gone by is like the man who says that the age for happiness is not yet come to him, or has passed away. Wherefore both when young and old a man must study philosophy, that as he grows old he may be young in blessings through the grateful recollection of what has been, and that in youth he may be old as well, since he will know no fear of what is to come. We must then meditate on the things that make our happiness, seeing that when that is with us we have all, but when it is absent we do all to win it.

The things which I used unceasingly to commend to you, these do and practise, considering them to be the first principles of the good life. First of all believe that God is a being immortal and blessed, even as the common idea of a god is engraved on men's minds, and do not assign to Him anything alien to His immortality or ill-suited to His blessedness, but believe about Him everything that can uphold His blessedness and immortality. For gods there are, since the knowledge of them is by clear vision. But they are not such as the many believe them to be, for indeed they do not consistently represent them as they believe them to be. And the impious man is not he who denies the gods of the many, but he who attaches to the gods the beliefs of the many. For the statements of the many about the gods are not conceptions derived from sensation, but false suppositions, according to which the greatest misfortunes befall the wicked and the greatest blessings the good by the gift of the gods. For men being accustomed always to their own virtues welcome those like themselves, but regard all that is not of their nature as alien.

Become accustomed to the belief that death is nothing to us. For all good and evil consists in sensation, but death is deprivation of sensation. And therefore a right understanding that death is nothing to us makes the mortality of life enjoyable, not because it adds to it an infinite span of time, but because it takes away the craving for immortality. For there is nothing terrible in life for the man who has truly comprehended that there is nothing terrible in not living. So that the man speaks but idly who says that he fears death not because it will be painful when it comes, but because it is painful in anticipation. For that which gives no trouble when it comes is but an empty pain in anticipation. So death, the most terrifying of ills, is nothing to us, since so long as we exist, death is not with us; but when death comes, then we do not exist. It does not then concern either the living or the dead, since for the former it is not, and the latter are no more.

But the many at one moment shun death as the greatest of evils, at another yearn for it as a respite from the evils in life. But the wise man neither seeks to escape life nor fears the cessation of life, for neither does life offend him nor does the absence of life seem to be any evil. And just as with food he does not seek simply the larger share and nothing else, but rather the most pleasant, so he seeks to enjoy not the longest period of time, but the most pleasant.

And he who counsels the young man to live well, but the old man to make a good end, is foolish, not merely because of the desirability of life, but also because it is the same training which teaches to live well and to die well. Yet much worse still is the man who says it is good not to be born, but

> once born make haste to pass the gates of Death.
>
> [*Theognis, 427*]

For if he says this from conviction why does he not pass away out of life? For it is open to him to do so, if he had firmly made up his mind to this. But if he speaks in jest, his words are idle among men who cannot receive them.

We must then bear in mind that the future is neither ours, nor yet wholly not ours, so that we may not altogether expect it as sure to come, nor abandon hope of it, as if it will certainly not come.

We must consider that of desires some are natural, others vain, and of the natural some are necessary and others merely natural; and of the necessary some are necessary for happiness, others for the repose of the body, and others for very life. The right understanding of these facts enables us to refer all choice and avoidance to the health of the body and the soul's freedom from disturbance, since this is the aim of the life of blessedness. For it is to obtain this end that we always act, namely, to avoid pain and fear. And when this is once secured for us, all the tempest of the soul is dispersed, since the living creature has not to wander as though in search of something that is missing, and to look for some other thing by which he can fulfil the good of the soul and the good of the body. For it is then that we have need of pleasure, when we feel pain owing to the absence of pleasure; but when we do not feel pain, we no longer need pleasure. And for this cause we call pleasure the beginning and end of the blessed life. For we recognize pleasure as the first good innate in us, and from pleasure we begin every act of choice and avoidance, and to pleasure we return again, using the feeling as the standard by which we judge every good.

And since pleasure is the first good and natural to us, for this very reason we do not choose every pleasure, but sometimes we pass over many pleasures, when greater discomfort accrues to us as the result of them; and similarly we think many pains better than pleasures, since a greater pleasure comes to us when we have endured pains for a long time. Every pleasure then because of its natural kinship to us is good, yet not every pleasure is to be chosen; even as every pain also is an evil, yet not all are always of a nature to be avoided. Yet by a scale of comparison and by the consideration of advantages and disadvantages we must form our judgment on all these matters. For the good on certain occasions we treat as bad, and conversely the bad as good.

And again independence of desire we think a great good—not that we may at all times enjoy but a few things, but that, if we do not possess many, we may enjoy the few in the genuine persuasion that those have the sweetest pleasure in luxury who least need it, and that all that is natural is easy to be obtained, but that which is superfluous is hard. And so plain savours bring us a pleasure equal to a luxurious diet when all the pain due to want is removed; and bread and water produce the highest pleasure when one who needs them puts them to his lips. To grow accustomed therefore to simple and not luxurious diet gives us health to the full, and makes a man alert for the needful employments of life, and, when after long intervals we approach luxuries, disposes us better towards them, and fits us to be fearless of fortune.

When, therefore, we maintain that pleasure is the end, we do not mean the pleasures of profligates and those that consist in sensuality, as is supposed by some who are either ignorant or disagree with us or do not understand, but freedom from pain in the body and from trouble in the mind. For it is not continuous drinkings and revellings, nor the satisfaction of lusts, nor the enjoyment of fish and other luxuries of the wealthy table which produce a pleasant life, but sober reasoning, searching out the motives for all choice and avoidance, and banishing mere opinions, to which are due the greatest disturbance of the spirit.

Of all this the beginning and the greatest good is prudence. Wherefore prudence is a more precious thing even than philosophy; for from prudence are sprung all the other virtues, and it teaches us that it is not possible to live pleasantly without living prudently and honourably and justly, nor, again, to live a life of prudence, honour, and justice without living pleasantly. For the virtues are by nature bound up with the pleasant life, and the pleasant life is inseparable from them. For indeed who, think you, is a better man than he who holds reverent opinions concerning the gods, and is at all times free from fear of death, and has reasoned out the end ordained by nature? He understands that the limit of good things is easy to fulfil and easy to attain, whereas the course of ills is either short in time or slight in pain: he laughs at Destiny, whom some have introduced as the mistress of all things. He thinks that with us lies the chief power in determining events, some of which happen by necessity and some by chance, and some are within our control; for while necessity cannot be called to account, he sees that chance is inconstant, but that which is in our control is subject to no master, and to it are naturally attached praise and blame. For, indeed, it were better to follow the myths about the gods than to become a slave to the Destiny of the natural philosophers; for the former suggests a hope of placating the gods by worship, whereas the latter involves a necessity which knows no placation. As to chance, he does not regard it as a god as most men do (for in a god's acts there is no disorder), nor as an uncertain cause of all things; for he does not believe that good and evil are given by chance to man for the framing of a blessed life, but that opportunities for great good and great evil are afforded by it. He therefore thinks it better to be unfortunate in reasonable action than to prosper in unreason. For it is better in a man's actions that what is well chosen should fail, rather than that what is ill chosen should be successful owing to chance.

Meditate therefore on these things and things akin to them night and day by yourself, and with a companion like to yourself, and never shall you be disturbed waking or asleep, but you shall live like a god among men. For a man who lives among immortal blessings is not like to a mortal being.

Epictetus

c. 60–c. 138

Epictetus, the son of a slave woman, was born about A.D. 60 in central Asia Minor, in Hierapolis, Phrygia. As a boy he was a slave in Rome to Epaphroditus, the secretary of Nero and himself a former slave. While still in servitude, Epictetus attended the lectures of the fashionable Stoic philosopher Musonius Rufus. Obtaining his freedom about the year 89, he set up as a street-corner teacher, but was unsuccessful. His first success came when, along with many other philosophers suspected of republicanism, he was exiled from Rome by the Emperor Domitian. He withdrew to northern Greece, to the city of Nicopolis, where he established a school. He remained there, teaching until his death, about 138. His fame as a teacher became so great that the town was known for being the site of his school.

Epictetus did no writing, but taught entirely by word of mouth. But among his pupils, who came from all parts of the empire, was Flavius Arrian, the later historian of Alexander. From what must have been the careful notes he took of his master's teaching, he published the doctrine of Epictetus in the eight books of the *Discourses*, of which four survive, and the *Enchiridion*, or *Manual*, which is printed here.

Stoicism was the most influential and also the most popular of the ancient schools of philosophy. It had its origin in Athens during the generation following the death of Plato. Zeno of Citium was its founder, and since he taught in a covered portico (*Stoa* in Greek), his teaching came to be known as the philosophy of the Porch, or Stoicism. It achieved its greatest triumph in Rome, where, in the persons of Epictetus and of Marcus Aurelius, it proved its capacity to reach from a slave to an emperor.

Following a tradition that goes back to Aristotle, the Stoics divided their teaching into logic, physics, and ethics. It was thus a complete philosophy and there was no part of the intellectual world that it did not claim to touch. It won great fame for its logic, and the second leader of the school, Chrysippus, was often referred to simply as The Logician. The Stoics developed in the logic of propositions a branch of logic which Aristotle, the father of logic, had not investigated. However, of the great many works in logic and physics, or natural philosophy, that were written by Stoic philosophers, all but a few fragments have disappeared. The only complete works that have come down to us from the Stoics are restricted almost entirely to the field of ethics or morals. These are the works of Epictetus and Marcus Aurelius.[1]

From the *Enchiridion* it is easy to see why "stoic" has become the word for a person who can endure pain without flinching. Socrates is frequently held up by the Stoics as the model for imitation. But it is not so much the Socrates of the Platonic dialogues who delights in intellectual controversy as the Socrates who is indifferent to pleasure and pain and possesses an interior freedom that is unmoved by imprisonment and death.

The Stoic philosopher as presented by Epictetus has many of the characteristics of the saint: he is ascetic, disciplined in will, resigned to whatever may befall him, fond of meditating on death, yet compassionate of others whom he recognizes as his brothers. However, to such a Christian as Pascal the teaching of Epictetus is an abomination. Convinced of the weakness and misery of man without God, he is affronted by the claim that there are things within man's power, and that the philosopher is one who "looks to himself for all help or harm." It is upon what the Stoic claims are "our own," such as "opinion, aim, desire, aversion," that Epictetus builds his moral teaching. By controlling our attitude toward what happens, he claims that it is possible for man to achieve freedom and a secure peace of mind.

---

[1] See *Great Books of the Western World*, Vol. 12, pp. 105–310.

The Enchiridion

I

There are things which are within our power, and there are things which are beyond our power. Within our power are opinion, aim, desire, aversion, and, in one word, whatever affairs are our own. Beyond our power are body, property, reputation, office, and, in one word, whatever are not properly our own affairs.

Now the things within our power are by nature free, unrestricted, unhindered; but those beyond our power are weak, dependent, restricted, alien. Remember, then, that if you attribute freedom to things by nature dependent and take what belongs to others for your own, you will be hindered, you will lament, you will be disturbed, you will find fault both with gods and men. But if you take for your own only that which is your own and view what belongs to others just as it really is, then no one will ever compel you, no one will restrict you; you will find fault with no one, you will accuse no one, you will do nothing against your will; no one will hurt you, you will not have an enemy, nor will you suffer any harm.

Aiming, therefore, at such great things, remember that you must not allow yourself any inclination, however slight, toward the attainment of the others; but that you must entirely quit some of them, and for the present postpone the rest. But if you would have these, and possess power and wealth likewise, you may miss the latter in seeking the former; and you will certainly fail of that by which alone happiness and freedom are procured.

Seek at once, therefore, to be able to say to every unpleasing semblance, "You are but a semblance and by no means the real thing." And then examine it by those rules which you have; and first and chiefly by this: whether it concerns the things which are within our own power or those which are not; and if it concerns anything beyond our power, be prepared to say that it is nothing to you.

II

Remember that desire demands the attainment of that of which you are desirous; and aversion demands the avoidance of that to which you are averse; that he who fails of the object of his desires is disappointed; and he who incurs the object of his aversion is wretched. If, then, you shun only those undesirable things which you can control, you will never incur anything which you shun; but if you shun sickness, or death, or poverty, you will run the risk of wretchedness. Remove [the habit of] aversion, then, from all things that are not within our power, and apply it to things undesirable which are within our power. But for the present, altogether restrain desire; for if you desire any of the things not within our own power, you must necessarily be disappointed; and you are not yet secure of those which are within our power, and so are legitimate objects of desire. Where it is practically necessary for you to pursue or avoid anything, do even this with discretion and gentleness and moderation.

III

With regard to whatever objects either delight the mind or contribute to use or are tenderly beloved, remind yourself of what nature they are, beginning with the merest trifles: if you have a favorite cup, that it is but a cup of which you are fond of—for thus, if it is broken, you can bear it; if you embrace your child or your wife, that you embrace a mortal—and thus, if either of them dies, you can bear it.

IV

When you set about any action, remind yourself of what nature the action is. If you are going to bathe, represent to yourself the incidents usual in the bath—some persons pouring out, others pushing in, others scolding, others pilfering. And thus you will more safely go about this action if you say to yourself, "I will now go to bathe and keep my own will in harmony with nature." And so with regard to every other action. For thus, if any impediment arises in bathing, you will be able to say, "It was not only to bathe that I desired, but to keep my will in harmony with nature; and I shall not keep it thus if I am out of humor at things that happen."

V

Men are disturbed not by things, but by the views which they take of things. Thus death is nothing terrible, else it would have appeared so to Socrates. But the terror consists in our notion of death, that it is terrible. When, therefore, we are hindered or disturbed, or grieved, let us never impute it to others, but to ourselves—that is, to our own views. It is the action of an uninstructed person to reproach others for his own misfortunes; of one entering upon instruction, to reproach himself; and one perfectly instructed, to reproach neither others nor himself.

VI

Be not elated at any excellence not your own. If a horse should be elated, and say, "I am handsome," it might be endurable. But when you are elated and say, "I have a handsome horse," know that you are elated only on the merit of the horse. What then is your own? The use of the phenomena of existence. So that when you are in harmony with nature in this respect, you will be elated with some reason; for you will be elated at some good of your own.

VII

As in a voyage, when the ship is at anchor, if you go on shore to get water, you may amuse yourself with picking up a shellfish or a truffle in your way, but your thoughts ought to be bent toward the ship, and perpetually attentive, lest the captain should call, and then you must leave all these things, that you may not have to be carried on board the vessel, bound like a sheep; thus likewise in life, if, instead of a truffle or shellfish, such a thing as a wife or a child be granted you, there is no objection; but if the captain calls, run to the ship, leave all these things, and never look behind. But if you are old, never go far from the ship, lest you should be missing when called for.

VIII

Demand not that events should happen as you wish; but wish them to happen as they do happen, and you will go on well.

IX

Sickness is an impediment to the body, but not to the will unless itself pleases. Lameness is an impediment to the leg, but not to the will; and say this to yourself with regard to everything that happens. For you will find it to be an impediment to something else, but not truly to yourself.

X

Upon every accident, remember to turn toward yourself and inquire what faculty you have for its use. If you encounter a handsome person, you will find continence the faculty needed; if pain, then fortitude; if reviling, then patience. And when thus habituated, the phenomena of existence will not overwhelm you.

XI

Never say of anything, "I have lost it," but, "I have restored it." Has your child died? It is restored. Has your wife died? She is restored. Has your estate been taken away? That likewise is restored. "But it was a bad man who took it." What is it to you by whose hands he who gave it has demanded it again? While he permits you to possess it, hold it as something not your own, as do travelers at an inn.

XII

If you would improve, lay aside such reasonings as these: "If I neglect my affairs, I shall not have a maintenance; if I do not punish my servant, he will be good for nothing." For it were better to die of hunger, exempt from grief and fear, than to live in affluence with perturbation; and it is better that your servant should be bad than you unhappy.

Begin therefore with little things. Is a little oil spilled or a little wine stolen? Say to yourself, "This is the price paid for peace and tranquillity; and nothing is to be had for nothing." And when you call your servant, consider that it is possible he may not come at your call; or, if he does, that he may not do what you wish. But it is not at all desirable for him, and very undesirable for you, that it should be in his power to cause you any disturbance.

XIII

If you would improve, be content to be thought foolish and dull with regard to externals. Do not desire to be thought to know anything; and though you should appear to others to be somebody, distrust yourself. For be assured, it is not easy at once to keep your will in harmony with nature and to secure externals; but while you are absorbed in the one, you must of necessity neglect the other.

XIV

If you wish your children and your wife and your friends to live forever, you are foolish, for you wish things to be in your power which are not so, and what belongs to others to be your own. So likewise, if you wish your servant to be without fault, you are foolish, for you wish vice not to be vice but something else. But if you wish not to be disappointed in your desires, that is in your own power. Exercise, therefore, what is in your power. A man's master is he who is able to confer or remove whatever that man seeks or shuns. Whoever then would be free, let him wish nothing, let him decline nothing, which depends on others; else he must necessarily be a slave.

XV

Remember that you must behave as at a banquet. Is anything brought round to you? Put out your hand and take a moderate share. Does it pass by you? Do not stop it. Is it not yet come? Do not yearn in desire toward it, but wait till it reaches you. So with regard to children, wife, office, riches; and you will some time or other be worthy to feast with the gods. And if you do not so much as take the things which are set before you, but are able even to forego them, then you will not only be worthy to feast with the gods, but to rule with them also. For, by thus doing, Diogenes and Heraclitus, and others like them, deservedly became divine, and were so recognized.

XVI

When you see anyone weeping for grief, either that his son has gone abroad or that he has suffered in his affairs, take care not to be overcome by the apparent evil, but discriminate and be ready to say, "What hurts this man is not this occurrence itself—for another man might not be hurt by it—but the view he chooses to take of it." As far as conversation goes, however, do not disdain to accommodate yourself to him and, if need be, to groan with him. Take heed, however, not to groan inwardly, too.

XVII

Remember that you are an actor in a drama of such sort as the Author chooses—if short, then in a short one; if long, then in a long one. If it be his pleasure that you should enact a poor man, or a cripple, or a ruler, or a private citizen, see that you act it well. For this is your business—to act well the given part, but to choose it belongs to another.

XVIII

When a raven happens to croak unluckily, be not overcome by appearances, but discriminate and say, "Nothing is portended to *me*, either to my paltry body, or property, or reputation, or children, or wife. But to *me* all portents are lucky if I will. For whatsoever happens, it belongs to me to derive advantage therefrom."

XIX

You can be unconquerable if you enter into no combat in which it is not in your own power to conquer. When, therefore, you see anyone eminent in honors or power, or in high esteem on any other account, take heed not to be bewildered by appearances and to pronounce him happy; for if the essence of good consists in things within our own power, there will be no room for envy or emulation. But, for your part, do not desire to be a general, or a senator, or a consul, but to be free; and the only way to this is a disregard of things which lie not within our own power.

XX

Remember that it is not he who gives abuse or blows, who affronts, but the view we take of these things as insulting. When, therefore, anyone provokes you, be assured that it is your own opinion which provokes you. Try, therefore, in the first place, not to be bewildered by appearances. For if you once gain time and respite, you will more easily command yourself.

XXI

Let death and exile, and all other things which appear terrible, be daily before your eyes, but death chiefly; and you will never entertain an abject thought, nor too eagerly covet anything.

XXII

If you have an earnest desire toward philosophy, prepare yourself from the very first to have the multitude laugh and sneer, and say, "He is returned to us a philosopher all at once"; and, "Whence this supercilious look?" Now, for your part, do not have a supercilious look indeed, but keep steadily to those things which appear best to you, as one appointed by God to this particular station. For remember that, if you are persistent, those very persons who at first ridiculed will afterwards admire you. But if you are conquered by them, you will incur a double ridicule.

XXIII

If you ever happen to turn your attention to externals, for the pleasure of anyone, be assured that you have ruined your scheme of life. Be content, then, in everything, with being a philosopher; and if you wish to seem so likewise to anyone, appear so to yourself, and it will suffice you.

XXIV

Let not such considerations as these distress you: "I shall live in discredit and be nobody anywhere." For if discredit be an evil, you can no more be involved in evil through another than in baseness. Is it any business of yours, then, to get power or to be admitted to an entertainment? By no means. How then, after all, is this discredit? And how it is true that you will be nobody anywhere when you ought to be somebody in those things only which are within your own power, in which you may be of the greatest consequence? "But my friends will be unassisted." What do you mean by "unassisted"? They will not have money from you, nor will you make them Roman citizens. Who told you, then, that these are among the things within our own power, and not rather the affairs of others? And who can give to another the things which he himself has not? "Well, but get them, then, that we too may have a share." If I can get them with the preservation of my own honor and fidelity and self-respect, show me the way and I will get them; but if you require me to lose my own proper good, that you may gain what is no good, consider how unreasonable and foolish you are. Besides, which would you rather have, a sum of money or a faithful and honorable friend? Rather assist me, then, to gain this character than require me to do those things by which I may lose it. Well, but my country, say you, as far as depends upon me, will be unassisted. Here, again, what assistance is this you mean? It will not have porticos nor baths of your providing? And what signifies that? Why, neither does a smith provide it with shoes, nor a shoemaker with arms. It is enough if everyone fully performs his own proper business. And were you to supply it with another faithful and honorable citizen, would not he be of use to it? Yes. Therefore neither are you yourself useless to it. "What place, then," say you, "shall I hold in the state?" Whatever you can hold with the preservation of your fidelity and honor. But if, by desiring to be useful to that, you lose these, how can you serve your country when you have become faithless and shameless?

XXV

Is anyone preferred before you at an entertainment, or in courtesies, or in confidential intercourse? If these things are good, you ought to rejoice that he has them; and if they are evil, do not be grieved that you have them not. And remember that you cannot be permitted to rival others in externals without using the same means to obtain them. For how can he who will not haunt the door of any man, will not attend him, will not praise him have an equal share with him who does these things? You are unjust, then, and unreasonable if you are unwilling to pay the price for which these things are sold, and would have them for nothing. For how much are lettuces sold? An obulus, for instance. If another, then, paying an obulus, takes the lettuces, and you, not paying it, go without them, do not imagine that he has gained any advantage over you. For as he has the lettuces, so you have the obulus which you did not give. So, in the present case, you have not been invited to such a person's entertainment because you have not paid him the price for which a supper is sold. It is sold for praise; it is sold for attendance. Give him, then, the value if it be for your advantage. But if you would at the same time not pay the one, and yet receive the other, you are unreasonable and foolish. Have you nothing, then, in place of the supper? Yes, indeed, you have—not to praise him whom you do not like to praise; not to bear the insolence of his lackeys.

XXVI

The will of nature may be learned from things upon which we are all agreed. As when our neighbor's boy has broken a cup, or the like, we are ready at once to say, "These are casualties that will happen"; be assured, then, that when your own cup is likewise broken, you ought to be affected just as when another's cup was broken. Now apply this to greater things. Is the child or wife of another dead? There is no one who would not say, "This is an accident of mortality." But if anyone's own child happens to die, it is immediately, "Alas! how wretched am I!" It should be always remembered how we are affected on hearing the same thing concerning others.

XXVII

As a mark is not set up for the sake of missing the aim, so neither does the nature of evil exist in the world.

XXVIII

If a person had delivered up your body to some passer-by, you would certainly be angry. And do you feel no shame in delivering up your own mind to any reviler, to be disconcerted and confounded?

XXIX

In every affair consider what precedes and what follows, and then undertake it. Otherwise you will begin with spirit, indeed, careless of the consequences, and when these are developed, you will shamefully desist. "I would conquer at the Olympic Games." But consider what precedes and what follows, and then, if it be for your advantage, engage in the affair. You must conform to rules, submit to a diet, refrain from dainties; exercise your body, whether you choose it or not, at a stated hour, in heat and cold; you must drink no cold water, and sometimes no wine—in a word, you must give yourself up to your trainer as to a physician. Then, in the combat, you may be thrown into a ditch, dislocate your arm, turn your ankle, swallow an abundance of dust, receive stripes [for negligence], and, after all, lose the victory. When you have reckoned up all this, if your inclination still holds, set about the combat. Otherwise, take notice, you will behave like children who sometimes play wrestlers, sometimes gladiators, sometimes blow a trumpet, and sometimes act a tragedy, when they happen to have seen and admired these shows. Thus you too will be at one time a wrestler, and another a gladiator; now a philosopher, now an orator; but nothing in earnest. Like an ape you mimic all you see, and one thing after another is sure to please you, but is out of favor as soon as it becomes familiar. For you have never entered upon anything considerately; nor after having surveyed and tested the whole matter, but carelessly, and with a halfway zeal. Thus some, when they have seen a philosopher and heard a man speaking like Euphrates—though, indeed, who can speak like him?—have a mind to be philosophers, too. Consider first, man, what the matter is, and what your own nature is able to bear. If you would be a wrestler, consider your shoulders, your back, your thighs; for different persons are made for different things. Do you think that you can act as you do and be a philosopher, that you can eat, drink, be angry, be discontented, as you are now? You must watch, you must labor, you must get the better of certain appetites, must quit your acquaintances, be despised by your servant, be laughed at by those you meet; come off worse than others in everything—in offices, in honors, before tribunals. When you have fully considered all these things, approach, if you please—that is, if, by parting with them, you have a mind to purchase serenity, freedom, and tranquillity. If not, do not come hither; do not, like children, be now a philosopher, then a publican, then an orator, and then one of Caesar's officers. These things are not consistent. You must be one man, either good or bad. You must cultivate either your own reason or else externals; apply yourself either to things within or without you—that is, be either a philosopher or one of the mob.

XXX

Duties are universally measured by relations. Is a certain man your father? In this are implied taking care of him, submitting to him in all things, patiently receiving his reproaches, his correction. But he is a bad father. Is your natural tie, then, to a *good* father? No, but to a father. Is a brother unjust? Well, preserve your own just relation toward him. Consider not what *he* does, but what *you* are to do to keep your own will in a state conformable to nature, for another cannot hurt you unless you please. You will then be hurt when you consent to be hurt. In this manner, therefore, if you accustom yourself to contemplate the relations of neighbor, citizen, commander, you can deduce from each the corresponding duties.

XXXI

Be assured that the essence of piety toward the gods lies in this—to form right opinions concerning them, as existing and as governing the universe justly and well. And fix yourself in this resolution, to obey them, and yield to them, and willingly follow them amidst all events, as being ruled by the most perfect wisdom. For thus you will never find fault with the gods, nor accuse them of neglecting you. And it is not possible for this to be affected in any other way than by withdrawing yourself from things which are not within our own power, and by making good or evil to consist only in those which are. For if you suppose any other things to be either good or evil, it is inevitable that, when you are disappointed of what you wish or incur what you would avoid, you should reproach and blame their authors. For every creature is naturally formed to flee and abhor things that appear hurtful and that which causes them; and to pursue and admire those which appear beneficial and that which causes them. It is impracticable, then, that one who supposes himself to be hurt should rejoice in the person who, as he thinks, hurts him, just as it is impossible to rejoice in the hurt itself. Hence, also, a father is reviled by his son when he does not impart the things which seem to be good; and this made Polynices and Eteocles mutually enemies—that empire seemed good to both. On this account the husbandman reviles the gods; [and so do] the sailor, the merchant, or those who have lost wife or child. For where our interest is, there, too, is piety directed. So that whoever is careful to regulate his desires and aversions as he ought is thus made careful of piety likewise. But it also becomes incumbent on everyone to offer libations and sacrifices and first fruits, according to the customs of his country, purely, and not heedlessly nor negligently; not avariciously, nor yet extravagantly.

XXXII

When you have recourse to divination, remember that you know not what the event will be, and you come to learn it of the diviner; but of what nature it is you knew before coming; at least, if you are of philosophic mind. For if it is among the things not within our own power, it can by no means be either good or evil. Do not, therefore, bring with you to the diviner either desire or aversion—else you will approach him trembling—but first clearly understand that every event is indifferent and nothing to *you*, of whatever sort it may be; for it will be in your power to make a right use of it, and this no one can hinder. Then come with confidence to the gods as your counselors; and afterwards, when any counsel is given you, remember what counselors you have assumed, and whose advice you will neglect if you disobey. Come to divination as Socrates prescribed, in cases of which the whole consideration relates to the event, and in which no opportunities are afforded by reason or any other art to discover the matter in view. When, therefore, it is our duty to share the danger of a friend or of our country, we ought not to consult the oracle as to whether we shall share it with them or not. For though the diviner should forewarn you that the auspices are unfavorable, this means no more than that either death or mutilation or exile is portended. But we have reason within us; and it directs us, even with these hazards, to stand by our friend and our country. Attend, therefore, to the greater diviner, the Pythian God, who once cast out of the temple him who neglected to save his friend.[1]

XXXIII

Begin by prescribing to yourself some character and demeanor, such as you may preserve both alone and in company.

Be mostly silent, or speak merely what is needful, and in few words. We may, however, enter sparingly into discourse sometimes, when occasion calls for it; but let it not run on any of the common subjects, as gladiators, or horse races, or athletic champions, or food, or drink—the vulgar topics of conversation—and especially not on men, so as either to blame, or praise, or make comparisons. If you are able, then, by your own conversation, bring over that of your company to proper subjects; but if you happen to find yourself among strangers, be silent.

Let not your laughter be loud, frequent, or abundant.

Avoid taking oaths, if possible, altogether; at any rate, so far as you are able.

Avoid public and vulgar entertainments; but if ever an occasion calls you to them, keep your attention upon the stretch, that you may not

---

1. [This refers to an anecdote given in full by Simplicius, in his commentary on this passage, of a man assaulted and killed on his way to consult the oracle, while his companion, deserting him, took refuge in the temple till cast out by the Deity.—Tr.]

imperceptibly slide into vulgarity. For be assured that if a person be ever so pure himself, yet, if his companion be corrupted, he who converses with him will be corrupted likewise.

Provide things relating to the body no further than absolute need requires, as meat, drink, clothing, house, retinue. But cut off everything that looks toward show and luxury.

Before marriage guard yourself with all your ability from unlawful intercourse with women; yet be not uncharitable or severe to those who are led into this, nor boast frequently that you yourself do otherwise.

If anyone tells you that a certain person speaks ill of you, do not make excuses about what is said of you, but answer: "He was ignorant of my other faults, else he would not have mentioned these alone."

It is not necessary for you to appear often at public spectacles; but if ever there is a proper occasion for you to be there, do not appear more solicitous for any other than for yourself—that is, wish things to be only just as they are, and only the best man to win; for thus nothing will go against you. But abstain entirely from acclamations and derision and violent emotions. And when you come away, do not discourse a great deal on what has passed and what contributes nothing to your own amendment. For it would appear by such discourse that you were dazzled by the show.

Be not prompt or ready to attend private recitations; but if you do attend, preserve your gravity and dignity, and yet avoid making yourself disagreeable.

When you are going to confer with anyone, and especially with one who seems your superior, represent to yourself how Socrates or Zeno would behave in such a case, and you will not be at a loss to meet properly whatever may occur.

When you are going before anyone in power, fancy to yourself that you may not find him at home, that you may be shut out, that the doors may not be opened to you, that he may not notice you. If, with all this, it be your duty to go, bear what happens and never say to yourself, "It was not worth so much"; for this is vulgar, and like a man bewildered by externals.

In company, avoid a frequent and excessive mention of your own actions and dangers. For however agreeable it may be to yourself to allude to the risks you have run, it is not equally agreeable to others to hear your adventures. Avoid likewise an endeavor to excite laughter, for this may readily slide you into vulgarity, and, besides, may be apt to lower you in the esteem of your acquaintance. Approaches to indecent discourse are likewise dangerous. Therefore, when anything of this sort happens, use the first fit opportunity to rebuke him who makes advances that way, or, at least, by silence and blushing and a serious look show yourself to be displeased by such talk.

XXXIV

If you are dazzled by the semblance of any promised pleasure, guard yourself against being bewildered by it; but let the affair wait your leisure, and procure yourself some delay. Then bring to your mind both points of time—that in which you shall enjoy the pleasure, and that in which you will repent and reproach yourself, after you have enjoyed it—and set before you, in opposition to these, how you will rejoice and applaud yourself if you abstain. And even though it should appear to you a seasonable gratification, take heed that its enticements and allurements and seductions may not subdue you, but set in opposition to this how much better it is to be conscious of having gained so great a victory.

XXXV

When you do anything from a clear judgment that it ought to be done, never shrink from being seen to do it, even though the world should misunderstand it; for if you are not acting rightly, shun the action itself; if you are, why fear those who wrongly censure you?

XXXVI

As the proposition, "either it is day or it is night," has much force in a disjunctive argument, but none at all in a conjunctive one, so, at a feast, to choose the largest share is very suitable to the bodily appetite, but utterly inconsistent with the social spirit of the entertainment. Remember, then, when you eat with another, not only the value to the body of those things which are set before you, but also the value of proper courtesy toward your host.

XXXVII

If you have assumed any character beyond your strength, you have both demeaned yourself ill in that and quitted one which you might have supported.

XXXVIII

As in walking you take care not to tread upon a nail, or turn your foot, so likewise take care not to hurt the ruling faculty of your mind. And if we were to guard against this in every action, we should enter upon action more safely.

XXXIX

The body is to everyone the proper measure of its possessions, as the foot is of the shoe. If, therefore, you stop at this, you will keep the measure; but if you move beyond it, you must necessarily be carried forward, as down a precipice; as in the case of a shoe, if you go beyond its fitness to the foot, it comes first to be gilded, then purple, and then studded with jewels. For to that which once exceeds the fit measure there is no bound.

XL

Women from fourteen years old are flattered by men with the title of mistresses. Therefore, perceiving that they are regarded only as qualified to give men pleasure, they begin to adorn themselves, and in that to place all their hopes. It is worth while, therefore, to try that they may perceive themselves honored only so far as they appear beautiful in their demeanor and modestly virtuous.

XLI

It is a mark of want of intellect to spend much time in things relating to the body, as to be immoderate in exercises, in eating and drinking, and in the discharge of other animal functions. These things should be done incidentally and our main strength be applied to our reason.

XLII

When any person does ill by you, or speaks ill of you, remember that he acts or speaks from an impression that it is right for him to do so. Now it is not possible that he should follow what appears right to you, but only what appears so to himself. Therefore, if he judges from false appearances, he is the person hurt, since he, too, is the person deceived. For if anyone takes a true proposition to be false, the proposition is not hurt, but only the man is deceived. Setting out, then, from these principles, you will meekly bear with a person who reviles you, for you will say upon every occasion, "It seemed so to him."

XLIII

Everything has two handles: one by which it may be borne, another by which it cannot. If your brother acts unjustly, do not lay hold on the affair by the handle of his injustice, for by that it cannot be borne, but rather by the opposite—that he is your brother, that he was brought up with you; and thus you will lay hold on it as it is to be borne.

XLIV

These reasonings have no logical connection: "I am richer than you, therefore I am your superior." "I am more eloquent than you, therefore I am your superior." The true logical connection is rather this: "I am richer than you, therefore my possessions must exceed yours." "I am more eloquent than you, therefore my style must surpass yours." But you, after all, consist neither in property nor in style.

XLV

Does anyone bathe hastily? Do not say that he does it ill, but hastily. Does anyone drink much wine? Do not say that he does ill, but that he drinks a great deal. For unless you perfectly understand his motives, how should you know if he acts ill? Thus you will not risk yielding to any appearances but such as you fully comprehend.

XLVI

Never proclaim yourself a philosopher, nor make much talk among the ignorant about your principles, but show them by actions. Thus, at an entertainment, do not discourse how people ought to eat, but eat as you ought. For remember that thus Socrates also universally avoided all ostentation. And when persons came to him and desired to be introduced by him to philosophers, he took them and introduced them; so well did he bear being overlooked. So if ever there should be among the ignorant any discussion of principles, be for the most part silent. For there is great danger in hastily throwing out what is undigested. And if anyone tells you that you know nothing, and you are not nettled at it, then you may be sure that you have really entered on your work. For sheep do not hastily throw up the grass to show the shepherds how much they have eaten, but, inwardly digesting their food, they produce it outwardly in wool and milk. Thus, therefore, do you not make an exhibition before the ignorant of your principles, but of the actions to which their digestion gives rise.

XLVII

When you have learned to nourish your body frugally, do not pique yourself upon it; nor, if you drink water, be saying upon every occasion, "I drink water." But first consider how much more frugal are the poor than we, and how much more patient of hardship. If at any time you would inure yourself by exercise to labor and privation, for your own sake and not for the public, do not attempt great feats; but when you are violently thirsty, just rinse your mouth with water, and tell nobody.

XLVIII

The condition and characteristic of a vulgar person is that he never looks for either help or harm from himself, but only from externals. The condition and characteristic of a philosopher is that he looks to himself for all help or harm. The marks of a proficient are that he censures no one, praises no one, blames no one, accuses no one; says nothing concerning himself as being anybody or knowing anything. When he is in any instance hindered or restrained, he accuses himself; and if he is praised, he smiles to himself at the person who praises him; and if he is censured, he makes no defense. But he goes about with the caution of a convalescent, careful of interference with anything that is doing well but not yet quite secure. He restrains desire; he transfers his aversion to those things only which thwart the proper use of our own will; he employs his energies moderately in all directions; if he appears stupid or ignorant, he does not care; and, in a word, he keeps watch over himself as over an enemy and one in ambush.

XLIX

When anyone shows himself vain on being able to understand and interpret the works of Chrysippus, say to yourself: "Unless Chrysippus had written obscurely, this person would have had nothing to be vain of.

But what do I desire? To understand nature, and follow her. I ask, then, who interprets her; and hearing that Chrysippus does, I have recourse to him. I do not understand his writings. I seek, therefore, one to interpret *them.*" So far there is nothing to value myself upon. And when I find an interpreter, what remains is to make use of his instructions. This alone is the valuable thing. But if I admire merely the interpretation, what do I become more than a grammarian, instead of a philosopher, except, indeed, that instead of Homer I interpret Chrysippus? When anyone, therefore, desires me to read Chrysippus to him, I rather blush when I cannot exhibit actions that are harmonious and consonant with his discourse.

L

Whatever rules you have adopted, abide by them as laws, and as if you would be impious to transgress them; and do not regard what anyone says of you, for this, after all, is no concern of yours. How long, then, will you delay to demand of yourself the noblest improvements, and in no instance to transgress the judgments of reason? You have received the philosophic principles with which you ought to be conversant; and you have been conversant with them. For what other master, then, do you wait as an excuse for this delay in self-reformation? You are no longer a boy but a grown man. If, therefore, you will be negligent and slothful, and always add procrastination to procrastination, purpose to purpose, and fix day after day in which you will attend to yourself, you will insensibly continue to accomplish nothing and, living and dying, remain of vulgar mind. This instant, then, think yourself worthy of living as a man grown up and a proficient. Let whatever appears to be the best be to you an inviolable law. And if any instance of pain or pleasure, glory or disgrace, be set before you, remember that now is the combat, now the Olympiad comes on, nor can it be put off; and that by one failure and defeat honor may be lost or—won. Thus Socrates became perfect, improving himself by everything, following reason alone. And though you are not yet a Socrates, you ought, however, to live as one seeking to be a Socrates.

LI

The first and most necessary topic in philosophy is the practical application of principles, as, We *ought not to lie;* the second is that of demonstrations as, Why *it is that we ought not to lie;* the third, that which gives strength and logical connection to the other two, as, Why *this is a demon-*

stration. For what is demonstration? What is a consequence? What a contradiction? What truth? What falsehood? The third point is then necessary on account of the second; and the second on account of the first. But the most necessary, and that whereon we ought to rest, is the first. But we do just the contrary. For we spend all our time on the third point and employ all our diligence about that, and entirely neglect the first. Therefore, at the same time that we lie, we are very ready to show how it is demonstrated that lying is wrong.

Upon all occasions we ought to have these maxims ready at hand:

> Conduct me, Zeus, and thou, O Destiny,
> Wherever your decrees have fixed my lot.
> I follow cheerfully; and, did I not,
> Wicked and wretched, I must follow still.[2]

> Who'er yields properly to Fate is deemed
> Wise among men, and knows the laws of Heaven.[3]

And this third:

> O Crito, if it thus pleases the gods, thus let it be.[4]
> Anytus and Meletus may kill me indeed; but hurt me they cannot.[5]

---

2. Cleanthes, in Diogenes Laertius, quoted also by Seneca, *Epistle* 107.
3. Euripides, Fragment 965.
4. Plato, *Crito* [See *Great Books of the Western World*, Vol. 7, p. 213 (Ed.)].
5. Plato, *Apology* [See *Great Books of the Western World*, Vol. 7, p. 206 (Ed.)].

Translated by Thomas W. Higginson.

Walter Horatio Pater

1839–1894

Walter Pater was born in England on August 4, 1839. His father, Richard, came from a Dutch family and was born in New York; he had moved to England several years before Walter's birth. Walter was educated at the King's School, Canterbury, and at Queen's College, Oxford. He remained at Oxford as a private tutor until 1864, when he was elected a fellow of Brasenose College. In 1868 his essay *Aesthetic Poetry* appeared in the *Fortnightly Review;* it was followed by critical essays on Leonardo, Pico, Botticelli, Michelangelo, and others. These were collected in a volume, *Studies in the History of the Renaissance,* which appeared in 1873. The celebrated "Conclusion" to this work is reprinted below.

Pater now became the center of a small circle of critics and aestheticians; the Pre-Raphaelites were among his friends. He published a novel, *Marius the Epicurean,* in 1885. This was hailed by his followers as the gospel of a new movement; it advocated devotion to an aesthetic ideal of life, and its perfection of style and calm elevation of tone lent force to the claim. Pater continued to write, publishing a series of philosophical essays in fictional form in 1887 called *Imaginary Portraits,* and in 1893 the critical work *Plato and Platonism.* In his later life Pater returned to the religious fervor of his youth, and it is said that if he had lived he might have taken orders. He died, however, on July 30, 1894, at the age of fifty-four. Two volumes of his essays and a novel were published after his death, and the collected edition of his writings appeared in 1901.

The highest goal of human beings, according to Plato and Aristotle, is disinterested intellectual contemplation. For Epicurus and Lucretius, the ideal of life was mild pleasure exempt from pain and trouble. Neither ideal, as Pater saw, excluded a certain *intensity* of experience. Intellectual contemplation was for him no mere passive beholding of truth; it also involved the joy of discovery. There was an exquisite poise and ardor in the gentle, undemanding friendships of the Epicureans, and courage in their acceptance of nature, which was conceived to be indifferent to man and his fate.

Pater developed and exaggerated this element in Epicureanism in his *Marius the Epicurean*. In Plato's doctrine, Pater emphasized the soul's reckless ascent to the highest truth and beauty and to the most intense experience. What gives value to life, he insisted, are the ecstasies, the high moments of realization. Humdrum virtues and mediocre achievements are a weariness. "Hitch your wagon to a star," as Emerson said. Think nothing of the sacrifice; be contented only with the finest—the finest phrase, the finest composition and color—the most consummate style in whatever you do.

The Renaissance was a subject to Pater's taste. Never before in history, except for a short period in Athens, had so many geniuses accumulated in one small peninsula. In spite of the suffering due to disease, internal wars, and invasions, life reached a feverish pitch of creative achievement. Pater could point to Renaissance Italy as a living model of his ideal.

In the "Conclusion" of this book, he tells us that the way to success in life is to pass quickly from ecstasy to ecstasy. It is "to burn always with this hard, gemlike flame." Like Rousseau, in his *Émile*, Pater thinks it is the forming of habits which robs us of spontaneity. If we are to maintain ecstasy, he says, we must avoid these stereotypes.

---

*Notes from the artist: "The figure of Lorenzo de' Medici
and the quotation from* Studies in the History of the Renaissance
*surmount the portrait of Pater, while below, at the right,
is a small head of the Greek philosopher Heraclitus,
an important influence on Pater's thought."*

For art comes to you, proposing frankly to give nothing but the highest quality to your moments as they pass, and simply for those moments' sake.

Pater

The Art of Life

from *The Renaissance*

To regard all things and principles of things as inconstant modes or fashions has more and more become the tendency of modern thought. Let us begin with that which is without—our physical life. Fix upon it in one of its more exquisite intervals, the moment, for instance, of delicious recoil from the flood of water in summer heat. What is the whole physical life in that moment but a combination of natural elements to which science gives their names? But those elements, phosphorus and lime and delicate fibres, are present not in the human body alone: we detect them in places most remote from it. Our physical life is a perpetual motion of them—the passage of the blood, the waste and repairing of the lenses of the eye, the modification of the tissues of the brain under every ray of light and sound—processes which science reduces to simpler and more elementary forces. Like the elements of which we are composed, the action of these forces extends beyond us: it rusts iron and ripens corn. Far out on every side of us those elements are broadcast, driven in many currents; and birth and gesture and death and the springing of violets from the grave are but a few out of ten thousand resultant combinations. That clear, perpetual outline of face and limb is but an image of ours, under which we group them—a design in a web, the actual threads of which pass out beyond it. This at least of flame-like our life has, that it is but the concurrence, renewed from moment to moment, of forces parting sooner or later on their ways.

Or, if we begin with the inward world of thought and feeling, the whirlpool is still more rapid, the flame more eager and devouring. There it is no longer the gradual darkening of the eye, the gradual fading of colour from the wall—movements of the shore-side, where the water flows down indeed, though in apparent rest—but the race of the mid-stream, a drift of momentary acts of sight and passion and thought. At first sight experience seems to bury us under a flood of external objects, pressing upon us with a sharp and importunate reality, calling us out of ourselves in a thousand forms of action. But when reflection begins to play upon those objects they are dissipated under its influence; the cohesive force seems suspended like some trick of magic; each object is loosed into a group of impressions—colour, odour, texture—in the mind of the observer. And if we continue to dwell in thought on this world, not of objects in the solidity with which language invests them, but of impressions, unstable, flickering, inconsistent, which burn and are extinguished with our consciousness of them, it contracts still further; the whole scope of observation is dwarfed into the narrow chamber of the individual mind. Experience, already reduced to a group of impressions, is ringed round for each one of us by that thick wall of personality through which no real voice has ever pierced on its way to us, or from us to that which we can only conjecture to be without. Every one of those impressions is the impression of the individual in his isolation, each mind keeping as a solitary prisoner its own dream of a world. Analysis goes a step farther still, and assures us that those impressions of the individual mind to which, for each one of us, experience dwindles down, are in perpetual flight; that each of them is limited by time, and that as time is infinitely divisible, each of them is infinitely divisible also; all that is actual in it being a single moment, gone while we try to apprehend it, of which it may ever be more truly said that it has ceased to be than that it is. To such a tremulous wisp constantly reforming itself on the stream, to a single sharp impression, with a sense in it, a relic more or less fleeting, of such moments gone by, what is real in our life fines itself down. It is with this movement, with the passage and dissolution of impressions, images, sensations, that analysis leaves off—that continual vanishing away, that strange, perpetual weaving and unweaving of ourselves.

Philosophiren, says Novalis, *ist dephlegmatisiren, vivificiren*. The service of philosophy, of speculative culture, towards the human spirit, is to rouse, to startle it to a life of constant and eager observation. Every moment some form grows perfect in hand or face; some tone on the hills or the sea is choicer than the rest; some mood of passion or insight or intellectual excitement is irresistibly real and attractive to us—for that moment only. Not the fruit of experience, but experience itself, is the end. A counted number of pulses only is given to us of a variegated, dramatic life. How may we see in them all that is to be seen in them by the finest senses? How shall we pass most swiftly from point to point, and be present always at the focus where the greatest number of vital forces unite in their purest energy?

To burn always with this hard, gemlike flame, to maintain this ecstasy, is success in life. In a sense it might even be said that our failure is to form habits: for, after all, habit is relative to a stereotyped world, and meantime it is only the roughness of the eye that makes any two persons, things, situations, seem alike. While all melts under our feet, we may well grasp at any exquisite passion, or any contribution to knowledge that seems by a lifted horizon to set the spirit free for a moment, or any stirring of the senses, strange dyes, strange colours, and curious odours, or work of the artist's hands, or the face of one's friend. Not to discriminate every moment some passionate attitude in those about us, and in the very brilliancy of their gifts some tragic dividing of forces on their ways, is, on this short day of frost and sun, to sleep before evening. With this sense of the splendour of our experience and of its awful brevity, gathering all we are into one desperate effort to see and touch, we shall hardly have time to make theories about the things we see and touch. What we have to do is to be for ever curiously testing new opinions and courting new impressions, never acquiescing in a facile orthodoxy of Comte, or of Hegel, or of our own. Philosophical theories or ideas, as points of view, instruments of criticism, may help us to gather up what might otherwise pass unregarded by us. "Philosophy is the microscope of thought." The theory or idea or system which requires of us the sacrifice of any part of this experience, in consideration of some interest into which we cannot enter, or some abstract theory we have not identified with ourselves, or of what is only conventional, has no real claim upon us.

One of the most beautiful passages of Rousseau is that in the sixth book of the *Confessions*, where he describes the awakening in him of the literary sense. An undefinable taint of death had clung always about him, and now in early manhood he believed himself smitten by mortal disease. He asked himself how he might make as much as possible of the interval that remained; and he was not biased by anything in his previous life when he decided that it must be by intellectual excitement, which he found just then in the clear, fresh writings of Voltaire. Well! we are all *condamnés* as Victor Hugo says: we are all under sentence of death but with a sort of indefinite reprieve—*les hommes sont tous condamnés à mort avec des sursis indéfinis*—we have an interval, and then our place knows us no more. Some spend this interval in listlessness, some in high passions, the wisest, at least among "the children of this world," in art and song. For our one chance lies in expanding that interval in getting as many pulsations as possible into the given time. Great passions may give us this quickened sense of life, ecstasy and sorrow of love, the various forms of enthusiastic activity, disinterested or otherwise, which come naturally to many of us. Only be sure it is passion—that it does yield you this fruit of a quickened, multiplied consciousness. Of such wisdom, the poetic passion, the desire of beauty, the love of art for its own sake, has most. For art comes to you proposing frankly to give nothing but the highest quality to your moments as they pass, and simply for those moments' sake.

The foregoing is the concluding section of Walter Pater's THE RENAISSANCE.

Plutarch [1]

c. 46–120

The essay that follows is often titled *On Tranquillity*. But the tranquil person is, perhaps, a more passive and resigned one than the ideal of Plutarch. In any event, *Contentment* seems to be closer in meaning to the Greek title of the piece. That is, therefore, the title chosen by the present translator.

What is contentment? Who is the contented man? He is, first of all, what might be called a sensible person. He does not covet the impossible; he recognizes the limitations that exist in the world and in the human beings with whom he must deal if he is to live at all. "The business entrusted to your administration," Plutarch says to Paccius, the friend to whom he addresses the essay, "is in large part served not by straightforward and upright characters, like tools suited to a job, but by uneven and crooked tools." He urges Paccius to "use them for what they are." The man who constantly bewails the fact that the world is disappointing cannot be content. He is disappointed because he expected too much. He should have known that nothing is perfect.

On the other hand, one cannot be content, either, if he underestimates the world. Contentment is not to be found, Plutarch says, in total resignation, in retirement. One who avoids all public or private business for the sake of contentment is like the man in Euripides' *Orestes* who was ordered to go to bed and stay there, as if this would cure all his ailments. Or he would be like Achilles, sitting beside the ships, "a useless burden upon the earth." Contentment is not obtainable simply by avoiding trouble.

To retire from life is cowardly and, besides, involves a betrayal of

---

[1] For a biography of Plutarch, see Vol. 7, pp. 93–95, in this set.

one's friends. The truly contented man is one who is active in the world's and in his own business. He must, nevertheless, regard blessings as probably transitory, and he must be willing and able to accept their loss with equanimity. "No man alive can say," Plutarch quotes Menander as reminding us, " 'This shall not happen to me.' " It is nonsense to insist that no harm can befall the good man. Of course it can. But the good man can remain content even in the face of disaster. Even death should not be feared. Death is not something to be constantly worrying about. Anyone can imagine circumstances in which it would constitute a change for the better.

Contentment depends on reason and knowledge. The soul must be schooled; "sensible people should rehearse" arguments which are specifics for the passions "before the passions arise to have them in stock for greater effectiveness." Fundamentally, "the culprit is self-love." Reason tells us that we may expect bad things as well as good, but self-love deludes us into thinking that the universe was created for our sake alone. One who believes that will soon be disappointed.

There is only one emotion that reason cannot control and overcome, Plutarch says, and that is regret. But even regret can be lessened if we act well, for then we will have little to regret. Thus contentment is far from a passive state of the soul. The contented man, like the virtuous one, is the man who not only avoids bad deeds, but who also does good ones. To him, Plutarch ends by saying, life is everywhere and at all times a festival. He can "face the future without apprehension or misgivings but with hope glad and shining."

The task of telling us how to be contented is as important as it is difficult. We all want to be contented but are often impatient of advice, especially when we are told to steel ourselves for reverses and to be untroubled when they come. Young people, it is said, have to learn for themselves. But would we learn as well if not prepared by past warnings? On the other hand, does not Plutarch demand too much? How can we be expected to be contented in the midst of disaster or heartbreak? And perhaps discontent would show us a better way out of it than contentment can. In any case, Plutarch's recipe for contentment prompts us to face up to the subject ourselves.

Contentment

Greetings and good wishes, my dear Paccius. It is only a short while since I received your letter urging me to write you a piece on contentment and one on points in Plato's *Timaeus* which require careful exegesis. At the same time it happened that our friend Eros was obliged to make a trip to Rome; he had received a characteristically peremptory summons from that splendid fellow Fundanus. I hadn't the leisure I would have liked to comply with your request, and at the same time could not have a visitor from me call upon you empty handed, and so I have put together notes on contentment which I had made for my own use, in the conviction that what you desired was not a polished literary composition but something that would be serviceable and helpful. Happily, though you are on terms of intimacy with great personages and enjoy an unsurpassed reputation as a public speaker, you have not fared like Merops in the tragedy, whom "the admiring crowd made oblivious" to normal reactions. You bear in mind what you have repeatedly heard, that gout is not relieved by a fine shoe nor a hangnail by a costly ring nor migraine by a tiara. How can money or reputation or power at court contribute to serenity of spirit and untroubled life unless men find their presence agreeable and do not always miss their absence? And what but reason can train and habituate us promptly to arrest the irrational and passionate part of the soul as often as it rebels and not suffer it to overflow and be swept away because of a momentary situation? Xenophon counsels us to be particularly mindful of the gods and honor them when we prosper so that in time of need we can call upon them with the assurance that they are friendly and favorably disposed. It is the same with arguments which are specifics for the passions: sensible people should rehearse them before the passions arise to have them in stock for greater effectiveness. Mastiffs bristle at every voice and are quieted only by the one they are used to; similarly the passions of the soul are not easily laid when they grow restive unless there are familiar and firmly held arguments ready to check their rioting.

"A man who would attain contentment," it has been said, "must not become involved in business private or public." In the first place, contentment comes very dear if its price is inactivity. It is like the advice to the invalid, "Stay in bed and don't move, poor fellow"; [1] lethargy is a bad remedy for an ailing frame. But a psychiatrist does no better if he prescribes sloth and effeminacy and betrayal of friends and relatives and country as a cure for a perturbed and distressed soul. In the second place, it is not true that persons not involved in business are even tempered. In that case women, whose chief concern is housekeeping, should be more even tempered than men; but the fact is that though, as Hesiod says, the north wind "blows not upon the tender flesh of a maiden," the women's apartment is assailed by more distress and disturbance and depression than you could count because of their jealousy and superstition and ambition and empty notions. Laertes spent twenty years on a farm by himself "with a crone to serve him food and drink," [2] but though he forsook his country and house and kingship, distress, along with inactivity and depression, kept house with him. Some people idleness reduces to moping, as in this case:

> But he continued in anger, sitting beside the swift ships,
> The Zeus-descended son of Peleus, swift-footed Achilles.
> Nor ever would he attend the man-honoring assembly
> Nor ever go to war, but wasted his heart, remaining there
> And longed for the battle cry and for war.[3]

Achilles himself avows that it makes him uneasy and fidgety: "Here I sit beside the ships, a useless burden upon the earth." [4] That is why even Epicurus holds that men who are ambitious for distinction should not keep inactive but fulfill their nature by participating in politics and public business; such men are disposed to suffer greater perturbation by reason of inactivity if they fail to reach their goals. But the absurdity of the position lies in urging a public career not on those capable of it, but on those incapable of inactivity. Contentment or its reverse should be defined not by the volume of a man's occupations but by their noble or base

1. Euripides, *Orestes*, 258. [Cf. *Great Books of the Western World*, Vol. 5, p. 396 (Ed.).]
2. Odyssey, I, 191. [Cf. *Great Books of the Western World*, Vol. 4, p. 185 (Ed.).]
3. *Iliad*, I, 488 ff. [Cf. *Great Books of the Western World*, Vol. 4, p. 8 (Ed.).]
4. *Iliad*, XVIII, 104. [Cf. *Great Books of the Western World*, Vol. 4, p. 131 (Ed.).]

quality, for, as has been remarked, the omission of good is no less reprehensible than the commission of evil.

Some specify one particular life, such as the farmer's, the bachelor's, the king's, as being free of vexation. For such Menander's lines are sufficient admonition:

> I imagined, Phanias, that rich men
> Who need not borrow or groan
> Through the night and toss and turn
> And cry Alack! could sleep sweet
> And soft.

He goes on to observe that rich and poor fare exactly alike:

> Grief must be fused with life.
> It subsists with a luxurious life,
> It attends a famous life,
> It grows old with a needy life.

Timorous and seasick voyagers imagine their plight would be eased if they transferred from a sloop to a merchantman and then from a merchantman to a warship; but their efforts are futile because they carry their bile and their squeamishness with them. So changing one career for another does not relieve the soul of the factors which vex and perturb it—inexperience, unreasonableness, incapacity, and ineptitude in making proper use of what is available. Rich and poor alike are storm tossed by these factors, they infect the unmarried as well as the married. Because of them men avoid the forum, and then find inactivity intolerable; because of them men seek preferment at court, and when they have attained it find it a burden. "It is being at a loss makes the sick hard to please"; [5] their wives annoy them, they find fault with the doctor, they are dissatisfied with the bed, and "a visitor is a nuisance when he comes and a burden when he goes," as Ion puts it. But when the disease is broken and supplanted by a different condition, access of health makes everything welcome and agreeable; a man who choked on eggs and rusks and crisp rolls yesterday eagerly relishes a coarse loaf with olives and water cress today.

Just such a cheerful change can be introduced into any life by reason. Alexander burst into tears when he heard Anaxarchus speak of an infinity of worlds, and when his friends asked what the matter was, he said: "When worlds are infinite is not our failure to master even one worth

---

5. Euripides, *Orestes*, 232. [Cf. *Great Books of the Western World*, Vol. 5, p. 396 (Ed.).]

crying about?" Yet Crates, with only scrip and poncho, went through life jesting and laughing as if it were a frolic. Agamemnon himself found it troublesome to rule many subjects:

> Agamemnon you must know, Atreus' son, upon whom
> Beyond all men Zeus laid never-ending cares.[6]

But Diogenes sprawled on the block and jeered the auctioneer, and when he ordered him to stand, Diogenes laughed and teased him: "What if you were selling a fish?" Socrates in jail philosophized with his friends; Phaethon mounted to heaven wept because no one would give him his father's horses and chariot. A shoe turns with the foot, not vice versa, and likewise dispositions mold lives to their own fashion. It is not habit, as has been alleged, that makes the best life sweet to those who have chosen it, but it is intelligence which makes a life at once best and sweetest. We should therefore purge the source of contentment which is in ourselves, so that externals also, like familiar things which are our own and which we do not abuse, may profit us.

> It is futile to rail at circumstances
> For they are indifferent. He shall fare well
> Who confronts circumstances aright.

Plato likened life to a game of dice, where we must make an advantageous throw, and then make proper use of whatever falls. The first of these, the advantageous throw, is not in our discretion; but to receive what fate allots properly, to assign each item a place where what we like will do most good and what we dislike least harm—that *is* our function if we are wise. Men who approach life without craftsmanship and intelligence are like sick people who can tolerate neither heat nor cold; prosperity elates them and adversity dejects them. They are perturbed by either lot, or rather by themselves in either lot, and no less in so-called prosperity than in the other. Theodorus called the Atheist used to say that he offered his discourses with his right hand and his hearers received them with the left; the uncultured often show their awkwardness by giving Fortune a left-handed reception when she makes a dextrous presentation. But sensible people behave like bees; bees get honey from thyme, which is very tart and dry, and sensible people often get something appropriate and useful to themselves from the most untoward situation.

This should be the first exercise to practice—like the man who missed the dog with his throw but hit his stepmother: "Not so bad," said he. It *is*

---

6. *Iliad*, X, 88 f. [Cf. *Great Books of the Western World*, Vol. 4, p. 66 (Ed.).]

possible to divert Fortune from what is unwelcome. Diogenes was banished: "Not so bad"; after he was banished he began to philosophize. Zeno of Citium had one freighter left, and when he heard that it too had foundered with its cargo he remarked, "Well done, Fortune! You have driven me to Stoicism." What prevents us from imitating such models? Your election campaign has miscarried? You shall live in the country and mind your own business. You courted some grandee and were snubbed? You shall be free of jeopardy and distraction. Are you again in some activity which involves time and worry? "Hot water does not so soothe the joints," in the words of Pindar, as fame and respect, and a modicum of power makes "Exertion sweet and toil well spent."[7] Has malice or envy confronted you with insult and abuse? It is a tail wind that wafts you to the Muses and the Academy, as it was for Plato when Dionysius' friendship broke into a tempest.

This too—the example of famous men who were not affected by adversity—will contribute greatly to contentment. For example, is childlessness a vexation? Consider the kings of Rome, none of whom bequeathed his realm to a son. Are you irked by actual poverty? Is there any Boeotian you would prefer to be rather than Epaminondas, any Roman rather than Fabricius? "But my wife has been seduced." Have you not read the inscription at Delphi, "Placed by Agis, king of sea and land," and have you not heard that Alcibiades seduced Agis' wife Timaia, and that she whispered to her servants that her baby's name was Alcibiades? But this did not prevent Alcibiades from becoming the greatest and most illustrious of the Greeks. Nor did his daughter's debauchery prevent Stilpo from being the most cheerful philosopher of his day. When Metrocles took him to task he said, "Is it my fault or hers?" "Her fault," Metrocles replied, "but your misfortune." "How do you mean?" said Stilpo. "Are not faults slips?" "They are indeed," said Metrocles. "And are not slips debited to those who slip?" Metrocles agreed. "And are not the debits the misfortune of the person debited?" This gentle dialectic demonstrated that the Cynic's scolding was pointless barking.

But most people are irritated and exasperated by the derelictions not only of their friends and relatives but even of their enemies. Upbraiding, irascibility, envy, malevolence, and malignant jealousy pertain only to persons ridden by these pests, and they do burden and exacerbate thoughtless people—neighbors' squabbling, friends' moping, malfeasance of officials in the discharge of their office are examples. I place you high in the

---

7. Euripides, *The Bacchantes*, 66. [Cf. *Great Books of the Western World*, Vol. 5, p. 340 (Ed.).]

list of people bothered by such conduct; like the doctors in Sophocles who "Bitter bile with bitter medicine purge" so you show indignation and exasperation to match their passion and distemper. This is illogical. The business entrusted to your administration is in large part served not by straightforward and upright characters, like tools suited to a job, but by uneven and crooked tools. Do not imagine it is your responsibility to straighten them out, or that it is easy to do. But if you use them for what they are, as a doctor uses dental forceps or surgical clips, and comfort yourself with the calmness and moderation the situation requires, the pleasure you take in your own deportment will be greater than your vexation at the crudeness and depravity of others. You will think that they are only fulfilling their nature, like dogs that bark, and no longer unwillingly concentrate a mass of vexation in a petty and impotent spirit, like scum which flows into a low and hollow sink, and is bound to infect you with others' woes. Some philosophers reprehend even pity bestowed on unfortunates, arguing that to help a neighbor is charity, but that to share his sorrow and surrender to it is not. More than this, when we realize that we are at fault and in a bad state these philosophers forbid us to be disheartened or distressed but enjoin us to apply a proper and objective cure to our malady; consider how unreasonable it is, then, to allow ourselves to be grieved and dejected because not everyone who has business with us or calls on us is an honest gentleman! Take care, my dear Paccius, that our general repugnance to the wickedness we encounter be not an unwitting and timid pretext for love of self, rather than hatred of evil. Vehement concern for politics, and either excessive appetite and pursuit or excessive distaste and revulsion, beget brooding suspicions against men we think deprived us of some things or thrust us into others. The man who has learned to accommodate himself to public business easily and dispassionately turns out to be very affable and gentle in his intercourse with his fellow men.

But we must revert to our proper subject. In a state of fever anything we taste seems bitter and disagreeable, but when we see others relishing these things without a wry face we no longer blame the food and drink but ourselves and our distemper; so we shall desist from finding fault and being provoked with circumstances if we see others accepting the same conditions calmly and cheerfully. When things fall out not according to our liking it will contribute to our contentment if we bethink us of the agreeable and charming things that are ours; in the mixture the better will eclipse the worse. When our eyes are dazzled by excessive glare we soothe them by turning to green grass and flowers, but our mind we keep intent on what is painful and force it to brood over vexation without respite, all but violently wrenching it from more comforting thoughts. This is an apt context for the remark made to the busybody in the play:

> Why, evil-eyed fellow, look you so keen
> On another's evil and turn a blind eye
> To your own?

Why, my good man, do you stare at your own evil so narrowly and make it vivid and conspicuous, but fail to turn your attention to the good things you have? You concentrate the worst of your qualities against yourself as cupping concentrates the worst humors to draw them out of the body. You are no better than the Chian who sold fine old wine to other people but looked for sour to take with his meal; when one of his slaves asked another what the master was doing when he left, the reply was, "Looking for bad when good is available."

The majority do indeed pass by what is potable and good in their own circumstances and rush towards what is troublesome and vexatious. Not so Aristippus; he put the resources he had on the scale, like a good man, and so lightened his woe. He had lost a fine estate, but when a sham friend offered sympathy and condolence he asked the man, "I have three farms left, and you only a plot of ground, I believe?" When his interlocutor agreed, he said, "Then should I not rather condole with you?" To be distressed at what is lost and not rejoice at what is saved is crazy; only a baby will weep and bawl and throw the rest of his toys away if one is taken from him. That is how we behave if, when Fortune has tripped us in one detail, we make all the rest unprofitable by wailing and grieving.

"What do we possess?" a man may ask. What do we not possess? One man has reputation, another a family, another a marriage, another a friend. On his deathbed Antipater of Tarsus made an inventory of the good things that had befallen him, and even included the good trip from Cilicia to Athens. Ordinary things must not be overlooked but taken into account. We ought to be thankful that we are alive and well and see the sun, that there is no war or revolution, that earth and sea lie open for those who wish to till or sail, that we can speak and act or hold our peace and enjoy repose. The presence of these blessings will conduce to our contentment even more if we imagine how it would be if they were not present, if we keep reminding ourselves how the sick yearn for health, men at war for peace, a stranger in the city for friends and reputation, and of how distressing the loss of these things can be. If we do, then we shall not value and cherish these blessings only when we have lost them and depreciate them only when they are safe. Our not having a thing does not raise its value. It is wrong to acquire things in the belief that they are good, to be in constant fear of losing them in the belief that they are good, and yet when we hold them to disregard and despise them as if they were nothing worth. Rather should we use them with pleasure and satisfaction, so that we may easily bear their loss, if that should befall. The majority of men, Arcesilaus remarks, feel obliged to scrutinize other peoples' poems and paintings and statues very carefully, examining each part with mind and eye; but their own lives, which have many features for agreeable contemplation, they overlook. Always they look to other men's reputations and fortunes, as adulterers look to other men's wives, and themselves and their own qualities they despise.

Here is another practice conducive to contentment. It is best, of course, to look to oneself and one's own state, but if not we should contemplate inferiors, and not, as the majority do, compare ourselves with our superiors. Prisoners, for example, regard those released as happy, and these, in turn, freemen, and freemen citizens, and citizens, in turn, the rich, the rich satraps, satraps kings, and kings gods, all but coveting thunder and lightning. Always desiderating what is beyond them, they are never pleased with what they have.

> The wealth of gold-abounding Croesus
>   Is no concern to me;
> Ambition offers no temptation;
>   From envy I am free.
> The gods' affairs I do not question;
>   No monarch would I be.
> I am content, where'er I'm sent
>   With mediocrity.[8]

"A Thasian's sentiment," it will be objected. But there are Chians and Galatians and Bithynians who are dissatisfied with the reputation or power they have got among their countrymen and wail because they cannot sport the patrician badge, and if they can, because they are not praetors, and if they are, because they are not consuls, and if they are, because they were nominated second instead of first. What is this but scraping up excuses for ingratitude to Fortune and penalizing and tormenting oneself? But the sensible man whose thinking is wholesome knows that the sun looks down on untold myriads of men, "As many as enjoy the produce of broad earth" [Simonides], does not sit downhearted and

---

8. Archilochus 25, tr. N. H. Dole.

humiliated because there are some more famous and richer than he, but reflects that his life is better and more respectable than millions of others and goes his way singing hallelujahs to his tutelary deity and to his life.

At Olympia you cannot win by choosing your competitors, but the rules of life allow you to vaunt your superiority over many others, to be enviable rather than envious—unless you set yourself up to rival a Briareus or a Hercules. So whenever you admire a man carried in a sedan chair as being superior, stoop to look at the carriers too. And whenever you call Xerxes blessed, as the Hellespontine did when he saw him crossing the bridge, look at the poor devils digging at Athos under the knout and having their ears and noses cut off because the waves broke the bridge down, and reflect on what is in their mind: they call *your* life and *your* state blessed.

When Socrates heard one of his friends complain that the city was dear—"Chian wine a mina, purple cloth three minae, a dram of honey five drachmas"—he took hold of him and brought him to the grain vendors. "Half a peck for an obol—the city is cheap"; then to the oil men—"A quart for two coppers"; then to the clothing merchants—"A gown for ten drachmas—the city is cheap." So when we hear anyone remark that our situation is mean and irksome because we are not consuls or governors, we can say, "Our situation is brilliant, our life enviable: we are not beggars, or porters, or flatterers."

But folly has habituated us to live with a view to others rather than to ourselves, and our nature holds so much envy and malice that our pleasure in our own advantages is not so great as our distress at others'; it behooves you, therefore, to look not merely at the brilliance and fame of those you envy and admire but to roll back the spangled curtain of their reputation, as it were, strip the veneer off and get inside, and behold the many troublesome and disagreeable aspects of their being. The famous Pittacus, whose courage and wisdom and justice were so widely acclaimed, was entertaining guests when his wife came storming in and overturned the table. His guests were embarrassed, but Pittacus said: "Each of us has his trouble; a man with mine is to be congratulated."

> This man the market place counts happy
> Is a heap of misery when he opens his door:
> His wife is emperor and general and always embattled.
> He has much to vex him, I have naught.

Many such vexations, which wealth and fame and royalty entail, are imperceptible to the commonality, for they are benighted in a fog. For his extrinsic pomp, his arms and horses and warrior host, Agamemnon is felicitated as "Atreides, favored by Fortune's weird"; [9] but from within the voice of his own suffering bears witness against this empty glory: "Zeus son of Cronus has bound me fast in heavy doom," [10] and

> I envy you, old man;
> I envy any man who has passed through life
> Without danger, without fame, without glory.[11]

Such reflections as these will serve to skim off that carping at Fortune which humbles and forfeits our own assets by admiration of our neighbor's.

A very considerable handicap to contentment is our failure to temper our ambition, as a skipper reefs his sails, to the energy available. Our hopes reach out for too much, and when we fail we blame Fortune and doom instead of our own folly. It is not bad luck which prevents a man from practicing archery with a plow or hunting rabbits with an ox, it is not a malignant deity which keeps him from catching stag or boar with fishing tackle; to attempt the impossible is stupid and silly. The culprit is self-love, which impels men to crave primacy and victory in everything and to an irrepressible desire to lay hands on everything. Men not only claim the right to be at once rich and learned and strong and good fellows and agreeable companions and friends of kings and governors of a city, but they are dejected if they do not also own blue-ribbon dogs and horses and quails and cocks.

The elder Dionysius was not content with being the greatest dictator of his time, but because he could not rhyme better than the poet Philoxenus or down Plato in dialectic, he flew into a rage and in his exasperation threw Philoxenus into the stone quarries and sent Plato to Aegina to be sold into slavery. Not so Alexander; when the champion Crison seemed to slacken speed on purpose in a race with him he got very angry. When Achilles says,[12] "Of the bronze-armed Achaeans none is my peer," he subjoins, "In battle; in council others are better." When Megabyzus the Persian visited Apelles' studio and undertook to babble about art, Apelles shut his mouth with the remark: "So long as you held your peace you seemed to be somebody because of your gold and purple, but now the apprentices grinding the colors are laughing at your foolishness."

When some people hear that the Stoics call their sage not only wise and

9. *Iliad*, III, 182. [Cf. *Great Books of the Western World*, Vol. 4, p. 20 (Ed.).]
10. *Iliad*, II, 111. [Cf. *Great Books of the Western World*, Vol. 4, p. 11 (Ed.).]
11. Euripides, *Iphigenia at Aulis*, 16 ff. [Cf. *Great Books of the Western World*, Vol. 5, p. 425 (Ed.).]
12. *Iliad*, XVIII, 105. [Cf. *Great Books of the Western World*, Vol. 4, p. 131 (Ed.).]

just and brave but also an orator, poet, general, millionaire, king, they think it funny, and yet they themselves claim all these graces and are irked if they do not get them. But even among the gods each has his own province; one is styled "of war," another "of prophecy," another "of gain," and Zeus assigns Aphrodite to weddings and the bridal chamber "for that she hath no share in deeds of war."

It is in the nature of certain pursuits that they cannot exist side by side but must be in conflict with one another. For example, practicing declamations and studying mathematics require leisure and freedom from distraction, whereas success as a public official or courtier is impossible without preoccupation and activity. Again, "wine and a meat diet render the body stout and robust, but the soul weak." Constant care and vigilance in money matters augments wealth, but a detached disdain of wealth is an effective viaticum for the road to philosophy. Not everything is for everyone; one must heed the Pythian injunction to know himself and then occupy himself as Nature intended and not override her by compulsive emulation of one mode of life after another. [As Pindar says:]

> The horse is for the chariot, the ox for the plow,
> The dolphin swiftly skims the sea at the vessel's side;
> If a man would slay a boar he must find a rugged hound.

Only a lunatic is impatient and vexed because he is not at once a lion "Mountain-ranging, confident in his strength," [13] and a Maltese lap dog for a widow to pet. Equally silly is the man who would be an Empedocles or Plato or Democritus, writing on the universe and the nature of reality, and at the same time sleep beside an elderly heiress like Euphorion or tipple with Alexander's cronies like Medius, who is indignant and irritated if he is not admired for his wealth like Ismenias and for his courage like Epaminondas. Runners are not downhearted because they do not carry off the wrestler's crown, but take pride and pleasure in their own accomplishment. "Sparta is your portion: cultivate Sparta!" So Solon said:

> We shall not exchange our virtue for their wealth,
> For virtue is stable, whereas money now one has,
> Now another.

When the physicist Strato heard that Menedemus had many more pupils he said: "Is it strange that more people want baths than an athlete's rubdown?" In a letter to Antipater Aristotle writes: "Alexander is not the

---

13. *Odyssey*, VI, 130. [Cf. *Great Books of the Western World*, Vol. 4, p. 215 (Ed.).]

only one entitled to be proud, because he rules many subjects; those whose speculations on theology are correct also have an equal claim." Men who have so high a regard for their own attainments will not be disturbed by the attainments of their neighbors. We do not expect a vine to bear figs or an olive grapes, but when it comes to ourselves, if we do not possess the combined advantages of millionaire and scholar and general and philosopher, of the flatterer and the plain speaker, of the frugal and the extravagant, we calumniate ourselves and are irked with ourselves and despise ourselves as leading a drab and curtailed life.

There is another lesson, which Nature herself teaches. For diverse beasts she has provided diverse sustenance, and has not made them all flesh eaters or seed pickers or root grubbers; for mankind too she has vouchsafed various avenues to a livelihood—"Shepherd, plowman, fowler, him the sea sustains."

Men should choose the calling suited to them, concentrate upon it, and let the others be; they should not take exception to Hesiod's dictum: "Potter envies potter, builder builder."

Actually men do not limit their jealousy to fellow craftsmen and men of their own class, the rich envy the learned, the famous the rich, the lawyers the professors, and freemen and patricians, by Zeus, grow delirious in blessing deft comedians on the stage and ballet dancers and servants in royal courts, thus inflicting no small vexation and unhappiness upon themselves.

Differences in our emotions make it plain that each man holds the cellars of contentment and discontent within himself; the jugs of good things and bad are not deposited "on Zeus' threshold" but in the soul. The foolish overlook and neglect the good things that are there because their imagination is always straining towards the future, but the wise make even things of the past vividly present by recalling them. The present offers itself to our touch for only an instant of time and then eludes the senses; fools think that it is no longer ours, that it no longer pertains to us. There is a painting of a ropemaker in hell with an ass gobbling up all the rope he makes as he plays it out; so the multitude is overtaken and held fast by insensate and ingrate forgetfulness, which erases every deed and every success and every pleasant experience of ease and companionship and enjoyment. It never allows life to grow into a unity, with the past interwoven with the present, but separates yesterday from today as though it were a different substance, and today from tomorrow, as if it were not the same; forgetfulness transforms every occurrence into a nonoccurrence. The logic of the schoolmen who deny the principle of growth on the ground that being is in constant flux would continually transform each of us into a different man; so those who do not retain and cherish the past in memory but allow it to flow away actually make themselves empty and impoverished day by day and dependent upon the morrow, as though all that had occurred yesterday and the day before had not happened at all and had no relevance to them.

If this is one factor that confounds contentment, a greater is when men glide away from what is amiable and easygoing to entangle themselves in memories of disagreeable experiences, like flies that slip off the smooth parts of a mirror and cling to the rough places where there are cracks. Better, like the beetles in Olynthus, which, when they have fallen into a place called Beetles' Doom, cannot get out but twist and turn until they die, so men who have subsided into memory of their misfortunes have no wish to struggle up and breathe free again. We ought to put the bright and attractive in the foreground of our soul, as we do colors in a picture, and de-emphasize or suppress the gloomy; to blot them out or banish them altogether is impossible. "The harmony of the universe is alternately tensed and relaxed, like a lyre or a bow"; and in the affairs of men too nothing is pure and unmixed. In music there are deep notes and shrill, and in grammar vowels and consonants, and the musician or grammarian does not dislike and avoid one or the other but understands how to blend them for his own purpose and use them. In human affairs too there are opposing elements, for as Euripides says:

> Good and bad may not be dissevered;
> There is, as there should be, a commingling.

The one element ought not make us downhearted and despondent; rather like musicians who dull the edge of the bad with the better and swathe the inferior with the good, we ought to make our life a tuneful blend which is appropriate to ourselves.

Menander says,

> Beside each man at his birth there stands a daimon
> To be his good guide through life.

Menander is wrong, and Empedocles has it right: *pairs* of daimons or Norns receive each of us at birth and direct us:

> Earth maiden was there and Sun maiden who sees afar;
> Bloody Strife and stable Harmony,
> Beauty and Ugliness, Haste and Loitering,
> Charming Infallibility and darkling Dubiety.

At birth we receive the seeds of each of these traits in a mixture, which produces marked unevenness. A sensible man prays for the better but anticipates the other as well, and, avoiding extremes, makes use of both. Epicurus remarks that "the man least dependent upon the morrow goes to meet the morrow most cheerfully"; just so do wealth and reputation and power and preferment give the greatest satisfaction to those least apprehensive of their opposites. A vehement desire for these things begets a vehement fear of their not lasting, and this makes the enjoyment of them unstable, like a flickering flame. But if Reason has equipped a man to say to Fortune, without fear or trepidation, "Very nice, if you bring me something; no harm if you do not," his stoutheartedness, the fact that he does not fear that loss would be intolerable, enables him to enjoy his present blessings with the greatest satisfaction.

Upon the death of his son, Anaxagoras said, "I knew I had begotten a mortal." We may not only admire his composure but imitate it and say, when any adversity befalls, "I know that wealth is transitory and impermanent. I know that those who bestow office can take it away. I know that my wife is good, but a woman, and that my friend is a man, a creature naturally changeable, as Plato says." When unwanted (but not unexpected) accidents befall people who have schooled themselves to such composure there is no place for such protestations as, "I would never have thought it. I anticipated something different. I had not expected this." Such composure banishes the leaping and fluttering of the heart and quickly restores its excitement and confusion to stability. In affairs of moment it is solely the element of the unexpected, as Carneades reminds us, that reduces us to distress and despair. The Macedonian Kingdom was a tiny fraction of the size of the Roman Empire, yet when Perseus lost Macedonia he bewailed his loss most bitterly, and everyone regarded him as the most unfortunate and ill starred of men. His conqueror, Aemilius, handed his supreme command by land and sea to his successor, received a wreath and offered sacrifice, and was counted blessed, and rightly. He knew he would relinquish the office he had received, whereas Perseus lost his when he did not expect to. Well has our poet taught us the power of the unexpected: when Odysseus' dog fawned upon him he wept, but when he sat by his tearful wife he showed no such feeling. In the latter case he had come prepared in advance, keeping his emotion under the control of reason, but the former case was a contretemps into which he had fallen suddenly and unexpectedly.

Of unwelcome occurrences, generally speaking, some naturally entail grief and vexation, but in the case of most a false conception has schooled and habituated us to be irked by them. As a specific against the latter it is advisable to keep a line of Menander handy: "Nothing has happened to you unless you make much of it." His meaning is that your body and soul need not be affected if, for example, your father is lowborn, your wife taken in adultery, yourself deprived of some honorary crown or front-seat privilege, for none of these prevents a man from thriving in physique or psyche. For the former category—sickness, hardship, the death of friends or of children—which seem naturally to entail grief and vexation, the line of Euripides should be kept handy: "Alas!—but why Alas? It is the lot of mortality we experience." No logic can so effectively brake the descending spiral of our emotions as the reflection that it is only through the common compulsion of Nature, which is an element in his physical constitution, that man is vulnerable to Fortune; in his most essential and greatest aspects he stands secure.

When Demetrius took the Megarians' city he asked Stilpo whether any of his goods had been looted. "I saw no one going off with *my* goods," said Stilpo. When Fortune plunders and confiscates all else we still have within us a thing "such as Achaeans can neither rape nor plunder." It follows that we must not underrate and dismiss Nature as being incapable of prevailing over or even withstanding Fortune. On the contrary, we know that the corruptible and unresisting part of man which is vulnerable to Fortune is small, whereas we ourselves are masters of the better part in which are firmly fixed the greatest of our goods—right opinions and knowledge and reasoning whose consummation is virtue—which can neither be alienated nor destroyed. Undismayed and with hearts courageous we face what is to be and say to Fortune what Socrates said to his judges when he was ostensibly speaking to his accusers: "Anytus and Meletus can kill me, they cannot harm me." Fortune can infect a man with sickness, take his money away, malign him to his countrymen or a tyrant; but she cannot make a good and virile and high-spirited man a poltroon or mean spirited or ignoble or envious, nor can she rob us of the serenity whose permanent availability is more useful for facing life than a pilot is for facing the sea. No pilot can calm rough wave and wind, or find a haven at will for his need, nor abide what is to be without fear and trepidation. So long as he has not despaired, he uses his skill

> To escape the hellish sea,
> Mainsail lashed at mast's bottom;

but when the sea shows its strength he sits shivering and shaking. But a wise man's serenity affords an expanse of calm to the bodily factors. By self-control and a prudent way of life and moderate exertion, he banishes susceptibility to disease; and if trouble of an outside origin befalls he skims by the reefs "riding a poised and light beam," as Asclepiades says. But if some great and extraordinary calamity overtakes and masters him, then a haven is ready at hand and he can swim from his body as from a boat with seams opened.

It is fear of death, not craving for life, that makes a fool hang on to his body and wind himself about it as Odysseus clung to the fig tree for fear of lurking Charybdis. "The gale suffers him neither to halt nor sail"; he is displeased with what is, and afraid of the alternative. But a man who has attained an understanding of the soul and has calculated that death may be a change for the better, but certainly not for the worse, has in indifference to death no inconsiderable resource for facing life with contentment. A man who can lead an agreeable life when the satisfactory and congenial element is in the ascendant and depart fearlessly when the uncongenial and unnatural assail him and say, "The god will himself release me whensoever I will," [14] is impregnable to any imaginable difficulty or distemper or agitation. It was not bolts or bars or walls that gave his confidence to the man who said, "I have forestalled you, Fortune; I have blocked your every access to me"; it was by precepts and doctrines which are available to everyone. Utterances of this kind should not be dismissed or distrusted; one should admire and emulate and be inspired by them to put himself to the proof, testing himself in lesser matters as preparation for greater, not evading or thrusting away the care of the soul or taking refuge in the thought that "probably nothing too disagreeable will happen." The luxury-loving soul which is preoccupied with what is easiest and retreats from what it doesn't like to what is most agreeable begets nervelessness and undisciplined effeminacy. But the soul which devotes study and the inexorable force of logic to formulate a detailed conception of what disease and hardship and exile are will find much that is spurious and empty and unsound in things seemingly difficult and formidable. Reason will demonstrate this in every case.

And yet Menander's line—"No man alive can say, 'This shall not happen to me'"—terrifies many people because they do not realize how much it contributes to serenity to train oneself to be able to look Fortune in the face with eyes wide open and not to foster in oneself fancies dainty and soft, embowered in the shade of many hopes which yield to every pressure and offer resistance to none. We can indeed agree with Menander's "This

---

14. Euripides, *The Bacchantes*, 498. [Cf. *Great Books of the Western World*, Vol. 5, p. 344 (Ed.).]

shall not happen to me," and declare, while we are men alive, "This I shall not do: I shall not lie, nor cheat, nor defraud, nor conspire." This lies within our power, and it is no slight contribution to contentment but a very great one. On the other hand,

> My conscience, my own awareness
> That I have committed a wrong

leaves behind in the soul, like an ulcer in the flesh, a trauma which always aches and draws blood. Other pangs reason can allay, but reason is the very thing that produces regret; it is the soul and its sense of shame that gnaws and scourges itself. The shivering and burning caused by ague or fever are more annoying and distressing than heat or cold from an outside source; similarly the darts of Fortune inflict lighter pain for they assail us from without. But the dirge we keen over offenses that issue from within ourselves—

> None other than I is to blame for these things;
> I myself am guilty—

exacerbates the pain by compounding it with shame.

It follows that no costly mansion, no mass of gold, no pride of race, no grandeur of office, no charm or force of eloquence can bestow upon life so clear skied a serenity as a soul purged of evil deeds and thoughts which keeps as the fountain of life a character imperturbable and untainted. From this fountain flow fair deeds which combine inspired and glad activity carried on with a high heart and a memory sweeter and solider than that Pindar speaks of as sustaining old age. "Even when they are emptied," says Carneades, "censers retain their bouquet for a long while"; and in the soul of a sensible man fair deeds leave behind a memory always pleasing and always fresh. By this memory satisfaction in fair deeds is kept watered, so that it thrives and despises such as bewail life and complain of it as a domain of evil or a place of exile appointed for souls in this world.

I like what Diogenes said when he saw his Spartan host outdoing himself in preparing for a certain festival: "Isn't every day a festival in the sight of a good man?" And a very splendid festival if we have good sense. The universe is a temple of the highest holiness and sanctity. Into this temple his birth introduces man as a beholder not of images made by man and incapable of movement but of such as the divine intelligence has revealed as imitations of ideas perceptible to the senses, in Plato's language, with the source of life and movement inherent in them—the sun and the moon and the stars and the rivers which continually send forth new water and the earth which continually sends up sustenance for plants and animals. Life is an initiation and consummation of these mysteries and should therefore be filled with contentment and joy. We should not, like the crowd, wait for such occasions as the Cronia and Diasia and Panathenaea and the like to take pleasure and recreation, purchasing laughter of mimes and dancers for cash payment. We observe the proprieties as we sit there, to be sure, and watch our tongues, for no one complains while he is being initiated or laments while he is attending the Pythia or drinking at the Cronia; but they shame the festivals which the god organizes for us and initiates us into by passing the greater part of their time in complaints and heavyheartedness and crushing anxiety. Men take delight in the sweet strains of instrumental music and in the singing of birds, they take pleasure in the spectacle of animals frisking and frolicking and dislike it when they roar and bellow and scowl. But when they see that their own life is unsmiling and brooding and crushed and ground down by highly disagreeable and unending passions and preoccupations and worries, they find no respite or refreshment for themselves—how could they? Not only so, but when others invite them to do so they will heed no argument whose acceptance would enable them to tolerate the present without recrimination, recall the past with gratitude, and face the future without apprehension or misgivings but with hope glad and shining.

Translated by Moses Hadas.

Cicero [1]

106–43 B.C.

Marcus Tullius Cicero was not only the greatest orator of ancient Rome, he was also one of its leading statesmen. Born at Arpinum, in central Italy, in 106 B.C., he was educated in Rome. He studied rhetoric, law, and philosophy under some of the most famous teachers of his time, and, at the age of twenty-five, he was ready to begin his career as an advocate. His earliest efforts attracted considerable attention, but they also brought him into disfavor with the dictator Sulla. Out of fear for his safety, Cicero temporarily left Rome. He journeyed to Athens, where he spent much of his time perfecting his oratorical style.

When he was thirty, Cicero was appointed to the office of quaestor in a province in Sicily. He performed his duties well, and within a few years he was asked to serve as prosecutor in the case against Verres, a Sicilian official who had cruelly oppressed the people. His successful handling of this case made him famous throughout Rome and launched him on his political career. He rose to power rapidly, and less than seven years later he was elected to the consulship, the highest office in Rome.

Cicero's unsuccessful rival for the consulship was Catiline, a patrician who had fallen into disrepute. Upon his defeat, Catiline organ-

[1] See Plutarch's *Cicero* in *Great Books of the Western World*, Vol. 14, pp. 704–723.

Notes from the artist: "The strength of Cicero as an orator, poet, and public figure is emphasized by the reverse of blacks and whites in this portrait. The quotation, from De divinatione, is translated as: 'There is nothing so absurd but some philosopher has said it.' "

Nihil tam absurde
dici potest, quod
non dicatur ab
aliquo philosophor-
um.

CICERO

ized a conspiracy to seize the highest offices of the state by force. Cicero discovered the plot and acted boldly to prevent it. For his vigilance he was rewarded with the title "Father of His Country."

Cicero's good fortune did not last long, however. He was soon banished from Rome for executing members of Catiline's party without trial. Then, only a little more than a year later, the edict of banishment was lifted. Upon his return to Rome, Cicero was enthusiastically received by the populace.

During the next few years, Cicero devoted himself to his law practice and to literary composition. He did not completely neglect political affairs, however, and he viewed with concern the rising star of Julius Caesar. When Caesar provoked civil war by crossing the Rubicon, Cicero sided with Pompey against him. Pompey was eventually defeated, but Caesar made no attempt to punish Cicero.

Cicero returned to his literary pursuits until the murder of Caesar in 44 B.C. Then, in the ensuing struggle for power, he took the side of young Octavian Caesar against Mark Antony. He attacked Antony in a famous series of orations known as the "Philippics." When Antony and Octavian came to an agreement, Cicero was condemned to death. He was killed by agents of Antony in 43 B.C., and his head and hands were cut off and exhibited in Rome.

Cicero was a man of vast learning and a prolific writer. We are indebted to him for much of our knowledge of Greek philosophy after Aristotle. His complete works, which include treatises on rhetoric and many philosophical and political subjects, essays, dialogues, speeches, and letters, fill several volumes.

Friendship was an important subject for the great philosophers of antiquity. Plato devoted an early dialogue, *Lysis*,[2] to an attempt to define it; Aristotle exhaustively analyzed it in the *Nicomachean Ethics*;[3] Epictetus made it the subject of one of his discourses;[4] Seneca touched upon it frequently in his *Moral Essays*; and Cicero wrote the dialogue *De amicitia*, or *On Friendship*. In the early modern period, the subject was taken up again by Montaigne and Bacon, each of whom composed an essay on it. Since then, however, philosophers have paid less and less attention to friendship.

---

[2] See *Great Books of the Western World*, Vol. 7, pp. 14–25.
[3] See *Great Books of the Western World*, Vol. 9, pp. 406–426.
[4] See *Great Books of the Western World*, Vol. 12, pp. 167–170.

The decline of interest in friendship can probably be explained in several ways. The most obvious explanation is that the emphasis on romantic love and marriage, which is characteristic of our civilization, has made friendship seem less important. Yet, as we all know from our own experience, friendship remains a significant part of human life. We are still interested in what philosophers have to say about it. We still want to know what friendship is, what it means to *have* a good friend, and what it means to *be* a good friend. There is perhaps no better place for us to begin than with Cicero's *On Friendship*.

On Friendship is presented as a dialogue between Gaius Laelius and two of his sons-in-law. Gaius Laelius was the father-in-law of Scaevola, one of Cicero's early teachers, but he is best known as the intimate friend of Publius Scipio Africanus, one of the greatest of early Romans. It was Scipio Africanus who led the Roman armies that conquered Carthage, defeated Hannibal, and established Rome as the supreme power in the Mediterranean world. The companion selection to *On Friendship—On Old Age—*is a dialogue between the same Gaius Laelius, Scipio Africanus the younger (grandson of the elder Scipio), and Marcus Cato, a Roman renowned for his wisdom and patriotism.

Cicero's views on old age (as expressed through the character of Cato) are quite different from those that appear to be dominant in the twentieth century. The present emphasis is on the importance of remaining young, both in appearance and in spirit. Old age seems to be an object of universal dread. This is not the case with Cicero. He insists that old age can be as happy as any other period in life.

Cicero considers each of the four most frequently voiced criticisms of old age: (1) it withdraws us from active employments; (2) it enfeebles the body; (3) it deprives us of nearly all physical pleasures; and (4) it is the last step before death. Then, in the main body of the dialogue, he presents arguments to prove that the first of these criticisms is not valid, the second involves no serious disadvantage, the third results in more of a gain than a loss, and the fourth can be overcome by reason.

On Friendship

The augur Quintus Mucius Scaevola used to recount a number of
stories about his father-in-law, Gaius Laelius, accurately remembered and
charmingly told; and whenever he talked about him always gave him the
title of "the wise" without any hesitation. I had been introduced by my
father to Scaevola as soon as I had assumed the *toga virilis,* and I took
advantage of the introduction never to quit the venerable man's side as
long as I was able to stay and he was spared to us. The consequence was
that I committed to memory many disquisitions of his, as well as many
short pointed apophthegms, and, in short, took as much advantage of his
wisdom as I could. When he died, I attached myself to Scaevola the
Pontifex, whom I may venture to call quite the most distinguished of our
countrymen for ability and uprightness. But of this latter I shall take other
occasions to speak. To return to Scaevola the augur: Among many other
occasions I particularly remember one. He was sitting on a semicircular
garden-bench, as was his custom, when I and a very few intimate friends
were there, and he chanced to turn the conversation upon a subject which
about that time was in many people's mouths. You must remember,
Atticus, for you were very intimate with Publius Sulpicius, what expressions of astonishment, or even indignation, were called forth by his mortal
quarrel, as tribune, with the consul Quintus Pompeius, with whom he had
formerly lived on terms of the closest intimacy and affection. Well, on this
occasion, happening to mention this particular circumstance, Scaevola
detailed to us a discourse of Laelius on friendship delivered to himself
and Laelius' other son-in-law, Gaius Fannius, son of Marcus Fannius, a
few days after the death of Africanus. The points of that discussion I
committed to memory, and have arranged them in this book at my own
discretion. For I have brought the speakers, as it were, personally on to
my stage to prevent the constant "said I" and "said he" of a narrative, and
to give the discourse the air of being orally delivered in our hearing.

You have often urged me to write something on friendship, and I quite

286

acknowledged that the subject seemed one worth everybody's investigation, and specially suited to the close intimacy that has existed between you and me. Accordingly I was quite ready to benefit the public at your request.

As to the *dramatis personae:* In the treatise *On Old Age,* which I dedicated to you, I introduced Cato as chief speaker. No one, I thought, could with greater propriety speak on old age than one who had been an old man longer than any one else, and had been exceptionally vigorous in his old age. Similarly, having learnt from tradition that of all friendships that between Gaius Laelius and Publius Scipio was the most remarkable, I thought Laelius was just the person to support the chief part in a discussion on friendship which Scaevola remembered him to have actually taken. Moreover, a discussion of this sort gains somehow in weight from the authority of men of ancient days, especially if they happen to have been distinguished. So it comes about that in reading over what I have myself written I have a feeling at times that it is actually Cato that is speaking, not I.

Finally, as I sent the former essay to you as a gift from one old man to another, so I have dedicated this *On Friendship* as a most affectionate friend to his friend. In the former Cato spoke, who was the oldest and wisest man of his day; in this Laelius speaks on friendship—Laelius, who was at once a wise man (that was the title given him) and eminent for his famous friendship. Please forget me for a while; imagine Laelius to be speaking.

Gaius Fannius and Quintus Mucius come to call on their father-in-law after the death of Africanus. They start the subject; Laelius answers them. And the whole essay on friendship is his. In reading it you will recognize a picture of yourself.

Fannius. You are quite right, Laelius! there never was a better or more illustrious character than Africanus. But you should consider that at the present moment all eyes are on you. Everybody calls you "the wise" *par excellence,* and thinks you so. The same mark of respect was lately paid Cato, and we know that in the last generation Lucius Atilius was called "the wise." But in both cases the word was applied with a certain difference. Atilius was so called from his reputation as a jurist; Cato got the name as a kind of honorary title and in extreme old age because of his varied experience of affairs, and his reputation for foresight and firmness, and the sagacity of the opinions which he delivered in senate and forum. You, however, are regarded as "wise" in a somewhat different sense—not alone on account of natural ability and character, but also from your industry and learning; and not in the sense in which the vulgar, but that in which scholars, give that title. In this sense we do not read of any one being called wise in Greece except one man at Athens; and he, to be sure, had been declared by the oracle of Apollo also to be "the supremely wise man." For those who commonly go by the name of the Seven Sages are not admitted into the category of the wise by fastidious critics. Your wisdom people believe to consist in this, that you look upon yourself as self-sufficing and regard the changes and chances of mortal life as powerless to affect your virtue. Accordingly they are always asking me, and doubtless also our Scaevola here, how you bear the death of Africanus. This curiosity has been the more excited from the fact that on the Nones of this month, when we augurs met as usual in the suburban villa of Decimus Brutus for consultation, you were not present, though it had always been your habit to keep that appointment and perform that duty with the utmost punctuality.

Scaevola. Yes, indeed, Laelius, I am often asked the question mentioned by Fannius. But I answer in accordance with what I have observed: I say that you bear in a reasonable manner the grief which you have sustained in the death of one who was at once a man of the most illustrious character and a very dear friend. That of course you could not but be affected—anything else would have been wholly unnatural in a man of your gentle nature—but that the cause of your non-attendance at our college meeting was illness, not melancholy.

Laelius. Thanks, Scaevola! You are quite right; you spoke the exact truth. For in fact I had no right to allow myself to be withdrawn from a duty which I had regularly performed, as long as I was well, by any personal misfortune; nor do I think that anything that can happen will cause a man of principle to intermit a duty. As for your telling me, Fannius, of the honourable appellation given me (an appellation to which I do not recognize my title, and to which I make no claim), you doubtless act from feelings of affection; but I must say that you seem to me to do less than justice to Cato. If any one was ever "wise"—of which I have my doubts—he was. Putting aside everything else, consider how he bore his son's death! I had not forgotten Paulus; I had seen with my own eyes Gallus. But they lost their sons when mere children; Cato his when he was a full-grown man with an assured reputation. Do not therefore be in a hurry to reckon as Cato's superior even that same famous personage whom Apollo, as you say, declared to be "the wisest." Remember the former's reputation rests on deeds, the latter's on words.

Now, as far as I am concerned (I speak to both of you now), believe me, the case stands thus: If I were to say that I am not affected by regret for Scipio, I must leave the philosophers to justify my conduct, but in point of fact I should be telling a lie. Affected of course I am by the loss of a friend as I think there will never be again, such as I can fearlessly say there never was before. But I stand in no need of medicine. I can find my own consolation, and it consists chiefly in my being free from the mistaken notion which generally causes pain at the departure of friends. To Scipio I am convinced no evil has befallen: mine is the disaster, if disaster there be; and to be severely distressed at one's own misfortunes does not show that you love your friend, but that you love yourself.

As for him, who can say that all is not more than well? For, unless he had taken the fancy to wish for immortality, the last thing of which he ever thought, what is there for which mortal man may wish that he did not attain? In his early manhood he more than justified by extraordinary personal courage the hopes which his fellow-citizens had conceived of him as a child. He never was a candidate for the consulship, yet was elected consul twice: the first time before the legal age; the second at a time which, as far as he was concerned, was soon enough, but was near being too late for the interests of the state. By the overthrow of two cities which were the most bitter enemies of our empire, he put an end not only to the wars then raging, but also to the possibility of others in the future. What need to mention the exquisite grace of his manners, his dutiful devotion to his mother, his generosity to his sisters, his liberality to his relations, the integrity of his conduct to every one? You know all this already. Finally, the estimation in which his fellow-citizens held him has been shown by the signs of mourning which accompanied his obsequies. What could such a man have gained by the addition of a few years? Though age need not be a burden—as I remember Cato arguing in the presence of myself and Scipio two years before he died—yet it cannot but take away the vigour and freshness which Scipio was still enjoying. We may conclude therefore that his life, from the good fortune which had attended him and the glory he had obtained, was so circumstanced that it could not be bettered, while the suddenness of his death saved him the sensation of dying. As to the manner of his death it is difficult to speak; you see what people suspect. Thus much, however, I may say: Scipio in his lifetime saw many days of supreme triumph and exultation, but none more magnificent than his last, on which, upon the rising of the Senate, he was escorted by the senators and the people of Rome, by the allies, and by the Latins, to his own door. From such an elevation of popular esteem the next step seems naturally to be an ascent to the gods above, rather than a descent to Hades.

For I am not one of these modern philosophers who maintain that our souls perish with our bodies, and that death ends all. With me ancient opinion has more weight: whether it be that of our own ancestors, who attributed such solemn observances to the dead, as they plainly would not have done if they had believed them to be wholly annihilated; or that of the philosophers who once visited this country, and who by their maxims and doctrines educated Magna Graecia, which at that time was in a flourishing condition, though it has now been ruined; or that of the man who was declared by Apollo's oracle to be "most wise," and who used to teach without the variation which is to be found in most philosophers that "the souls of men are divine, and that when they have quitted the body a return to heaven is open to them, least difficult to those who have been most virtuous and just." This opinion was shared by Scipio. Only a few days before his death—as though he had a presentiment of what was coming—he discoursed for three days on the state of the republic. The company consisted of Philus and Manlius and several others, and I had brought you, Scaevola, along with me. The last part of his discourse referred principally to the immortality of the soul; for he told us what he had heard from the elder Africanus in a dream. Now if it be true that in proportion to a man's goodness the escape from what may be called the prison and bonds of the flesh is easiest, whom can we imagine to have had an easier voyage to the gods than Scipio? I am disposed to think, therefore, that in his case mourning would be a sign of envy rather than of friendship. If, however, the truth rather is that the body and soul perish together, and that no sensation remains, then though there is nothing good in death, at least there is nothing bad. Remove sensation, and a man is exactly as though he had never been born; and yet that this man *was* born is a joy to me, and will be a subject of rejoicing to this state to its last hour.

Wherefore, as I said before, all is as well as possible with him. Not so with me; for as I entered life before him, it would have been fairer for me to leave it also before him. Yet such is the pleasure I take in recalling our friendship, that I look upon my life as having been a happy one because I have spent it with Scipio. With him I was associated in public and private business; with him I lived in Rome and served abroad; and between us there was the most complete harmony in our tastes, our pursuits, and our sentiments, which is the true secret of friendship. It is not therefore in that reputation for wisdom mentioned just now by Fannius—especially as it happens to be groundless—that I find my happiness so much, as in the hope that the memory of our friendship will be lasting. What makes me care the more about this is the fact that in all history there are scarcely three or four pairs of friends on record; and it is classed with them that I cherish a hope of the friendship of Scipio and Laelius being known to posterity.

Fannius. Of course that must be so, Laelius. But since you have mentioned the word friendship, and we are at leisure, you would be doing me a great kindness, and I expect Scaevola also, if you would do as it is your habit to do when asked questions on other subjects, and tell us your sentiments about friendship, its nature, and the rules to be observed in regard to it.

Scaevola. I shall of course be delighted. Fannius has anticipated the very request I was about to make. So you will be doing us both a great favour.

Laelius. I should certainly have no objection if I felt confidence in myself. For the theme is a noble one, and we are (as Fannius has said) at leisure. But who am I? and what ability have I? What you propose is all very well for professional philosophers, who are used, particularly if Greeks, to have the subject for discussion proposed to them on the spur of the moment. It is a task of considerable difficulty, and requires no little practice. Therefore for a set discourse on friendship you must go, I think, to professional lecturers. All I can do is to urge on you to regard friendship as the greatest thing in the world; for there is nothing which so fits in with our nature, or is so exactly what we want in prosperity or adversity.

But I must at the very beginning lay down this principle—*friendship can only exist between good men.* I do not, however, press this too closely, like the philosophers who push their definitions to a superfluous accuracy. They have truth on their side, perhaps, but it is of no practical advantage. Those, I mean, who say that no one but the "wise" is "good." Granted, by all means. But the "wisdom" they mean is one to which no mortal ever yet attained. We must concern ourselves with the facts of everyday life as we find it—not imaginary and ideal perfections. Even Gaius Fannius, Manius Curius, and Tiberius Coruncanius, whom our ancestors decided to be "wise," I could never declare to be so according to their standard. Let them, then, keep this word "wisdom" to themselves. Everybody is irritated by it; no one understands what it means. Let them but grant that the men I mentioned were "good." No, they won't do that either. No one but the "wise" can be allowed that title, say they. Well, then, let us dismiss them and manage as best we may with our own poor mother wit, as the phrase is.

We mean then by the "good" *those whose actions and lives leave no question as to their honour, purity, equity, and liberality; who are free from greed, lust, and violence; and who have the courage of their convictions.* The men I have just named may serve as examples. Such men as these being generally accounted "good," let us agree to call them so, on the ground that to the best of human ability they follow nature as the most perfect guide to a good life.

Now this truth seems clear to me, that nature has so formed us that a certain tie unites us all, but that this tie becomes stronger from proximity. So it is that fellow-citizens are preferred in our affections to foreigners, relations to strangers; for in their case Nature herself has caused a kind of friendship to exist, though it is one which lacks some of the elements of permanence. Friendship excels relationship in this, that whereas you may eliminate affection from relationship, you cannot do so from friendship. Without it relationship still exists in name, friendship does not. You may best understand this friendship by considering that, whereas the merely natural ties uniting the human race are indefinite, this one is so concentrated, and confined to so narrow a sphere, that affection is ever shared by two persons only, or at most by a few.

Now friendship may be thus defined: *a complete accord on all subjects human and divine, joined with mutual good will and affection.* And with the exception of wisdom, I am inclined to think nothing better than this has been given to man by the immortal gods. There are people who give the palm to riches or to good health, or to power and office, many even to sensual pleasures. This last is the ideal of brute beasts; and of the others we may say that they are frail and uncertain, and depend less on our own prudence than on the caprice of fortune. Then there are those who find the "chief good" in virtue. Well, that is a noble doctrine. But the very virtue they talk of is the parent and preserver of friendship, and without it friendship cannot possibly exist.

Let us, I repeat, use the word virtue in the ordinary acceptation and meaning of the term, and do not let us define it in high-flown language. Let us account as good the persons usually considered so, such as Paulus, Cato, Gallus, Scipio, and Philus. Such men as these are good enough for everyday life; and we need not trouble ourselves about those ideal characters which are nowhere to be met with.

Well, between men like these the advantages of friendship are almost more than I can say. To begin with, how can life be worth living, to use the words of Ennius, which lacks that repose which is to be found in the mutual good will of a friend? What can be more delightful than to have some one to whom you can say everything with the same absolute confidence as to yourself? Is not prosperity robbed of half its value if you have no one to share your joy? On the other hand, misfortunes would be hard to bear if there were not some one to feel them even more acutely than yourself. In a word, other objects of ambition serve for particular ends—riches for use, power for securing homage, office for reputation, pleasure for enjoyment, health for freedom from pain and the full use of the functions of the body. But friendship embraces innumerable advantages. Turn which way you please, you will find it at hand. It is everywhere; and yet never out of place, never unwelcome. Fire and water themselves, to use a common expression, are not of more universal use than friendship. I am not now speaking of the common or modified form of it, though even that is a source of pleasure and profit, but of that true and complete friendship which existed between the select few who are known to fame. Such friendship enhances prosperity, and relieves adversity of its burden by halving and sharing it.

And great and numerous as are the blessings of friendship, this certainly is the sovereign one, that it gives us bright hopes for the future and forbids weakness and despair. In the face of a true friend a man sees as it were a second self. So that where his friend is he is; if his friend be rich, he is not poor; though he be weak, his friend's strength is his; and in his friend's life he enjoys a second life after his own is finished. This last is perhaps the most difficult to conceive. But such is the effect of the respect, the loving remembrance, and the regret of friends which follow us to the grave. While they take the sting out of death, they add a glory to the life of the survivors. Nay, if you eliminate from nature the tie of affection, there will be an end of house and city, nor will so much as the cultivation of the soil be left. If you don't see the virtue of friendship and harmony, you may learn it by observing the effects of quarrels and feuds. Was any family ever so well established, any state so firmly settled, as to be beyond the reach of utter destruction from animosities and factions? This may teach you the immense advantage of friendship.

They say that a certain philosopher of Agrigentum, in a Greek poem, pronounced with the authority of an oracle the doctrine that whatever in nature and the universe was unchangeable was so in virtue of the binding force of friendship; whatever was changeable was so by the solvent power of discord. And indeed this is a truth which everybody understands and practically attests by experience. For if any marked instance of loyal friendship in confronting or sharing danger comes to light, every one applauds it to the echo. What cheers there were, for instance, all over the theatre at a passage in the new play of my friend and guest Pacuvius; where, the king not knowing which of the two was Orestes, Pylades declared himself to be Orestes, that he might die in his stead, while the real Orestes kept on asserting that it was he. The audience rose *en masse* and clapped their hands. And this was at an incident in fiction: what would they have done, must we suppose, if it had been in real life? You can easily see what a natural feeling it is, when men who would not have had the resolution to act thus themselves, showed how right they thought it in another.

I don't think I have any more to say about friendship. If there is any more, and I have no doubt there is much, you must, if you care to do so, consult those who profess to discuss such matters.

Fannius. We would rather apply to you. Yet I have often consulted such persons, and have heard what they had to say with a certain satisfaction. But in your discourse one somehow feels that there is a different strain.

Scaevola. You would have said that still more, Fannius, if you had been present the other day in Scipio's pleasure-grounds when we had the discussion about the state. How splendidly he stood up for justice against Philus' elaborate speech!

Fannius. Ah! it was naturally easy for the justest of men to stand up for justice.

Scaevola. Well, then, what about friendship? Who could discourse on it more easily than the man whose chief glory is a friendship maintained with the most absolute fidelity, constancy, and integrity?

Laelius. Now you are really using force. It makes no difference what kind of force you use: force it is. For it is neither easy nor right to refuse a wish of my sons-in-law, particularly when the wish is a creditable one in itself.

Well, then, it has very often occurred to me when thinking about friendship, that the chief point to be considered was this: is it weakness and want of means that make friendship desired? I mean, is its object an interchange of good offices, so that each may give that in which he is strong, and receive that in which he is weak? Or is it not rather true that, although this is an advantage naturally belonging to friendship, yet its original cause is quite other, prior in time, more noble in character, and springing more directly from our nature itself? The Latin word for friendship—*amicitia*—is derived from that for love—*amor;* and love is certainly the prime mover in contracting mutual affection. For as to material advantages, it often happens that those are obtained even by men who are courted by a mere show of friendship and treated with respect from interested motives. But friendship by its nature admits of no feigning, no pretence: as far as it goes it is both genuine and spontaneous. Therefore I gather that friendship springs from a natural impulse rather than a wish for help: from an inclination of the heart, combined with a certain instinctive feeling of love, rather than from a deliberate calculation of the material advantage it was likely to confer. The strength of this feeling you may notice in certain animals. They show such love to their offspring for a certain period, and are so beloved by them, that they clearly have a share in this natural, instinctive affection. But of course it is more evident in the case of man: first, in the natural affection between children and their parents, an affection which only shocking wickedness can sunder; and next, when the passion of love has attained to a like strength—on our finding, that is, some one person with whose character and nature we are in full sympathy, because we think that we perceive in him what I may call the beacon-light of virtue. For nothing inspires love, nothing conciliates affection, like virtue. Why, in a certain sense we may be said to feel affection even for men we have never seen, owing to their honesty and virtue. Who, for instance, fails to dwell on the memory of Gaius Fabricius and Manius Curius with some affection and warmth of feeling, though he has never seen them? Or who but loathes Tarquinius Superbus, Spurius Cassius, Spurius Maelius? We have fought for empire in Italy with two great generals, Pyrrhus and Hannibal. For the former, owing to his probity, we entertain no great feelings of enmity: the latter, owing to his cruelty, our country has detested and always will detest.

Now, if the attraction of probity is so great that we can love it not only in those whom we have never seen, but, what is more, actually in an enemy, we need not be surprised if men's affections are roused when they fancy that they have seen virtue and goodness in those with whom a close intimacy is possible. I do not deny that affection is strengthened by the actual receipt of benefits, as well as by the perception of a wish to render service, combined with a closer intercourse. When these are added to the original impulse of the heart, to which I have alluded, a quite surprising warmth of feeling springs up. And if any one thinks that this comes from a sense of weakness, that each may have some one to help him to his particular need, all I can say is that, when he maintains it to be born of want and poverty, he allows to friendship an origin very base, and a pedigree, if I may be allowed the expression, far from noble. If this had been the case, a man's inclination to friendship would be exactly in proportion to his low opinion of his own resources. Whereas the truth is quite the other way. For when a man's confidence in himself is greatest, when he is so fortified by virtue and wisdom as to want nothing and to feel absolutely self-dependent, it is then that he is most conspicuous for seeking out and keeping up friendships. Did Africanus, for example, want anything of me? Not the least in the world! Neither did I of him. In my case it was an admiration of his virtue, in his an opinion, maybe, which he entertained of my character, that caused our affection. Closer intimacy added to the warmth of our feelings. But though many great material advantages did ensue, they were not the source from which our affection proceeded. For as we are not beneficent and liberal with any view of extorting gratitude, and do not regard an act of kindness as an investment, but follow a natural inclination to liberality; so we look on friendship as worth trying for, not because we are attracted to it by the expectation of ulterior gain, but in the conviction that what it has to give us is from first to last included in the feeling itself.

Far different is the view of those who, like brute beasts, refer everything to sensual pleasure. And no wonder. Men who have degraded all their powers of thought to an object so mean and contemptible can of course raise their eyes to nothing lofty, to nothing grand and divine. Such persons indeed let us leave out of the present question. And let us accept the doctrine that the sensation of love and the warmth of inclination have their origin in a spontaneous feeling which arises directly the presence of probity is indicated. When once men have conceived the inclination, they of course try to attach themselves to the object of it, and move themselves nearer and nearer to him. Their aim is that they may be on the same footing and the same level in regard to affection, and be more inclined to do a good service than to ask a return, and that there should be this noble rivalry between them. Thus both truths will be established. We shall get the most important material advantages from friendship; and its origin from a natural impulse rather than from a sense of need will be at once more dignified and more in accordance with fact. For if it were true that its material advantages cemented friendship, it would be equally true that any change in them would dissolve it. But nature being incapable of change, it follows that genuine friendships are eternal.

So much for the origin of friendship. But perhaps you would not care to hear any more.

Fannius. Nay, pray go on; let us have the rest, Laelius. I take on myself to speak for my friend here as his senior.

Scaevola. Quite right! Therefore, pray let us hear.

Laelius. Well, then, my good friends, listen to some conversations about friendship which very frequently passed between Scipio and myself. I must begin by telling you, however, that he used to say that the most difficult thing in the world was for a friendship to remain unimpaired to the end of life. So many things might intervene: conflicting interests; differences of opinion in politics; frequent changes in character, owing sometimes to misfortunes, sometimes to advancing years. He used to illustrate these facts from the analogy of boyhood, since the warmest affections between boys are often laid aside with the boyish toga; and even if they did manage to keep them up to adolescence, they were sometimes broken by a rivalry in courtship, or for some other advantage to which their mutual claims were not compatible. Even if the friendship was prolonged beyond that time, yet it frequently received a rude shock should the two happen to be competitors for office. For while the most fatal blow to friendship in the majority of cases was the lust of gold, in the case of the best men it was a rivalry for office and reputation, by which it had often happened that the most violent enmity had arisen between the closest friends.

Again, wide breaches and, for the most part, justifiable ones were caused by an immoral request being made of friends, to pander to a man's unholy desires or to assist him in inflicting a wrong. A refusal, though perfectly right, is attacked by those to whom they refuse compliance as a violation of the laws of friendship. Now the people who have no scruples as to the requests they make to their friends, thereby allow that they are ready to have no scruples as to what they will do *for* their friends; and it is the recriminations of such people which commonly not only quench friendships, but give rise to lasting enmities. "In fact," he used to say, "these fatalities overhang friendship in such numbers that it requires not only wisdom but good luck also to escape them all."

With these premises, then, let us first, if you please, examine the question—how far ought personal feeling to go in friendship? For instance: suppose Coriolanus to have had friends, ought they to have joined him in invading his country? Again, in the case of Vecellinus or Spurius Maelius, ought their friends to have assisted them in their attempt to establish a tyranny? Take two instances of either line of conduct. When Tiberius Gracchus attempted his revolutionary measures he was deserted, as we saw, by Quintus Tubero and the friends of his own standing. On the other hand, a friend of your own family, Scaevola, Gaius Blossius of Cumae, took a different course. I was acting as assessor to the consuls Laenus and

Rupilius to try the conspirators, and Blossius pleaded for my pardon on the ground that his regard for Tiberius Gracchus had been so high that he looked upon his wishes as law. "Even if he had wished you to set fire to the Capitol?" said I. "That is a thing," he replied, "that he never would have wished." "Ah, but if he had wished it?" said I. "I would have obeyed." The wickedness of such a speech needs no comment. And in point of fact he was as good and better than his word; for he did not wait for orders in the audacious proceedings of Tiberius Gracchus, but was the head and front of them, and was a leader rather than an abettor of his madness. The result of his infatuation was that he fled to Asia, terrified by the special commission appointed to try him, joined the enemies of his country, and paid a penalty to the republic as heavy as it was deserved. I conclude, then, that the plea of having acted in the interests of a friend is not a valid excuse for a wrong action. For, seeing that a belief in a man's virtue is the original cause of friendship, friendship can hardly remain if virtue be abandoned. But if we decide it to be right to grant our friends whatever they wish, and to ask them for whatever we wish, perfect wisdom must be assumed on both sides if no mischief is to happen. But we cannot assume this perfect wisdom; for we are speaking only of such friends as are ordinarily to be met with, whether we have actually seen them or have been told about them—men, that is to say, of everyday life. I must quote some examples of such persons, taking care to select such as approach nearest to our standard of wisdom. We read, for instance, that Papus Aemilius was a close friend of Gaius Luscinus. History tells us that they were twice consuls together, and colleagues in the censorship. Again, it is on record that Manius Curius and Tiberius Coruncanius were on the most intimate terms with them and with each other. Now, we cannot even suspect that any one of these men ever asked of his friend anything that militated against his honour or his oath or the interests of the republic. In the case of such men as these there is no point in saying that one of them would not have obtained such a request if he had made it; for they were men of the most scrupulous piety, and the making of such a request would involve a breach of religious obligation no less than the granting it. However, it is quite true that Gaius Carbo and Gaius Cato did follow Tiberius Gracchus; and though his brother Gaius Gracchus did not do so at the time, he is now the most eager of them all.

We may then lay down this rule of friendship—*neither ask nor consent to do what is wrong*. For the plea "for friendship's sake" is a discreditable one, and not to be admitted for a moment. This rule holds good for all wrong-doing, but more especially in such as involves disloyalty to the republic. For things have come to such a point with us, my dear Fannius and Scaevola, that we are bound to look somewhat far ahead to what is likely to happen to the republic. The constitution, as known to our ancestors, has already swerved somewhat from the regular course and the lines marked out for it. Tiberius Gracchus made an attempt to obtain the power of a king, or, I might rather say, enjoyed that power for a few months. Had the Roman people ever heard or seen the like before? What the friends and connections that followed him, even after his death, have succeeded in doing in the case of Publius Scipio I cannot describe without tears. As for Carbo, thanks to the punishment recently inflicted on Tiberius Gracchus, we have by hook or by crook managed to hold out against his attacks. But what to expect of the tribuneship of Gaius Gracchus I do not like to forecast. One thing leads to another; and once set going, the downward course proceeds with ever increasing velocity. There is the case of the ballot: what a blow was inflicted first by the lex Gabinia, and two years afterwards by the lex Cassia! I seem already to see the people estranged from the Senate, and the most important affairs at the mercy of the multitude. For you may be sure that more people will learn how to set such things in motion than how to stop them. What is the point of these remarks? This: no one ever makes any attempt of this sort without friends to help him. We must therefore impress upon good men that, should they become inevitably involved in friendships with men of this kind, they ought not to consider themselves under any obligation to stand by friends who are disloyal to the republic. Bad men must have the fear of punishment before their eyes: a punishment not less severe for those who follow than for those who lead others to crime. Who was more famous and powerful in Greece than Themistocles? At the head of the army in the Persian War he had freed Greece; he owed his exile to personal envy: but he did not submit to the wrong done him by his ungrateful country as he ought to have done. He acted as Coriolanus had acted among us twenty years before. But no one was found to help them in their attacks upon their fatherland. Both of them accordingly committed suicide.

We conclude, then, not only that no such confederation of evilly disposed men must be allowed to shelter itself under the plea of friendship, but that, on the contrary, it must be visited with the severest punishment, lest the idea should prevail that fidelity to a friend justifies even making war upon one's country. And this is a case which I am inclined to think, considering how things are beginning to go, will sooner or later arise. And I care quite as much what the state of the constitution will be after my death as what it is now.

Let this, then, be laid down as the first law of friendship, that *we should ask from friends, and do for friends, only what is good.* But do not let us wait to be asked either: let there be ever an eager readiness, and an absence of hesitation. Let us have the courage to give advice with candour. In friendship, let the influence of friends who give good advice be paramount; and let this influence be used to enforce advice not only in plain-spoken terms, but sometimes, if the case demands it, with sharpness; and when so used, let it be obeyed.

I give you these rules because I believe that some wonderful opinions are entertained by certain persons who have, I am told, a reputation for wisdom in Greece. There is nothing in the world, by the way, beyond the reach of their sophistry. Well, some of them teach that we should avoid very close friendships, for fear that one man should have to endure the anxieties of several. Each man, say they, has enough and to spare on his own hands; it is too bad to be involved in the cares of other people. The wisest course is to hold the reins of friendship as loose as possible; you can then tighten or slacken them at your will. For the first condition of a happy life is freedom from care, which no one's mind can enjoy if it has to travail, so to speak, for others besides itself. Another sect, I am told, gives vent to opinions still less generous. I briefly touched on this subject just now. They affirm that friendships should be sought solely for the sake of the assistance they give, and not at all from motives of feeling and affection; and that therefore just in proportion as a man's power and means of support are lowest, he is most eager to gain friendships: thence it comes that weak women seek the support of friendship more than men, the poor more than the rich, the unfortunate rather than those esteemed prosperous. What noble philosophy! You might just as well take the sun out of the sky as friendship from life; for the immortal gods have given us nothing better or more delightful.

But let us examine the two doctrines. What is the value of this "freedom from care"? It is very tempting at first sight, but in practice it has in many cases to be put on one side. For there is no business and no course of action demanded from us by our honour which you can consistently decline, or lay aside when begun, from a mere wish to escape from anxiety. Nay, if we wish to avoid anxiety we must avoid virtue itself, which necessarily involves some anxious thoughts in showing its loathing and abhorrence for the qualities which are opposite to itself—as kindness for ill nature, self-control for licentiousness, courage for cowardice. Thus you may notice that it is the just who are most pained at injustice, the brave at cowardly actions, the temperate at depravity. It is then characteristic of a rightly ordered mind to be pleased at what is good and grieved at the reverse. Seeing then that the wise are not exempt from the heart-ache (which must be the case unless we suppose all human nature rooted out of their hearts), why should we banish friendship from our lives, for fear of being involved by it in some amount of distress? If you take away emotion, what difference remains I don't say between a man and a beast, but between a man and a stone or a log of wood, or anything else of that kind?

Neither should we give any weight to the doctrine that virtue is some-thing rigid and unyielding as iron. In point of fact it is in regard to friendship, as in so many other things, so supple and sensitive that it expands, so to speak, at a friend's good fortune, contracts at his misfor-tunes. We conclude then that mental pain which we must often encounter on a friend's account is not of sufficient consequence to banish friendship from our life, any more than it is true that the cardinal virtues are to be dispensed with because they involve certain anxieties and distresses.

Let me repeat then, "the clear indication of virtue, to which a mind of like character is naturally attracted, is the beginning of friendship." When that is the case the rise of affection is a necessity. For what can be more irrational than to take delight in many objects incapable of response, such as office, fame, splendid buildings, and personal decoration, and yet to take little or none in a sentient being endowed with virtue, which has the faculty of loving or, if I may use the expression, loving back? For nothing is really more delightful than a return of affection, and the mutual inter-change of kind feeling and good offices. And if we add, as we may fairly do, that nothing so powerfully attracts and draws one thing to itself as likeness does to friendship, it will at once be admitted to be true that the good love the good and attach them to themselves as though they were united by blood and nature. For nothing can be more eager, or rather greedy, for what is like itself than nature. So, my dear Fannius and Scaevola, we may look upon this as an established fact, that between good men there is, as it were of necessity, a kindly feeling, which is the source of friendship ordained by nature. But this same kindliness affects the many also. For that is no unsympathetic or selfish or exclusive virtue, which protects even whole nations and consults their best interests. And that certainly it would not have done had it disdained all affection for the common herd.

Again, the believers in the "interest" theory appear to me to destroy the most attractive link in the chain of friendship. For it is not so much what one gets by a friend that gives one pleasure, as the warmth of his feeling;

and we only care for a friend's service if it has been prompted by affection. And so far from its being true that lack of means is a motive for seeking friendship, it is usually those who, being most richly endowed with wealth and means, and above all with virtue (which, after all, is a man's best support), are least in need of another, that are most open handed and beneficent. Indeed I am inclined to think that friends ought at times to be in want of something. For instance, what scope would my affections have had if Scipio had never wanted my advice or co-operation at home or abroad? It is not friendship, then, that follows material advantage, but material advantage friendship.

We must not therefore listen to these superfine gentlemen when they talk of friendship, which they know neither in theory nor in practice. For who, in heaven's name, would choose a life of the greatest wealth and abundance on condition of neither loving nor being beloved by any creature? That is the sort of life tyrants endure. They, of course, can count on no fidelity, no affection, no security for the good will of any one. For them all is suspicion and anxiety; for them there is no possibility of friendship. Who can love one whom he fears, or by whom he knows that he is feared? Yet such men have a show of friendship offered them, but it is only a fair-weather show. If it ever happen that they fall, as it generally does, they will at once understand how friendless they are. So they say Tarquin observed in his exile that he never knew which of his friends were real and which sham, until he had ceased to be able to repay either. Though what surprises me is that a man of his proud and overbearing character should have a friend at all. And as it was his character that prevented his having genuine friends, so it often happens in the case of men of unusually great means—their very wealth forbids faithful friendships. For not only is Fortune blind herself; but she generally makes those blind also who enjoy her favours. They are carried, so to speak, beyond themselves with self-conceit and self-will; nor can anything be more perfectly intolerable than a successful fool. You may often see it. Men who before had pleasant manners enough undergo a complete change on attaining power of office. They despise their old friends: devote themselves to new.

Now, can anything be more foolish than that men who have all the opportunities which prosperity, wealth, and great means can bestow, should secure all else which money can buy—horses, servants, splendid upholstering, and costly plate—but do not secure friends, who are, if I may use the expression, the most valuable and beautiful furniture of life? And yet, when they acquire the former, they know not who will enjoy them, nor for whom they may be taking all this trouble; for they will one and all eventually belong to the strongest: while each man has a stable and inalienable ownership in his friendships. And even if those possessions, which are, in a manner, the gifts of fortune, do prove permanent, life can never be anything but joyless which is without the consolations and companionship of friends.

To turn to another branch of our subject: We must now endeavour to ascertain what limits are to be observed in friendship—what is the boundary-line, so to speak, beyond which our affection is not to go. On this point I notice three opinions, with none of which I agree. One is *that we should love our friend just as much as we love ourselves, and no more;* another, *that our affection to friends should exactly correspond and equal theirs to us;* a third, *that a man should be valued at exactly the same rate as he values himself.* To not one of these opinions do I assent. The first, which holds that our regard for ourselves is to be the measure of our regard for our friend, is not true; for how many things there are which we would never have done for our own sakes, but do for the sake of a friend! We submit to make requests from unworthy people, to descend even to supplication; to be sharper in invective, more violent in attack. Such actions are not creditable in our own interests, but highly so in those of our friends. There are many advantages too which men of upright character voluntarily forgo, or of which they are content to be deprived, that their friends may enjoy them rather than themselves.

The second doctrine is that which limits friendship to an exact equality in mutual good offices and good feelings. But such a view reduces friendship to a question of figures in a spirit far too narrow and illiberal, as though the object were to have an exact balance in a debtor and creditor account. True friendship appears to me to be something richer and more generous than that comes to; and not to be so narrowly on its guard against giving more than it receives. In such a matter we must not be always afraid of something being wasted or running over in our measure, or of more than is justly due being devoted to our friendship.

But the last limit proposed is the worst, namely, that a friend's estimate of himself is to be the measure of our estimate of him. It often happens that a man has too humble an idea of himself, or takes too despairing a view of his chance of bettering his fortune. In such a case a friend ought not to take the view of him which he takes of himself. Rather he should do all he can to raise his drooping spirits, and lead him to more cheerful hopes and thoughts.

We must then find some other limit. But I must first mention the sentiment which used to call forth Scipio's severest criticism. He often said that no one ever gave utterance to anything more diametrically opposed to the spirit of friendship than the author of the dictum, "You should love your friend with the consciousness that you may one day hate him." He could not be induced to believe that it was rightfully attributed to Bias, who was counted as one of the Seven Sages. It was the sentiment of some person with sinister motives or selfish ambition, or who regarded everything as it affected his own supremacy. How can a man be friends with another, if he thinks it possible that he may be his enemy? Why, it will follow that he must wish and desire his friend to commit as many mistakes as possible, that he may have all the more handles against him; and, conversely, that he must be annoyed, irritated, and jealous at the right actions or good fortune of his friends. This maxim, then, let it be whose it will, is the utter destruction of friendship. The true rule is to take such care in the selection of our friends as never to enter upon a friendship with a man whom we could under any circumstances come to hate. And even if we are unlucky in our choice, we must put up with it— according to Scipio—in preference to making calculations as to a future breach.

The real limit to be observed in friendship is this: the characters of two friends must be stainless. There must be complete harmony of interests, purpose, and aims, without exception. Then if the case arises of a friend's wish (not strictly right in itself) calling for support in a matter involving his life or reputation, we must make some concession from the straight path—on condition, that is to say, that extreme disgrace is not the consequence. Something must be conceded to friendship. And yet we must not be entirely careless of our reputation, nor regard the good opinion of our fellow-citizens as a weapon which we can afford to despise in conducting the business of our life, however lowering it may be to tout for it by flattery and smooth words. We must by no means abjure virtue, which secures us affection.

But to return again to Scipio, the sole author of the discourse on friendship: He used to complain that there was nothing on which men bestowed so little pains: that every one could tell exactly how many goats or sheep he had, but not how many friends; and while they took pains in procuring the former, they were utterly careless in selecting friends, and possessed no particular marks, so to speak, or tokens by which they might judge of their suitability for friendship. Now the qualities we ought to look out for in making our selection are firmness, stability, constancy. There is a plentiful lack of men so endowed, and it is difficult to form a judgment without testing. Now this testing can only be made during the actual existence of the friendship; for friendship so often precedes the formation of a judgment, and makes a previous test impossible. If we are prudent then, we shall rein in our impulse to affection as we do chariot horses. We make a preliminary trial of horses. So we should of friendship; and should test our friends' characters by a kind of tentative friendship. It may often happen that the untrustworthiness of certain men is completely displayed in a small money matter; others who are proof against a small sum are detected if it be large. But even if some *are* found who think it mean to prefer money to friendship, where shall we look for those who put friendship before office, civil or military promotions, and political power, and who, when the choice lies between these things on the one side and the claims of friendship on the other, do not give a strong preference to the former? It is not in human nature to be indifferent to political power; and if the price men have to pay for it is the sacrifice of friendship, they think their treason will be thrown into the shade by the magnitude of the reward. This is why true friendship is very difficult to find among those who engage in politics and the contest for office. Where can you find the man to prefer his friend's advancement to his own? And to say nothing of that, think how grievous and almost intolerable it is to most men to share political disaster. You will scarcely find any one who can bring himself to do that. And though what Ennius says is quite true—"the hour of need shows the friend indeed"—yet it is in these two ways that most people betray their untrustworthiness and inconstancy, by looking down on friends when they are themselves prosperous, or deserting them in their distress. A man, then, who has shown a firm, unshaken, and unvarying friendship in both these contingencies we must reckon as one of a class the rarest in the world, and all but superhuman.

Now what is the quality to look out for as a warrant for the stability and permanence of friendship? It is loyalty. Nothing that lacks this can be stable. We should also in making our selection look out for simplicity, a social disposition, and a sympathetic nature, moved by what moves us. These all contribute to maintain loyalty. You can never trust a character which is intricate and tortuous. Nor, indeed, is it possible for one to be trustworthy and firm who is unsympathetic by nature and unmoved by what affects ourselves. We may add, that he must neither take pleasure in bringing accusations against us himself, nor believe them when they are brought. All these contribute to form that constancy which I have been endeavouring to describe. And the result is, what I started by saying, that friendship is only possible between good men.

Now there are two characteristic features in his treatment of his friends that a good (which may be regarded as equivalent to a wise) man will always display. First, he will be entirely without any make-believe or pretence of feeling; for the open display even of dislike is more becoming to an ingenuous character than a studied concealment of sentiment. Secondly, he will not only reject all accusations brought against his friend by another, but he will not be suspicious himself either, nor be always thinking that his friend has acted improperly. Besides this, there should be a certain pleasantness in word and manner which adds no little flavour to friendship. A gloomy temper and unvarying gravity may be very impressive; but friendship should be a little less unbending, more indulgent and gracious, and more inclined to all kinds of good-fellowship and good nature.

But here arises a question of some little difficulty. Are there any occasions on which, assuming their worthiness, we should prefer new to old friends, just as we prefer young to aged horses? The answer admits of no doubt whatever. For there should be no satiety in friendship, as there is in other things. The older the sweeter, as in wines that keep well. And the proverb is a true one, "You must eat many a peck of salt with a man to be thorough friends with him." Novelty, indeed, has its advantage, which we must not despise. There is always hope of fruit, as there is in healthy blades of corn. But age too must have its proper position; and, in fact, the influence of time and habit is very great. To recur to the illustration of the horse which I have just now used: Every one likes *ceteris paribus* [other things being equal] to use the horse to which he has been accustomed, rather than one that is untried and new. And it is not only in the case of a living thing that this rule holds good, but in inanimate things also; for we like places where we have lived the longest, even though they are mountainous and covered with forest. But here is another golden rule in friendship: *put yourself on a level with your friend*. For it often happens that there are certain superiorities, as for example Scipio's in what I may call our set. Now he never assumed any airs of superiority over Philus, or Rupilius, or Mummius, or over friends of a lower rank still. For instance, he always showed a deference to his brother Quintus Maximus because he was his senior, who, though a man no doubt of eminent character, was by no means his equal. He used also to wish that all his friends should be the better for his support. This is an example we should all follow. If any of us have any advantage in personal character, intellect, or fortune, we should be ready to make our friends sharers and partners in it with ourselves. For instance, if their parents are in humble circumstances, if their relations are powerful neither in intellect nor means, we should supply their deficiencies and promote their rank and dignity.

You know the legends of children brought up as servants in ignorance of their parentage and family. When they are recognized and discovered to be the sons of gods or kings, they still retain their affection for the shepherds whom they have for many years looked upon as their parents. Much more ought this to be so in the case of real and undoubted parents. For the advantages of genius and virtue, and in short of every kind of superiority, are never realized to their fullest extent until they are bestowed upon our nearest and dearest.

But the converse must also be observed. For in friendship and relationship, just as those who possess any superiority must put themselves on an equal footing with those who are less fortunate, so these latter must not be annoyed at being surpassed in genius, fortune, or rank. But most people of that sort are for ever either grumbling at something, or harping on their claims; and especially if they consider that they have services of their own to allege involving zeal and friendship and some trouble to themselves. People who are always bringing up their services are a nuisance. The recipient ought to remember them; the performer should never mention them. In the case of friends, then, as the superior are bound to descend, so are they bound in a certain sense to raise those below them. For there are people who make their friendship disagreeable by imagining themselves undervalued. This generally happens only to those who think that they deserve to be so; and they ought to be shown by deeds as well as by words the groundlessness of their opinion. Now the measure of your benefits should be in the first place your own power to bestow, and in the second place the capacity to bear them on the part of him on whom you are bestowing affection and help. For, however great your personal prestige may be, you cannot raise all your friends to the highest offices of the state. For instance, Scipio was able to make Publius Rupilius consul, but not his brother Lucius. But granting that you can give any one anything you choose, you must have a care that it does not prove to be beyond his powers.

As a general rule, we must wait to make up our mind about friendships till men's characters and years have arrived at their full strength and development. People must not, for instance, regard as fast friends all whom in their youthful enthusiasm for hunting or football they liked for having the same tastes. By that rule, if it were a mere question of time, no one would have such claims on our affections as nurses and slave-tutors. Not that they are to be neglected, but they stand on a different ground. It is only these mature friendships that can be permanent. For difference of character leads to difference of aims, and the result of such diversity is to estrange friends. The sole reason, for instance, which prevents good men from making friends with bad, or bad with good, is that the divergence of their characters and aims is the greatest possible.

Another good rule in friendship is this: do not let an excessive affection hinder the highest interests of your friends. This very often happens. I will go again to the region of fable for an instance. Neoptolemus could never have taken Troy if he had been willing to listen to Lycomedes, who had brought him up, and with many tears tried to prevent his going there. Again, it often happens that important business makes it necessary to part from friends: the man who tries to balk it, because he thinks that he cannot endure the separation, is of a weak and effeminate nature, and on that very account makes but a poor friend. There are, of course, limits to what you ought to expect from a friend and to what you should allow him to demand of you. And these you must take into calculation in every case.

Again, there is such a disaster, so to speak, as having to break off friendship. And sometimes it is one we cannot avoid. For at this point the stream of our discourse is leaving the intimacies of the wise and touching on the friendship of ordinary people. It will happen at times that an outbreak of vicious conduct affects either a man's friends themselves or strangers, yet the discredit falls on the friends. In such cases friendships should be allowed to die out gradually by an intermission of intercourse. They should, as I have been told that Cato used to say, rather be un-stitched than torn in twain; unless, indeed, the injurious conduct be of so violent and outrageous a nature as to make an instant breach and separation the only possible course consistent with honour and rectitude. Again, if a change in character and aim takes place, as often happens, or if party politics produces an alienation of feeling (I am now speaking, as I said a short time ago, of ordinary friendships, not of those of the wise), we shall have to be on our guard against appearing to embark upon active enmity while we only mean to resign a friendship. For there can be nothing more discreditable than to be at open war with a man with whom you have been intimate. Scipio, as you are aware, had abandoned his friendship for Quintus Pompeius on my account; and again, from differences of opinion in politics, he became estranged from my colleague Metellus. In both cases he acted with dignity and moderation, showing that he was offended indeed, but without rancour.

Our first object, then, should be to prevent a breach; our second, to secure that, if it does occur, our friendship should seem to have died a natural rather than a violent death. Next, we should take care that friend-ship is not converted into active hostility, from which flow personal quarrels, abusive language, and angry recriminations. These last, however, provided that they do not pass all reasonable limits of forbearance, we ought to put up with, and, in compliment to an old friendship, allow the party that inflicts the injury, not the one that submits to it, to be in the wrong. Generally speaking, there is but one way of securing and providing oneself against faults and inconveniences of this sort—not to be too hasty in bestowing our affection, and not to bestow it at all on unworthy objects.

Now, by "worthy of friendship" I mean those who have in themselves the qualities which attract affection. This sort of man is rare; and indeed all excellent things *are* rare; and nothing in the world is so hard to find as a thing entirely and completely perfect of its kind. But most people not only recognize nothing as good in our life unless it is profitable, but look upon friends as so much stock, caring most for those by whom they hope to make most profit. Accordingly they never possess that most beautiful and most spontaneous friendship which must be sought solely for itself without any ulterior object. They fail also to learn from their own feelings the nature and the strength of friendship. For every one loves himself, not for any reward which such love may bring, but because he is dear to himself independently of anything else. But unless this feeling is transferred to another, what a real friend is will never be revealed; for he is, as it were, a second self. But if we find these two instincts showing themselves in animals—whether of the air or the sea or the land, whether wild or tame—first, a love of self, which in fact is born in everything that lives alike; and, secondly, an eagerness to find and attach themselves to other creatures of their own kind; and if this natural action is accompanied by desire and by something resembling human love, how much more must this be the case in man by the law of his nature? For man not only loves himself, but seeks another whose spirit he may so blend with his own as almost to make one being of two.

But most people unreasonably, not to speak of modesty, want such a friend as they are unable to be themselves, and expect from their friends what they do not themselves give. The fair course is first to be good yourself, and then to look out for another of like character. It is between such that the stability in friendship of which we have been talking can be secured; when, that is to say, men who are united by affection learn, first of all, to rule those passions which enslave others, and in the next place to take delight in fair and equitable conduct, to bear each other's burdens, never to ask each other for anything inconsistent with virtue and rectitude, and not only to serve and love but also to respect each other. I say "respect"; for if respect is gone, friendship has lost its brightest jewel. And this shows the mistake of those who imagine that friendship gives a privilege to licentiousness and sin. Nature has given us friendship as the handmaid of virtue, not as a partner in guilt: to the end that virtue, being powerless when isolated to reach the highest objects, might succeed in doing so in union and partnership with another. Those who enjoy in the present, or have enjoyed in the past, or are destined to enjoy in the future such a partnership as this, must be considered to have secured the most excellent and auspicious combination for reaching nature's highest good. This is the partnership, I say, which combines moral rectitude, fame, peace of mind, serenity: all that men think desirable because with them life is happy, but without them cannot be so. This being our best and highest object, we must, if we desire to attain it, devote ourselves to virtue; for without virtue we can obtain neither friendship nor anything else desirable. In fact, if virtue be neglected, those who imagine themselves to possess friends will find out their error as soon as some grave disaster forces them to make trial of them. Wherefore, I must again and again repeat, you must satisfy your judgment before engaging your affections: not love first and judge afterwards. We suffer from carelessness in many of our undertakings: in none more than in selecting and cultivating our friends. We put the cart before the horse, and shut the stable door when the steed is stolen, in defiance of the old proverb. For, having mutually involved ourselves in a long-standing intimacy or by actual obligations, all on a sudden some cause of offence arises and we break off our friendships in full career.

It is this that makes such carelessness in a matter of supreme importance all the more worthy of blame. I say "supreme importance," because friendship is the one thing about the utility of which everybody with one accord is agreed. That is not the case in regard even to virtue itself; for many people speak slightingly of virtue as though it were mere puffing and self-glorification. Nor is it the case with riches. Many look down on riches, being content with a little and taking pleasure in poor fare and dress. And as to the political offices for which some have a burning desire—how many entertain such a contempt for them as to think nothing in the world more empty and trivial!

And so on with the rest; things desirable in the eyes of some are regarded by very many as worthless. But of friendship all think alike to a man, whether those who have devoted themselves to politics, or those who delight in science and philosophy, or those who follow a private way of life and care for nothing but their own business, or those lastly who have given themselves body and soul to sensuality—they all think, I say, that without friendship life is no life, if they want some part of it, at any rate, to be noble. For friendship, in one way or another, penetrates into the lives of us all, and suffers no career to be entirely free from its influence. Though a man be of so churlish and unsociable a nature as to loathe and shun the company of mankind, as we are told was the case with a certain Timon at Athens, yet even he cannot refrain from seeking some one in whose hearing he may disgorge the venom of his bitter temper. We should see this most clearly, if it were possible that some god should carry us away from these haunts of men, and place us somewhere in perfect solitude, and then should supply us in abundance with everything necessary to our nature, and yet take from us entirely the opportunity of looking upon a human being. Who could steel himself to endure such a life? Who would not lose in his loneliness the zest for all pleasures? And indeed this is the point of the observation of, I think, Archytas of Tarentum. I have it third hand; men who were my seniors told me that their seniors had told them. It was this: "If a man could ascend to heaven and get a clear view of the natural order of the universe, and the beauty of the heavenly bodies, that wonderful spectacle would give him small pleasure, though nothing could be conceived more delightful if he had but had some one to whom to tell what he had seen." So true it is that Nature abhors isolation, and ever leans upon something as a stay and support; and this is found in its most pleasing form in our closest friend.

But though Nature also declares by so many indications what her wish and object and desire is, we yet in a manner turn a deaf ear and will not hear her warnings. The intercourse between friends is varied and complex, and it must often happen that causes of suspicion and offence arise, which a wise man will sometimes avoid, at other times remove, at others treat with indulgence. The one possible cause of offence that must be faced is when the interests of your friend and your own sincerity are at stake. For instance, it often happens that friends need remonstrance and even reproof. When these are administered in a kindly spirit they ought to be taken in good part. But somehow or other there is truth in what my friend Terence says in his *Andria*:

Compliance gets us friends, plain speaking hate.

Plain speaking is a cause of trouble, if the result of it is resentment, which is poison of friendship; but compliance is really the cause of much more trouble, because by indulging his faults it lets a friend plunge into headlong ruin. But the man who is most to blame is he who resents plain speaking and allows flattery to egg him on to his ruin. On this point, then, from first to last there is need of deliberation and care. If we remonstrate, it should be without bitterness; if we reprove, there should be no word of insult. In the matter of compliance (for I am glad to adopt Terence's word), though there should be every courtesy, yet that base kind which assists a man in vice should be far from us, for it is unworthy of a free-born man, to say nothing of a friend. It is one thing to live with a tyrant, another with a friend. But if a man's ears are so closed to plain speaking that he cannot bear to hear the truth from a friend, we may give him up in despair. This remark of Cato's, as so many of his did, shows great acuteness: "There are people who owe more to bitter enemies than to apparently pleasant friends: the former often speak the truth, the latter never." Besides, it is a strange paradox that the recipients of advice should feel no annoyance where they ought to feel it, and yet feel so much where they ought not. They are not at all vexed at having committed a fault, but very angry at being reproved for it. On the contrary, they ought to be grieved at the crime and glad of the correction.

Well, then, if it is true that to give and receive advice—the former with freedom and yet without bitterness, the latter with patience and without irritation—is peculiarly appropriate to genuine friendship, it is no less true that there can be nothing more utterly subversive of friendship than flattery, adulation, and base compliance. I use as many terms as possible to brand this vice of light-minded, untrustworthy men, whose sole object in speaking is to please without any regard to truth. In everything false pretence is bad, for it suspends and vitiates our power of discerning the truth. But to nothing is it so hostile as to friendship; for it destroys that frankness without which friendship is an empty name. For the essence of friendship being that two minds become as one, how can that ever take place if the mind of each of the separate parties to it is not single and uniform, but variable, changeable, and complex? Can anything be so pliable, so wavering, as the mind of a man whose attitude depends not only on another's feeling and wish, but on his very looks and nods?

> If one says "No," I answer "No"; if "Yes," I answer "Yes."
> In fine, I've laid this task upon myself,
> To echo all that's said—

to quote my old friend Terence again. But he puts these words into the mouth of a Gnatho. To admit such a man into one's intimacy at all is a sign of folly. But there are many people like Gnatho, and it is when they are superior either in position or fortune or reputation that their flatteries become mischievous, the weight of their position making up for the lightness of their character. But if we only take reasonable care, it is as easy to separate and distinguish a genuine from a specious friend as anything else that is coloured and artificial from what is sincere and genuine. A public assembly, though composed of men of the smallest possible culture, nevertheless will see clearly the difference between a mere demagogue (that is, a flatterer and untrustworthy citizen) and a man of principle, standing, and solidity. It was by this kind of flattering language that Gaius Papirius the other day endeavoured to tickle the ears of the assembled people, when proposing his law to make the tribunes re-eligible. I spoke against it. But I will leave the personal question. I prefer speaking of Scipio. Good heavens! how impressive his speech was, what a majesty there was in it! You would have pronounced him, without hesitation, to be no mere henchman of the Roman people, but their leader. However, you were there, and moreover have the speech in your hands. The result was that a law meant to please the people was by the people's votes rejected. Once more to refer to myself, you remember how apparently popular was the law proposed by Gaius Licinius Crassus "about the election to the College of Priests" in the consulship of Quintus Maximus, Scipio's brother, and Lucius Mancinus. For the power of filling up their own vacancies on the part of the colleges was by this proposal to be transferred to the people. It was this man, by the way, who began the practice of turning towards the forum when addressing the people. In spite of this, however, upon my speaking on the conservative side, religion gained an easy victory over his plausible speech. This took place in my praetorship, five years before I was elected consul, which shows that the cause was successfully maintained more by the merits of the case than by the prestige of the highest office.

Now, if on a stage, such as a public assembly essentially is, where there is the amplest room for fiction and half-truths, truth nevertheless prevails if it be but fairly laid open and brought into the light of day, what ought to happen in the case of friendship, which rests entirely on truthfulness? Friendship, in which, unless you both see and show an open breast, to use a common expression, you can neither trust nor be certain of anything—no, not even of mutual affection, since you cannot be sure of its sincerity. However, this flattery, injurious as it is, can hurt no one but the man who takes it in and likes it. And it follows that the man to open his ears widest to flatterers is he who first flatters himself and is fondest of himself. I grant you that Virtue naturally loves herself; for she knows herself and perceives how worthy of love she is. But I am not now speaking of absolute virtue, but of the belief men have that they possess virtue. The fact is that fewer people are endowed with virtue than wish to be thought to be so. It is such people that take delight in flattery. When they are addressed in language expressly adapted to flatter their vanity, they look upon such empty persiflage as a testimony to the truth of their own praises. It is not then properly friendship at all when the one will not listen to the truth, and the other is prepared to lie. Nor would the servility of parasites in comedy have seemed humorous to us had there been no such things as braggart captains. "Is Thaïs really much obliged to me?" It would have been quite enough to answer, "Much," but he must needs say, "Immensely." Your servile flatterer always exaggerates what his victim wishes to be put strongly. Wherefore, though it is with those who catch at and invite it that this flattering falsehood is especially powerful, yet men even of solider and steadier character must be warned to be on the watch against being taken in by cunningly disguised flattery. An open flatterer any one can detect, unless he is an absolute fool: the covert insinuation of the cunning and the sly is what we have to be studiously on our guard against. His detection is not by any means the easiest thing in the world, for he often covers his servility under the guise of contradiction, and flatters by pretending to dispute, and then at last giving in and allowing himself to be beaten, that the person hoodwinked may think himself to have been the clearer sighted. Now what can be more degrading than to be thus hoodwinked? You must be on your guard against this happening to you, like the man in the *Heiress:*

> How have I been befooled! no drivelling dotards
> On any stage were e'er so played upon.

For even on the stage we have no grosser representation of folly than that of short-sighted and credulous old men. But somehow or other I have strayed away from the friendship of the perfect, that is, of the "wise" (meaning, of course, such "wisdom" as human nature is capable of), to the subject of vulgar, unsubstantial friendships. Let us then return to our original theme, and at length bring that, too, to a conclusion.

Well, then, Fannius and Mucius, I repeat what I said before. It is virtue, virtue, which both creates and preserves friendship. On it depends harmony of interest, permanence, fidelity. When Virtue has reared her head and shown the light of her countenance, and seen and recognized the same light in another, she gravitates towards it, and in her turn welcomes that which the other has to show; and from it springs up a flame which you may call love or friendship as you please. Both words are from the same root in Latin; and love is just the cleaving to him whom you love without the prompting of need or any view to advantage—though this latter blossoms spontaneously on friendship, little as you may have looked for it. It is with such warmth of feeling that I cherished Lucius Paulus, Marcus Cato, Gaius Gallus, Publius Nasica, Tiberius Gracchus, my dear Scipio's father-in-law. It shines with even greater warmth when men are of the same age, as in the case of Scipio and Lucius Furius, Publius Rupilius, Spurius Mummius, and myself. *En revanche,* in my old age I find comfort in the affection of young men, as in the case of yourselves and Quintus Tubero: nay more, I delight in the intimacy of such a very young man as Publius Rutilius and Aulus Verginius. And since the law of our nature and of our life is that a new generation is for ever springing up, the most desirable thing is that along with your contemporaries, with whom you started in the race, you may also reach what is to us the goal. But in view of the instability and perishableness of mortal things, we should be continually on the look-out for some to love and by whom to be loved; for if we lose affection and kindliness from our life, we lose all that gives it charm. For me, indeed, though torn away by a sudden stroke, Scipio still lives and ever will live. For it was the virtue of the man that I loved, and that has not suffered death. And it is not my eyes only, because I had all my life a personal experience of it, that never lose sight of it: it will shine to posterity also with undimmed glory. No one will ever cherish a nobler ambition or a loftier hope without thinking his memory and his image the best to put before his eyes. I declare that of all the blessings which either fortune or nature has bestowed upon me I know none to compare with Scipio's friendship. In it I found sympathy in public, counsel in private business; in it too a means of spending my leisure with unalloyed delight. Never, to the best of my knowledge, did I offend him even in the most trivial point; never did I hear a word from him I could have wished unsaid. We had one house, one table, one style of living; and not only were we together on foreign service, but in our tours also and country sojourns. Why speak of our eagerness to be ever gaining some knowledge, to be ever learning something, on which we spent all our leisure hours far from the gaze of the world? If the recollection and memory of these things had perished with the man, I could not possibly have endured the regret for one so closely united with me in life and affection. But these things have not perished; they are rather fed and strengthened by reflection and memory. Even supposing me to have been entirely bereft of them, still my time of life of itself brings me no small consolation: for I cannot have much longer now to bear this regret; and everything that is brief ought to be endurable, however severe.

This is all I had to say on friendship. One piece of advice on parting. Make up your minds to this: virtue (without which friendship is impossible) is first; but next to it, and to it alone, the greatest of all things is friendship.

On Old Age

And should my service, Titus, ease the weight
Of care that wrings your heart, and draw the sting
Which rankles there, what guerdon shall there be?

For I may address you, Atticus, in the lines in which Flamininus was addressed by the man

who, poor in wealth, was rich in honour's gold,

though I am well assured that you are not, as Flamininus was,

kept on the rack of care by night and day.

For I know how well-ordered and equable your mind is, and am fully aware that it was not a surname alone which you brought home with you from Athens, but its culture and good sense. And yet I have an idea that you are at times stirred to the heart by the same circumstances as myself. To console you for these is a more serious matter, and must be put off to another time. For the present I have resolved to dedicate to you an essay on old age. For from the burden of impending or at least advancing age, common to us both, I would do something to relieve us both: though as to yourself I am fully aware that you support and will support it, as you do everything else, with calmness and philosophy. But directly I resolved to write on old age, you at once occurred to me as deserving a gift of which both of us might take advantage. To myself, indeed, the composition of this book has been so delightful that it has not only wiped away all the disagreeables of old age, but has even made it luxurious and delightful too. Never, therefore, can philosophy be praised as highly as it deserves, considering that its faithful disciple is able to spend every period of his life with unruffled feelings. However, on other subjects I have spoken at large, and shall often speak again: this book which I herewith send you is on old age. I have put the whole discourse not, as Alisto of Cos did, in the mouth of Tithonus—for a mere fable would have lacked conviction—but in that of Marcus Cato when he was an old man, to give my essay greater weight. I represent Laelius and Scipio at his house expressing surprise at his carrying his years so lightly, and Cato answering them. If he shall seem to show somewhat more learning in this discourse than he generally did in his own books, put it down to the Greek literature of which it is known that he became an eager student in his old age. But what need of more? Cato's own words will at once explain all I feel about old age.

M. CATO. PUBLIUS CORNELIUS SCIPIO AFRICANUS (*the younger*). GAIUS LAELIUS.

Scipio. Many a time have I in conversation with my friend Gaius Laelius here expressed my admiration, Marcus Cato, of the eminent, nay perfect, wisdom displayed by you indeed at all points, but above everything because I have noticed that old age never seemed a burden to you, while to most old men it is so hateful that they declare themselves under a weight heavier than Aetna.

Cato. Your admiration is easily excited, it seems, my dear Scipio and Laelius. Men, of course, who have no resources in themselves for securing a good and happy life find every age burdensome. But those who look for all happiness from within can never think anything bad which Nature makes inevitable. In that category before anything else comes old age, to which all wish to attain, and at which all grumble when attained. Such is Folly's inconsistency and unreasonableness! They say that it is stealing upon them faster than they expected. In the first place, who compelled them to hug an illusion? For in what respect did old age steal upon manhood faster than manhood upon childhood? In the next place, in what way would old age have been less disagreeable to them if they were in their eight-hundredth year than in their eightieth? For their past, however long, when once it was past, would have no consolation for a stupid old age. Wherefore, if it is your wont to admire my wisdom—and I would that it were worthy of your good opinion and of my own surname of Sapiens—it really consists in the fact that I follow Nature, the best of guides, as I would a god, and am loyal to her commands. It is not likely, if she has written the rest of the play well, that she has been careless about the last act like some idle poet. But after all some "last" was inevitable, just as to the berries of a tree and the fruits of the earth there comes in the fullness of time a period of decay and fall. A wise man will not make a grievance of this. To rebel against Nature—is not that to fight like the giants with the gods?

Laelius. And yet, Cato, you will do us a very great favour (I venture to speak for Scipio as for myself) if—since we all hope, or at least wish, to become old men—you would allow us to learn from you in good time before it arrives, by what methods we may most easily acquire the strength to support the burden of advancing age.

Cato. I will do so without doubt, Laelius, especially if, as you say, it will be agreeable to you both.

Laelius. We do wish very much, Cato, if it is no trouble to you, to be allowed to see the nature of the bourne which you have reached after completing a long journey, as it were, upon which we too are bound to embark.

Cato. I will do the best I can, Laelius. It has often been my fortune to hear the complaints of my contemporaries—like will to like, you know, according to the old proverb—complaints to which men like C. Salinator and Sp. Albinus, who were of consular rank and about my time, used to give vent. They were, first, that they had lost the pleasures of the senses, without which they did not regard life as life at all; and, secondly, that they were neglected by those from whom they had been used to receive attentions. Such men appear to me to lay the blame on the wrong thing. For if it had been the fault of old age, then these same misfortunes would have befallen me and all other men of advanced years. But I have known many of them who never said a word of complaint against old age; for they were only too glad to be freed from the bondage of passion, and were not at all looked down upon by their friends. The fact is that the blame for all complaints of that kind is to be charged to character, not to a particular time of life. For old men who are reasonable and neither cross-grained nor churlish find old age tolerable enough: whereas unreason and churlishness cause uneasiness at every time of life.

Laelius. It is as you say, Cato. But perhaps some one may suggest that it is your large means, wealth, and high position that make you think old age tolerable: whereas such good fortune only falls to few.

Cato. There is something in that, Laelius, but by no means all. For instance, the story is told of the answer of Themistocles in a wrangle with a certain Seriphian, who asserted that he owed his brilliant position to the reputation of his country, not to his own. "If I had been a Seriphian," said he, "even I should never have been famous, nor would you if you had been an Athenian." Something like this may be said of old age. For the philosopher himself could not find old age easy to bear in the depths of poverty, nor the fool feel it anything but a burden though he were a millionaire. You may be sure, my dear Scipio and Laelius, that the arms best adapted to old age are culture and the active exercise of the virtues. For if they have been maintained at every period—if one has lived much as well as long—the harvest they produce is wonderful, not only because they never fail us even in our last days (though that in itself is supremely important), but also because the consciousness of a well-spent life and the recollection of many virtuous actions are exceedingly delightful.

Take the case of Q. Fabius Maximus, the man, I mean, who recovered Tarentum. When I was a young man and he an old one, I was as much attached to him as if he had been my contemporary. For that great man's serious dignity was tempered by courteous manners, nor had old age made any change in his character. True, he was not exactly an old man when my devotion to him began, yet he was nevertheless well on in life; for his first consulship fell in the year after my birth. When quite a stripling I went with him in his fourth consulship as a soldier in the ranks, on the expedition against Capua, and in the fifth year after that against Tarentum. Four years after that I was elected quaestor, holding office in the consulship of Tuditanus and Cethegus, in which year, indeed, he as a very old man spoke in favour of the Cincian law "on gifts and fees."

Now this man conducted wars with all the spirit of youth when he was far advanced in life, and by his persistence gradually wearied out Hannibal, when rioting in all the confidence of youth. How brilliant are those lines of my friend Ennius on him!

> For us, down beaten by the storms of fate,
> One man by wise delays restored the State.
> Praise or dispraise moved not his constant mood,
> True to his purpose, to his country's good!
> Down ever-lengthening avenues of fame
> Thus shines and shall shine still his glorious name.

Again, what vigilance, what profound skill did he show in the capture of Tarentum! It was indeed in my hearing that he made the famous retort to Salinator, who had retreated into the citadel after losing the town: "It was owing to me, Quintus Fabius, that you retook Tarentum." "Quite so," he replied with a laugh; "for had you not lost it, I should never have recovered it." Nor was he less eminent in civil life than in war. In his second consulship, though his colleague would not move in the matter, he resisted as long as he could the proposal of the tribune C. Flaminius to divide the territory of the Picenians and Gauls in free allotments in defiance of a resolution of the Senate. Again, though he was an augur, he ventured to say that whatever was done in the interests of the state was done with the best possible auspices, that any laws proposed against its interest were proposed against the auspices. I was cognizant of much that was admirable in that great man, but nothing struck me with greater astonishment than the way in which he bore the death of his son—a man of brilliant character and who had been consul. His funeral speech over him is in wide circulation, and when we read it, is there any philosopher of whom we do not think meanly? Nor in truth was he only great in the light of day and in the sight of his fellow-citizens; he was still more eminent in private and at home. What a wealth of conversation! What weighty maxims! What a wide acquaintance with ancient history! What an accurate knowledge of the science of augury! For a Roman, too, he had a great tincture of letters. He had a tenacious memory for military history of every sort, whether of Roman or foreign wars. And I used at that time to enjoy his conversation with a passionate eagerness, as though I already divined, what actually turned out to be the case, that when he died there would be no one to teach me anything.

What then is the purpose of such a long disquisition on Maximus? It is because you now see that an old age like his cannot conscientiously be called unhappy. Yet it is after all true that everybody cannot be a Scipio or a Maximus, with stormings of cities, with battles by land and sea, with wars in which they themselves commanded, and with triumphs to recall. Besides this there is a quiet, pure, and cultivated life which produces a calm and gentle old age, such as we have been told Plato's was, who died at his writing-desk in his eighty-first year; or like that of Isocrates, who says that he wrote the book called *The Panegyric* in his ninety-fourth year, and who lived for five years afterwards; while his master Gorgias of Leontini completed a hundred and seven years without ever relaxing his diligence or giving up work. When some one asked him why he consented to remain so long alive—"I have no fault," said he, "to find with old age." That was a noble answer, and worthy of a scholar. For fools impute their own frailties and guilt to old age, contrary to the practice of Ennius, whom I mentioned just now. In the lines—

> Like some brave steed that oft before
> The Olympic wreath of victory bore,
> Now by the weight of years oppressed,
> Forgets the race, and takes his rest—

he compares his own old age to that of a high-spirited and successful race-horse. And him indeed you may very well remember. For the present consuls Titus Flamininus and Manius Acilius were elected in the nineteenth year after his death; and his death occurred in the consulship of Caepio and Philippus, the latter consul for the second time: in which year I, then sixty-six years old, spoke in favour of the Voconian law in a voice that was still strong and with lungs still sound; while he, though seventy years old, supported two burdens considered the heaviest of all—poverty and old age—in such a way as to be all but fond of them.

The fact is that when I come to think it over, I find that there are four reasons for old age being thought unhappy: First, that it withdraws us from active employments; second, that it enfeebles the body; third, that it deprives us of nearly all physical pleasures; fourth, that it is the next step to death. Of each of these reasons, if you will allow me, let us examine the force and justice separately.

OLD AGE WITHDRAWS US FROM ACTIVE EMPLOYMENTS. From which of them? Do you mean from those carried on by youth and bodily strength? Are there then no old men's employments to be after all conducted by the intellect, even when bodies are weak? So then Q. Maximus did nothing; nor L. Aemilius—your father, Scipio, and my excellent son's father-in-law! So with other old men—the Fabricii, the Curii and Coruncanii—when they were supporting the state by their advice and influence, they were doing nothing! To old age Appius Claudius had the additional disadvantage of being blind; yet it was he who, when the Senate was inclining towards a peace with Pyrrhus and was for making a treaty, did not hesitate to say what Ennius has embalmed in the verses:

> Whither have swerved the souls so firm of yore?
> Is sense grown senseless? Can feet stand no more?

And so on in a tone of the most passionate vehemence. You know the poem, and the speech of Appius himself is extant. Now, he delivered it seventeen years after his second consulship, there having been an interval of ten years between the two consulships, and he having been censor before his previous consulship. This will show you that at the time of the war with Pyrrhus he was a very old man. Yet this is the story handed down to us.

There is therefore nothing in the arguments of those who say that old age takes no part in public business. They are like men who would say that a steersman does nothing in sailing a ship, because, while some of the crew are climbing the masts, others hurrying up and down the gangways, others pumping out the bilge water, he sits quietly in the stern holding the tiller. He does not do what young men do; nevertheless he does what is much more important and better. The great affairs of life are not performed by physical strength, or activity, or nimbleness of body, but by deliberation, character, expression of opinion. Of these old age is not only not deprived, but, as a rule, has them in a greater degree. Unless by any chance I, who as a soldier in the ranks, as military tribune, as legate, and as consul have been employed in various kinds of war, now appear to you to be idle because not actively engaged in war. But I enjoin upon the Senate what is to be done, and how. Carthage has long been harbouring evil designs, and I accordingly proclaim war against her in good time. I shall never cease to entertain fears about her till I hear of her having been levelled with the ground. The glory of doing that I pray that the immortal gods may reserve for you, Scipio, so that you may complete the task begun by your grandfather, now dead more than thirty-two years ago; though all years to come will keep that great man's memory green. He died in the year before my censorship, nine years after my consulship, having been returned consul for the second time in my own consulship. If then he had lived to his hundredth year, would he have regretted having lived to be old? For he would of course not have been practising rapid marches, nor dashing on a foe, nor hurling spears from a distance, nor using swords at close quarters—but only counsel, reason, and senatorial eloquence. And if those qualities had not resided in us *seniors,* our ancestors would never have called their supreme council a *Senate.* At Sparta, indeed, those who hold the highest magistracies are in accordance with the fact actually called "elders." But if you will take the trouble to read or listen to foreign history, you will find that the mightiest states have been brought into peril by young men, have been supported and restored by old. The question occurs in the poet Naevius' *Sport:*

> Pray, who are those who brought your state
> With such despatch to meet its fate?

There is a long answer, but this is the chief point:

> A crop of brand-new orators we grew,
> And foolish, paltry lads who thought they knew.

For of course rashness is the note of youth, prudence of old age.

But, it is said, memory dwindles. No doubt, unless you keep it in practice, or if you happen to be somewhat dull by nature. Themistocles had the names of all his fellow-citizens by heart. Do you imagine that in his old age he used to address Aristides as Lysimachus? For my part, I know not only the present generation, but their fathers also, and their grandfathers. Nor have I any fear of losing my memory by reading tombstones, according to the vulgar superstition. On the contrary, by reading them I renew my memory of those who are dead and gone. Nor, in point of fact, have I ever heard of any old man forgetting where he had hidden his money. They remember everything that interests them: when to answer to their bail, business appointments, who owes them money, and to whom they owe it. What about lawyers, pontiffs, augurs, philosophers, when old? What a multitude of things they remember! Old men retain their intellects well enough, if only they keep their minds active and fully employed. Nor is that the case only with men of high position and great office: it applies equally to private life and peaceful pursuits. Sophocles composed tragedies to extreme old age; and being believed to neglect the care of his property owing to his devotion to his art, his sons brought him into court to get a judicial decision depriving him of the management of his property on the ground of weak intellect—just as in our law it is customary to deprive a paterfamilias of the management of his property if he is squandering it. Thereupon the old poet is said to have read to the judges the play he had on hand and had just composed—the *Oedipus Coloneus*—and to have asked them whether they thought that the work of a man of weak intellect. After the reading he was acquitted by the jury. Did old age then compel this man to become silent in his particular art, or Homer, Hesiod, Simonides, or Isocrates and Gorgias, whom I mentioned before, or the founders of schools of philosophy, Pythagoras, Democritus, Plato, Xenocrates, or later Zeno and Cleanthus, or Diogenes the Stoic, whom you too saw at Rome? Is it not rather the case with all these that the active pursuit of study only ended with life?

But, to pass over these sublime studies, I can name some rustic Romans from the Sabine district, neighbours and friends of my own, without whose presence farm work of importance is scarcely ever performed —whether sowing, or harvesting or storing crops. And yet in other things this is less surprising; for no one is so old as to think that he may not live a year. But they bestow their labour on what they know does not affect them in any case:

> He plants his trees to serve a race to come,

as our poet Statius says in his *Comrades*. Nor indeed would a farmer, however old, hesitate to answer any one who asked him for whom he was planting: "For the immortal gods, whose will it was that I should not merely receive these things from my ancestors, but should also hand them on to the next generation."

That remark about the old man is better than the following:

> If age brought nothing worse than this,
> It were enough to mar our bliss,
> That he who bides for many years
> Sees much to shun and much for tears.

Yes, and perhaps much that gives him pleasure too. Besides, as to subjects for tears, he often comes upon them in youth as well.

A still more questionable sentiment in the same Caecilius is:

> No greater misery can of age be told
> Than this: be sure, the young dislike the old.

Delight in them is nearer the mark than dislike. For just as old men, if they are wise, take pleasure in the society of young men of good parts, and as old age is rendered less dreary for those who are courted and liked by the youth, so also do young men find pleasure in the maxims of the old, by which they are drawn to the pursuit of excellence. Nor do I perceive that you find my society less pleasant than I do yours. But this is enough to show you how, so far from being listless and sluggish, old age is even a busy time, always doing and attempting something, of course of the same nature as each man's taste had been in the previous part of his life. Nay, do not some even add to their stock of learning? We see Solon, for instance, boasting in his poems that he grows old "daily learning something new." Or again in my own case, it was only when an old man that I became acquainted with Greek literature, which in fact I absorbed with such avidity—in my yearning to quench, as it were, a long-continued thirst—that I became acquainted with the very facts which you see me now using as precedents. When I heard what Socrates had done about the lyre I should have liked for my part to have done that too, for the ancients used to learn the lyre, but, at any rate, I worked hard at literature.

Nor, again, do I now MISS THE BODILY STRENGTH OF A YOUNG MAN (for that was the second point as to the disadvantages of old age) any more than as a young man I missed the strength of a bull or an elephant. You should use what you have, and whatever you may chance to be doing, do it with all your might. What could be weaker than Milo of Croton's exclamation? When in his old age he was watching some athletes practising in the course, he is said to have looked at his arms and to have exclaimed with tears in his eyes: "Ah, well! these are now as good as dead." Not a bit more so than yourself, you trifler! For at no time were you made famous by your real self, but by chest and biceps. Sext. Aelius never gave vent to such a remark, nor, many years before him, Titus Coruncanius, nor, more recently, P. Crassus—all of them learned jurisconsults in active practice, whose knowledge of their profession was maintained to their last breath. I am afraid an orator does lose vigour by old age, for his art is not a matter of the intellect alone, but of lungs and bodily strength. Though as a rule that musical ring in the voice even gains in brilliance in a certain way as one grows old—certainly I have not yet lost it, and you see my years. Yet after all the style of speech suitable to an old man is the quiet and unemotional, and it often happens that the chastened and calm delivery of an old man eloquent secures a hearing. If you cannot attain to that yourself, you might still instruct a Scipio and a Laelius. For what is more charming than old age surrounded by the enthusiasm of youth? Shall we not allow old age even the strength to teach the young, to train and equip them for all the duties of life? And what can be a nobler employment? For my part, I used to think Publius and Gnaeus Scipio and your two grandfathers, L. Aemilius and P. Africanus, fortunate men when I saw them with a company of young nobles about them. Nor should we think any teachers of the fine arts otherwise than happy, however much their bodily forces may have decayed and failed. And yet that same failure of the bodily forces is more often brought about by the vices of youth than of old age; for a dissolute and intemperate youth hands down the body to old age in a worn-out state. Xenophon's Cyrus, for instance, in his discourse delivered on his death-bed and at a very advanced age, says that he never perceived his old age to have become weaker than his youth had been. I remember as a boy Lucius Metellus, who, having been created Pontifex Maximus four years after his second consulship, held that office twenty-two years, enjoying such excellent strength of body in the very last hours of his life as not to miss his youth. I need not speak of myself; though that indeed is an old man's way and is generally allowed to my time of life. Don't you see in Homer how frequently Nestor talks of his own good qualities? For he was living through a third generation; nor had he any reason to fear that upon saying what was true about himself he should appear either over vain or talkative. For, as Homer says, "from his lips flowed discourse sweeter than honey," for which sweet breath he wanted no bodily strength. And yet, after all, the famous leader of the Greeks nowhere wishes to have ten men like Ajax, but like Nestor: if he could get them, he feels no doubt of Troy shortly falling.

But to return to my own case: I am in my eighty-fourth year. I could wish that I had been able to make the same boast as Cyrus; but, after all, I can say this: I am not indeed as vigorous as I was as a private soldier in the Punic War, or as quaestor in the same war, or as consul in Spain, and four years later when as a military tribune I took part in the engagement at Thermopylae under the consul Manius Acilius Glabrio; but yet, as you see, old age has not entirely destroyed my muscles, has not quite brought me to the ground. The Senate-house does not find all my vigour gone, nor the rostra, nor my friends, nor my clients, nor my foreign guests. For I have never given in to that ancient and much praised proverb:

> Old when young
> Is old for long.

For myself, I had rather be an old man a somewhat shorter time than an old man *before* my time. Accordingly, no one up to the present has wished to see me, to whom I have been denied as engaged. But, it may be said, I have less strength than either of you. Neither have you the strength of the centurion T. Pontius: is he the more eminent man on that account? Let there be only a proper husbanding of strength, and let each man proportion his efforts to his powers. Such an one will assuredly not be possessed with any great regret for his loss of strength. At Olympia Milo is said to have stepped into the course carrying a live ox on his shoulders. Which then of the two would you prefer to have given to you—bodily strength like that, or intellectual strength like that of Pythagoras? In fine, enjoy that blessing when you have it; when it is gone, don't wish it back—unless we are to think that young men should wish their childhood back, and those somewhat older their youth! The course of life is fixed, and nature admits of its being run but in one way, and only once; and to each part of our life there is something specially seasonable; so that the feebleness of children, as well as the high spirit of youth, the soberness of maturer years, and the ripe wisdom of old age—all have a certain natural advantage which should be secured in its proper season. I think you are informed, Scipio, what your grandfather's foreign friend Masinissa does to this day, though ninety years old. When he has once begun a journey on foot he does not mount his horse at all; when on horseback he never gets off his horse. By no rain or cold can he be induced to cover his head. His body is absolutely free from unhealthy humours, and so he still performs all the duties and functions of a king. Active exercise, therefore, and temperance can preserve some part of one's former strength even in old age.

Bodily strength is wanting to old age; but neither is bodily strength demanded from old men. Therefore, both by law and custom, men of my time of life are exempt from those duties which cannot be supported without bodily strength. Accordingly not only are we not forced to do what we cannot do; we are not even obliged to do as much as we can. But, it will be said, many old men are so feeble that they cannot perform any duty in life of any sort or kind. That is not a weakness to be set down as peculiar to old age: it is one shared by ill health. How feeble was the son of P. Africanus, who adopted you! What weak health he had, or rather no health at all! If that had not been the case, we should have had in him a second brilliant light in the political horizon; for he had added a wider cultivation to his father's greatness of spirit. What wonder then, that old men are eventually feeble, when even young men cannot escape it? My dear Laelius and Scipio, we must stand up against old age and make up for its drawbacks by taking pains. We must fight it as we should an illness. We must look after our health, use moderate exercise, take just enough food and drink to recruit, but not to overload, our strength. Nor is it the body alone that must be supported, but the intellect and soul much more. For they are like lamps: unless you feed them with oil, they too go out from old age. Again, the body is apt to get gross from exercise; but the intellect becomes nimbler by exercising itself. For what Caecilius means by "old dotards of the comic stage" are the credulous, the forgetful, and the slipshod. These are faults that do not attach to old age as such, but to a sluggish, spiritless, and sleepy old age. Young men are more frequently wanton and dissolute than old men; but yet, as it is not all young men that are so, but the bad set among them, even so senile folly—usually called imbecility—applies to old men of unsound character, not to all. Appius governed four sturdy sons, five daughters, that great establishment, and all those clients, though he was both old and blind. For he kept his mind at full stretch like a bow, and never gave in to old age by growing slack. He maintained not merely an influence but an absolute command over his family: his slaves feared him, his sons were in awe of him, all loved him. In that family, indeed, ancestral custom and discipline were in full vigour. The fact is that old age is respectable just as long as it asserts itself, maintains its proper rights, and is not enslaved to any one. For as I admire a young man who has something of the old man in him, so do I an old one who has something of a young man. The man who aims at this may possibly become old in body—in mind he never will. I am now engaged in composing the seventh book of my *Origins*. I collect all the records of antiquity. The speeches delivered in all the celebrated cases which I have defended I am at this particular time getting into shape for publication. I am writing treatises on augural, pontifical, and civil law. I am, besides, studying hard at Greek, and after the manner of the Pythagoreans—to keep my memory in working order—I repeat in the evening whatever I have said, heard, or done in the course of each day. These are the exercises of the intellect, these the training-grounds of the mind: while I sweat and labour on these I don't much feel the loss of bodily strength. I appear in court for my friends; I frequently attend the Senate and bring motions before it on my own responsibility, prepared after deep and long reflection. And these I support by my intellectual, not my bodily forces. And if I were not strong enough to do these things, yet I should enjoy my sofa—imagining the very operations which I was now unable to perform. But what makes me capable of doing this is my past life. For a man who is always living in the midst of these studies and labours does not perceive when old age creeps upon him. Thus, by slow and imperceptible degrees life draws to its end. There is no sudden breakage; it just slowly goes out.

The third charge against old age is that it LACKS SENSUAL PLEASURES. What a splendid service does old age render, if it takes from us the greatest blot of youth! Listen, my dear young friends, to a speech of Archytas of Tarentum, among the greatest and most illustrious of men, which was put into my hands when as a young man I was at Tarentum with Q. Maximus. "No more deadly curse than sensual pleasure has been inflicted on mankind by nature, to gratify which our wanton appetites are roused beyond all prudence or restraint. It is a fruitful source of treasons, revolutions, secret communications with the enemy. In fact, there is no crime, no evil deed, to which the appetite for sensual pleasures does not impel us. Fornications and adulteries, and every abomination of that kind, are brought about by the enticements of pleasure and by them alone. Intellect is the best gift of nature or God: to this divine gift and endowment there is nothing so inimical as pleasure. For when appetite is our master, there is no place for self-control; nor where pleasure reigns supreme can virtue hold its ground. To see this more vividly, imagine a man excited to the highest conceivable pitch of sensual pleasure. It can be doubtful to no one that such a person, so long as he is under the influence of such excitation of the senses, will be unable to use to any purpose either intellect, reason, or thought. Therefore nothing can be so execrable and so fatal as pleasure; since, when more than ordinarily violent and lasting, it darkens all the light of the soul."

These were the words addressed by Archytas to the Samnite Gaius Pontius, father of the man by whom the consuls Spurius Postumius and

Titus Veturius were beaten in the battle of Caudium. My friend Nearchus of Tarentum, who had remained loyal to Rome, told me that he had heard them repeated by some old men; and that Plato the Athenian was present, who visited Tarentum, I find, in the consulship of L. Camillus and Appius Claudius.

What is the point of all this? It is to show you that, if we were unable to scorn pleasure by the aid of reason and philosophy, we ought to have been very grateful to old age for depriving us of all inclination for that which it was wrong to do. For pleasure hinders thought, is a foe to reason, and, so to speak, blinds the eyes of the mind. It is, moreover, entirely alien to virtue. I was sorry to have to expel Lucius, brother of the gallant Titus Flamininus, from the Senate seven years after his consulship; but I thought it imperative to affix a stigma on an act of gross sensuality. For when he was in Gaul as consul, he had yielded to the entreaties of his paramour at a dinner-party to behead a man who happened to be in prison condemned on a capital charge. When his brother Titus was Censor, who preceded me, he escaped; but I and Flaccus could not countenance an act of such criminal and abandoned lust, especially as, besides the personal dishonour, it brought disgrace on the government.

I have often been told by men older than myself, who said that they had heard it as boys from old men, that Gaius Fabricius was in the habit of expressing astonishment at having heard, when envoy at the headquarters of King Pyrrhus, from the Thessalian Cineas, that there was a man of Athens who professed to be a "philosopher," and affirmed that everything we did was to be referred to pleasure. When he told this to Manius Curius and Publius Decius, they used to remark that they wished that the Samnites and Pyrrhus himself would hold the same opinion. It would be much easier to conquer them, if they had once given themselves over to sensual indulgences. Manius Curius had been intimate with P. Decius, who four years before the former's consulship had devoted himself to death for the republic. Both Fabricius and Coruncanius knew him also, and from the experience of their own lives, as well as from the action of P. Decius, they were of opinion that there did exist something intrinsically noble and great, which was sought for its own sake, and at which all the best men aimed, to the contempt and neglect of pleasure. Why then do I spend so many words on the subject of pleasure? Why, because, far from being a charge against old age, that it does not much feel the want of any pleasures, it is its highest praise.

But, you will say, it is deprived of the pleasures of the table, the heaped-up board, the rapid passing of the wine-cup. Well, then, it is also free from headache, disordered digestion, broken sleep. But if we must grant pleasure something, since we do not find it easy to resist its charms—for Plato, with happy inspiration, calls pleasure "vice's bait," because of course men are caught by it as fish by a hook—yet, although old age has to abstain from extravagant banquets, it is still capable of enjoying modest festivities. As a boy I often used to see Gaius Duilius, the son of Marcus, then an old man, returning from a dinner-party. He thoroughly enjoyed the frequent use of torch and flute-player, distinctions which he had assumed though unprecedented in the case of a private person. It was the privilege of his glory. But why mention others? I will come back to my own case. To begin with, I have always remained a member of a "club"—clubs, you know, were established in my quaestorship on the reception of the Magna Mater from Ida. So I used to dine at their feast with the members of my club—on the whole with moderation, though there was a certain warmth of temperament natural to my time of life; but as that advances there is a daily decrease of all excitement. Nor was I, in fact, ever wont to measure my enjoyment even of these banquets by the physical pleasures they gave more than by the gathering and conversation of friends. For it was a good idea of our ancestors to style the presence of guests at a dinner-table—seeing that it implied a community of enjoyment—a *convivium*, "a living together." It is a better term than the Greek words which mean "a drinking together" or "an eating together." For they would seem to give the preference to what is really the least important part of it.

For myself, owing to the pleasure I take in conversation, I enjoy even banquets that begin early in the afternoon, and not only in company with my contemporaries—of whom very few survive—but also with men of your age and with yourselves. I am thankful to old age, which has increased my avidity for conversation, while it has removed that for eating and drinking. But if any one does enjoy these—not to seem to have proclaimed war against all pleasure without exception, which is perhaps a feeling inspired by nature—I fail to perceive even in these very pleasures that old age is entirely without the power of appreciation. For myself, I take delight even in the old-fashioned appointment of master of the feast; and in the arrangement of the conversation, which according to ancestral custom is begun from the last place on the left-hand couch when the wine is brought in; as also in the cups which, as in Xenophon's banquet, are small and filled by driblets; and in the contrivance for cooling in summer, and for warming by the winter sun or winter fire. These things I keep up even among my Sabine countrymen, and every day have a full dinner-party of neighbours, which we prolong as far into the night as we can with varied conversation.

But you may urge—there is not the same tingling sensation of pleasure in old men. No doubt; but neither do they miss it so much. For nothing gives you uneasiness which you do not miss. That was a fine answer of Sophocles to a man who asked him, when in extreme old age, whether he was still a lover. "Heaven forbid!" he replied; "I was only too glad to escape from that, as though from a boorish and insane master." To men indeed who are keen after such things it may possibly appear disagreeable and uncomfortable to be without them; but to jaded appetites it is pleasanter to lack than to enjoy. However, he cannot be said to lack who does not want: my contention is that not to want is the pleasanter thing.

But even granting that youth enjoys these pleasures with more zest; in the first place, they are insignificant things to enjoy, as I have said; and in the second place, such as age is not entirely without, if it does not possess them in profusion. Just as a man gets greater pleasure from Ambivius Turpio if seated in the front row at the theatre than if he was in the last, yet, after all, the man in the last row does get pleasure; so youth, because it looks at pleasures at closer quarters, perhaps enjoys itself more, yet even old age, looking at them from a distance, does enjoy itself well enough. Why, what blessings are these—that the soul, having served its time, so to speak, in the campaigns of desire and ambition, rivalry and hatred, and all the passions, should live in its own thoughts, and, as the expression goes, should dwell apart! Indeed, if it has in store any of what I may call the food of study and philosophy, nothing can be pleasanter than an old age of leisure. We were witnesses to C. Gallus—a friend of your father's, Scipio—intent to the day of his death on mapping out the sky and land. How often did the light surprise him while still working out a problem begun during the night! How often did night find him busy on what he had begun at dawn! How he delighted in predicting for us solar and lunar eclipses long before they occurred! Or again in studies of a lighter nature, though still requiring keenness of intellect, what pleasure Naevius took in his *Punic War!* Plautus in his *Truculentus* and *Pseudolus!* I even saw Livius Andronicus, who, having produced a play six years before I was born—in the consulship of Cento and Tuditanus—lived till I had become a young man. Why speak of Publius Licinius Crassus' devotion to pontifical and civil law, or of the Publius Scipio of the present time, who within these last few days has been created Pontifex Maximus? And yet I have seen all whom I have mentioned ardent in these pursuits when old men. Then there is Marcus Cethegus, whom Ennius justly called "Persuasion's Marrow"—with what enthusiasm did we see him exert himself in oratory even when quite old! What pleasures are there in feasts, games, or mistresses comparable to pleasures such as these? And they are all tastes, too, connected with learning, which in men of sense and good education grow with their growth. It is indeed an honourable sentiment which Solon expresses in a verse which I have quoted before—that he grew old learning many a fresh lesson every day. Than that intellectual pleasure none certainly can be greater.

I come now to the pleasures of the farmer, in which I take amazing delight. These are not hindered by any extent of old age, and seem to me to approach nearest to the ideal wise man's life. For he has to deal with the earth, which never refuses its obedience, nor ever returns what it has received without usury; sometimes, indeed, with less, but generally with greater interest. For my part, however, it is not merely the thing produced, but the earth's own force and natural productiveness that delight me. For having received in its bosom the seed scattered broadcast upon it, softened and broken up, she first keeps it concealed therein (hence the harrowing which accomplishes this gets its name from a word meaning "to hide"); next, when it has been warmed by her heat and close pressure, she splits it open and draws from it the greenery of the blade. This, supported by the fibres of the root, little by little grows up, and held upright by its jointed stalk is enclosed in sheaths, as being still immature. When it has emerged from them it produces an ear of corn arranged in order, and is defended against the pecking of the smaller birds by a regular palisade of spikes.

Need I mention the starting, planting, and growth of vines? I can never have too much of this pleasure—to let you into the secret of what gives my old age repose and amusement. For I say nothing here of the natural force which all things propagated from the earth possess—the earth which from that tiny grain in a fig, or the grapestone in a grape, or the most minute seeds of the other cereals and plants, produces such huge trunks and boughs. Mallet-shoots, slips, cuttings, quicksets, layers—are they not enough to fill any one with delight and astonishment? The vine by nature is apt to fall, and unless supported drops down to the earth; yet in order to keep itself upright it embraces whatever it reaches with its tendrils as though they were hands. Then as it creeps on, spreading itself in intricate and wild profusion, the dresser's art prunes it with the knife and prevents it growing a forest of shoots and expanding to excess in every direction. Accordingly at the beginning of spring in the shoots which have been left there protrudes at each of the joints what is termed an "eye." From this the grape emerges and shows itself; which, swollen by the juice of the earth and the heat of the sun, is at first very bitter to the taste, but afterwards grows sweet as it matures; and being covered with tendrils is never without a moderate warmth, and yet is able to ward off the fiery heat of the sun. Can anything be richer in product or more beautiful to contemplate? It is not its utility only, as I said before, that charms me, but the method of its cultivation and the natural process of its growth: the rows of uprights, the cross-pieces for the tops of the plants, the tying up of the vines and their propagation by layers, the pruning, to which I have already referred, of some shoots, the setting of others. I need hardly mention irrigation, or trenching and digging the soil, which much increase its fertility. As to the advantages of manuring I have spoken in my book on agriculture. The learned Hesiod did not say a single word on this subject, though he was writing on the cultivation of the soil; yet Homer, who in my opinion was many generations earlier, represents Laertes as softening his regret for his son by cultivating and manuring his farm. Nor is it only in cornfields and meadows and vineyards and plantations that a farmer's life is made cheerful. There are the garden and the orchard, the feeding of sheep, the swarms of bees, endless varieties of flowers. Nor is it only planting out that charms: there is also grafting—surely the most ingenious invention ever made by husbandmen.

I might continue my list of the delights of country life; but even what I have said I think is somewhat overlong. However, you must pardon me; for farming is a very favourite hobby of mine, and old age is naturally rather garrulous—for I would not be thought to acquit it of all faults.

Well, it was in a life of this sort that Manius Curius, after celebrating triumphs over the Samnites, the Sabines, and Pyrrhus, spent his last days. When I look at his villa—for it is not far from my own—I never can enough admire the man's own frugality or the spirit of the age. As Curius was sitting at his hearth the Samnites, who brought him a large sum of gold, were repulsed by him; for it was not, he said, a fine thing in his eyes to possess gold, but to rule those who possessed it. Could such a high spirit fail to make old age pleasant?

But to return to farmers—not to wander from my own *métier*. In those days there were senators, *i.e.*, old men, on their farms. For L. Quinctius Cincinnatus was actually at the plough when word was brought him that he had been named dictator. It was by his order as dictator, by the way, that C. Servilius Ahala, the master of the horse, seized and put to death Spurius Maelius when attempting to obtain royal power. Curius as well as other old men used to receive their summonses to attend the Senate in their farm-houses, from which circumstances the summoners were called *viatores* or "travellers." Was these men's old age an object of pity who found their pleasure in the cultivation of the land? In my opinion, scarcely any life can be more blessed, not alone from its utility (for agriculture is beneficial to the whole human race), but also as much from the mere pleasure of the thing, to which I have already alluded, and from the rich abundance and supply of all things necessary for the food of man and for the worship of the gods above. So, as these are objects of *desire* to certain people, let us make our peace with pleasure. For the good and hard-working farmer's wine-cellar and oil-store, as well as his larder, are always well filled, and his whole farm-house is richly furnished. It abounds in pigs, goats, lambs, fowls, milk, cheese, and honey. Then there is the garden, which the farmers themselves call their "second flitch." A zest and flavour is added to all these by hunting and fowling in spare hours. Need I mention the greenery of meadows, the rows of trees, the beauty of vineyard and olive grove? I will put it briefly: nothing can either furnish necessaries more richly, or present a fairer spectacle, than well-cultivated land. And to the enjoyment of that, old age does not merely present no hindrance—it actually invites and allures to it. For where else can it better warm itself, either by basking in the sun or by sitting by the fire, or at the proper time cool itself more wholesomely by the help of shade or water? Let the young keep their arms then to themselves, their horses, spears, their foils and ball, their swimming-baths and running-path. To us old men let them, out of the many forms of sport, leave dice and counters; but even that as they choose, since old age can be quite happy without them.

Xenophon's books are very useful for many purposes. Pray go on reading them with attention, as you have ever done. In what ample terms is agriculture lauded by him in the book about husbanding one's property, which is called *Oeconomicus!* But to show you that he thought nothing so worthy of a prince as the taste for cultivating the soil, I will translate what Socrates says to Critobulus in that book:

"When that most gallant Lacedaemonian, Lysander, came to visit the Persian prince Cyrus at Sardis, so eminent for his character and the glory of his rule, bringing him presents from his allies, he treated Lysander in all ways with courteous familiarity and kindness, and, among other things, took him to see a certain park carefully planted. Lysander expressed admiration of the height of the trees and the exact arrangement of their rows in the quincunx, the careful cultivation of the soil, its freedom from weeds, and the sweetness of the odours exhaled from the flowers, and went on to say that what he admired was not the industry only, but also the skill of the man by whom this had been planned and laid out. Cyrus replied: 'Well, it was I who planned the whole thing; these rows are my doing, the laying out is all mine; many of the trees were even planted by my own hand.' Then Lysander, looking at his purple robe, the brilliance of his person, and his adornment Persian fashion with gold and many jewels, said: 'People are quite right, Cyrus, to call you happy, since the advantages of high fortune have been joined to an excellence like yours.'"

This kind of good fortune, then, it is in the power of old men to enjoy; nor is age any bar to our maintaining pursuits of every other kind, and especially of agriculture, to the very extreme verge of old age. For instance, we have it on record that M. Valerius Corvus kept it up to his hundredth year, living on his land and cultivating it after his active career was over, though between his first and sixth consulships there was an interval of six and forty years. So that he had an official career lasting the number of years which our ancestors defined as coming between birth and the beginning of old age. Moreover, that last period of his old age was more blessed than that of his middle life, inasmuch as he had greater influence and less labour. For the crowning grace of old age is influence.

How great was that of L. Caecilius Metellus! How great that of Atilius Calatinus, over whom the famous epitaph was placed, "Very many classes agree in deeming this to have been the very first man of the nation"! The line cut on his tomb is well known. It is natural, then, that a man should have had influence, in whose praise the verdict of history is unanimous. Again, in recent times, what a great man was Publius Crassus, Pontifex Maximus, and his successor in the same office, M. Lepidus! I need scarcely mention Paulus or Africanus, or, as I did before, Maximus. It was not only their senatorial utterances that had weight: their least gesture had it also. In fact, old age, especially when it has enjoyed honours, has an influence worth all the pleasures of youth put together.

But throughout my discourse remember that my panegyric applies to an old age that has been established on foundations laid by youth. From which may be deduced what I once said with universal applause, that it was a wretched old age that had to defend itself by speech. Neither white hairs nor wrinkles can at once claim influence in themselves: it is the honourable conduct of earlier days that is rewarded by possessing influence at the last. Even things generally regarded as trifling and matters of course—being saluted, being courted, having way made for one, people rising when one approaches, being escorted to and from the forum, being referred to for advice—all these are marks of respect, observed among us and in other states—always most sedulously where the moral tone is highest. They say that Lysander the Spartan, whom I have mentioned before, used to remark that Sparta was the most dignified home for old age; for that nowhere was more respect paid to years, nowhere was old age held in higher honour. Nay, the story is told of how when a man of advanced years came into the theatre at Athens when the games were going on, no place was given him anywhere in that large assembly by his own countrymen; but when he came near the Lacedaemonians, who as ambassadors had a fixed place assigned to them, they rose as one man out of respect for him, and gave the veteran a seat. When they were greeted with rounds of applause from the whole audience, one of them remarked: "The Athenians know what is right, but will not do it."

There are many excellent rules in our augural college, but among the best is one which affects our subject—that precedence in speech goes by seniority; and augurs who are older are preferred not only to those who have held higher office, but even to those who are actually in possession of *imperium*. What then are the physical pleasures to be compared with the reward of influence? Those who have employed it with distinction appear to me to have played the drama of life to its end, and not to have broken down in the last act like unpractised players.

But, it will be said, old men are fretful, fidgety, ill tempered, and disagreeable. If you come to that, they are also avaricious. But these are faults of character, not of the time of life. And, after all, fretfulness and the other faults I mentioned admit of some excuse—not, indeed, a complete one, but one that may possibly pass muster: they think themselves neglected, looked down upon, mocked. Besides, with bodily weakness every rub is a source of pain. Yet all these faults are softened both by good character and good education. Illustrations of this may be found in real life, as also on the stage in the case of the brothers in the *Adelphi*. What harshness in the one, what gracious manners in the other! The fact is that, just as it is not every wine, so it is not every life, that turns sour from keeping. Serious gravity I approve of in old age, but, as in other things, it must be within due limits: bitterness I can in no case approve. What the object of senile avarice may be I cannot conceive. For can there be anything more absurd than to seek more journey money, the less there remains of the journey?

There remains the fourth reason, which more than anything else appears to torment men of my age and keep them in a flutter—THE NEARNESS OF DEATH, which, it must be allowed, cannot be far from an old man. But what a poor dotard must he be who has not learnt in the course of so long a life that death is not a thing to be feared? Death, that is either to be totally disregarded, if it entirely extinguishes the soul, or is even to be desired, if it brings him where he is to exist forever. A third alternative, at any rate, cannot possibly be discovered. Why then should I be afraid if I am destined either not to be miserable after death or even to be happy? After all, who is such a fool as to feel certain—however young he may be—that he will be alive in the evening? Nay, that time of life has many more chances of death than ours. Young men more easily contract diseases; their illnesses are more serious; their treatment has to be more severe. Accordingly, only a few arrive at old age. If that were not so, life would be conducted better and more wisely; for it is in old men that thought, reason, and prudence are to be found; and if there had been no old men, states would never have existed at all. But I return to the subject of the imminence of death. What sort of charge is this against old age, when you see that it is shared by youth? I had reason in the case of my excellent son—as you had, Scipio, in that of your brothers, who were expected to attain the highest honours—to realize that death is common to every time of life. Yes, you will say; but a young man expects to live long; an old man cannot expect to do so. Well, he is a fool to expect it. For what can be more foolish than to regard the uncertain as certain, the false as true? "An old man has nothing even to hope." Ah, but it is just there that he is in a better position than a young man, since what the latter only hopes he has obtained. The one wishes to live long; the other has lived long.

And yet, good heavens! what is "long" in a man's life? For grant the utmost limit: let us expect an age like that of the King of the Tartessi. For there was, as I find recorded, a certain Agathonius at Gades who reigned eighty years and lived a hundred and twenty. But to my mind nothing seems even long in which there is any "last," for when that arrives, then all the past has slipped away—only that remains to which you have attained by virtue and righteous actions. Hours indeed, and days and months and years depart, nor does past time ever return, nor can the future be known. Whatever time each is granted for life, with that he is bound to be content. An actor, in order to earn approval, is not bound to perform the play from beginning to end; let him only satisfy the audience in whatever act he appears. Nor need a wise man go on to the concluding "plaudite." For a short term of life is long enough for living well and honourably. But if you go farther, you have no more right to grumble than farmers do because the charm of the spring season is past and the summer and autumn have come. For the word "spring" in a way suggests youth, and points to the harvest to be: the other seasons are suited for the reaping and storing of the crops. Now the harvest of old age is, as I have often said, the memory and rich store of blessings laid up in earlier life.

Again, all things that accord with nature are to be counted as good. But what can be more in accordance with nature than for old men to die? A thing, indeed, which also befalls young men, though Nature revolts and fights against it. Accordingly, the death of young men seems to me like putting out a great fire with a deluge of water; but old men die like a fire going out because it has burnt down of its own nature without artificial means. Again, just as apples when unripe are torn from trees, but when ripe and mellow drop down, so it is violence that takes life from young men, ripeness from old. This ripeness is so delightful to me that, as I approach nearer to death, I seem, as it were, to be sighting land, and to be coming to port at last after a long voyage.

Again, there is no fixed border-line for old age, and you are making a good and proper use of it as long as you can satisfy the call of duty and disregard death. The result of this is, that old age is even more confident and courageous than youth. That is the meaning of Solon's answer to the tyrant Pisistratus. When the latter asked him what he relied upon in opposing him with such boldness, he is said to have replied, "On my old age." But that end of life is the best when, without the intellect or senses being impaired, Nature herself takes to pieces her own handiwork which she also put together. Just as the builder of a ship or a house can break them up more easily than any one else, so the Nature that knit together the human frame can also best unfasten it. Moreover, a thing freshly glued together is always difficult to pull asunder; if old, this is easily done.

The result is that the short time of life left to them is not to be grasped at by old men with greedy eagerness, or abandoned without cause. Pythagoras forbids us, without an order from our commander, that is God, to desert life's fortress and outpost. Solon's epitaph, indeed, is that of a wise man, in which he says that he does not wish his death to be unaccompanied by the sorrow and lamentations of his friends. He wants, I suppose, to be beloved by them. But I rather think Ennius says better:

> None grace me with their tears, nor weeping loud
> Make sad my funeral rites!

He holds that a death is not a subject for mourning when it is followed by immortality.

Again, there may possibly be some sensation of dying—and that only for a short time, especially in the case of an old man: *after* death, indeed, sensation is either what one would desire, or it disappears altogether. But to disregard death is a lesson which must be studied from our youth up; for unless that is learnt, no one can have a quiet mind. For die we certainly must, and that too without being certain whether it may not be this very day. As death, therefore, is hanging over our head every hour, how can a man ever be unshaken in soul if he fears it?

But on this theme I don't think I need much enlarge: when I remember what Lucius Brutus did, who was killed while defending his country; or the two Decii, who spurred their horses to a gallop and met a voluntary death; or M. Atilius Regulus, who left his home to confront a death of torture, rather than break the word which he had pledged to the enemy; or the two Scipios, who determined to block the Carthaginian advance even with their own bodies; or your grandfather Lucius Paulus, who paid with his life for the rashness of his colleague in the disgrace at Cannae; or M. Marcellus, whose death not even the most bloodthirsty of enemies would allow to go without the honour of burial. It is enough to recall that our legions (as I have recorded in my *Origins*) have often marched with cheerful and lofty spirit to ground from which they believed that they would never return. That, therefore, which young men—not only uninstructed, but absolutely ignorant—treat as of no account, shall men who are neither young nor ignorant shrink from in terror? As a general truth, as it seems to me, it is weariness of all pursuits that creates weariness of life. There are certain pursuits adapted to childhood: do young men miss them? There are others suited to early manhood: does that settled time of life called "middle age" ask for them? There are others, again, suited to that age, but not looked for in old age. There are, finally, some which belong to old age. Therefore, as the pursuits of the earlier ages have their time for disappearing, so also have those of old age. And when that takes place, a satiety of life brings on the ripe time for death.

For I do not see why I should not venture to tell you my personal opinion as to death, of which I seem to myself to have a clearer vision in proportion as I am nearer to it. I believe, Scipio and Laelius, that your fathers—those illustrious men and my dearest friends—are still alive, and that too with a life which alone deserves the name. For as long as we are imprisoned in this framework of the body, we perform a certain function and laborious work assigned us by fate. The soul, in fact, is of heavenly origin, forced down from its home in the highest, and, so to speak, buried in earth, a place quite opposed to its divine nature and its immortality. But I suppose the immortal gods to have sown souls broadcast in human bodies, that there might be some to survey the world, and while contemplating the order of the heavenly bodies to imitate it in the unvarying regularity of their life. Nor is it only reason and arguments that have brought me to this belief, but the great fame and authority of the most distinguished philosophers. I used to be told that Pythagoras and the Pythagoreans—almost natives of our country, who in old times had been called the Italian school of philosophers—never doubted that we had souls drafted from the universal divine intelligence. I used besides to have pointed out to me the discourse delivered by Socrates on the last day of his life upon the immortality of the soul—Socrates, who was pronounced by the oracle at Delphi to be the wisest of men. I need say no more. I have convinced myself, and I hold—in view of the rapid movement of the soul, its vivid memory of the past and its prophetic knowledge of the future, its many accomplishments, its vast range of knowledge, its numerous discoveries—that a nature embracing such varied gifts cannot itself be mortal. And since the soul is always in motion and yet has no external source of motion, for it is self-moved, I conclude that it will also have no end to its motion, because it is not likely ever to abandon itself. Again, since the nature of the soul is not composite, nor has in it any admixture that is not homogeneous and similar, I conclude that it is indivisible, and, if indivisible, that it cannot perish. It is again a strong proof of men knowing most things before birth, that when mere children they grasp innumerable facts with such speed as to show that they are not then taking them in for the first time, but remembering and recalling them. This is roughly Plato's argument.

Once more in Xenophon we have the elder Cyrus on his death-bed speaking as follows:

"Do not suppose, my dearest sons, that when I have left you I shall be nowhere and no one. Even when I was with you, you did not see my soul, but knew that it was in this body of mine from what I did. Believe then that it is still the same, even though you see it not. The honours paid to illustrious men had not continued to exist after their death, had the souls of these very men not done something to make us retain our recollection of them beyond the ordinary time. For myself, I never could be persuaded that souls while in mortal bodies were alive, and died directly they left them; nor, in fact, that the soul only lost all intelligence when it left the unintelligent body. I believe rather that when, by being liberated from all corporeal admixture, it has begun to be pure and undefiled, it is then that it becomes wise. And again, when man's natural frame is resolved into its elements by death, it is clearly seen whither each of the other elements departs: for they all go to the place from which they came: but the soul alone is invisible alike when present and when departing. Once more, you see that nothing is so like death as sleep. And yet it is in sleepers that souls most clearly reveal their divine nature; for they foresee many events when they are allowed to escape and are left free. This shows what they are likely to be when they have completely freed themselves from the fetters of the body. Wherefore, if these things are so, obey me as a god. But if my soul is to perish with my body, nevertheless do you from awe of the gods, who guard and govern this fair universe, preserve my memory by the loyalty and piety of your lives."

Such are the words of the dying Cyrus. I will now, with your good leave, look at home. No one, my dear Scipio, shall ever persuade me that your father, Paulus, and your two grandfathers, Paulus and Africanus, or the father of Africanus, or his uncle, or many other illustrious men not necessary to mention, would have attempted such lofty deeds as to be remembered by posterity, had they not seen in their minds that future ages concerned them. Do you suppose—to take an old man's privilege of a little self-praise—that I should have been likely to undertake such heavy labours by day and night, at home and abroad, if I had been destined to have the same limit to my glory as to my life? Had it not been much better to pass an age of ease and repose without any labour or exertion? But my soul, I know not how, refusing to be kept down, ever fixed its eyes upon future ages, as though from a conviction that it would begin to live only when it had left the body. But had it not been the case that souls were immortal, it would not have been the souls of all the best men that made the greatest efforts after an immortality of fame.

Again, is there not the fact that the wisest man ever dies with the greatest cheerfulness, the most unwise with the least? Don't you think that the soul which has the clearer and longer sight sees that it is starting for better things, while the soul whose vision is dimmer does not see it? For my part, I am transported with the desire to see your fathers, who were the object of my reverence and affection. Nor is it only those whom I knew that I long to see; it is those also of whom I have been told and have read, whom I have myself recorded in my history. When I am setting out for that, there is certainly no one who will find it easy to draw me back, or boil me up again like second Pelios. Nay, if some god should grant me to renew my childhood from my present age and once more to be crying in my cradle, I would firmly refuse; nor should I in truth be willing, after having, as it were, run the full course, to be recalled from the winning-crease to the barriers. For what blessing has life to offer? Should we not rather say, what labour? But granting that it has, at any rate it has after all a limit either to enjoyment or to existence. I don't wish to depreciate life, as many men and good philosophers have often done; nor do I regret having lived, for I have done so in a way that lets me think that

I was not born in vain. But I quit life as I would an inn, not as I would a home. For nature has given us a place of entertainment, not of residence.

Oh, glorious day when I shall set out to join that heavenly conclave and company of souls, and depart from the turmoil and impurities of this world! For I shall not go to join only those whom I have before mentioned, but also my son Cato, than whom no better man was ever born, nor one more conspicuous for piety. His body was burnt by me, though mine ought, on the contrary, to have been burnt by him; but his spirit, not abandoning, but ever looking back upon me, has certainly gone whither he saw that I too must come. I was thought to bear that loss heroically, not that I really bore it without distress, but I found my own consolation in the thought that the parting and separation between us was not to be for long.

It is by these means, my dear Scipio—for you said that you and Laelius were wont to express surprise on this point—that my old age sits lightly on me, and is not only not oppressive but even delightful. But if I am wrong in thinking the human soul immortal, I am glad to be wrong; nor will I allow the mistake which gives me so much pleasure to be wrested from me as long as I live. But if when dead, as some insignificant philosophers think, I am to be without sensation, I am not afraid of dead philosophers deriding my errors. Again, if we are not to be immortal, it is nevertheless what a man must wish—to have his life end at its proper time. For nature puts a limit to living as to everything else. Now, old age is, as it were, the playing out of the drama, the full fatigue of which we should shun, especially when we also feel that we have had more than enough of it.

This is all I had to say on old age. I pray that you may arrive at it, that you may put my words to a practical test.

Translated by E. S. Shuckburgh.

Sir Francis Bacon [1]

1561–1626

Of the fixed things in Bacon's fixed world, nothing is more stable than mankind, nor did Bacon need to wait half a century for Locke to tell him that "human nature is always and everywhere the same." No doubt men are always different too, as between one individual and another, but as a whole they are all alike, and it is with the whole that Bacon is concerned in these essays on moral subjects. Hence his talk is generalized—stripped to the bone of common truth.

Of truth itself, he says candidly: "A mixture of a lie doth ever add pleasure." On other moral matters, he speaks with equal if chilling realism. "Men fear Death as children fear to go in the dark," he tells us, "and as that natural fear in children is increased with tales, so is the other." Bacon does not seek to change men, but to govern them. "To seek to extinguish Anger utterly is but a bravery of the Stoics," he says. "We have better oracles: 'Be angry, but sin not. Let not the sun go down upon your anger.' Anger must be limited and confined," he suggests instead, meaning that we must live with it.

Bacon does not reach noble heights, or try to. His talk is of the middle ground, where good and evil are always mixed—where men are what they are, not what they ought to be. They might act better than they do, certainly; nor does Bacon fail to suggest how. But he mostly has in mind their satisfaction and their safety rather than their souls. The reader should not decide too quickly that this is cynical. Perhaps souls are not much the business of the civil lawyer, who is concerned with something nearer than salvation—with this world rather than the next. Goodness is not impossible in the world,

---

[1] For a biography of Sir Francis Bacon, see Vol. 5, pp. 90–92, in this set.

except as the iniquity of the world is not recognized or faced. The point simply is—as Bacon might be taken to imply, following every philosopher since Plato—that the best man is in the end the wisest, and the one most knowing of humankind.

Of Truth

W hat is Truth?" said jesting Pilate; and would not stay for an answer. Certainly there be that delight in giddiness, and count it a bondage to fix a belief, affecting free will in thinking, as well as in acting. And though the sects of philosophers of that kind be gone, yet there remain certain discoursing wits which are of the same veins, though there be not so much blood in them as was in those of the ancients. But it is not only the difficulty and labour which men take in finding out of truth, nor again that when it is found it imposeth upon men's thoughts, that doth bring lies in favour, but a natural though corrupt love of the lie itself. One of the later school of the Grecians examineth the matter, and is at a stand to think what should be in it that men should love lies, where neither they make for pleasure, as with poets, nor for advantage, as with the merchant, but for the lie's sake. But I cannot tell: this same truth is a naked and open daylight, that doth not show the masks and mummeries and triumphs of the world half so stately and daintily as candlelights.

Truth may perhaps come to the price of a pearl, that showeth best by day; but it will not rise to the price of a diamond or carbuncle [ruby], that showeth best in varied lights. A mixture of a lie doth ever add pleasure. Doth any man doubt that if there were taken out of men's minds vain opinions, flattering hopes, false valuations, imaginations as one would, and the like, but it would leave the minds of a number of men poor shrunken things, full of melancholy and indisposition, and unpleasing to themselves? One of the Fathers, in great severity, called poesy *vinum daemonum* [devils' wine], because it filleth the imagination; and yet it is but with the shadow of a lie. But it is not the lie that passeth through the mind, but the lie that sinketh in and settleth in it, that doth the hurt; such as we spake of before. But howsoever these things are thus in men's depraved judgments and affections, yet truth, which only doth judge itself, teacheth that the inquiry of truth, which is the love-making or wooing of it, the knowledge of truth, which is the presence of it, and the

belief of truth, which is the enjoying of it, is the sovereign good of human
nature.

The first creature of God, in the works of the days, was the light of the
sense; the last was the light of reason; and his sabbath work ever since is
the illumination of his Spirit. First he breathed light upon the face of the
matter or chaos; then he breathed light into the face of man; and still he
breatheth and inspireth light into the face of his chosen. The poet that
beautified the sect that was otherwise inferior to the rest saith yet excel-
lently well: "It is a pleasure to stand upon the shore, and to see ships
tossed upon the sea; a pleasure to stand in the window of a castle, and to
see a battle and the adventures thereof below; but no pleasure is comparable to the standing upon the vantage ground of truth (a hill not to be
commanded, and where the air is always clear and serene), and to see the
errors, and wanderings, and mists, and tempests, in the vale below"; so
always that this prospect be with pity, and not with swelling or pride.
Certainly, it is heaven upon earth to have a man's mind move in charity,
rest in providence, and turn upon the poles of truth.

To pass from theological and philosophical truth to the truth of civil
business, it will be acknowledged even by those that practise it not that
clear and round dealing is the honour of man's nature; and that mixture of
falsehood is like alloy in coin of gold and silver, which may make the
metal work the better, but it embaseth it. For these winding and crooked
courses are the goings of the serpent, which goeth basely upon the belly,
and not upon the feet. There is no vice that doth so cover a man with shame
as to be found false and perfidious. And therefore Montaigne saith pret-
tily, when he inquired the reason, why the word of the lie should be such
a disgrace and such an odious charge. Saith he, "If it be well weighed, to
say that a man lieth is as much to say as that he is brave towards God and
a coward towards men." For a lie faces God, and shrinks from man. Surely
the wickedness of falsehood and breach of faith cannot possibly be so
highly expressed as in that it shall be the last peal to call the judgments of
God upon the generations of men; it being foretold that when Christ
cometh, "He shall not find faith upon the earth."

Of Death

Men fear death as children fear to go in the dark; and as that natural fear in children is increased with tales, so is the other. Certainly, the contemplation of death, as the wages of sin and passage to another world, is holy and religious; but the fear of it, as a tribute due unto nature, is weak. Yet in religious meditations there is sometimes mixture of vanity and of superstition. You shall read in some of the friars' books of mortification that a man should think with himself what the pain is if he have but his finger's end pressed or tortured, and thereby imagine what the pains of death are, when the whole body is corrupted and dissolved; when many times death passeth with less pain than the torture of a limb, for the most vital parts are not the quickest of sense. And by him that spake only as a philosopher and natural man, it was well said, *Pompa mortis magis terret quam mors ipsa* [The funeral procession is more terrible than death itself]. Groans and convulsions, and a discoloured face, and friends weeping, and blacks, and obsequies, and the like, show death terrible.

It is worthy the observing that there is no passion in the mind of man so weak but it mates and masters the fear of death; and therefore death is no such terrible enemy when a man hath so many attendants about him that can win the combat of him. Revenge triumphs over death; love slights it; honour aspireth to it; grief flieth to it; fear pre-occupateth it; nay we read, after Otho the emperor had slain himself, pity (which is the tenderest of affections) provoked many to die, out of mere compassion to their sovereign, and as the truest sort of followers. Nay Seneca adds niceness and satiety: *Cogita quamdiu eadem feceris; mori velle, non tantum fortis, aut miser, sed etiam fastidiosus potest* [Take thought, as long as you will do the same: not only the strong, not only the wretched, but also the fastidious man can welcome death]. A man would die, though he were neither valiant nor miserable, only upon a weariness to do the same thing so oft over and over.

348

It is no less worthy to observe how little alteration in good spirits the approaches of death make, for they appear to be the same men till the last instant. Augustus Caesar died in a compliment: *Livia, conjugii nostri memor, vive et vale* [Live and prosper, Livia, in remembrance of our marriage]. Tiberius in dissimulation, as Tacitus saith of him: *Jam Tiberium vires et corpus, non dissimulatio, deserebant* [For now his strength and his body, but not his duplicity, were deserting him]. Vespasian in a jest, sitting upon the stool: *Ut puto Deus fio* [As I see it, I am becoming a god]. Galba with a sentence: *Feri, si ex re sit populi Romani* [Strike, if it profits the Roman people]; holding forth his neck. Septimius Severus in despatch: *Adeste si quid mihi restat agendum* [Come, then, if there is still anything that I must do]. And the like. Certainly the Stoics bestowed too much cost upon death, and by their great preparations made it appear more fearful. Better saith he, *qui finem vitae extremum inter munera ponat naturae* [. . . , who counts the end of life among the gifts of nature]. It is as natural to die as to be born; and to a little infant, perhaps, the one is as painful as the other. He that dies in an earnest pursuit is like one that is wounded in hot blood; who, for the time, scarce feels the hurt; and therefore a mind fixed and bent upon somewhat that is good doth avert the dolours of death. But above all, believe it, the sweetest canticle [1] is, *Nunc dimittis* [Lord, now lettest thou thy servant depart in peace] when a man hath obtained worthy ends and expectations. Death hath this also: that it openeth the gate to good fame, and extinguisheth envy. *Extinctus amabitur idem* [That same man (who was envied while he was alive) shall be loved when he is dead].

---

1. The Canticle of Simeon, Luke 2:29 [Ed.].

Of Adversity

I t was a high speech of Seneca (after the manner of the Stoics), "that the good things which belong to prosperity are to be wished; but the good things that belong to adversity are to be admired." *Bona rerum secundarum optabilia; adversarum mirabilia.* Certainly if miracles be the command over nature, they appear most in adversity. It is yet a higher speech of his than the other (much too high for a heathen), "It is true greatness to have in one the frailty of a man, and the security of a God." *Vere magnum habere fragilitatem hominis, securitatem Dei.* This would have done better in poesy, where transcendences are more allowed. And the poets indeed have been busy with it; for it is in effect the thing which is figured in that strange fiction of the ancient poets, which seemeth not to be without mystery; nay, and to have some approach to the state of a Christian; that "Hercules, when he went to unbind Prometheus (by whom human nature is represented), sailed the length of the great ocean in an earthen pot or pitcher"; lively describing Christian resolution, that saileth in the frail bark of the flesh thorough the waves of the world.

But to speak in a mean. The virtue of prosperity is temperance; the virtue of adversity is fortitude, which in morals is the more heroical virtue. Prosperity is the blessing of the Old Testament; adversity is the blessing of the New, which carrieth the greater benediction, and the clearer revelation of God's favour. Yet even in the Old Testament, if you listen to David's harp, you shall hear as many hearse-like airs as carols; and the pencil of the Holy Ghost hath laboured more in describing the afflictions of Job than the felicities of Solomon. Prosperity is not without many fears and distastes; and adversity is not without comforts and hopes. We see in needleworks and embroideries it is more pleasing to have a lively work upon a sad and solemn ground than to have a dark and melancholy work upon a lightsome ground: judge therefore of the pleasure of the heart by the pleasure of the eye. Certainly virtue is like precious odours, most fragrant when they are incensed or crushed; for prosperity doth best discover vice, but adversity doth best discover virtue.

Of Love

The stage is more beholding to love than the life of man. For as to the stage, love is ever matter of comedies, and now and then of tragedies; but in life it doth much mischief, sometimes like a siren, sometimes like a fury. You may observe that amongst all the great and worthy persons (whereof the memory remaineth, either ancient or recent) there is not one that hath been transported to the mad degree of love, which shows that great spirits and great business do keep out this weak passion. You must except nevertheless Marcus Antonius, the half-partner of the empire of Rome, and Appius Claudius, the decemvir and lawgiver; whereof the former was indeed a voluptuous man, and inordinate; but the latter was an austere and wise man; and therefore it seems (though rarely) that love can find entrance not only into an open heart but also into a heart well fortified, if watch be not well kept.

It is a poor saying of Epicurus, *Satis magnum alter alteri theatrum sumus* [We are each for one another a theatre large enough]; as if man, made for the contemplation of heaven and all noble objects, should do nothing but kneel before a little idol, and make himself a subject, though not of the mouth (as beasts are), yet of the eye, which was given him for higher purposes. It is a strange thing to note the excess of this passion, and how it braves the nature and value of things, by this: that the speaking in a perpetual hyperbole is comely in nothing but in love. Neither is it merely in the phrase; for whereas it hath been well said that the arch-flatterer, with whom all the petty flatterers have intelligence, is a man's self, certainly the lover is more. For there was never proud man thought so absurdly well of himself as the lover doth of the person loved; and therefore it was well said, "That it is impossible to love and to be wise." Neither doth this weakness appear to others only, and not to the party loved; but to the loved most of all, except the love be reciprocal. For it is a true rule that love is ever rewarded either with the reciprocal or with an inward and secret contempt. By how much the more men ought to beware of this passion, which loseth not only other things, but itself. As for the other losses, the poet's relation doth well figure them: that he that preferred Helena quitted the gifts of Juno and Pallas. For whosoever esteemeth too much of amorous affection quitteth both riches and wisdom.

This passion hath his floods in the very times of weakness, which are great prosperity and great adversity, though this latter hath been less observed; both which times kindle love, and make it more fervent, and therefore show it to be the child of folly. They do best who, if they cannot but admit love, yet make it keep quarter, and sever it wholly from their serious affairs and actions of life; for if it check once with business, it troubleth men's fortunes, and maketh men that they can no ways be true to their own ends. I know not how, but martial men are given to love; I think it is but as they are given to wine, for perils commonly ask to be paid in pleasures. There is in man's nature a secret inclination and motion towards love of others, which, if it be not spent upon some one or a few, doth naturally spread itself towards many, and maketh men become humane and charitable; as it is seen sometimes in friars. Nuptial love maketh mankind; friendly love perfecteth it; but wanton love corrupteth and embaseth it.

Of Friendship

I t had been hard for him that spake it to have put more truth and untruth together in few words than in that speech, "Whosoever is delighted in solitude is either a wild beast or a god." For it is most true that a natural and secret hatred and aversation towards society in any man hath somewhat of the savage beast; but it is most untrue that it should have any character at all of the divine nature, except it proceed, not out of a pleasure in solitude, but out of a love and desire to sequester a man's self for a higher conversation, such as is found to have been falsely and feignedly in some of the heathen, as Epimenides the Candian, Numa the Roman, Empedocles the Sicilian, and Apollonius of Tyana, and truly and really in divers of the ancient hermits and holy fathers of the church. But little do men perceive what solitude is, and how far it extendeth. For a crowd is not company; and faces are but a gallery of pictures; and talk but a tinkling cymbal, where there is no love. The Latin adage meeteth with it a little: *Magna civitas, magna solitudo* [A great city is a great solitude]; because in a great town friends are scattered; so that there is not that fellowship, for the most part, which is in less neighbourhoods. But we may go further, and affirm most truly that it is a mere and miserable solitude to want true friends, without which the world is but a wilderness; and even in this sense also of solitude, whosoever in the frame of his nature and affections is unfit for friendship, he taketh it of the beast, and not from humanity.

A principal fruit of friendship is the ease and discharge of the fullness and swellings of the heart, which passions of all kinds do cause and induce. We know diseases of stoppings and suffocations are the most dangerous in the body; and it is not much otherwise in the mind. You may take sarza to open the liver, steel to open the spleen, flower of sulphur for the lungs, castoreum for the brain; but no receipt openeth the heart but a true friend, to whom you may impart griefs, joys, fears, hopes, suspicions,

353

counsels, and whatsoever lieth upon the heart to oppress it, in a kind of civil shrift or confession.

It is a strange thing to observe how high a rate great kings and monarchs do set upon this fruit of friendship whereof we speak: so great as they purchase it many times at the hazard of their own safety and greatness. For princes, in regard of the distance of their fortune from that of their subjects and servants, cannot gather this fruit except (to make themselves capable thereof) they raise some persons to be as it were companions and almost equals to themselves, which many times sorteth to inconvenience. The modern languages give unto such persons the name of favourites, or privadoes, as if it were matter of grace, or conversation. But the Roman name attaineth the true use and cause thereof, naming them *participes curarum* [those who share in troubles], for it is that which tieth the knot. And we see plainly that this hath been done, not by weak and passionate princes only, but by the wisest and most politic that ever reigned; who have oftentimes joined to themselves some of their servants; whom both themselves have called friends, and allowed others likewise to call them in the same manner, using the word which is received between private men.

L. Sylla, when he commanded Rome, raised Pompey (after surnamed the Great) to that height, that Pompey vaunted himself for Sylla's overmatch. For when he had carried the consulship for a friend of his against the pursuit of Sylla, and that Sylla did a little resent thereat, and began to speak great, Pompey turned upon him again, and in effect bade him be quiet, for that more men adored the sun rising than the sun setting. With Julius Caesar, Decimus Brutus had obtained that interest, as he set him down in his testament for heir in remainder after his nephew. And this was the man that had power with him to draw him forth to his death. For when Caesar would have discharged the Senate, in regard of some ill presages, and specially a dream of Calpurnia, this man lifted him gently by the arm out of his chair, telling him he hoped he would not dismiss the Senate till his wife had dreamt a better dream. And it seemeth his favour was so great as Antonius, in a letter which is recited verbatim in one of Cicero's *Philippics,* calleth him *venefica,* "witch," as if he had enchanted Caesar. Augustus raised Agrippa (though of mean birth) to that height, as when he consulted with Maecenas about the marriage of his daughter Julia, Maecenas took the liberty to tell him, "that he must either marry his daughter to Agrippa, or take away his life: there was no third way, he had made him so great." With Tiberius Caesar, Sejanus had ascended to that height, as they two were termed and reckoned as a pair of friends.

Tiberius in a letter to him saith, *haec pro amicitia nostra non occultavi* [I have not concealed these things on account of our friendship]; and the whole Senate dedicated an altar to friendship, as to a goddess, in respect of the great dearness of friendship between them two. The like or more was between Septimius Severus and Plautianus. For he forced his eldest son to marry the daughter of Plautianus; and would often maintain Plautianus in doing affronts to his son; and did write also in a letter to the Senate by these words: "I love the man so well as I wish he may overlive me." Now if these princes had been as a Trajan or a Marcus Aurelius, a man might have thought that this had proceeded of an abundant goodness of nature; but being men so wise, of such strength and severity of mind, and so extreme lovers of themselves, as all these were, it proveth most plainly that they found their own felicity (though as great as ever happened to mortal men) but as a half piece except they might have a friend to make it entire; and yet, which is more, they were princes that had wives, sons, nephews; and yet all these could not supply the comfort of friendship.

It is not to be forgotten what Commineus observeth of his first master, Duke Charles the Hardy; namely, that he would communicate his secrets with none; and least of all, those secrets which troubled him most. Whereupon he goeth on and saith that towards his latter time that closeness did impair and a little perish his understanding. Surely Commineus might have made the same judgment also, if it had pleased him, of his second master, Louis XI, whose closeness was indeed his tormentor. The parable of Pythagoras is dark, but true: *Cor ne edito,* "Eat not the heart." Certainly, if a man would give it a hard phrase, those that want friends to open themselves unto are cannibals of their own hearts. But one thing is most admirable (wherewith I will conclude this first fruit of friendship), which is that this communicating of a man's self to his friend works two contrary effects: for it redoubleth joys and cutteth griefs in halves. For there is no man that imparteth his joys to his friend but he joyeth the more; and no man that imparteth his griefs to his friend but he grieveth the less. So that it is in truth of operation upon a man's mind, of like virtue as the alchemists use to attribute to their stone for man's body, that it worketh all contrary effects, but still to the good and benefit of nature. But yet, without praying in aid of alchemists, there is a manifest image of this in the ordinary course of nature. For in bodies, union strengtheneth and cherisheth any natural action, and on the other side weakeneth and dulleth any violent impression, and even so it is of minds.

The second fruit of friendship is healthful and sovereign for the understanding, as the first is for the affections. For friendship maketh indeed a fair day in the affections, from storm and tempests; but it maketh daylight in the understanding, out of darkness and confusion of thoughts. Neither is this to be understood only of faithful counsel, which a man receiveth from his friend; but before you come to that, certain it is that whosoever hath his mind fraught with many thoughts, his wits and understanding do clarify and break up in the communicating and discoursing with another; he tosseth his thoughts more easily; he marshalleth them more orderly; he seeth how they look when they are turned into words; finally, he waxeth wiser than himself, and that more by an hour's discourse than by a day's meditation. It was well said by Themistocles to the king of Persia, "That speech was like cloth of Arras, opened and put abroad; whereby the imagery doth appear in figure; whereas in thoughts they lie but as in packs." Neither is this second fruit of friendship, in opening the under-standing, restrained only to such friends as are able to give a man counsel (they indeed are best); but even without that, a man learneth of himself, and bringeth his own thoughts to light, and whetteth his wits as against a stone, which itself cuts not. In a word, a man were better relate himself to a statue or picture than to suffer his thoughts to pass in smother.

Add now, to make this second fruit of friendship complete, that other point which lieth more open and falleth within vulgar observation, which is faithful counsel from a friend. Heraclitus saith well in one of his enigmas, "Dry light is ever the best." And certain it is that the light that a man receiveth by counsel from another is drier and purer than that which cometh from his own understanding and judgment, which is ever infused and drenched in his affections and customs. So there is as much difference between the counsel that a friend giveth and that a man giveth himself as there is between the counsel of a friend and of a flatterer. For there is no such flatterer as is a man's self; and there is no such remedy against flattery of a man's self as the liberty of a friend. Counsel is of two sorts: the one concerning manners, the other concerning business. For the first, the best preservative to keep the mind in health is the faithful admonition of a friend. The calling of a man's self to a strict account is a medicine, sometime, too piercing and corrosive. Reading good books of morality is a little flat and dead. Observing our faults in others is sometimes improper for our case. But the best receipt (best, I say, to work, and best to take) is the admonition of a friend.

It is a strange thing to behold what gross errors and extreme absurdities many (especially of the greater sort) do commit for want of a friend to tell them of them, to the great damage both of their fame and fortune; for, as St. James saith, they are as men "that look sometimes into a glass, and presently forget their own shape and favour." As for business, a man may think, if he will, that two eyes see no more than one; or that a gamester seeth always more than a looker-on; or that a man in anger is as wise as he that hath said over the four and twenty letters; or that a musket may be shot off as well upon the arm as upon a rest; and such other fond and high imaginations, to think himself all in all. But when all is done, the help of good counsel is that which setteth business straight. And if any man think that he will take counsel, but it shall be by pieces, asking counsel in one business of one man, and in another business of another man, it is well (that is to say, better perhaps than if he asked none at all); but he runneth two dangers: one, that he shall not be faithfully counselled; for it is a rare thing, except it be from a perfect and entire friend, to have counsel given but such as shall be bowed and crooked to some ends which he hath that giveth it. The other, that he shall have counsel given hurtful and unsafe (though with good meaning), and mixed partly of mischief and partly of remedy; even as if you would call a physician that is thought good for the cure of the disease you complain of, but is unacquainted with your body; and therefore may put you in way for a present cure, but overthroweth your health in some other kind; and so cure the disease and kill the patient. But a friend that is wholly acquainted with a man's estate will beware, by furthering any present business, how he dasheth upon other inconvenience. And therefore rest not upon scattered counsels; they will rather distract and mislead than settle and direct.

After these two noble fruits of friendship (peace in the affections and support of the judgment), followeth the last fruit, which is like the pomegranate, full of many kernels; I mean aid and bearing a part in all actions and occasions. Here the best way to represent to life the manifold use of friendship is to cast and see how many things there are which a man cannot do himself; and then it will appear that it was a sparing speech of the ancients to say, "that a friend is another himself"; for that a friend is far more than himself. Men have their time, and die many times in desire of some things which they principally take to heart: the bestowing of a child, the finishing of a work, or the like. If a man have a true friend, he may rest almost secure that the care of those things will continue after him. So that a man hath, as it were, two lives in his desires. A man hath a body, and that body is confined to a place; but where friendship is, all offices of life are as it were granted to him and his deputy. For he may exercise them by his friend. How many things are there which a man cannot, with any face or comeliness, say or do himself? A man can scarce allege his own merits with modesty, much less extol them; a man cannot sometimes brook to supplicate or beg; and a number of the like. But all these things are graceful in a friend's mouth, which are blushing in a man's own. So again, a man's person hath many proper relations which he cannot put off. A man cannot speak to his son but as a father, to his wife but as a husband, to his enemy but upon terms; whereas a friend may speak as the case requires, and not as it sorteth with the person. But to enumerate these things were endless; I have given the rule where a man cannot fitly play his own part; if he have not a friend, he may quit the stage.

Of Anger

To seek to extinguish anger utterly is but a bravery of the Stoics. We have better oracles: "Be angry, but sin not. Let not the sun go down upon your anger." Anger must be limited and confined both in race and in time. We will first speak how the natural inclination and habit to be angry may be attempered and calmed. Secondly, how the particular motions of anger may be repressed, or at least refrained from doing mischief. Thirdly, how to raise anger or appease anger in another.

For the first, there is no other way but to meditate and ruminate well upon the effects of anger, how it troubles man's life. And the best time to do this is to look back upon anger when the fit is thoroughly over. Seneca saith well, "That anger is like ruin, which breaks itself upon that it falls." The Scripture exhorteth us, "To possess our souls in patience." Whosoever is out of patience is out of possession of his soul. Men must not turn bees;

> . . . *animasque in vulnere ponunt.*
>
> [. . . and give up their lives in the sting.]

Anger is certainly a kind of baseness, as it appears well in the weakness of those subjects in whom it reigns: children, women, old folks, sick folks. Only men must beware that they carry their anger rather with scorn than with fear, so that they may seem rather to be above the injury than below it, which is a thing easily done if a man will give law to himself in it.

For the second point, the causes and motives of anger are chiefly three. First, to be too sensible of hurt; for no man is angry that feels not himself hurt; and therefore tender and delicate persons must needs be oft angry; they have so many things to trouble them, which more robust natures have little sense of. The next is the apprehension and construction of the injury offered to be, in the circumstances thereof, full of contempt; for contempt is that which putteth an edge upon anger, as much or more than the hurt itself. And therefore when men are ingenious in picking out cir-

359

cumstances of contempt, they do kindle their anger much. Lastly, opinion of the touch of a man's reputation doth multiply and sharpen anger. Wherein the remedy is that a man should have, as Consalvo was wont to say, *telam honoris crassiorem* [somewhat thickly woven honour]. But in all refrainings of anger, it is the best remedy to win time; and to make a man's self believe that the opportunity of his revenge is not yet come, but that he foresees a time for it, and so to still himself in the mean time and reserve it.

To contain anger from mischief, though it take hold of a man, there be two things whereof you must have special caution. The one, of extreme bitterness of words, especially if they be aculeate and proper, for *communia maledicta* [general railing accusations] are nothing so much; and again, that in anger a man reveal no secrets, for that makes him not fit for society. The other, that you do not peremptorily break off, in any business, in a fit of anger; but howsoever you show bitterness, do not act anything that is not revocable.

For raising and appeasing anger in another, it is done chiefly by choosing of times, when men are frowardest and worst disposed, to incense them. Again, by gathering (as was touched before) all that you can find out to aggravate the contempt. And the two remedies are by the contraries. The former to take good times when first to relate to a man an angry business, for the first impression is much; and the other is to sever, as much as may be, the construction of the injury from the point of contempt, imputing it to misunderstanding, fear, passion, or what you will.

The foregoing essays are from a collection of Bacon's essays entitled ESSAYS: CIVIL AND MORAL.

George Santayana

1863–1952

George Santayana, poet and philosopher, was born in Madrid, Spain, in 1863. At the age of nine he was brought to the United States, where, at Boston, he was reared and educated. At Harvard College, in the 1880's, he was at once a promising poet and a young philosopher—a favorite student of William James and Josiah Royce. And though Santayana joined the faculty as a teacher of philosophy in 1889, his productions for the next dozen years included three volumes of poems, a play in verse, and a treatise on aesthetics.

Santayana left Harvard and his adopted country in 1912 and spent the remainder of his long life abroad. His last years were spent in Italy, where he died in 1952. He never married; indeed, after his retirement from teaching he lived in virtual seclusion, content to be known by the many writings that were his only occupation. Among these were *The Life of Reason* (5 vols., 1905–06), in which he surveyed the progress of systematic thought since the Greeks, and *The Realms of Being* (4 vols., 1927–40), in which he indicated both a total skepticism as to the possibility of knowledge and at the same time what he called an "animal faith" in the existence of things. This anti-philosophical conclusion may, with some reservations, be called his ultimate one, though his complex and sophisticated mind defies summary.

Perhaps it is enough to say that he was both various and subtle in his judgments of the world and of ideas, and that these were always expressed in language of exquisite if somewhat chilly grace, so that Santayana has come to be known less for any doctrines he held than for the felicity with which he uttered them.

The two essays which follow, on Lucretius[1] and on Goethe's *Faust*,[2] were first published in a volume called *Three Philosophical Poets* (1910). (The third poet was Dante.[3]) The title is important, for it was because his three poets were philosophical that Santayana studied them. By philosophical he appears to mean that they were concerned to find nothing less than the order of the world. He did not study them in the narrow terms of literary criticism, which might have been content with the poems they wrote. Instead it is with the poets themselves that Santayana is concerned, not in the sense of their biographies but in terms of the speculative minds their works reveal. It was Santayana's belief that each of those minds was "typical of an age," and that "taken together they sum up all European philosophy."

What he means by this he explains in the Introduction to *Three Philosophical Poets*. In the philosophy of Lucretius—"materialism in natural science, humanism in ethics"—Santayana finds not only "the gist of all Greek philosophy before Socrates" but the precedent for "what may be called the philosophy of the Renaissance, the reassertion of science and liberty in the modern world, by Bacon, by Spinoza, by the whole contemporary school that looks to science for its view of facts, and to the happiness of men on earth for its ideal." Such a system, Santayana says, "is called naturalism; and of this Lucretius is the unrivalled poet."

Goethe, too, is seen in the context of his age, or rather *Faust* is. The age was 1800, and it was one, Santayana says, in which "the

---

[1] See *Great Books of the Western World*, Vol. 12, pp. 1–97.
[2] See *Great Books of the Western World*, Vol. 47.
[3] For Dante's *Divine Comedy*, see *Great Books of the Western World*, Vol. 21. For a selection from his *De Monarchia*, see Vol. 7, pp. 383–399, in this set.

Notes from the artist: "Santayana with some of the people that were prominent in his life. The three complete figures are those of Goethe and Lucretius at the top, and Dante at the left, all alluding to Santayana's Three Philosophical Poets.

Santayana

Teutonic races that have previously conquered Europe have begun to dominate themselves. They have become Protestants, or protesters against the Roman world. An infinite fountain of life seems to be unlocked within their bosom. They turn successively to the Bible, to learning, to patriotism, to industry, for new objects to love and fresh worlds to conquer; but they have too much vitality, or too little maturity, to rest in any of these things. A demon drives them on; and this demon, divine and immortal in its apparent waywardness, is their inmost self. It is their insatiable will, their radical courage. . . . This is romanticism. . . . The greatest monument to this romanticism is Goethe's *Faust*."

Santayana was a very learned man and had a wide knowledge of history and philosophy; he thus had as much right as anyone, perhaps, to epitomize an age in such terms as those above. But it should be recognized that Santayana really does not claim to have read or realized all that men have said and done. All that he claims to do is to attempt to find the center of the age, whereby, though he cannot see all its multitudinous parts, he can place the most important of them in relation to each other. That is what Lucretius did, in his *On the Nature of Things*, with the universe of nature. He sought a theory of it that would make it comprehensible. Santayana would seem in his book to be doing much the same thing with the history of philosophy. Through his poetic subjects he is seeking a theory that will make comprehensible the universe of thought.

No reader should be disappointed, upon reading the essays, to discover that the theory is difficult to grasp. Of course it is, as any such comprehensive idea—certainly "the sum of all European philosophy"—must be. It may even be allowed that Santayana is not wholly successful in what he tried to do. But neither was Lucretius, nor Goethe.

Santayana is remarkable, nevertheless, not so much for what he found, or even for what he sought, but for the place in which he sought it. In studying European philosophy, he turned not to the philosophers but to the poets. His idea was that the greatest poetry is philosophical, and in its eloquence perhaps the best philosophy there is. "Can it be accident," he asks, "that the most adequate and probably the most lasting exposition of these three schools of philosophy should have been made by poets?" His book gives a clear answer to the question: it is no accident. And Santayana gives the impression beyond a doubt that he believes any philosopher should realize that.

Lucretius

There is perhaps no important poem the antecedents of which can be traced so exhaustively as can those of the work of Lucretius, *De rerum natura*. These antecedents, however, do not lie in the poet himself. If they did, we should not be able to trace them, since we know nothing, or next to nothing, about Lucretius the man. In a chronicon, compiled by St. Jerome largely out of Suetonius, in which miscellaneous events are noted which occurred in each successive year, we read for the year 94 B.C.: "Titus Lucretius, poet, is born. After a love-philtre had turned him mad, and he had written, in the intervals of his insanity, several books which Cicero revised, he killed himself by his own hand in the forty-fourth year of his age."

The love-philtre in this report sounds apocryphal; and the story of the madness and suicide attributes too edifying an end to an atheist and Epicurean not to be suspected. If anything lends color to the story it is a certain consonance which we may feel between its tragic incidents and the genius of the poet as revealed in his work, where we find a strange scorn of love, a strange vehemence, and a high melancholy. It is by no means incredible that the author of such a poem should have been at some time the slave of a pathological passion, that his vehemence and inspiration should have passed into mania, and that he should have taken his own life. But the untrustworthy authority of St. Jerome cannot assure us whether what he repeats is a tradition founded on fact or an ingenious fiction.

Our ignorance of the life of Lucretius is not, I think, much to be regretted. His work preserves that part of him which he himself would have wished to preserve. Perfect conviction ignores itself, proclaiming the public truth. To reach this no doubt requires a peculiar genius which is called intelligence; for intelligence is quickness in seeing things as they are. But where intelligence is attained, the rest of a man, like the scaffolding to a finished building, becomes irrelevant. We do not wish it to intercept our view of the solid structure, which alone was intended by the artist—if he was building for others, and was not a coxcomb. It is his intellectual vision that the naturalist in particular wishes to hand down to posterity, not the shabby incidents that preceded that vision in his own person. These incidents, even if they were by chance interesting, could not be repeated in us; but the vision into which the thinker poured his faculties, and to which he devoted his vigils, is communicable to us also, and may become a part of ourselves.

Since Lucretius is thus identical for us with his poem, and is lost in his philosophy, the antecedents of Lucretius are simply the stages by which his conception of nature first shaped itself in the human mind. To retrace these stages is easy; some of them are only too familiar; yet the very triteness of the subject may blind us to the grandeur and audacity of the intellectual feat involved. A naturalistic conception of things is a great work of imagination—greater, I think, than any dramatic or moral mythology: it is a conception fit to inspire great poetry, and in the end, perhaps, it will prove the only conception able to inspire it.

We are told of the old Xenophanes that he looked up into the round heaven and cried, "The All is One." What is logically a truism may often be, imaginatively, a great discovery, because no one before may have thought of the obvious analogy which the truism registers. So, in this case, the unity of all things is logically an evident, if barren, truth; for the most disparate and unrelated worlds would still be a multitude, and so an aggregate, and so, in some sense, a unity. Yet it was a great imaginative feat to cast the eye deliberately round the entire horizon, and to draw mentally the sum of all reality, discovering that reality makes such a sum, and may be called one; as any stone or animal, though composed of many parts, is yet called one in common parlance. It was doubtless some prehistoric man of genius, long before Xenophanes, who first applied in this way to all things together that notion of unity and wholeness which everybody had gained by observation of things singly, and who first ventured to speak of "the world." To do so is to set the problem for all natural philosophy, and in a certain measure to anticipate the solution of that problem; for it is to ask how things hang together, and to assume that they do hang together in one way or another.

To cry "The All is One," and to perceive that all things are in one landscape and form a system by their juxtaposition, is the rude beginning of wisdom in natural philosophy. But it is easy to go farther, and to see that things form a unity in a far deeper and more mysterious way. One of the first things, for instance, that impresses the poet, the man of feeling and reflection, is that these objects that people the world all pass away, and that the place thereof knows them no more. Yet, when they vanish, nothingness does not succeed; other things arise in their stead. Nature remains always young and whole in spite of death at work everywhere; and what takes the place of what continually disappears is often remarkably like it in character. Universal instability is not incompatible with a great monotony in things; so that while Heraclitus lamented that everything was in flux, Ecclesiastes, who was also entirely convinced of that truth, could lament that there was nothing new under the sun.

This double experience of mutation and recurrence, an experience at once sentimental and scientific, soon brought with it a very great thought, perhaps the greatest thought that mankind has ever hit upon, and which was the chief inspiration of Lucretius. It is that all we observe about us, and ourselves also, may be so many passing forms of a permanent substance. This substance, while remaining the same in quantity and in inward quality, is constantly redistributed; in its redistribution it forms those aggregates which we call things, and which we find constantly disappearing and reappearing. All things are dust, and to dust they return; a dust, however, eternally fertile, and destined to fall perpetually into new, and doubtless beautiful, forms. This notion of substance lends a much greater unity to the outspread world; it persuades us that all things pass into one another, and have a common ground from which they spring successively, and to which they return.

The spectacle of inexorable change, the triumph of time, or whatever we may call it, has always been a favorite theme for lyric and tragic poetry, and for religious meditation. To perceive universal mutation, to feel the vanity of life, has always been the beginning of seriousness. It is the condition for any beautiful, measured, or tender philosophy. Prior to that, everything is barbarous, both in morals and in poetry; for until then mankind has not learned to renounce anything, has not outgrown the instinctive egotism and optimism of the young animal, and has not removed the center of its being, or of its faith, from the will to the imagination.

To discover substance, then, is a great step in the life of reason, even if substance be conceived quite negatively as a term that serves merely to mark, by contrast, the unsubstantiality, the vanity, of all particular moments and things. That is the way in which Indian poetry and philosophy conceived substance. But the step taken by Greek physics, and by the poetry of Lucretius, passes beyond. Lucretius and the Greeks, in observing universal mutation and the vanity of life, conceived behind appearance a great intelligible process, an evolution in nature. The reality became interesting, as well as the illusion. Physics became scientific, which had previously been merely spectacular.

Here was a much richer theme for the poet and philosopher, who was launched upon the discovery of the ground and secret causes of this gay or melancholy flux. The understanding that enabled him to discover these causes did for the European what no Indian mystic, what no despiser of understanding anywhere, suffers himself to do; namely, to dominate, foretell, and transform this changing show with a virile, practical intelligence. The man who discovers the secret springs of appearances opens to contemplation a second positive world, the workshop and busy depths of nature, where a prodigious mechanism is continually supporting our life, and making ready for it from afar by the most exquisite adjustments. The march of this mechanism, while it produces life and often fosters it, yet as often makes it difficult and condemns it to extinction. This truth, which the conception of natural substance first makes intelligible, justifies the elegies which the poets of illusion and disillusion have always written upon human things. It is a truth with a melancholy side; but being a truth, it satisfies and exalts the rational mind, that craves truth as truth, whether it be sad or comforting, and wishes to pursue a possible, not an impossible, happiness.

So far, Greek science had made out that the world was one, that there was a substance, that this was a physical substance, distributed and moving in space. It was matter. The question remained, What is the precise nature of matter, and how does it produce the appearances we observe? The only answer that concerns us here is that given by Lucretius; an answer he accepted from Epicurus, his master in everything, who in turn had accepted it from Democritus. Now Democritus had made a notable advance over the systems that selected one obvious substance, like water, or collected all the obvious substances, as Anaxagoras had done, and tried to make the world out of them. Democritus thought that the substance of everything ought not to have any of the qualities present in some things and absent in others; it ought to have only the qualities present in all things. It should be *merely* matter. Materiality, according to him, consisted of extension, figure, and solidity; in the thinnest ether, if we looked sharp enough, we should find nothing but particles possessing these properties. All other qualities of things were apparent only, and imputed to them by a convention of the mind. The mind was a born mythologist, and projected its feelings into their causes. Light, color, taste, warmth, beauty, excellence were such imputed and conventional qualities; only space and matter were real. But empty space was no less real than matter. Consequently, although the atoms of matter never changed their form, real changes could take place in nature, because their position might change in a real space.

Unlike the useless substance of the Indians, the substance of Democritus could offer a calculable ground for the flux of appearances; for this substance was distributed unequally in the void, and was constantly moving. Every appearance, however fleeting, corresponded to a precise configuration of substance; it arose with that configuration and perished with it. This substance, accordingly, was physical, not metaphysical. It was no dialectical term, but a scientific anticipation, a prophecy as to what an observer who should be properly equipped would discover in the interior of bodies. Materialism is not a system of metaphysics; it is a speculation in chemistry and physiology, to the effect that, if analysis could go deep enough, it would find that all substance was homogeneous, and that all motion was regular.

Though matter was homogeneous, the forms of the ultimate particles, according to Democritus, were various; and sundry combinations of them constituted the sundry objects in nature. Motion was not, as the vulgar (and Aristotle) supposed, unnatural, and produced magically by some moral cause; it had been eternal and was native to the atoms. On striking, they rebounded; and the mechanical currents or vortexes which these contacts occasioned formed a multitude of stellar systems, called worlds, with which infinite space was studded.

Mechanism as to motion, atomism as to structure, materialism as to substance, that is the whole system of Democritus. It is as wonderful in its insight, in its sense for the ideal demands of method and understanding, as it is strange and audacious in its simplicity. Only the most convinced rationalist, the boldest prophet, could embrace it dogmatically; yet time has largely given it the proof. If Democritus could look down upon the present state of science, he would laugh, as he was in the habit of doing, partly at the confirmation we can furnish to portions of his philosophy, and partly at our stupidity that cannot guess the rest.

There are two maxims in Lucretius that suffice, even to this day, to distinguish a thinker who is a naturalist from one who is not. "Nothing," he says, "arises in the body in order that we may use it, but what arises brings forth its use." [1] This is that discarding of final causes on which all progress in science depends. The other maxim runs: "One thing will grow

---

1. Lucretius, IV. 834, 835. [Cf. *Great Books of the Western World*, Vol. 12, p. 55 (Ed.).]

plain when compared with another: and blind night shall not obliterate the path for thee, before thou hast thoroughly scanned the ultimate things of nature; so much will things throw light on things." [2] Nature is her own standard; and if she seems to us unnatural, there is no hope for our minds.

The ethics of Democritus, insofar as we may judge from scanty evidence, were merely descriptive or satirical. He was an aristocratic observer, a scorner of fools. Nature was laughing at us all; the wise man considered his fate and, by knowing it, raised himself in a measure above it. All living things pursued the greatest happiness they could see their way to; but they were marvellously shortsighted; and the business of the philosopher was to foresee and pursue the greatest happiness that was really possible. This, in so rough a world, was to be found chiefly in abstention and retrenchment. If you asked for little, it was more probable that the event would not disappoint you. It was important not to be a fool, but it was very hard.

The system of Democritus was adopted by Epicurus, but not because Epicurus had any keenness of scientific vision. On the contrary, Epicurus, the Herbert Spencer of antiquity, was in his natural philosophy an encyclopaedia of secondhand knowledge. Prolix and minute, vague and inconsistent, he gathered his scientific miscellany with an eye fixed not on nature, but on the exigencies of an inward faith—a faith accepted on moral grounds, deemed necessary to salvation, and defended at all costs with any available weapon. It is instructive that materialism should have been adopted at that juncture on the same irrelevant moral grounds on which it has usually been rejected.

Epicurus, strange as it may sound to those who have heard, with horror or envy, of wallowing in his sty, Epicurus was a saint. The ways of the world filled him with dismay. The Athens of his time, which some of us would give our eyes to see, retained all its splendor amid its political decay; but nothing there interested or pleased Epicurus. Theaters, porches, gymnasiums, and above all the agora, reeked, to his sense, with vanity and folly. Retired in his private garden, with a few friends and disciples, he sought the ways of peace; he lived abstemiously; he spoke gently; he gave alms to the poor; he preached against wealth, against ambition, against passion. He defended free will because he wished to exercise it in withdrawing from the world, and in not swimming with the current. He denied the supernatural, since belief in it would have a

---

2. *Ibid.*, I. 1115–18. [Cf. *Great Books of the Western World*, Vol. 12, p. 14 (Ed.).]

disquieting influence on the mind, and render too many things compulsory and momentous. There was no future life: the art of living wisely must not be distorted by such wild imaginings.

All things happened in due course of nature; the gods were too remote and too happy, secluded like good Epicureans, to meddle with earthly things. Nothing ruffled what Wordsworth calls their "voluptuous unconcern." Nevertheless, it was pleasant to frequent their temples. There, as in the spaces where they dwelt between the worlds, the gods were silent and beautiful, and wore the human form. Their statues, when an unhappy man gazed at them, reminded him of happiness; he was refreshed and weaned for a moment from the senseless tumult of human affairs. From those groves and hallowed sanctuaries the philosopher returned to his garden strengthened in his wisdom, happier in his isolation, more friendly and more indifferent to all the world. Thus the life of Epicurus, as St. Jerome bears witness, was "full of herbs, fruits, and abstinences." There was a hush in it, as of bereavement. His was a philosophy of the decadence, a philosophy of negation, and of flight from the world.

Although science for its own sake could not interest so monkish a nature, yet science might be useful in buttressing the faith, or in removing objections to it. Epicurus therefore departed from the reserve of Socrates, and looked for a natural philosophy that might support his ethics. Of all the systems extant—and they were legion—he found that of Democritus the most helpful and edifying. Better than any other it would persuade men to renounce the madness that must be renounced and to enjoy the pleasures that may be enjoyed. But, since it was adopted on these external and pragmatic grounds, the system of Democritus did not need to be adopted entire. In fact, one change at least was imperative. The motion of the atoms must not be wholly regular and mechanical. Chance must be admitted, that Fate might be removed. Fate was a terrifying notion. It was spoken of by the people with superstitious unction. Chance was something humbler, more congenial to the man in the street. If only the atoms were allowed to deflect a little now and then from their courses, the future might remain unpredictable, and free will might be saved. Therefore, Epicurus decreed that the atoms deflected, and fantastic arguments were added to show that this intrusion of chance would aid in the organization of nature; for the declension of the atoms, as it is called, would explain how the original parallel downpour of them might have yielded to vortexes, and so to organized bodies. Let us pass on.

Materialism, like any system of natural philosophy, carries with it no commandments and no advice. It merely describes the world, including the aspirations and consciences of mortals, and refers all to a material ground. The materialist, being a man, will not fail to have preferences, and even a conscience, of his own; but his precepts and policy will express, not the logical implications of his science, but his human instincts, as inheritance and experience may have shaped them. Any system of ethics might accordingly coexist with materialism; for if materialism declares certain things (like immortality) to be impossible, it cannot declare them to be undesirable. Nevertheless, it is not likely that a man so constituted as to embrace materialism will be so constituted as to pursue things which he considers unattainable. There is therefore a psychological, though no logical, bond between materialism and a homely morality.

The materialist is primarily an observer; and he will probably be such in ethics also; that is, he will have no ethics, except the emotion produced upon him by the march of the world. If he is an *esprit fort* and really disinterested, he will love life; as we all love perfect vitality, or what strikes us as such, in gulls and porpoises. This, I think, is the ethical sentiment psychologically consonant with a vigorous materialism: sympathy with the movement of things, interest in the rising wave, delight at the foam it bursts into, before it sinks again. Nature does not distinguish the better from the worse, but the lover of nature does. He calls better what, being analogous to his own life, enhances his vitality and probably possesses some vitality of its own. This is the ethical feeling of Spinoza, the greatest of modern naturalists in philosophy; and we shall see how Lucretius, in spite of his fidelity to the ascetic Epicurus, is carried by his poetic ecstasy in the same direction.

But mark the crux of this union: the materialist will love the life of nature when he loves his own life; but if he should hate his own life, how should the life of nature please him? Now Epicurus, for the most part, hated life. His moral system, called hedonism, recommends that sort of pleasure which has no excitement and no risk about it. This ideal is modest, and even chaste, but it is not vital. Epicurus was remarkable for his mercy, his friendliness, his utter horror of war, of sacrifice, of suffering. These are not sentiments that a genuine naturalist would be apt to share. Pity and repentance, Spinoza said, were vain and evil; what increased a man's power and his joy increased his goodness also. The naturalist will believe in a certain hardness, as Nietzsche did; he will incline to a certain scorn, as the laughter of Democritus was scornful. He will not count too scrupulously the cost of what he achieves; he will be an imperialist, rapt in the joy of achieving something. In a word, the moral hue of materialism in a formative age, or in an aggressive mind, would be aristocratic and

imaginative; but in a decadent age, or in a soul that is renouncing everything, it would be, as in Epicurus, humanitarian and timidly sensual.

We have now before us the antecedents and components of Lucretius'
poem on nature. There remains the genius of the poet himself. The
greatest thing about this genius is its power of losing itself in its object, its
impersonality. We seem to be reading not the poetry of a poet about
things, but the poetry of things themselves. That things have their poetry,
not because of what we make them symbols of, but because of their own
movement and life, is what Lucretius proves once for all to mankind.

Of course, the poetry we see in nature is due to the emotion the
spectacle produces in us; the life of nature might be as romantic and
sublime as it chose, it would be dust and ashes to us if there were nothing
sublime and romantic in ourselves to be stirred by it to sympathy. But our
emotion may be ingenuous; it may be concerned with what nature really
is and does, has been and will do forever. It need not arise from a selfish
preoccupation with what these immense realities involve for our own
persons or may be used to suggest to our self-indulgent fancy. No, the
poetry of nature may be discerned merely by the power of intuition which
it awakens and the understanding which it employs. These faculties,
more, I should say, than our moodiness or stuffy dreams, draw taut the
strings of the soul, and bring out her full vitality and music. Naturalism is
a philosophy of observation, and of an imagination that extends the
observable; all the sights and sounds of nature enter into it, and lend it
their directness, pungency, and coercive stress. At the same time, naturalism is an intellectual philosophy; it divines substance behind appearance,
continuity behind change, law behind fortune. It therefore attaches all
those sights and sounds to a hidden background that connects and explains them. So understood, nature has depth as well as surface, force and
necessity as well as sensuous variety. Before the sublimity of this insight,
all forms of the pathetic fallacy seem cheap and artificial. Mythology, that
to a childish mind is the only possible poetry, sounds like bad rhetoric in
comparison. The naturalistic poet abandons fairy land, because he has
discovered nature, history, the actual passions of man. His imagination
has reached maturity; its pleasure is to dominate, not to play.

Poetic dominion over things as they are is seen best in Shakespeare for
the ways of men, and in Lucretius for the ways of nature. Unapproachably
vivid, relentless, direct in detail, he is unflinchingly grand and serious in
his grouping of the facts. It is the truth that absorbs him and carries him
along. He wishes us to be convinced and sobered by the fact, by the
overwhelming evidence of thing after thing, raining down upon us, all
bearing witness with one voice to the nature of the world.

Suppose, however—and it is a tenable supposition—that Lucretius is quite wrong in his science, and that there is no space, no substance, and no nature. His poem would then lose its pertinence to our lives and personal convictions; it would not lose its imaginative grandeur. We could still conceive a world composed as he describes. Fancy what emotions those who lived in such a world would have felt on the day when a Democritus or a Lucretius revealed to them their actual situation. How great the blindness or the madness dissipated, and how wonderful the vision gained! How clear the future, how intelligible the past, how marvelous the swarming atoms, in their unintentional, perpetual fertility! What the sky is to our eyes on a starry night, that every nook and cranny of nature would resemble, with here and there the tentative smile of life playing about those constellations. Surely that universe, for those who lived in it, would have had its poetry. It would have been the poetry of naturalism. Lucretius, thinking he lived in such a world, heard the music of it, and wrote it down.

And yet, when he set himself to make his poem out of the system of Epicurus, the greatness of that task seems to have overwhelmed him. He was to unfold for the first time, in sonorous but unwieldy Latin, the birth and nature of all things, as Greek subtlety had discerned them. He was to dispel superstition, to refute antagonists, to lay the sure foundations of science and of wisdom, to summon mankind compellingly from its cruel passions and follies to a life of simplicity and peace. He was himself combative and distracted enough—as it is often our troubles, more than our attainments, that determine our ideals. Yet in heralding the advent of human happiness, and in painting that of the gods, he was to attain his own, soaring upon the strong wings of his hexameters into an ecstasy of contemplation and enthusiasm. When it is so great an emotion to read these verses, what must it have been to compose them? Yet could he succeed? Could such great things fall to his lot? Yes, they might, if only the creative forces of nature, always infinite and always at hand, could pass into his brain and into his spirit; if only the seeds of corruption and madness, which were always coursing through the air, could be blown back for a moment; and if the din of civil conflicts could be suspended while he thought and wrote. To a fortunate conjunction of atoms, a child owes his first being. To a propitious season and atmosphere, a poet owes his inspiration and his success. Conscious that his undertaking hangs upon these chance conjunctions, Lucretius begins by invoking the powers he is about to describe, that they may give him breath and genius enough to describe them. And at once these powers send him a happy inspiration,

perhaps a happy reminiscence of Empedocles. There are two great perspectives which the moralist may distinguish in the universal drift of
atoms—a creative movement, producing what the moralist values, and a
destructive movement, abolishing the same. Lucretius knows very well
that this distinction is moral only, or as people now say, subjective. No one
else has pointed out so often and so clearly as he that nothing arises in this
world not helped to life by the death of some other thing; [3] so that the
destructive movement creates and the creative movement destroys. Yet
from the point of view of any particular life or interest, the distinction
between a creative force and a destructive force is real and all-important.
To make it is not to deny the mechanical structure of nature, but only to
show how this mechanical structure is fruitful morally, how the outlying
parts of it are friendly or hostile to me or to you, its local and living
products.

This double coloring of things is supremely interesting to the philosopher; so much so that before his physical science has reached the mechanical stage, he will doubtless regard the double aspect which things present
to him as a dual principle in these things themselves. So Empedocles had
spoken of Love and Strife as two forces which respectively gathered and
disrupted the elements, so as to carry on between them the Penelope's
labor of the world, the one perpetually weaving fresh forms of life, and
the other perpetually undoing them.[4]

It needed but a slight concession to traditional rhetoric in order to
exchange these names, Love and Strife, which designated divine powers
in Empedocles, into the names of Venus and Mars, which designated the
same influences in Roman mythology. The Mars and Venus of Lucretius
are not moral forces, incompatible with the mechanism of atoms; they are
this mechanism itself, insofar as it now produces and now destroys life, or
any precious enterprise, like this of Lucretius in composing his saving
poem. Mars and Venus, linked in each other's arms, rule the universe
together; nothing arises save by the death of some other thing. Yet when
what arises is happier in itself, or more congenial to us, than what is
destroyed, the poet says that Venus prevails, that she woos her captive
lover to suspend his unprofitable raging. At such times it is spring on
earth; the storms recede (I paraphrase the opening passage),[5] the fields
are covered with flowers, the sunshine floods the serene sky, and all the

---

3. Lucretius, I. 264, 265. [Cf. *Great Books of the Western World*, Vol. 12, p. 4 (Ed.).]
4. An excellent expression of this view is put by Plato into the mouth of the physician
Eryximachus in the *Symposium*. [See *Great Books of the Western World*, Vol. 7,
pp. 155–156 (Ed.).]
5. Lucretius, I. 1–13. [Cf. *Great Books of the Western World*, Vol. 12, p. 1 (Ed.).]

tribes of animals feel the mighty impulse of Venus in their hearts. The corn ripens in the plains, and even the sea bears in safety the fleets that traverse it.

Not least, however, of these works of Venus is the Roman people. Never was the formative power of nature better illustrated than in the vitality of this race, which conquered so many other races, or than in its assimilative power, which civilized and pacified them. Legend had made Venus the mother of Aeneas, and Aeneas the progenitor of the Romans. Lucretius seizes on this happy accident and identifies the Venus of fable with the true Venus, the propitious power in all nature, of which Rome was indeed a crowning work. But the poet's work, also, if it is to be accomplished worthily, must look to the same propitious movement for its happy issue and for its power to persuade. Venus must be the patron of his art and philosophy. She must keep Memmius from the wars, that he may read, and be weaned from frivolous ambitions; and she must stop the tumult of constant sedition, that Lucretius may lend his undivided mind to the precepts of Epicurus, and his whole heart to a sublime friendship, which prompts him to devote to intense study all the watches of the starry night, plotting the course of each invisible atom, and mounting almost to the seat of the gods.[6]

This impersonation in the figure of Venus of whatever makes for life would not be legitimate—it would really contradict a mechanical view of nature—if it were not balanced by a figure representing the opposite tendency, the no less universal tendency towards death.

The Mars of the opening passage, subdued for a moment by the blandishments of love, is raging in all the rest of the poem in his irrepressible fury. These are the two sides of every transmutation, that in creating, one thing destroys another; and this transmutation being perpetual—nothing being durable except the void, the atoms, and their motion—it follows that the tendency towards death is, for any particular thing, the final and victorious tendency. The names of Venus and Mars, not being essential to the poet's thought, are allowed to drop out, and the actual processes they stand for are described nakedly; yet, if the poem had ever been finished, and Lucretius had wished to make the end chime with the beginning, and represent, as it were, one great cycle of the world, it is conceivable that he might have placed at the close a mythical passage to match that at the beginning; and we might have seen Mars aroused from his luxurious lethargy, reasserting his immortal nature, and rushing, firebrand in hand,

---

6. Lucretius, I. 24, 28–30, 41–43, 140–44. [Cf. *Great Books of the Western World*, Vol. 12, pp. 1–2 (Ed.).]

from the palace of love to spread destruction throughout the universe, till all things should burn fiercely, and be consumed together. Yet not quite all; for the goddess herself would remain, more divine and desirable than ever in her averted beauty. Instinctively into her bosom the God of War would sink again, when weary and drunk with slaughter; and a new world would arise from the scattered atoms of the old.

These endless revolutions, taken in themselves, exactly balance; and I am not sure that, impartially considered, it is any sadder that new worlds should arise than that this world should always continue. Besides, nature cannot take from us more than she has given, and it would be captious and thankless in us to think of her as destructive only, or destructive essentially, after the unspeculative fashion of modern pessimists. She destroys to create, and creates to destroy, her interest (if we may express it so) being not in particular things, nor in their continuance, but solely in the movement that underlies them, in the flux of substance beneath. Life, however, belongs to form, and not to matter; or in the language of Lucretius, life is an *eventum*, a redundant ideal product or incidental aspect, involved in the equilibration of matter; as the throw of sixes is an *eventum*, a redundant ideal product or incidental aspect, occasionally involved in shaking a dicebox. Yet, as this throw makes the acme and best possible issue of a game of dice, so life is the acme and best possible issue of the dance of atoms; and it is from the point of view of this *eventum* that the whole process is viewed by us, and is judged. Not until that happy chance has taken place, do we exist morally, or can we reflect or judge at all. The philosopher is at the top of the wave, he is the foam in the rolling tempest; and as the wave must have risen before he bursts into being, all that he lives to witness is the fall of the wave. The decadence of all he lives by is the only prospect before him; his whole philosophy must be a prophecy of death. Of the life that may come after, when the atoms come together again, he can imagine nothing; the life he knows and shares, all that is life to him, is waning and almost spent.

Therefore Lucretius, who is nothing if not honest, is possessed by a profound melancholy. Vigorous and throbbing as are his pictures of spring, of love, of ambition, of budding culture, of intellectual victory, they pale before the vivid strokes with which he paints the approach of death—fatigue of the will, lassitude in pleasure, corruption and disintegration in society, the soil exhausted, the wild animals tamed or exterminated, poverty, pestilence, and famine at hand; and for the individual, almost at once, the final dissipation of the atoms of his soul, escaping from a relaxed body, to mingle and lose themselves in the universal flaw. Nothing comes out of nothing, nothing falls back into nothing, if we consider substance; but everything comes from nothing and falls back into nothing if we consider things—the objects of love and experience. Time can make no impression on the void or on the atoms; nay, time is itself an *eventum* created by the motion of atoms in the void; but the triumph of time is absolute over persons, and nations, and worlds.[7]

In treating of the soul and of immortality Lucretius is an imperfect psychologist and an arbitrary moralist. His zeal to prove that the soul is mortal is inspired by the wish to dispel all fear of future punishments, and so to liberate the mind for the calm and tepid enjoyment of this world. There is something to be gained in this direction, undoubtedly, especially if tales about divine vengeance to come are used to sanction irrational practices, and to prevent poor people from improving their lot. At the same time, it is hardly fair to assume that hell is the only prospect which immortality could possibly open to any of us; and it is also unfair not to observe that the punishments which religious fables threaten the dead with are, for the most part, symbols for the actual degradation which evil-doing brings upon the living; so that the fear of hell is not more deterrent or repressive than experience of life would be if it were clearly brought before the mind.

There is another element in this polemic against immortality which, while highly interesting and characteristic of a decadent age, betrays a very one-sided and, at bottom, untenable ideal. This element is the fear of life. Epicurus had been a pure and tender moralist, but pusillanimous. He was so afraid of hurting and of being hurt, so afraid of running risks or tempting fortune, that he wished to prove that human life was a brief business, not subject to any great transformations, nor capable of any great achievements. He taught accordingly that the atoms had produced already all the animals they could produce, for though infinite in number the atoms were of few kinds. Consequently the possible sorts of being were finite and soon exhausted; this world, though on the eve of destruction, was of recent date. The worlds around it, or to be produced in future, could not afford anything essentially different. All the suns were much alike, and there was nothing new under them. We need not, then, fear the world; it is an explored and domestic scene—a home, a little garden, six feet of earth for a man to stretch in. If people rage and make a great noise, it is not because there is much to win, or much to fear, but because people are mad. Let me not be mad, thought Epicurus; let me be

---

7. Lucretius, II. 1139–41, 1148–49, 1164–74. [Cf. *Great Books of the Western World*, Vol. 12, pp. 29–30 (Ed.).]

reasonable, cultivating sentiments appropriate to a mortal who inhabits a world morally comfortable and small, and physically poor in its infinite monotony. The well-known lines of Fitzgerald echo this sentiment perfectly:

> A Book of Verses underneath the Bough,
> A Jug of Wine, a Loaf of Bread—and Thou
>   Beside me singing in the Wilderness—
> Oh, Wilderness were Paradise enow!

But what if the shadow of incalculable possibilities should fall across this sunny retreat? What if after death we should awake in a world to which the atomic philosophy might not in the least apply? Observe that this suggestion is not in the least opposed to any of the arguments by which science might prove the atomic theory to be correct. All that Epicurus taught about the universe now before us might be perfectly true of it; but what if tomorrow a new universe should have taken its place? The suggestion is doubtless gratuitous, and no busy man will be much troubled by it; yet when the heart is empty it fills itself with such attenuated dreams. The muffled pleasures of the wise man, as Epicurus conceived him, were really a provocation to supernaturalism. They left a great void; and before long supernaturalism—we shall see it in Dante—actually rushed in to quicken the pulses of life with fresh hopes and illusions, or at least (what may seem better than nothing) with terrors and fanatical zeal. With such tendencies already afoot as the myths and dogmas of Plato had betrayed, it was imperative for Epicurus to banish anxiously all thought of what might follow death. To this end are all his arguments about the material nature of the soul and her incapacity to survive the body.

To say that the soul is material has a strange and barbarous sound to modern ears. We live after Descartes, who taught the world that the essence of the soul was consciousness; and to call consciousness material would be to talk of the blackness of white. But ancient usage gave the word soul a rather different meaning. The essence of the soul was not so much to be conscious as to govern the formation of the body, to warm, move, and guide it. And if we think of the soul exclusively in this light, it will not seem a paradox, it may even seem a truism, to say that the soul must be material. For how are we to conceive that pre-existing consciousness should govern the formation of the body, move, warm, or guide it? A spirit capable of such a miracle would in any case not be human, but altogether divine. The soul that Lucretius calls material should not, then, be identified with consciousness, but with the ground of consciousness, which is at the same time the cause of life in the body. This he conceives to be a swarm of very small and volatile atoms, a sort of ether, resident in all living seeds, breathed in abundantly during life and breathed out at death.

Even if this theory were accepted, however, it would not prove the point which Lucretius has chiefly at heart, namely, that an afterlife is impossible. The atoms of the soul are indestructible, like all atoms; and if consciousness were attached to the fortunes of a small group of them, or of one only (as Leibniz afterwards taught), consciousness would continue to exist after these atoms had escaped from the body and were shooting through new fields of space. Indeed, they might be the more aroused by that adventure, as a bee might find the sky or the garden more exciting than the hive. All that Lucretius urges about the divisibility of the soul, its diffused bodily seat, and the perils it would meet outside fails to remove the ominous possibility that troubles him.

To convince us that we perish at death he has to rely on vulgar experience and inherent probability: what changes is not indestructible; what begins, ends; mental growth, health, sanity accompany the fortunes of the body as a whole (not demonstrably those of the soul-atoms); the passions are relevant to bodily life and to an earthly situation; we should not be ourselves under a different mask or in a new setting; we remember no previous existence if we had one, and so, in a future existence, we should not remember this. These reflections are impressive, and they are enforced by Lucretius with his usual vividness and smack of reality. Nothing is proved scientifically by such a deliverance, yet it is good philosophy and good poetry; it brings much experience together and passes a loftly judgment upon it. The artist has his eye on the model; he is painting death to the life.

If these considerations succeed in banishing the dread of an afterlife, there remains the distress which many feel at the idea of extinction; and if we have ceased to fear death, like Hamlet, for the dreams that may come after it, we may still fear death instinctively, like a stuck pig. Against this instinctive horror of dying Lucretius has many brave arguments. Fools, he says to us, why do you fear what never can touch you? While you still live, death is absent; and when you are dead, you are so dead that you cannot know you are dead, nor regret it. You will be as much at ease as before you were born. Or is what troubles you the childish fear of being cold in the earth, or feeling its weight stifling you? But you will not be there; the atoms of your soul—themselves unconscious—will be dancing in some sunbeam far away, and you yourself will be nowhere; you will absolutely not exist. Death is by definition a state that excludes experience. If you fear it, you fear a word.

To all this, perhaps, Memmius, or some other recalcitrant reader, might retort that what he shrank from was not the metaphysical state of being dead, but the very real agony of dying. Dying is something ghastly, as being born is something ridiculous; and, even if no pain were involved in quitting or entering this world, we might still say what Dante's Francesca says of it: *Il modo ancor m' offende*—"I shudder at the way of it." Lucretius, for his part, makes no attempt to show that everything is as it should be; and if our way of coming into this life is ignoble, and our way of leaving it pitiful, that is no fault of his nor of his philosophy. If the fear of death were merely the fear of dying, it would be better dealt with by medicine than by argument. There is, or there might be, an art of dying well, of dying painlessly, willingly, and in season—as in those noble partings which Attic gravestones depict—especially if we were allowed, as Lucretius would allow us, to choose our own time.

But the radical fear of death, I venture to think, is something quite different. It is the love of life. Epicurus, who feared life, seems to have missed here the primordial and colossal force he was fighting against. Had he perceived that force, he would have been obliged to meet it in a more radical way, by an enveloping movement, as it were, and an attack from the rear. The love of life is not something rational, or founded on experience of life. It is something antecedent and spontaneous. It is that Venus Genetrix which covers the earth with its flora and fauna. It teaches every animal to seek its food and its mate, and to protect its offspring; as also to resist or fly from all injury to the body, and most of all from threatened death. It is the original impulse by which good is discriminated from evil, and hope from fear.

Nothing could be more futile, therefore, than to marshal arguments against that fear of death which is merely another name for the energy of life, or the tendency to self-preservation. Arguments involve premises, and these premises, in the given case, express some particular form of the love of life; whence it is impossible to conclude that death is in no degree evil and not at all to be feared. For what is most dreaded is not the agony of dying, nor yet the strange impossibility that when we do not exist we should suffer for not existing. What is dreaded is the defeat of a present will directed upon life and its various undertakings. Such a present will cannot be argued away, but it may be weakened by contradictions arising within it, by the irony of experience, or by ascetic discipline. To introduce ascetic discipline, to bring out the irony of experience, to expose the self-contradictions of the will, would be the true means of mitigating the love of life; and if the love of life were extinguished, the fear of death, like smoke rising from that fire, would have vanished also.

Indeed, the force of the great passage against the fear of death, at the end of the third book of Lucretius, comes chiefly from the picture it draws of the madness of life. His philosophy deprecates covetousness, ambition, love, and religion; it takes a long step towards the surrender of life, by surrendering all in life that is ardent, on the ground that it is painful in the end and ignominious. To escape from it all is a great deliverance. And since genius must be ardent about something, Lucretius pours out his enthusiasm on Epicurus, who brought this deliverance and was the savior of mankind. Yet this was only a beginning of salvation, and the same principles carried further would have delivered us from the Epicurean life and what it retained that was Greek and naturalistic: science, friendship, and the healthy pleasures of the body. Had it renounced these things also, Epicureanism would have become altogether ascetic, a thorough system of mortification, or the pursuit of death. To those who sincerely pursue death, death is no evil, but the highest good. No need in that case of elaborate arguments to prove that death should not be feared, because it is nothing; for in spite of being nothing—or rather because it is nothing—death can be loved by a fatigued and disillusioned spirit, just as in spite of being nothing—or rather because it is nothing—it must be hated and feared by every vigorous animal.

One more point, and I have done with this subject. Ancient culture was rhetorical. It abounded in ideas that are verbally plausible, and pass muster in a public speech, but that, if we stop to criticize them, prove at once to be inexcusably false. One of these rhetorical fallacies is the maxim that men cannot live for what they cannot witness. What does it matter to you, we may say in debate, what happened before you were born, or what may go on after you are buried? And the orator who puts such a challenge may carry the audience with him, and raise a laugh at the expense of human sincerity. Yet the very men who applaud are proud of their ancestors, care for the future of their children, and are very much interested in securing legally the execution of their last will and testament. What may go on after their death concerns them deeply, not because they expect to watch the event from hell or heaven, but because they are interested ideally in what that event shall be, although they are never to witness it. Lucretius himself, in his sympathy with nature, in his zeal for human enlightenment, in his tears for Iphigenia, long since dead, is not moved by the hope of observing, or the memory of having observed, what excites his emotion. He forgets himself. He sees the whole universe spread out in its true movement and proportions; he sees mankind freed from the incubus of superstition, and from the havoc of passion. The vision kindles his enthusiasm, exalts his imagination, and swells his verse into unmistakable earnestness.

If we follow Lucretius, therefore, in narrowing the sum of our personal fortunes to one brief and partial glimpse of earth, we must not suppose that we need narrow at all the sphere of our moral interests. On the contrary, just in proportion as we despise superstitious terrors and sentimental hopes, and as our imagination becomes self-forgetful, we shall strengthen the direct and primitive concern which we feel in the world and in what may go on there, before us, after us, or beyond our ken. If, like Lucretius and every philosophical poet, we range over all time and all existence, we shall forget our own persons, as he did, and even wish them to be forgotten, if only the things we care for may subsist or arise. He who truly loves God, says Spinoza, cannot wish that God should love him in return. One who lives the life of the universe cannot be much concerned for his own. After all, the life of the universe is but the locus and extension of ours. The atoms that have once served to produce life remain fit to reproduce it; and although the body they might animate later would be a new one, and would have a somewhat different career, it would not, according to Lucretius, be of a totally new species; perhaps not more unlike ourselves than we are unlike one another, or than each of us is unlike himself at the various stages of his life.

The soul of nature, in the elements of it, is then, according to Lucretius, actually immortal; only the human individuality, the chance composition of those elements, is transitory; so that, if a man could care for what happens to other men, for what befell him when young or what may overtake him when old, he might perfectly well care, on the same imaginative principle, for what may go on in the world forever. The finitude and injustice of his personal life would be broken down; the illusion of selfishness would be dissipated; and he might say to himself, I have imagination, and nothing that is real is alien to me.

The word nature has many senses; but if we preserve the one which etymology justifies, and which is the most philosophical as well, nature should mean the principle of birth or genesis, the universal mother, the great cause, or system of causes, that brings phenomena to light. If we take the word nature in this sense, it may be said that Lucretius, more than any other man, is the poet of nature. Of course, being an ancient, he is not particularly a poet of landscape. He runs deeper than that; he is a poet of the source of landscape, a poet of matter. A poet of landscape might try to suggest, by well-chosen words, the sensations of light, movement, and form which nature arouses in us; but in this attempt he would encounter the insuperable difficulty which Lessing long ago pointed out, and warned poets of: I mean the unfitness of language to render what is spatial and material; its fitness to render only what, like language itself, is bodiless and flowing—action, feeling, and thought.

It is noticeable, accordingly, that poets who are fascinated by pure sense and seek to write poems about it are called not impressionists, but symbolists; for in trying to render some absolute sensation they render rather the field of association in which that sensation lies, or the emotions and half-thoughts that shoot and play about it in their fancy. They become—against their will, perhaps—psychological poets, ringers of mental chimes, and listeners for the chance overtones of consciousness. Hence we call them symbolists, mixing perhaps some shade of disparagement in the term, as if they were symbolists of an empty, supersubtle, or fatuous sort. For they play with things luxuriously, making them symbols for their thoughts, instead of mending their thoughts intelligently, to render them symbols for things.

A poet might be a symbolist in another sense—if he broke up nature, the object suggested by landscape to the mind, and reverted to the elements of landscape, not in order to associate these sensations lazily together, but in order to build out of them in fancy a different nature, a better world, than that which they reveal to reason. The elements of landscape, chosen, emphasized, and recombined for this purpose, would then be symbols for the ideal world they were made to suggest, and for the ideal life that might be led in that paradise. Shelley is a symbolic landscape poet in this sense. To Shelley, as Francis Thompson has said, nature was a toyshop; his fancy took the materials of the landscape and wove them into a gossamer world, a bright ethereal habitation for newborn irresponsible spirits. Shelley was the musician of landscape; he traced out its unrealized suggestions; transformed the things he saw into the things he would fain have seen. In this idealization it was spirit that guided him, the bent of his wild and exquisite imagination, and he fancied sometimes that the grosser landscapes of earth were likewise the work of some half-spiritual stress, of some restlessly dreaming power. In this sense, earthly landscape seemed to him the symbol of the earth spirit, as the starlit crystal landscapes of his verse, with their pensive flowers, were symbols in which his own fevered spirit was expressed, images in which his passion rested.

Another sort of landscape poetry is to be found in Wordsworth, for whom the title of poet of nature might perhaps be claimed. To him the landscape is an influence. What he renders, beyond such pictorial touches as language is capable of, is the moral inspiration which the scene brings to him. This moral inspiration is not drawn at all from the real processes of nature which every landscape manifests in some aspect and for one moment. Such would have been the method of Lucretius; he would have passed imaginatively from the landscape to the sources of the landscape; he would have disclosed the poetry of matter, not of spirit. Wordsworth, on the contrary, dwells on adventitious human matters. He is no poet of genesis, evolution, and natural force in its myriad manifestations. Only a part of the cosmic process engages his interest, or touches his soul—the strengthening or chastening of human purposes by the influences of landscape. These influences are very real; for as food or wine keeps the animal heart beating, or quickens it, so large spaces of calm sky, or mountains, or dells, or solitary stretches of water, expand the breast, disperse the obsessions that cramp a man's daily existence, and even if he be less contemplative and less virtuous than Wordsworth, make him, for the moment, a friend to all things, and a friend to himself.

Yet these influences are vague and for the most part fleeting. Wordsworth would hardly have felt them so distinctly and so constantly had he not found a further link to bind landscape to moral sentiment. Such a link exists. The landscape is the scene of human life. Every spot, every season, is associated with the sort of existence which falls to men in that environment. Landscape for Wordsworth's age and in his country was seldom without figures. At least, some visible trace of man guided the poet and set the key for his moral meditation. Country life was no less dear to Wordsworth than landscape was; it fitted into every picture; and while the march of things, as Lucretius conceived it, was not present to Wordsworth's imagination, the revolutions of society—the French Revolution, for instance—were constantly in his thoughts. Insofar as he was a poet of human life, Wordsworth was truly a poet of nature. Insofar, however, as he was a poet of landscape, he was still fundamentally a poet of human life, or merely of his personal experience. When he talked of nature he was generally moralizing, and altogether subject to the pathetic fallacy; but when he talked of man, or of himself, he was unfolding a part of nature, the upright human heart, and studying it in its truth.

Lucretius, a poet of universal nature, studied everything in its truth. Even moral life, though he felt it much more narrowly and coldly than Wordsworth did, was better understood and better sung by him for being seen in its natural setting. It is a fault of idealists to misrepresent idealism, because they do not view it as a part of the world. Idealism *is* a part of the world, a small and dependent part of it. It is a small and dependent part even in the life of men. This fact is nothing against idealism taken as a moral energy, as a faculty of idealization and a habit of living in the familiar presence of an image of what would, in everything, be best. But it is the ruin of idealism taken as a view of the central and universal power in the world. For this reason Lucretius, who sees human life and human idealism in their natural setting, has a saner and maturer view of both than has Wordsworth, for all his greater refinement. Nature, for the Latin poet, is really nature. He loves and fears her, as she deserves to be loved and feared by her creatures. Whether it be a wind blowing, a torrent rushing, a lamb bleating, the magic of love, genius achieving its purpose, or a war, or a pestilence, Lucretius sees everything in its causes, and in its total career. One breath of lavish creation, one iron law of change, runs through the whole, making all things kin in their inmost elements and in their last end. Here is the touch of nature indeed, her largeness and eternity. Here is the true echo of the life of matter.

Any comprehensive picture of nature and destiny, if the picture be credited, must arouse emotion, and in a reflective and vivid mind must inspire poetry—for what is poetry but emotion, fixing and coloring the objects from which it springs? The sublime poem of Lucretius, expounding the least poetical of philosophies, proves this point beyond a doubt. Yet Lucretius was far from exhausting the inspiration which a poet might draw from materialism. In the philosophy of Epicurus, even, which had but a sickly hold on materialism, there were two strains which Lucretius did not take up, and which are naturally rich in poetry, the strain of piety and the strain of friendship. It is usual and, in one sense, legitimate to speak of the Epicureans as atheists, since they denied providence and any government of God in the world. Yet they admitted the existence of gods, living in the quiet spaces between those celestial whirlpools which form the various worlds. To these gods they atttributed the human form, and the serene life to which Epicurus aspired. Epicurus himself was so sincere in this belief, and so much affected by it, that he used to frequent the temples, keep the feasts of the gods, and often spend hours before their images in contemplation and prayer.

In this, as in much else, Epicurus was carrying out to its logical conclusion the rational and reforming essence of Hellenism. In Greek religion, as in all other religions, there was a background of vulgar superstitions. Survivals and revivals of totem worship, taboo, magic, ritual barter, and objectified rhetoric are to be found in it to the very end; yet if we consider in Greek religion its characteristic tendency, and what rendered it distinctively Greek, we see that it was its unprecedented ideality, disinterestedness, and aestheticism. To the Greek, insofar as he was a Greek, religion was an aspiration to grow like the gods by invoking their companionship, rehearsing their story, feeling vicariously the glow of their splendid prerogatives, and placing them, in the form of beautiful and very human statues, constantly before his eyes. This sympathetic interest in the immortals took the place, in the typical Greek mind, of any vivid hope of human immortality; perhaps it made such a hope seem superfluous and inappropriate. Mortality belonged to man, as immortality to the gods; and the one was the complement of the other. Imagine a poet who, to the freedom and simplicity of Homer, should have added the more reverent idealism of a later age; and what an inexhaustible fund of poetry might he not have found in this conception of the immortals leading a human life, without its sordid contrarieties and limitations, eternally young, and frank, and different!

Hints of such poetry are to be found in Plato, myths that present the ideal suggestions of human life in pictures. These he sometimes leaves general and pale, calling them ideas; but at other times he embodies them in deities, or in detailed imaginary constructions, like that of his *Republic*. This Platonic habit of mind might have been carried further by some franker and less reactionary poet than Plato was, or tended to become, as the years turned his wine into vinegar. But the whole world was then getting sour. Imagination flagged, or was diverted from the Greek into the Hebrew channel. Nevertheless, the hymns of modern poets to the ancient gods, and the irrepressible echoes of classic mythology in our literature, show how easy it would have been for the later ancients themselves, had they chosen, to make immortal poetry out of their dying superstitions. The denials of Epicurus do not exclude this ideal use of religion; on the contrary, by excluding all the other uses of it—the commercial, the mock scientific, and the selfish—they leave the moral interpretative aspect of religion standing alone, ready to the poet's hand, if any poet could be found pure and fertile enough to catch and to render it. Rationalized paganism might have had its Dante, a Dante who should have been the pupil not of Virgil and Aquinas, but of Homer and Plato. Lucretius was too literal, positivistic, and insistent for such a delicate task. He was a Roman. Moral mythology and ideal piety, though his philosophy had room for them, formed no part of his poetry.

What the other neglected theme, friendship, might have supplied, we may see in the tone of another Epicurean, the poet Horace. Friendship was highly honored in all ancient states; and the Epicurean philosophy, in banishing so many traditional forms of sentiment, could only intensify the emphasis on friendship. It taught men that they were an accident in the universe, comrades afloat on the same raft together with no fate not common to them all, and no possible helpers but one another. Lucretius does speak, in a passage to which I have already referred,[8] about the hope of sweet friendship that supports him in his labors; and elsewhere [9] he repeats the Epicurean idyl about picnicking together on the green grass by a flowing brook; but the little word "together" is all he vouchsafes us to mark what must be the chief ingredient in such rural happiness.

Horace, usually so much slighter than Lucretius, is less cursory here. Not only does he strike much oftener the note of friendship, but his whole mind and temper breathe of friendliness and expected agreement. There is, in the very charm and artifice of his lines, a sort of confidential joy in tasting with the kindred few the sweet or pungent savor of human things. To be brief and gently ironical is to assume mutual intelligence; and to assume mutual intelligence is to believe in friendship. In Lucretius, on the other hand, zeal is mightier than sympathy, and scorn mightier than humor. Perhaps it would be asking too much of his uncompromising fervor that he should have unbent now and then and shown us in some detail what those pleasures of life may be which are without care and fear. Yet, if it were impossible for him not to be always serious and austere, he might at least have noted the melancholy of friendship—for friendship, where nature has made minds isolated and bodies mortal, is rich also in melancholy. This again we may find in Horace, where once or twice he lets the "something bitter" bubble up from the heart even of this flower, when he feels a vague need that survives satiety, and yearns perversely for the impossible.[10] Poor Epicureans, when they could not learn, like their master, to be saints!

So far the decadent materialism of Epicurus might have carried a poet; but a materialist in our days might find many other poetic themes to weave into his system. To the picture which Lucretius sketches of primitive civilization, we might add the whole history of mankind. To a consistent and vigorous materialism all personal and national dramas, with the beauties of all the arts, are no less natural and interesting than are flowers or animal bodies. The moral pageantry of this world, surveyed scientifically, is calculated wonderfully to strengthen and refine the philosophy of

8. Cf. page 375.
9. Lucretius, II. 29–33. [Cf. *Great Books of the Western World,* Vol. 12, p. 15 (Ed.).]
10. Horace, *Odes,* IV. 1.

abstention suggested to Epicurus by the flux of material things and by the illusions of vulgar passion. Lucretius studies superstition, but only as an enemy; and the naturalistic poet should be the enemy of nothing. His animus blinds him to half the object, to its more beautiful half, and makes us distrust his version of the meaner half he is aware of. Seen in its totality, and surrounded by all the other products of human imagination, superstition is not only moving in itself, a capital subject for tragedy and for comedy, but it reinforces the materialistic way of thinking, and shows that it may be extended to the most complex and emotional spheres of existence. At the same time, a naturalism extended impartially over moral facts brings home a lesson of tolerance, scepticism, and independence which, without contradicting Epicurean principles, would very much enlarge and transform Epicurean sentiment. History would have opened to the Epicurean poet a new dimension of nature and a more varied spectacle of folly. His imagination would have been enriched and his maxims fortified.

The emotions which Lucretius associated with his atoms and void, with his religious denials and his abstentions from action, are emotions necessarily involved in life. They will exist in any case, though not necessarily associated with the doctrines by which this poet sought to clarify them. They will remain standing, whatever mechanism we put in the place of that which he believed in—that is, if we are serious, and not trying to escape from the facts rather than to explain them. If the ideas embodied in a philosophy represent a comprehensive survey of the facts, and a mature sentiment in the presence of them, any new ideas adopted instead will have to acquire the same values, and nothing will be changed morally except the language or euphony of the mind.

Of course one theory of the world must be true and the rest false, at least if the categories of any theory are applicable to reality; but the true theory like the false resides in imagination, and the truth of it which the poet grasps is its truth to life. If there are no atoms, at least there must be habits of nature, or laws of evolution, or dialectics of progress, or decrees of providence, or intrusions of chance; and before these equally external and groundless powers we must bow, as Lucretius bowed to his atoms. It will always be important and inevitable to recognize *something* external, something that generates or surrounds us; and perhaps the only difference between materialism and other systems in this respect is that materialism has studied more scrupulously the detail and method of our dependence.

Similarly, even if Lucretius were wrong, and the soul is immortal, it is

nevertheless steadily changing its interests and its possessions. Our lives
are mortal if our soul is not; and the sentiment which reconciled Lucretius
to death is as much needed if we are to face many deaths, as if we are to
face only one. The gradual losing of what we have been and are, Emerson
says:

> This losing is true dying;
> This is lordly man's down-lying,
> This his slow but sure reclining,
> Star by star his world resigning.

The maxim of Lucretius, that nothing arises save by the death of something else, meets us still in our crawling immortality. And his art of
accepting and enjoying what the conditions of our being afford also has a
perennial application. Dante, the poet of faith, will tell us that we must
find our peace in the will that gives us our limited portion. Goethe, the
poet of romantic experience, will tell us that we must renounce, renounce
perpetually. Thus wisdom clothes the same moral truth in many cosmic
parables. The doctrines of philosophers disagree where they are literal
and arbitrary—mere guesses about the unknown; but they agree or complete one another where they are expressive or symbolic, thoughts wrung
by experience from the hearts of poets. Then all philosophies alike are ways
of meeting and recording the same flux of images, the same vicissitudes of
good and evil, which will visit all generations, while man is man.

Goethe's Faust

In approaching the third of our philosophical poets, there is a scruple that may cross the mind. Lucretius was undoubtedly a philosophical poet; his whole poem is devoted to expounding and defending a system of philosophy. In Dante the case is almost as plain. The *Divine Comedy* is a moral and personal fable; yet not only are many passages explicitly philosophical, but the whole is inspired and controlled by the most definite of religious systems and of moral codes. Dante, too, is unmistakably a philosophical poet. But was Goethe a philosopher? And is *Faust* a philosophical poem?

If we say so, it must be by giving a certain latitude to our terms. Goethe was the wisest of mankind; too wise, perhaps, to be a philosopher in the technical sense, or to try to harness this wild world in a brain-spun terminology. It is true that he was all his life a follower of Spinoza, and that he may be termed, without hesitation, a naturalist in philosophy and a pantheist. His adherence to the general attitude of Spinoza, however, did not exclude a great plasticity and freedom in his own views, even on the most fundamental points. Thus Goethe did not admit the mechanical interpretation of nature advocated by Spinoza. He also assigned, at least to privileged souls like his own, a more personal sort of immortality than Spinoza allowed. Moreover, he harbored a generous sympathy with the dramatic explanations of nature and history current in the Germany of his day. Yet such transcendental idealism, making the world the expression of a spiritual endeavor, was a total reversal of that conviction, so profound in Spinoza, that all moral energies are resident in particular creatures, themselves sparks in an absolutely infinite and purposeless world. In a word, Goethe was not a systematic philosopher. His feeling for the march of things and for the significance of great personages and great ideas was indeed philosophical, although more romantic than scientific. His thoughts upon life were fresh and miscellaneous. They voiced the genius and learning of his age. They did not express a firm personal attitude, radical and unified, and transmissible to other times and persons. For philosophers, after all, have this advantage over men of letters, that their minds, being more organic, can more easily propagate themselves. They scatter less influence, but more seeds.

If from Goethe we turn to *Faust*—and it is as the author of *Faust* only that we shall consider him—the situation is not less ambiguous. In the play, as the young Goethe first wrote it, philosophy appeared in the first line—*Hab nun ach die Philosophey* [I have (studied), alas, philosophy]; but it appeared there, and throughout the piece, merely as a human experience, a passion or an illusion, a fund of images or an ambitious art. Later, it is true, under the spell of fashion and of Schiller, Goethe surrounded his original scenes with others, like the prologue in heaven, or the apotheosis of Faust, in which a philosophy of life was indicated; namely, that he who strives strays, yet in that straying finds his salvation. This idea left standing all that satirical and Mephistophelian wisdom with which the whole poem abounds, the later parts no less than the earlier. Frankly, it was a moral that adorned the tale, without having been the seed of it, and without even expressing fairly the spirit which it breathes. *Faust* remained an essentially romantic poem, written to give vent to a pregnant and vivid genius, to touch the heart, to bewilder the mind with a carnival of images, to amuse, to thrill, to humanize; and, if we must speak of philosophy, there were many express maxims in the poem, and many insights, half betrayed, that exceeded in philosophic value the belated and official moral which the author affixed to it, and which he himself warned us not to take too seriously.

Faust is, then, no philosophical poem, after an open or deliberate fashion; and yet it offers a solution to the moral problem of existence as truly as do the poems of Lucretius and Dante. Heard philosophies are sweet, but those unheard may be sweeter. They may be more unmixed and more profound for being adopted unconsciously, for being lived rather than taught. This is not merely to say what might be said of every work of art and of every natural object, that it could be made the starting point for a chain of inferences that should reveal the whole universe, like the flower in the crannied wall. It is to say, rather, that the vital straining towards an ideal, definite but latent, when it dominates a whole life, may express that ideal more fully than could the best-chosen words.

Now *Faust* is the foam on the top of two great waves of human aspiration, merging and heaping themselves up together—the wave of romanticism rising from the depths of northern traditions and genius, and the wave of a new paganism coming from Greece over Italy. These are not philosophies to be read into *Faust* by the critic; they are passions seething in the drama. It is the drama of a philosophical adventure; a rebellion against convention; a flight to nature, to tenderness, to beauty; and then a return to convention again, with a feeling that nature, tenderness, and beauty, unless found there, will not be found at all. Goethe never depicts, as Dante does, the object his hero is pursuing; he is satisfied with depicting the pursuit. Like Lessing, in his famous apologue, he prefers the pursuit of the ideal to the ideal itself; perhaps, as in the case of Lessing, because the hope of realizing the ideal, and the interest in realizing it, were beginning to forsake him.

The case is somewhat as that of Dante would have been if, instead of recognizing and loving Beatrice at first sight and rising into a vision of the eternal world, ready-made and perfectly ordered, Dante had passed from love to love, from *donna gentile* to *donna gentile*, always longing for the eyes of Beatrice without ever meeting them. The *Divine Comedy* would then have been only human, yet it might have suggested and required the very consummation that the *Divine Comedy* depicts; and without expressing this consummation, our human comedy might have furnished materials and momentum for it, such that, if ever that consummation came to be expressed, it would be more deeply felt and more adequately understood. Dante gives us a philosophical goal, and we have to recall and retrace the journey; Goethe gives us a philosophic journey, and we have to divine the goal.

Goethe is a romantic poet; he is a novelist in verse. He is a philosopher of experience as it comes to the individual; the philosopher of life, as action, memory, or soliloquy may put life before each of us in turn. Now the zest of romanticism consists in taking what you know is an independent and ancient world as if it were material for your private emotions. The savage or the animal, who should not be aware of nature or history at all, could not be romantic about them, nor about himself. He would be blandly idiotic, and take everything quite unsuspectingly for what it was in him. The romanticist, then, should be a civilized man, so that his primitiveness and egotism may have something paradoxical and conscious about them; and so that his life may contain a rich experience, and his reflection may play with all varieties of sentiment and thought. At the same time, in his inmost genius, he should be a barbarian, a child, a transcendentalist, so that his life may seem to him absolutely fresh, self-determined, unforeseen, and unforeseeable. It is part of his inspiration to believe that he creates a new heaven and a new earth with each revolution in his moods or in his purposes. He ignores, or seeks to ignore, all the conditions of life, until perhaps by living he personally discovers them. Like Faust, he flouts science, and is minded to make trial of magic, which renders a man's will master of the universe in which he seems to live. He disowns all authority, save that mysteriously exercised over him by his deep faith in himself. He is always honest and brave; but he is always different, and absolves himself from his past as soon as he has outgrown or forgotten it. He is inclined to be wayward and foolhardy, justifying himself on the ground that all experience is interesting, that the springs of it are inexhaustible and always pure, and that the future of his soul is infinite. In the romantic hero the civilized man and the barbarian must be combined; he should be the heir to all civilization, and, nevertheless, he should take life arrogantly and egotistically, as if it were an absolute personal experiment.

This singular combination was strikingly exemplified in Doctor Johannes Faustus, a figure half historical, half legendary, familiar to Goethe in his boyhood in puppet shows and chapbooks. An adventurer in the romantic as well as in the vulgar sense of the word, somewhat like Paracelsus or Giordano Bruno, Doctor Faustus had felt the mystery of nature, had scorned authority, had credited magic, had lived by imposture, and had fled from the police. His blasphemous boasts and rascally conduct, together with his magic arts, had made him even in his lifetime a scandalous and interesting personage. He was scarcely dead when legends gathered about his name. It was published abroad that he had sold his soul to the devil, in exchange for twenty-four years of wild pleasures upon earth.

This legend purported to offer a terrible and edifying example, a warning to all Christians to avoid the snares of science, of pleasure, and of ambition. These things had sent Doctor Faustus into hell-fire; his corpse, found face downward, could not be turned over upon its back. Nevertheless, we may suspect that even at the beginning people recognized in Doctor Faustus a braver brother, a somewhat enviable reprobate who had dared to relish the good things of this life above the sad joys vaguely promised for the other. All that the Renaissance valued was here represented as in the devil's gift; and the man in the street might well doubt whether it was religion or worldly life that was thereby made the more unlovely. Doubtless the Lutheran authors of the first chapbook felt, and felt rightly, that those fine things which tempted Faustus were unevangelical, pagan, and popish; yet they could not cease altogether to admire and even to covet them, especially when the first ardors of the Old Christian revival had had time to cool.

Marlowe, who wrote only a few years later, made a beginning in the rehabilitation of the hero. His Faustus is still damned, but he is transformed into the sort of personage that Aristotle approves of for the hero of tragedy, essentially human and noble, but led astray by some excusable vice or error. Marlowe's public would see in Doctor Faustus a man and a Christian like themselves, carried a bit too far by ambition and the love of pleasure. He is no radical unbeliever, no natural mate for the devil, conscienceless and heathen, like the typical villain of the Renaissance. On the contrary, he has become a good Protestant, and holds manfully to all those parts of the creed which express his spontaneous affections. A good angel is often overheard whispering in his ear; and if the bad angel finally prevails, it is in spite of continual remorse and hesitation on the Doctor's part. This excellent Faustus is damned by accident or by predestination; he is brow-beaten by the devil and forbidden to repent when he has really repented. The terror of the conclusion is thereby heightened; we see an essentially good man, because in a moment of infatuation he had signed away his soul, driven against his will to despair and damnation. The alternative of a happy solution lies almost at hand; and it is only a lingering taste for the lurid and the horrible, ingrained in this sort of melodrama, that sends him shrieking to hell.

What makes Marlowe's conclusion the more violent and the more unphilosophical is the fact that, to anyone not dominated by convention, the good angel, in the dialogue, seems to have so much the worse of the argument. All he has to offer is sour admonition and external warnings:

> O Faustus, lay that damnèd book aside,
> And gaze not on it lest it tempt thy soul,
> And heap God's heavy wrath upon thy head.
> Read, read, the Scriptures; that is blasphemy. . . .
> Sweet Faustus, think of heaven, and heavenly things.

To which the evil angel replies:

> No, Faustus, think of honour and of wealth.

And in another place:

> Go forward, Faustus, in that famous art,
> Wherein all nature's treasure is contained.
> Be thou on earth as Jove is in the sky,
> Lord and commander of these elements.

There can be no doubt that the devil here represents the natural ideal of Faustus, or of any child of the Renaissance; he appeals to the vague but healthy ambitions of a young soul, that would make trial of the world. In other words, this devil represents the true good, and it is no wonder if the honest Faustus cannot resist his suggestions. We like him for his love of life, for his trust in nature, for his enthusiasm for beauty. He speaks for us all when he cries:

> Was this the face that launched a thousand ships
> And burnt the topless towers of Ilium?

Even his irreverent pranks, being directed against the pope, endear him the more to an anti-clerical public; and he appeals to courtiers and cavaliers by his lofty poetical scorn for such crabbed professions as the law, medicine, or theology. In a word, Marlowe's Faustus is a martyr to everything that the Renaissance prized,—power, curious knowledge, enterprise, wealth, and beauty.

How thoroughly Marlowe and Goethe are on the way towards reversing the Christian philosophy of life may be seen if we compare *Faust* for a moment (as, in other respects, has often been done) with *The Wonder-working Magician* of Calderón. This earlier hero, St. Cyprian of Antioch, is like Faust in being a scholar, signing away his soul to the devil, practising magic, embracing the ghost of beauty, and being ultimately saved. Here the analogy ends. Cyprian, far from being disgusted with all theory, and particularly with theology, is a pagan philosopher eagerly seeking God, and working his way, with full faith in his method, toward Christian orthodoxy. He floors the devil in scholastic argument about the unity of God, his power, wisdom, and goodness. He falls in love, and sells his soul merely in the hope of satisfying his passion. He studies magic chiefly for the same reason; but magic cannot overrule the free will of the Christian lady he loves (a modern and very Spanish one, though supposed to adorn ancient Antioch). The devil can supply only a false phantasm of her person, and as Cyprian approaches her and lifts her veil, he finds a hideous death's-head beneath; for God can work miracles to cap those of any magician, and can beat the devil at his own game. Thunderstruck at this portent, Cyprian becomes a Christian. Half-naked, ecstatic, taken for a madman, he bears witness loudly and persistently to the power, wisdom, and goodness of the one true God; and, since the persecution of Decius is then going on, he is hurried away to martyrdom. His lady, sentenced also for the same cause, encourages him by her heroic attitude and words. Their earthly passion is dead; but their souls are united in death and in immortality.

In this drama we see magic checkmated by miracles, doubt yielding to faith, purity resisting temptation, passion transformed into zeal, and all the glories of the world collapsing before disillusion and asceticism. These glories are nothing, the poet tells us, but dust, ashes, smoke, and air.

The contrast with Goethe's *Faust* could not be more complete. Both poets take the greatest liberties with their chronology, yet the spirit of their dramas is remarkably true to the respective ages in which they are supposed to occur. Calderón glorifies the movement from paganism to Christianity. The philosophy in which that movement culminated—Catholic orthodoxy—still dominates the poet's mind, not in a perfunctory way, but so as to kindle his imagination, and render his personages sublime and his verses rapturous. Goethe's *Faust,* on the contrary, glorifies the return from Christianity to paganism. It shows the spirit of the Renaissance liberating the soul, and bursting the bonds of traditional faith and traditional morals. This spirit, after manifesting itself brilliantly at the time of the historical Faust, had seemed to be smothered in the great world during the seventeenth century. Men's characters and laws had reaffirmed their old allegiance to Christianity, and the Renaissance survived only abstractly, in scholarship or the fine arts, to which it continued to lend a certain classic or pseudoclassic elegance. In Goethe's time, however, a second Renaissance was taking place in the souls of men. The love of life, primal and adventurous, was gathering head in many an individual. In the romantic movement and in the French Revolution, this love of life freed itself from the politic compromises and conventions that had been stifling it for two hundred years. Goethe's hero embodies this second, romantic emancipation of the mind, too long an unwilling pupil of Christian tradition. He cries for air, for nature, for all experience. Cyprian, on the other hand, an unwilling pupil of paganism, had yearned for truth, for solitude, and for heaven.

Such was the legend that, to the great good fortune of mankind, fascinated the young Goethe, and took root in his fancy. Around it gathered the experiences and insights of sixty well-filled years: *Faust* became the poetical autobiography and the philosophic testament of Goethe. He stuffed it with every enthusiasm that diversified his own life, from the great alternative of romantic or classical art, down to the controversy between Neptunism and Vulcanism in geology, and to his fatherly admiration for Lord Byron. Yet in spite of the liberties he took with the legend, and the personal turn he gave it, nothing in its historical associations escaped him. His life in Frankfurt and in Strasbourg had made the medieval scene familiar to his fancy; Herder had communicated to him an imaginative cult for all that was national and characteristic in art and manners; the spell of Gothic architecture had fallen on him; and he had learned to feel in Shakespeare the infinite strength of suggestion in details, in multitudinous glimpses, in lifelike medleys of sadness and mirth, in a humble realism in externals, amid lyric and metaphysical outpourings of the passions. The sense for classic beauty which had inspired Marlowe with immortal lines, and was later to inspire his own *Helena*, was as yet dormant; but instead he had caught the humanitarian craze, then prevalent, for defending and idealizing the victims of law and society, among others, the poor girl who, to escape disgrace, did away with her newborn child. Such a victim of a selfish seducer and a Pharisaical public was to add a desirable touch of femininity and pathos to the story of Faust: Gretchen was to take the place, at least for the nonce, of the coveted Helen.

This Gretchen was to be no common creature, but one endowed with all the innocence, sweetness, intelligence, fire, and fortitude which Goethe was finding, or thought he was finding, in his own Gretchens, Kätchens, and Frederickes. For the young Goethe, though very learned, was no mere student of books; to his human competence and power to succeed, he joined the gusts of feeling, the irresponsible raptures, the sudden sorrows, of a genuine poet. He was a true lover, and a wayward one. He could delve into magic with awe, in a Faust-like spirit of adventure; he could burn offerings in his attic to the rising sun; he could plunge into Christian mysticism; and there could well up, on occasion, from the deep store of his unconscious mind, floods of words, of images, and of tears. He was a genius, if ever there was one; and this genius, in all its freshness, was poured into the composition of *Faust*—the most kindred of themes, the most picturesque and magical of romances.

In Goethe's first version of the poem, before the story of Gretchen, we find the studious Faust, as in Marlowe, soliloquizing on the vanity of the sciences. They grasp nothing of the genuine truth; they are verbal shams. They have not even brought Faust fame or riches. Perhaps magic might do better. The air was full of spirits; could they be summoned to our aid, possibly the secrets of nature might be unlocked. We might reach true science, and through it undreamt-of power over the material world. For Nature, according to Goethe, really has secrets. She is not all open to eventual inspection; she is no mere mechanism of minute parts and statable laws. Our last view of her, like our first glimpse, must be interpreted; from the sum of her manifestations we must divine her soul. Therefore only a poetic and rhetorical art, like magic, has any chance of unveiling her, and of bringing us face to face with the truth.

In this invocation of spirits, as Goethe's Faust makes it, there is no question of selling, or even of risking, the soul. This Faust, unlike Marlowe's, has no faith and no fear. From the point of view of the church he is damned already as an unbeliever; but, as an unbeliever, he is looking for salvation in another quarter. Like the bolder spirits of the Renaissance, he is hoping to find in universal nature, infinite, placid, noncensorious, an escape from the prison house of Christian doctrine and Christian law. His magic arts are the sacrament that will initiate him into his new religion, the religion of nature. He turns to nature also in another sense, more characteristic of the age of Goethe than of that of Faust. He longs for grandiose solitudes. He feels that moonlight, caves, mountains, driving clouds would be his best medicine and his best counselors. The souls of Rousseau, Byron, and Shelley are preincarnate in this Faust, the epitome of all romantic rebellions. They coexist there with the souls of Paracelsus and Giordano Bruno. The wild aspects of nature, he thinks, will melt and renew his heart, while magic reveals the mysteries of cosmic law and helps him to exploit them.

Full of these hopes, Faust opens his book of magic at the sign of the Macrocosm: it shows him the mechanism of the world, all forces and events playing into one another and forming an infinite chain. The spectacle entrances him; he seems to have attained one of his dearest ambitions. But here he comes at once upon the other half, or, as Hegel would call it, the other moment, of the romantic life. Every romantic ideal, once realized, disenchants. No matter what we attain, our dissatisfaction must be perpetual. Thus the vision of the universe, which Faust now has before him, is, he remembers, only a vision; it is a theory or conception. It is not a rendering of the inner life of the world as Shakespeare, for instance, feels and renders it. Experience, as it comes to him who lives and works, is not given by that theoretical vision; in science experience is turned into so many reviewed events, the passage of so much substance through so many forms. But Faust does not want an image or description of reality; he yearns to enact and to become the reality itself.

In this new search, he fixes his eye on the sign of the Earth-Spirit, which seems more propitious to his present wish. This sign is the key to all experience. All experience tempts Faust; he shrinks from nothing that any mortal may have endured; he is ready to undertake everything that any mortal may have done. In all men he would live; and with the last man he will be content to die. So mighty is his yearning for experience that the Earth-Spirit is softened and appears at his bidding. In a red flame he sees its monstrous visage, and his enthusiasm is turned to horror. Outspread before him is the furious, indiscriminate cataract of life, the merciless flux, the infinite variety, the absolute inconstancy of it. This general life is not for any individual to rehearse; it bursts all bounds of personality. Each man may assimilate that part only which falls within his understanding, only that aspect which things wear from his particular angle, and to his particular interests. *Du gleichst*, the Earth-Spirit cries to him—*du gleichst dem Geist den du begreifst, nicht mir* [You resemble the spirit you comprehend, not me].

This saying—that the life possible and good for man is the life of reason, not the life of nature—is a hard one to the romantic, unintellectual, insatiable Faust. He thinks, like many another philosopher of feeling, that since his is a part of the sum of experience, the whole of experience should be akin to his. But in fact the opposite is far nearer the truth. Man is constituted by his limitations, by his station contrasted with all other stations, and his purposes chosen from amongst all other purposes. Any great scope he can attain must be due to his powers of representation. His understanding may render him universal; his life never can. Faust, as he hears this sentence from the departing Earth-Spirit, collapses under it. He feels impotent to gainsay what the tumult of the world is thundering at him, but he will not accept on authority so unwelcome and chastening a truth. All his long experience to come will scarcely suffice to convince him of it.

These are the chief philosophical ideas that appear in the two earlier versions of Goethe's *Faust*—the *Urfaust* and the *Fragment*. What Mephistopheles says to the young student is only a clever expansion of what Faust had said in his first monologue about the vanity of science and of the learned professions. Mephistopheles, too, finds theory ashen, and the tree of life green and full of golden fruit; only, having more experience than Faust of the second disenchanting moment in the romantic dialectic, he foresees that this golden fruit also will turn to ashes in the mouth, as it did in the garden of Eden. Science is folly, but life is no better; for after all is not science a part of life?

When we turn to the first part in its final shape, or to the entire drama, we find many changes and additions that seem to transform the romantic picture of the opening scene, and to offer us a rounded philosophy. The changes, however, are more in expression than in ultimate substance, and the additions are chiefly new illustrations of the ancient theme. Critics who study the *Entstehungsgeschichte* [story of the Genesis] of works of art help us to analyze them more intelligently and reproduce more accurately what, at various times, may have been the intention of their authors. Yet these bits of information would be dearly bought if we were distracted by them from what gives poetic value and individual character to the result—its total idiosyncrasy, its place in the moral world. The place in the moral world of Goethe's *Faust* as a whole is just the place which the opening scene gave it in the beginning. It fills more space, it touches more historical and poetic matters; but its center is the old center, and its result the old result. It remains romantic in its pictures and in its philosophy.

The first addition that promises to throw new light on the idea of the drama is the *Prologue in Heaven.* In imitation of *The Book of Job,* we find the morning stars—the three archangels—singing together; and then follows a very agreeable and humorous conversation between the Lord and Mephistopheles. The scene is in the style of medieval religious plays, and this circumstance might lead us to suppose that the point at issue was the salvation of Faust's soul. But that, in the literal sense, is far from being the case. As in *Job,* the question is what sentiments the tempted mortal will maintain during this life, not what fate will afterwards overtake his disembodied spirit. Dead men, Mephistopheles observes, do not interest him. He is not a devil from a subterranean hell, concerned, out of pique or ambition, to increase the population of tortured shades in that fabulous region. He dwells in the atmosphere of earth; he knows nothing of the suns or the worlds—the life of man is his element. He remains—what he was in the first versions of the play—a part of the Earth-Spirit, one of its embodiments. His particular office, as we shall see presently, is to precipitate that continual destruction which is involved in the continual renewal of life. He finds it very foolish of Faust to demand everything and be satisfied with nothing; and his wager is that Faust may be brought to demand nothing and be satisfied with what chance throws in his way, that he shall lick the dust, and lick it with pleasure, that he shall renounce the dignity of willing what is not and cannot be, and crawl about, like the serpent, basking in the comforts of the moment.

Against this, the Lord pronounces Faust to be his servant—the servant, that is, of an ideal—and declares that whoever strives after an ideal must needs go astray; yet in his necessary errors, the good man never misses the right road. In other words, to have an ideal to strive for, and, like Faust, never to be satisfied, is itself the salvation of man. Faust does not yet know this. He half believes there is some concrete and ultimate good beyond, and so is bitter and violent in his dissatisfaction; but in due season he will come to clearness on this subject, and understand that only he deserves freedom and life who must daily win them afresh. Mephistopheles himself, with his mockeries and seductions, helps to keep the world moving and men wide awake. Imperfection is all that is possible in the world of action;

but the angels may gather up and fix in thought the perfect forms approached or suggested by existence.

In the two earlier versions of *Faust*, Mephistopheles appears without introduction; we find him amusing himself by giving ambiguous advice to an innocent scholar, and accompanying Faust in his wanderings. His mocking tone and miraculous powers mark him at once as the devil of the legend; but several passages prove that he is a deputy of the Earth-Spirit evoked by Faust in the beginning. That he should be both devil and world-demon ought not to surprise the learned. The devils of popular medieval religion were not cut out of whole cloth: they were simply the Neoplatonic demons of the air, together with the gods of Olympus and the more ancient chthonian deities, blackened by sectarian zeal, and degraded by a coarse and timid imagination. Many of these pagan sprites, indeed, had been originally impish and mischievous, since not all the aspects of nature are lovely or propitious, nor all the dreams of men. But as a whole they were without malice in their irresponsible, elemental life—winged powers darting through space between the earth and the moon. They were not dwellers in a subterranean hell; they were not tormentors nor tormented. Often they swarmed and sang blithely, as they do in *Faust* and even in the *Wonder-working Magician;* and if at other times they croaked or hooted, it was like frogs and owls, less lovely creatures than hummingbirds, but not less natural.

One of these less amiable spirits of the atmosphere, especially of its ambient fire, is the Mephistopheles of Goethe. Why he delighted in evil rather than in good he himself explains in a profound and ingenious fashion. Darkness or nothingness, he says, existed alone before the birth of light. Nothingness or darkness still remains the fundamental and, to his mind, the better part of that mixture of being and privation which we call existence. Nothing that exists can be preserved, nor does it deserve to be; therefore it would have been better if nothing had ever existed. To deny the value of whatever is, and to wish to destroy it, according to him, is the only rational ambition; he is the spirit that denies continually, he is the everlasting No. This spirit—which we might compare with the Mars of Lucretius—has great power in the world; every change, in one of its aspects, expresses it, since in one of its aspects, every change is the destruction of something. This spirit is always willing evil, for it wills death, with all the folly, crime, and despair that minister to death. But in willing evil, it is always accomplishing good; for these evils make for nothingness, and nothingness is the true good. The famous couplet—

Ein Teil von jener Kraft
Die stets das Böse will, und stets das Gute schafft—

[A part of that force which always wants evil and always creates good]

is far from expressing the Hegelian commonplace with which it is usually identified. It does not mean that destruction serves a good purpose after all because it clears the way for "something higher." Mephistopheles is not one of those philosophers who think change and evolution a good in themselves. He does not admit that his activity, while aiming at evil, contributes unintentionally to the good. It contributes to the good intentionally, because the evil it does is, in his opinion, less than the evil it cures. He is the cruel surgeon to the disease of life.

If he admitted the other interpretation, he would be *ipso facto* converted to the view of the Lord in the *Prologue*. His naughtiness would become, in his own eyes, a needful service in the cause of life—a condition of life being really vital and worth living. He might then continue his sly operations and biting witticisms, without one drop more of kindness, and yet be sanctioned in everything by the Absolute, and adopt the smile and halo of the optimist. He would have perceived that he was the spice of life, the yeast and red pepper of the world, necessary to the perfect savor of the providential concoction. As it is, Mephistopheles is far more modest. He says that he wills evil, because what he wills is contrary to what his victims will; he is the great contradictor, the blaster of young hopes. Yet he does good, because these young hopes, if let alone, would lead to misery and absurdity. His contradiction nips the folly of living in the bud. To be sure, as he goes on to acknowledge, the destructive power never wins a decisive victory. While everything falls successively beneath his sickle, the seeds of life are being scattered perpetually behind his back. The Lucretian Venus has her innings, as well as the Lucretian Mars. The eternal seesaw, the ancient flux, continues without end and without abatement.

Thus Mephistopheles has a philosophy, and is justified and consistent in his own eyes; yet in the course of the drama he wears various masks and has various moods. All he says and does cannot be made altogether compatible with the essence of his mind, as Goethe finally conceived it. The dramatic figure of Mephistopheles had been fixed long before in its graphic characteristics. Mephistopheles, for instance, is extremely old; he feels older than the universe. There is nothing new for him; he has no illusions. His feeling for anyone he sees is choked, as happens to old people, by his feelings for the infinite number of persons he remembers.

He is heartless, because he is impersonal and universal. He is altogether inhuman; he has not the shames nor the tastes of man. He often assumes the form of a dog—it is his favorite mask in this earthly carnival. He is not averse to the witches' kitchen, with its senseless din and obscenity. He puts up good-naturedly with the grotesque etiquette of the spirit world, observes all the rules about signing contracts in blood, knocking thrice, and respecting pentagrams. Why should he not? Dogs and demons of the air are forms of the Earth-Spirit as much as man; man has no special dignity that Mephistopheles should respect. Man's morality is one of the moralities, his conventions are not less absurd than the conventions of other monkeys. Mephistopheles has no prejudice against the snake; he understands and he despises his cousin, the snake, also. He understands and he despises himself; he has had time to know himself thoroughly.

His understanding, however, is not impartial, because he is the advocate of death; he cannot sympathize with the other half of the Earth-Spirit, which he does not represent—the creative, propulsive, enamoured side, the side that worships the ideal, the love that makes the world go round. What enchants an ingenuous soul can only amuse Mephistopheles; what torments it gives him a sardonic satisfaction. Thus he comes to be in fact a sour and mocking devil. At other times, when he opposes the silliness and romanticism of Faust, he seems to be the spokesman of all experience and reason; as when he warns Faust that to be at all you must be something in particular. Yet even this he says by way of checking and denying Faust's passion for the infinite. The soberest truth, when unwelcome, may seem to the sentimental as diabolical as the most cynical lie; so that in spite of the very unequal justness of his various sentiments, Mephistopheles retains his dramatic unity. We recognize his tone and, under whatever mask, we think him a villain and find him delightful.

Such is the spirit, and such are the conditions, in which Faust undertakes his adventures. He thirsts for all experience, including all experience of evil; he fears no hell; and he hopes for no happiness. He trusts in magic; that is, he believes, or is willing to make believe, that apart from any settled conditions laid down by nature or God, personal will can evoke the experience it covets by its sheer force and assurance. His bond with Mephistopheles is an expression of this romantic faith. It is no bargain to buy pleasures on earth at the cost of torments hereafter; for neither Goethe, nor Faust, nor Mephistopheles believes that such pleasures are worth having, or such torments possible.

The first taste Faust gets of the world is in Auerbach's cellar, and he finds it at once unpalatable. His mature and disdainful mind cannot be amused by the sodden merriment he sees there. He is without that simplicity and heartiness which might find even drunken gaiety attractive; to put up with such follies, one must know nothing, like Brander, or everything, like Mephistopheles. Faust still feels the "pathos of distance"; he is acutely conscious of something incomparably noble just out of reach. In the witches' kitchen, which he next visits, pleasure is still more ugly and shallow; here the din is even more nonsensical, and the fancy more obscene. Yet Faust comes forth with two points gained in his romantic rehabilitation; he has taken the elixir of youth and he has seen the image of Helen in a mirror. He is henceforth in love with ideal beauty, and being young again, he is able to find ideal beauty in the first woman he sees.

The great episode of Gretchen follows; and when he leaves her (after the duel with her brother) to view the wild revels of the Walpurgisnacht, his youth for a moment catches the contagion of that orgy. His love of ideal beauty, which remains unsatisfied, saves him, however, from any lasting illusion. He sees a little red mouse running out of the mouth of a nymph he is pursuing, and his momentary inclination turns to aversion. When he goes back to Gretchen in her prison, it is too late for him to do more than recognize the ruin he has brought about—Gretchen dishonored, her mother poisoned, her brother killed, her child drowned by her in a pond, and she herself about to be executed. Gretchen, who is the only true Christian in this poem, refuses to be rescued, because she wishes to offer her voluntary death in propitiation for her grave, though almost involuntary, offences.

This is the end of Faust's career through the world of private interests—the little world—and we may well ask what has been the fruit of his experiments so far. What strength or experience has he amassed for his further adventures? The answer is to be found in the first scene of the second part, where Goethe reaches his highest potency as a poet and as a philosopher. We are transported to a remote, magnificent, virgin country. It is evening, and Faust is lying, weary but restless, on a flowering hillside. Kindly spirits of nature are hovering above his head. Ariel, their leader, bids them bring solace to the troubled hero. It is enough he was unfortunate—they make no question whether he was a saint or a sinner. The spirits in chorus then sing four lovely stanzas, one for each watch of the night. The first invokes peace, forgetfulness, surrender to the healing influence of sleep. Pity and remorse, they seem to say, in the words of Spinoza, are evil and vain; failure is incidental; error is innocent. Nature has no memory; forgive yourself, and you are forgiven. The song of the second watch merges the unhappy soul again in the infinite incorruptible substance of nature. The stars, great or little, twinkling or pure, fill the sky with their ordered peace, and the sea with their trembling reflection. In this universal circulation there is no private will, no permanent division. In the next watch we find the plastic stress of nature beginning to reassert itself; seeds swell, sap mounts up the thawing branches, buds grow full; everything recovers a fresh individuality and a tender, untried will. Finally, the song of the fourth watch bids the flowers open their petals and Faust his eyes. Forces renewed in repose should tempt a new career. Nature is open to the brave, to the intelligent; all may be noble, who dare to be so.

Soothed by these ministrations, Faust awakes full of new strength and ambition. He watches with rapture the sunlight touch the mountaintops and creep down gradually into the valleys. When it reaches him, he turns to look directly at the sun; but he is dazzled. He seems to remember the Earth-Spirit that had once allured and then rejected him. We wish, he says, to kindle our torch of life, and we produce a conflagration, a monstrous medley of joy and sorrow, love and hate. Let us turn our backs upon the sun, upon infinite force and infinite existence. Fitter for our eyes the waterfall over against it, the torrent of human affairs, broken into a myriad rills. Upon the mists that rise from it the sunlight paints a rainbow, always vanishing, but always restored. This is the true image of rational human achievement. We have our life in the iridescence of the world. Or, as Shelley has said it for us—

> Life, like a dome of many-coloured glass,
> Stains the white radiance of eternity,
> Until death tramples it to fragments.

This death, however, is itself unstable. The Lucretian Venus, by reshaping our senses and instincts, builds that colored dome once more. The rainbow is renewed, as the mists rise again or the wind dies down, and creation is glorious as on the first day.

This is Goethe's theory of rejuvenation and immortality. It is thoroughly naturalistic. There is a life after death, but only for such souls as have enough scope to identify themselves with those forms which nature, in her uncertain oscillations, always tends to reproduce. A deep mind has deep roots in nature—it will bloom many times over. But what a deep mind carries over into its next incarnation—perhaps in some remote sphere—is not its conventional merits and demerits, its load of remorse, or its sordid memories. These are washed away in its new baptism. What remains is only what was deep in that deep mind, so deep that new situations may again imply and admit it.

When, after the scene with the Earth-Spirit, Faust thought of suicide, he regarded it as a means to escape from oppressive conditions and to begin a fresh life under conditions wholly different and unknown. It was as if a man in middle life, disgusted with his profession, should abandon it to take up another. Such a resolution is serious. It expresses a great dissatisfaction with things as they stand, but it also expresses a great hope. Death, for Faust, is an adventure, like any other; and if, contrary to his presumption, this adventure should prove the last, that, too, is a risk he is willing to run. Accordingly, as he lifted the poison to his lips, he drank to the dawn, to a new springtime of existence. It was by no means the saddest nor the weakest moment of his life.

Although the sound of an Easter hymn checked him, bringing sentimental memories of a religion in which he no longer believed, the transformation scene he looked for was only postponed. There is not much difference between dying as he had thought to die and living as he was about to live. Venomous essences, artificially brewed, were hardly necessary to bring him to a new life; the adventures he was entering upon were suicidal enough, for he was to strive without hope of attainment, and to proceed by passionate willfulness or magic, without accepting the discipline of art or reason. Now, at the close of the first part, he has drained this poisoned life to the dregs, and the fever into which he falls carries him of itself into a new existence. He is not grown better or more reasonable; he is simply starting afresh, like a new day or a new person. He retains, however, the fundamental part of his character; his will remains wayward, but indomitable, and his achievements remain fruitless. Only he will henceforth be romantic on a broader stage, that of history and civilization; and his magic will summon before him illusions somewhat more intellectual, counterfeits of beauty and of power. His old loves have blown over, like the storms of a bygone year; and with only a dreamlike memory of his past errors, he goes forth to meet a new day.

Among the allurements which, in the old legend, prompted Faust to sell his soul to the devil, one was the beauty of woman. The poor recluse, grown gray among his parchments, had never noticed real women, or had not found them beautiful. Pedantic child that he was, when he thought of the beauty of woman, he thought only of Helen of Troy. And Helen, to the Faust of the legend, was simply what Venus might be to Tannhäuser—a woman more ravishing than other ravishing women. She was the supreme instance of a vulgar thing. The young Goethe, however, who was a poet and a true German, and loved with his soul, was not attracted by this ideal. He gave his Faust a tenderer love—a love of the heart as well as of the senses. Later, also, when Goethe took up the old legend again in a more antiquarian spirit, and restored Helen to her place in it, he transformed her from a symbol of feminine beauty alone into a symbol for all beauty, and especially for the highest beauty, that of Hellas. The second love of Faust is the passion for classicism.

This passion in a romantic age is not so paradoxical as it may sound. Winckelmann and the philologians were restoring something ancient. It was the romantic passion for all experience—for the faded experience of the ancients also—that made, for them, the poetry and the charm of antiquity. How dignified everything was in those heroic days! How noble, serene, and abstracted! How pure the blind eyes of statues, how chaste the white folds of the marble drapery! Greece was a remote, fascinating vision, the most romantic thing in the history of mankind. The sad, delicious emotion one felt before a ruined temple was as sentimental as anything one could feel before a ruined castle, but more elegant and more choice. It was sentimentality in marble. The heroes of the *Iliad* were idealized in the same way as the savages of Rousseau were idealized, or as the robbers of Schiller.

The romantic classicism of the Napoleonic era lies between the polite classicism of the French seventeenth century and the archaeological classicism of our present Grecians. French classicism had been quite indifferent to the picturesque aspects of ancient life; it could tolerate on the stage an Achilles in a periwig and laces. What the French tragedians had adopted from the ancients was something inward, a standard of character and motive, or a criterion of taste. They studied harmony and restraint, not because these had been Greek qualities, but because they were qualities essentially reasonable and beautiful, naturally belonging, even in modern times, to a cultivated society and a cultivated poet. Again, the admiration for Greece which is common in our time among people of judgement differs from that of Goethe and his age; for if we admire the artistic expression of ancient life in poetry or sculpture, we know that these manifestations were made possible by a long political and moral discipline, and that, in spite of that discipline, ancient art remained very mixed, and often grotesque and impure.

For Goethe, however, as for Byron, Greece was less a past civilization, to be studied scientifically, than a living idea, a summons to new forms of art and of sentiment. Goethe was never so romantic as when he was classical. His distichs are like theatrical gestures; he feels the sweep of his toga as he rounds them off. His Iphigenia is a sentimental dream—*verflucht human* [accursedly humane], as he himself came to feel; and his Helena is an evocation of magic, magical not merely by accident and in the story, but essentially so, in her ghostly semiconsciousness and glassy beauty. The apparent incongruities of the scenes in which she appears, surrounded by German knights in the court of a feudal castle, are not real incongruities. For this Helen is not a thing of the past; she is the present dream and affectation of things classical in a romantic era. Faust and his vassals offer Helen the most chivalrous and exaggerated homage; they introduce her, as a play queen, into their society. Faust retires with her to Arcadia—the land of intentional and midsummer idleness. Here a son, Euphorion, is born to them, a young genius, classic in aspect, but wildly romantic and ungovernable in temper. He scales the highest peaks, pursues by preference the nymphs that flee from him, loves violence and unreason, and finally, thinking to fly, falls headlong, like Icarus, and perishes. His last words call his mother after him, and she follows, leaving her veil and mantle behind, as Euphorion had left his lyre. On the mantle of Helen, which swells into a cloud, Faust is borne back again to his native Germany; its virtue, as he learns, is to lift him above all commonness.

This long allegory is charming enough, as a series of pictures and melodies, to leave the reader content not to interpret it; yet the intention of the poet is clear, if we care to disentangle it. By going down into the bowels of nature, where the earth goddesses dwell, who are the first mothers of all life and of all civilizations alike, we may gather intelligence to comprehend even the most alien existence. Greece, after such a reversion to the elemental, will appear to us in her unmatched simplicity and beauty. The vision will be granted us, although the object we see belongs to a distant past; and if our enthusiasm, like that of Faust, is passionate and indomitable, we may actually persuade the Queen of the Dead to yield up Helen that we may wed her. Our scholarship and philosophy, our faithful imitation of Greek art and literature, may actually render the Greek scene familiar to us. Yet the setting of this recovered genius will still be modern; it will become half modern itself; we shall have to teach Helen to rhyme. The product of this hybrid inspiration will be a romantic soul in the garb of classicism, a lovely wild thing, fated to die young. When this enthusiasm has dashed itself against the hard conditions of life, the beauty of Greece, that was its mother, will also pale before our eyes. We shall be, perforce, content to let it return to the realm of irrevocable past things. Only its garment, the monuments of its art and thought, will remain to raise us, if we have loved them, above all vulgarity in taste and in moral allegiance.

It is an evidence of Goethe's great wisdom that he felt that romantic classicism must be subordinated or abandoned; that Helen must evaporate, while Faust returned to Germany and to the feeling that after all Gretchen was his true love. At the same time the issue of this wonderful episode is a little disappointing. At the beginning, the vision of Helen in a mirror had inspired Faust with renewed enthusiasm. The sight of her again, in the magic play, had altogether enraptured and overwhelmed him; and this inspiration had come just when, after the death of Gretchen, he had resolved to pursue not all experience, as at first, but rather the best experience—a hint that the transformations of Faust's will were expected somehow to constitute a real progress. There was, indeed, among mortals such an infinite need of this incomparable and symbolic Helen, that it could move the very guardians of the dead to mercy and to tears. When we remember all this, we have some reason to expect that a great and permanent improvement in the life and heart of our hero should follow on his obtaining so rare a boon. But to live within Arcadia Helen was not needed; any Phyllis would have served.

Helen, to be sure, leaves some relics behind, by which we may understand that the influence of Greek history, literature, and sculpture may still avail to cultivate the mind and give it an air of distinction. Perhaps in the commonwealth he is about to found, Faust would wish to establish not only dikes and freedom, but also professorships of Greek and archaeological museums. And the lyre of Euphorion, which is also left us, may signify that poems like Byron's *Isle of Greece*, Keats's *Grecian Urn, Die Götter Griechenlands* of Schiller, and Goethe's own classical pieces will continue to enrich European literature. This is something, but not enough to lift Faust's immense enthusiasm for Helen above a crass illusion. That dream of a perfect beauty to be achieved, of a perfect life to be lived according to nature and reason, would have ended in a little scholarship and a little pedantry. Faust would have won Helen in order to hand her over to Wagner.

Helen was queen of Sparta; and although of course the Doric Sparta of Lycurgus was something much later, and had nothing to do with the Sparta of Homer, yet taken symbolically it is the happiest accident that Helen, the type of Greek perfection in beauty, should have been queen of Sparta, the type of Greek perfection in discipline. A Faust that had truly deserved and understood Helen would have built her a Hellenic city; he would have become himself an [*anax andron*], a master of men, one of those poets in things, those shapers of well-bred generations and wise laws, of which Plato speaks, contrasting them with Homer and other poets in words only. For the beauty of mind and body that fascinates the romantic classicist, and which inspired the ancient poets themselves, was not a product of idleness and sentimentality, nor of material and forced activity; it was a product of orderly war, religion, gymnastics, and deliberate self-government.

The next turn in Faust's fortunes actually finds him a trader, a statesman, an empire builder; and if such a rolling stone could gather any moss, we should expect to see here, if anywhere, the fruits of that "aesthetic education of mankind" which Helen represented. We should expect Faust, who had lain in the lap of absolute beauty, to understand its nature. We should expect him, in eager search after perfection, to establish his state on the distinction between the better and the worse—a distinction never to be abolished or obscured for one who has loved beauty. In other words, he might have established a moral society, founding it on great renunciations and on enlightened heroisms, so that the highest beauty might really come down and dwell within that city. But we find nothing of the sort. Faust founds his kingdom because he must do something; and his only ideal of what he hopes to secure for his subjects is that they shall always have something to do. Thus the will to live, in Faust, is not in the least educated by his experience. It changes its objects because it must; the passions of youth yield to those of age; and among all the illusions of his life the most fatuous is the illusion of progress.

It is characteristic of the absolute romantic spirit that when it has finished with something it must invent a new interest. It beats the bush for fresh game; it is always on the verge of being utterly bored. So now that Helen is flown, Mephistopheles must come to the rescue, like an amiable nurse, and propose all sorts of pastimes. Frankfurt, Leipzig, Paris, Versailles are described, with the entertainments that life there might afford; but Faust, who was always *difficile,* has been rendered more so by his recent splendid adventures. However, a new impulse suddenly arises in his breast. From the mountaintop to which Helen's mantle has borne him, he can see the German Ocean, with its tides daily covering great stretches of the flat shore, and rendering them brackish and uninhabitable. It would be a fine thing to reclaim those wastes, to plant there a prosperous population. After Greece, Faust has a vision of Holland.

This last ambition of Faust's is as romantic as the others. He feels the prompting towards political art, as he had felt the prompting towards love or beauty. The notion of transforming things by his will, of leaving for ages his mark upon nature and upon human society, fascinates him; but this passion for activity and power, which some simple-minded commentators dignify with the name of altruism and of living for others, has no steady purpose or standard about it. Goethe is especially lavish in details to prove this point. Magic, the exercise of an unteachable will, is still Faust's instrument. Mephistopheles, by various arts of illusion, secures the triumph of the emperor in a desperate war which he is carrying on against a justifiable insurrection. As a reward for the aid rendered, Faust receives the shore marches in fief. The necessary dikes and canals are built by magic; the spirits that Mephistopheles commands dig and build them with strange incantations. The commerce that springs up is also illegitimate: piracy is involved in it.

Nor is this all. On some sand dunes that diversified the original beach, an old man and his wife, Philemon and Baucis, lived before the advent of Faust and his improvements. On the hillock, besides their cottage, there stood a small chapel, with a bell which disturbed Faust in his newly built palace, partly by its importunate sound, partly by its Christian suggestions, and partly by reminding him that he was not master of the country altogether, and that something existed in it not the product of his magical will. The old people would not sell out; and in a fit of impatience Faust orders that they should be evicted by force, and transferred to a better dwelling elsewhere. Mephistopheles and his minions execute these orders somewhat roughly: the cottage and chapel are set on fire, and Philemon and Baucis are consumed in the flames, or buried in the ruins.

Faust regrets this accident; but it is one of those inevitable developments of action which a brave man must face, and forget as soon as possible. He had regretted in the same way the unhappiness of Gretchen, and, presumably, the death of Euphorion; but such is romantic life. His will, though shaken, is not extinguished by such misadventures. He would continue, if life could last, doing things that, in some respect, he would be obliged to regret: but he would banish that regret easily, in the pursuit of some new interest, and, on the whole, he would not regret having been obliged to regret them. Otherwise, he would not have shared the whole experience of mankind, but missed the important experience of self-accusation and of self-recovery.

It is impossible to suppose that the citizens he is establishing behind leaky dikes, so that they may always have something to keep them busy, would have given him unmixed satisfaction if he could really have foreseen their career in its concrete details. Holland is an interesting country, but hardly a spectacle which would long entrance an idealist like Faust, so exacting that he has found the arts and sciences wholly vain, domesticity impossible and kitchens and beer cellars beneath consideration. The career of Faust himself had been far more free and active than that of his industrious burghers could ever hope to be. His interest in establishing them is a masterful, irresponsible interest. It is one more arbitrary passion, one more selfish illusion. As he had no conscience in his love, and sought and secured nobody's happiness, so he has no conscience in his ambition and in his political architecture; but if only his will is done, he does not ask whether, judged by its fruits, it will be worth doing. As his immense dejection at the beginning, when he was a doctor in his laboratory, was not founded on any real misfortune, but on restlessness and a vague infinite ambition, so his ultimate satisfaction in his work is not founded on any good done, but on a passionate wilfulness. He calls the thing he wants for others good, because he now wants to bestow it on them, not because they naturally want it for themselves. Incapable of sympathy, he has a momentary pleasure in policy; and in the last and "highest" expression of his will, in his statesmanship and supposed public spirit, he remains romantic and, if need be, aggressive and criminal.

Meantime, his end is approaching. The smoke from that poor little conflagration turns into shadowy shapes of want, guilt, care, and death, which come and hover about him. Want is kept off by his wealth, and guilt is transcended by his romantic courage. But care slips through the keyhole, breathes upon him, and blinds him; while death, though he does not see it, follows close upon his heels. Nevertheless, the old man—Faust is in his hundredth year—is undaunted, and all his thoughts are intent on the future, on the work to which he has set his hand. He orders the digging to proceed on the canals he is building; but the spirits that seem to obey him are getting out of hand, and dig his grave instead.

When he feels death upon him, Faust has one of his most splendid moments of self-assertion. He has stormed through the world, he says, taking with equal thanks the buffets and rewards of fortune; and the last word of wisdom he has learned is that no man deserves life or freedom who does not daily win them anew. He will leave the dikes he has thrown up against the sea to protect the nation he has established; a symbol that their health and freedom must consist in perpetual striving against an indomitable foe. The thought of many generations living in that wholesome danger and labor fills him with satisfaction; he could almost say to this moment, in which that prospect opens before his mind's eye, "Stay, thou art so fair." And with these words—a last challenge and mock surrender to Mephistopheles—he sinks into the grave open at his feet.

Who has won the wager? Faust has almost, though not quite, pronounced the words which were to give Mephistopheles the victory; but the sense of them is new, and Mephistopheles has not succeeded in making Faust surrender his will to will, his indefinite idealism. Since what satisfies Faust is merely the consciousness that this will to will is to be maintained, and that neither he, nor the colonists he has brought into being, will ever lick the dust, and take comfort, without any further aspiration, in the chance pleasures of the moment. Faust has maintained his enthusiasm for a stormy, difficult, and endless life. He has been true to his romantic philosophy.

He is therefore saved, in the sense in which salvation is defined in the *Prologue in Heaven,* and presently again in the song of the angels that receive his soul when they say: "Whosoever is unflagging in his striving forever, him we can redeem." This salvation does not hang on any improvement in Faust's character—he was sinful to the end, and had been God's unwitting servant from the very beginning—nor does it lie in any revolution in his fortunes, as if in heaven he were to be differently employed than on earth. He is going to teach life to the souls of young boys who have died too soon to have had in their own persons any experience of Rathskellers, Gretchens, Helens, and Walpurgisnachts. Teaching (though not exactly in these subjects) had been Doctor Faustus' original profession; and the weariness of it was what had driven him to magic and almost to suicide, until he had escaped into the great world of adventure outside. Certainly, with his new pupils he will not be more content; his romantic restlessness will not forsake him in heaven. Some fine day he will throw his celestial schoolbooks out of the window, and with his pupils after him, go forth to taste life in some windier region of the clouds.

No, Faust is not saved in the sense of being sanctified or brought to a final, eternal state of bliss. The only improvement in his nature has been that he has passed, at the beginning of the second part, from private to public activities. If, at the end of this part, he expresses a wish to abandon magic and to live like a man among men, in the bosom of real nature, that wish remains merely Platonic. It is a thought that visited Goethe often during his long career, that it is the part of wisdom to accept life under natural conditions rather than to pretend to evoke the conditions of life out of the will to live. This thought, were it held steadfastly, would constitute an advance from transcendentalism to naturalism. But the spirit of nature is itself romantic. It lives spontaneously, bravely, without premeditation, and for the sake of living rather than of enjoying or attaining anything final. And under natural conditions, the vicissitudes of an endless life would be many; and there could be no question of an ultimate goal, nor even of an endless progress in any particular direction. The veering of life is part of its vitality—it is essential to romantic irony and to romantic pluck.

The secret of what is serious in the moral of *Faust* is to be looked for in Spinoza—the source of what is serious in the philosophy of Goethe. Spinoza has an admirable doctrine, or rather insight, which he calls seeing things under the form of eternity. This faculty is fundamental in the human mind; ordinary perception and memory are cases of it. Therefore, when we use it to deal with ultimate issues, we are not alienated from experience, but, on the contrary, endowed with experience and with its fruits. A thing is seen under the form of eternity when all its parts or stages are conceived in their true relations, and thereby conceived together. The complete biography of Caesar is Caesar seen under the form of eternity. Now the complete biography of Faust, Faust seen under the form of eternity, shows forth his salvation. God and Faust himself, in his last moment of insight, see that to have led such a life, in such a spirit, *was* to be saved; it was to be the sort of man a man should be. The blots on that life were helpful and necessary blots; the passions of it were necessary and creative passions. To have felt such perpetual dissatisfaction is truly satisfactory; such desire for universal experience is the right experience. You are saved in that you lived well; saved not after you have stopped living well, but during the whole process. Your destiny has been to be the servant of God. That God and your own conscience should pronounce this sentence is your true salvation. Your worthiness is thereby established under the form of eternity.

The play, in its philosophic development, ends here; but Goethe added several more details and scenes, with that abundance, that love, of symbolic pictures and poetic epigrams which characterizes the whole second part. As Faust expires, or rather before he does so, Mephistopheles posts one of his little demons at each aperture of the hero's body, lest the soul should slip out without being caught. At the same time a bevy of angels descends, scattering the red roses of love and singing its praises. These roses, if they touch Mephistopheles and his demons, turn to balls of fire; and although fire is their familiar element, they are scorched and scared away. The angels are thus enabled to catch the soul of Faust at their leisure, and bear it away triumphantly.

It goes without saying that this fight of little boys over a fluttering butterfly cannot be what really determines the issue of the wager and the salvation of Faust; but Goethe, in his conversations with Eckermann, justifies this intervention of a sort of mechanical accident, by the analogy of Christian doctrine. Grace is needed, besides virtue; and the intercession of Gretchen and the Virgin Mary, like that of the Virgin Mary, Lucia, and Beatrice, in Dante's case, and the stratagem of the balls of fire, all stand for this external condition of salvation.

This intervention of grace is, at bottom, only a new symbol for the essential justification, under the form of eternity, of what is imperfect and insufficient in time. The checkered and willful life of Faust is not righteous in any of its parts; yet righteousness is imputed to it as a whole; divine love accepts it as sufficient; speculative reason declares that to be the best possible life which, to humdrum understanding, seems a series of faults and of failures. If the foretaste of his new Holland fills, from a distance, the dying Faust with satisfaction, how much more must the wonderful career of Faust himself deserve to be accepted and envied, and proclaimed to be its own excuse for being! The faults of Faust in time are not counted against him in eternity. His crimes and follies were blessings in disguise. Did they not render his life interesting and fit to make a poem of? Was it not by falling into them, and rising out of them, that Faust was Faust at all? This insight is the higher reason, the divine love, supervening to save him. What ought to be imperfect in time is, because of its very imperfection there, perfect when viewed under the form of eternity. To live, to live just as we do, that—if we could only realize it—is the purpose and the crown of living. We must seek improvement; we must be dissatisfied with ourselves; that is the appointed attitude, the histrionic pose, that is to keep the ball rolling. But while we feel this dissatisfaction we are perfectly satisfactory, and while we play our game and constantly lose it, we are winning the game for God.

Even this scene, however, did not satisfy the prolific fancy of the poet, and he added a final one—the apotheosis or *Himmelfahrt* [ascension] of Faust. In the Campo Santo at Pisa Goethe had seen a fresco representing various anchorites dwelling on the flanks of some sacred mountain—Sinai, Carmel, or Athos—each in his little cave or hermitage; and above them, in the large space of sky, flights of angels were seen rising towards the Madonna. Through such a landscape the poet now shows us the soul of Faust carried slowly upwards.

This scene has been regarded as inspired by Catholic ideas, whereas the *Prologue in Heaven* was Biblical and Protestant; and Goethe himself says that his "poetic intention" could best be rendered by images borrowed from the tradition of the medieval church. But in truth there is nothing Catholic about the scene, except the names or titles of the personages. What they say is all sentimental landscape painting or vague mysticism, such as might go with any somewhat nebulous piety; and much is actually borrowed from Swedenborg. What is Swedenborgian, however—such as the notion of heavenly instruction, passage from sphere to sphere, and looking through other people's eyes—is in turn a mere form of expression. The "poetic intention" of the author is, as we have seen, altogether Spinozitic. Undoubtedly he conceives that the soul of Faust is to pass, in another world, through some new series of experiences. But that destiny is not his salvation; it is the continuance of his trial. The famous chorus at the very end repeats, with an interesting variation, the same contrast we have seen before between the point of view of time and that of eternity. Everything transitory, says the mystic chorus, is only an image; here (that is, under the form of eternity) the insufficient is turned into something actual and complete; and what seemed in experience an endless pursuit becomes to speculation a perfect fulfillment. The ideal of something infinitely attractive and essentially inexhaustible—the eternal feminine, as Goethe calls it—draws life on from stage to stage.

Gretchen and Helen had been symbols of this ideal; Goethe's green old age had felt, to the very last, the charm of woman, the sweetness and the sorrow of loving what he could not hope to possess, and what, in its ideal perfection, necessarily eludes possession. He had reconciled himself, not without tears, to this desire without hope, and, like Piccarda in the *Paradiso*, he had blessed the hand that gave the passion and denied the happiness. Thus, in dreaming of one satisfaction and renouncing it, he had found a satisfaction of another kind. *Faust* ends on the same philosophical level on which it began—the level of romanticism. The worth of life lies in pursuit, not in attainment; therefore, everything is worth pursuing, and nothing brings satisfaction—save this endless destiny itself.

Such is the official moral of *Faust,* and what we may call its general philosophy. But, as we saw just now, this moral is only an afterthought, and is far from exhausting the philosophic ideas which the poem contains. Here is a scheme for experience; but experience, in filling it out, opens up many vistas; and some of these reveal deeper and higher things than experience itself. The path of the pilgrim and the inns he stops at are neither the whole landscape he sees as he travels, nor the true shrine he is making for. And the incidental philosophy or philosophies of Goethe's *Faust* are, to my mind, often better than its ultimate philosophy. The first scene of the second part, for instance, is better, poetically and philosophically, than the last. It shows a deeper sense for the realities of nature and of the soul, and it is more sincere. Goethe there is interpreting nature with Spinoza; he is not dreaming with Swedenborg, nor talking equivocal paradoxes with Hegel.

In fact, the great merit of the romantic attitude in poetry, and of the transcendental method in philosophy, is that they put us back at the beginning of our experience. They disintegrate convention, which is often cumbrous and confused, and restore us to ourselves, to immediate perception and primordial will. That, as it would seem, is the true and inevitable starting point. Had we not been born, had we not peeped into this world, each out of his personal eggshell, this world might indeed have existed without us, as a thousand undiscoverable worlds may now exist; but for us it would not have existed. This obvious truth would not need to be insisted on but for two reasons: one that conventional knowledge, such as our notions of science and morality afford, is often top-heavy; asserts and imposes on us much more than our experience warrants—our experience, which is our only approach to reality. The other reason is the reverse or counterpart of this; for conventional knowledge often ignores and seems to suppress parts of experience no less actual and important for us as those parts on which the conventional knowledge itself is reared. The public world is too narrow for the soul, as well as too mythical and fabulous. Hence the double critical labor and reawakening which romantic reflection is good for—to cut off the dead branches and feed the starving shoots. This philosophy, as Kant said, is a cathartic: it is purgative and liberating; it is intended to make us start afresh and start right.

It follows that one who has no sympathy with such a philosophy is a comparatively conventional person. He has a secondhand mind. Faust has a firsthand mind, a truly free, sincere, courageous soul. It follows also, however, that one who has no philosophy but this has no wisdom; he can say nothing that is worth carrying away; everything in him is attitude and nothing is achievement. Faust, and especially Mephistopheles, do have other philosophies on top of their transcendentalism; for this is only a method, to be used in reaching conclusions that shall be critically safeguarded and empirically grounded. Such outlooks, such vistas into nature, are scattered liberally through the pages of *Faust*. Words of wisdom diversify this career of folly, as exquisite scenes fill this tortuous and overloaded drama. The mind has become free and sincere, but it has remained bewildered.

The literary merits of Goethe's *Faust* correspond accurately with its philosophical excellences. In the prologue in the theater Goethe himself has described them; much scenery, much wisdom, some folly, great wealth of incident and characterization; and behind, the soul of a poet singing with all sincerity and fervor the visions of his life. Here is profundity, inwardness, honesty, waywardness; here are the most touching accents of nature, and the most varied assortment of curious lore and grotesque fancies. This work, says Goethe (in a quatrain intended as an epilogue, but not ultimately inserted in the play)—this work is like human life: it has a beginning, it has an end; but it has no totality, it is not one whole. How, indeed, should we draw the sum of an infinite experience that is without conditions to determine it, and without goals in which it terminates? Evidently all a poet of pure experience can do is to represent some snatches of it, more or less prolonged; and the more prolonged the experience represented is the more it will be a collection of snatches, and the less the last part of it will have to do with the beginning. Any character which we may attribute to the whole of what we have surveyed would fail to dominate it, if that whole had been larger, and if we had had memory or foresight enough to include other parts of experience differing altogether in kind from the episodes we happen to have lived through. To be miscellaneous, to be indefinite, to be unfinished, is essential to the romantic life. May we not say that it is essential to all life, in its immediacy; and that only in reference to what is not life—to objects, ideals, and unanimities that cannot be experienced but may only be conceived—can life become rational and truly progressive? Herein we may see the radical and inalienable excellence of romanticism; its sincerity, freedom, richness, and infinity. Herein, too, we may see its limitations, in that it cannot fix or trust any of its ideals, and blindly believes the universe to be as wayward as itself, so that nature and art are always slipping through its fingers. It is obstinately empirical, and will never learn anything from experience.

The foregoing consists of Chapters I and III from Santayana's THREE PHILOSOPHICAL POETS.

Henry Adams [1]

1838–1918

In his *Letter to American Teachers of History* Henry Adams records his dark vision of mankind at the mercy of the law of entropy—the gradual running down of the universe. In Adams' time —roughly the early twentieth century—science could offer no alternative to this process, nor, in his opinion, could any other discipline. Hence his interest in the thirteenth century, when an alternative existed in men's conception of themselves as part not only of a natural order but also of a divine one that, being eternal, cannot pass away. These two orders were reconciled by medieval theology, of which Adams treats in this discussion of St. Thomas Aquinas, whose *Summa Theologica* is the great medieval statement.

Actually the discussion, which is taken from a longer work by Adams called *Mont-Saint-Michel and Chartres* (1913), is as much about buildings as it is about books. For Adams' approach to St. Thomas is through the architecture of the Gothic cathedrals, which were constructed in the same age that conceived the *Summa* and which are looked upon by Adams as products of the same general effort.

The effort was to see the whole universe in relation to God and to understand the law by which the universe is governed. But it was also to determine the place of man under that law. Indeed, the relation between man and God was the heart of the medieval structure. This relation was asserted first in the eleventh century by force, Adams says earlier in his book, and the symbol of that is the fortress church of Mont-Saint-Michel. It was developed in the twelfth century as a matter of faith, and the symbol of that is the Cathedral of

---

[1] For a biography of Henry Adams see Vol. 6, pp. 318–319, in this set.

Chartres. Then at last, as Adams here points out, came the thirteenth-century attempt of St. Thomas to treat the relation in terms of reason —to climb heaven with the mind.

While the attempt perhaps was bound to fail, it was, Adams suggests, a magnificent intellectual flight. Its symbol is the thirteenth-century Cathedral of Beauvais, which like the *Summa* was never finished. Only the choir of Beauvais stands, but its columns rise in one unbroken dizzy sweep to the highest vaulted roof ever reached.

St. Thomas Aquinas

Long before St. Francis' death, in 1226, the French mystics had exhausted their energies and the *siècle* had taken new heart. Society could not remain forever balancing between thought and act. A few gifted natures could absorb themselves in the absolute, but the rest lived for the day, and needed shelter and safety. So the Church bent again to its task, and bade the Spaniard Dominic arm new levies with the best weapons of science, and flaunt the name of Aristotle on the Church banners along with that of St. Augustine. The year 1215, which happened to be the date of Magna Carta and other easily fixed events, like the birth of St. Louis, may serve to mark the triumph of the schools. The pointed arch reveled at Rheims and the Gothic architects reached perfection at Amiens just as Francis died at Assisi and Thomas was born at Aquino. The Franciscan Order itself was swept with the stream that Francis tried to dam, and the great Franciscan schoolman, Alexander Hales, in 1222, four years before the death of Francis, joined the order and began lecturing as though Francis himself had lived only to teach scholastic philosophy.

The rival Dominican champion, Albertus Magnus, began his career a little later, in 1228. Born of the noble Swabian family of Bollstädt, in 1193, he drifted, like other schoolmen, to Paris, and the Rue Maître Albert, opposite Notre Dame, still records his fame as a teacher there. Thence he passed to a school established by the order at Cologne, where he was lecturing with great authority in 1243 when the general superior of the order brought up from Italy a young man of the highest promise to be trained as his assistant.

Thomas, the new pupil, was born under the shadow of Monte Cassino in 1226 or 1227. His father, the Count of Aquino, claimed descent from the imperial line of Swabia; his mother, from the Norman princes of Sicily; so that in him the two most energetic strains in Europe met. His social rank was royal, and the order set the highest value on it. He took the vows in 1243, and went north at once to help Albertus at Cologne. In 1245, the order sent Albertus back to Paris, and Thomas with him. There he remained till 1248 when he was ordered to Cologne as assistant lecturer, and only four years afterwards, at twenty-five years old, he was made full professor at Paris. His industry and activity never rested till his death in 1274, not yet fifty years old, when he bequeathed to the Church a mass of manuscript that tourists will never know enough to estimate except by weight. His complete works, repeatedly printed, fill between twenty and thirty quarto volumes. For so famous a doctor, this is almost meagre. Unfortunately his greatest work, the *Summa Theologica,* is unfinished —like Beauvais Cathedral.

Perhaps Thomas' success was partly due to his memory which is said to have been phenomenal; for, in an age when cyclopedias were unknown, a cyclopedic memory must have counted for half the battle in these scholastic disputes where authority could be met only by authority; but in this case, memory was supported by mind. Outwardly Thomas was heavy and slow in manner, if it is true that his companions called him "the big dumb ox of Sicily"; and in fashionable or court circles he did not enjoy reputation for acute sense of humor. St. Louis' household offers a picture not wholly clerical, least of all among the King's brothers and sons; and perhaps the dinner table was not much more used then than now to abrupt interjections of theology into the talk about hunting and hounds; but however it happened, Thomas one day surprised the company by solemnly announcing—"I have a decisive argument against the Manichaeans!" No wit or humor could be more to the point—between two saints that were to be—than a decisive argument against enemies of Christ, and one greatly regrets that the rest of the conversation was not reported, unless, indeed, it is somewhere in the twenty-eight quarto volumes; but it probably lacked humor for courtiers.

The twenty-eight quarto volumes must be closed books for us. None but Dominicans have a right to interpret them. No Franciscan—or even Jesuit—understands St. Thomas exactly or explains him with authority. For summer tourists to handle these intricate problems in a theological spirit would be altogether absurd; but, for us, these great theologians were also architects who undertook to build a Church Intellectual, corresponding bit by bit to the Church Administrative, both expressing—and expressed by—the Church Architectural. Alexander Hales, Albert the Great, Thomas Aquinas, Duns Scotus, and the rest, were artists; and if St. Thomas happens to stand at their head as type, it is not because we choose him or understand him better than his rivals, but because his order chose him rather than his master Albert to impose as authority on the Church;

and because Pope John XXII canonized him on the ground that his decisions were miracles; and because the Council of Trent placed his *Summa* among the sacred books on their table; and because Innocent VI said that his doctrine alone was sure; and finally, because Leo XIII very lately made a point of declaring that, on the wings of St. Thomas' genius, human reason has reached the most sublime height it can probably ever attain.

Although the Franciscans, and, later, the Jesuits, have not always shown as much admiration as the Dominicans for the genius of St. Thomas, and the mystics have never shown any admiration whatever for the philosophy of the schools, the authority of Leo XIII is final, at least on one point and the only one that concerns us. St. Thomas is still alive and overshadows as many schools as he ever did; at all events, as many as the Church maintains. He has outlived Descartes and Leibnitz and a dozen other schools of philosophy more or less serious in their day. He has mostly outlived Hume, Voltaire, and the militant skeptics. His method is typical and classic; his sentences, when interpreted by the Church, seem, even to an untrained mind, intelligible and consistent; his Church Intellectual remains practically unchanged, and, like the Cathedral of Beauvais, erect, although the storms of six or seven centuries have prostrated, over and over again, every other social or political or juristic shelter. Compared with it, all modern systems are complex and chaotic, crowded with self-contradictions, anomalies, impracticable functions and outworn inheritances; but beyond all their practical shortcomings is their fragmentary character. An economic civilization troubles itself about the universe much as a hive of honeybees troubles about the ocean, only as a region to be avoided. The hive of St. Thomas sheltered God and man, mind and matter, the universe and the atom, the one and the multiple, within the walls of an harmonious home.

Theologians, like architects, were supposed to receive their Church complete in all its lines; they were modern judges who interpreted the law, but never invented it. St. Thomas merely selected between disputed opinions, but he allowed himself to wander very far afield, indeed, in search of opinions to dispute. The field embraced all that existed, or might have existed, or could never exist. The immense structure rested on Aristotle and St. Augustine at the last, but as a work of art it stood alone, like Rheims or Amiens Cathedral, as though it had no antecedents. Then, although, like Rheims, its style was never meant to suit modern housekeeping and is ill seen by the École des Beaux Arts, it reveals itself in its great mass and intelligence as a work of extraordinary genius; a system as admirably proportioned as any cathedral and as complete; a success not universal either in art or science.

St. Thomas' architecture, like any other work of art, is best studied by itself as though he created it outright; otherwise a tourist would never get beyond its threshold. Beginning with the foundation which is God and God's active presence in His Church, Thomas next built God into the walls and towers of His Church, in the Trinity and its creation of mind and matter in time and space; then finally he filled the Church by uniting mind and matter in man, or man's soul, giving to humanity a free will that rose, like the flèche, to heaven. The foundation—the structure—the congregation—are enough for students of art; his ideas of law, ethics, and politics; his vocabulary, his syllogisms, his arrangement are, like the drawings of Villard de Honnecourt's sketchbook, curious but not vital. After the eleventh-century Romanesque Church of St. Michael came the twelfth-century Transition Church of the Virgin, and all merged and ended at last in the thirteenth-century Gothic Cathedral of the Trinity. One wants to see the end.

The foundation of the Christian Church should be—as the simple deist might suppose—always the same, but St. Thomas knew better. His foundation was Norman, not French; it spoke the practical architect who knew the mathematics of his art, and who saw that the foundation laid by St. Bernard, St. Victor, St. Francis, the whole mystical, semimystical, Cartesian, Spinozan foundation, past or future, could not bear the weight of the structure to be put on it. Thomas began by sweeping the ground clear of them. God must be a concrete thing, not a human thought. God must be proved by the senses like any other concrete thing; *nihil est in intellectu quin prius fuerit in sensu* [there is nothing in the mind which was not first in the senses]; even if Aristotle had not affirmed the law, Thomas would have discovered it. He admitted at once that God could not be taken for granted.

The admission, as every boy student of the Latin Quarter knew, was exceedingly bold and dangerous. The greatest logicians commonly shrank from proving unity by multiplicity. Thomas was one of the greatest logicians that ever lived; the question had always been at the bottom of theology; he deliberately challenged what every one knew to be an extreme peril. If his foundation failed, his Church fell. Many critics have thought that he saw dangers four hundred years ahead. The time came, about 1650–1700, when Descartes, deserting St. Thomas, started afresh with the idea of God as concept, and at once found himself charged with a deity that contained the universe; nor did the Cartesians—until Spinoza made it clear—seem able or willing to see that the Church could not accept this deity because the Church required a God who caused the universe. The two deities destroyed each other. One was passive; the other active. Thomas warned Descartes of a logical quicksand which must necessarily swallow up any Church, and which Spinoza explored to the bottom. Thomas said truly that every true cause must be proved as a cause, not merely as a sequence; otherwise they must end in a universal energy or substance without causality—a source.

Whatever God might be to others, to His Church he could not be a sequence or a source. That point had been admitted by William of Champeaux, and made the division between Christians and infidels. On the other hand, if God must be proved as a true cause in order to warrant the Church or the State in requiring men to worship Him as Creator, the student became the more curious—if a churchman, the more anxious—to be assured that Thomas succeeded in his proof, especially since he did not satisfy Descartes and still less Pascal. That the mystics should be dissatisfied was natural enough, since they were committed to the contrary view, but that Descartes should desert was a serious blow which threw the French Church into consternation from which it never quite recovered.

"I see motion," said Thomas: "I infer a motor!" This reasoning, which may be fifty thousand years old, is as strong as ever it was; stronger than some more modern inferences of science; but the average mechanic stated it differently. "I see motion," he admitted: "I infer energy. I see motion everywhere; I infer energy everywhere." St. Thomas barred this door to materialism by adding: "I see motion; I cannot infer an infinite series of motors: I can only infer, somewhere at the end of the series, an intelligent, fixed motor." The average modern mechanic might not dissent but would certainly hesitate. "No doubt!" he might say; "we can conduct our works as well on that as on any other theory, or as we could on no theory at all; but, if you offer it as proof, we can only say that we have not yet reduced all motion to one source or all energies to one law, much less to one act of creation, although we have tried our best." The result of some centuries of experiment tended to raise rather than silence doubt, although, even in his own day, Thomas would have been scandalized beyond the resources of his Latin had St. Bonaventure met him at St. Louis' dinner table and complimented him, in the King's hearing, on having proved, beyond all Franciscan cavils, that the Church Intellectual had necessarily but one first cause and creator—himself.

The Church Intellectual, like the Church Architectural, implied not one architect, but myriads, and not one fixed, intelligent architect at the end of the series, but a vanishing vista without a beginning at any definite moment; and if Thomas pressed his argument, the twentieth-century mechanic who should attend his conferences at the Sorbonne would be apt to say so. "What is the use of trying to argue me into it? Your inference may be sound logic, but is not proof. Actually we know less about it than you did. All we know is the thing we handle, and we cannot handle your fixed, intelligent prime motor. To your old ideas of form we have added what we call force, and we are rather further than ever from reducing the complex to unity. In fact, if you are aiming to convince me, I will tell you flatly that I know only the multiple, and have no use for unity at all."

In the thirteenth century men did not depend so much as now on actual experiment, but the nominalist said in effect the same thing. Unity to him was a pure concept, and anyone who thought it real would believe that a triangle was alive and could walk on its legs. Without proving unity, philosophers saw no way to prove God. They could only fall back on an attempt to prove that the concept of unity proved itself, and this phantasm drove the Cartesians to drop Thomas' argument and assert that "the mere fact of having within us the idea of a thing more perfect than ourselves, proves the real existence of that thing." Four hundred years earlier St. Thomas had replied in advance that Descartes wanted to prove altogether too much, and Spinoza showed mathematically that St. Thomas had been in the right. The finest religious mind of the time—Pascal—admitted it and gave up the struggle, like the mystics of St. Victor.

Thus some of the greatest priests and professors of the Church, including Duns Scotus himself, seemed not wholly satisfied that Thomas' proof was complete, but most of them admitted that it was the safest among possible foundations, and that it showed, as architecture, the Norman temper of courage and caution. The Norman was ready to run great risks, but he would rather grasp too little than too much; he narrowed the spacing of his piers rather than spread them too wide for safe vaulting. Between Norman blood and Breton blood was a singular gap, as Renan and every other Breton has delighted to point out. Both Abelard and Descartes were Breton. The Breton seized more than he could hold; the Norman took less than he would have liked.

God, then, is proved. What the schools called form, what science calls energy, and what the intermediate period called the evidence of design made the foundation of St. Thomas' cathedral. God is an intelligent, fixed prime motor—not a concept, or proved by concepts—a concrete fact, proved by the senses of sight and touch. On that foundation Thomas built. The walls and vaults of his Church were more complex than the foundation; especially the towers were troublesome. Dogma, the vital purpose of the Church, required support. The most weighty dogma, the central tower of the Norman cathedral, was the Trinity, and between the Breton solution which was too heavy, and the French solution which was too light, the Norman Thomas found a way. Remembering how vehemently the French Church, under St. Bernard, had protected the Trinity from all interference whatever, one turns anxiously to see what Thomas said about it; and unless one misunderstands him—as is very likely, indeed, to be the case, since no one may even profess to understand the Trinity—Thomas treated it as simply as he could. "God, being conscious of Himself, thinks Himself; his thought is Himself, his own reflection in the verb—the so-called Son." *Est in Deo intelligente seipsum Verbum Dei quasi Deus intellectus.* The idea was not new, and as ideas went it was hardly a mystery; but the next step was naïve: God, as a double consciousness, loves Himself, and realizes Himself in the Holy Ghost. The third side of the triangle is love or grace.

Many theologians have found fault with this treatment of the subject, which seemed open to every objection that had been made to Abelard, Gilbert de la Porrée, or a thousand other logicians. They commonly asked why Thomas stopped the Deity's self-realizations at love, or inside the triangle, since these realizations were real, not symbolic, and the square was at least as real as any other combination of line. Thomas replied that knowledge and will—the verb and the Holy Ghost—were alone essential. The reply did not suit every one, even among doctors, but since St. Thomas rested on this simple assertion, it is no concern of ours to argue the theology. Only as art, one can afford to say that the form is more architectural than religious; it would surely have been suspicious to St. Bernard. Mystery there was none, and logic little. The concept of the Holy Ghost was childlike; for a pupil of Aristotle it was inadmissible, since it led to nothing and helped no step toward the universe.

Admitting, if necessary, the criticism, Thomas need not admit the blame, if blame there were. Every theologian was obliged to stop the pursuit of logic by force, before it dragged him into paganism and pantheism. Theology begins with the universal—God—who must be a reality, not a symbol; but it is forced to limit the process of God's realizations somewhere, or the priest soon becomes a worshiper of God in sticks and stones. Theologists had commonly chosen, from time immemorial, to stop at the Trinity; within the triangle they were wholly realist; but they could not admit that God went on to realize Himself in the square and circle, or that the third member of the Trinity contained multiplicity, because the

Trinity was a restless weight on the Church piers, which, like the central tower, constantly tended to fall, and needed to be lightened. Thomas gave it the lightest form possible, and there fixed it.

Then came his great tour de force, the vaulting of his broad nave; and, if ignorance is allowed an opinion, even a lost soul may admire the grand simplicity of Thomas' scheme. He swept away the horizontal lines altogether, leaving them barely as a part of decoration. The whole weight of his arches fell, as in the latest Gothic, where the eye sees nothing to break the sheer spring of the nervures, from the rosette on the keystone a hundred feet above down to the church floor. In Thomas' creation nothing intervened between God and his world; secondary causes became ornaments; only two forces, God and man, stood in the Church.

The chapter of Creation is so serious, and Thomas' creation, like every other, is open to so much debate, that no student can allow another to explain it; and certainly no man whatever, either saint or skeptic, can ever yet have understood Creation aright unless divinely inspired; but whatever Thomas' theory was as he meant it, he seems to be understood as holding that every created individual—animal, vegetable, or mineral—was a special, divine act. Whatever has form is created, and whatever is created takes form directly from the will of God, which is also his act. The intermediate universals—the secondary causes—vanish as causes; they are, at most, sequences or relations; all merge in one universal act of will; instantaneous, infinite, eternal.

St. Thomas saw God, much as Milton saw him, resplendent in

> That glorious form, that light unsufferable,
> And that far-beaming blaze of Majesty,
> Wherewith he wont, at Heaven's high council table,
> To sit the midst of Trinal Unity;

except that, in Thomas' thought, the council table was a worktable, because God did not take counsel; He was an act. The Trinity was an infinite possibility of will; nothing within but

> The baby image of the giant mass
> Of things to come at large.

Neither time nor space, neither matter nor mind, not even force existed, nor could any intelligence conceive how, even though they should exist, they could be united in the lowest association. A crystal was as miraculous as Socrates. Only abstract force, or what the schoolmen called form, existed undeveloped from eternity, like the abstract line in mathematics.

Fifty or a hundred years before St. Thomas settled the Church dogma, a monk of Citeaux or some other abbey, a certain Alain of Lille, had written a Latin poem, as abstruse an allegory as the best, which had the merit of painting the scene of man's creation as far as concerned the mechanical process much as Thomas seems to have seen it. M. Hauréau has printed an extract. Alain conceded to the weakness of human thought, that God was working in time and space, or rather on His throne in heaven, when Nature, proposing to create a new and improved man, sent Reason and Prudence up to ask Him for a soul to fit the new body. Having passed through various adventures and much scholastic instruction, the messenger Prudence arrived, after having dropped her dangerous friend Reason by the way. The request was respectfully presented to God, and favorably received. God promised the soul, and at once sent His servant Noys—Thought—to the storehouse of ideas, to choose it:

Ipse Deus rem prosequitur, producit in actum	God Himself pursues the task, and sets in act
Quod pepigit. Vocat ergo Noym quae praepaert illi	What He promised. So he calls Noys to seek
Numinis exemplar, humanae mentis Idaeam,	A copy of His will, Idea of the human mind,
Ad cujus formam formetur spiritus omni	To whose form the spirit should be shaped,
Munere virtutum dives, qui, nube caducae	Rich in every virtue, which, veiled in garb
Carnis odumbratus veletur corporis umbra.	Of frail flesh, is to be hidden in a shade of body,
Tunc Noys ad regis praeceptum singula rerum	Then Noys, at the King's order, turning one by one
Vestigans exempla, novam perquirit Idaeam.	Each sample, seeks the new Idea.
Inter tot species, speciem vix invenit illam	Among so many images she hardly finds that
Quam petit; offertur tandem quaesita petenti.	Which she seeks; at last the sought one appears.
Hanc formam Noys ipsa Deo praesentat ut ejus	This form Noys herself brings to God for Him
Formet ad exemplar animam. Tunc ille sigillum	To form a soul to its pattern. He takes the seal,
Sumit, ad ipsius formae vestigia formam	And gives form to the soul after the model
Dans animae, vultum qualem deposcit Idaea	Of the form itself, stamping on the sample
Imprimit exemplo; totas usurpat imago	The figure such as the Idea requires. The seal
Exemplaris opes, loquiturque figura sigillum.	Covers the whole field, and the impression expresses the stamp.

The translation is probably full of mistakes; indeed, one is permitted to doubt whether Alain himself accurately understood the process; but in substance he meant that God contained a storehouse of ideas, and stamped each creation with one of these forms. The poets used a variety of figures to help out their logic, but that of the potter and his pot was one of the most common. Omar Khayyam was using it at the same time with Alain of Lille, but with a difference: for his pot seems to have been matter alone, and his soul was the wine it received from God; while Alain's soul seems to have been the form and not the contents of the pot.

The figure matters little. In any case God's act was the union of mind with matter by the same act or will which created both. No intermediate cause or condition intervened; no secondary influence had anything whatever to do with the result. Time had nothing to do with it. Every individual that has existed or shall exist was created by the same instantaneous act, for all time. "When the question regards the universal agent who produces beings *and* time, we cannot consider him as acting *now* and *before,* according to the succession of time." God emanated time, force, matter, mind, as He might emanate gravitation, not as a part of His substance but as an energy of His will, and maintains them in their activity by the same act, not by a new one. Every individual is a part of the direct act; not a secondary outcome. The soul has no father or mother. Of all errors one of the most serious is to suppose that the soul descends by generation. "Having life and action of its own, it subsists without the body; . . . it must therefore be produced directly, and since it is not a material substance, it cannot be produced by way of generation; it must necessarily be created by God. Consequently to suppose that the intelligence [or intelligent soul] is the effect of generation is to suppose that it is not a pure and simple substance but corruptible like the body. It is therefore heresy to say that this soul is transmitted by generation." What is true of the soul should be true of all other form, since no form is a material substance. The utmost possible relation between any two individuals is that God may have used the same stamp or mold for a series of creations, and especially for the less spiritual: "God is the first model for all things. One may also say that, among His creatures some serve as types or models for others because there are some which are made in the image of others"; but generation means sequence, not cause. The only true cause is God. Creation is His sole act, in which no second cause can share. "Creation is more perfect and loftier than generation, because it aims at producing the whole substance of the being, though it starts from absolute nothing."

Thomas Aquinas, when he pleased, was singularly lucid, and on this point he was particularly positive. The architect insisted on the controlling idea of his structure. The Church was God, and its lines excluded interference. God and the Church embraced all the converging lines of the universe, and the universe showed none but lines that converged. Between God and man, nothing whatever intervened. The individual was a compound of form, or soul, and matter; but both were always created together, by the same act, out of nothing. *Simpliciter fatendum est animas simul cum corporibus creari et infundi.* It must be distinctly understood that souls were not created before bodies, but that they were created at the same time as the bodies they animate. Nothing whatever preceded this union of two substances which did not exist: *Creatio est productio alicujus rei secundum suam totam substantiam, nullo praesupposito, quod sit vel increatum vel ab aliquo creatum.* Language can go no further in exclusion of every possible preceding, secondary, or subsequent cause, *Productio universalis entis a Deo non est motus nec mutatio, sed est quaedam simplex emanatio.* The whole universe is, so to speak, a simple emanation from God.

The famous junction, then, is made—that celebrated fusion of the universal with the individual, of unity with multiplicity, of God and nature, which had broken the neck of every philosophy ever invented; which had ruined William of Champeaux and was to ruin Descartes; this evolution of the finite from the infinite was accomplished. The supreme triumph was as easily effected by Thomas Aquinas as it was to be again effected, four hundred years later, by Spinoza. He had merely to assert the fact: "It is so! it cannot be otherwise!" "For the thousandth and hundred-thousandth time; what is the use of discussing this prime motor, this Spinozan substance, any longer? We know it is there!" that—as Professor Haeckel very justly repeats for the millionth time—is enough.

One point, however, remained undetermined. The Prime Motor and His action stood fixed, and no one wished to disturb Him; but this was not the point that had disturbed William of Champeaux. Abelard's question still remained to be answered. How did Socrates differ from Plato—Judas from John—Thomas Aquinas from Professor Haeckel? Were they, in fact, two, or one? What made an individual? What was God's centimeter measure? The abstract form or soul which existed as a possibility in God, from all time—was it one or many? To the Church, this issue overshadowed all else, for, if humanity was one and not multiple, the Church, which dealt only with individuals, was lost. To the schools, also, the issue was vital, for, if the soul or form was already multiple from the first, unity was lost; the ultimate substance and prime motor itself became multiple; the whole issue was reopened.

To the consternation of the Church, and even of his own order, Thomas, following closely his masters, Albert and Aristotle, asserted that the soul was measured by matter. "Division occurs in substances in ratio of quantity, as Aristotle says in his *Physics*. And so dimensional quantity is a principle of individuation." The soul is a fluid absorbed by matter in proportion to the absorptive power of the matter. The soul is an energy existing in matter proportionately to the dimensional quantity of the matter. The soul is a wine, greater or less in quantity according to the size of the cup. In our report of the great debate of 1110, between Champeaux and Abelard, we have seen William persistently tempting Abelard to fall into this admission that matter made the man; that the universal equilateral triangle became an individual if it were shaped in metal, the matter giving it reality which mere form could not give; and Abelard evading the issue as though his life depended on it. In fact, had Abelard dared to follow Aristotle into what looked like an admission that Socrates and Plato were identical as form and differed only in weight, his life might have been the forfeit. How St. Thomas escaped is a question closely connected with the same inquiry about St. Francis of Assisi. A Church which embraced, with equal sympathy, and within a hundred years, the Virgin, St. Bernard, William of Champeaux and the School of St. Victor, Peter the Venerable, St. Francis of Assisi, St. Dominic, St. Thomas Aquinas, and St. Bonaventure was more liberal than any modern State can afford to be. Radical contradictions the State may perhaps tolerate, though hardly, but never embrace or profess. Such elasticity long ago vanished from human thought.

Yet only Dominicans believe that the Church adopted this law of individualization, or even assented to it. If M. Jourdain is right, Thomas was quickly obliged to give it another form: that, though all souls belonged to the same species, they differed in their aptitudes for uniting with particular bodies. "This soul is commensurate with this body, and not with that other one." The idea is double; for either the souls individualized themselves, and Thomas abandoned his doctrine of their instantaneous creation, with the bodies, out of nothing; or God individualized them in the act of creation, and matter had nothing to do with it. The difficulty is no concern of ours, but the great scholars who took upon themselves to explain it made it worse, until at last one gathers only that St. Thomas held one of three views: either the soul of humanity was individualized by God, or it individualized itself, or it was divided by ratio of quantity, that is, by matter. This amounts to saying that one knows nothing about it, which we knew before and may admit with calmness; but Thomas Aquinas was not so happily placed, between the Church and the schools. Humanity had a form common to itself, which made it what it was. By some means this form was associated with matter; in fact, matter was only known as associated with form. If, then, God, by an instantaneous act, created matter and gave it form according to the dimensions of the matter, innocent ignorance might infer that there was, in the act of God, one world soul and one world matter, which He united in different proportions to make men and things. Such a doctrine was fatal to the Church. No greater heresy could be charged against the worst Arab or Jew, and Thomas was so well aware of his danger that he recoiled from it with a vehemence not at all in keeping with his supposed phlegm. With feverish eagerness to get clear of such companions, he denied and denounced, in all companies, in season and out of season, the idea that intellect was one and the same for all men, differing only with the quantity of matter it accompanied. He challenged the adherent of such a doctrine to battle; "let him take the pen if he dares!" No one dared, seeing that even Jews enjoyed a share of common sense and had seen some of their friends burn at the stake not very long before for such opinions, not even openly maintained; while uneducated people, who are perhaps incapable of receiving intellect at all, but for whose instruction and salvation the great work of St. Thomas and his scholars must chiefly exist, cannot do battle because they cannot understand Thomas' doctrine of matter and form which to them seems frank pantheism.

So it appeared to Duns Scotus also, if one may assert in the *Doctor Subtilis* any opinion without qualification. Duns began his career only about 1300, after Thomas' death, and stands, therefore, beyond our horizon; but he is still the pride of the Franciscan Order and stands second in authority to the great Dominican alone. In denying Thomas' doctrine that matter individualizes mind, Duns laid himself open to the worse charge of investing matter with a certain embryonic, independent, shadowy soul of its own. Scotus' system, compared with that of Thomas, tended toward liberty. Scotus held that the excess of power in Thomas' prime motor neutralized the power of his secondary causes, so that these appeared altogether superfluous. This is a point that ought to be left to the Church to decide, but there can be no harm in quoting, on the other hand, the authority of some of Scotus' critics within the Church, who have thought that his doctrine tended to deify matter and to keep open the road to Spinoza. Narrow and dangerous was the border line always between pantheism and materialism, and the chief interest of the schools was in finding fault with each other's paths.

The opinions in themselves need not disturb us, although the question is as open to dispute as ever it was and perhaps as much disputed; but the turn of Thomas' mind is worth study. A century or two later, his passion to be reasonable, scientific, architectural would have brought him within range of the Inquisition. Francis of Assisi was not more archaic and cave dweller than Thomas of Aquino was modern and scientific. In his effort to be logical he forced his Deity to be as logical as himself, which hardly suited Omnipotence. He hewed the Church dogmas into shape as though they were rough stones. About no dogma could mankind feel interest more acute than about that of immortality, which seemed to be the single point vitally necessary for any Church to prove and define as clearly as light itself. Thomas trimmed down the soul to half its legitimate claims as an immortal being by insisting that God created it from nothing in the same act or will by which He created the body and united the two in time and space. The soul existed as form for the body, and had no previous existence. Logic seemed to require that when the body died and dissolved, after the union which had lasted, at most, only an instant or two of eternity, the soul, which fitted that body and no other, should dissolve with it. In that case the Church dissolved, too, since it had no reason for existence except the soul. Thomas met the difficulty by suggesting that the body's form might take permanence from the matter to which it gave form. That matter should individualize mind was itself a violent wrench of logic, but that it should also give permanence—the one quality it did not possess—to this individual mind seemed to many learned doctors a scandal. Perhaps Thomas meant to leave the responsibility on the Church, where it belonged as a matter not of logic but of revealed truth. At all events, this treatment of mind and matter brought him into trouble which few modern logicians would suspect.

The human soul having become a person by contact with matter, and having gained eternal personality by the momentary union, was finished, and remains to this day for practical purposes unchanged; but the angels and devils, a world of realities then more real than man, were never united with matter, and therefore could not be persons. Thomas admitted and insisted that the angels, being immaterial—neither clothed in matter, nor stamped on it, nor mixed with it—were universals; that is, each was a species in himself, a class, or perhaps what would be now called an energy, with no other individuality than he gave himself.

The idea seems to modern science reasonable enough. Science has to deal, for example, with scores of chemical energies which it knows little about except that they always seem to be constant to the same conditions;

but every one knows that in the particular relation of mind to matter the battle is as furious as ever. The soul has always refused to live in peace with the body. The angels, too, were always in rebellion. They insisted on personality, and the devils even more obstinately than the angels. The dispute was—and is—far from trifling. Mind would rather ignore matter altogether. In the thirteenth century mind did, indeed, admit that matter was something—which it quite refuses to admit in the twentieth—but treated it as a nuisance to be abated. To the pure in spirit one argued in vain that spirit must compromise; that nature compromised; that God compromised; that man himself was nothing but a somewhat clumsy compromise. No argument served. Mind insisted on absolute despotism. Schoolmen as well as mystics would not believe that matter was what it seemed—if, indeed, it existed—unsubstantial, shifty, shadowy; changing with incredible swiftness into dust, gas, flame; vanishing in mysterious lines of force into space beyond hope of recovery; whirled about in eternity and infinity by that mind, form, energy, or thought which guides and rules and tyrannizes and is the universe. The Church wanted to be pure spirit; she regarded matter with antipathy as something foul, to be held at arms' length lest it should stain and corrupt the soul; the most she would willingly admit was that mind and matter might travel side by side, like a double-headed comet, on parallel lines that never met, with a pre-established harmony that existed only in the prime motor.

Thomas and his master Albert were almost alone in imposing on the Church the compromise so necessary for its equilibrium. The balance of matter against mind was the same necessity in the Church Intellectual as the balance of thrusts in the arch of the Gothic cathedral. Nowhere did Thomas show his architectural obstinacy quite so plainly as in thus taking matter under his protection. Nothing would induce him to compromise with the angels. He insisted on keeping man wholly apart, as a complex of energies in which matter shared equally with mind. The Church must rest firmly on both. The angels differed from other beings below them precisely because they were immaterial and impersonal. Such rigid logic outraged the spiritual Church. Perhaps Thomas' sudden death in 1274 alone saved him from the fate of Abelard, but it did not save his doctrine. Two years afterwards, in 1276, the French and English churches combined to condemn it. Étienne Tempier, Bishop of Paris, presided over the French Synod; Robert Kilwardby, of the Dominican Order, Archbishop of Canterbury, presided over the Council at Oxford. The synods were composed of schoolmen as well as churchmen, and seem to have been the result of a serious struggle for power between the Dominican and Franciscan Orders.

Apparently the Church compromised between them by condemning the errors of both. Some of these errors, springing from Alexander Hales and his Franciscan schools, were in effect the foundation of another Church. Some were expressly charged against Brother Thomas. *Contra fratrem Thomam* the councils forbade teaching that—*quia intelligentiae non habent materiam, Deus non potest plures ejusdem speciei facere; et quod materia non est in angelis* [because intelligences do not have matter, God cannot make more of the same sort; that the angels are not material]; further, the councils struck at the vital center of Thomas' system—*quod Deus non potest individua multiplicare sub una specie sine materia* [that God cannot multiply individual things under one species without matter]; and again in its broadest form—*quod formae non accipiunt divisionem nisi secundam materiam.* These condemnations made a great stir. Old Albertus Magnus, who was the real victim of attack, fought for himself and for Thomas. After a long and earnest effort, the Thomists rooted out opposition in the order, and carried their campaign to Rome. After fifty years of struggle, by use of every method known in Church politics, the Dominican Order, in 1323, caused John XXII to canonize Thomas and in effect affirm his doctrine.

The story shows how modern, how heterodox, how material, how altogether new and revolutionary the system of St. Thomas seemed at first even in the schools; but that was the affair of the Church and a matter of pure theology. We study only his art. Step by step, stone by stone, we see him build his church building like a stonemason, "with the care that the twelfth-century architects put into" their work, as Viollet-le-Duc saw some similar architect at Rouen, building the tower of St. Romain: "He has thrown over his work the grace and finesse, the study of detail, the sobriety in projections, the perfect harmony," which belongs to his school, and yet he was rigidly structural and Norman. The foundation showed it; the elevation, which is God, developed it; the vaulting, with its balance of thrusts in mind and matter, proved it; but he had still the hardest task in art, to model man.

The cathedral, then, is built, and God is built into it, but, thus far, God is there alone, filling it all, and maintains the equilibrium by balancing created matter separately against created mind. The proportions of the building are superb; nothing so lofty, so large in treatment, so true in scale, so eloquent of multiplicity in unity, has ever been conceived elsewhere; but it was the virtue or the fault of superb structures like Bourges and Amiens and the Church universal that they seemed to need man more than man needed them; they were made for crowds, for thousands and tens of thousands of human beings; for the whole human race, on its knees, hungry for pardon and love. Chartres needed no crowd, for it was meant as a palace of the Virgin, and the Virgin filled it wholly; but the Trinity made their church for no other purpose than to accommodate man, and made man for no other purpose than to fill their church; if man failed to fill it, the church and the Trinity seemed equally failures. Empty, Bourges and Beauvais are cold; hardly as religious as a wayside cross; and yet, even empty, they are perhaps more religious than when filled with cattle and machines. St. Thomas needed to fill his Church with real men, and although he had created his own God for that special purpose, the task was, as every boy knew by heart, the most difficult that Omnipotence had dealt with.

God, as Descartes justly said, we know! but what is man? The schools answered: Man is a rational animal! So was apparently a dog, or a bee, or a beaver, none of which seemed to need churches. Modern science, with infinite effort, has discovered and announced that man is a bewildering complex of energies, which helps little to explain his relations with the ultimate substance or energy or prime motor whose existence both science and schoolmen admit; which science studies in laboratories and religion worships in churches. The man whom God created to fill His Church must be an energy independent of God; otherwise God filled His own Church with His own energy. Thus far, the God of St. Thomas was alone in His Church. The beings He had created out of nothing—Omar's pipkins of clay and shape—stood against the walls, waiting to receive the wine of life, a life of their own. Of that life, energy, will, or wine—whatever the poets or professors called it—God was the only cause, as He was also the immediate cause, and support. Thomas was emphatic on that point. God is the cause of energy as the sun is the cause of color: *prout sol dicitur causa manifestationis coloris.* He not only gives forms to his pipkins, or energies to his agents, but He also maintains those forms in being: *dat formas creaturis agentibus et eas tenet in esse.* He acts directly, not through secondary causes, on everything and every one: *Deus in omnibus intime operatur.* If, for an instant, God's action, which is also His will, were to stop, the universe would not merely fall to pieces, but would vanish, and must then be created anew from nothing: *Quia non habet radicem in aere, statim cessat lumen, cessante actione solis. Sic autem se habet omnis creatura ad Deum sicut aer ad solem illuminantem.* God radiates energy as the sun radiates light, and "the whole fabric of nature would return to nothing" if that radiation ceased even for an instant. Everything is created by one instantaneous, eternal, universal act of will, and by the same act is maintained in being.

Where, then—in what mysterious cave outside of creation—could man, and his free will, and his private world of responsibilities and duties, lie hidden? Unless man was a free agent in a world of his own beyond constraint, the Church was a fraud, and it helped little to add that the State was another. If God was the sole and immediate cause and support of everything in His creation, God was also the cause of its defects, and could not—being Justice and Goodness in essence—hold man responsible for His own omissions. Still less could the State or Church do it in His name.

Whatever truth lies in the charge that the schools discussed futile questions by faulty methods, one cannot decently deny that in this case the question was practical and the method vital. Theist or atheist, monist or anarchist must all admit that society and science are equally interested with theology in deciding whether the universe is one or many, a harmony or a discord. The Church and State asserted that it was a harmony, and that they were its representatives. They say so still. Their claim led to singular but unavoidable conclusions, with which society has struggled for seven hundred years, and is still struggling.

Freedom could not exist in nature, or even in God, after the single, unalterable act or will which created. The only possible free will was that of God before the act. Abelard with his rigid logic averred that God had no freedom; being Himself whatever is most perfect, He produced necessarily the most perfect possible world. Nothing seemed more logical, but if God acted necessarily, His world must also be of necessity the only possible product of His act, and the Church became an impertinence, since man proved only fatuity by attempting to interfere. Thomas dared not disturb the foundations of the Church, and therefore began by laying down the law that God—previous to His act—could choose, and had chosen, whatever scheme of creation He pleased, and that the harmony of the actual scheme proved His perfections. Thus he saved God's free will.

This philosophical apse would have closed the lines and finished the plan of his church choir had the universe not shown some divergencies or discords needing to be explained. The student of the Latin Quarter was then harder to convince than now that God was Infinite Love and His world a perfect harmony, when perfect love and harmony showed them, even in the Latin Quarter, and still more in revealed truth, a picture of suffering, sorrow, and death; plague, pestilence, and famine; inundations, droughts, and frosts; catastrophes world-wide and accidents in corners; cruelty, perversity, stupidity, uncertainty, insanity; virtue begetting vice; vice working for good; happiness without sense, selfishness without gain, misery without cause, and horrors undefined. The students in public dared not ask, as Voltaire did, *avec son hideux sourire* [with his grotesque grin], whether the Lisbon earthquake was the final proof of God's infinite goodness, but in private they used the *argumentum ad personam divinam* [argument to the divine person] freely enough, and when the Church told them that evil did not exist, the ribalds laughed.

St. Augustine certainly tempted Satan when he fastened the Church to this doctrine that evil is only the privation of good, an *amissio boni;* and that good alone exists. The point was infinitely troublesome. Good was order, law, unity. Evil was disorder, anarchy, multiplicity. Which was truth? The Church had committed itself to the dogma that order and unity were the ultimate truth, and that the anarchist should be burned. She could do nothing else, and society supported her—still supports her; yet the Church, who was wiser than the State, had always seen that St. Augustine dealt with only half the question. She knew that evil might be an excess of good as well as absence of it; that good leads to evil, evil to good; and that, as Pascal says, "three degrees of polar elevation upset all jurisprudence; a meridian decides truth; fundamental laws change; rights have epochs. Pleasing Justice! bounded by a river or a mountain! truths on this side the Pyrenees! errors beyond!" Thomas conceded that God Himself, with the best intentions, might be the source of evil, and pleaded only that His action might in the end work benefits. He could offer no proof of it, but he could assume as probable a plan of good which became the more perfect for the very reason that it allowed great liberty in detail.

One hardly feels St. Thomas here in all his force. He offers suggestion rather than proof; apology—the weaker because of obvious effort to apologize—rather than defense, for infinite goodness, justice, and power; scoffers might add that he invented a new proof *ab defectu* [from the defect], or argument for proving the perfection of a machine by the number of its imperfections; but at all events, society has never done better by way of proving its right to enforce morals or unity of opinion. Unless it asserts law, it can only assert force. Rigid theology went much further. In God's providence, man was as nothing. With a proper sense of duty, every solar system should be content to suffer, if thereby the efficiency of the Milky Way were improved. Such theology shocked St. Thomas, who never wholly abandoned man in order to exalt God. He persistently brought God and man together, and if he erred, the Church rightly pardons him because he erred on the human side. Whenever the path lay through the valley of despair he called God to his aid, as though he felt the moral obligation of the Creator to help His creation.

At best the vision of God, sitting forever at His worktable, willing the existence of mankind exactly as it is, while conscious that, among these myriad arbitrary creations of His will, hardly one in a million could escape temporary misery or eternal damnation, was not the best possible background for a Church, as the Virgin and the Saviour frankly admitted by taking the foreground; but the Church was not responsible for it. Mankind could not admit an anarchical—a dual or a multiple—universe. The world was there, staring them in the face, with all its chaotic conditions, and society insisted on its unity in self-defense. Society still insists on treating it as unity, though no longer affecting logic. Society insists on its free will, although free will has never been explained to the satisfaction of any but those who much wish to be satisfied, and although the words in any common sense implied not unity but duality in creation. The Church had nothing to do with inventing this riddle—the oldest that fretted mankind. Apart from all theological interferences—fall of Adam or fault of Eve, Atonement, Justification, or Redemption—either the universe was one, or it was two, or it was many; either energy was one, seen only in powers of itself, or it was several; either God was harmony, or He was discord. With practical unanimity, mankind rejected the dual or multiple scheme; it insisted on unity. Thomas took the question as it was given him. The unity was full of defects; he did not deny them; but he claimed that they might be incidents, and that the admitted unity might even prove their beneficence. Granting this enormous concession, he still needed a means of bringing into the system one element which vehemently refused to be brought: that is, man himself, who insisted that the universe was a unit, but that he was a universe; that energy was one, but that he was another energy; that God was omnipotent, but that man was free. The contradiction had always existed, exists still, and always must exist, unless man either admits that he is a machine, or agrees that anarchy and chaos are the habit of nature, and law and order its accident. The agreement may become possible, but it was not possible in the thirteenth century nor is it now. St. Thomas' settlement could not be a simple one or final, except for practical use, but it served, and it holds good still.

No one ever seriously affirmed the literal freedom of will. Absolute liberty is absence of restraint; responsibility is restraint; therefore, the ideally free individual is responsible only to himself. This principle is the philosophical foundation of anarchism, and, for anything that science has yet proved, may be the philosophical foundation of the universe; but it is fatal to all society and is especially hostile to the State. Perhaps the

Church of the thirteenth century might have found a way to use even this principle for a good purpose; certainly, the influence of St. Bernard was sufficiently unsocial and that of St. Francis was sufficiently unselfish to conciliate even anarchists of the militant class; but St. Thomas was working for the Church and the State, not for the salvation of souls, and his chief object was to repress anarchy. The theory of absolute free will never entered his mind, more than the theory of material free will would enter the mind of an architect. The Church gave him no warrant for discussing the subject in such a sense. In fact, the Church never admitted free will, or used the word when it could be avoided. In Latin, the term used was *liberum arbitrium*—free choice—and in French to this day it remains in strictness *libre arbitre* still. From St. Augustine downwards the Church was never so unscientific as to admit of liberty beyond the faculty of choosing between paths, some leading through the Church and some not, but all leading to the next world; as a criminal might be allowed the liberty of choosing between the guillotine and the gallows, without infringing on the supremacy of the judge.

Thomas started from that point, already far from theoretic freedom. "We are masters of our acts," he began, "in the sense that we can choose such and such a thing; now, we have not to choose our end, but the means that relate to it, as Aristotle says." Unfortunately, even this trenchant amputation of man's free energies would not accord with fact or with logic. Experience proved that man's power of choice in action was very far from absolute, and logic seemed to require that every choice should have some predetermining cause which decided the will to act. Science affirmed that choice was not free—could not be free—without abandoning the unity of force and the foundation of law. Society insisted that its choice must be left free, whatever became of science or unity. St. Thomas was required to illustrate the theory of *liberum arbitrium* by choosing a path through these difficulties, where path there was obviously none.

Thomas' method for treating this problem was sure to be as scientific as the vaulting of a Gothic arch. Indeed, one follows it most easily by translating his school vocabulary into modern technical terms. With very slight straining of equivalents, Thomas might now be written thus:

By the term God is meant a prime motor which supplies all energy to the universe, and acts directly on man as well as on all other creatures, moving him as a mechanical motor might do; but man, being specially provided with an organism more complex than the organisms of other creatures, enjoys an exceptional capacity for reflex action—a power of reflection—which enables him within certain limits to choose between paths; and this singular capacity is called free choice or free will. Of course, the reflection is not choice, and though a man's mind reflected as perfectly as the facets of a lighthouse lantern, it would never reach a choice without an energy which impels it to act.

Now let us read St. Thomas:

> Some kind of an agent is required to determine one's choice; that agent is reflection. Man reflects, then, in order to learn what choice to make between the two acts which offer themselves. But reflection is, in its turn, a faculty of doing opposite things, for we can reflect or not reflect; and we are no further forward than before. One cannot carry back this process infinitely, for in that case one would never decide. The fixed point is not in man, since we meet in him, as a being apart by himself, only the alternative faculties; we must, therefore, recur to the intervention of an exterior agent who shall impress on our will a movement capable of putting an end to its hesitations: That exterior agent is nothing else than God!

The scheme seems to differ little, and unwillingly, from a system of dynamics as modern as the dynamo. Even in the prime motor, from the moment of action, freedom of will vanished. Creation was not successive; it was one instantaneous thought and act, identical with the will, and was complete and unchangeable from end to end, including time as one of its functions. Thomas was as clear as possible on that point: "Supposing God wills anything in effect; He cannot will not to will it, because His will cannot change." He wills that some things shall be contingent and others necessary, but He wills in the same act that the contingency shall be necessary. "They are contingent because God has willed them to be so, and with this object has subjected them to causes which are so." In the same way He wills that His creation shall develop itself in time and space and sequence, but He creates these conditions as well as the events. He creates the whole, in one act, complete, unchangeable, and it is then unfolded like a rolling panorama, with its predetermined contingencies.

Man's free choice—*liberum arbitrium*—falls easily into place as a predetermined contingency. God is the first cause, and acts in all secondary causes directly; but while He acts mechanically on the rest of creation—as far as is known—He acts freely at one point, and this free action remains free as far as it extends on that line. Man's freedom derives from this source, but it is simply apparent, as far as he is a cause; it is a reflex action determined by a new agency of the first cause.

However abstruse these ideas may once have sounded, they are far from seeming difficult in comparison with modern theories of energy.

Indeed, measured by that standard, the only striking feature of St. Thomas' motor is its simplicity. Thomas' prime motor was very powerful, and its lines of energy were infinite. Among these infinite lines, a certain group ran to the human race, and, as long as the conduction was perfect, each man acted mechanically. In cases where the current, for any reason, was for a moment checked—that is to say, produced the effect of hesitation or reflection in the mind—the current accumulated until it acquired power to leap the obstacle. As St. Thomas expressed it, the Prime Motor, Who was nothing else than God, intervened to decide the channel of the current. The only difference between man and a vegetable was the reflex action of the complicated mirror which was called mind, and the mark of mind was reflective absorption or choice. The apparent freedom was an illusion arising from the extreme delicacy of the machine, but the motive power was in fact the same—that of God.

This exclusion of what men commonly called freedom was carried still further in the process of explaining dogma. Supposing the conduction to be insufficient for a given purpose; a purpose which shall require perfect conduction? Under ordinary circumstances, in ninety-nine cases out of a hundred, the conductor will be burned out, so to speak; condemned, and thrown away. This is the case with most human beings. Yet there are cases where the conductor is capable of receiving an increase of energy from the prime motor, which enables it to attain the object aimed at. In dogma, this store of reserved energy is technically called Grace. In the strict, theological sense of the word, as it is used by St. Thomas, the exact, literal meaning of Grace is "a motion which the Prime Motor, as a supernatural cause, produces in the soul, perfecting free will." It is a reserved energy, which comes to aid and reinforce the normal energy of the battery.

To religious minds this scientific inversion of solemn truths seems, and is, sacrilege; but Thomas' numerous critics in the Church have always brought precisely this charge against his doctrine, and are doing so still. They insist that he has reduced God to a mechanism and man to a passive conductor of force. He has left, they say, nothing but God in the universe. The terrible word which annihilates all other philosophical systems against which it is hurled, has been hurled freely against his for six hundred years and more, without visibly affecting the Church; and yet its propriety seems, to the vulgar, beyond reasonable cavil. To Father de Régnon, of the extremely learned and intelligent Society of Jesus, the difference between pantheism and Thomism reduces itself to this: "Pantheism, starting from the notion of an infinite substance which is the plenitude of being, concludes that there can exist no other beings than *the* being; no other realities than the absolute reality. Thomism, starting from the efficacy of the first cause, tends to reduce more and more the efficacy of second causes, and to replace it by a passivity which receives without producing, which is determined without determining." To students of architecture, who know equally little about pantheism and about Thomism—or, indeed, for that matter, about architecture, too—the quality that rouses most surprise in Thomism is its astonishingly scientific method. The Franciscans and the Jesuits call it pantheism, but science, too, is pantheism, or has till very recently been wholly pantheistic. Avowedly science has aimed at nothing but the reduction of multiplicity to unity, and has excommunicated, as though it were itself a Church, anyone who doubted or disputed its object, its method, or its results. The effort is as evident and quite as laborious in modern science, starting as it does from multiplicity, as in Thomas Aquinas, who started from unity; and it is necessarily less successful, for its true aims, as far as it is science and not disguised religion, were equally attained by reaching infinite complexity; but the assertion or assumption of ultimate unity has characterized the law of energy as emphatically as it has characterized the definition of God in theology. If it is a reproach to St. Thomas, it is equally a reproach to Clerk Maxwell. In truth, it is what men most admire in both—the power of broad and lofty generalization.

Under any conceivable system the process of getting God and man under the same roof—of bringing two independent energies under the same control—required a painful effort, as science has much cause to know. No doubt, many good Christians and some heretics have been shocked at the tour de force by which they felt themselves suddenly seized, bound hand and foot, attached to each other, and dragged into the Church, without consent or consultation. To religious mystics, whose skepticism concerned chiefly themselves and their own existence, St. Thomas' man seemed hardly worth herding, at so much expense and trouble, into a Church where he was not eager to go. True religion felt the nearness of God without caring to see the mechanism. Mystics like St. Bernard, St. Francis, St. Bonaventure, or Pascal had a right to make this objection, since they got into the Church, so to speak, by breaking through the windows; but society at large accepted and retains St. Thomas' man much as St. Thomas delivered him to the Government; a two-sided being, free or unfree, responsible or irresponsible, an energy or a victim of energy, moved by choice or moved by compulsion, as the interests of society seemed for the moment to need. Certainly St. Thomas lavished no excess of liberty on the man he created, but still he was more generous than the State has ever been. St. Thomas asked little from man, and gave much; even as much freedom of will as the State gave or now gives; he added immortality hereafter and eternal happiness under reasonable restraints; his God watched over man's temporal welfare far more anxiously than the State has ever done, and assigned him space in the Church which he never can have in the galleries of Parliament or Congress; more than all this, St. Thomas and his God placed man in the center of the universe, and made the sun and the stars for his uses. No statute law ever did as much for man, and no social reform ever will try to do it; yet man bitterly complained that he had not his rights, and even in the Church is still complaining, because St. Thomas set a limit, more or less vague, to what the man was obstinate in calling his freedom of will.

Thus St. Thomas completed his work, keeping his converging lines clear and pure throughout, and bringing them together, unbroken, in the curves that gave unity to his plan. His sense of scale and proportion was that of the great architects of his age. One might go on studying it for a lifetime. He showed no more hesitation in keeping his Deity in scale than in adjusting man to it. Strange as it sounds, although man thought himself hardly treated in respect to freedom, yet, if freedom meant superiority, man was in action much the superior of God, Whose freedom suffered, from St. Thomas, under restraints that man never would have tolerated. St. Thomas did not allow God even an undetermined will; He was pure Act, and as such He could not change. Man alone was allowed, in act, to change direction. What was more curious still, man might absolutely prove his freedom by refusing to move at all; if he did not like his life he could stop it, and habitually did so, or acquiesced in its being done for him; while God could not commit suicide or even cease for a single instant His continuous action. If man had the singular fancy of making himself absurd—a taste confined to himself but attested by evidence exceedingly strong—he could be as absurd as he liked; but God could not be absurd. St. Thomas did not allow the Deity the right to contradict Himself, which is one of man's chief pleasures. While man enjoyed what was, for his purposes, an unlimited freedom to be wicked—a privilege which, as both Church and State bitterly complained and still complain, he has outrageously abused—God was Goodness, and could be nothing else. While man moved about his relatively spacious prison with a certain degree of ease, God, being everywhere, could not move. In one respect, at least, man's freedom seemed to be not relative but absolute, for his thought was an energy paying no regard to space or time or order or object or sense; but God's thought was His act and will at once; speaking correctly, God could not think; He is. St. Thomas would not, or could not, admit that God was Necessity, as Abelard seems to have held, but he refused to tolerate the idea of a divine maniac, free from moral obligation to himself. The atmosphere of St. Louis surrounds the God of St. Thomas, and its pure ether shuts out the corruption and pollution to come—the Valois and Bourbons, the Occams and Hobbeses, the Tudors and the Medicis, of an enlightened Europe.

The theology turns always into art at the last, and ends in aspiration. The spire justifies the church. In St. Thomas' Church, man's free will was the aspiration to God, and he treated it as the architects of Chartres and Laon had treated their famous flèches. The square foundation tower, the expression of God's power in act—His Creation—rose to the level of the Church façade as a part of the normal unity of God's energy; and then, suddenly, without show of effort, without break, without logical violence, became a many-sided, voluntary, vanishing human soul, and neither Villard de Honnecourt nor Duns Scotus could distinguish where God's power ends and man's free will begins. All they saw was the soul vanishing into the skies. How it was done, one does not care to ask; in a result so exquisite, one has not the heart to find fault with *adresse* [skill].

About St. Thomas' theology we need not greatly disturb ourselves; it can matter now not much, whether he put more pantheism than the law allowed or more materialism than Duns Scotus approved—or less of either—into his universe, since the Church is still on the spot, responsible for its own doctrines; but his architecture is another matter. So scientific and structural a method was never an accident or the property of a single mind even with Aristotle to prompt it. Neither his Church nor the architect's church was a sketch, but a completely studied structure. Every relation of parts, every disturbance of equilibrium, every detail of construction was treated with infinite labor, as the result of two hundred years of experiment and discussion among thousands of men whose minds and whose instincts were acute, and who discussed little else. Science and art were one. Thomas Aquinas would probably have built a better cathedral at Beauvais than the actual architect who planned it; but it is quite likely that the architect might have saved Thomas some of his errors, as pointed out by the Councils of 1276. Both were great artists; perhaps in their professions, the greatest that ever lived; and both must have been great students beyond their practice. Both were subject to constant criticism from men and bodies of men whose minds were as acute and whose learning was as great as their own. If the Archbishop of Canterbury and the Bishop of Paris condemned Thomas, the Bernardines had, for nearly two hundred years, condemned Beauvais in advance. Both the *Summa Theologica* and Beauvais Cathedral were excessively modern, scientific, and technical, marking the extreme points reached by Europe on the lines of scholastic science. This is all we need to know. If we like, we can go on to study, inch by inch, the slow decline of the art. The essence of it—the despotic central idea—was that of organic unity both in the thought and the building. From that time, the universe has steadily become more complex and less reducible to a central control. With as much obstinacy as though it were human, it has insisted on expanding its parts; with as much elusiveness as though it were feminine, it has evaded the attempt to impose on it a single will. Modern science, like modern art, tends, in practice, to drop the dogma of organic unity. Some of the medieval habit of mind survives, but even that is said to be yielding before the daily evidence of increasing and extending complexity. The fault, then, was not in man, if he no longer looked at science or art as an organic whole or as the expression of unity. Unity turned itself into complexity, multiplicity, variety, and even contradiction. All experience, human and divine, assured man in the thirteenth century that the lines of the universe converged. How was he to know that these lines ran in every conceivable and inconceivable direction, and that at least half of them seemed to diverge from any imaginable center of unity! Dimly conscious that his Trinity required in logic a fourth dimension, how was the schoolman to supply it, when even the mathematician of today can only infer its necessity? Naturally man tended to lose his sense of scale and relation. A straight line, or a combination of straight lines, may have still a sort of artistic unity, but what can be done in art with a series of negative symbols? Even if the negative were continuous, the artist might express at least a negation; but supposing that Omar's kinetic analogy of the ball and the players turned out to be a scientific formula! supposing that the highest scientific authority, in order to obtain any unity at all, had to resort to the Middle Ages for an imaginary demon to sort his atoms! how could art deal with such problems, and what wonder that art lost unity with philosophy and science! Art had to be confused in order to express confusion; but perhaps it was truest, so.

Some future summer, when you are older, and when I have left, like Omar, only the empty glass of my scholasticism for you to turn down, you can amuse yourself by going on with the story after the death of St. Louis, St. Thomas, and William of Lorris, and after the failure of Beauvais. The pathetic interest of the drama deepens with every new expression, but at least you can learn from it that your parents in the nineteenth century were not to blame for losing the sense of unity in art. As early as the fourteenth century, signs of unsteadiness appeared, and, before the eighteenth century, unity became only a reminiscence. The old habit of centralizing a strain at one point, and then dividing and subdividing it, and distributing it on visible lines of support to a visible foundation, disappeared in architecture soon after 1500, but lingered in theology two centuries longer, and even, in very old-fashioned communities, far down to our own time; but its values were forgotten, and it survived chiefly as a stock jest against the clergy. The passage between the two epochs is as beautiful as the "Slave" of Michelangelo; but, to feel its beauty, you should see it from above, as it came from its radiant source. Truth, indeed, may not exist; science avers it to be only a relation; but what men took for truth stares one everywhere in the eye and begs for sympathy. The architects of the twelfth and thirteenth centuries took the Church and the universe for truths, and tried to express them in a structure which should be final. Knowing by an enormous experience precisely where the strains were to come, they enlarged their scale to the utmost point of material endurance, lightening the load and distributing the burden until the gutters and gargoyles that seem mere ornament, and the grotesques that seem rude absurdities, all do work either for the arch or for the eye; and every inch of material, up and down, from crypt to vault, from man to God, from the universe to the atom, had its task, giving support where support was needed, or weight where concentration was felt, but always with the condition of showing conspicuously to the eye the great lines which led to unity and the curves which controlled divergence; so that, from the cross on the flèche and the keystone of the vault, down through the ribbed nervures, the columns, the windows, to the foundation of the flying buttresses far beyond the walls, one idea controlled every line; and this is true of St. Thomas' Church as it is of Amiens Cathedral. The method was the same for both, and the result was an art marked by singular unity, which endured and served its purpose until man changed his attitude toward the universe. The trouble was not in the art or the method or the structure, but in the universe itself which presented different aspects as man moved. Granted a Church, St. Thomas' Church was the most expressive that man has made, and the great Gothic cathedrals were its most complete expression.

Perhaps the best proof of it is their apparent instability. Of all the elaborate symbolism which has been suggested for the Gothic cathedral, the most vital and most perfect may be that the slender nervure, the springing motion of the broken arch, the leap downwards of the flying buttress—the visible effort to throw off a visible strain—never let us forget that faith alone supports it, and that, if faith fails, heaven is lost. The equilibrium is visibly delicate beyond the line of safety; danger lurks in every stone. The peril of the heavy tower, of the restless vault, of the vagrant buttress; the uncertainty of logic, the inequalities of the syllogism, the irregularities of the mental mirror—all these haunting nightmares of the Church are expressed as strongly by the Gothic cathedral as though it had been the cry of human suffering, and as no emotion had ever been expressed before or is likely to find expression again. The delight of its aspirations is flung up to the sky. The pathos of its self-distrust and anguish of doubt is buried in the earth as its last secret. You can read out of it whatever else pleases your youth and confidence; to me, this is all.

The foregoing consists of Chapter XVI
from Adams' MONT-SAINT-MICHEL AND CHARTRES.

Voltaire [1]

1694–1778

Voltaire apparently first conceived the idea of the *Philosophical Dictionary* while he was at the court of Frederick the Great during 1751–1753. He thought of it as "an account in alphabetical order of all that I ought to think about this world and the next." By the time he first published it in 1764 he had included many of the articles which he had originally written for the great French Encyclopedia of Diderot and d'Alembert. The selection offered here thus provides an opportunity to study one of the conceptions of philosophy for which the Encyclopedia is famous. It may well be looked upon as constituting a particular type of popular philosophy.

More is involved than writing clearly in a simple style that an educated reader can understand. This much is generally true of Plato, Berkeley, and of Bertrand Russell in our own day. Voltaire agrees with these writers in denying that philosophy has to develop a highly technical terminology such as is found, for example, in Aristotle, Aquinas, and Whitehead. Yet it cannot be claimed that Voltaire shares the same concept of philosophy which is found among the first group. He seldom raises the kind of difficult and puzzling problems that they deal with. It seems that the clarity at which Voltaire aims is as much a question of matter as of form.

Essays in Popular Philosophy is a title William James used for one of his works. The same title might be used for these pieces of Voltaire's. Both are agreed that the matters on which they write are too important to be left to the professionals alone. They concern all men and should be considered by all. Yet compared with the tenor of their work as a whole, this agreement stands out as an exception. In

---

[1] For a biography of Voltaire, see Vol. 2, pp. 237–238, in this set.

other respects it cannot be said that they share the same concept of philosophy.

Perhaps the briefest way of describing how Voltaire differs from all the philosophers who have been mentioned is to note that he is at once more literary and more political. The imaginative tales for which he is also famous he once described as "philosophical stories." [2] This interest in story also appears in the *Philosophical Dictionary*. It is seen, for example, in the article on truth, which is organized about the story of Pontius Pilate. Yet in this Voltaire is more than just a storyteller. He is obviously concerned to distinguish and analyze different meanings of truth.

Voltaire's political intent is apparent throughout. He is always attacking the establishment of church and state. The French Encyclopedia, for which Voltaire wrote many of the pieces in the *Philosophical Dictionary*, has been described as a weapon. It was written as much to form opinion as to provide information. It is widely credited with contributing to the events and the climate of opinion that resulted in the French Revolution. Thus for Voltaire philosophy is always practical. He would agree with Marx that it is a tool with which to change the world.

---

[2] See *Micromégas*, Vol. 2, pp. 241–256, in this set.

The Philosophy of Common Sense
from *Philosophical Dictionary*

*That the Recent Birth of the Arts Does Not Prove
the Recent Formation of the Globe.*

All philosophers have thought matter eternal; but the arts appear to be new. Even the art of making bread is of recent origin. The first Romans ate pap; and those conquerors of so many nations had neither windmills nor watermills. This truth seems, at first sight, to contradict the doctrine of the antiquity of the globe as it now is, or to indicate that our earth has suffered terrible revolutions. Irruptions of barbarians can hardly annihilate arts which have become necessary. Suppose that an army of Negroes were to come upon us, like locusts, from the mountains of southern Africa, through Monomotapa, Monoemugi, etc., traversing Abyssinia, Nubia, Egypt, Syria, Asia Minor, and all Europe, ravaging and overturning everything in its way; there would still be a few bakers, tailors, shoemakers, and carpenters left; the necessary arts would revive; luxury alone would be annihilated. This was what happened at the fall of the Roman Empire; even the art of writing became very rare; nearly all those arts which contributed to render life agreeable were for a long time extinct. Now, we are inventing new ones every day.

From all this, no well-grounded inference can be drawn against the antiquity of the globe. For, supposing that a flood of barbarians had entirely swept away the arts of writing and making bread; supposing even that we had had bread, or pens, ink, and paper, only for ten years—the country which could exist for ten years without eating bread or writing down its thoughts could exist for an age, or a hundred thousand ages, without these resources.

It is quite clear that man and the other animals can very well subsist without bakers, without romance-writers, and without divines, as witness America, and as witness also three-fourths of our own continent. The recent birth of the arts among us does not prove the recent formation of the globe, as was pretended by Epicurus, one of our predecessors in speculation, who supposed that the eternal atoms in their declination one day formed our earth by pure chance. Pomponatius used to say: *"Se il mondo non e eterno, per tutti santi e molto vecchio"*—"If this world be not eternal, by all the saints, it is very old."

ASTROLOGY

Astrology may rest on better foundations than magic. For if no one has ever seen either goblins, or lemurs, or goddesses, or peris, or demons, or cacodemons, the predictions of astrologers have often been seen to succeed. If, of two astrologers consulted on the life of a child and on the weather, one says that the child will live to manhood, the other not; if one announces rain, and the other fine weather, it is clear that one of them will be a prophet.

The prime misfortune of the astrologers is that the sky has changed since the rules of the art were established. The sun, which at the equinox was in Aries in the time of the Argonauts, is today in Taurus; and the astrologers, to the great hurt of their art, today attribute to one house of the sun what belongs visibly to another. This, however, is not a conclusive argument against astrology. The masters of the art deceive themselves; but it is not demonstrated that the art cannot exist.

There is no absurdity in saying: Such and such a child is born in the waxing of the moon, during stormy weather, at the rising of such and such star; his constitution has been feeble, and his life unhappy and short, which is the ordinary lot of poor constitutions: whereas this child, on the contrary, was born when the moon was full, the sun strong, the weather calm, at the rising of such and such star; his constitution has been good, his life long and happy. If these observations had been repeated, if they had been found accurate, experience would have been able after some thousands of centuries to form an art which it would have been difficult to doubt. One would have thought, with some reason, that men are like trees and vegetables which must be planted and sown only in certain seasons. It would have been of no avail against the astrologers to say: My son was born at a fortunate time, and nevertheless died in his cradle. The astrologer would have replied: It often happens that trees planted in the proper season perish; I answered to you for the stars, but I did not answer for the malformation you communicated to your child. Astrology operates only when no cause opposes itself to the good the stars can do.

One would have succeeded no better in discrediting the astrologer by saying: Of two children who were born in the same minute, one has been king, the other has been only churchwarden of his parish. For the astrologer could very well have defended himself by pointing out that the peasant made his fortune when he became churchwarden, as the prince when he became king.

And if one alleged that a bandit hanged by Sixtus V was born at the same time as Sixtus V himself, who from a pig-herd became Pope, the astrologers would say there had been a mistake of a few seconds, and that it is impossible, according to the rules, for the same star to bestow the triple crown and the gallows. Only because a host of experiences belied predictions, did men at last perceive that the art is illusory; but, before being undeceived, they were long credulous.

One of the most famous mathematicians in Europe, named Stoffler, who flourished in the fifteenth and sixteenth centuries, and who worked for a long time on the calendar reform which was proposed at the Council of Constance, foretold a universal flood for the year 1524. This flood was supposed to arrive in the month of February, and nothing was more plausible; for Saturn, Jupiter, and Mars were then in conjunction in the sign of Pisces. All the peoples of Europe, Asia and Africa, who heard of the prediction, were dismayed. Everyone expected the flood, rainbows to the contrary. Several contemporary authors record that the inhabitants of the maritime provinces of Germany hastened to sell their lands dirt-cheap to those who had the most money, and who were less credulous than they. Everyone provided himself with a boat to serve as an ark. A Toulouse doctor, named Auriol, had a great ark made for himself, his family, and his friends; the same precautions were taken throughout a large part of Italy. At last the month of February arrived, and not a drop of water fell. Never was there a drier month, and never were the astrologers more embarrassed. Nevertheless they were neither discouraged nor neglected, and almost all princes continued to consult them.

I have not the honour of being a prince; but the celebrated Count of Boulainvilliers, and an Italian named Colonna, who was highly thought of in Paris, both foretold that I should most certainly die at the age of thirty-two. I have been malicious enough to outwit them by nearly thirty years already, wherefore I humbly beg their pardon.

AUTHORITY

Wretched human beings, whether you wear green robes, turbans, black robes or surplices, cloaks and clerical bands, never seek to use authority where it is only a question of reason, unless you wish to be scoffed at throughout the centuries as the most impertinent of men, and to suffer public hatred as the most unjust.

You have been spoken to a hundred times of the insolent absurdity with which you condemned Galileo, and I speak to you for the hundred and first, and I hope you will keep the anniversary of that event for ever. Would that there might be graved on the door of your Holy Office: "Here seven cardinals, assisted by minor brethren, had the finest thinker of Italy thrown into prison at the age of seventy; made him fast on bread and water because he instructed the human race, and because they were ignorant."

In the same place there was pronounced a sentence in favour of Aristotle's categories, and the penalty of the galleys was learnedly and equitably decreed for anyone who should be sufficiently daring as to hold an opinion different from those of the Stagyrite, whose books were formerly burned by two councils.

Still later a faculty—which was possessed of no great faculties—issued a decree condemning innate ideas, and later a decree in favour of innate ideas, without the said faculty being informed by its beadles what an idea is.

In the neighbouring schools judicial proceedings were instituted against the circulation of the blood.

An action has been started against inoculation, and parties have been subpoenaed.

At the Customs of Thought twenty-one folio volumes were seized, in which it was treacherously and wickedly stated that triangles always have three angles; that a father is older than his son; that Rhea Silvia lost her virginity before giving birth to her child; and that flour is not an oak leaf.

On another occasion the action: *Utrum chimera bombinans in vacuo possit comedere secundas intentiones* [whether a chimera buzzing in a vacuum can feed on good intentions], came up for judgment; and it was decided in the affirmative.

The result was that everyone thought himself far superior to Archimedes, Euclid, Cicero, and Pliny, and strutted proudly about the University Quarter.

AUTHORS

Do you wish to be an author? Do you wish to make a book? Remember that it must be new and useful, or at least have great charm. Why from your provincial retreat should you slay me with another quarto, to teach me that a king ought to be just, and that Trajan was more virtuous than Caligula? You insist upon printing the sermons which have lulled your little obscure town to sleep, and you put all our histories under contributions to extract from them the life of a prince of whom you can say nothing new.

If you have written a history of your own time, doubt not but you will find some learned chronologist, or newspaper commentator, who will catch you up on a date, a Christian name, or a squadron which you have wrongly placed at the distance of three hundred paces from the place where it was really posted. Be grateful, and correct these important errors forthwith.

If an ignoramus, or an empty fool, pretend to criticize this thing or the other, you may properly confute him; but name him rarely, for fear of soiling your writings. If you are attacked on your style, never answer; your work alone should reply.

If you are said to be sick, content yourself that you are well, without wishing to prove to the people that you are in perfect health; and, above all, remember that the world cares very little whether you are well or ill.

A hundred authors compile to get their bread, and twenty fools extract, criticize, apologize, and satirize these compilations to get bread also, because they have no profession. All these people repair on Fridays to the lieutenant of the police at Paris to demand permission to sell their drugs. They have their audience immediately after the prostitutes, who pay no attention to them, because they know that they are poor customers.

They return with a tacit permission to sell and distribute throughout the kingdom their stories; their collection of bon mots; the life of the blessed Regis; the translation of a German poem; new discoveries on eels; a new copy of verses; a treatise on the origin of bells, or on the loves of the toads. A bookseller buys their productions for ten crowns; they give five of them to a corner pamphleteer, on condition that he will speak well of them in his sheet. The scribbler takes their money, and says all the ill he can of their books. The aggrieved parties go to complain to the Jew, who is keeping the wife of the journalist, and the scene closes by the critic being carried to Fort-Evêque; and these are they who call themselves authors!

These poor people are divided into two or three bands, and go begging like mendicant friars; but not having taken vows, their society lasts only for a few days, for they betray one another like priests who run after the same benefice, though they have no benefice to hope for. But they still call themselves authors!

The misfortune of these men is that their fathers did not make them learn a trade, which is a great fault of our modern system. Every man of the people who can bring up his son in a useful art, and does not do so, merits punishment. The son of a mason becomes a Jesuit at seventeen; he is chased from society at four-and-twenty, because the looseness of his habits has become too notorious. Behold him without bread! He turns journalist, he cultivates the lowest kind of literature, and is scorned even by the mob. And such as these, again, call themselves authors!

The only authors are they who have succeeded in a genuine art, be it epic poetry, tragedy, comedy, history, or philosophy, and who teach or delight mankind. The others, of whom we have spoken, are, among men of letters, like bats among the birds.

CONCATENATION OF EVENTS

It is said that the present is pregnant with the future. Events are linked to each other by an invincible fatality: Homer puts Destiny above even Jupiter. This master of gods and men declares roundly that he cannot stop his son Sarpedon dying at his appointed time. Sarpedon was born at the moment when he had to be born, and could not be born at another moment; he could not die otherwise than before Troy; he could not be buried elsewhere than in Lycia; he had at the appointed time to produce vegetables which had to be changed into the substance of a few Lycians; his heirs had to establish a new order in his states; this new order had to exert an influence over the neighbouring kingdoms; from it necessarily resulted a new arrangement of war and peace with the neighbours of the neighbours of Lycia: thus, step by step, the destiny of the whole world has been dependent on Sarpedon's death, which depended on Helen being carried off; and this carrying-off was necessarily linked to Hecuba's marriage, which when traced back to other events was linked to the origin of things.

If only one of these facts had been arranged differently, another universe would have resulted: but it was not possible for the present universe not to exist; therefore it was not possible for Jupiter to save his son's life, for all that he was Jupiter.

This system of necessity and fatality according to report has been invented in our time by Leibnitz, under the name of *self-sufficient reason*. It is, however, very ancient: that there is no effect without a cause, and that often the smallest cause produces the greatest effects, is not a recent idea.

Lord Bolingbroke avows that the little quarrels of Madame Marlborough and Madame Masham gave birth to his chance of making Queen Anne's private treaty with Louis XIV; this treaty led to the Peace of Utrecht; this Peace of Utrecht established Philip V on the throne of Spain. Philip V took Naples and Sicily from the house of Austria; the Spanish prince who is today King of Naples clearly owes his kingdom to my lady Masham: and he would not have had it, he would not perhaps even have been born, if the Duchess of Marlborough had been more complaisant towards the Queen of England. His existence at Naples depended on one foolishness more or less at the court of London.

Examine the position of all the peoples of the universe. They are established like this on a sequence of facts which appear to be connected with nothing and which are connected with everything. Everything is cog, pulley, cord, spring, in this vast machine.

It is likewise in the physical sphere. A wind which blows from the depths of Africa and the southern seas brings with it a portion of the African atmosphere, which falls in rain in the valleys of the Alps. These rains fertilize our lands, while our north wind in its turn sends our vapours among the Negroes. We do good to Guinea, and Guinea does good to us. The chain stretches from one end of the universe to the other.

But it seems to me that the truth of this principle is strangely abused. From it some people conclude that there is not a sole minute atom whose movement has not exerted its influence in the present arrangement of the world; that there is not a single minute accident, among either men or animals, which is not an essential link in the great chain of fate.

Let us understand each other: every effect clearly has its cause, going back from cause to cause in the abyss of eternity; but every cause has not its effect going forward to the end of the centuries. All events are produced by each other, I admit; if the past is delivered of the present, the present is delivered of the future; every being has a father, but every being does not always have children. Here it is precisely as with a genealogical tree: each house goes back, as we say, to Adam; but in the family there are many persons who have died without issue.

There is a genealogical tree of the events of this world. It is incontestable that the inhabitants of Gaul and Spain are descended from Gomer, and the Russians from Magog, his younger brother: one finds this genealogy in so many fat books! On this basis one cannot deny that the Great Turk, who is also descended from Magog, was bound to be well beaten in 1769 by Catherine II, Empress of Russia. This adventure is clearly connected with other great adventures. But that Magog spat to right or left, near Mount Caucasus, and that he made two circles in a well or three, that he slept on the left side or on the right, are matters which, in my opinion, had little influence on present affairs.

One must conclude that everything is not complete in nature, as Newton has demonstrated, and that every movement is not communicated step by step, until it makes a circuit of the world, as he has demonstrated still further. Throw into water a body of like density: You calculate easily that after a short time the movement of this body, and the movement it has communicated to the water, will be destroyed. The movement disappears and is effaced. In the same way, the movement that Magog might have produced by spitting in a well cannot influence what is passing today in Moldavia and Walachia; therefore present events are not the children of *all* past events: they have their direct lines; but a thousand little collateral lines do not serve them at all. Once more, every being has a father, but every being does not have children.

DEMOCRACY

As a rule there is no comparison between the crimes of great men, who are always ambitious, and the crimes of the people, who always want, and can only want, liberty and equality. These two sentiments, Liberty and Equality, do not lead straight to calumny, rapine, assassination, poisoning, the devastation of one's neighbours' lands, etc. But ambitious might and the mania for power plunge men into all these crimes, whatever the time, whatever the place.

Popular government is in itself, therefore, less iniquitous, less abominable than despotic power.

The great vice of democracy is certainly not tyranny and cruelty. There have been mountain-dwelling republicans who were savage and ferocious; but it was not the republican spirit that made them so, it was nature.

The real vice of a civilized republic is expressed in the Turkish fable of the dragon with many heads and the dragon with many tails. The many heads injured one another, and the many tails obeyed a single head which sought to devour everything.

Democracy seems suitable only to a very little country, and one that is happily situated. However small it may be, it will make many mistakes, because it will be composed of men. Discord will reign there as in a monastery; but there will be no St. Bartholomew, no Irish massacres, no Sicilian vespers, no Inquisition, no condemnation to the galleys for having taken some water from the sea without paying for it—unless one assumes that this republic is composed of devils in a corner of hell.

Which is better—runs the endless question—a republic or a monarchy? The dispute always resolves itself into an agreement that it is a very difficult business to govern men. The Jews had God Himself for their master, and see what has happened to them as a result: nearly always have they been oppressed and enslaved and even today they do not appear to cut a very pretty figure.

EQUALITY

It is clear that men, in the enjoyment of their natural faculties, are equal: they are equal when they perform animal functions, and when they exercise their understanding. The King of China, the Great Mogul, the Padishah of Turkey, cannot say to the least of men: "I forbid you to digest, to go to the privy, or to think." All the animals of each species are equal among themselves. Animals, by nature, have over us the advantage of independence. If a bull which is wooing a heifer is driven away with the blows of the horns by a stronger bull, it goes in search of another mistress in another field, and lives free. A cock, beaten by a cock, consoles itself in another poultry-house. It is not so with us. A little vizier exiles a bostanji to Lemnos: the vizier Azem exiles the little vizier to Tenedos: the padishah exiles the vizier Azem to Rhodes: the Janissaries put the padishah in prison, and elect another who will exile good Mussulmans as he chooses; people will still be very obliged to him if he limits his sacred authority to this small exercise.

If this world were what it seems it should be, if man could find everywhere in it an easy subsistence, and a climate suitable to his nature, it is clear that it would be impossible for one man to enslave another. If this globe were covered with wholesome fruits; if the air, which should contribute to our life, gave us no diseases and no premature deaths; if man had no need of lodging and bed other than those of the buck and the deer; then the Jenghiz Khans and the Tamerlanes would have no servants other than their children, who would be decent enough to help them in their old age.

In the natural state enjoyed by all untamed quadrupeds, birds and reptiles, man would be as happy as they. Domination would then be a chimera, an absurdity of which no one would think; for why seek servants when you have no need of their service?

If it came into the head of some individual of tyrannous mind and brawny arm to enslave a neighbour less strong than he, the thing would be impossible; the oppressed would be on the Danube before the oppressor had taken his measures on the Volga.

All men then would be necessarily equal, if they were without needs. It is the poverty connected with our species which subordinates one man to another. It is not the inequality which is the real misfortune, it is the dependence. It matters very little that So-and-so calls himself "His Highness," and So-and-so "His Holiness"; but to serve the one or the other is hard.

A big family has cultivated fruitful soil; two little families nearby have thankless and rebellious fields; the two poor families have to serve the opulent family, or slaughter it. There is no difficulty in that. But one of the two indigent families offers its arms to the rich family in exchange for bread, while the other attacks and is defeated. The subservient family is the origin of the servants and the workmen; the beaten family is the origin of the slaves.

In our unhappy world it is impossible for men living in society not to be divided into two classes, the one the rich who command, the other the poor who serve; and these two classes are subdivided into a thousand, and these thousand still have different gradations.

When the lots are drawn you come to us and say:"I am a man like you. I have two hands and two feet, as much pride as you, nay more, a mind as disordered, at least, as inconsequent, as contradictory as yours. I am a citizen of San Marino, or of Ragusa, or Vaugirard: give me my share of the land. In our known hemisphere there are about fifty thousand million *arpents* to cultivate, some passable, some sterile. We are only about a thousand million featherless bipeds in this continent; that makes fifty *arpents* apiece: be just; give me my fifty *arpents*."

"Go and take them in the land of the Kaffirs," we answer, "or the Hottentots, or the Samoyeds; come to an amicable arrangement with them; here all the shares are taken. If you want to eat, be clothed, lodged, and warmed among us, work for us as your father did; serve us or amuse us, and you will be paid; otherwise you will be obliged to ask charity, which would be too degrading to your sublime nature, and would stop your being really the equal of kings, and even of country parsons, according to the pretensions of your noble pride."

All the poor are not unhappy. The majority were born in that state, and continual work keeps them from feeling their position too keenly; but when they do feel it, then one sees wars, like that of the popular party against the senate party in Rome, like those of the peasants in Germany, England, and France. All these wars finish sooner or later with the subjection of the people, because the powerful have money, and money is master of everything in a state. I say in a state, for it is not the same between nations. The nation which makes the best use of the sword will always subjugate the nation which has more gold and less courage.

All men are born with a sufficiently violent liking for domination, wealth, and pleasure, and with a strong taste for idleness; consequently, all men covet the money, the wives, or the daughters of other men; they wish to be their master, to subject them to all their caprices, and to do nothing, or at least to do only very agreeable things. You see clearly that with these fine inclinations it is as impossible for men to be equal as it is impossible for two preachers or two professors of theology not to be jealous of each other.

The human race, such as it is, cannot subsist unless there is an infinity of useful men who possess nothing at all; for it is certain that a man who is well off will not leave his own land to come to till yours, and if you have need of a pair of shoes, it is not the Secretary to the Privy Council who will make them for you. Equality, therefore, is at once the most natural thing and the most fantastic.

As men go to excess in everything when they can, this inequality has been exaggerated. It has been maintained in many countries that it was not permissible for a citizen to leave the country where chance has caused him to be born. The sense of this law is obviously: "This land is so bad and so badly governed, that we forbid any individual to leave it, for fear that everyone will leave it." Do better: make all your subjects wish to live in your country, and foreigners wish to come to it.

All men have the right in the bottom of their hearts to think themselves entirely equal to other men. It does not follow from this that the cardinal's cook should order his master to prepare him his dinner, but the cook can say: "I am a man like my master; like him I was born crying; like me he will die with the same pangs and the same ceremonies. Both of us perform the same animal functions. If the Turks take possession of Rome, and if then I am cardinal and my master cook, I shall take him into my service." This discourse is reasonable and just, but while waiting for the Great Turk to take possession of Rome, the cook must do his duty, or else all human society is disordered.

As regards a man who is neither a cardinal's cook, nor endowed with any other employment in the state; as regards a private person who is connected with nothing, but who is vexed at being received everywhere with an air of being patronized or scorned, who sees quite clearly that many monseigneurs have no more knowledge, wit, or virtue than he, and who at times is bored at waiting in their antechambers, what should he decide to do? Why, to take himself off.

FRIENDSHIP

Friendship is the marriage of souls, and this marriage is subject to divorce. It is a tacit contract between two sensitive and virtuous persons. I say sensitive, because a monk, a recluse, can be innocent of evil and still live without knowing the meaning of friendship. I say virtuous, because the wicked have only accomplices; voluptuaries have companions in debauch, self-seekers have partners, politicians attract partisans; the generality of idle men have attachments; princes have courtiers; while virtuous men alone have friends. Cethegus was the accomplice of Catiline, and Maecenas the courtier of Octavius; but Cicero was the friend of Atticus.

LAWS

Sheep live very placidly together, and they are considered very easygoing, because we do not see the prodigious quantity of animals they devour. It is possible, of course, that they eat them innocently and without knowing it, as we do when we eat a Sassenage cheese. The republic of the sheep is a faithful representation of the golden age.

A chicken-run is obviously the most perfect monarchic state. There is no king comparable to a cock. If he marches proudly in the midst of his people, it is not out of vanity. If an enemy approaches, he does not order his subjects to go forth to kill themselves for his sake, by virtue of his infallible wisdom and plenary power; he goes to battle himself, ranges his chickens behind him and fights to the death. If he is the victor, he himself sings the *Te Deum*. In civil life there is no one so gallant, so honest, so disinterested. The cock has all the virtues. If his royal beak holds a grain of corn, or a grub, he gives it to the first lady among his subjects who presents herself. Solomon in his harem did not even approach a barnyard cock.

If it is true that bees are governed by a queen to whom all her subjects make love, then the bees enjoy a still more perfect government.

Ants are considered to be excellent democrats. Democracy is above all the other states, because in a democracy everyone is equal, and each individual works for the good of all. The republic of the beavers is superior to even that of the ants, at least if we judge by their masonry work. As for the monkeys, they resemble strolling players rather than a civilized people; and they do not appear to be united under fixed, fundamental laws, as are the species previously mentioned.

We resemble the monkeys more than any other animal, by virtue of our gift of mimicry, the frivolity of our ideas, and the inconstancy which has never permitted us to establish uniform and durable laws.

When nature formed our species, she gave us certain instincts: self-esteem for our preservation, benevolence for the preservation of others, love which is common to all species, and the inexplicable gift of combining more ideas than all the animals together. Then, having given us our portion, she said to us: "Do as you can."

No country has a good code of laws. The reason for this is evident: the laws have been made according to the time, the place, the need, etc.

When the needs have changed, the laws which have remained have become ridiculous. Thus the law which forbade the eating of pig and the drinking of wine was very reasonable in Arabia, where pig and wine are injurious. But it is absurd at Constantinople.

The law which gives the whole estate to the eldest son is very good in times of anarchy and pillage. Then the eldest son is the captain of the castle which the brigands will attack sooner or later; the younger sons will be his chief officers, the husbandmen his soldiers. The only danger is that the younger son may assassinate or poison the Salian lord, his elder brother, in order to become in his turn the master of the hovel; but these cases are rare, because nature has so combined our instincts and our passions that our horror of assassinating our elder brother is stronger than our envy of his position. But this law, suitable for the owners of dungeons in Chilperic's time, is detestable when it is a question of sharing revenues in a city.

To the shame of mankind, it is well known that the laws which govern our games are the only ones which are completely just, clear, inviolable and enforced. Why is the Indian who gave us the rules of the game of chess willingly obeyed all over the world, and why are the popes' decretals, for example, today an object of horror and scorn? The reason is that the inventor of chess arranged everything with precision for the satisfaction of the players, while the popes, in their decretals, had nothing in view but their own interest. The Indian wished to exercise men's minds equally, and give them pleasure; the popes wished to besot men's minds. Also, the essence of the game of chess has remained the same for five thousand years, it is common to all the inhabitants of the earth; and the decretals are known only at Spoletto, Orvieto, Loretto, where the shallowest lawyer secretly hates and despises them.

Full of all these reflections, I like to think that there is a natural law independent of all human conventions: the fruit of my work must belong to me; I must honour my father and my mother; I have no right over my fellow's life, and my fellow has none over mine, etc. But when I reflect that from the days of Chedorlaomer to those of Mentzel [1] everyone has gone about loyally killing and pillaging his neighbours, with a licence in his pocket, I am very sad.

I am told that there are laws among thieves, and also laws of war. I ask what are these laws of war. I learn that they mean hanging a brave officer who has stood fast in a bad post without cannon against a royal army; that they mean having a prisoner hanged, if the enemy has hanged one of yours; that they mean putting to fire and sword villages which have not made their required contributions on an appointed day, according to the orders of the gracious sovereign of the district. "Good," say I, "this is the *Spirit of the Laws.*"

It seems to me that almost everyone has received from nature enough common sense to make laws, but that no one is just enough to make good laws.

MAN, GENERAL REFLECTION ON

It requires twenty years for man to rise from the vegetable state in which he is within his mother's womb, and from the pure animal state which is the lot of his early childhood, to the state when the maturity of reason begins to appear. It has required thirty centuries to learn a little about his structure. It would need eternity to learn something about his soul. It takes an instant to kill him.

MOUNTAIN

It is a very old, universal fable that tells of the mountain which, having frightened all the country-side by its outcry that it was in labour, was

---

1. Chedorlaomer was king of the Elamites, and contemporary with Abraham. See Genesis 14.

   Mentzel was a famous chief of Austrian partisans in the war of 1741. At the head of five thousand men, he made Munich capitulate on February 13, 1742.

hissed by all present when it brought into the world a mere mouse. The people in the pit were not philosophers. Those who hissed should have admired. It was as remarkable for the mountain to give birth to a mouse, as for the mouse to give birth to a mountain. A rock which produces a rat is a very prodigious thing; and never has the world seen anything approaching this miracle. All the globes of the universe could not call a fly into existence. Where the vulgar laugh, the philosopher admires; and he laughs where the vulgar open their big, stupid eyes in astonishment.

NEW NOVELTIES

It seems that the first words of Ovid's *Metamorphoses, In nova fert animus* [the mind is carried away by novelty], are the motto of the human race. Nobody is moved by the wonderful spectacle of the sun which rises, or rather appears to rise, every day; everybody runs to see the tiniest meteor which flames for an instant in that accumulation of vapours, called the sky, which surrounds the earth.

An itinerant bookseller does not burden himself with a Virgil, with a Horace, but with a new book, even though it be detestable. He draws you aside and says to you: "Sir, do you want some books from Holland?"

From the beginning of time, women have complained that men have been unfaithful to them for the sake of novelty, for the sake of other women whose novelty was their only merit. Many ladies (it must be confessed, despite the infinite respect we have for them) have treated men as they complain they have themselves been treated; and the story of Gioconda is much older than Ariosto.

Perhaps this universal taste for novelty is one of nature's blessings. People cry to us: "Be content with what you have, desire nothing that is above your station, restrain your curiosity, curb your intellectual activity." These are excellent maxims, but if we had always followed them, we should still be eating acorns, we should still be sleeping in the open air, and we should not have had Corneille, Racine, Molière, Poussin, Lebrun, Lemoine, or Pigalle.

REASON

At the time when all France was mad over the Mississippi Bubble, and John Law was controller-general, there came to him a man who was always right, who always had reason on his side. Said he to Law, in the presence of a large crowd:

"Sir, you are the biggest madman, the biggest fool, or the biggest rogue who has yet appeared among us, and that is saying a great deal. This is how I prove it. You have imagined that a state's wealth can be increased ten-fold with paper, but as this paper can represent only the money that is representative of true wealth—the products of the land and industry—you should have begun by giving us ten times more corn, wine, cloth, canvas, etc. That is not enough, you must be sure of your market. But you make ten times as many notes as we have of silver and commodities, therefore you are ten times more extravagant, or more inept, or more of a rogue than all the comptrollers who have preceded you. Now this is how I prove the major term of my thesis."

But he had hardly started his major when he was led off to a lunatic asylum.

When he came out of the asylum, where he studied hard and strengthened his reason, he went to Rome, where he asked for a public audience with the Pope, on condition that he would not be interrupted in his harangue. And he spoke to the Pope in these terms: "Holy Father, you are an antichrist and this is how I prove it to Your Holiness. I call antichrist the man who does the contrary to what Christ did and commanded. Now Christ was poor, and you are very rich; he paid tribute, and you exact tribute; he submitted to the powers that were, and you have become a power yourself; he walked on foot, and you go to Castel Gandolfo in a sumptuous equipage; he ate whatever anyone was good enough to give him, and you want us to eat fish on Friday and Saturday, when we live far from sea and river; he forbade Simon Barjona to use a sword, and you have swords in your service, etc., etc., etc. Therefore in this sense Your Holiness is antichrist. In every other sense I hold you in great veneration, and I ask you for an indulgence *in articulo mortis* [at the moment of death]."

My man was put in the Castello St. Angelo.

When he came out of the Castello St. Angelo, he rushed to Venice, and asked to speak to the doge.

"Your Serenity," he said, "must be a very extravagant person to marry the sea every year: for, in the first place, one only marries the same person once; secondly, your marriage resembles Harlequin's which was half made, seeing that it lacked but the consent of the bride; thirdly, how do you know that other maritime powers will not one day declare you incapable of consummating the marriage?"

Having spoken, he was shut up in the Tower of St. Mark's.

When he came out of the Tower of St. Mark's, he went to Constantinople, where he had an audience with the mufti, and spoke to him in these terms: "Your religion, although it has some good points, such as worship of a supreme Being, and the rule of being just and charitable, is otherwise nothing but a rehash of Judaism and a tedious collection of fairy tales. If the archangel Gabriel had brought the leaves of the Koran to Mohammed from some planet, all Arabia would have seen Gabriel come down; but nobody saw him. Therefore Mohammed was a brazen impostor who deceived imbeciles."

Hardly had he pronounced these words than he was run through with a sword. Nevertheless he had always been right, and had always had reason on his side.

SELF-LOVE

Nicole in his *Essais de Morale*—written on top of two or three thousand other volumes of ethics—says that "by means of the wheels and gibbets which people erect in common, the tyrannous thoughts and designs of each individual's self-love are repressed."

I shall not inquire whether or not people have gibbets in common, as they have meadows and woods in common, and a common purse, or if one represses ideas with wheels; but it seems very strange to me that Nicole should take highway robbery and assassination for self-love. One should distinguish shades of difference a little better. The man who said that Nero had his mother assassinated through self-love, and that Cartouche had an excess of self-love, would not be expressing himself very correctly. Self-love is not wickedness, it is a sentiment that is natural to all men; it is much nearer vanity than crime.

A beggar in the suburbs of Madrid was nobly begging charity. A passer-by said to him: "Are you not ashamed to practice this infamous calling when you are able to work?"

"Sir," answered the beggar, "I ask for money, not advice." And he turned on his heel with full Castilian dignity.

This gentleman was a proud beggar, his vanity was wounded by a trifle. He asked charity out of love for himself, and could not tolerate the reprimand out of further love for himself.

A missionary traveling in India met a fakir laden with chains, naked as a monkey, lying on his stomach, who was having himself whipped for the sins of his compatriots, the Indians, who gave him a few farthings.

"What self-denial!" said one of the spectators.

"Self-denial!" answered the fakir. "I have myself flogged in this world in order to give this flogging back to you in the next world, when you will be horses and I a horseman."

Those who have said that love of ourselves is the basis of all our opinions and all our actions, have therefore been quite right in India, Spain, and all the habitable world: and as one does not write to prove to men that they have faces, it is not necessary to prove to them that they have self-love. Self-love is our instrument of preservation; it resembles the instrument which perpetuates the species. It is necessary, it is dear to us, it gives us pleasure, and it has to be hidden.

SOCRATES

One day, two citizens of Athens, returning from the temple of Mercury, perceived Socrates in the public square. One said to the other: "Is not that the rascal who says that one can be virtuous without going every day to offer up sheep and geese?" "Yes," said the other, "that is the sage who has no religion; that is the atheist who says there is only one God." Socrates approached them with his simple air, his daemon, and his irony, which Madame Dacier has so highly extolled. "My friends," said he to them, "one word, if you please: a man who prays to God, who adores Him, who seeks to resemble Him as much as human weakness can do, and who does all the good which lies in his power, what would you call him?" "A very religious soul," said they. "Very well; we may therefore adore the Supreme Being, and have a great deal of religion?" "Granted," said the two Athenians. "But do you believe," pursued Socrates, "that when the Divine Architect of the world arranged all the spheres which revolve above our heads, when He gave motion and life to so many different beings, He made use of the arm of Hercules, the lyre of Apollo, or the flute of Pan?" "It is not probable," said they. "But if it is not probable that He called in the aid of others to construct that which we see, it is not credible that He preserves it through others rather than through Himself. If Neptune were the absolute master of the sea, Juno of the air, Aeolus of the winds, Ceres of harvests—and if one desired a calm, when another wanted wind and rain—you see clearly, that the order of nature could not exist as it is. You will confess, that all depends upon Him who has made all. You attribute four white horses to the sun, and four black ones to the moon; but is it not more likely, that day and night are the effect of the motion given to the stars by their Master, than that they were produced by eight horses?" The two citizens looked at him, but answered nothing. In short, Socrates concluded by proving to them that they might have harvests without giving money to the priests of Ceres; go to the chase without offering little silver statues to the temple of Diana; that Pomona gave not fruits; that Neptune gave not horses; and that they should thank the Sovereign who had made all.

His discourse was most exactly logical. Xenophon, his disciple, a man who knew the world, and who afterwards sacrificed to the wind, during the retreat of the ten thousand, took Socrates by the sleeve, and said to him: "Your discourse is admirable; you have spoken better than an oracle; and you are lost. One of these good people to whom you speak is a butcher, who sells sheep and geese for sacrifices; and the other a goldsmith, who profits by making little gods of silver and brass for women. They will accuse you of being a blasphemer, who would diminish their trade. They will depose against you to Melitus and Anitus, your enemies, who have resolved upon your ruin. Have a care of hemlock; your familiar spirit should have warned you not to say to a butcher and a goldsmith what you should say only to Plato and Xenophon."

Some time after, the enemies of Socrates caused him to be condemned by the council of five hundred. He had two hundred and twenty voices in his favour, by which it may be presumed that there were two hundred and twenty philosophers in this tribunal; but it shows that, in all companies, the number of philosophers is always the minority.

Socrates therefore drank hemlock, for having spoken in favour of the unity of God; and the Athenians afterward consecrated a temple to Socrates—to him who disputed against all temples dedicated to inferior beings.

TRUTH

"Pilate therefore said unto him, Art thou a king then? Jesus answered, Thou sayest that I am a king. To this end was I born, and for this cause came I into the world, that I should bear witness unto the truth. Everyone that is of the truth heareth my voice.

"Pilate saith unto Him, What is truth? And when he had said this he went out, etc."

It is a sad thing for the human race that Pilate went out without waiting for the answer; we should know what truth is. Pilate had very little curiosity. The accused led before him says he is king, that he was born to be king; and Pilate does not inquire how these things can be. He is supreme judge in Caesar's name, he has power of life and death; his duty is to probe the sense of these words. He ought to say: "Tell me what you understand by being king. How were you born to be king and to bear witness to the truth? It is maintained that it is hard for truth to reach the ears of kings. I am a judge, and I have always had great trouble in finding it. While your enemies are howling against you outside, give me some information on the point; you will be doing me the greatest service that has ever been done a judge; and I much prefer to learn to recognize truth, than to accede to the Jews' clamourous demand to have you hanged."

Of course, we cannot dare to imagine what the author of all truth would have been able to reply to Pilate.

Would he have said: "Truth is an abstract word which most men use indifferently, in their books and judgments, for error and falsehood?" This definition would have been marvelously appropriate to all makers of systems. Similarly the word "wisdom" is often taken for folly, and "wit" for nonsense.

Humanly speaking, let us define truth, while waiting for a better definition, as *a statement of the facts as they are.*

I suppose that if one had given only six months to teaching Pilate the truths of logic, he would assuredly have made this conclusive syllogism: One must not take away a man's life for simply good morality. Well, the accused man has, even on the showing of his enemies, often preached excellent morality. Therefore he should not be punished with death.

He might have drawn this further argument. My duty is to disperse the riotous assemblage of a seditious people who demand a man's death, unreasonably and without legal form. Very well. This is the exact position of the Jews in this instance; therefore I must drive them away and break up their meeting.

We suppose that Pilate knew arithmetic; hence we will not speak of those forms of truth.

As regards mathematical truths, I think it would have taken at least three years before he could have learned higher geometry. The truths of physics combined with those of geometry would have demanded more than four years. We spend six, ordinarily, in studying theology; but I ask twelve for Pilate, seeing that he was pagan; on the ground that six years would not have been too much for eradicating all his old errors, and six years more would be required to fit him to receive a doctor's hood.

If Pilate had had a well-balanced mind, I should have asked only two years to teach him metaphysical truth; and as metaphysical truth is necessarily allied to moral truth, I flatter myself that in less than nine years he would have become a real scholar and a perfectly virtuous man.

I should then have said to Pilate: Historical truths are merely probabilities. If you fought at the battle of Philippi, that is for you a truth which you know by intuition, by perception. But for us who dwell near the Syrian desert, it is merely a very probable thing, which we know by hearsay. How much hearsay is necessary to form a conviction equal to that of a man who, having seen the thing, can flatter himself that he has a sort of certainty?

He who has heard the thing told by twelve thousand eyewitnesses, has only twelve thousand probabilities, equal to one strong probability, which is not equal to certainty. If you have the thing from only one of these witnesses, you know nothing; you should be skeptical. If the witness is dead, you should be still more skeptical, for you cannot enlighten yourself. If from several witnesses who are dead, you are in the same plight. If from those to whom the witnesses have spoken, your skepticism should increase still more.

From generation to generation skepticism increases, and probability diminishes; and soon probability is reduced to zero.

TYRANNY

One gives the name of tyrant to the sovereign who knows no laws but those of his caprice, who takes his subjects' property, and then mobilizes them to take the property of his neighbours. There are none of these tyrants in Europe.

One distinguishes between the tyranny of one man and that of many. The tyranny of one man is comparable to that of a body which has invaded the rights of other bodies, and which exercises despotism under cover of laws which it has itself corrupted. Nor are there any tyrants of this sort in Europe.

Under which tyranny would you like to live? Under neither, but if I had to choose, I should detest the tyranny of one man less than that of many. A despot always has his good moments; an assembly of despots never. If a tyrant does me an injustice, I can disarm him through his mistress, his confessor, or his page; but a company of solemn tyrants is inaccessible to all seductions. When it is not unjust, it is at the least harsh, and never does it bestow favours.

If I have only one despot, I am quit of him by drawing myself up against a wall when I see him pass, or by bowing low, or by striking the ground with my forehead, according to the custom of the country. But if there is a company of a hundred despots, I may have to repeat this ceremony a hundred times a day, which in the long run can be very annoying if one's hams are not supple. If I have a farm in the neighbour-hood of one of our nobles, I am wiped out. If I plead against a relation of the relations of one of our noblemen, I am ruined. What is to be done? I fear that in this world one must be either hammer or anvil; for it is indeed a lucky man who escapes these alternatives!

The foregoing consists of selected articles from Voltaire's PHILOSOPHICAL DICTIONARY, *translated by H. I. Woolf.*

John Stuart Mill [1]

1806–1873

J ohn Stuart Mill worked hard for reform through political action. Yet he was convinced that "no great improvements in the lot of mankind are possible until a great change takes place in the fundamental constitution of their modes of thought." He lamented the lack of an accepted standard of the right and good in human action and the consequent want of certitude in moral and political matters. He knew but rejected the long tradition that Nature provides such a standard. In antiquity both Stoics and Epicureans, the most popular schools of philosophy, had proposed "Follow Nature" as their motto for moral action. In the doctrine of natural law, as found for example in Thomas Aquinas,[2] the concept of nature provides the basis for a highly elaborated system of morality and justice.

Mill presents his reasons for rejecting these traditions in the following essay, entitled *Nature*. Nature is one of the great and key ideas of human thought; it constitutes Chapter 60 in *The Great Ideas*.[3] From the wide range of meanings that the term has acquired, Mill concentrates upon two: "It either denotes the entire system of things . . . or it denotes things as they would be, apart from human intervention." In neither sense, Mill argues, does nature provide a standard for human action.

He claims that to follow nature is poor advice in any sense other than that the study and observation of nature is necessary as a prelude to intelligent action. He flatly denies that nature unmodified by man can offer anything that man should imitate. For the injunction "Follow Nature" he proposes to substitute "Control and Amend

---

[1] For a biography of John Stuart Mill, see Vol. 6, pp. 1–3, in this set.
[2] See *Great Books of the Western World*, Vol. 20, pp. 220–226.
[3] See *Great Books of the Western World*, Vol. 3, pp. 225–250.

Nature." In this, he sets himself against Thoreau and Wordsworth, who find in nature their greatest teacher; and also against Rousseau and Freud, who claim that the repression of man's natural inclinations is perhaps the greatest source of discontent.

The essay on nature is one of the *Three Essays on Religion,* published posthumously in 1874. It has important bearings on questions of religion, besides its rejection of natural law, which for Aquinas is a participation in the eternal law of God. It also questions whether the order and design of nature can afford evidence for the existence of a just and benevolent creator. Mill touches upon the problem of evil. This, as is known from Augustine's story of his conversion,[4] is often a stumbling block in man's search for God.

---

[4] See his *Confessions* in *Great Books of the Western World,* Vol. 18, pp. 43–52.

Nature

Nature, natural, and the group of words derived from them, or allied to them in etymology, have at all times filled a great place in the thoughts and taken a strong hold on the feelings of mankind. That they should have done so is not surprising when we consider what the words, in their primitive and most obvious signification, represent; but it is unfortunate that a set of terms which play so great a part in moral and metaphysical speculation should have acquired many meanings different from the primary one, yet sufficiently allied to it to admit of confusion. The words have thus become entangled in so many foreign associations, mostly of a very powerful and tenacious character, that they have come to excite, and to be the symbols of, feelings which their original meaning will by no means justify; and which have made them one of the most copious sources of false taste, false philosophy, false morality, and even bad law.

The most important application of the Socratic *elenchus*, as exhibited and improved by Plato, consists in dissecting large abstractions of this description, fixing down to a precise definition the meaning which as popularly used they merely shadow forth, and questioning and testing the common maxims and opinions in which they bear a part. It is to be regretted that among the instructive specimens of this kind of investigation which Plato has left, and to which subsequent times have been so much indebted for whatever intellectual clearness they have attained, he has not enriched posterity with a dialogue *Of Nature*. If the idea denoted by the word had been subjected to his searching analysis, and the popular commonplaces in which it figures had been submitted to the ordeal of his powerful dialectics, his successors probably would not have rushed, as they speedily did, into modes of thinking and reasoning of which the fallacious use of that word formed the corner-stone—a kind of fallacy from which he was himself singularly free.

According to the Platonic method, which is still the best type of such investigations, the first thing to be done with so vague a term is to ascertain precisely what it means. It is also a rule of the same method, that the meaning of an abstraction is best sought for in the concrete—of a universal in the particular. Adopting this course with the word nature, the first question must be, what is meant by the "nature" of a particular object—as of fire, of water, or of some individual plant or animal? Evidently the ensemble or aggregate of its powers or properties: the modes in which it acts on other things (counting among those things the senses of the observer) and the modes in which other things act upon it; to which, in the case of a sentient being, must be added its own capacities of feeling or being conscious. The nature of the thing means all this, means its entire capacity of exhibiting phenomena. And since the phenomena which a thing exhibits, however much they vary in different circumstances, are always the same in the same circumstances, they admit of being described in general forms of words, which are called the *laws* of the thing's nature. Thus it is a law of the nature of water that, under the mean pressure of the atmosphere at the level of the sea, it boils at 212° Fahrenheit.

As the nature of any given thing is the aggregate of its powers and properties, so nature in the abstract is the aggregate of the powers and properties of all things. Nature means the sum of all phenomena together with the causes which produce them, including not only all that happens but all that is capable of happening, the unused capabilities of causes being as much a part of the idea of nature as those which take effect. Since all phenomena which have been sufficiently examined are found to take place with regularity, each having certain fixed conditions, positive and negative, on the occurrence of which it invariably happens, mankind have been able to ascertain, either by direct observation or by reasoning processes grounded on it, the conditions of the occurrence of many phenomena; and the progress of science mainly consists in ascertaining those conditions. When discovered, they can be expressed in general propositions, which are called laws of the particular phenomenon and also, more generally, laws of nature. Thus the truth that all material objects tend toward one another with a force directly as their masses and inversely as the square of their distance is a law of nature. The proposition that air and food are necessary to animal life, if it be, as we have good reason to believe, true without exception, is also a law of nature, though the phenomenon of which it is the law is special and not, like gravitation, universal.

Nature, then, in this its simplest acceptation, is a collective name for all facts, actual and possible, or (to speak more accurately) a name for the mode, partly known to us and partly unknown, in which all things take place. For the word suggests not so much the multitudinous detail of the phenomena as the conception which might be formed of their manner of existence as a mental whole by a mind possessing a complete knowledge of them, to which conception it is the aim of science to raise itself by successive steps of generalization from experience.

Such, then, is a correct definition of the word nature. But this definition corresponds only to one of the senses of that ambiguous term. It is evidently inapplicable to some of the modes in which the word is familiarly employed. For example, it entirely conflicts with the common form of speech by which nature is opposed to art, and natural to artificial. For in the sense of the word nature which has just been defined, and which is the true scientific sense, art is as much nature as anything else; and everything which is artificial is natural—art has no independent powers of its own: art is but the employment of the powers of nature for an end. Phenomena produced by human agency, no less than those which as far as we are concerned are spontaneous, depend on the properties of the elementary forces, or of the elementary substances and their compounds. The united powers of the whole human race could not create a new property of matter in general, or of any one of its species. We can only take advantage for our purposes of the properties which we find. A ship floats by the same laws of specific gravity and equilibrium as a tree uprooted by the wind and blown into the water. The corn which men raise for food grows and produces its grain by the same laws of vegetation by which the wild rose and the mountain strawberry bring forth their flowers and fruit. A house stands and holds together by the natural properties, the weight and cohesion, of the materials which compose it. A steam-engine works by the natural expansive force of steam, exerting a pressure upon one part of a system of arrangements, which pressure, by the mechanical properties of the lever, is transferred from that to another part where it raises the weight or removes the obstacle brought into connection with it. In these and all other artificial operations the office of man is, as has often been remarked, a very limited one; it consists in moving things into certain places. We move objects, and by doing this bring some things into contact which were separate, or separate others which were in contact; and, by this simple change of place, natural forces previously dormant are called into action and produce the desired effect. Even the volition which designs, the intelligence which contrives, and the muscular force which executes these movements are themselves powers of nature.

It thus appears that we must recognize at least two principal meanings

in the word nature. In one sense, it means all the powers existing in either
the outer or the inner world and everything which takes place by means of
those powers. In another sense it means not everything which happens
but only what takes place without the agency, or without the voluntary
and intentional agency, of man. This distinction is far from exhausting
the ambiguities of the word; but it is the key to most of those on which
important consequences depend.

Such, then, being the two principal senses of the word nature, in which
of these is it taken, or is it taken in either, when the word and its
derivatives are used to convey ideas of commendation, approval, and
even moral obligation?

It has conveyed such ideas in all ages. *Naturam sequi* [Follow nature]
was the fundamental principle of morals in many of the most admired
schools of philosophy. Among the ancients, especially in the declining
period of ancient intellect and thought, it was the test to which all ethical
doctrines were brought. The Stoics and the Epicureans, however irrecon-
cilable in the rest of their systems, agreed in holding themselves bound to
prove that their respective maxims of conduct were the dictates of nature.
Under their influence the Roman jurists, when attempting to systematize
jurisprudence, placed in the front of their exposition a certain *jus naturae,
quod natura*, as Justinian declares in the *Institutes, omnia animalia
docuit* [what nature taught to all animals]; and as the modern systematic writers, not only on law but on moral philosophy, have generally taken the Roman jurists for their models, treatises on the so-called law
of nature have abounded; and references to this law as a supreme rule and
ultimate standard have pervaded literature. The writers on international
law have done more than any others to give currency to this style of
ethical speculation, inasmuch as, having no positive law to write about
and yet being anxious to invest the most approved opinions respecting
international morality with as much as they could of the authority of law,
they endeavored to find such an authority in nature's imaginary code. The
Christian theology during the period of its greatest ascendancy opposed
some, though not a complete, hindrance to the modes of thought which
erected nature into the criterion of morals, inasmuch as, according to the
creed of most denominations of Christians (though assuredly not
of Christ), a man is by nature wicked. But this very doctrine, by the
reaction which it provoked, has made the deistical moralists almost unanimous in proclaiming the divinity of nature and setting up its fancied
dictates as an authoritative rule of action. A reference to that supposed
standard is the predominant ingredient in the vein of thought and feeling

which was opened by Rousseau, and which has infiltrated itself most widely into the modern mind, not excepting that portion of it which calls itself Christian. The doctrines of Christianity have in every age been largely accommodated to the philosophy which happened to be prevalent, and the Christianity of our day has borrowed a considerable part of its colour and flavour from sentimental deism. At the present time it cannot be said that nature, or any other standard, is applied as it was wont to be to deduce rules of action with juridical precision, and with an attempt to make its application coextensive with all human agency. The people of this generation do not commonly apply principles with any such studious exactness, nor own such binding allegiance to any standard, but live in a kind of confusion of many standards—a condition not propitious to the formation of steady moral convictions but convenient enough to those whose moral opinions sit lightly on them, since it gives them a much wider range of arguments for defending the doctrine of the moment. But though perhaps no one could now be found who, like the institutional writers of former times, adopts the so-called law of nature as the foundation of ethics, and endeavours consistently to reason from it, the word and its cognates must still be counted among those which carry great weight in moral argumentation. That any mode of thinking, feeling, or acting is "according to nature" is usually accepted as a strong argument for its goodness. If it can be said with any plausibility that "nature enjoins" anything, the propriety of obeying the injunction is by most people considered to be made out; and conversely, the imputation of being contrary to nature is thought to bar the door against any pretension on the part of the thing so designated to be tolerated or excused, and the word "unnatural" has not ceased to be one of the most vituperative epithets in the language. Those who deal in these expressions may avoid making themselves responsible for any fundamental theorem respecting the standard of moral obligation, but they do not the less imply such a theorem, and one which must be the same in substance with that on which the more logical thinkers of a more laborious age grounded their systematic treatises on natural law.

Is it necessary to recognize in these forms of speech another distinct meaning of the word nature? Or can they be connected, by any rational bond of union, with either of the two meanings already treated of? At first it may seem that we have no option but to admit another ambiguity in the term. All inquiries are either into what is, or into what ought to be; science and history belonging to the first division, art, morals, and politics to the second. But the two senses of the word nature first pointed out agree in referring only to what is. In the first meaning, nature is a collective name for everything which is. In the second, it is a name for everything which is of itself, without voluntary human intervention. But the employment of the word nature as a term of ethics seems to disclose a third meaning, in which nature does not stand for what is but for what ought to be, or for the rule or standard of what ought to be. A little consideration, however, will show that this is not a case of ambiguity; there is not here a third sense of the word. Those who set up nature as a standard of action do not intend a merely verbal proposition; they do not mean that the standard, whatever it be, should be *called* nature; they think they are giving some information as to what the standard of action really is. Those who say that we ought to act according to nature do not mean the mere identical proposition that we ought to do what we ought to do. They think that the word nature affords some external criterion of what we should do; and if they lay down as a rule for what ought to be a word which in its proper signification denotes what is, they do so because they have a notion, either clearly or confusedly, that what is constitutes the rule and standard of what ought to be.

The examination of this notion is the object of the present essay. It is proposed to inquire into the truth of the doctrines which make nature a test of right and wrong, good and evil, or which in any mode or degree attach merit or approval to following, imitating, or obeying nature. To this inquiry the foregoing discussion respecting the meaning of terms was an indispensable introduction. Language is, as it were, the atmosphere of philosophical investigation, which must be made transparent before anything can be seen through it in the true figure and position. In the present case it is necessary to guard against a further ambiguity, which, though abundantly obvious, has sometimes misled even sagacious minds, and of which it is well to take distinct note before proceeding further. No word is more commonly associated with the word nature than law; and this last word has distinctly two meanings, in one of which it denotes some definite portion of what is, in the other, of what ought to be. We speak of the law of gravitation, the three laws of motion, the law of definite proportions in chemical combination, the vital laws of organized beings. All these are portions of what is. We also speak of the criminal law, the civil law, the law of honour, the law of veracity, the law of justice—all of which are portions of what ought to be, or of somebody's suppositions, feelings, or commands respecting what ought to be. The first kind of laws, such as the laws of motion and of gravitation, are neither more nor less than the observed uniformities in the occurrence of phenomena: partly uniformities of antecedence and sequence, partly of concomitance. These are what in science, and even in ordinary parlance, are meant by laws of nature. Laws in the other sense are the laws of the land, the law of nations, or moral laws; among which, as already noticed, is dragged in by jurists and publicists something which they think proper to call the law of nature. Of the liability of these two meanings of the word to be confounded there can be no better example than the first chapter of Montesquieu, where he remarks that the material world has its laws, the inferior animals have their laws, and man has his laws; and calls attention to the much greater strictness with which the first two sets of laws are observed than the last; as if it were an inconsistency and a paradox that things always are what they are, but men not always what they ought to be. A similar confusion of ideas pervades the writings of Mr. George Combe, from whence it has overflowed into a large region of popular literature, and we are now continually reading injunctions to obey the physical laws of the universe as being obligatory in the same sense and manner as the moral. The conception which the ethical use of the word nature implies, of a close relation if not absolute identity between what is and what ought to be, certainly derives part of its hold on the mind from the custom of designating what is by the expression "laws of nature," while the same word law is also used, and even more familiarly and emphatically, to express what ought to be.

When it is asserted or implied that nature, or the laws of nature, should be conformed to, is the nature which is meant nature in the first sense of the term, meaning all which is—the powers and properties of all things? But in this signification there is no need of a recommendation to act according to nature, since it is what nobody can possibly help doing, and equally whether he acts well or ill. There is no mode of acting which is not conformable to nature in this sense of the term, and all modes of acting are so in exactly the same degree. Every action is the exertion of some natural power, and its effects of all sorts are so many phenomena of nature, produced by the powers and properties of some of the objects of nature, in exact obedience to some law or laws of nature. When I voluntarily use my organs to take in food, the act and its consequences take place according to laws of nature; if instead of food I swallow poison, the case is exactly the same. To bid people conform to the laws of nature when they have no power but what the laws of nature give them, when it is a physical impossibility for them to do the smallest thing otherwise than through some law of nature, is an absurdity. The thing they need to be told is what particular law of nature they should make use of in a particular case. When, for example, a person is crossing a river by a narrow bridge to which there is no parapet, he will do well to regulate his proceedings by the laws of equilibrium in moving bodies, instead of conforming only to the law of gravitation and falling into the river.

Yet idle as it is to exhort people to do what they cannot avoid doing, and absurd as it is to prescribe as a rule of right conduct what agrees exactly as well with wrong, nevertheless a rational rule of conduct *may* be constructed out of the relation which it ought to bear to the laws of nature in this widest acceptation of the term. Man necessarily obeys the laws of nature, or, in other words, the properties of things, but he does not necessarily *guide* himself by them. Though all conduct is in conformity to laws of nature, all conduct is not grounded on knowledge of them and intelligently directed to the attainment of purposes by means of them. Though we cannot emancipate ourselves from the laws of nature as a whole, we can escape from any particular law of nature if we are able to withdraw ourselves from the circumstances in which it acts. Though we can do nothing except through laws of nature, we can use one law to counteract another. According to Bacon's maxim, we can obey nature in such a manner as to command it. Every alteration of circumstances alters more or less the laws of nature under which we act; and by every choice which we make, either of ends or of means, we place ourselves to a greater or less extent under one set of laws of nature instead of another. If, therefore, the useless precept to follow nature were changed into a precept to study nature—to know and take heed of the properties of the things we have to deal with, so far as these properties are capable of forwarding or obstructing any given purpose—we should have arrived at the first principle of all intelligent action, or rather at the definition of intelligent action itself. And a confused notion of this true principle is, I doubt not, in the minds of many of those who set up the unmeaning doctrine which superficially resembles it. They perceive that the essential difference between wise and foolish conduct consists in attending, or not attending, to the particular laws of nature on which some important result depends. And they think that a person who attends to a law of nature in order to shape his conduct by it may be said to obey it, while a person who practically disregards it and acts as if no such law existed may be said to disobey it; the circumstance being overlooked that what is thus called disobedience to a law of nature is obedience to some other or perhaps to the very law itself. For example, a person who goes into a powder-magazine either not knowing, or carelessly omitting to think of, the explosive force of gunpowder is likely to do some act which will cause him to be blown to atoms in obedience to the very law which he has disregarded.

But however much of its authority the *naturam sequi* doctrine may owe to its being confounded with the rational precept *naturam observare* [to observe nature], its favourers and promoters unquestionably intend much more by it than that precept. To acquire knowledge of the properties of things and make use of the knowledge for guidance is a rule of prudence for the adaptation of means to ends, for giving effect to our wishes and intentions, whatever they may be. But the maxim of obedience to nature, or conformity to nature, is held up not as a simply prudential but as an ethical maxim, and by those who talk of *jus naturae*, even as a law, fit to be administered by tribunals and enforced by sanctions. Right action must mean something more and other than merely intelligent action; yet no precept beyond this last can be connected with the word nature in the wider and more philosophical of its acceptations. We must try it, therefore, in the other sense, that in which nature stands distinguished from art and denotes, not the whole course of the phenomena which come under our observation, but only their spontaneous course.

Let us then consider whether we can attach any meaning to the supposed practical maxim of following nature in this second sense of the word, in which nature stands for that which takes place without human intervention. In nature as thus understood, is the spontaneous course of things when left to themselves the rule to be followed in endeavouring to adapt things to our use? But it is evident at once that the maxim, taken in this sense, is not merely, as it is in the other sense, superfluous and unmeaning, but palpably absurd and self-contradictory. For while human action cannot help conforming to nature in the one meaning of the term, the very aim and object of action is to alter and improve nature in the other meaning. If the natural course of things were perfectly right and satisfactory, to act at all would be a gratuitous meddling, which, as it could not make things better, must make them worse. Or if action at all could be justified, it would only be when in direct obedience to instincts, since these might perhaps be accounted part of the spontaneous order of nature; but to do anything with forethought and purpose would be a violation of that perfect order. If the artificial is not better than the natural, to what end are all the arts of life? To dig, to plough, to build, to wear clothes are direct infringements of the injunction to follow nature.

Accordingly it would be said by everyone, even of those most under the influence of the feelings which prompt the injunction, that to apply it to such cases as those just spoken of would be to push it too far. Everybody professes to approve and admire many great triumphs of art over nature: the junction by bridges of shores which Nature had made separate, the draining of Nature's marshes, the excavation of her wells, the dragging to light of what she has buried at immense depths in the earth; the turning away of her thunderbolts by lightning-rods, of her inundations by embankments, of her ocean by breakwaters. But to commend these and similar feats is to acknowledge that the ways of Nature are to be conquered, not obeyed; that her powers are often toward man in the position of enemies, from whom he must wrest, by force and ingenuity, what little he can for his own use, and deserves to be applauded when that little is rather more than might be expected from his physical weakness in comparison to those gigantic powers. All praise of civilization, or art, or contrivance is so much dispraise of nature, an admission of imperfection which it is man's business and merit to be always endeavouring to correct or mitigate.

The consciousness that whatever man does to improve his condition is in so much a censure and a thwarting of the spontaneous order of nature has in all ages caused new and unprecedented attempts at improvement to be generally at first under a shade of religious suspicion as being in any case uncomplimentary, and very probably offensive, to the powerful beings (or, when polytheism gave place to monotheism, to the all-powerful Being) supposed to govern the various phenomena of the universe, and of whose will the course of nature was conceived to be the expression. Any attempt to mould natural phenomena to the convenience of mankind might easily appear an interference with the government of those superior beings; and though life could not have been maintained, much less made pleasant, without perpetual interferences of the kind, each new one was doubtless made with fear and trembling until experience had shown that it could be ventured on without drawing down the vengeance of the gods. The sagacity of priests showed them a way to reconcile the impunity of particular infringements with the maintenance of the general dread of encroaching on the divine administration. This was effected by representing each of the principal human inventions as the gift and favour of some god. The old religions also afforded many resources for consulting the gods and obtaining their express permission for what would otherwise have appeared a breach of their prerogative. When oracles had ceased, any religion which recognized a revelation afforded expedients for the same purpose. The Catholic religion had the resource of an infallible Church, authorized to declare what exertions of human spontaneity were permitted or forbidden; and in default of this the case was always open to argument from the Bible whether any particular practice had expressly or by implication been sanctioned. The notion remained that this liberty to control nature was conceded to man only by special indulgence, and as far as required by his necessities; and there was always a tendency, though a diminishing one, to regard any attempt to exercise power over nature, beyond a certain degree and a certain admitted range, as an impious effort to usurp divine power and dare more than was permitted to man. The lines of Horace in which the familiar arts of shipbuilding and navigation are reprobated as *vetitum nefas* [impious and forbidden] indicate even in that sceptical age a still unexhausted vein of the old sentiment. The intensity of the corresponding feeling in the Middle Ages is not a precise parallel, on account of the superstition about dealing with evil spirits with which it was complicated; but the imputation of prying into the secrets of the Almighty long remained a powerful weapon of attack against unpopular inquirers into nature; and the charge of presumptuously attempting to defeat the designs of Providence still retains enough of its original force to be thrown in as a make-weight along with other objections when there is a desire to find fault with any new exertion of human forethought and contrivance. No one, indeed, asserts it to be the intention of the Creator that the spontaneous order of the creation should not be altered, or even that it should not be altered in any new way. But there still exists a vague notion that, though it is very proper to control this or the other natural phenomenon, the general scheme of nature is a model for us to imitate; that with more or less liberty in details we should on the whole be guided by the spirit and general conception of nature's own ways: that they are God's work, and as such perfect; that man cannot rival their unapproachable excellence, and can best show his skill and piety by attempting, in however imperfect a way, to reproduce their likeness; and that if not the whole, yet some particular parts of the spontaneous order of nature, selected according to the speaker's predilections, are in a peculiar sense manifestations of the Creator's will, a sort of finger-posts pointing out the direction which things in general, and therefore our voluntary actions, are intended to take. Feelings of this sort, though repressed on ordinary occasions by the contrary current of life, are ready to break out whenever custom is silent and the native promptings of the mind have nothing opposed to them but reason; and appeals are continually made to them by rhetoricians, with the effect, if not of convincing opponents, at least of making those who already hold the opinion which the rhetorician desires to recommend better satisfied with it. For in the present day it probably seldom happens that any one is persuaded to approve any course of action because it appears to him to bear an analogy to the divine government of the world, though the argument tells on him with great force, and is felt by him to be a great support, in behalf of anything which he is already inclined to approve.

If this notion of imitating the ways of Providence as manifested in nature is seldom expressed plainly and downrightly as a maxim of general application, it also is seldom directly contradicted. Those who find it on their path prefer to turn the obstacle rather than to attack it, being often themselves not free from the feeling, and in my case afraid of incurring the charge of impiety by saying anything which might be held to disparage the works of the Creator's power. They therefore, for the most part, rather endeavour to show that they have as much right to the religious argument as their opponents, and that, if the course they recommend seems to conflict with some part of the ways of Providence, there is some other part with which it agrees better than what is contended for on the other side. In this mode of dealing with the great *a priori* fallacies, the progress of improvement clears away particular errors while the causes of errors are still left standing and very little weakened by each conflict; yet by a long series of such partial victories precedents are accumulated to which an appeal may be made against these powerful prepossessions, and which afford a growing hope that the misplaced feeling, after having so often learned to recede, may some day be compelled to an unconditional surrender. For however offensive the proposition may appear to many religious persons, they should be willing to look in the face the undeniable fact that the order of nature, in so far as unmodified by man, is such as no Being whose attributes are justice and benevolence would have made with the intention that his rational creatures should follow it as an example. If made wholly by such a Being, and not partly by beings of very different qualities, it could only be as a designedly imperfect work which man, in his limited sphere, is to exercise justice and benevolence in amending. The best persons have always held it to be the essence of religion that the paramount duty of man upon earth is to amend himself; but all except monkish quietists have annexed to this in their inmost minds (though seldom willing to enunciate the obligation with the same clearness) the additional religious duty of amending the world, and not solely the human part of it but the material, the order of physical nature.

In considering this subject it is necessary to divest ourselves of certain preconceptions which may justly be called natural prejudices, being grounded on feelings which, in themselves natural and inevitable, intrude into matters with which they ought to have no concern. One of these feelings is the astonishment, rising into awe, which is inspired (even independently of all religious sentiment) by any of the greater natural phenomena. A hurricane, a mountain precipice, the desert, the ocean either agitated or at rest, the solar system and the great cosmic forces which hold it together, the boundless firmament and to an educated mind any single star excite feelings which make all human enterprises and powers appear so insignificant that to a mind thus occupied it seems insufferable presumption in so puny a creature as man to look critically on things so far above him, or dare to measure himself against the grandeur of the universe. But a little interrogation of our own consciousness will suffice to convince us that what makes these phenomena so impressive is simply their vastness. The enormous extension in space and time, or the enormous power they exemplify, constitutes their sublimity—a feeling in all cases more allied to terror than to any moral emotion. And though the vast scale of these phenomena may well excite wonder, and sets at defiance all idea of rivalry, the feeling it inspires is of a totally different character from admiration of excellence. Those in whom awe produces admiration may be aesthetically developed, but they are morally uncultivated. It is one of the endowments of the imaginative part of our mental nature that conceptions of greatness and power, vividly realized, produce a feeling which, though in its higher degrees closely bordering on pain, we prefer to most of what are accounted pleasures. But we are equally capable of experiencing this feeling toward maleficent power; and we never experience it so strongly toward most of the powers of the universe as when we have most present to our consciousness a vivid sense of their capacity of inflicting evil. Because these natural powers have what we cannot imitate, enormous might, and overawe us by that one attribute, it would be a great error to infer that their other attributes are such as we ought to emulate, or that we should be justified in using our small powers after the example which Nature sets us with her vast forces.

For how stands the fact? That next to the greatness of these cosmic forces, the quality which most forcibly strikes everyone who does not avert his eyes from it is their perfect and absolute recklessness. They go straight to their end, without regarding what or whom they crush on the road. Optimists, in their attempts to prove that "whatever is is right," are obliged to maintain, not that Nature ever turns one step from her path to avoid trampling us into destruction, but that it would be very unreasonable in us to expect that she should. Pope's "Shall gravitation cease when you go by?" may be a just rebuke to anyone who should be so silly as to expect common human morality from nature. But if the question were between two men, instead of between a man and a natural phenomenon, that triumphant apostrophe would be thought a rare piece of impudence. A man who should persist in hurling stones or firing cannon when another man "goes by," and having killed him should urge a similar plea in exculpation, would very deservedly be found guilty of murder.

In sober truth, nearly all the things which men are hanged or imprisoned for doing to one another are Nature's everyday performances. Killing, the most criminal act recognized by human laws, Nature does once to every being that lives, and in a large proportion of cases after protracted tortures such as only the greatest monsters whom we read of ever purposely inflicted on their living fellow creatures. If by an arbitrary reservation we refuse to account anything murder but what abridges a certain term supposed to be allotted to human life, Nature also does this to all but a small percentage of lives, and does it in all the modes, violent or insidious, in which the worst human beings take the lives of one another. Nature impales men, breaks them as if on the wheel, casts them to be devoured by wild beasts, burns them to death, crushes them with stones like the first Christian martyr, starves them with hunger, freezes them with cold, poisons them by the quick or slow venom of her exhalations, and has hundreds of other hideous deaths in reserve such as the ingenious cruelty of a Nabis or a Domitian never surpassed. All this Nature does with the most supercilious disregard both of mercy and of justice, emptying her shafts upon the best and noblest indifferently with the meanest and worst; upon those who are engaged in the highest and worthiest enterprises, and often as the direct consequence of the noblest acts; and it might almost be imagined as a punishment for them. She mows down those on whose existence hangs the well-being of a whole people, perhaps the prospects of the human race for generations to come, with as little compunction as those whose death is a relief to themselves or a blessing to those under their noxious influence. Such are Nature's dealings with life. Even when she does not intend to kill, she inflicts the same tortures in apparent wantonness. In the clumsy provision which she has made for that perpetual renewal of animal life, rendered necessary by the prompt termination she puts to it in every individual instance, no human being ever comes into the world but another human being is literally stretched on the rack for hours or days, not unfrequently issuing in death. Next to taking life (equal to it, according to a high authority) is taking the means by which we live; and Nature does this, too, on the largest scale and with the most callous indifference. A single hurricane destroys the hopes of a season; a flight of locusts, or an inundation, desolates a district; a trifling chemical change in an edible root starves a million of people. The waves of the sea, like banditti, seize and appropriate the wealth of the rich and the little all of the poor with the same accompaniments of stripping, wounding, and killing as their human antitypes. Everything, in short, which the worst men commit either against life or property is perpetrated on a larger scale by natural agents. Nature has *noyades* more fatal than those of Carrier; her explosions of fire-damp are as destructive as human artillery; her plague and cholera far surpass the poison cups of the Borgias. Even the love of "order" which is thought to be a following of the ways of Nature is in fact a contradiction of them. All which people are accustomed to deprecate as "disorder" and its consequences is precisely a counterpart of Nature's ways. Anarchy and the reign of terror are overmatched in injustice, ruin, and death by a hurricane and a pestilence.

But, it is said, all these things are for wise and good ends. On this I must first remark that whether they are so or not is altogether beside the point. Supposing it is true that, contrary to appearances, these horrors when perpetrated by Nature promote good ends, still, as no one believes that good ends would be promoted by our following the example, the course of Nature cannot be a proper model for us to imitate. Either it is right that we should kill because Nature kills, torture because Nature tortures, ruin and devastate because Nature does the like, or we ought not to consider at all what Nature does, but what it is good to do. If there is such a thing as a *reductio ad absurdum,* this surely amounts to one. If it is a sufficient reason for doing one thing that Nature does it, why not another thing? If not all things, why any thing? The physical government of the world being full of the things which when done by men are deemed the greatest enormities, it cannot be religious or moral in us to guide our actions by the analogy of the course of nature. This proposition remains true whatever occult quality of producing good may reside in those facts of nature which to our perceptions are most noxious, and which no one considers it other than a crime to produce artificially.

But, in reality, no one consistently believes in any such occult quality. The phrases which ascribe perfection to the course of nature can only be considered as the exaggerations of poetic or devotional feeling, not intended to stand the test of a sober examination. No one, either religious or irreligious, believes that the hurtful agencies of nature, considered as a whole, promote good purposes in any other way than by inciting human rational creatures to rise up and struggle against them. If we believed that those agencies were appointed by a benevolent Providence as the means of accomplishing wise purposes which could not be compassed if they did not exist, then everything done by mankind which tends to chain up these natural agencies or to restrict their mischievous operation, from draining a pestilential marsh down to curing the toothache or putting up an umbrella, ought to be accounted impious; which assuredly nobody does account them, notwithstanding an undercurrent of sentiment setting in that direction which is occasionally perceptible. On the contrary, the improvements on which the civilized part of mankind most pride themselves consist in more successfully warding off those natural calamities which, if we really believed what most people profess to believe, we should cherish as medicines provided for our earthly state by infinite wisdom. Inasmuch, too, as each generation greatly surpasses its predecessors in the amount of natural evil which it succeeds in averting, our condition, if the theory were true, ought by this time to have become a terrible manifestation of some tremendous calamity against which the physical evils we have learned to overmaster had previously operated as a preservative. Anyone, however, who acted as if he supposed this to be the case would be more likely, I think, to be confined as a lunatic than reverenced as a saint.

It is undoubtedly a very common fact that good comes out of evil, and, when it does occur, it is far too agreeable not to find people eager to dilate on it. But in the first place, it is quite as often true of human crimes as of natural calamities. The fire of London, which is believed to have had so salutary an effect on the healthiness of the city, would have produced that effect just as much if it had been really the work of the *furor papisticus* so long commemorated on the monument. The deaths of those whom tyrants or persecutors have made martyrs in any noble cause have done a service to mankind which would not have been obtained if they had died by accident or disease. Yet whatever incidental and unexpected benefits may result from crimes, they are crimes nevertheless. In the second place, if good frequently comes out of evil, the converse fact, evil coming out of good, is equally common. Every event, public or private, which, regretted on its occurrence, was declared providential at a later period on account of some unforeseen good consequence, might be matched by some other event, deemed fortunate at the time, but which proved calamitous or fatal to those whom it appeared to benefit. Such conflicts between the beginning and the end, or between the event and the expectation, are not only as frequent but as often held up to notice in the painful cases as in the agreeable, but there is not the same inclination to generalize on them or at all events they are not regarded by the moderns (though they were by the ancients) as similarly an indication of the divine purposes: men satisfy themselves with moralizing on the imperfect nature of our foresight, the uncertainty of events, and the vanity of human expectations. The simple fact is, human interests are so complicated, and the effects of any incident whatever so multitudinous, that if it touches mankind at all its influence on them is, in the great majority of cases, both good and bad. If the greater number of personal misfortunes have their good side, hardly any good fortune ever befell anyone which did not give either to the same or to some other person something to regret; and unhappily there are many misfortunes so overwhelming that their favourable side, if it exist, is entirely overshadowed and made insignificant, while the corresponding statement can seldom be made concerning blessings. The effects, too, of every cause depend so much on the circumstances which accidentally accompany it that many cases are sure to occur in which even the total result is markedly opposed to the predominant tendency; and thus not only evil has its good and good its evil side, but good often produces an overbalance of evil and evil an overbalance of good. This, however, is by no means the general tendency of either phenomenon. On the contrary, both good and evil naturally tend to fructify, each in its own kind, good producing good, and evil, evil. It is one of Nature's general rules and part of her habitual injustice that "to him that hath shall be given, but from him that hath not shall be taken even that which he hath." The ordinary and predominant tendency of good is toward more good. Health, strength, wealth, knowledge, virtue are not only good in themselves but facilitate and promote the acquisition of good, both of the same and of other kinds. The person who can learn easily is he who already knows much; it is the strong and not the sickly person who can do everything which most conduces to health; those who find it easy to gain money are not the poor but the rich; while health, strength, knowledge, talents are all means of acquiring riches, and riches are often an indispensable means of acquiring these. Again, e converso [conversely], whatever may be said of evil turning into good, the general tendency of evil is toward further evil. Bodily illness renders the body more susceptible of disease; it produces incapacity of exertion, sometimes debility of mind, and often the loss of means of subsistence. All severe pain, either bodily or mental, tends to increase the susceptibilities of pain forever after. Poverty is the parent of a thousand mental and moral evils. What is still worse, to be injured or oppressed, when habitual, lowers the whole tone of the character. One bad action leads to others, both in the agent himself, in the bystanders, and in the sufferers. All bad qualities are strengthened by habit, and all vices and follies tend to spread. Intellectual defects generate moral, and moral, intellectual; and every intellectual or moral defect generates others, and so on without end.

That much applauded class of authors, the writers on natural theology, have, I venture to think, entirely lost their way and missed the sole line of argument which could have made their speculations acceptable to anyone who can perceive when two propositions contradict one another. They have exhausted the resources of sophistry to make it appear that all the suffering in the world exists to prevent greater—that misery exists for fear lest there should be misery: a thesis which, if ever so well maintained, could only avail to explain and justify the works of limited beings, compelled to labour under conditions independent of their own will, but could have no application to a Creator assumed to be omnipotent who, if he bends to a supposed necessity, himself makes the necessity which he bends to. If the maker of the world *can* all that he will, he wills misery, and there is no escape from the conclusion. The more consistent of those who have deemed themselves qualified to "vindicate the ways of God to man" have endeavoured to avoid the alternative by hardening their hearts and denying that misery is an evil. The goodness of God, they say, does not consist in willing the happiness of his creatures but their virtue; and the universe, if not a happy, is a just universe. But waiving the objections to this scheme of ethics, it does not at all get rid of the difficulty. If the Creator of mankind willed that they should all be virtuous, His designs are as completely baffled as if He had willed that they should all be happy; and the order of nature is constructed with even less regard to the requirements of justice than to those of benevolence. If the law of all creation were justice and the Creator omnipotent, then, in whatever amount suffering and happiness might be dispensed to the world, each person's share of them would be exactly proportioned to that person's good or evil deeds; no human being would have a worse lot than another without worse deserts; accident or favouritism would have no part in such a world, but every human life would be the playing out of a drama constructed like a perfect moral tale. No one is able to blind himself to the fact that the world we live in is totally different from this, insomuch that the necessity of redressing the balance has been deemed one of the strongest arguments for another life after death, which amounts to an admission that the order of things in this life is often an example of injustice, not justice. If it be said that God does not take sufficient account of pleasure and pain to make them the reward or punishment of the good or the wicked, but that virtue is itself the greatest good and vice the greatest evil, then these at least ought to be dispensed to all according to what they have done to deserve them; instead of which every kind of moral depravity is entailed upon multitudes by the fatality of their birth, through the fault of their parents, of society, or of uncontrollable circumstances, certainly through no fault of their own. Not even on the most distorted and contracted theory of good which ever was framed by religious or philosophical fanaticism can the government of nature be made to resemble the work of a being at once good and omnipotent.

The only admissible moral theory of Creation is that the Principle of Good *cannot* at once and altogether subdue the powers of evil, either physical or moral; could not place mankind in a world free from the necessity of an incessant struggle with the maleficent powers, or make them always victorious in that struggle, but could and did make them capable of carrying on the fight with vigour and with progressively increasing success. Of all the religious explanations of the order of nature, this alone is neither contradictory to itself nor to the facts for which it attempts to account. According to it, man's duty would consist, not in simply taking care of his own interests by obeying irresistible power, but in standing forward a not ineffectual auxiliary to a Being of perfect beneficence—a faith which seems much better adapted for nerving him to exertion than a vague and inconsistent reliance on an Author of Good who is supposed to be also the author of evil. And I venture to assert that such has really been, though often unconsciously, the faith of all who have drawn strength and support of any worthy kind from trust in a superintending Providence. There is no subject on which men's practical belief is more incorrectly indicated by the words they use to express it than religion. Many have derived a base confidence from imagining themselves to be favourites of an omnipotent but capricious and despotic Deity. But those who have been strengthened in goodness by relying on the sympathizing support of a powerful and good governor of the world have, I am satisfied, never really believed that governor to be, in the strict sense of the term, omnipotent. They have always saved his goodness at the expense of his power. They have believed, perhaps, that he could, if he willed, remove all the thorns from their individual path, but not without causing greater harm to someone else, or frustrating some purpose of greater importance to the general well-being. They have believed that he could do any one thing, but not any combination of things; that his government, like human government, was a system of adjustments and compromises; that the world is inevitably imperfect, contrary to his intention.[1] And since the exertion of all his power to make it as little imperfect as possible leaves it

---

1. This irresistible conviction comes out in the writings of religious philosophers in exact proportion to the general clearness of their understanding. It nowhere shines forth so distinctly as in Leibniz's famous *Théodicée*, so strangely mistaken for a system of optimism and, as such, satirized by Voltaire on grounds which do not even touch the author's argument. Leibniz does not maintain that this world is the best of all imaginable, but only of all possible, worlds; which, he argues, it cannot but be inasmuch as God, who is absolute goodness, has chosen it and not another. In every page of the work he tacitly assumes an abstract possibility and impossibility, independent of the divine power; and though his pious feelings make him continue to designate that power by the word Omnipotence, he so explains that term as to make it mean power extending to all that is within the limits of that abstract possibility.

no better than it is, they cannot but regard that power, though vastly beyond human estimate, yet as in itself not merely finite but extremely limited. They are bound, for example, to suppose that the best he could do for his human creatures was to make an immense majority of all who have yet existed be born (without any fault of their own) Patagonians, or Eskimos, or something nearly as brutal and degraded, but to give them capacities which, by being cultivated for very many centuries in toil and suffering and after many of the best specimens of the race have sacrificed their lives for the purpose, have at last enabled some chosen portions of the species to grow into something better, capable of being improved in centuries more into something really good, of which hitherto there are only to be found individual instances. It may be possible to believe with Plato that perfect goodness, limited and thwarted in every direction by the intractableness of the material, has done this because it could do no better. But that the same perfectly wise and good Being had absolute power over the material and made it, by voluntary choice, what it is—to admit this might have been supposed impossible to anyone who has the simplest notions of moral good and evil. Nor can any such person, whatever kind of religious phrases he may use, fail to believe that if nature and man are both the works of a Being of perfect goodness, that Being intended nature as a scheme to be amended, not imitated, by man.

But even though unable to believe that nature, as a whole, is a realization of the designs of perfect wisdom and benevolence, men do not willingly renounce the idea that some part of Nature, at least, must be intended as an exemplar or type; that on some portion or other of the Creator's works the image of the moral qualities which they are accustomed to ascribe to him must be impressed; that if not all which is, yet something which is, must not only be a faultless model of what ought to be, but must be intended to be our guide and standard in rectifying the rest. It does not suffice them to believe that what tends to good is to be imitated and perfected, and what tends to evil is to be corrected; they are anxious for some more definite indication of the Creator's designs, and, being persuaded that this must somewhere be met with in his works, undertake the dangerous responsibility of picking and choosing among them in quest of it—a choice which, except so far as directed by the general maxim that he intends all the good and none of the evil, must of necessity be perfectly arbitrary, and, if it leads to any conclusions other than such as can be deduced from that maxim, must be, exactly in that proportion, pernicious.

It has never been settled by any accredited doctrine what particular departments of the order of nature shall be reputed to be designed for our moral instruction and guidance; and accordingly each person's individual predilections, or momentary convenience, have decided to what parts of the divine government the practical conclusions that he was desirous of establishing should be recommended to approval as being analogous. One such recommendation must be as fallacious as another, for it is impossible to decide that certain of the Creator's works are more truly expressions of his character than the rest; and the only selection which does not lead to immoral results is the selection of those which most conduce to the general good—in other words, of those which point to an end which, if the entire scheme is the expression of a single omnipotent and consistent will, is evidently not the end intended by it.

There is, however, one particular element in the construction of the world which, to minds on the look-out for special indication of the Creator's will, has appeared, not without plausibility, peculiarly fitted to afford them, viz., the active impulses of human and other animated beings. One can imagine such persons arguing that when the Author of Nature only made circumstances, he may not have meant to indicate the manner in which his rational creatures were to adjust themselves to those circumstances; but that when he implanted positive stimuli in the creatures themselves, stirring them up to a particular kind of action, it is impossible to doubt that he intended that sort of action to be practised by them. This reasoning, followed out consistently, would lead to the conclusion that the Deity intended, and approves, whatever human beings do; since all that they do being the consequence of some of the impulses with which their Creator must have endowed them, all must equally be considered as done in obedience to his will. As this practical conclusion was shrunk from, it was necessary to draw a distinction and to pronounce that not the whole but only parts of the active nature of mankind point to a special intention of the Creator in respect to their conduct. These parts, it seemed natural to suppose, must be those in which the Creator's hand is manifested rather than the man's own, and hence the frequent antithesis between man as God made him and man as he has made himself. Since what is done with deliberation seems more the man's own act, and he is held more completely responsible for it than for what he does from sudden impulse, the considerate part of human conduct is apt to be set down as man's share in the business and the inconsiderate as God's. The result is the vein of sentiment so common in the modern world (though unknown to the philosophic ancients) which exalts instinct at the expense of reason, an aberration rendered still more mischievous by the opinion commonly held in conjunction with it that every, or almost every, feeling or impulse which acts promptly without waiting to ask questions is an instinct. Thus almost every variety of unreflecting and uncalculating impulse receives a kind of consecration except those which, though unreflecting at the moment, owe their origin to previous habits of reflection; these, being evidently not instinctive, do not meet with the favour accorded to the rest, so that all unreflecting impulses are invested with authority over reason except the only ones which are most probably right. I do not mean, of course, that this mode of judgment is even pretended to be consistently carried out; life could not go on if it were not admitted that impulses must be controlled, and that reason ought to govern our actions. The pretension is not to drive reason from the helm but rather to bind her by articles to steer only in a particular way. Instinct is not to govern, but reason is to practise some vague and unassignable amount of deference to instinct. Though the impression in favour of instinct as being a peculiar manifestation of the divine purposes has not been cast into the form of a consistent general theory, it remains a standing prejudice, capable of being stirred up into hostility to reason in any case in which the dictate of the rational faculty has not acquired the authority of prescription.

I shall not here enter into the difficult psychological question, what are or are not instincts; the subject would require a volume to itself. Without touching upon any disputed theoretical points, it is possible to judge how little worthy is the instinctive part of human nature to be held up as its chief excellence—as the part in which the hand of infinite goodness and wisdom is peculiarly visible. Allowing everything to be an instinct which anybody has ever asserted to be one, it remains true that nearly every respectable attribute of humanity is the result, not of instinct, but of a victory over instinct; and that there is hardly anything valuable in the natural man except capacities—a whole world of possibilities, all of them dependent upon eminently artificial discipline for being realized.

It is only in a highly artificialized condition of human nature that the notion grew up, or, I believe, ever could have grown up, that goodness was natural; because only after a long course of artificial education did good sentiments become so habitual, and so predominant over bad, as to arise unprompted when occasion called for them. In the times when mankind were nearer to their natural state, cultivated observers regarded the natural man as a sort of wild animal, distinguished chiefly by being craftier than the other beasts of the field; and all worth of character was deemed the result of a sort of taming, a phrase often applied by the ancient philosophers to the appropriate discipline of human beings. The truth is that there is hardly a single point of excellence belonging to human character which is not decidedly repugnant to the untutored feelings of human nature.

If there be a virtue which more than any other we expect to find, and really do find, in an uncivilized state, it is the virtue of courage. Yet this is from first to last a victory achieved over one of the most powerful emotions of human nature. If there is any one feeling or attribute more natural than all others to human beings it is fear; and no greater proof can be given of the power of artificial discipline than the conquest which it has at all times and places shown itself capable of achieving over so mighty and so universal a sentiment. The widest difference no doubt exists between one human being and another in the facility or difficulty with which they acquire this virtue. There is hardly any department of human excellence in which difference of original temperament goes so far. But it may fairly be questioned if any human being is naturally courageous. Many are naturally pugnacious, or irascible, or enthusiastic, and these passions when strongly excited may render them insensible to fear. But take away the conflicting emotion, and fear reasserts its dominion; consistent courage is always the effect of cultivation. The courage which is occasionally, though by no means generally, found among tribes of savages is as much the result of education as that of the Spartans or Romans. In all such tribes there is a most emphatic direction of the public sentiment into every channel of expression through which honour can be paid to courage and cowardice held up to contempt and derision. It will perhaps be said that, as the expression of a sentiment implies the sentiment itself, the training of the young to courage presupposes an originally courageous people. It presupposes only what all good customs presuppose—that there must have been individuals better than the rest who set the customs going. Some individuals who, like other people, had fears to conquer must have had strength of mind and will to conquer them for themselves. These would obtain the influence belonging to heroes, for that which is at once astonishing and obviously useful never fails to be admired; and partly through this admiration, partly through the fear they themselves excite, they would obtain the power of legislators and could establish whatever customs they pleased.

Let us next consider a quality which forms the most visible and one of the most radical of the moral distinctions between human beings and most of the lower animals, that of which the absence, more than of anything else, renders men bestial—the quality of cleanliness. Can anything be more entirely artificial? Children, and the lower classes of most countries, seem to be actually fond of dirt; the vast majority of the human race are indifferent to it; whole nations of otherwise civilized and cultivated human beings tolerate it in some of its worst forms, and only a very small minority are consistently offended by it. Indeed, the universal law of the subject appears to be that uncleanliness offends only those to whom it is unfamiliar, so that those who have lived in so artificial a state as to be unused to it in any form are the sole persons whom it disgusts in all forms. Of all virtues this is the most evidently not instinctive, but a triumph over instinct. Assuredly neither cleanliness nor the love of cleanliness is natural to man, but only the capacity of acquiring a love of cleanliness.

Our examples have thus far been taken from the personal or, as they are called by Bentham, the self-regarding virtues, because these, if any, might be supposed to be congenial even to the uncultivated mind. Of the social virtues it is almost superfluous to speak, so completely is it the verdict of all experience that selfishness is natural. By this I do not in any wise mean to deny that sympathy is natural also; I believe, on the contrary, that on that important fact rests the possibility of any cultivation of goodness and nobleness, and the hope of their ultimate entire ascendancy. But sympathetic characters, left uncultivated and given up to their sympathetic instincts, are as selfish as others. The difference is in the *kind* of selfishness: theirs is not solitary but sympathetic selfishness—*l'egoîsme à deux, à trois,* or *à quatre*—and they may be very amiable and delightful to those with whom they sympathize, and grossly unjust and unfeeling to the rest of the world. Indeed, the finer nervous organizations which are most capable of and most require sympathy have, from their fineness, so much stronger impulses of all sorts that they often furnish the most striking examples of selfishness, though of a less repulsive kind than that of colder natures. Whether there ever was a person in whom, apart from all teaching of instructors, friends, or books, and from all intentional self-modeling according to an ideal, natural benevolence was a more powerful attribute than selfishness in any of its forms may remain undecided. That such cases are extremely rare everyone must admit, and this is enough for the argument.

But (to speak no further of self-control for the benefit of others) the commonest self-control for one's own benefit—that power of sacrificing a present desire to a distant object or a general purpose which is indispensable for making the actions of the individual accord with his own notions of his individual good—even this is most unnatural to the undisciplined human being, as may be seen by the long apprenticeship which children serve to it, the very imperfect manner in which it is acquired by persons born to power whose will is seldom resisted, and by all who have been early and much indulged; and the marked absence of the quality in savages, in soldiers and sailors, and in a somewhat less degree in nearly the whole of the poorer classes in this and many other countries. The principal difference on the point under consideration between this virtue and others is that, although, like them, it requires a course of teaching, it is more susceptible than most of them of being self-taught. The axiom is trite that self-control is only learned by experience; and this endowment is only thus much nearer to being natural than the others we have spoken of, inasmuch as personal experience, without external inculcation, has a certain tendency to engender it. Nature does not of herself bestow this, any more than other virtues; but Nature often administers the rewards and punishments which cultivate it, and which in other cases have to be created artificially for the express purpose.

Veracity might seem, of all virtues, to have the most plausible claim to being natural, since in the absence of motives to the contrary speech usually conforms to, or at least does not intentionally deviate from, fact. Accordingly this is the virtue with which writers like Rousseau delight in decorating savage life and setting it in advantageous contrast with the treachery and trickery of civilization. Unfortunately this is a mere fancy picture, contradicted by all the realities of savage life. Savages are always liars. They have not the faintest notion of truth as a virtue. They have a notion of not betraying to their hurt, as of not hurting in any other way, persons to whom they are bound by some special tie of obligation: their chief, their guest, perhaps, or their friend—these feelings of obligation being the taught morality of the savage state, growing out of its characteristic circumstances. But of any point of honour respecting truth for truth's sake they have not the remotest idea, no more than the whole East and the greater part of Europe; and, in the few countries which are sufficiently improved to have such a point of honour, it is confined to a small minority who alone, under any circumstances of real temptation, practise it.

From the general use of the expression "natural justice" it must be presumed that justice is a virtue generally thought to be directly implanted by nature. I believe, however, that the sentiment of justice is entirely of artificial origin, the idea of natural justice not preceding but following that of conventional justice. The farther we look back into the early modes of thinking of the human race, whether we consider ancient times (including those of the Old Testament) or the portions of mankind who are still in no more advanced a condition than that of ancient times, the more completely do we find men's notions of justice defined and bounded by the express appointment of law. A man's just rights meant the rights which the law gave him; a just man was he who never infringed, or sought to infringe, the legal property or other legal rights of others. The notion of a higher justice, to which laws themselves are amenable and by which the conscience is bound without a positive prescription of law, is a later extension of the idea suggested by and following the analogy of legal justice, to which it maintains a parallel direction through all the shades and varieties of the sentiment, and from which it borrows nearly the whole of its phraseology. The very words *justus* and *justitia* are derived from *jus*, law. Courts of justice, administration of justice, always mean the tribunals.

If it be said that there must be the germs of all these virtues in human nature, otherwise mankind would be incapable of acquiring them, I am ready, with a certain amount of explanation, to admit the fact. But the weeds that dispute the ground with these beneficent germs are themselves not germs but rankly luxuriant growths and would, in all but some one case in a thousand, entirely stifle and destroy the former, were it not so strongly the interest of mankind to cherish the good germs in one another that they always do so in as far as their degree of intelligence (in this as in other respects still very imperfect) allows. It is through such fostering, commenced early and not counteracted by unfavourable influences, that, in some happily circumstanced specimens of the human race, the most elevated sentiments of which humanity is capable become a second nature, stronger than the first, and not so much subduing the original nature as merging it into itself. Even those gifted organizations which have attained the like excellence by self-culture owe it essentially to the same cause; for what self-culture would be possible without aid from the general sentiment of mankind delivered through books, and from the contemplation of exalted characters real or ideal? This artificially created or at least artificially perfected nature of the best and noblest human beings is the only nature which it is ever commendable to follow. It is almost superfluous to say that even this cannot be erected into a standard of conduct, since it is itself the fruit of a training and culture the choice of which, if rational and not accidental, must have been determined by a standard already chosen.

This brief survey is amply sufficient to prove that the duty of man is the same in respect to his own nature as in respect to the nature of all other things, namely, not to follow but to amend it. Some people, however, who do not attempt to deny that instinct ought to be subordinate to reason, pay deference to nature so far as to maintain that every natural inclination must have some sphere of action granted to it, some opening left for its gratification. All natural wishes, they say, must have been implanted for a purpose; and this argument is carried so far that we often hear it maintained that every wish which it is supposed to be natural to entertain must have a corresponding provision in the order of the universe for its gratification; insomuch (for instance) that the desire of an indefinite prolongation of existence is believed by many to be in itself a sufficient proof of the reality of a future life.

I conceive that there is a radical absurdity in all these attempts to discover, in detail, what are the designs of Providence, in order when they are discovered to help Providence in bringing them about. Those who argue, from particular indications, that Providence intends this or that either believe that the Creator can do all that he will or that he cannot. If the first supposition is adopted—if Providence is omnipotent—Providence intends whatever happens, and the fact of its happening proves that Providence intended it. If so, everything which a human being can do is predestined by Providence and is a fulfillment of its designs. But if, as is the more religious theory, Providence intends not all which happens, but only what is good, then indeed man has it in his power, by his voluntary actions, to aid the intentions of Providence; but he can only learn those intentions by considering what tends to promote the general good, and not what man has a natural inclination to; for, limited as, on this showing, the divine power must be by inscrutable but insurmountable obstacles, who knows that man *could* have been created without desires which never are to be, and even which never ought to be, fulfilled? The inclinations with which man has been endowed, as well as any of the other contrivances which we observe in nature, may be the expression, not of the divine will, but of the fetters which impede its free action; and to take hints from these for the guidance of our own conduct may be falling into a trap laid by the enemy. The assumption that everything which infinite goodness can desire actually comes to pass in this universe, or at least that we must never say or suppose that it does not, is worthy only of those whose slavish fears make them offer the homage of lies to a Being who, they profess to think, is incapable of being deceived and holds all falsehood in abomination.

With regard to this particular hypothesis, that all natural impulses, all propensities sufficiently universal and sufficiently spontaneous to be capable of passing for instincts, must exist for good ends and ought to be only regulated, not repressed—this is of course true of the majority of them, for the species could not have continued to exist unless most of its inclinations had been directed to things needful or useful for its preservation. But unless the instincts can be reduced to a very small number indeed, it must be allowed that we have also bad instincts which it should be the aim of education not simply to regulate but to extirpate, or rather (what can be done even to an instinct) to starve them by disuse. Those who are inclined to multiply the number of instincts usually include among them one which they call destructiveness, an instinct to destroy for destruction's sake. I can conceive no good reason for preserving this, no more than another propensity which if not an instinct is very like one, what has been called the instinct of domination, a delight in exercising despotism, in holding other beings in subjection to our will. The man who takes pleasure in the mere exertion of authority, apart from the purpose for which it is to be employed, is the last person in whose hands one would willingly entrust it. Again, there are persons who are cruel by character, or as the phrase is, naturally cruel, who have a real pleasure in inflicting or seeing the infliction of pain. This kind of cruelty is not mere hardheartedness, absence of pity or remorse; it is a positive thing, a particular kind of voluptuous excitement. The East and southern Europe have afforded, and probably still afford, abundant examples of this hateful propensity. I suppose it will be granted that this is not one of the natural inclinations which it would be wrong to suppress. The only question would be whether it is not a duty to suppress the man himself along with it.

But even if it were true that every one of the elementary impulses of human nature has its good side and may by a sufficient amount of artificial training be made more useful than hurtful, how little would this amount to when it must in any case be admitted that, without such training, all of them, even those which are necessary to our preservation, would fill the world with misery, making human life an exaggerated likeness of the odious scene of violence and tyranny which is exhibited by the rest of the animal kingdom, except in so far as tamed and disciplined by man. There, indeed, those who flatter themselves with the notion of reading the purposes of the Creator in His works ought in consistency to have seen grounds for inferences from which they have shrunk. If there are any marks at all of special design in creation, one of the things most evidently designed is that a large proportion of all animals should pass their existence in tormenting and devouring other animals. They have been lavishly fitted out with the instruments necessary for that purpose; their strongest instincts impel them to it, and many of them seem to have been constructed incapable of supporting themselves by any other food. If a tenth part of the pains which have been expended in finding benevolent adaptations in all nature had been employed in collecting evidence to blacken the character of the Creator, what scope for comment would not have been found in the entire existence of the lower animals, divided with scarcely an exception into devourers and devoured, and a prey to a thousand ills from which they are denied the faculties necessary for protecting themselves! If we are not obliged to believe the animal creation to be the work of a demon it is because we need not suppose it to have been made by a Being of infinite power. But if imitation of the Creator's will as revealed in nature were applied as a rule of action in this case, the most atrocious enormities of the worst men would be more than justified by the apparent intention of Providence that throughout all animated nature the strong should prey upon the weak.

The preceding observations are far from having exhausted the almost infinite variety of modes and occasions in which the idea of conformity to nature is introduced as an element into the ethical appreciation of actions and dispositions. The same favourable prejudgment follows the word nature through the numerous acceptations in which it is employed as a distinctive term for certain parts of the constitution of humanity as contrasted with other parts. We have hitherto confined ourselves to one of these acceptations, in which it stands as a general designation for those parts of our mental and moral constitution which are supposed to be innate, in contradistinction to those which are acquired: as when nature is contrasted with education; or when a savage state, without laws, arts, or knowledge, is called a state of nature; or when the question is asked whether benevolence, or the moral sentiment, is natural or acquired; or whether some persons are poets or orators by nature and others not. But in another and a more lax sense, any manifestations by human beings are often termed natural when it is merely intended to say that they are not studied or designedly assumed in the particular case, as when a person is said to move or speak with natural grace, or when it is said that a person's natural manner or character is so and so, meaning that it is so when he does not attempt to control or disguise it. In a still looser acceptation, a person is said to be naturally that which he was until some special cause had acted upon him, or which it is supposed he would be if some such cause were withdrawn. Thus a person is said to be naturally dull but to have made himself intelligent by study and perseverance; to be naturally cheerful but soured by misfortune; naturally ambitious but kept down by want of opportunity. Finally, the word natural, applied to feelings or conduct, often seems to mean no more than that they are such as are ordinarily found in human beings: as when it is said that a person acted on some particular occasion as it was natural to do; or that to be affected in a particular way by some sight, or sound, or thought, or incident in life is perfectly natural.

In all these senses of the term the quality called natural is very often confessedly a worse quality than the one contrasted with it; but whenever its being so is not too obvious to be questioned the idea seems to be entertained that by describing it as natural something has been said amounting to a considerable presumption in its favour. For my part I can perceive only one sense in which nature, or naturalness, in a human being are really terms of praise, and then the praise is only negative, namely, when used to denote the absence of affectation. Affectation may be defined the effort to appear what one is not, when the motive or the occasion is not such as either to excuse the attempt or to stamp it with the more odious name of hypocrisy. It must be added that the deception is often attempted to be practised on the deceiver himself as well as on others; he imitates the external signs of qualities which he would like to have, in hopes to persuade himself that he has them. Whether in the form of deception or of self-deception, or of something hovering between the two, affectation is very rightly accounted a reproach, and naturalness, understood as the reverse of affectation, a merit. But a more proper term by which to express this estimable quality would be sincerity, a term which has fallen from its original elevated meaning and popularly denotes only a subordinate branch of the cardinal virtue it once designated as a whole.

Sometimes also, in cases where the term affectation would be inappropriate, since the conduct or demeanor spoken of is really praiseworthy, people say in disparagement of the person concerned that such conduct or demeanor is not natural to him, and make uncomplimentary comparisons between him and some other person to whom it is natural, meaning that what in the one seemed excellent was the effect of temporary excitement, or of a great victory over himself, while in the other it is the result to be expected from the habitual character. This mode of speech is not open to censure, since nature is here simply a term for the person's ordinary disposition, and if he is praised it is not for being natural but for being naturally good.

Conformity to nature has no connection whatever with right and wrong. The idea can never be fitly introduced into ethical discussions at all, except occasionally and partially into the question of degrees of culpability. To illustrate this point let us consider the phrase by which the greatest intensity of condemnatory feeling is conveyed in connection with the idea of nature—the word unnatural. That a thing is unnatural, in any precise meaning which can be attached to the word, is no argument for its being blamable, since the most criminal actions are, to a being like man, not more unnatural than most of the virtues. The acquisition of virtue has in all ages been accounted a work of labour and difficulty, while the *descensus Averni* on the contrary is of proverbial facility; and it assuredly requires in most persons a greater conquest over a greater number of natural inclinations to become eminently virtuous than transcendently vicious. But if an action or an inclination has been decided on other grounds to be blamable, it may be a circumstance in aggravation that it is unnatural, that is, repugnant to some strong feeling usually found in human beings; since the bad propensity, whatever it be, has afforded evidence of being both strong and deeply rooted by having overcome that repugnance. This presumption, of course, fails if the individual never had the repugnance, and the argument, therefore, is not fit to be urged unless the feeling which is violated by the act is not only justifiable and reasonable but is one which it is blamable to be without.

The corresponding plea in extenuation of a culpable act because it was natural, or because it was prompted by a natural feeling, never, I think, ought to be admitted. There is hardly a bad action ever perpetrated which is not perfectly natural, and the motives to which are not perfectly natural feelings. In the eye of reason, therefore, this is no excuse, but it is quite "natural" that it should be so in the eyes of the multitude because the meaning of the expression is that they have a fellow feeling with the offender. When they say that something which they cannot help admitting to be blamable is nevertheless natural, they mean that they can imagine the possibility of their being themselves tempted to commit it. Most people have a considerable amount of indulgence toward all acts of which they feel a possible source within themselves, reserving their rigour for those which, though perhaps really less bad, they cannot in any way understand how it is possible to commit. If an action convinces them (which it often does on very inadequate grounds) that the person who does it must be a being totally unlike themselves, they are seldom particular in examining the precise degree of blame due to it, or even if blame is properly due to it at all. They measure the degree of guilt by the strength of their antipathy; and hence differences of opinion, and even differences of tastes, have been objects of as intense moral abhorrence as the most atrocious crimes.

It will be useful to sum up in a few words the leading conclusions of this essay.

The word nature has two principal meanings: it either denotes the entire system of things, with the aggregate of all their properties, or it denotes things as they would be, apart from human intervention.

In the first of these senses, the doctrine that man ought to follow nature is unmeaning, since man has no power to do anything else than follow nature; all his actions are done through and in obedience to some one or many of nature's physical or mental laws.

In the other sense of the term, the doctrine that men ought to follow nature or, in other words, ought to make the spontaneous course of things the model of his voluntary actions is equally irrational and immoral: irrational, because all human action whatever consists in altering, and all useful action in improving, the spontaneous course of nature; immoral, because the course of natural phenomena being replete with everything which when committed by human beings is most worthy of abhorrence, any one who endeavoured in his actions to imitate the natural course of things would be universally seen and acknowledged to be the wickedest of men.

The scheme of nature regarded in its whole extent cannot have had, for its sole or even principal object, the good of human or other sentient beings. What good it brings to them is mostly the result of their own exertions. Whatsoever in nature gives indication of beneficent design proves this beneficence to be armed only with limited power; and the duty of man is to co-operate with the beneficent powers, not by imitating but by perpetually striving to amend the course of nature—and bringing that part of it over which we can exercise control more nearly into conformity with a high standard of justice and goodness.

Ralph Waldo Emerson [1]

1803–1882

It has been said that Plato had no doctrines. His thought was rich, complex and elusive, and above all irreducible to a system, to a set of easily comprehended propositions and theses. Plato was Emerson's master, and Emerson had no doctrines either. Emerson was far from being an Aristotle. Dante could never have said of Emerson, as he said of Aristotle, that he was "the master of those who know."

On the contrary, it can almost be said that Emerson did not *know* anything, in the systematic, scientific sense in which we use the word nowadays. Emerson was a kind of sage, a kind of lay preacher on moral and metaphysical matters; because of this, perhaps, he was widely read and was a person of unique force in his day. His books were in every American home, and he lectured all over the United States, so that his words were heard, as well as read, by a vast number of his countrymen. In his books and lectures he was most concerned with the infinitude of the human soul and the inexhaustible wonder of nature; in a sense these were his only subjects. They are great subjects, but it is doubtful if any man can be systematic about them. One cannot *know* infinity and wonder.

The early essay called *Nature* reveals his inability to make a system of his mind, which he later had the wisdom to allow the freedom it needed. Emerson is most interesting on what a true theory of nature would explain if it were found, such as the mysteries of language, sleep, madness, dreams, beasts, and sex. But Emerson does not claim to offer us a true theory of nature. He is content to consider the uses of nature so far as men are concerned, and even these are difficult to grasp.

---

[1] For a biography of Ralph Waldo Emerson, see Vol. 6, pp. 146–148, in this set.

If Emerson's thought had any center, it was what came to be expressed in the essay *Self-reliance*, a term that for him seemed to describe the essential human virtue. Not that he meant to praise an unrestrained or ignorant egotism in anyone, least of all himself. "To believe your own thought, to believe that what is true for you in your private heart is true for all men—that is genius," the essay proclaims, but the private heart of which it speaks is the soul that all men share, and reliance upon this is obedience to the good that all men by their reason know. Nor did Emerson mean thereby to scorn the world, except as men rely instead on its example. For the world in his view is but the leavings—called variously by such names as society, opinion, tradition, and history—of genius which has gone before, and those who allow themselves to be ruled by that are content with the shadow of human possibility rather than the substance.

Emerson could not bring himself to reject the world, even though he often thought he should. The essay on Montaigne makes clear how much he loved that worldliest of men—loved him for his very matter-of-factness, his constant concern with everyday things. There was something inconsistent in Emerson's affection for such a man. True, the skeptic which Emerson admired in Montaigne had some of the quality of the self-reliant soul. He permitted nothing the world could say to dominate his intellect. But he achieved this mastery by giving full attention to what he heard, not by ignoring it.

The skeptic, Emerson says (and he was partly one himself), is a man who believes everything rather than nothing. He listens to the talk of other men and supposes that all of it may be true, which means that no part of it can be all the truth there is. Like self-reliance, skepticism as Emerson understands it is superior to the world, but the superiority is gained by experience in and of the world.

Whether to withdraw from the world or immerse himself in it was, for Emerson, the great problem. He could never decide which to do. And because the problem was never resolved within himself, his mind was essentially paradoxical. He said that inspiration was everything—but he was an omnivorous reader. He preached the virtues of self-communion—but he spent his time talking to other men. His essays praised the spirit—but at the same time they insisted on the importance of facts. And his style is alternately the haziest and the most pungent, often in the same paragraph, of any writer who ever lived. Throughout his life, Emerson sought company yet found it distracting, sought privacy yet found it enervating. "Solitude is impracticable and society fatal," he once admitted. It was as near a resolution of his problem as he ever got.

Despite the haziness and the lack of systematic resolutions, Emerson is worth reading again and again. He is more than just worthwhile. Emerson's words are sometimes exalting. They make us jump. We are overwhelmed and changed in our very hearts by the suddenly seen truth of a sentence or even a phrase. They make us realize that system is not everything. They even suggest that the world cannot be systematized. In an age of science, there may be no more important insight than this.

Nature

The rounded world is fair to see,
Nine times folded in mystery:
Though baffled seers cannot impart
The secret of its laboring heart,
Throb thine with Nature's throbbing breast,
And all is clear from east to west.
Spirit that lurks each form within
Beckons to spirit of its kin;
Self-kindled every atom glows,
And hints the future which it owes.

There are days which occur in this climate, at almost any season of the year, wherein the world reaches its perfection; when the air, the heavenly bodies and the earth make a harmony, as if Nature would indulge her offspring; when, in these bleak upper sides of the planet, nothing is to desire that we have heard of the happiest latitudes, and we bask in the shining hours of Florida and Cuba; when everything that has life gives sign of satisfaction, and the cattle that lie on the ground seem to have great and tranquil thoughts. These halcyons may be looked for with a little more assurance in that pure October weather which we distinguish by the name of the Indian summer. The day, immeasurably long, sleeps over the broad hills and warm wide fields. To have lived through all its sunny hours seems longevity enough. The solitary places do not seem quite lonely. At the gates of the forest, the surprised man of the world is forced to leave his city estimates of great and small, wise and foolish. The knapsack of custom falls off his back with the first step he takes into these precincts. Here is sanctity which shames our religions, and reality which discredits our heroes. Here we find Nature to be the circumstance which dwarfs every other circumstance, and judges like a god all men that come to her. We have crept out of our close and crowded houses into the night and morning, and we see what majestic beauties daily wrap us in their bosom. How willingly we would escape the barriers which render them comparatively impotent, escape the sophistication and second thought, and suffer nature to entrance us. The tempered light of the woods is like a perpetual morning, and is stimulating and heroic. The anciently reported spells of these places creep on us. The stems of pines, hemlocks and oaks almost gleam like iron on the excited eye. The incommunicable trees begin to persuade us to live with them, and quit our life of solemn trifles. Here no history, or church, or state is interpolated on the divine sky and the immortal year. How easily we might walk onward into the opening landscape, absorbed by new pictures and by thoughts fast succeeding each other, until by degrees the recollection of home was crowded out of the mind, all memory obliterated by the tyranny of the present, and we were led in triumph by Nature.

These enchantments are medicinal, they sober and heal us. These are plain pleasures, kindly and native to us. We come to our own, and make friends with matter, which the ambitious chatter of the schools would persuade us to despise. We never can part with it; the mind loves its old home: as water to our thirst, so is the rock, the ground, to our eyes and hands and feet. It is firm water; it is cold flame; what health, what affinity! Ever an old friend, ever like a dear friend and brother when we chat affectedly with strangers, comes in this honest face, and takes a grave liberty with us, and shames us out of our nonsense. Cities give not the human senses room enough. We go out daily and nightly to feed the eyes on the horizon, and require so much scope, just as we need water for our bath. There are all degrees of natural influence, from these quarantine powers of Nature, up to her dearest and gravest ministrations to the imagination and the soul. There is the bucket of cold water from the spring, the wood fire to which the chilled traveler rushes for safety—and there is the sublime moral of autumn and of noon. We nestle in Nature, and draw our living as parasites from her roots and grains, and we receive glances from the heavenly bodies, which call us to solitude and foretell the remotest future. The blue zenith is the point in which romance and reality meet. I think if we should be rapt away into all that and dream of heaven, and should converse with Gabriel and Uriel, the upper sky would be all that would remain of our furniture.

It seems as if the day was not wholly profane in which we have given heed to some natural object. The fall of snowflakes in a still air, preserving to each crystal its perfect form; the blowing of sleet over a wide sheet of water, and over plains; the waving rye field; the mimic waving of acres of houstonia, whose innumerable florets whiten and ripple before the eye;

the reflections of trees and flowers in glassy lakes; the musical, steaming, odorous south wind, which converts all trees to wind harps; the crackling and spurting of hemlock in the flames, or of pine logs, which yield glory to the walls and faces in the sitting room—these are the music and pictures of the most ancient religion. My house stands in low land, with limited outlook, and on the skirt of the village. But I go with my friend to the shore of our little river, and with one stroke of the paddle I leave the village politics and personalities, yes, and the world of villages and person-alities, behind, and pass into a delicate realm of sunset and moonlight, too bright almost for spotted man to enter without novitiate and probation. We penetrate bodily this incredible beauty; we dip our hands in this painted element; our eyes are bathed in these lights and forms. A holiday, a *villeggiatura*, a royal revel, the proudest, most heart-rejoicing festival that valor and beauty, power and taste ever decked and enjoyed, estab-lishes itself on the instant. These sunset clouds, these delicately emerging stars, with their private and ineffable glances, signify it and proffer it. I am taught the poorness of our invention, the ugliness of towns and palaces. Art and luxury have early learned that they must work as enhancement and sequel to this original beauty. I am overinstructed for my return. Henceforth I shall be hard to please. I cannot go back to toys. I am grown expensive and sophisticated. I can no longer live without elegance, but a countryman shall be my master of revels. He who knows the most, he who knows what sweets and virtues are in the ground, the waters, the plants, the heavens, and how to come at these enchantments, is the rich and royal man. Only as far as the masters of the world have called in nature to their aid, can they reach the height of magnificence. This is the meaning of their hanging gardens, villas, garden houses, islands, parks and preserves, to back their faulty personality with these strong accessories. I do not wonder that the landed interest should be invincible in the state with these dangerous auxiliaries. These bribe and invite; not kings, not palaces, not men, not women, but these tender and poetic stars, eloquent of secret promises. We heard what the rich man said, we knew of his villa, his grove, his wine and his company, but the provocation and point of the invitation came out of these beguiling stars. In their soft glances I see what men strove to realize in some Versailles, or Paphos, or Ctesiphon. Indeed, it is the magical lights of the horizon and the blue sky for the background which save all our works of art, which were otherwise baubles. When the rich tax the poor with servility and obsequiousness, they should consider the effect of men reputed to be the possessors of nature, on imaginative minds. Ah! if the rich were rich as the poor fancy riches! A boy hears a military band play on the field at night, and he has kings and queens and famous chivalry palpably before him. He hears the echoes of a horn in a hill country, in the Notch Mountains, for example, which converts the mountains into an Aeolian harp—and this supernatural *tiralira* restores to him the Dorian mythology, Apollo, Diana, and all divine hunters and huntresses. Can a musical note be so lofty, so haughtily beautiful! To the poor young poet, thus fabulous is his picture of society; he is loyal; he respects the rich; they are rich for the sake of his imagination; how poor his fancy would be if they were not rich! That they have some high-fenced grove which they call a park; that they live in larger and better-garnished saloons than he has visited, and go in coaches, keeping only the society of the elegant, to watering places and to distant cities—these make the groundwork from which he has delineated estates of romance, compared with which their actual possessions are shanties and paddocks. The muse herself betrays her son, and enhances the gifts of wealth and well-born beauty by a radiation out of the air, and clouds, and forests that skirt the road—a certain haughty favor, as if from patrician genii to patricians, a kind of aristocracy in nature, a prince of the power of the air.

The moral sensibility which makes Edens and Tempes so easily may not be always found, but the material landscape is never far off. We can find these enchantments without visiting the Como Lake, or the Madeira Islands. We exaggerate the praises of local scenery. In every landscape the point of astonishment is the meeting of the sky and the earth, and that is seen from the first hillock as well as from the top of the Alleghenies. The stars at night stoop down over the brownest, homeliest common with all the spiritual magnificence which they shed on the Campagna, or on the marble deserts of Egypt. The uprolled clouds and the colors of morning and evening will transfigure maples and alders. The difference between landscape and landscape is small, but there is great difference in the beholders. There is nothing so wonderful in any particular landscape as the necessity of being beautiful under which every landscape lies. Nature cannot be surprised in undress. Beauty breaks in everywhere.

But it is very easy to outrun the sympathy of readers on this topic, which schoolmen called *natura naturata*, or nature passive. One can hardly speak directly of it without excess. It is as easy to broach in mixed companies what is called "the subject of religion." A susceptible person does not like to indulge his tastes in this kind without the apology of some trivial necessity: he goes to see a wood lot, or to look at the crops, or to fetch a plant or a mineral from a remote locality, or he carries a fowling piece or a fishing rod. I suppose this shame must have a good reason. A dilettanteism in nature is barren and unworthy. The fop of fields is no better than his brother of Broadway. Men are naturally hunters and inquisitive of woodcraft, and I suppose that such a gazetteer as woodcutters and Indians should furnish facts for would take place in the most sumptuous drawing rooms of all the "Wreaths" and "Flora's chaplets" of the bookshops; yet ordinarily, whether we are too clumsy for so subtle a topic, or from whatever cause, as soon as men begin to write on nature, they fall into euphuism. Frivolity is a most unfit tribute to Pan, who ought to be represented in the mythology as the most continent of gods. I would not be frivolous before the admirable reserve and prudence of time, yet I cannot renounce the rights of returning often to this old topic. The multitude of false churches accredits the true religion. Literature, poetry, science are the homage of man to this unfathomed secret, concerning which no sane man can affect an indifference or incuriosity. Nature is loved by what is best in us. It is loved as the city of God, although, or rather because, there is no citizen. The sunset is unlike anything that is underneath it: it wants men. And the beauty of nature must always seem unreal and mocking, until the landscape has human figures that are as good as itself. If there were good men, there would never be this rapture in nature. If the king is in the palace, nobody looks at the walls. It is when he is gone, and the house is filled with grooms and gazers, that we turn from the people to find relief in the majestic men that are suggested by the pictures and the architecture. The critics who complain of the sickly separation of the beauty of nature from the thing to be done must consider that our hunting of the picturesque is inseparable from our protest against false society. Man is fallen; nature is erect, and serves as a differential thermometer, detecting the presence or absence of the divine sentiment in man. By fault of our dullness and selfishness we are looking up to nature, but when we are convalescent, nature will look up to us. We see the foaming brook with compunction: if our own life flowed with the right energy, we should shame the brook. The stream of zeal sparkles with real fire, and not with reflex rays of sun and moon. Nature may be as selfishly studied as trade. Astronomy to the selfish becomes astrology; psychology, mesmerism (with intent to show where our spoons are gone); and anatomy and physiology become phrenology and palmistry.

But taking timely warning, and leaving many things unsaid on this topic, let us not longer omit our homage to the efficient nature, *natura naturans*, the quick cause before which all forms flee as the driven snows; itself secret, its works driven before it in flocks and multitudes (as the ancients represented nature by Proteus, a shepherd) and in undescribable variety. It publishes itself in creatures, reaching from particles and spiculae through transformation on transformation to the highest symmetries, arriving at consummate results without a shock or a leap. A little heat, that is a little motion, is all that differences the bald, dazzling white and deadly cold poles of the earth from the prolific tropical climates. All changes pass without violence, by reason of the two cardinal conditions of boundless space and boundless time. Geology has initiated us into the secularity of nature, and taught us to disuse our dame-school measures, and exchange our Mosaic and Ptolemaic schemes for her large style. We knew nothing rightly, for want of perspective. Now we learn what patient periods must round themselves before the rock is formed; then before the rock is broken, and the first lichen race has disintegrated the thinnest external plate into soil, and opened the door for the remote Flora, Fauna, Ceres, and Pomona to come in. How far off yet is the trilobite! how far the quadruped! how inconceivably remote is man! All duly arrive, and then race after race of men. It is a long way from granite to the oyster; farther yet to Plato and the preaching of the immortality of the soul. Yet all must come, as surely as the first atom has two sides.

Motion or change and identity or rest are the first and second secrets of Nature: motion and rest. The whole code of her laws may be written on the thumbnail, or the signet of a ring. The whirling bubble on the surface of a brook admits us to the secret of the mechanics of the sky. Every shell on the beach is a key to it. A little water made to rotate in a cup explains the formation of the simpler shells; the addition of matter from year to year arrives at last at the most complex forms; and yet so poor is Nature with all her craft that from the beginning to the end of the universe she has but one stuff—but one stuff with its two ends, to serve up all her dreamlike variety. Compound it how she will, star, sand, fire, water, tree, man, it is still one stuff, and betrays the same properties.

Nature is always consistent, though she feigns to contravene her own laws. She keeps her laws, and seems to transcend them. She arms and equips an animal to find its place and living in the earth, and at the same time she arms and equips another animal to destroy it. Space exists to divide creatures; but by clothing the sides of a bird with a few feathers she gives him a petty omnipresence. The direction is forever onward, but the artist still goes back for materials and begins again with the first elements on the most advanced stage; otherwise all goes to ruin. If we look at her work, we seem to catch a glance of a system in transition. Plants are the young of the world, vessels of health and vigor; but they grope ever upward towards consciousness; the trees are imperfect men, and seem to bemoan their imprisonment, rooted in the ground. The animal is the novice and probationer of a more advanced order. The men, though young, having tasted the first drop from the cup of thought, are already dissipated; the maples and ferns are still uncorrupt; yet no doubt when they come to consciousness they too will curse and swear. Flowers so strictly belong to youth that we adult men soon come to feel that their beautiful generations concern not us: we have had our day; now let the children have theirs. The flowers jilt us, and we are old bachelors with our ridiculous tenderness.

Things are so strictly related that, according to the skill of the eye, from any one object the parts and properties of any other may be predicted. If we had eyes to see it, a bit of stone from the city wall would certify us of the necessity that man must exist, as readily as the city. That identity makes us all one, and reduces to nothing great intervals on our customary scale. We talk of deviations from natural life, as if artificial life were not also natural. The smoothest curled courtier in the boudoirs of a palace has an animal nature, rude and aboriginal as a white bear, omnipotent to its own ends, and is directly related, there amid essences and billets-doux, to Himalaya mountain chains and the axis of the globe. If we consider how much we are nature's, we need not be superstitious about towns, as if that terrific or benefic force did not find us there also, and fashion cities. Nature, who made the mason, made the house. We may easily hear too much of rural influences. The cool disengaged air of natural objects makes them enviable to us, chafed and irritable creatures with red faces, and we think we shall be as grand as they if we camp out and eat roots; but let us be men instead of woodchucks and the oak and the elm shall gladly serve us, though we sit in chairs of ivory on carpets of silk.

This guiding identity runs through all the surprises and contrasts of the piece, and characterizes every law. Man carries the world in his head, the whole astronomy and chemistry suspended in a thought. Because the history of nature is charactered in his brain, therefore is he the prophet and discoverer of her secrets. Every known fact in natural science was divined by the presentiment of somebody, before it was actually verified. A man does not tie his shoe without recognizing laws which bind the farthest regions of nature: moon, plant, gas, crystal are concrete geometry and numbers. Common sense knows its own, and recognizes the fact at first sight in chemical experiment. The common sense of Franklin, Dalton, Davy and Black is the same common sense which made the arrangements which now it discovers.

If the identity expresses organized rest, the counter action runs also into organization. The astronomers said, "Give us matter and a little motion and we will construct the universe. It is not enough that we should have matter, we must also have a single impulse, one shove to launch the mass and generate the harmony of the centrifugal and centripetal forces. Once heave the ball from the hand, and we can show how all this mighty order grew." "A very unreasonable postulate," said the metaphysicians, "and a plain begging of the question. Could you not prevail to know the genesis of projection, as well as the continuation of it?" Nature, meanwhile, had not waited for the discussion, but, right or wrong, bestowed the impulse, and the balls rolled. It was no great affair, a mere push, but the astronomers were right in making much of it, for there is no end to the consequences of the act. That famous aboriginal push propagates itself through all the balls of the system, and through every atom of every ball; through all the races of creatures, and through the history and performances of every individual. Exaggeration is in the course of things. Nature sends no creature, no man into the world without adding a small excess of his proper quality. Given the planet, it is still necessary to add the impulse; so to every creature nature added a little violence of direction in its proper path, a shove to put it on its way; in every instance a slight generosity, a drop too much. Without electricity the air would rot, and without this violence of direction which men and women have, without a spice of bigot and fanatic, no excitement, no efficiency. We aim above the mark to hit the mark. Every act hath some falsehood of exaggeration in it. And when now and then comes along some sad, sharp-eyed man, who sees how paltry a game is played, and refuses to play but blabs the secret, how then? Is the bird flown? O no, the wary Nature sends a new troop of fairer forms, of lordlier youths, with a little more excess of direction to hold them fast to their several aim; makes them a little wrong-headed in that direction in which they are rightest, and on goes the game again with new whirl, for a generation or two more. The child with his sweet pranks, the fool of his senses, commanded by every sight and sound, without any power to compare and rank his sensations, abandoned to a whistle or a painted chip, to a lead dragoon or a gingerbread dog, individualizing everything, generalizing nothing, delighted with every new thing, lies down at night overpowered by the fatigue which this day of continual pretty madness has incurred. But Nature has answered her purpose with the curly, dimpled lunatic. She has tasked every faculty, and has secured the symmetrical growth of the bodily frame by all these attitudes and exertions—an end of the first importance, which could not be trusted to any care less perfect than her own. This glitter, this opaline luster plays round the top of every toy to his eye to insure his fidelity, and he is deceived to his good. We are made alive and kept alive by the same arts. Let the stoics say what they please, we do not eat for the good of living, but because the meat is savory and the appetite is keen. The vegetable life does not content itself with casting from the flower or the tree a single seed, but it fills the air and earth with a prodigality of seeds, that, if thousands perish, thousands may plant themselves; that hundreds may come up, that tens may live to maturity; that at least one may replace the parent. All things betray the same calculated profusion. The excess of fear with which the animal frame is hedged round, shrinking from cold, starting at sight of a snake or at a sudden noise, protects us, through a multitude of groundless alarms, from some one real danger at last. The lover seeks in marriage his private felicity and perfection, with no prospective end; and Nature hides in his happiness her own end, namely progeny, or the perpetuity of the race.

But the craft with which the world is made runs also into the mind and character of men. No man is quite sane; each has a vein of folly in his composition, a slight determination of blood to the head, to make sure of holding him hard to some one point which Nature had taken to heart. Great causes are never tried on their merits; but the cause is reduced to particulars to suit the size of the partisans, and the contention is ever hottest on minor matters. Not less remarkable is the overfaith of each man in the importance of what he has to do or say. The poet, the prophet, has a higher value for what he utters than any hearer, and therefore it gets spoken. The strong, self-complacent Luther declares with an emphasis not to be mistaken that "God himself cannot do without wise men." Jacob Behmen and George Fox betray their egotism in the pertinacity of their controversial tracts, and James Naylor once suffered himself to be worshipped as the Christ. Each prophet comes presently to identify himself with his thought, and to esteem his hat and shoes sacred. However this may discredit such persons with the judicious, it helps them with the people, as it gives heat, pungency and publicity to their words. A similar experience is not infrequent in private life. Each young and ardent person writes a diary, in which, when the hours of prayer and penitence arrive, he inscribes his soul. The pages thus written are to him burning and fragrant; he reads them on his knees by midnight and by the morning star; he wets them with his tears; they are sacred; too good for the world, and hardly yet to be shown to the dearest friend. This is the man-child that is born to the soul, and her life still circulates in the babe. The umbilical cord has not yet been cut. After some time has elapsed, he begins to wish to admit his friend to this hallowed experience, and with hesitation, yet with firmness, exposes the pages to his eye. Will they not burn his eyes? The friend coldly turns them over, and passes from the writing to conversation, with easy transition, which strikes the other party with astonishment and vexation. He cannot suspect the writing itself. Days and nights of fervid life, of communion with angels of darkness and of light have engraved their shadowy characters on their tear-stained book. He suspects the intelligence or the heart of his friend. Is there then no friend? He cannot yet credit that one may have impressive experience and yet may not know how to put his private fact into literature: and perhaps the discovery that wisdom has other tongues and ministers than we, that though we should hold our peace the truth would not the less be spoken, might check injuriously the flames of our zeal. A man can only speak so long as he does not feel his speech to be partial and inadequate. It is partial, but he does not see it to be so while he utters it. As soon as he is released from the instinctive and particular and sees its partiality, he shuts his mouth in disgust. For no man can write anything who does not think that what he writes is for the time the history of the world; or do anything well who does not esteem his work to be of importance. My work may be of none, but I must not think it of none, or I shall not do it with impunity.

In like manner, there is throughout nature something mocking, something that leads us on and on, but arrives nowhere, keeps no faith with us. All promise outruns the performance. We live in a system of approximations. Every end is prospective of some other end, which is also temporary; a round and final success nowhere. We are encamped in nature, not domesticated. Hunger and thirst lead us on to eat and to drink; but bread and wine, mix and cook them how you will, leave us hungry and thirsty, after the stomach is full. It is the same with all our arts and performances. Our music, our poetry, our language itself are not satisfactions, but suggestions. The hunger for wealth, which reduces the planet to a garden, fools the eager pursuer. What is the end sought? Plainly to secure the ends of good sense and beauty from the intrusion of deformity or vulgarity of any kind. But what an operose method! What a train of means to secure a little conversation! This palace of brick and stone, these servants, this kitchen, these stables, horses and equipage, this bank stock and file of mortgages; trade to all the world, country house and cottage by the waterside, all for a little conversation, high, clear and spiritual! Could it not be had as well by beggars on the highway? No, all these things came from successive efforts of these beggars to remove friction from the wheels of life, and give opportunity. Conversation, character were the avowed ends; wealth was good as it appeased the animal cravings, cured the smoky chimney, silenced the creaking door, brought friends together in a warm and quiet room, and kept the children and the dinner table in a different apartment. Thought, virtue, beauty were the ends; but it was known that men of thought and virtue sometimes had the headache, or wet feet, or could lose good time while the room was getting warm in winter days. Unluckily, in the exertions necessary to remove these inconveniences, the main attention has been diverted to this object; the old aims have been lost sight of, and to remove friction has come to be the end. That is the ridicule of rich men; and Boston, London, Vienna, and now the governments generally of the world, are cities and governments of the rich; and the masses are not men, but *poor* men, that is, men who would be rich; this is the ridicule of the class, that they arrive with pains and sweat and fury nowhere; when all is done, it is for nothing. They are like one who has interrupted the conversation of a company to make his speech, and now has forgotten what he went to say. The appearance strikes the eye everywhere of an aimless society, of aimless nations. Were the ends of nature so great and cogent as to exact this immense sacrifice of men?

Quite analogous to the deceits in life, there is, as might be expected, a similar effect on the eye from the face of external nature. There is in woods and waters a certain enticement and flattery, together with a failure to yield a present satisfaction. This disappointment is felt in every landscape. I have seen the softness and beauty of the summer clouds floating feathery overhead, enjoying, as it seemed, their height and privilege of motion, while yet they appeared not so much the drapery of this place and hour, as forelooking to some pavilions and gardens of festivity beyond. It is an odd jealousy, but the poet finds himself not near enough to his object. The pine tree, the river, the bank of flowers before him, does not seem to be nature. Nature is still elsewhere. This or this is but outskirt and a far-off reflection and echo of the triumph that has passed by and is now at its glancing splendor and heyday, perchance in the neighboring fields, or, if you stand in the field, then in the adjacent woods. The present object shall give you this sense of stillness that follows a pageant which has just gone by. What splendid distance, what recesses of ineffable pomp and loveliness in the sunset! But who can go where they are, or lay his hand or plant his foot thereon? Off they fall from the round world forever and ever. It is the same among the men and women as among the silent trees; always a referred existence, an absence, never a presence and satisfaction. Is it that beauty can never be grasped? in persons and in landscape is equally inaccessible? The accepted and betrothed lover has lost the wildest charm of his maiden in her acceptance of him. She was heaven while he pursued her as a star: she cannot be heaven if she stoops to such a one as he.

What shall we say of this omnipresent appearance of that first projectile impulse, of this flattery and balking of so many well-meaning creatures? Must we not suppose somewhere in the universe a slight treachery and derision? Are we not engaged to a serious resentment of this use that is made of us? Are we tickled trout, and fools of nature? One look at the face of heaven and earth lays all petulance at rest, and soothes us to wiser convictions. To the intelligent, nature converts itself into a vast promise, and will not be rashly explained. Her secret is untold. Many and many an Oedipus arrives; he has the whole mystery teeming in his brain. Alas! the same sorcery has spoiled his skill; no syllable can he shape on his lips. Her mighty orbit vaults like the fresh rainbow into the deep, but no archangel's wing was yet strong enough to follow it and report of the return of the curve. But it also appears that our actions are seconded and disposed to greater conclusions than we designed. We are escorted on every hand through life by spiritual agents, and a beneficent purpose lies in wait for us. We cannot bandy words with Nature, or deal with her as we deal with persons. If we measure our individual forces against hers we may easily feel as if we were the sport of an insuperable destiny. But if, instead of identifying ourselves with the work, we feel that the soul of the workman streams through us, we shall find the peace of the morning dwelling first in our hearts, and the fathomless powers of gravity and chemistry, and, over them, of life, pre-existing within us in their highest form.

The uneasiness which the thought of our helplessness in the chain of causes occasions us results from looking too much at one condition of nature, namely, motion. But the drag is never taken from the wheel. Wherever the impulse exceeds, the rest or identity insinuates its compensation. All over the wide fields of earth grows the prunella or self-heal. After every foolish day we sleep off the fumes and furies of its hours; and though we are always engaged with particulars, and often enslaved to them, we bring with us to every experiment the innate universal laws These, while they exist in the mind as ideas, stand around us in nature forever embodied, a present sanity to expose and cure the insanity of men. Our servitude to particulars betrays us into a hundred foolish expectations. We anticipate a new era from the invention of a locomotive, or a balloon; the new engine brings with it the old checks. They say that by electromagnetism your salad shall be grown from the seed while your fowl is roasting for dinner; it is a symbol of our modern aims and endeavors, of our condensation and acceleration of objects; but nothing is gained; nature cannot be cheated; man's life is but seventy salads long, grow they swift or grow they slow. In these checks and impossibilities, however, we find our advantage, not less than in the impulses. Let the victory fall where it will, we are on that side. And the knowledge that we traverse the whole scale of being, from the center to the poles of nature, and have some stake in every possibility, lends that sublime luster to death, which philosophy and religion have too outwardly and literally striven to express in the popular doctrine of the immortality of the soul. The reality is more excellent than the report. Here is no ruin, no discontinuity, no spent ball. The divine circulations never rest nor linger. Nature is the incarnation of a thought, and turns to a thought again, as ice becomes water and gas. The world is mind precipitated, and the volatile essence is forever escaping again into the state of free thought. Hence the virtue and pungency of the influence on the mind of natural objects, whether inorganic or organized. Man imprisoned, man crystallized, man vegetative, speaks to man impersonated. That power which does not respect quantity, which makes the whole and the particle its equal channel, delegates its smile to the morning, and distills its essence into every drop of rain. Every moment instructs, and every object; for wisdom is infused into every form. It has been poured into us as blood; it convulsed us as pain; it slid into us as pleasure; it enveloped us in dull, melancholy days, or in days of cheerful labor; we did not guess its essence until after a long time.

Self-Reliance

Ne te quæsiveris extra.[1]

Man is his own star; and the soul that can
Render an honest and a perfect man,
Commands all light, all influence, all fate;
Nothing to him falls early or too late.
Our acts our angels are, or good or ill,
Our fatal shadows that walk by us still.

Epilogue to Beaumont and Fletcher's
Honest Man's Fortune.

Cast the bantling on the rocks,
Suckle him with the she-wolf's teat,
Wintered with the hawk and fox,
Power and speed be hands and feet.

I read the other day some verses written by an eminent painter which were original and not conventional. The soul always hears an admonition in such lines, let the subject be what it may. The sentiment they instill is of more value than any thought they may contain. To believe your own thought, to believe that what is true for you in your private heart is true for all men—that is genius. Speak your latent conviction, and it shall be the universal sense; for the inmost in due time becomes the outmost, and our first thought is rendered back to us by the trumpets of the Last Judgment. Familiar as the voice of the mind is to each, the highest merit we ascribe to Moses, Plato and Milton is that they set at naught books and traditions, and spoke not what men, but what *they*, thought. A man should learn to detect and watch that gleam of light which flashes across his mind from within, more than the luster of the firmament of bards and sages. Yet he dismisses without notice his thought,

---

1. "If you seek yourself, look not without."

because it is his. In every work of genius we recognize our own rejected thoughts; they come back to us with a certain alienated majesty. Great works of art have no more affecting lesson for us than this. They teach us to abide by our spontaneous impression with good-humored inflexibility than most when the whole cry of voices is on the other side. Else tomorrow a stranger will say with masterly good sense precisely what we have thought and felt all the time, and we shall be forced to take with shame our own opinion from another.

There is a time in every man's education when he arrives at the conviction that envy is ignorance; that imitation is suicide; that he must take himself for better for worse as his portion; that though the wide universe is full of good, no kernel of nourishing corn can come to him but through his toil bestowed on that plot of ground which is given to him to till. The power which resides in him is new in nature, and none but he knows what that is which he can do, nor does he know until he has tried. Not for nothing one face, one character, one fact, makes much impression on him, and another none. This sculpture in the memory is not without pre-established harmony. The eye was placed where one ray should fall, that it might testify of that particular ray. We but half express ourselves, and are ashamed of that divine idea which each of us represents. It may be safely trusted as proportionate and of good issues, so it be faithfully imparted, but God will not have his work made manifest by cowards. A man is relieved and gay when he has put his heart into his work and done his best; but what he has said or done otherwise shall give him no peace. It is a deliverance which does not deliver. In the attempt his genius deserts him; no muse befriends; no invention, no hope.

Trust thyself: every heart vibrates to that iron string. Accept the place the divine providence has found for you, the society of your contemporaries, the connection of events. Great men have always done so, and confided themselves childlike to the genius of their age, betraying their perception that the absolutely trustworthy was seated at their heart, working through their hands, predominating in all their being. And we are now men, and must accept in the highest mind the same transcendent destiny; and not minors and invalids in a protected corner, not cowards fleeing before a revolution, but guides, redeemers and benefactors, obeying the Almighty effort and advancing on chaos and the dark.

What pretty oracles nature yields us on this text in the face and behavior of children, babes, and even brutes! That divided and rebel mind, that distrust of a sentiment because our arithmetic has computed the strength and means opposed to our purpose, these have not. Their mind being whole, their eye is as yet unconquered; and when we look in their faces we are disconcerted. Infancy conforms to nobody; all conform to it; so that one babe commonly makes four or five out of the adults who prattle and play to it. So God has armed youth and puberty and manhood no less with its own piquancy and charm, and made it enviable and gracious and its claims not to be put by, if it will stand by itself. Do not think the youth has no force, because he cannot speak to you and me. Hark! in the next room his voice is sufficiently clear and emphatic. It seems he knows how to speak to his contemporaries. Bashful or bold then, he will know how to make us seniors very unnecessary.

The nonchalance of boys who are sure of a dinner, and would disdain as much as a lord to do or say aught to conciliate one, is the healthy attitude of human nature. A boy is in the parlor what the pit is in the playhouse; independent, irresponsible, looking out from his corner on such people and facts as pass by, he tries and sentences them on their merits, in the swift, summary way of boys, as good, bad, interesting, silly, eloquent, troublesome. He cumbers himself never about consequences, about interests; he gives an independent, genuine verdict. You must court him; he does not court you. But the man is as it were clapped into jail by his consciousness. As soon as he has once acted or spoken with éclat he is a committed person, watched by the sympathy or the hatred of hundreds, whose affections must now enter into his account. There is no Lethe for this. Ah, that he could pass again into his neutrality! Who can thus avoid all pledges and, having observed, observe again from the same unaffected, unbiased, unbribable, unaffrighted innocence must always be formidable. He would utter opinions on all passing affairs, which being seen to be not private but necessary, would sink like darts into the ear of men and put them in fear.

These are the voices which we hear in solitude, but they grow faint and inaudible as we enter into the world. Society everywhere is in conspiracy against the manhood of every one of its members. Society is a joint-stock company, in which the members agree, for the better securing of his bread to each shareholder, to surrender the liberty and culture of the eater. The virtue in most request is conformity. Self-reliance is its aversion. It loves not realities and creators, but names and customs.

Whoso would be a man must be a nonconformist. He who would gather immortal palms must not be hindered by the name of goodness, but must explore if it be goodness. Nothing is at last sacred but the integrity of your own mind. Absolve you to yourself, and you shall have the suffrage of the world. I remember an answer which when quite young I was prompted to make to a valued adviser who was wont to importune me with the dear old doctrines of the church. On my saying, "What have I to do with the sacredness of traditions, if I live wholly from within?" my friend suggested—"But these impulses may be from below, not from above." I replied, "They do not seem to me to be such; but if I am the Devil's child, I will live then from the Devil." No law can be sacred to me but that of my nature. Good and bad are but names very readily transferable to that or this; the only right is what is after my constitution; the only wrong what is against it. A man is to carry himself in the presence of all opposition as if everything were titular and ephemeral but he. I am ashamed to think how easily we capitulate to badges and names, to large societies and dead institutions. Every decent and well-spoken individual affects and sways me more than is right. I ought to go upright and vital, and speak the rude truth in all ways. If malice and vanity wear the coat of philanthropy, shall that pass? If an angry bigot assumes this bountiful cause of Abolition, and comes to me with his last news from Barbados, why should I not say to him, "Go love thy infant; love thy wood chopper; be good natured and modest; have that grace; and never varnish your hard, uncharitable ambition with this incredible tenderness for black folk a thousand miles off. Thy love afar is spite at home." Rough and graceless would be such greeting, but truth is handsomer than the affectation of love. Your goodness must have some edge to it—else it is none. The doctrine of hatred must be preached, as the counteraction of the doctrine of love, when that pules and whines. I shun father and mother and wife and brother when my genius calls me. I would write on the lintels of the doorpost, *Whim.* I hope it is somewhat better than whim at last, but we cannot spend the day in explanation. Expect me not to show cause why I seek or why I exclude company. Then again, do not tell me, as a good man did today, of my obligation to put all poor men in good situations. Are they *my* poor? I tell thee, thou foolish philanthropist, that I grudge the dollar, the dime, the cent I give to such men as do not belong to me and to whom I do not belong. There is a class of persons to whom by all spiritual affinity I am bought and sold; for them I will go to prison if need be; but your miscellaneous popular charities; the education at college of fools; the building of meetinghouses to the vain end to which many now stand; alms to sots, and the thousandfold relief societies; though I confess with shame I sometimes succumb and give the dollar, it is a wicked dollar, which by and by I shall have the manhood to withhold.

Virtues are, in the popular estimate, rather the exception than the rule. There is the man *and* his virtues. Men do what is called a good action, as some piece of courage or charity, much as they would pay a fine in expiation of daily nonappearance on parade. Their works are done as an apology or extenuation of their living in the world—as invalids and the insane pay a high board. Their virtues are penances. I do not wish to expiate, but to live. My life is for itself and not for a spectacle. I much prefer that it should be of a lower strain, so it be genuine and equal, than that it should be glittering and unsteady. I wish it to be sound and sweet, and not to need diet and bleeding. I ask primary evidence that you are a man, and refuse this appeal from the man to his actions. I know that for myself it makes no difference whether I do or forbear those actions which are reckoned excellent. I cannot consent to pay for a privilege where I have intrinsic right. Few and mean as my gifts may be, I actually am, and do not need for my own assurance or the assurance of my fellows any secondary testimony.

What I must do is all that concerns me, not what the people think. This rule, equally arduous in actual and in intellectual life, may serve for the whole distinction between greatness and meanness. It is the harder because you will always find those who think they know what is your duty better than you know it. It is easy in the world to live after the world's opinion; it is easy in solitude to live after our own; but the great man is he who in the midst of the crowd keeps with perfect sweetness the independence of solitude.

The objection to conforming to usages that have become dead to you is that it scatters your force. It loses your time and blurs the impression of your character. If you maintain a dead church, contribute to a dead Bible society, vote with a great party either for the government or against it, spread your table like base housekeepers—under all these screens I have difficulty to detect the precise man you are: and of course so much force is withdrawn from your proper life. But do your work, and I shall know you. Do your work, and you shall reinforce yourself. A man must consider what a blindman's buff is this game of conformity. If I know your sect I anticipate your argument. I hear a preacher announce for his text and topic the expediency of one of the institutions of his church. Do I not know beforehand that not possibly can he say a new and spontaneous word? Do I not know that with all this ostentation of examining the grounds of the institution he will do no such thing? Do I not know that he is pledged to himself not to look but at one side, the permitted side, not as a man, but as a parish minister? He is a retained attorney, and these airs of the bench are the emptiest affectation. Well, most men have bound their eyes with one or another handkerchief, and attached themselves to some one of these communities of opinion. This conformity makes them not false in a few particulars, authors of a few lies, but false in all particulars. Their every truth is not quite true. Their two is not the real two, their four not the real four; so that every word they say chagrins us and we know not where to begin to set them right. Meantime nature is not slow to equip us in the prison uniform of the party to which we adhere. We come to wear one cut of face and figure, and acquire by degrees the gentlest asinine expression. There is a mortifying experience in particular, which does not fail to wreak itself also in the general history; I mean "the foolish face of praise," the forced smile which we put on in company where we do not feel at ease, in answer to conversation which does not interest us. The muscles, not spontaneously moved but moved by a low usurping willfulness, grow tight about the outline of the face, with the most disagreeable sensation.

For nonconformity the world whips you with its displeasure. And therefore a man must know how to estimate a sour face. The bystanders look askance on him in the public street or in the friend's parlor. If this aversion had its origin in contempt and resistance like his own he might well go home with a sad countenance; but the sour faces of the multitude, like their sweet faces, have no deep cause, but are put on and off as the wind blows and a newspaper directs. Yet is the discontent of the multitude more formidable than that of the senate and the college. It is easy enough for a firm man who knows the world to brook the rage of the cultivated classes. Their rage is decorous and prudent, for they are timid, as being very vulnerable themselves. But when to their feminine rage the indignation of the people is added, when the ignorant and the poor are aroused, when the unintelligent brute force that lies at the bottom of society is made to growl and mow, it needs the habit of magnanimity and religion to treat it godlike as a trifle of no concernment.

The other terror that scares us from self-trust is our consistency; a reverence for our past act or word because the eyes of others have no other data for computing our orbit than our past acts, and we are loath to disappoint them.

But why should you keep your head over your shoulder? Why drag about this corpse of your memory, lest you contradict somewhat you have stated in this or that public place? Suppose you should contradict yourself; what then? It seems to be a rule of wisdom never to rely on your memory alone, scarcely even in acts of pure memory, but to bring the past for judgment into the thousand-eyed present, and live ever in a new day. In your metaphysics you have denied personality to the Deity, yet when the devout motions of the soul come, yield to them heart and life, though they should clothe God with shape and color. Leave your theory, as Joseph his coat in the hand of the harlot, and flee.

A foolish consistency is the hobgoblin of little minds, adored by little statesmen and philosophers and divines. With consistency a great soul has simply nothing to do. He may as well concern himself with his shadow on the wall. Speak what you think now in hard words and tomorrow speak what tomorrow thinks in hard words again, though it contradict everything you said today.—"Ah, so you shall be sure to be misunderstood."—Is it so bad then to be misunderstood? Pythagoras was misunderstood, and Socrates, and Jesus, and Luther, and Copernicus, and Galileo, and Newton, and every pure and wise spirit that ever took flesh. To be great is to be misunderstood.

I suppose no man can violate his nature. All the sallies of his will are rounded in by the law of his being, as the inequalities of Andes and Himalaya are insignificant in the curve of the sphere. Nor does it matter how you gauge and try him. A character is like an acrostic or Alexandrian stanza; read it forward, backward, or across, it still spells the same thing. In this pleasing contrite wood life which God allows me, let me record day by day my honest thought without prospect or retrospect, and, I cannot doubt, it will be found symmetrical, though I mean it not and see it not. My book should smell of pines and resound with the hum of insects. The swallow over my window should interweave that thread or straw he carries in his bill into my web also. We pass for what we are. Character teaches above our wills. Men imagine that they communicate their virtue or vice only by overt actions, and do not see that virtue or vice emit a breath every moment.

There will be an agreement in whatever variety of actions, so they be each honest and natural in their hour. For of one will, the actions will be harmonious, however unlike they seem. These varieties are lost sight of at a little distance, at a little height of thought. One tendency unites them all. The voyage of the best ship is a zigzag line of a hundred tacks. See the line from a sufficient distance, and it straightens itself to the average tendency. Your genuine action will explain itself and will explain your other genuine actions. Your conformity explains nothing. Act singly, and what you have already done singly will justify you now. Greatness appeals to the future. If I can be firm enough today to do right and scorn eyes, I must have done so much right before as to defend me now. Be it how it will, do right now. Always scorn appearances and you always may. The force of character is cumulative. All the foregone days of virtue work their

health into this. What makes the majesty of the heroes of the senate and
the field, which so fills the imagination? The consciousness of a train of
great days and victories behind. They shed a united light on the advancing
actor. He is attended as by a visible escort of angels. That is it which
throws thunder into Chatham's voice, and dignity into Washington's port,
and America into Adams' eye. Honor is venerable to us because it is no
ephemera. It is always ancient virtue. We worship it today because it is
not of today. We love it and pay it homage because it is not a trap for our
love and homage, but is self-dependent, self-derived, and therefore of an
old immaculate pedigree, even if shown in a young person.

I hope in these days we have heard the last of conformity and consistency. Let the words be gazetted and ridiculous henceforward. Instead of
the gong for dinner, let us hear a whistle from the Spartan fife. Let us
never bow and apologize more. A great man is coming to eat at my house.
I do not wish to please him; I wish that he should wish to please me. I will
stand here for humanity, and though I would make it kind, I would make
it true. Let us affront and reprimand the smooth mediocrity and squalid
contentment of the times, and hurl in the face of custom and trade and
office, the fact which is the upshot of all history, that there is a great
responsible thinker and actor working wherever a man works; that a true
man belongs to no other time or place, but is the center of things. Where
he is, there is nature. He measures you and all men and all events.
Ordinarily, everybody in society reminds us of somewhat else, or of some
other person. Character, reality, reminds you of nothing else; it takes
place of the whole creation. The man must be so much that he must make
all circumstances indifferent. Every true man is a cause, a country, and an
age; requires infinite spaces and numbers and time fully to accomplish his
design; and posterity seem to follow his steps as a train of clients. A man
Caesar is born, and for ages after we have a Roman Empire. Christ is
born, and millions of minds so grow and cleave to his genius that he is
confounded with virtue and the possible of man. An institution is the
lengthened shadow of one man; as, Monachism, of the Hermit Antony;
the Reformation, of Luther; Quakerism, of Fox; Methodism, of Wesley;
Abolition, of Clarkson. Scipio, Milton called "the height of Rome"; and
all history resolves itself very easily into the biography of a few stout and
earnest persons.

Let a man then know his worth, and keep things under his feet. Let him
not peep or steal, or skulk up and down with the air of a charity boy, a
bastard, or an interloper in the world which exists for him. But the man in
the street, finding no worth in himself which corresponds to the force

which built a tower or sculptured a marble god, feels poor when he looks on these. To him a palace, a statue, or a costly book have an alien and forbidding air, much like a gay equipage, and seem to say like that, "Who are you, Sir?" Yet they all are his, suitors for his notice, petitioners to his faculties that they will come out and take possession. The picture waits for my verdict; it is not to command me, but I am to settle its claims to praise. That popular fable of the sot who was picked up dead-drunk in the street, carried to the duke's house, washed and dressed and laid in the duke's bed, and, on his waking, treated with all obsequious ceremony like the duke, and assured that he had been insane owes its popularity to the fact that it symbolizes so well the state of man, who is in the world a sort of sot, but now and then wakes up, exercises his reason and finds himself a true prince.

Our reading is mendicant and sycophantic. In history our imagination plays us false. Kingdom and lordship, power and estate, are a gaudier vocabulary than private John and Edward in a small house and common day's work; but the things of life are the same to both; the sum total of both is the same. Why all this deference to Alfred and Scanderbeg and Gustavus? Suppose they were virtuous; did they wear out virtue? As great a stake depends on your private act today as followed their public and renowned steps. When private men shall act with original views, the luster will be transferred from the actions of kings to those of gentlemen.

The world has been instructed by its kings, who have so magnetized the eyes of nations. It has been taught by this colossal symbol the mutual reverence that is due from man to man. The joyful loyalty with which men have everywhere suffered the king, the noble, or the great proprietor to walk among them by a law of his own, make his own scale of men and things and reverse theirs, pay for benefits not with money but with honor, and represent the law in his person was the hieroglyphic by which they obscurely signified their consciousness of their own right and comeliness, the right of every man.

The magnetism which all original action exerts is explained when we inquire the reason of self-trust. Who is the trustee? What is the aboriginal self, on which a universal reliance may be grounded? What is the nature and power of that science-baffling star, without parallax, without calculable elements, which shoots a ray of beauty even into trivial and impure actions, if the least mark of independence appear? The inquiry leads us to that source, at once the essence of genius, of virtue, and of life, which we call spontaneity or instinct. We denote this primary wisdom as intuition, while all later teachings are tuitions. In that deep force, the last fact behind which analysis cannot go, all things find their common origin. For the sense of being which in calm hours rises, we know not how, in the soul is not diverse from things, from space, from light, from time, from man, but one with them and proceeds obviously from the same source whence their life and being also proceed. We first share the life by which things exist and afterwards see them as appearances in nature and forget that we have shared their cause. Here is the fountain of action and of thought. Here are the lungs of that inspiration which giveth man wisdom and which cannot be denied without impiety and atheism. We lie in the lap of immense intelligence, which makes us receivers of its truth and organs of its activity. When we discern justice, when we discern truth, we do nothing of ourselves, but allow a passage to its beams. If we ask whence this comes, if we seek to pry into the soul that causes, all philosophy is at fault. Its presence or its absence is all we can affirm. Every man discriminates between the voluntary acts of his mind and his involuntary perceptions, and knows that to his involuntary perceptions a perfect faith is due. He may err in the expression of them, but he knows that these things are so, like day and night, not to be disputed. My willful actions and acquisitions are but roving; the idlest reverie, the faintest native emotion command my curiosity and respect. Thoughtless people contradict as readily the statement of perceptions as of opinions, or rather much more readily; for they do not distinguish between perception and notion. They fancy that I choose to see this or that thing. But perception is not whimsical, but fatal. If I see a trait, my children will see it after me, and in course of time all mankind—although it may chance that no one has seen it before me. For my perception of it is as much a fact as the sun.

The relations of the soul to the divine spirit are so pure that it is profane to seek to interpose helps. It must be that when God speaketh he should communicate, not one thing, but all things; should fill the world with his voice; should scatter forth light, nature, time, souls, from the center of the present thought; and new date and new create the whole. Whenever a mind is simple and receives a divine wisdom, old things pass away—means, teachers, texts, temples fall; it lives now, and absorbs past and future into the present hour. All things are made sacred by relation to it—one as much as another. All things are dissolved to their center by their cause, and in the universal miracle petty and particular miracles disappear. If therefore a man claims to know and speak of God and carries you backward to the phraseology of some old moldered nation in another country, in another world, believe him not. Is the acorn better than the oak which is its fullness and completion? Is the parent better than the child into whom he has cast his ripened being? Whence then this worship of the past? The centuries are conspirators against the sanity and authority of the soul. Time and space are but physiological colors which the eye makes, but the soul is light: where it is, is day; where it was, is night; and history is an impertinence and an injury if it be anything more than a cheerful apologue or parable of my being and becoming.

Man is timid and apologetic; he is no longer upright; he dares not say "I think," "I am," but quotes some saint or sage. He is ashamed before the blade of grass or the blowing rose. These roses under my window make no reference to former roses or to better ones; they are for what they are; they exist with God today. There is no time to them. There is simply the rose; it is perfect in every moment of its existence. Before a leaf bud has burst, its whole life acts; in the full-blown flower there is no more; in the leafless root there is no less. Its nature is satisfied and it satisfies nature in all moments alike. But man postpones or remembers; he does not live in the present, but with reverted eye laments the past, or, heedless of the riches that surround him, stands on tiptoe to foresee the future. He cannot be happy and strong until he too lives with nature in the present, above time.

This should be plain enough. Yet see what strong intellects dare not yet hear God himself unless he speak the phraseology of I know not what David, or Jeremiah, or Paul. We shall not always set so great a price on a few texts, on a few lives. We are like children who repeat by rote the sentences of grandames and tutors, and, as they grow older, of the men of talents and character they chance to see—painfully recollecting the exact words they spoke; afterwards, when they come into the point of view which those had who uttered these sayings, they understand them and are willing to let the words go; for at any time they can use words as good when occasion comes. If we live truly, we shall see truly. It is as easy for the strong man to be strong as it is for the weak to be weak. When we have new perception, we shall gladly disburden the memory of its hoarded treasures as old rubbish. When a man lives with God, his voice shall be as sweet as the murmur of the brook and the rustle of the corn.

And now at last the highest truth on this subject remains unsaid; probably cannot be said; for all that we say is the far-off remembering of the intuition. That thought by what I can now nearest approach to say it is this: When good is near you, when you have life in yourself, it is not by any known or accustomed way; you shall not discern the footprints of any other; you shall not see the face of man; you shall not hear any name; the way, the thought, the good shall be wholly strange and new. It shall exclude example and experience. You take the way from man, not to man. All persons that ever existed are its forgotten ministers. Fear and hope are alike beneath it. There is somewhat low even in hope. In the hour of vision there is nothing that can be called gratitude, nor properly joy. The soul raised over passion beholds identity and eternal causation, perceives the self-existence of Truth and Right, and calms itself with knowing that all things go well. Vast spaces of nature, the Atlantic Ocean, the South Sea; long intervals of time, years, centuries, are of no account. This which I think and feel underlay every former state of life and circumstances, as it does underlie my present, and what is called life and what is called death.

Life only avails, not the having lived. Power ceases in the instant of repose; it resides in the moment of transition from a past to a new state, in the shooting of the gulf, in the darting to an aim. This one fact the world hates; that the soul *becomes;* for that forever degrades the past, turns all riches to poverty, all reputation to a shame, confounds the saint with the rogue, shoves Jesus and Judas equally aside. Why then do we prate of self-reliance? Inasmuch as the soul is present there will be power not confident but agent. To talk of reliance is a poor external way of speaking. Speak rather of that which relies because it works and is. Who has more obedience than I masters me, though he should not raise his finger. Round him I must revolve by the gravitation of spirits. We fancy it rhetoric when we speak of eminent virtue. We do not yet see that virtue is height, and that a man or a company of men, plastic and permeable to principles, by the law of nature must overpower and ride all cities, nations, kings, rich men, poets who are not.

This is the ultimate fact which we so quickly reach on this, as on every topic, the resolution of all into the ever-blessed One. Self-existence is the attribute of the Supreme Cause, and it constitutes the measure of good by the degree in which it enters into all lower forms. All things real are so by so much virtue as they contain. Commerce, husbandry, hunting, whaling, war, eloquence, personal weight are somewhat, and engage my respect as examples of its presence and impure action. I see the same law working in nature for conservation and growth. Power is, in nature, the essential measure of right. Nature suffers nothing to remain in her kingdoms which cannot help itself. The genesis and maturation of a planet, its poise and orbit, the bended tree recovering itself from the strong wind, the vital resources of every animal and vegetable are demonstrations of the self-sufficing and therefore self-relying soul.

Thus all concentrates: let us not rove; let us sit at home with the cause. Let us stun and astonish the intruding rabble of men and books and institutions by a simple declaration of the divine fact. Bid the invaders take the shoes from off their feet, for God is here within. Let our simplicity judge them, and our docility to our own law demonstrate the poverty of nature and fortune beside our native riches.

But now we are a mob. Man does not stand in awe of man, nor is his genius admonished to stay at home, to put itself in communication with the internal ocean, but it goes abroad to beg a cup of water of the urns of other men. We must go alone. I like the silent church before the service begins, better than any preaching. How far off, how cool, how chaste the persons look, begirt each one with a precinct or sanctuary! So let us always sit. Why should we assume the faults of our friend, or wife, or father, or child, because they sit around our hearth, or are said to have the same blood? All men have my blood and I all men's. Not for that will I adopt their petulance or folly, even to the extent of being ashamed of it. But your isolation must not be mechanical, but spiritual, that is, must be elevation. At times the whole world seems to be in conspiracy to importune you with emphatic trifles. Friend, client, child, sickness, fear, want, charity, all knock at once at thy closet door and say—"Come out unto us." But keep thy state; come not into their confusion. The power men possess to annoy me I give them by a weak curiosity. No man can come near me but through my act. "What we love that we have, but by desire we bereave ourselves of the love."

If we cannot at once rise to the sanctities of obedience and faith, let us at least resist our temptations; let us enter into the state of war and wake Thor and Woden, courage and constancy, in our Saxon breasts. This is to be done in our smooth times by speaking the truth. Check this lying hospitality and lying affection. Live no longer to the expectation of these deceived and deceiving people with whom we converse. Say to them, "O father, O mother, O wife, O brother, O friend, I have lived with you after appearances hitherto. Henceforward I am the truth's. Be it known unto you that henceforward I obey no law less than the eternal law. I will have no covenants but proximities. I shall endeavor to nourish my parents, to support my family, to be the chaste husband of one wife—but these relations I must fill after a new and unprecedented way. I appeal from your customs. I must be myself. I cannot break myself any longer for you, or you. If you can love me for what I am, we shall be the happier. If you cannot, I will still seek to deserve that you should. I will not hide my tastes or aversions. I will so trust that what is deep is holy that I will do strongly before the sun and moon whatever inly rejoices me and the heart appoints. If you are noble, I will love you; if you are not, I will not hurt you and myself by hypocritical attentions. If you are true, but not in the same truth with me, cleave to your companions; I will seek my own. I do this not selfishly but humbly and truly. It is alike your interest, and mine, and all men's, however long we have dwelt in lies, to live in truth. Does this sound harsh today? You will soon love what is dictated by your nature as well as mine, and if we follow the truth it will bring us out safe at last." But so may you give these friends pain. Yes, but I cannot sell my liberty and my power to save their sensibility. Besides, all persons have their moments of reason, when they look out into the region of absolute truth; then will they justify me and do the same thing.

The populace think that your rejection of popular standards is a rejection of all standard, and mere antinomianism; and the bold sensualist will use the name of philosophy to gild his crimes. But the law of consciousness abides. There are two confessionals, in one or the other of which we must be shriven. You may fulfill your round of duties by clearing yourself in the direct, or in the reflex way. Consider whether you have satisfied your relations to father, mother, cousin, neighbor, town, cat and dog—whether any of these can upbraid you. But I may also neglect this reflex standard and absolve me to myself. I have my own stern claims and perfect circle. It denies the name of duty to many offices that are called duties. But if I can discharge its debts it enables me to dispense with the popular code. If anyone imagines that this law is lax, let him keep its commandment one day.

And truly it demands something godlike in him who has cast off the common motives of humanity and has ventured to trust himself for a taskmaster. High be his heart, faithful his will, clear his sight, that he may in good earnest be doctrine, society, law to himself, that a simple purpose may be to him as strong as iron necessity is to others!

If any man consider the present aspects of what is called by distinction society, he will see the need of these ethics. The sinew and heart of man seem to be drawn out, and we are become timorous, desponding whimperers. We are afraid of truth, afraid of fortune, afraid of death, and afraid of each other. Our age yields no great and perfect persons. We want men and women who shall renovate life and our social state, but we see that most natures are insolvent, cannot satisfy their own wants, have an ambition out of all proportion to their practical force and do lean and beg day and night continually. Our housekeeping is mendicant, our arts, our occupations, our marriages, our religion we have not chosen, but society has chosen for us. We are parlor soldiers. We shun the rugged battle of fate, where strength is born.

If our young men miscarry in their first enterprises they lose all heart. If the young merchant fails, men say he is ruined. If the finest genius studies at one of our colleges and is not installed in an office within one year afterwards in the cities or suburbs of Boston or New York, it seems to his friends and to himself that he is right in being disheartened and in complaining the rest of his life. A sturdy lad from New Hampshire or Vermont who in turn tries all the professions, who teams it, farms it, peddles, keeps a school, preaches, edits a newspaper, goes to Congress, buys a township, and so forth, in successive years, and always like a cat falls on his feet, is worth a hundred of these city dolls. He walks abreast with his days and feels no shame in not "studying a profession," for he does not postpone his life, but lives already. He has not one chance, but a hundred chances. Let a Stoic open the resources of man and tell men they are not leaning willows, but can and must detach themselves; that with the exercise of self-trust, new powers shall appear; that a man is the word made flesh, born to shed healing to the nations; that he should be ashamed of our compassion, and that the moment he acts from himself, tossing the laws, the books, idolatries and customs out of the window, we pity him no more but thank and revere him; and that teacher shall restore the life of man to splendor and make his name dear to all history.

It is easy to see that a greater self-reliance must work a revolution in all the offices and relations of men; in their religion; in their education; in their pursuits; their modes of living; their association; in their property; in their speculative views.

In what prayers do men allow themselves! That which they call a holy office is not so much as brave and manly. Prayer looks abroad and asks for some foreign addition to come through some foreign virtue, and loses itself in endless mazes of natural and supernatural, and mediatorial and miraculous. Prayer that craves a particular commodity, anything less than all good, is vicious. Prayer is the contemplation of the facts of life from the highest point of view. It is the soliloquy of a beholding and jubilant soul. It is the spirit of God pronouncing his works good. But prayer as a means to effect a private end is meanness and theft. It supposes dualism and not unity in nature and consciousness. As soon as the man is at one with God, he will not beg. He will then see prayer in all action. The prayer of the farmer kneeling in his field to weed it, the prayer of the rower kneeling with the stroke of his oar are true prayers heard throughout nature, though for cheap ends. Caratach, in Fletcher's *Bonduca,* when admonished to inquire the mind of the god Audate, replies—

> His hidden meaning lies in our endeavors;
> Our valors are our best gods.

Another sort of false prayers are our regrets. Discontent is the want of self-reliance: it is infirmity of will. Regret calamities if you can thereby help the sufferer; if not, attend your own work and already the evil begins to be repaired. Our sympathy is just as base. We come to them who weep foolishly and sit down and cry for company, instead of imparting to them truth and health in rough electric shocks, putting them once more in communication with their own reason. The secret of fortune is joy in our hands. Welcome evermore to gods and men is the self-helping man. For him all doors are flung wide; him all tongues greet, all honors crown, all eyes follow with desire. Our love goes out to him and embraces him because he did not need it. We solicitously and apologetically caress and celebrate him because he held on his way and scorned our disapprobation. The gods love him because men hated him. "To the persevering mortal," said Zoroaster, "the blessed Immortals are swift."

As men's prayers are a disease of the will, so are their creeds a disease of the intellect. They say with those foolish Israelites, "Let not God speak to us, lest we die. Speak thou, speak any man with us, and we will obey." Everywhere I am hindered of meeting God in my brother, because he has shut his own temple doors and recites fables merely of his brother's, or his brother's brother's God. Every new mind is a new classification. If it prove a mind of uncommon activity and power, a Locke, a Lavoisier, a Hutton, a Bentham, a Fourier, it imposes its classification on other men, and lo! a new system. In proportion to the depth of the thought, and so to the number of the objects it touches and brings within reach of the pupil, is his complacency. But chiefly is this apparent in creeds and churches, which are also classifications of some powerful mind acting on the elemental thought of duty and man's relation to the Highest. Such is Calvinism, Quakerism, Swedenborgism. The pupil takes the same delight in subordinating everything to the new terminology as a girl who has just learned botany in seeing a new earth and new seasons thereby. It will happen for a time that the pupil will find his intellectual power has grown by the study of his master's mind. But in all unbalanced minds the classification is idolized, passes for the end and not for a speedily exhaustible means, so that the walls of the system blend to their eye in the remote horizon with the walls of the universe; the luminaries of heaven seem to them hung on the arch their master built. They cannot imagine how you aliens have any right to see—how you can see: "It must be somehow that you stole the light from us." They do not yet perceive that light, unsystematic, indomitable, will break into any cabin, even into theirs. Let them chirp awhile and call it their own. If they are honest and do well, presently their neat new pinfold will be too strait and low, will crack, will lean, will rot and vanish, and the immortal light, all young and joyful, million orbed, million colored, will beam over the universe as on the first morning.

It is for want of self-culture that the superstition of traveling, whose idols are Italy, England, Egypt, retains its fascination for all educated Americans. They who made England, Italy, or Greece venerable in the imagination did so by sticking fast where they were, like an axis of the earth. In manly hours we feel that duty is our place. The soul is no traveler; the wise man stays at home, and when his necessities, his duties on any occasion call him from his house, or into foreign lands, he is at home still and shall make men sensible by the expression of his countenance that he goes, the missionary of wisdom and virtue, and visits cities and men like a sovereign and not like an interloper or a valet.

I have no churlish objection to the circumnavigation of the globe for the purposes of art, of study, and benevolence, so that the man is first domesticated, or does not go abroad with the hope of finding somewhat greater than he knows. He who travels to be amused, or to get somewhat which he does not carry, travels away from himself, and grows old even in youth among old things. In Thebes, in Palmyra, his will and mind have become old and dilapidated as they. He carries ruins to ruins.

Traveling is a fool's paradise. Our first journeys discover to us the indifference of places. At home I dream that at Naples, at Rome, I can be intoxicated with beauty and lose my sadness. I pack my trunk, embrace my friends, embark on the sea and at last wake up in Naples, and there beside me is the stern fact, the sad self, unrelenting, identical, that I fled from. I seek the Vatican and the palaces. I affect to be intoxicated with sights and suggestions, but I am not intoxicated. My giant goes with me wherever I go.

But the rage of traveling is a symptom of a deeper unsoundness affecting the whole intellectual action. The intellect is vagabond, and our system of education fosters restlessness. Our minds travel when our bodies are forced to stay at home. We imitate; and what is imitation but the traveling of the mind? Our houses are built with foreign taste; our shelves are garnished with foreign ornaments; our opinions, our tastes, our faculties lean, and follow the past and the distant. The soul created the arts wherever they have flourished. It was in his own mind that the artist sought his model. It was an application of his own thought to the thing to be done and the conditions to be observed. And why need we copy the Doric or the Gothic model? Beauty, convenience, grandeur of thought and quaint expression are as near to us as to any, and if the American artist will study with hope and love the precise thing to be done by him, considering the climate, the soil, the length of the day, the wants of the people, the habit and form of the government, he will create a house in which all these will find themselves fitted, and taste and sentiment will be satisfied also.

Insist on yourself; never imitate. Your own gift you can present every moment with the cumulative force of a whole life's cultivation; but of the adopted talent of another you have only an extemporaneous half possession. That which each can do best, none but his Maker can teach him. No man yet knows what it is, nor can, till that person has exhibited it. Where is the master who could have taught Shakespeare? Where is the master who could have instructed Franklin, or Washington, or Bacon, or Newton? Every great man is a unique. The Scipionism of Scipio is precisely that part he could not borrow. Shakespeare will never be made by the study of Shakespeare. Do that which is assigned you, and you cannot hope too much or dare too much. There is at this moment for you an utterance brave and grand as that of the colossal chisel of Phidias, or trowel of the Egyptians, or the pen of Moses or Dante, but different from all these. Not possibly will the soul, all rich, all eloquent, with thousand-cloven tongue, deign to repeat itself; but if you can hear what these patriarchs say, surely you can reply to them in the same pitch of voice; for the ear and the tongue are two organs of one nature. Abide in the simple and noble regions of thy life, obey thy heart, and thou shalt reproduce the foreworld again.

As our religion, our education, our art look abroad, so does our spirit of society. All men plume themselves on the improvement of society, and no man improves.

Society never advances. It recedes as fast on one side as it gains on the other. It undergoes continual changes: it is barbarous, it is civilized, it is Christianized, it is rich, it is scientific; but this change is not amelioration. For everything that is given something is taken. Society acquires new arts and loses old instincts. What a contrast between the well-clad, reading, writing, thinking American, with a watch, a pencil and a bill of exchange in his pocket, and the naked New Zealander, whose property is a club, a spear, a mat and an undivided twentieth of a shed to sleep under! But compare the health of the two men and you shall see that the white man has lost his aboriginal strength. If the traveler tell us truly, strike the savage with a broadaxe and in a day or two the flesh shall unite and heal as if you struck the blow into soft pitch, and the same blow shall send the white to his grave.

The civilized man has built a coach, but has lost the use of his feet. He is supported on crutches, but lacks so much support of muscle. He has a fine Geneva watch, but he fails of the skill to tell the hour by the sun. A Greenwich nautical almanac he has, and so being sure of the information when he wants it, the man in the street does not know a star in the sky. The solstice he does not observe; the equinox he knows as little; and the whole bright calendar of the year is without a dial in his mind. His notebooks impair his memory; his libraries overload his wit; the insurance office increases the number of accidents; and it may be a question whether machinery does not encumber; whether we have not lost by refinement some energy, by a Christianity, entrenched in establishments and forms, some vigor of wild virtue. For every Stoic was a Stoic; but in Christendom where is the Christian?

There is no more deviation in the moral standard than in the standard of height or bulk. No greater men are now than ever were. A singular equality may be observed between the great men of the first and of the last ages; nor can all the science, art, religion, and philosophy of the nineteenth century avail to educate greater men than Plutarch's heroes, three or four and twenty centuries ago. Not in time is the race progressive. Phocion, Socrates, Anaxagoras, Diogenes are great men, but they leave no class. He who is really of their class will not be called by their name, but will be his own man, and in his turn the founder of a sect. The arts and inventions of each period are only its costume and do not invigorate men. The harm of the improved machinery may compensate its good. Hudson and Behring accomplished so much in their fishing boats as to astonish Parry and Franklin, whose equipment exhausted the resources of science and art. Galileo, with an opera glass, discovered a more splendid series of celestial phenomena than anyone since. Columbus found the New World in an undecked boat. It is curious to see the periodical disuse and perishing of means and machinery which were introduced with loud laudation a few years or centuries before. The great genius returns to essential man. We reckoned the improvements of the art of war among the triumphs of science, and yet Napoleon conquered Europe by the bivouac, which consisted of falling back on naked valor and disencumbering it of all aids. The Emperor held it impossible to make a perfect army, says Las Cases, "without abolishing our arms, magazines, commissaries and carriages, until, in imitation of the Roman custom, the soldier should receive his supply of corn, grind it in his hand mill and bake his bread himself."

Society is a wave. The wave moves onward, but the water of which it is composed does not. The same particle does not rise from the valley to the ridge. Its unity is only phenomenal. The persons who make up a nation today next year die, and their experience dies with them.

And so the reliance on property, including the reliance on governments which protect it, is the want of self-reliance. Men have looked away from themselves and at things so long that they have come to esteem the religious, learned and civil institutions as guards of property, and they deprecate assaults on these, because they feel them to be assaults on property. They measure their esteem of each other by what each has, and not by what each is. But a cultivated man becomes ashamed of his property, out of new respect for his nature. Especially he hates what he has if he see that it is accidental—came to him by inheritance, or gift, or crime; then he feels that it is not having; it does not belong to him, has no root in him and merely lies there because no revolution or no robber takes it away. But that which a man is does always by necessity acquire; and what the man acquires is living property, which does not wait the beck of rulers, or mobs, or revolutions, or fire, or storm, or bankruptcies, but perpetually renews itself wherever the man breathes. "Thy lot or portion of life," said the Caliph Ali, "is seeking after thee; therefore be at rest from seeking after it." Our dependence on these foreign goods leads us to our slavish respect for numbers. The political parties meet in numerous conventions; the greater the concourse and with each new uproar of announcement, The delegation from Essex! The Democrats from New Hampshire! The Whigs of Maine! the young patriot feels himself stronger than before by a new thousand of eyes and arms. In like manner the reformers summon conventions and vote and resolve in multitude. Not so, O friends! will the God deign to enter and inhabit you, but by a method precisely the reverse. It is only as a man puts off all foreign support and stands alone that I see him to be strong and to prevail. He is weaker by every recruit to his banner. Is not a man better than a town? Ask nothing of men, and, in the endless mutation, thou only firm column must presently appear the upholder of all that surrounds thee. He who knows that power is inborn, that he is weak because he has looked for good out of him and elsewhere, and, so perceiving, throws himself unhesitatingly on his thought, instantly rights himself, stands in the erect position, commands his limbs, works miracles; just as a man who stands on his feet is stronger than a man who stands on his head.

So use all that is called Fortune. Most men gamble with her, and gain all, and lose all, as her wheel rolls. But do thou leave as unlawful these winnings, and deal with Cause and Effect, the chancellors of God. In the Will work and acquire, and thou hast chained the wheel of Chance, and shall sit hereafter out of fear from her rotations. A political victory, a rise of rents, the recovery of your sick, or the return of your absent, friend, or some other favorable event raises your spirits, and you think good days are preparing for you. Do not believe it. Nothing can bring you peace but yourself. Nothing can bring you peace but the triumph of principles.

Montaigne;
or, the Skeptic

Every fact is related on one side to sensation, and, on the other, to morals. The game of thought is, on the appearance of one of these two sides, to find the other: given the upper, to find the under side. Nothing so thin, but has these two faces; and, when the observer has seen the obverse, he turns it over to see the reverse. Life is a pitching of this penny—heads or tails. We never tire of this game, because there is still a slight shudder of astonishment at the exhibition of the other face, at the contrast of the two faces. A man is flushed with success, and bethinks himself what this good luck signifies. He drives his bargain in the street; but it occurs that he also is bought and sold. He sees the beauty of a human face, and searches the cause of that beauty, which must be more beautiful. He builds his fortunes, maintains the laws, cherishes his children; but he asks himself, why? And whereto? This head and this tail are called, in the language of philosophy, infinite and finite; relative and absolute; apparent and real; and many fine names beside.

Each man is born with a predisposition to one or the other of these sides of nature; and it will easily happen that men will be found devoted to one or the other. One class has the perception of difference, and is conversant with facts and surfaces; cities and persons; and the bringing certain things to pass—the men of talent and action. Another class has the perception of identity, and are men of faith and philosophy, men of genius.

Each of these riders drives too fast. Plotinus believes only in philosophers; Fénelon in saints; Pindar and Byron in poets. Read the haughty language in which Plato and the Platonists speak of all men who are not devoted to their own shining abstractions: other men are rats and mice. The literary class is usually proud and exclusive. The correspondence of Pope and Swift describes mankind around them as monsters; and that of Goethe and Schiller, in our own time, is scarcely more kind.

It is easy to see how this arrogance comes. The genius is a genius by the first look he casts on any object. Is his eye creative? Does he not rest in angles and colors, but beholds the design—he will presently undervalue the actual object. In powerful moments, his thought has dissolved the works of art and nature into their causes, so that the works appear heavy and faulty. He has a conception of beauty which the sculptor cannot embody. Picture, statue, temple, railroad, steam engine existed first in an artist's mind, without flaw, mistake, or friction, which impair the executed models. So did the church, the state, college, court, social circle, and all the institutions. It is not strange that these men, remembering what they have seen and hoped of ideas, should affirm disdainfully the superiority of ideas. Having at some time seen that the happy soul will carry all the arts in power, they say, Why cumber ourselves with superfluous realizations? and, like dreaming beggars, they assume to speak and act as if these values were already substantiated.

On the other part, the men of toil and trade and luxury—the animal world, including the animal in the philosopher and poet also—and the practical world, including the painful drudgeries which are never excused to philosopher or poet any more than to the rest—weigh heavily on the other side. The trade in our streets believes in no metaphysical causes, thinks nothing of the force which necessitated traders and a trading planet to exist: no; but sticks to cotton, sugar, wool, and salt. The ward meetings, on election days, are not softened by any misgiving of the value of these ballotings. Hot life is streaming in a single direction. To the men of this world, to the animal strength and spirits, to the men of practical power, while immersed in it, the man of ideas appears out of his reason. They alone have reason.

Things always bring their own philosophy with them, that is, prudence. No man acquires property without acquiring with it a little arithmetic, also. In England, the richest country that ever existed, property stands for more, compared with personal ability, than in any other. After dinner, a man believes less, denies more: verities have lost some charm. After dinner, arithmetic is the only science: ideas are disturbing, incendiary, follies of young men, repudiated by the solid portion of society; and a man comes to be valued by his athletic and animal qualities. Spence relates that Mr. Pope was with Sir Godfrey Kneller, one day, when his nephew, a Guinea trader, came in. "Nephew," said Sir Godfrey, "you have the honor of seeing the two greatest men in the world." "I don't know how great men you may be," said the Guinea man, "but I don't like your looks. I have often bought a man much better than both of you, all muscles and bones, for ten guineas." Thus, the men of the senses revenge themselves on the professors, and repay scorn for scorn. The first had leaped to conclusions not yet ripe, and say more than is true; the others make themselves merry with the philosopher, and weigh man by the pound. They believe that mustard bites the tongue, that pepper is hot, friction matches are incendiary, revolvers to be avoided, and suspenders hold up pantaloons; that there is much sentiment in a chest of tea; and a man will be eloquent if you give him good wine. Are you tender and scrupulous—you must eat more mince pie. They hold that Luther had milk in him when he said,

> *Wer nicht liebt Wein, Weib, und Gesang,*
> *Der bleibt ein Narr sein Leben lang;*

> [He who loves not wine, women, and song,
> Stays a fool his whole life long.]

and when he advised a young scholar perplexed with foreordination and free will to get well drunk. "The nerves," says Cabanis, "they are the man." My neighbor, a jolly farmer, in the tavern barroom, thinks that the use of money is sure and speedy spending. "For his part," he says, "he puts his down his neck, and gets the good of it."

The inconvenience of this way of thinking is that it runs into indifferentism, and then into disgust. Life is eating us up. We shall be fables presently. Keep cool: it will be all one a hundred years hence. Life's well enough; but we shall be glad to get out of it, and they will all be glad to have us. Why should we fret and drudge? Our meat will taste tomorrow as it did yesterday, and we may at last have had enough of it. "Ah," said my languid gentleman at Oxford, "there's nothing new or true—and no matter."

With a little more bitterness, the cynic moans: our life is like an ass led to market by a bundle of hay being carried before him: he sees nothing but the bundle of hay. "There is so much trouble in coming into the world," said Lord Bolingbroke, "and so much more, as well as meanness, in going out of it, that 'tis hardly worthwhile to be here at all." I knew a philosopher of this kidney, who was accustomed briefly to sum up his experience of human nature in saying, "Mankind is a damned rascal": and the natural corollary is pretty sure to follow—"The world lives by humbug, and so will I."

The abstractionist and the materialist thus mutually exasperating each other, and the scoffer expressing the worst of materialism, there arises a third party to occupy the middle ground between these two, the skeptic, namely. He finds both wrong by being in extremes. He labors to plant his feet, to be the beam of the balance. He will not go beyond his card. He sees the one-sidedness of these men of the street; he will not be a Gibeon-ite; he stands for the intellectual faculties, a cool head, and whatever serves to keep it cool: no unadvised industry, no unrewarded self-devotion, no loss of the brains in toil. Am I an ox, or a dray? You are both in extremes, he says. You that will have all solid, and a world of pig lead, deceive yourselves grossly. You believe yourselves rooted and grounded on adamant; and yet, if we uncover the last facts of our knowledge, you are spinning like bubbles in a river, you know not whither or whence, and you are bottomed and capped and wrapped in delusions.

Neither will he be betrayed to a book, and wrapped in a gown. The studious class are their own victims: they are thin and pale, their feet are cold, their heads are hot, the night is without sleep, the day a fear of interruption—pallor, squalor, hunger, and egotism. If you come near them, and see what conceits they entertain—they are abstractionists, and spend their days and nights in dreaming some dream; in expecting the homage of society to some precious scheme built on a truth, but destitute of proportion in its presentment, of justness in its application, and of all energy of will in the schemer to embody and vitalize it.

But I see plainly, he says, that I cannot see. I know that human strength is not in extremes, but in avoiding extremes. I, at least, will shun the weakness of philosophizing beyond my depth. What is the use of pretend-ing to powers we have not? What is the use of pretending to assurances we have not, respecting the other life? Why exaggerate the power of virtue? Why be an angel before your time? These strings, wound up too high, will snap. If there is a wish for immortality, and no evidence, why not say just that? If there are conflicting evidences, why not state them? If there is not ground for a candid thinker to make up his mind, yea or nay—why not suspend the judgment? I weary of these dogmatizers. I tire of these hacks of routine, who deny the dogmas. I neither affirm nor deny. I stand here to try the case. I am here to consider [*skeptein*], to consider how it is. I will try to keep the balance true. Of what use to take the chair, and glibly rattle off theories of society, religion, and nature, when I know that practical objections lie in the way, insurmountable by me and by my mates? Why so talkative in public when each of my neighbors can pin me to my seat by arguments I cannot refute? Why pretend that life is so simple a game, when we know how subtle and elusive the Proteus is? Why think to shut up all things in your narrow coop, when we know there are not one or two only, but ten, twenty, a thousand things, and unlike? Why fancy that you have all the truth in your keeping? There is much to say on all sides.

Who shall forbid a wise skepticism, seeing that there is no practical question on which anything more than an approximate solution can be had? Is not marriage an open question, when it is alleged, from the beginning of the world, that such as are in the institution wish to get out, and such as are out wish to get in? And the reply of Socrates, to him who asked whether he should choose a wife, still remains reasonable, "that, whether he should choose one or not, he would repent it." Is not the state a question? All society is divided in opinion on the subject of the state. Nobody loves it; great numbers dislike it, and suffer concientious scruples to allegiance: and the only defense set up is the fear of doing worse in disorganizing. Is it otherwise with the church? Or, to put any of the questions which touch mankind nearest—shall the young man aim at a leading part in law, in politics, in trade? It will not be pretended that a success in either of these kinds is quite coincident with what is best and inmost in his mind. Shall he, then, cutting the stays that hold him fast to the social state, put out to sea with no guidance but his genius? There is much to say on both sides. Remember the open question between the present order of "competition," and the friends of "attractive and associated labor." The generous minds embrace the proposition of labor shared by all; it is the only honesty; nothing else is safe. It is from the poor man's hut alone that strength and virtue come; and yet, on the other side, it is alleged that labor impairs the form, and breaks the spirit of man, and the laborers cry unanimously, "We have no thoughts." Culture, how indispensable! I cannot forgive you the want of accomplishments: and yet, culture will instantly destroy that chiefest beauty of spontaneousness. Excellent is culture for a savage; but once let him read in the book, and he is no longer able not to think of Plutarch's heroes. In short, since true fortitude of understanding consists "in not letting what we know be embarrassed by what we do not know," we ought to secure those advantages which we can command, and not risk them by clutching after the airy and unattainable. Come, no chimeras! Let us go abroad; let us mix in affairs; let us learn, and get, and have, and climb. "Men are a sort of moving plants, and, like trees, receive a great part of their nourishment from the air. If they keep too much at home, they pine." Let us have a robust, manly life; let us know what we know, for certain; what we have, let it be solid, and seasonable, and our own. A world in the hand is worth two in the bush. Let us have to do with real men and women, and not with skipping ghosts.

This, then, is the right ground of the skeptic—this of consideration, of self-containing; not at all of unbelief; not at all of universal denying, nor of universal doubting—doubting even that he doubts; least of all, of scoffing and profligate jeering at all that is stable and good. These are no more his moods than are those of religion and philosophy. He is the considerer, the prudent, taking in sail, counting stock, husbanding his means, believing that a man has too many enemies than that he can afford to be his own; that we cannot give ourselves too many advantages, in this unequal conflict, with powers so vast and unweariable ranged on one side, and this little, conceited, vulnerable popinjay that a man is, bobbing up and down into every danger, on the other. It is a position taken up for better defense, as of more safety, and one that can be maintained; and it is one of more opportunity and range, as, when we build a house, the rule is to set it not too high nor too low, under the wind, but out of the dirt.

The philosophy we want is one of fluxions and mobility. The Spartan and Stoic schemes are too stark and stiff for our occasion. A theory of St. John, and of nonresistance, seems, on the other hand, too thin and aerial. We want some coat woven of elastic steel, stout as the first, and limber as the second. We want a ship in these billows we inhabit. An angular, dogmatic house would be rent to chips and splinters in this storm of many elements. No, it must be tight, and fit to the form of man, to live at all; as a shell is the architecture of a house founded on the sea. The soul of man must be the type of our scheme, just as the body of man is the type after which a dwelling house is built. Adaptiveness is the peculiarity of human nature. We are golden averages, volitant stabilities, compensated or periodic errors, houses founded on the sea. The wise skeptic wishes to have a near view of the best game, and the chief players; what is best in the planet; art and nature, places and events, but mainly men. Everything that is excellent in mankind—a form of grace, an arm of iron, lips of persuasion, a brain of resources, everyone skillful to play and win—he will see and judge.

The terms of admission to this spectacle are that he have a certain solid and intelligible way of living of his own; some method of answering the inevitable needs of human life; proof that he had played with skill and success; that he has evinced the temper, stoutness, and the range of qualities which, among his contemporaries and countrymen, entitle him to fellowship and trust. For, the secrets of life are not shown except to sympathy and likeness. Men do not confide themselves to boys, or coxcombs, or pedants, but to their peers. Some wise limitation, as the modern phrase is; some condition between the extremes, and having itself a positive quality; some stark and sufficient man, who is not salt or sugar, but sufficiently related to the world to do justice to Paris or London, and, at the same time, a vigorous and original thinker, whom cities cannot overawe, but who uses them, is the fit person to occupy this ground of speculation.

These qualities meet in the character of Montaigne. And yet, since the personal regard which I entertain for Montaigne may be unduly great, I will, under the shield of this prince of egotists, offer, as an apology for electing him as the representative of skepticism, a word or two to explain how my love began and grew for this admirable gossip.

A single odd volume of Cotton's translation of the Essays remained to me from my father's library, when a boy. It lay long neglected, until, after many years, when I was newly escaped from college, I read the book, and procured the remaining volumes. I remember the delight and wonder in which I lived with it. It seemed to me as if I had myself written the book, in some former life, so sincerely it spoke to my thought and experience. It happened, when in Paris, in 1833, that, in the cemetery of Père le Chaise, I came to a tomb of Auguste Collignon, who died in 1830, aged sixty-eight years, and who, said the monument, "lived to do right, and had formed himself to virtue on the Essays of Montaigne." Some years later, I became acquainted with an accomplished English poet, John Sterling; and, in prosecuting my correspondence, I found that, from a love of Montaigne, he had made a pilgrimage to his château, still standing near Castellan, in Perigord, and, after two hundred and fifty years, had copied from the walls of his library the inscriptions which Montaigne had written there. That journal of Mr. Sterling's, published in the *Westminster Review*, Mr. Hazlitt has reprinted in the *Prolegomena* to his edition of the *Essays*. I heard with pleasure that one of the newly discovered autographs of William Shakespeare was in a copy of Florio's translation of Montaigne. It is the only book which we certainly know to have been in the poet's library. And, oddly enough, the duplicate copy of Florio, which the British Museum purchased, with a view of protecting the Shakespeare autograph (as I was informed in the Museum), turned out to have the autograph of Ben Jonson in the flyleaf. Leigh Hunt relates of Lord Byron that Montaigne was the only great writer of past times whom he read with avowed satisfaction. Other coincidences, not needful to be mentioned here, concurred to make this old Gascon still new and immortal for me.

In 1571, on the death of his father, Montaigne, then thirty-eight years old, retired from the practice of law, at Bordeaux, and settled himself on his estate. Though he had been a man of pleasure, and sometimes a courtier, his studious habits now grew on him, and he loved the compass, staidness, and independence of the country gentleman's life. He took up his economy in good earnest, and made his farms yield the most. Downright and plain-dealing, and abhorring to be deceived or to deceive, he was esteemed in the country for his sense and probity. In the civil wars of the League, which converted every house into a fort, Montaigne kept his gates open, and his house without defense. All parties freely came and went, his courage and honor being universally esteemed. The neighboring lords and gentry brought jewels and papers to him for safe keeping. Gibbon reckons, in these bigoted times, but two men of liberality in France—Henry IV and Montaigne.

Montaigne is the frankest and honestest of all writers. His French freedom runs into grossness; but he has anticipated all censure by the bounty of his own confessions. In his times, books were written to one sex only, and almost all were written in Latin; so that, in a humorist, a certain nakedness of statement was permitted, which our manners, of a literature addressed equally to both sexes, do not allow. But though a biblical plainness, coupled with a most uncanonical levity, may shut his pages to many sensitive readers, yet the offense is superficial. He parades it; he makes the most of it; nobody can think or say worse of him than he does. He pretends to most of the vices; and, if there be any virtue in him, he says, it got in by stealth. There is no man, in his opinion, who has not deserved hanging five or six times; and he pretends no exception in his own behalf. "Five or six as ridiculous stories," too, he says, "can be told of me, as of any man living." But with all this really superfluous frankness, the opinion of an invincible probity grows into every reader's mind.

"When I the most strictly and religiously confess myself, I find that the best virtue I have has in it some tincture of vice; and I am afraid that Plato, in his purest virtue (I, who am as sincere and perfect a lover of virtue of that stamp as any other whatever), if he had listened, and laid his ear close to himself, would have heard some jarring sound of human mixture, but faint and remote, and only to be perceived by himself."

Here is an impatience and fastidiousness at color or pretense of any kind. He has been in courts so long as to have conceived a furious disgust at appearances; he will indulge himself with a little cursing and swearing; he will talk with sailors and gypsies, use flash and street ballads: he has stayed indoors till he is deadly sick; he will to the open air, though it rain bullets. He has seen too much of gentlemen of the long robe, until he wishes for cannibals; and is so nervous, by factitious life, that he thinks the more barbarous man is, the better he is. He likes his saddle. You may read theology, and grammar, and metaphysics elsewhere. Whatever you get here shall smack of the earth and of real life, sweet, or smart, or stinging. He makes no hesitation to entertain you with the records of his disease; and his journey to Italy is quite full of that matter. He took and kept this position of equilibrium. Over his name, he drew an emblematic pair of scales, and wrote *Que sçais je?* under it. As I look at his effigy opposite the title page, I seem to hear him say, "You may play old Poz, if you will; you may rail and exaggerate—I stand here for truth, and will not, for all the states, and churches, and revenues, and personal reputations of Europe, overstate the dry fact, as I see it; I will rather mumble and prose about what I certainly know—my house and barns; my father, my wife, and my tenants; my old lean bald pate; my knives and forks; what meats I eat, and what drinks I prefer; and a hundred straws just as ridiculous— than I will write, with a fine crow-quill, a fine romance. I like gray days, and autumn and winter weather. I am gray and autumnal myself, and think an undress, and old shoes that do not pinch my feet, and old friends who do not constrain me, and plain topics where I do not need to strain myself and pump my brains the most suitable. Our condition as men is risky and ticklish enough. One cannot be sure of himself and his fortune an hour, but he may be whisked off into some pitiable or ridiculous plight. Why should I vapor and play the philosopher, instead of ballasting, the best I can, this dancing balloon? So, at least, I live within compass, keep myself ready for action, and can shoot the gulf, at last, with decency. If there be anything farcical in such a life, the blame is not mine: let it lie at fate's and nature's door."

The *Essays*, therefore, are an entertaining soliloquy on every random topic that comes into his head, treating everything without ceremony, yet with masculine sense. There have been men with deeper insight; but, one would say, never a man with such abundance of thoughts; he is never dull, never insincere, and has the genius to make the reader care for all that he cares for.

The sincerity and marrow of the man reaches to his sentences. I know not anywhere the book that seems less written. It is the language of conversation transferred to a book. Cut these words, and they would bleed; they are vascular and alive. One has the same pleasure in it that we have in listening to the necessary speech of men about their work, when any unusual circumstance gives momentary importance to the dialogue. For blacksmiths and teamsters do not trip in their speech; it is a shower of bullets. It is Cambridge men who correct themselves, and begin again at every half sentence, and, moreover, will pun, and refine too much, and swerve from the matter to the expression. Montaigne talks with shrewd- ness, knows the world, and books, and himself, and uses the positive degree: never shrieks, or protests, or prays; no weakness, no convulsion, no superlative; does not wish to jump out of his skin, or play any antics, or annihilate space or time; but is stout and solid; tastes every moment of the day; like pain, because it makes him feel himself, and realize things, as we pinch ourselves to know that we are awake. He keeps the plain; he rarely mounts or sinks; likes to feel solid ground, and the stones underneath. His writing has no enthusiasms, no aspiration; contented, self-respecting, and keeping the middle of the road. There is but one exception—in his love for Socrates. In speaking of him, for once his cheek flushes, and his style rises to passion.

Montaigne died of a quinsy, at the age of sixty, in 1592. When he came to die, he caused the mass to be celebrated in his chamber. At the age of thirty-three, he had been married. "But," he says, "might I have had my own will, I would not have married Wisdom herself, if she would have me: but 'tis to much purpose to evade it, the common custom and use of life will have it so. Most of my actions are guided by example, not choice." In the hour of death, he gave the same weight to custom. *Que sçais je?* What do I know?

This book of Montaigne the world has endorsed, by translating it into all tongues, and printing seventy-five editions of it in Europe: and that, too, a circulation somewhat chosen, namely, among courtiers, soldiers, princes, men of the world, and men of wit and generosity.

Shall we say that Montaigne has spoken wisely, and given the right and permanent expression of the human mind, on the conduct of life?

We are natural believers. Truth, or the connection between cause and effect, alone interests us. We are persuaded that a thread runs through all things: all worlds are strung on it, as beads, and men, and events, and life come to us only because of that thread; they pass and repass only that we may know the direction and continuity of that line. A book or statement which goes to show that there is no line, but random and chaos, a calamity out of nothing, a prosperity and no account of it, a hero born from a fool, a fool from a hero—dispirits us. Seen or unseen, we believe the tie exists. Talent makes counterfeit ties; genius finds the real ones. We hearken to the man of science, because we anticipate the sequence in natural phenomena which he uncovers. We love whatever affirms, connects, preserves; and dislike what scatters or pulls down. One man appears whose nature is to all men's eyes conserving and constructive: his presence supposes a well-ordered society, agriculture, trade, large institutions, and empire. If these did not exist, they would begin to exist through his endeavors. Therefore, he cheers and comforts men, who feel all this in him very readily. The nonconformist and the rebel say all manner of unanswerable things against the existing republic, but discover to our sense no plan of house or state of their own. Therefore, though the town, and state, and way of living which our counselor contemplated might be a very modest or musty prosperity, yet men rightly go for him, and reject the reformer, so long as he comes only with ax and crowbar.

But though we are natural conservers and causationists, and reject a sour, dumpish unbelief, the skeptical class, which Montaigne represents, has reason, and every man, at some time, belongs to it. Every superior mind will pass through this domain of equilibration—I should rather say, will know how to avail himself of the checks and balances in nature, as a natural weapon against the exaggeration and formalism of bigots and blockheads.

Skepticism is the attitude assumed by the student in relation to the particulars which society adores, but which he sees to be reverend only in their tendency and spirit. The ground occupied by the skeptic is the vestibule of the temple. Society does not like to have any breath of question blown on the existing order. But the interrogation of custom at all points is an inevitable stage in the growth of every superior mind, and is the evidence of its perception of the flowing power which remains itself in all changes.

The superior mind will find itself equally at odds with the evils of society, and with the projects that are offered to relieve them. The wise skeptic is a bad citizen; no conservative; he sees the selfishness of property, and the drowsiness of institutions. But neither is he fit to work with any democratic party that ever was constituted; for parties wish every one committed, and he penetrates the popular patriotism. His politics are those of the "Soul's Errand" of Sir Walter Raleigh; or of Krishna, in the Bhagavat, "There is none who is worthy of my love or hatred"; while he sentences law, physic, divinity, commerce, and custom. He is a reformer; yet he is no better member of the philanthropic association. It turns out that he is not the champion of the operative, the pauper, the prisoner, the slave. It stands in his mind that our life in this world is not of quite so easy interpretation as churches and schoolbooks say. He does not wish to take ground against these benevolences, to play the part of devil's attorney, and blazon every doubt and sneer that darkens the sun for him. But he says, "There are doubts."

I mean to use the occasion, and celebrate the calendar day of our St. Michael de Montaigne, by counting and describing these doubts or negations. I wish to ferret them out of their holes, and sun them a little. We must do with them as the police do with old rogues who are shown up to the public at the marshal's office. They will never be so formidable when once they have been identified and registered. But I mean honestly by them—that justice shall be done to their terrors. I shall not take Sunday objections, made up on purpose to be put down. I shall take the worst I can find, whether I can dispose of them, or they of me.

I do not press the skepticism of the materialist. I know the quadruped opinion will not prevail. 'Tis of no importance what bats and oxen think. The first dangerous symptom I report is the levity of intellect, as if it were fatal to earnestness to know much. Knowledge is the knowing that we cannot know. The dull pray; the geniuses are light mockers. How respectable is earnestness on every platform! but intellect kills it. Nay, San Carlo, my subtle and admirable friend, one of the most penetrating of men, finds that all direct ascension, even of lofty piety, leads to this ghastly insight, and sends back the votary orphaned. My astonishing San Carlo thought the lawgivers and saints infected. They found the ark empty; saw, and would not tell; and tried to choke off their approaching followers, by saying, "Action, action, my dear fellows, is for you!" Bad as was to me this detection by San Carlo, this frost in July, this blow from a bride, there was still a worse, namely, the cloy or satiety of the saints. In the mount of vision, ere they have yet risen from their knees, they say, "We discover that this our homage and beatitude is partial and deformed: we must fly for relief to the suspected and reviled Intellect, to the Understanding, the Mephistopheles, to the gymnastics of talent."

This is hobgoblin the first; and, though it has been the subject of much elegy, in our nineteenth century, from Byron, Goethe, and other poets of less fame, not to mention many distinguished private observers, I confess it is not very affecting to my imagination; for it seems to concern the shattering of babyhouses and crockery shops. What flutters the church of Rome, or of England, or of Geneva, or of Boston may yet be very far from touching any principle of faith. I think that the intellect and moral sentiment are unanimous; and that, though philosophy extirpates bugbears, yet it supplies the natural checks of vice, and polarity to the soul. I think that the wiser a man is, the more stupendous he finds the natural and moral economy, and lifts himself to a more absolute reliance.

There is the power of moods, each setting at nought all but its own tissue of facts and beliefs. There is the power of complexions, obviously modifying the dispositions and sentiments. The beliefs and unbeliefs appear to be structural; and, as soon as each man attains the poise and vivacity which allow the whole machinery to play, he will not need extreme examples, but will rapidly alternate all opinions in his own life. Our life is March weather, savage and serene in one hour. We go forth austere, dedicated, believing in the iron links of Destiny, and will not turn on our heel to save our life; but a book, or a bust, or only the sound of a name, shoots a spark through the nerves, and we suddenly believe in will: my finger ring shall be the seal of Solomon; fate is for imbeciles; all is possible to the resolved mind. Presently, a new experience gives a new turn to our thoughts: common sense resumes its tyranny; we say, "Well, the army, after all, is the gate to fame, manners, and poetry; and, look you—on the whole, selfishness plants best, prunes best, makes the best commerce, and the best citizen." Are the opinions of a man on right and wrong, on fate and causation, at the mercy of a broken sleep or an indigestion? Is his belief in God and Duty no deeper than a stomach evidence? And what guarantee for the permanence of his opinions? I like not the French celerity—a new church and state once a week. This is the second negation; and I shall let it pass for what it will. As far as it asserts rotation of states of mind, I suppose it suggests its own remedy, namely, in the record of larger periods. What is the mean of many states; of all the states? Does the general voice of ages affirm any principle, or is no community of sentiment discoverable in distant times and places? And when it shows the power of self-interest, I accept that as part of the divine law, and must reconcile it with aspiration the best I can.

The word Fate, or Destiny, expresses the sense of mankind, in all ages—that the laws of the world do not always befriend, but often hurt and crush us. Fate, in the shape of *Kinde* or nature, grows over us like grass. We paint Time with a scythe; Love and Fortune, blind; and Destiny, deaf. We have too little power of resistance against this ferocity which champs us up. What front can we make against these unavoidable, victorious, maleficent forces? What can I do against the influence of race, in my history? What can I do against hereditary and constitutional habits, against scrofula, lymph, impotence? against climate, against barbarism, in my country? I can reason down or deny everything, except this perpetual Belly; feed he must and will, and I cannot make him respectable.

But the main resistance which the affirmative impulse finds, and one including all others, is in the doctrine of the illusionists. There is a painful rumor in circulation that we have been practiced upon in all the principal performances of life, and free agency is the emptiest name. We have been sopped and drugged with the air, with food, with woman, with children, with sciences, with events, which leave us exactly where they found us.

The mathematics, 'tis complained, leave the mind where they find it; so do all sciences; and so do all events and actions. I find a man who has passed through all the sciences, the churl he was; and, through all the offices, learned, civil, and social, can detect the child. We are not the less necessitated to dedicate life to them. In fact, we may come to accept it as the fixed rule and theory of our state of education that God is a substance, and his method is illusion. The eastern sages owned the goddess Yoganidra, the great illusory energy of Vishnu, by whom, as utter ignorance, the whole world is beguiled.

Or shall I state it thus?—The astonishment of life is the absence of any appearance of reconciliation between the theory and practice of life. Reason, the prized reality, the law, is apprehended, now and then, for a serene and profound moment, amidst the hubbub of cares and works which have no direct bearing on it; is then lost, for months or years, and again found, for an interval, to be lost again. If we compute it in time, we may, in fifty years, have half a dozen reasonable hours. But what are these cares and works the better? A method in the world we do not see, but this parallelism of great and little, which never react on each other, nor discover the smallest tendency to converge. Experiences, fortunes, governings, readings, writings are nothing to the purpose; as when a man comes into the room, it does not appear whether he has been fed on yams or buffalo—he has contrived to get so much bone and fiber as he wants, out of rice or out of snow. So vast is the disproportion between the sky of law and the pismire of performance under it that whether he is a man of worth or a sot is not so great a matter as we say. Shall I add, as one juggle of this enchantment, the stunning nonintercourse law which makes co-operation impossible? The young spirit pants to enter society. But all the ways of culture and greatness lead to solitary imprisonment. He has been often balked. He did not expect a sympathy with his thought from the village, but he went with it to the chosen and intelligent, and found no entertainment for it, but mere misapprehension, distaste, and scoffing. Men are strangely mistimed and misapplied; and the excellence of each is an inflamed individualism which separates him more.

There are these, and more than these diseases of thought, which our ordinary teachers do not attempt to remove. Now shall we, because a good nature inclines us to virtue's side, say, There are no doubts,—and lie for the right? Is life to be led in a brave or in a cowardly manner? and is not the satisfaction of the doubts essential to all manliness? Is the name of virtue to be a barrier to that which is virtue? Can you not believe that a man of earnest and burly habit may find small good in tea, essays, and catechism, and want a rougher instruction, want men, labor, trade, farm-ing, war, hunger, plenty, love, hatred, doubt, and terror to make things plain to him, and has he not a right to insist on being convinced in his own way? When he is convinced, he will be worth the pains.

Belief consists in accepting the affirmations of the soul; unbelief, in denying them. Some minds are incapable of skepticism. The doubts they profess to entertain are rather a civility or accommodation to the common discourse of their company. They may well give themselves leave to speculate, for they are secure of a return. Once admitted to the heaven of thought, they see no relapse into night, but infinite invitation on the other side. Heaven is within heaven, and sky over sky, and they are encom-passed with divinities. Others there are, to whom the heaven is brass, and it shuts down to the surface of the earth. It is a question of temperament, or of more or less immersion in nature. The last class must needs have a reflex or parasite faith; not a sight of realities, but an instinctive reliance on the seers and believers of realities. The manners and thoughts of believers astonish them, and convince them that these have seen some-thing which is hid from themselves. But their sensual habit would fix the believer to his last position, while he as inevitably advances; and presently the unbeliever, for love of belief, burns the believer.

Great believers are always reckoned infidels, impracticable, fantastic, atheistic, and really men of no account. The spiritualist finds himself driven to express his faith by a series of skepticisms. Charitable souls come with their projects, and ask his co-operation. How can he hesitate? It is the rule of mere comity and courtesy to agree where you can, and to turn your sentence with something auspicious, and not freezing and sinis-ter. But he is forced to say, "Oh, these things will be as they must be: what can you do? These particular griefs and crimes are the foliage and fruit of such trees as we see growing. It is vain to complain of the leaf or the berry: cut it off; it will bear another just as bad. You must begin your cure lower down." The generosities of the day prove an intractable element for him. The people's questions are not his; their methods are not his; and, against all the dictates of good nature, he is driven to say he has no pleasure in them.

Even the doctrines dear to the hope of man, of the divine Providence, and of the immortality of the soul, his neighbors cannot put the statement so that he shall affirm it. But he denies out of more faith, and not less. He denies out of honesty. He had rather stand charged with the imbecility of skepticism than with untruth. I believe, he says, in the moral design of the universe; it exists hospitably for the weal of souls; but your dogmas seem to me caricatures: why should I make believe them? Will any say, this is cold and infidel? The wise and magnanimous will not say so. They will exult in his farsighted good will, that can abandon to the adversary all the ground of tradition and common belief, without losing a jot of strength. It sees to the end of all transgression. George Fox saw "that there was an ocean of darkness and death; but withal, an infinite ocean of light and love which flowed over that of darkness."

The final solution in which skepticism is lost is in the moral sentiment, which never forfeits its supremacy. All moods may be safely tried, and their weight allowed to all objections: the moral sentiment as easily outweighs them all, as any one. This is the drop which balances the sea. I play with the miscellany of facts, and take those superficial views which we call skepticism; but I know that they will presently appear to me in that order which makes skepticism impossible. A man of thought must feel the thought that is parent of the universe: that the masses of nature do undulate and flow.

This faith avails to the whole emergency of life and objects. The world is saturated with deity and with law. He is content with just and unjust, with sots and fools, with the triumph of folly and fraud. He can behold with serenity the yawning gulf between the ambition of man and his power of performance, between the demand and supply of power, which makes the tragedy of all souls.

Charles Fourier announced that "the attractions of man are proportioned to his destinies"; in other words, that every desire predicts its own satisfaction. Yet, all experience exhibits the reverse of this; the incompetency of power is the universal grief of young and ardent minds. They accuse the divine providence of a certain parsimony. It has shown the heaven and earth to every child, and filled him with a desire for the whole; a desire raging, infinite; a hunger, as of space to be filled with planets; a cry of famine, as of devils for souls. Then for the satisfaction—to each man is administered a single drop, a bead of dew of vital power, per day—a cup as large as space, and one drop of the water of life in it. Each man woke in the morning, with an appetite that could eat the solar system like a cake; a spirit for action and passion without bounds; he could lay his hand on the morning star; he could try conclusions with gravitation or chemistry; but, on the first motion to prove his strength, hands, feet, senses gave way, and would not serve him. He was an emperor deserted by his states, and left to whistle by himself, or thrust into a mob of emperors, all whistling; and still the sirens sang, "The attractions are proportioned to the destinies." In every house, in the heart of each maiden, and of each boy, in the soul of the soaring saint, this chasm is found—between the largest promise of ideal power, and the shabby experience.

The expansive nature of truth comes to our succor, elastic, not to be surrounded. Man helps himself by larger generalizations. The lesson of life is practically to generalize; to believe what the years and the centuries say against the hours; to resist the usurpation of particulars; to penetrate to their catholic sense. Things seem to say one thing, and say the reverse. The appearance is immoral; the result is moral. Things seem to tend downwards, to justify despondency, to promote rogues, to defeat the just; and, by knaves, as by martyrs, the just cause is carried forward. Although knaves win in every political struggle, although society seems to be delivered over from the hands of one set of criminals into the hands of another set of criminals, as fast as the government is changed, and the march of civilization is a train of felonies, yet, general ends are somehow answered. We see, now, events forced on, which seem to retard or retrograde the civility of ages. But the world spirit is a good swimmer, and storms and waves cannot drown him. He snaps his finger at laws: and so, throughout history, heaven seems to affect low and poor means. Through the years and the centuries, through evil agents, through toys and atoms, a great and beneficent tendency irresistibly streams.

Let a man learn to look for the permanent in the mutable and fleeting; let him learn to bear the disappearance of things he was wont to reverence, without losing his reverence; let him learn that he is here, not to work, but to be worked upon; and that, though abyss open under abyss, and opinion displace opinion, all are at last contained in the Eternal Cause—

If my bark sink, 'tis to another sea.

William Hazlitt [1]

1778-1830

Like any other good writer, Hazlitt often tells us things we know but did not know we knew. His *On the Feeling of Immortality in Youth* provides some excellent examples. We are all young or have been. Thus we are all capable of judging the truth of the feelings he describes, though perhaps in different and limited ways. Hazlitt's subject is not youth in itself but youth in the light of its opposite age, and seen from that viewpoint. Youth, as he says, can hardly imagine age; and age, though it has its own youth to remember, will more often than not gild that youth out of all resemblance to itself.

Hazlitt begins with an aphorism of his brother's: "No young man believes he shall ever die." Though we think of exceptions at once—Keats dying of tuberculosis, a young infantryman who has done too much fighting—we are struck with its general truth of feeling. We see how it makes a keynote for the whole essay. Moreover, we are reminded of that saying of Marlow's, in Conrad's *Youth*,[2] that he had felt as if he "could last for ever, outlast the sea, the earth, and all men. . . ." It is the same feeling. "Youth" is an abstract noun; "being young" is the thing itself. Conrad creates a sequence of events that will symbolize this feeling; Hazlitt generalizes, but so warmly that he too manages to give us the sense of the thing itself.

And how well he does it, with what a wealth of example! In youth, he says, "we are rocked in the cradle of our desires, and hushed into fancied security by the roar of the universe around us," so that we have "no room for the thoughts of death." Death—and how truly that poet's phrase catches the feeling—is no more than a "dim shadow lingering for us in the distance." We are alive and young.

[1] For a biography of William Hazlitt, see Vol. 5, pp. 260–262, in this set.
[2] See Vol. 2, pp. 210–236, in this set.

That is enough for us. To be young is to be the citizen of a universal and immortal country, in which every man in his youth—everyone who has ever been young or will be—is our contemporary. For the romantic, and Hazlitt was that, the rest of life is a long exile from that country.

Hazlitt was well acquainted with the Elizabethans, and there is a touch of Elizabethan eagerness and splendor about the passage that begins: "To see the golden sun. . . ." It turns dark as it confronts the paradox of death in the midst of this brightness. He tells us about his own youth, how it caught fire in the ardor of the French Revolution, the common hope of liberty for all men. But when that hope "set once more in the night of despotism," he felt that his youth was ended and turned back to the past.

If we are young, or if we remember our own early years with some exactness, we may perhaps feel that Hazlitt idealizes youth a little. Did he forget its troubles? Did he forget that to be young is often to be anxious, to be confused about which way we are going, to attempt things we do not quite understand, things we are not quite sure we can do? Did he forget that when we are young the world is very big and very strong, that it is sometimes hostile or indifferent to the best and truest of our wishes?

On the Feeling of Immortality
in Youth

No young man believes he shall ever die. It was a saying of my brother's, and a fine one. There is a feeling of eternity in youth which makes us amends for everything. To be young is to be as one of the immortals. One half of time indeed is spent—the other half remains in store for use with all its countless treasures, for there is no line drawn, and we see no limit to our hopes and wishes. We make the coming age our own—

> The vast, the unbounded prospect lies before us.

Death, old age are words without a meaning, a dream, a fiction, with which we have nothing to do. Others may have undergone, or may still undergo them—we "bear a charmed life," which laughs to scorn all such idle fancies. As, in setting out on a delightful journey, we strain our eager sight forward,

> Bidding the lovely scenes at distance hail,

and see no end to prospect after prospect, new objects presenting themselves as we advance, so in the outset of life we see no end to our desires nor to the opportunities of gratifying them. We have as yet found no obstacle, no disposition to flag, and it seems that we can go on so for ever. We look round in a new world, full of life and motion, and ceaseless progress, and feel in ourselves all the vigour and spirit to keep pace with it, and do not foresee from any present signs how we shall be left behind in the race, decline into old age, and drop into the grave. It is the simplicity and, as it were, abstractedness of our feelings in youth that (so to speak) identifies us with nature and (our experience being weak and our passions strong) makes us fancy ourselves immortal like it. Our short-lived connection with being, we fondly flatter ourselves, is an indissoluble and lasting union. As infants smile and sleep, we are rocked in the cradle of our desires, and hushed into fancied security by the roar of the universe around us—we quaff the cup of life with eager thirst without draining it, and joy and hope seem ever mantling to the brim—objects press around us, filling the mind with their magnitude and with the throng of desires that wait upon them, so that there is no room for the thoughts of death. We are too much dazzled by the gorgeousness and novelty of the bright waking dream about us to discern the dim shadow lingering for us in the distance. Nor would the hold that life has taken of us permit us to detach our thoughts that way, even if we could. We are too much absorbed in present objects and pursuits. While the spirit of youth remains unimpaired, ere "the wine of life is drunk," we are like people intoxicated or in a fever, who are hurried away by the violence of their own sensations: it is only as present objects begin to pall upon the sense, as we have been disappointed in our favourite pursuits, cut off from our closest ties, that we by degrees become weaned from the world, that passion loosens its hold upon futurity, and that we begin to contemplate as in a glass darkly the possibility of parting with it for good. Till then, the example of others has no effect upon us. Casualties we avoid; the slow approaches of age we play at hide-and-seek with. Like the foolish fat scullion in Sterne, who hears that Master Bobby is dead, our only reflection is, "So am not I!" The idea of death, instead of staggering our confidence, only seems to strengthen and enhance our sense of the possession and enjoyment of life. Others may fall around us like leaves, or be mowed down by the scythe of Time like grass: these are but metaphors to the unreflecting, buoyant ears and overweening presumption of youth. It is not till we see the flowers of love, hope, and joy withering around us that we give up the flattering delusions that before led us on, and that the emptiness and dreariness of the prospect before us reconciles us hypothetically to the silence of the grave.

Life is indeed a strange gift, and its privileges are most mysterious. No wonder when it is first granted to us that our gratitude, our admiration, and our delight should prevent us from reflecting on our own nothingness, or from thinking it will ever be recalled. Our first and strongest impressions are borrowed from the mighty scene that is opened to us, and we unconsciously transfer its durability as well as its splendour to ourselves. So newly found, we cannot think of parting with it yet, or at least put off that consideration *sine die*. Like a rustic at a fair, we are full of amazement and rapture, and have no thought of going home, or that it will soon be night. We know our existence only by ourselves, and confound our knowledge with the objects of it. We and nature are therefore one. Otherwise the illusion, the "feast of reason and the flow of soul," to which we are invited, is a mockery and a cruel insult. We do not go from a play till the last act is ended, and the lights are about to be extinguished. But the fairy face of Nature still shines on: shall we be called away before the curtain falls, or ere we have scarce had a glimpse of what is going on? Like children, our stepmother Nature holds us up to see the raree-show of the universe, and then, as if we were a burden to her to support, lets us fall down again. Yet what brave sublunary things does not this pageant present, like a ball or fête of the universe!

To see the golden sun, the azure sky, the outstretched ocean; to walk upon the green earth, and be lord of a thousand creatures; to look down yawning precipices or over distant sunny vales; to see the world spread out under one's feet on a map; to bring the stars near; to view the smallest insects through a microscope; to read history, and consider the revolutions of empire and the successions of generations; to hear of the glory of Tyre, of Sidon, of Babylon, and of Susa, and to say all these were before me and are now nothing; to say I exist in such a point of time, and in such a point of space; to be a spectator and a part of its ever moving scene; to witness the change of season, of spring and autumn, of winter and summer; to feel hot and cold, pleasure and pain, beauty and deformity, right and wrong; to be sensible to the accidents of nature; to consider the mighty world of eye and ear; to listen to the stock-dove's notes amid the forest deep; to journey over moor and mountain; to hear the midnight sainted choir; to visit lighted halls, or the cathedral's gloom, or sit in crowded theatres and see life itself mocked; to study the works of art and refine the sense of beauty to agony; to worship fame, and to dream of immortality; to look upon the Vatican, and to read Shakespeare; to gather up the wisdom of the ancients, and to pry into the future; to listen to the trump of war, the shout of victory; to question history as to the movements of the human heart; to seek for truth; to plead the cause of humanity; to overlook the world as if Time and Nature poured their treasures at our feet—to be and to do all this, and then in a moment to be nothing—to have it all snatched from us as by a juggler's trick, or a phantasmagoria! There is something in this transition from all to nothing that shocks us and damps the enthusiasm of youth new flushed with hope and pleasure, and we cast the comfortless thought as far from us as we can. In the first enjoyment of the estate of life we discard the fear of debts and duns, and never think of the final payment of our great debt to nature. Art we know is long; life, we flatter

ourselves, should be so too. We see no end of the difficulties and delays
we have to encounter: perfection is slow of attainment, and we must have
time to accomplish it in. The fame of the great names we look up to is
immortal: and shall not we who contemplate it imbibe a portion of
ethereal fire, the *divinae particula aurae,* which nothing can extinguish? A
wrinkle in Rembrandt or in nature takes whole days to resolve itself into
its component parts, its softenings and its sharpnesses; we refine upon our
perfections, and unfold the intricacies of nature. What a prospect for the
future! What a task have we not begun! And shall we be arrested in the
middle of it? We do not count our time thus employed lost, or our pains
thrown away; we do not flag or grow tired, but gain new vigour at our
endless task. Shall Time, then, grudge us to finish what we have begun,
and have formed a compact with Nature to do? Why not fill up the blank
that is left us in this manner? I have looked for hours at a Rembrandt
without being conscious of the flight of time, but with ever new wonder
and delight, have thought that not only my own but another existence I
could pass in the same manner. This rarefied, refined existence seemed to
have no end, nor stint, nor principle of decay in it. The print would
remain long after I who looked on it had become the prey of worms. The
thing seems in itself out of all reason: health, strength, appetite are
opposed to the idea of death, and we are not ready to credit it till we have
found our illusions vanished, and our hopes grown cold. Objects in youth,
from novelty, etc., are stamped upon the brain with such force and
integrity that one thinks nothing can remove or obliterate them. They are
riveted there, and appear to us as an element of our nature. It must be a
mere violence that destroys them, not a natural decay. In the very strength
of this persuasion we seem to enjoy an age by anticipation. We melt down
years into a single moment of intense sympathy, and by anticipating the
fruits defy the ravages of time. If, then, a single moment of our lives is
worth years, shall we set any limits to its total value and extent? Again,
does it not happen that so secure do we think ourselves of an indefinite
period of existence that at times, when left to ourselves, and impatient of
novelty, we feel annoyed at what seems to us the slow and creeping
progress of time, and argue that if it always moves at this tedious snail's
pace it will never come to an end? How ready are we to sacrifice any
space of time which separates us from a favourite object, little thinking
that before long we shall find it moves too fast?

For my part, I started in life with the French Revolution, and I have
lived, alas! to see the end of it. But I did not foresee this result. My sun
arose with the first dawn of liberty, and I did not think how soon both

must set. The new impulse to ardour given to men's minds imparted a congenial warmth and glow to mine; we were strong to run a race together, and I little dreamed that long before mine was set, the sun of liberty would turn to blood, or set once more in the night of despotism. Since then, I confess, I have no longer felt myself young, for with that my hopes fell.

I have since turned my thoughts to gathering up some of the fragments of my early recollections, and putting them into a form to which I might occasionally revert. The future was barred to my progress, and I turned for consolation and encouragement to the past. It is thus that, while we find our personal and substantial identity vanishing from us, we strive to gain a reflected and vicarious one in our thoughts: we do not like to perish wholly, and wish to bequeath our names, at least, to posterity. As long as we can make our cherished thoughts and nearest interests live in the minds of others, we do not appear to have retired altogether from the stage. We still occupy the breasts of others, and exert an influence and power over them, and it is only our bodies that are reduced to dust and powder. Our favourite speculations still find encouragement, and we make as great a figure in the eye of the world, or perhaps a greater than in our lifetime. The demands of our self-love are thus satisfied, and these are the most imperious and unremitting. Besides, if by our intellectual superiority we survive ourselves in this world, by our virtues and faith we may attain an interest in another, and a higher state of being, and may thus be recipients at the same time of men and of angels.

> E'en from the tomb the voice of Nature cries,
> E'en in our ashes live their wonted fires.

As we grow old, our sense of the value of time becomes vivid. Nothing else, indeed, seems of any consequence. We can never cease wondering that that which has ever been should cease to be. We find many things remain the same: why then should there be change in us. This adds a convulsive grasp of whatever is, a sense of fallacious hollowness in all we see. Instead of the full, pulpy feeling of youth tasting existence and every object in it, all is flat and vapid—a whited sepulchre, fair without but full of ravening and all uncleanness within. The world is a witch that puts us off with false shows and appearances. The simplicity of youth, the confiding expectation, the boundless raptures are gone: we only think of getting out of it as well as we can, and without any great mischance or annoyance. The flush of illusion, even the complacent retrospect of past joys and hopes, is over: if we can slip out of life without indignity, can escape with little bodily infirmity, and frame our minds to the calm and respectable composure of still life before we return to absolute nothingness, it is as much as we can expect. We do not die wholly at our deaths: we have mouldered away gradually long before. Faculty after faculty, interest after interest, attachment after attachment disappear: we are torn from ourselves while living, year after year sees us no longer the same, and death only consigns the last fragment of what we were to the grave. That we should wear out by slow stages, and dwindle at last into nothing, is not wonderful, when even in our prime our strongest impressions leave little trace but for the moment, and we are the creatures of petty circumstance. How little effect is made on us in our best days by the books we have read, the scenes we have witnessed, the sensations we have gone through! Think only of the feelings we experience in reading a fine romance (one of Sir Walter's, for instance); what beauty, what sublimity, what interest, what heart-rending emotions! You would suppose the feelings you then experienced would last for ever, or subdue the mind to their own harmony and tone: while we are reading it seems as if nothing could ever put us out of our way, or trouble us—the first splash of mud that we get on entering the street, the first twopence we are cheated out of, the feeling vanishes clean out of our minds, and we become the prey of petty and annoying circumstance. The mind soars to the lofty; it is at home in the groveling, the disagreeable, and the little. And yet we wonder that age should be feeble and querulous—that the freshness of youth should fade away. Both worlds would hardly satisfy the extravagance of our desires and of our presumption.

Sir Thomas Browne

1605–1682

Sir Thomas Browne was one of those amateurs in the arts who end up outdoing the professionals. He was born in London on October 19, 1605. His father, a Cheapside cloth merchant, died when Thomas was eight. His mother then married Sir Thomas Sutton. Young Browne was educated at Winchester and at Oxford, where he took a B.A. in 1626 and an M.A. in 1629. He visited Ireland and later studied medicine at the University of Montpellier, at Padua, and finally in Leiden, where he took his M.D. in 1633.

He settled in Norwich, England. There he developed a large practice and lived for the rest of his life. His friend Whitefoot says that "his complexion and hair was [*sic*] answerable to his name; his stature was moderate, and habit of body neither fat nor lean," but fleshy. His first book, *Religio Medici* (*The Religion of a Doctor*), was published without his consent. Brought out in an authorized edition, it at once became popular and remained so. It is still his most famous work. A second book, *Pseudodoxia Epidemica* (*Common Errors*), was a large and fascinating compilation of popular superstitions. This, too, was very popular. In it Browne confutes scores of false notions that some educated persons even today do not question.

Browne was a Royalist in his sympathies, yet he lived through the English Civil War without suffering any persecutions. He never let public disturbances deflect him from his practice and from his antiquarian researches. He married in 1641 and had twelve children. In 1671 he was knighted. The circumstances are worth recounting. The King, Charles II, was to make a royal visit to Norwich, and let it be known that one citizen of the town would be knighted. The choice would ordinarily have fallen upon the mayor. But the latter, a remarkably generous man, deferred to Browne, on the grounds that he was the town's most illustrious citizen.

In 1664 Browne testified at the trial of two women charged as witches. He was a deeply religious man who, like most of his contemporaries, believed in a personal Satan and in witches as Satan's agents. The accusation that his testimony was the decisive factor in their condemnation, though still sometimes made, has several times been proved to be unfounded. He died in Norwich in 1682, at the age of seventy-seven.

Our selection is the famous fifth and last chapter of *Hydriotaphia: Urne-buriall, or, A Discourse of the Sepulchrall Urnes lately found in Norfolk.* Taking as his starting place some ancient funeral urns dug up in Norfolk, in which human remains were found but no sign of the names of their originals, Browne meditates grandly on the theme of death and plays variations on such other related themes as methods of burial in other countries and ages, and the means whereby a man may hope to preserve the memory of himself—and the folly of trying to do so.

Try this experiment. Read the selection through as if it were something in a foreign language that you could pronounce but understood very little of. This is prose that is meant to be read aloud; indeed, its closest relatives are the sermons of such contemporaries of Browne as Donne, Andrewes, and Jeremy Taylor. Browne lived in an age of great and fashionable preachers.

Can you catch the noble rolling of that prose in such phrases as "the iniquity of oblivion blindly scattereth her poppy" or "the famous nations of the dead"? Browne was an organist of language. But he did not keep his work under the control of a formal musical logic. He was more like an organist in an empty church, improvising without self-consciousness on some great theme, turning it this way and that, calling up references from all the music of the past.

---

*Notes from the artist: "Browne is shown standing by a table of medical
and surgical instruments of his time. The Greek inscription
on the Aesculapian wand reads 'Life is short; art is long; experience
difficult.' The background is from the title page
of an early edition of* Religio Medici.*"*

Religio
Medici

ΒΙΟΣ
ΒΡΑΧΥΣ
Η ΤΕΧΝΗ
ΜΑΚΡΗ
Ο ΚΑΙΡΟΣ

Thomas Browne

But you do not understand all that you have read? Even a very learned man might be hard put to it to catch all the Greek and Latin and other allusions the first time. Browne was a prodigious reader, and he had a prodigious memory. Learning was fashionable in his time. Among other things, it was a kind of game. There might even be a certain one-upmanship in producing a Latin tag from a source no one else could guess. Even so, it is easy enough to look up "diuturnity" and find that it means the quality of being long lasting, or that "ossuaries" are receptacles for the bones of the dead. We discover that Jerome Cardan was a famous sixteenth-century physician, and that Herostratus was a man who burned the temple of Diana on the night Alexander the Great was born, hoping that this act would cause his name to be remembered. You can go on and on. *Urn-Burial* is a scholar's paradise.

There are better things to do with Browne than to look up his references. The best thing is to read him—over and over. When this is done, whole sentences and passages begin to come alive. Some mystery remains. Like any good poet, Browne reserves the right to be difficult. He knows that all men's minds do not work in the same way, nor do they have the same emotional references. Beyond simple things, in some obscurity, the true emotional depths may lie. Far from depressing us, this great meditation on death has the effect of coloring the simplest death with glory.

That is the real point of the selection. Browne was a fervent Christian. For him, death was but the entry into a better life, and the true Christian should not wish to perpetuate his earthly existence. "To subsist in lasting monuments," he writes, in one of the most famous passages in all English prose, "to live in their productions, to exist in their names . . . was large satisfaction unto old expectations. . . . But all this is nothing in the metaphysics of true belief. To live indeed is to be again ourselves, which being not only a hope, but an evidence, in noble believers, 'tis all one to lie in St. Innocent's churchyard as in the sands of Egypt; ready to be anything, in the ecstasy of being ever, and as content with six foot as the *moles* of Adrianus."

Immortality

from *Urn-Burial*

Now since these dead bones have already outlasted the living ones of Methuselah, and in a yard underground, and thin walls of clay, outworn all the strong and specious buildings above it, and quietly rested under the drums and tramplings of three conquests, what prince can promise such diuturnity unto his relics, or might not gladly say,

> *"Sic ego componi versus in ossa velim"*?
> [Thus turned to stone should I wish to be]

Time, which antiquates antiquities, and hath an art to make dust of all things, hath yet spared these minor monuments.

In vain we hope to be known by open and visible conservatories, when to be unknown was the means of their continuation, and obscurity their protection. If they died by violent hands and were thrust into their urns, these bones become considerable, and some old philosophers would honour them, whose souls they conceived most pure which were thus snatched from their bodies, and to retain a stronger propension unto them; whereas they weariedly left a languishing corpse, and with faint desires of reunion. If they fell by long and aged decay, yet, wrapt up in the bundle of time, they fall into indistinction and make but one blot with infants. If we begin to die when we live, and long life be but a prolongation of death, our life is a sad composition; we live with death, and die not in a moment. How many pulses made up the life of Methuselah were work for Archimedes: common counters sum up the life of Moses his man. Our days become considerable, like petty sums, by minute accumulations, where numerous fractions make up but small round numbers; and our days of a span long make not one little finger.

If the nearness of our last necessity brought a nearer conformity into it, there were a happiness in hoary hairs and no calamity in half senses. But the long habit of living indisposeth us for dying; when avarice makes us the sport of death, when even David grew politicly cruel, and Solomon could hardly be said to be the wisest of men. But many are too early old, and before the date of age. Adversity stretcheth our days, misery makes Alcmena's nights, and time hath no wings unto it. But the most tedious being is that which can unwish itself, content to be nothing or never to have been, which was beyond the malcontent of Job, who cursed not the day of his life but his nativity, content to have so far been as to have a title to future being, although he had lived here but in a hidden state of life, and, as it were, an abortion.

What song the Sirens sang, or what name Achilles assumed when he hid himself among women, though puzzling questions, are not beyond all conjecture. What time the persons of these ossuaries entered the famous nations of the dead, and slept with princes and counsellors, might admit a wide solution. But who were the proprietaries of these bones, or what bodies these ashes made up, were a question above antiquarianism; not to be resolved by man, nor easily perhaps by spirits, except we consult the provincial guardians or tutelary observators. Had they made as good provision for their names as they have done for their relics, they had not so grossly erred in the art of perpetuation. But to subsist in bones, and be but pyramidally extant, is a fallacy in duration. Vain ashes, which in the oblivion of names, persons, times, and sexes have found unto themselves a fruitless continuation, and only arise unto late posterity as emblems of mortal vanities, antidotes against pride, vainglory, and madding vices! Pagan vainglories, which thought the world might last for ever, had encouragement for ambition; and, finding no *Atropos* unto the immortality of their names, were never dampt with the necessity of oblivion. Even old ambitions had the advantage of ours, in the attempts of their vainglories, who, acting early and before the probable meridian of time, have by this time found great accomplishment of their designs, whereby the ancient heroes have already outlasted their monuments and mechanical preservations. But in this latter scene of time we cannot expect such mummies unto our memories, when ambition may fear the prophecy of Elias, and Charles V can never hope to live within two Methuselahs of Hector.

And, therefore, restless inquietude for the diuturnity of our memories unto present considerations seems a vanity almost out of date and super-annuated piece of folly. We cannot hope to live so long in our names as some have done in their persons. One face of Janus holds no proportion unto the other. 'Tis too late to be ambitious. The great mutations of the world are acted, or time may be too short for our designs. To extend our memories by monuments whose death we daily pray for, and whose duration we cannot hope without injury to our expectations in the advent of the Last Day, were a contradiction to our beliefs. We whose generations are ordained in this setting part of time are providentially taken off from such imaginations, and, being necessitated to eye the remaining particle of futurity, are naturally constituted unto thoughts of the next world, and cannot excusably decline the consideration of that duration which maketh pyramids pillars of snow and all that's past a moment.

Circles and right lines limit and close all bodies, and the mortal right-lined circle must conclude and shut up all. There is no antidote against the opium of time, which temporally considereth all things: our fathers find their graves in our short memories, and sadly tell us how we may be buried in our survivors. Gravestones tell truth scarce forty years. Generations pass while some trees stand, and old families last not three oaks. To be read by bare inscriptions like many in Gruter, to hope for eternity by enigmatical epithets or first letters of our names, to be studied by antiquaries, who we were, and have new names given us like many of the mummies, are cold consolations unto the students of perpetuity, even by everlasting languages.

To be content that times to come should only know there was such a man, not caring whether they knew more of him, was a frigid ambition in Cardan, disparaging his horoscopal inclination and judgment of himself. Who cares to subsist like Hippocrates' patients, or Achilles' horses in Homer, under naked nominations, without deserts and noble acts, which are the balsam of our memories, the entelecheia and soul of our subsistences? To be nameless in worthy deeds exceeds an infamous history. The Canaanitish woman lives more happily without a name than Herodias with one. And who had not rather have been the good thief than Pilate?

But the iniquity of oblivion blindly scattereth her poppy, and deals with the memory of men without distinction to merit of perpetuity. Who can but pity the founder of the pyramids? Herostratus lives that burnt the temple of Diana; he is almost lost that built it. Time hath spared the epitaph of Adrian's horse, confounded that of himself. In vain we compute our felicities by the advantage of our good names, since bad have equal durations and Thersites is like to live as long as Agamemnon. Who knows whether the best of men be known, or whether there be not more remarkable persons forgot than any that stand remembered in the known account of time? Without the favour of the everlasting register, the first man had been as unknown as the last, and Methuselah's long life had been his only chronicle.

Oblivion is not to be hired. The greater part must be content to be as though they had not been, to be found in the register of God, not in the record of man. Twenty-seven names make up the first story before the

Flood, and the recorded names ever since contain not one living century. The number of the dead long exceedeth all that shall live. The night of time far surpasseth the day, and who knows when was the equinox? Every hour adds unto that current arithmetic, which scarce stands one moment. And since death must be the *Lucina* of life, and even pagans could doubt whether thus to live were to die; since our longest sun sets at right descensions and makes but winter arches, and therefore it cannot be long before we lie down in darkness and have our light in ashes; since the brother of death daily haunts us with dying mementos, and time, that grows old in itself, bids us hope no long duration, diuturnity is a dream and folly of expectation.

Darkness and light divide the course of time, and oblivion shares with memory a great part even of our living beings; we slightly remember our felicities, and the smartest strokes of affliction leave but short smart upon us. Sense endureth no extremities, and sorrows destroy us or themselves. To weep into stones are fables. Afflictions induce callosities; miseries are slippery, or fall like snow upon us, which notwithstanding is no unhappy stupidity. To be ignorant of evils to come and forgetful of evils past is a merciful provision in nature, whereby we digest the mixture of our few and evil days, and, our delivered senses not relapsing into cutting remembrances, our sorrows are not kept raw by the edge of repetitions. A great part of antiquity contented their hopes of subsistency with a transmigration of their souls—a good way to continue their memories, while, having the advantage of plural successions, they could not but act something remarkable in such variety of beings, and, enjoying the fame of their passed selves, make accumulation of glory unto their last durations. Others, rather than be lost in the uncomfortable night of nothing, were content to recede into the common being and make one particle of the public soul of all things, which was no more than to return into their unknown and divine original again. Egyptian ingenuity was more unsatisfied, contriving their bodies in sweet consistencies, to attend the return of their souls. But all was vanity, feeding the wind, and folly. The Egyptian mummies, which Cambyses or time hath spared, avarice now consumeth. Mummy is become merchandise, Mizraim cures wounds, and Pharaoh is sold for balsams.

In vain do individuals hope for immortality or any patent from oblivion, in preservations below the moon; men have been deceived even in their flatteries, above the sun, and studied conceits to perpetuate their names in heaven. The various cosmography of that part hath already varied the names of contrived constellations; Nimrod is lost in Orion, and Osiris in the Dog-star. While we look for incorruption in the heavens, we find they are but like the earth—durable in their main bodies, alterable in their parts; whereof, beside comets and new stars, perspectives begin to tell tales, and the spots that wander about the sun, with Phaeton's favour, would make clear conviction.

There is nothing strictly immortal but immortality. Whatever hath no beginning may be confident of no end; which is the peculiar of that necessary essence that cannot destroy itself, and the highest strain of omnipotency, to be so powerfully constituted as not to suffer even from the power of itself: all others have a dependent being and within the reach of destruction. But the sufficiency of Christian immortality frustrates all earthly glory, and the quality of either state, after death, makes a folly of posthumous memory. God, who can only destroy our souls and hath assured our resurrection, either of our bodies or names hath directly promised no duration. Wherein there is so much of chance that the boldest expectants have found unhappy frustration; and to hold long subsistence seems but a scape in oblivion. But man is a noble animal, splendid in ashes and pompous in the grave, solemnizing nativities and deaths with equal lustre, nor omitting ceremonies of bravery in the infamy of his nature.

Life is a pure flame, and we live by an invisible sun within us. A small fire sufficeth for life; great flames seemed too little after death, while men vainly affected precious pyres and to burn like Sardanapalus: but the wisdom of funeral laws found the folly of prodigal blazes, and reduced undoing fires unto the rule of sober obsequies, wherein few could be so mean as not to provide wood, pitch, a mourner, and an urn.

Five languages secured not the epitaph of Gordianus. The man of God lives longer without a tomb than any by one, invisibly interred by angels and adjudged to obscurity, though not without some marks directing human discovery. Enoch and Elias, without either tomb or burial, in an anomalous state of being, are the great examples of perpetuity, in their long and living memory, in strict account being still on this side death and having a late part yet to act upon this stage of earth. If in the decretory term of the world we shall not all die but be changed, according to received translation, the Last Day will make but few graves; at least, quick resurrections will anticipate lasting sepultures. Some graves will be opened before they be quite closed, and Lazarus be no wonder. When many that feared to die shall groan that they can die but once, the dismal state is the second and living death, when life puts despair on the damned, when men shall wish the coverings of mountains, not of monuments, and annihilations shall be courted.

While some have studied monuments, others have studiously declined them, and some have been so vainly boisterous that they durst not acknowledge their graves; wherein Alaricus seems most subtle, who had a river turned to hide his bones at the bottom. Even Sylla, that thought himself safe in his urn, could not prevent revenging tongues, and stones thrown at his monument. Happy are they whom privacy makes innocent, who deal so with men in this world that they are not afraid to meet them in the next, who, when they die, make no commotion among the dead, and are not touched with that poetical taunt of Isaiah.

Pyramids, arches, obelisks were but the irregularities of vainglory, and wild enormities of ancient magnanimity. But the most magnanimous resolution rests in the Christian religion, which trampleth upon pride and sits on the neck of ambition, humbly pursuing that infallible perpetuity unto which all others must diminish their diameters and be poorly seen in angles of contingency.

Pious spirits who passed their days in raptures of futurity made little more of this world than the world that was before it, while they lay obscure in the chaos of pre-ordination and night of their fore-beings. And if any have been so happy as truly to understand Christian annihilation, ecstasies, exolution, liquefaction, transformation, the kiss of the spouse, gustation of God, and ingression into the divine shadow, they have already had a handsome anticipation of heaven; the glory of the world is surely over, and the earth in ashes unto them.

To subsist in lasting monuments, to live in their productions, to exist in their names and predicament of chimaeras, was large satisfaction unto old expectations, and made one part of their Elysiums. But all this is nothing in the metaphysics of true belief. To live indeed is to be again ourselves, which being not only a hope, but an evidence, in noble believers, 'tis all one to lie in St. Innocent's churchyard as in the sands of Egypt; ready to be anything, in the ecstasy of being ever, and as content with six foot as the moles of Adrianus.

> . . . *tabesne cadavera solvat,*
> *An rogus, haud refert.*

[It matters not whether putrefaction or the pyre destroys our bodies.]

Lucan

The foregoing is Chapter V
of Sir Thomas Browne's HYDRIOTAPHIA: URN-BURIAL.